Photograph by Mervin S. Stewart, M.D.

SELECTED WRITINGS
of
BERTRAM D. LEWIN

Edited by

JACOB A. ARLOW, M.D.

Library of Congress Catalog Card Number 72-94802

PUBLISHED BY

THE PSYCHOANALYTIC QUARTERLY, INC.

57 WEST 57TH STREET

NEW YORK, N. Y., 10019

PRINTED IN U.S.A. FOR THE PUBLISHERS

BY THE WILLIAM BYRD PRESS, INC., RICHMOND, VA.

CONTENTS

Clinical Applications of Dream Psychology

The Pursuit of Knowledge and the Nature of the Mind

Psychoanalysis and Education

INTRODUCTION

Of all American psychoanalysts, Bertram D. Lewin in his teaching, writing, and personality influenced psychoanalysis in the United States the most. He was a man of exceptional intellectual gifts and charismatic personality. The combination of these qualities made him unique as psychoanalyst and educator.

For Lewin nothing was more exciting than exploring the world of the mind, his own as well as that of others. To this discipline he brought the introspective intuition of the poet, the objectivity of the scientist, and the adventuresomeness of the explorer. He enjoyed this quest with a merry wit and infectious enthusiasm. Erudite and scholarly, imaginative and creative, a bit of whimsey with a touch of genius—such was Bertram D. Lewin.

Words, language, and ideas were his natural métier. Fluent in German, French, and Spanish, he also read Russian, Portuguese, Italian, and Swedish. With his colleagues he would exchange versified quips and parodies in Latin and other languages. Sometimes, he would playfully compose verses and then render them into four additional languages.

This gift was only one aspect of an extraordinary capacity to empathize intellectually as well as emotionally with the inner logic of systematized structures. With the same ease that he could shift from one language to another, Lewin could switch from the logic of mathematics to that of poetry, philosophy, the primary process, the psychology of a dream, a symptom, or an institute. Many of his creative insights grew out of this ability to describe data from one realm of experience in terms of the logic of another. Lewin's analysis of Descartes's philosophy, his elucidation of the meaning of reality, his etymological contributions, the explanation of the ecology of psychoanalytic institutes and training programs, the dream screen, and the metaphor all illustrate the wide range of phenomena to which he applied his prodigious ability.

This thoroughgoing fluency with the inner logic of unconscious mental processes emerged in every aspect of Lewin's work. He once said, 'The most important discoveries you ever make in psychoanalysis are the ones you have first discovered in yourself'. In the same spirit he also said, 'If you are listening to a patient and you get an idea for a paper, put it down. The proof is sure to come later.' This was not scientific adventurousness, nor was it loose disregard of methodology. Rather, it reflected Lewin's recognition of the creative, intuitive leap which precedes and anticipates scientific discovery; it derived from his appreciation of the unconscious forces at work in creativity, a concept for which he acknowledged his indebtedness to Hanns Sachs.

Lewin demonstrated his disciplined openness to unconscious mental processes during seminars on clinical methodology. These seminars were a real tour de force and have become a legend to those who had the good fortune to attend them. Given no more than the first communications made by the patient at the beginning of a session, he would proceed to anticipate the rest of the material, pursuing relentlessly the inexorable logic of the data. The ability to pursue the implications of observations to their ultimate logical culmination made possible Lewin's discoveries about sleep, mania, psychoanalytic technique, and the oral triad.

For Lewin the quest for knowledge was never a tedious or ponderous task. On the contrary, it was a joyful enterprise which he was only too glad to share with others. He gave respectful attention to every new idea put to him, from whatever source, and afterwards communicated to the authors further thoughts on the subject together with useful biographical references. Generous giving to his colleagues in every possible way epitomizes Lewin's relation to psychoanalysis.

The American Psychoanalytic Association chose Lewin to direct its survey of psychoanalytic education. This study, conducted in collaboration with Helen Ross, is summarized in their book, *Psychoanalytic Education in the United States.* The true impact of their efforts, however, cannot be encompassed in any publication. During the years 1956 to 1959, Lewin and Miss Ross created an intellectual and educational ferment in the institutes. By their tactful, patient, stimulating, and inspiring visits they helped break down the prevalent parochialism and suspicion. Every psychoanalyst in the United States, present and future, is and will be affected by the Lewin-Ross survey.

There is a unity in Lewin's published work which has an almost æsthetic quality. The themes of incorporation into the body, fusion, and transformation run like scarlet threads through his writings. These themes may be found in his early works on the compulsive character, the body as phallus, claustrophobia, hypomania, and learning, as well as in his later works on depression, elation, dreams, omniscience and education.

As the reader of this volume will find, no matter how bold his imagination or how speculative his ideas, Bertram Lewin's work always begins and ends with introspection and with solid psychoanalytic data.

JACOB A. ARLOW

ACKNOWLEDGMENTS

The idea of publishing the Selected Writings of Bertram D. Lewin was first suggested by Mary Crowther, executive assistant of The Psychoanalytic Quarterly and a long-time associate of Dr. Lewin's. The editors of The Quarterly readily agreed that this would be the appropriate tribute to Lewin who was one of the founders of The Quarterly and who served continuously on its staff as associate editor and editor for almost forty years from its inception in 1932 until the time of his death.

The volume could not have been published without the help and encouragement of Dr. Lewin's daughter, Barbara L. Schwartz, and his son, Professor David Lewin, who made available to us the complete files of their father's works.

We also express our thanks to the many friends and colleagues of Bertram Lewin who have given us invaluable help. Miss Helen Ross and Dr. Lawrence S. Kubie have been especially generous in giving us many useful ideas and suggestions as the work on the volume progressed.

Dr. Werner Nathan graciously donated his services as the translator of *Kotschmieren, Menses und Weibliches Über-Ich,* which is published in this volume for the first time in English under the title, Smearing of Feces, Menstruation, and Female Superego.

We are grateful to the following publishers who granted permission to reprint papers from journals and chapters from books:

American Medical Association
American Psychoanalytic Association
Bond Wheelwright Company
Bulletin of the Menninger Clinic
Bulletin of the Philadelphia Association for Psychoanalysis
International Journal of Psycho-Analysis
International Universities Press, Inc.
Journal of Nervous and Mental Disease
Psychoanalytic Review
Psychosomatic Medicine
University of Pittsburgh Press
W. W. Norton & Co., Inc.

Mary Crowther and Josephine Shapiro of The Psychoanalytic Quarterly office staff are due thanks for their painstaking work on the References and Index. They, with Elisabeth King, also proofread the material.

J. A. A.

EARLY CLINICAL STUDIES

Lewin's early clinical papers constitute a remarkable group. In dramatic progression, they foreshadow all the essential themes of his subsequent work. In the 1930 paper, *Smearing of Feces, Menstruation, and Female Superego,* Lewin demonstrated how, in fantasy, fecal smearing may be a variant of coprophagy by which, in fantasy, an act of incorporation may serve to undo the loss of the penis and the father. The result of this incorporation is an alteration in the subject, namely, the consolidation of the superego. His two papers, *The Body as Phallus* and *Claustrophobia,* advanced the theme of oral incorporation, but this time into the claustrum of the mother's body. Eating a phallus and thereby being transformed into a phallus makes it possible for one to realize a childhood wish of re-entering the mother's body and being reunited with her. In fantasy such reunion may be effected either through incorporation by way of intercourse or incorporation by being devoured. Safely incorporated in the body of the mother, the body as phallus becomes the body as foetus, and in this way the rivals for the mother's love—the father and siblings—may be set aside and displaced.

In these papers, Lewin also introduces a variant of the idea of claustrophobia, namely, the fear of being dislodged from the claustrum by the intruding penis, by siblings, or during birth. This latter idea played an important role in his concept of the dream screen, sleep, and elation.

J. A. A.

I. THE COMPULSIVE CHARACTER*

With the term compulsive character or compulsive personality (*Zwangscharakter*), we designate those individuals who, though showing few or no symptoms of a compulsion neurosis in the narrower sense, have a character and a way of life identical with or similar to the compulsion neurotic.

It will be seen at once that this definition is entirely descriptive, for it tells us only two things about these individuals: they are like patients with a compulsion neurosis in a general way, but differ from them in not having a feeling that they are ill, in not having what they consider symptoms. Plainly such a conception as the 'compulsive personality' is a derived one—derived in fact from our experience with compulsion neurotics—and can make no claim to special theoretical value. Indeed, there are physicians who would make no distinction between compulsion neurotics and compulsive personalities; for them the latter have rationalized neuroses, or compulsion neuroses under cover: '*rationalisierte oder verhüllte Zwangsneurosen*' (Alexander, 1927a). They represent, to use the same author's terminology, 'asymptomatic neuroses'.

Persons with this character rarely come to the physician because of dissatisfaction with it, but like individuals with an unsuspected diabetes who present themselves to the physician with an infection, they will consult him for some disharmony in their work or marriage, and the physician will find that he can do no more for their presenting difficulty without 'treating' their character than his colleague in internal medicine could do for the infection without treating the 'laboratory' diabetes. It soon becomes evident that the character is as intimately related to the problems as the diabetic tissue alteration is to the infection. In both cases it is the patient as an individual, with all that is amiss, who must be treated.

* [No. 5 in Bibliography.]

Numbers used for this and all following papers refer to Lewin's complete bibliography. *See*, pp. 555-564 [Ed.].

The analytic approach to the character is no different than the analytic approach to the symptom. Character traits, or at any rate many character traits, have the same psychologic structure as neurotic symptoms; they are modifications of the ego set up to repress or ward off unwelcome instinctual urges. They are known as reaction-formations. Other character traits represent ego-acceptable modifications of these same urges—the sublimations. It is indeed a generally known fact that during psychoanalysis character traits may be modified, may disappear, or may be replaced by others, and these alterations in the character can be correlated with alterations in the symptomatology and sexuality of the patient. Ferenczi's (1925) epigram is quite just: from the standpoint of the psychoanalyst, the character is a neurosis.

To learn the deep psychological meaning of the character traits in a compulsive personality, we can best begin by considering the deep psychology of the compulsive symptoms. The compulsion neurotic feels cravings, or is obsessed by ideas foreign to his conscious personality: they are either pointless, or are such as offend moral or æsthetic feelings. Fantasies of killing some beloved person, of having sexual relations with a near relative, or of putting feces in the mouth would be outspoken examples of such obsessions. On the other hand, other obsessive impulses are outspokenly moral or social; they frequently exaggerate the demands made on the individual during his upbringing. The compulsion to wash the hands countless times during the day is an example of this class. Apparently pointless actions on analysis turn out to be symbolic of one or the other type of compulsion. To use our present-day terminology, the first type of compulsion is carried out by the ego at the behest of the asocial instinctual part of the personality—the id.

The second overmoral or overæsthetic activity is executed by the same ego at the behest of the individual's unconscious conscience—the superego. To run counter to the superego and omit, for example, the ritual hand washing, would throw the individual into a state of fear or anxiety. Carrying out this act allays or wards off the anxiety, which is really bad conscience for gratifying unconscious instinctual urges. Behind the fear of the superego, genetically, is a fear of the father, the earliest prototype of conscience, the first upholder of the demands of society. Sometimes instinctual gratification and conscience gratification will be condensed into one act; for example, symmetrical washing of the knees, which is 'cleansing', may at the same time be a substitutive masturbation; or a moral compulsion may precede or follow one of the other type in order to cancel or repeal it. As the neurosis progresses, more and more compulsions come to give gratification, and ultimately the victory goes to the id.

The neurosis begins as an attempt at defense against the libidinal wishes represented in the œdipus complex; in spite of the castration threat the incestuous objects of these strivings remain, but the genital quality of the relations is lost, and supplanted by the older sadistic and anal strivings—or to put it more technically, there is a regression from the genital to a pregenital level, the anal-sadistic one. It is assumed that constitutional factors have been operative in these persons so that pregenital interest in sadistic and anal functions was unusually well developed. Such persons were trained to neatness, propriety, and gentleness either with great difficulty or very harshly. When confronted by genital urges, they try to bring to bear against these the prohibitions found useful in their training in neatness; they also try to get around these prohibitions as they sought to overcome the will of those who trained them in cleanliness. Thus it is that the compulsion neurotic can clean himself from masturbatory (i.e., genital) guilt by washing his hands, a method he learned when dealing with his pleasure in getting dirty. This regression to the anal-sadistic level, with its substitutions of the pregenital strivings for the genital ones, causes hate impulses and impulses to soil or debase to appear wherever there would be, at the genital level, a purely positive attitude to the object. In this way, the libidinal relations of the compulsion neurotic, whether to persons or to more abstract objects, are ambivalent; those he loves, he also hates. The overmoral and overæsthetic character traits or symptoms are built up to help ward off the anal erotic and sadistic urges, represent in some way the opposite of these, and are reaction-formations or overcompensations for them.

The person with a compulsive character but without true compulsions or obsessions as such has been through this same development, perhaps less quantitatively pronounced than in the neurotic; his ego too has become altered and shows the character traits which, as reaction-formations, serve to ward off sadistic and anal erotic strivings. However, he has been able to a greater extent to sublimate his id tendencies, that is, to modify them to conform with the demands of his own ego and with the demands of his environment. In studying the character of such a person, then, we should see how these reaction-formations and sublimations affect his attitude to his work, to abstract questions, to standards of behavior, to money, to authority, and to other persons generally.

It is a striking fact that, to speak from a purely descriptive standpoint, compulsive personalities are usually above the average in intelligence. They are also usually very ethical in their principles, sometimes to the point of being ascetics. They are under fortunate circumstances hard workers, conscientious, formal, punctual; yet in spite of this, they show a tendency to procrastinate and draw out their labors as long as they can. Nor are they, in spite of meritorious and apparently useful traits, apt to be successful financially, for it is their tendency to choose unremunerative occupations, either those in which routine plays a large part or else those in which the immediate result is not directly well rewarded economically, such as pure scientific research. It is their hope, however, that ultimately, perhaps posthumously, recognition will come to them, or that some prestige and power will accrue to them.

We are all acquainted among our medical colleagues with persons of the compulsive type. They prolong their internship and hospital training indefinitely, and then perhaps choose some poorly paying research position. Though irked by hospital routine they nevertheless write long detailed histories, and employ all possible methods of investigation, even though they may merely be obviously time-wasting and beside the point. In clinical practice these persons are surgeons who are meticulous in regard to the details of technique, internists who never quite finish a physical examination, repeating their auscultation, etc., perhaps without coming to a definite diagnosis, neurologists who can never quite decide whether a reflex is slightly exaggerated or not. Laboratory men may become lost in perfecting some trivial point in technique which, when perfected, brings them no gain in the way of increased efficiency or knowledge. A tendency to indulge in irrelevant detail may also delay the practical execution or decision. A lawyer will be meticulous as to the details of his documents, correct and recorrect them, look up the law on cases having only a remote connection with his immediate problem, and, in spite of great correctness and perfection in technicalities, still not have found the law appropriate to the case.

Such instances show very well some of the sublimations and character formations of the compulsive personalities. Their occupation represents a sublimation of instinctual (id) tendencies. In both the physician and the lawyer, these sublimations give the individual a chance to manifest ego-acceptable sadistic urges. The physician is permitted by his own standards and by society even to inflict pain in a good cause; the lawyer is permitted to 'fight' his legal colleague or the party of the opposite side. At the same time they must serve their patient, client, or society, or even more generally the internalized representative of society, the superego. The fact that they 'do good', 'promote justice', etc., is this service to the superego.

In an entirely successful sublimation the ego's duty to the superego and to the id is happily settled in smooth efficient activity. But in the persons in question, this is not quite the case. The work must satisfy a larger quantity of id strivings than usual, and it is consequently treated to a certain extent as if it were really the unsublimated pleasure striving: the over-conscientious, meticulous, burdensome features are therefore accentuated so that the complementary demand of the superego for penance may be satisfied. At the same time the obvious triviality of the work may represent an unconscious persiflage of the demands of the superego, as if to say, 'this is the silly sort of thing required of me'.

Psychoanalysis has shown that work is a homosexual sublimation; a man, in obeying his superego, in doing his duty, is using those energies which as a child were included in his passive relation to his father. But the sadistic anal relation to objects which maintains in the compulsive personality brings with it an ambivalent object relation to the father also, and this is manifested by signs of unconscious hostility to the work, resistance to obeying the superego, and to doing one's duty. It is thus that we may understand the double attitude to work. A sense of the unconscious hostility lurking behind the work leads to the constant perfecting and correcting, technical compliance with rules, to make sure that the hostility does not really break through in some unconscious slip. The procrastination and detailed work also serve to lengthen the time put on the work: work also holds libidinal gratification and therefore is prolonged through as many means as possible. Since the work is usually a sublimation of anal strivings the procrastination may well be compared with the infantile attitude toward the 'work' of defecating—in both instances the aim is pleasure through retention.

Compulsive personalities always have an attitude to money that goes beyond any rational principle. They carry with them some of the psychology of the child, who does not earn money (that function being a prerogative of the father), and to whom money either comes as a gift or as something stolen. In other words, an unconscious sense of guilt may attach to the entirely necessary desire to earn money. As is well known, this represents an anal erotic manifestation. Compulsive personalities therefore choose professions, or in their work demean themselves, so that they may remain free from 'dirtying themselves' with filthy lucre, and not compete against the father. A frequent habit of such persons is to accumulate money without investing it usefully; thus they avoid competing (i.e., fighting), and at the same time indulge their anal erotic wish to amass.

Their relation to authority is usually quite characteristic. They ask advice of some person (usually a father figure) before making decisions, even though this person is not necessarily more competent than themselves. They usually engineer it so that this person's opinion will be the one they themselves wish. For the moment this person is put in place of the superego so that he may give them authoritative permission to carry out some piece of behavior about which otherwise they would have scruples. The scruples were based on the fact that the decision in question would lead to an unconscious sense of guilt—which is relieved by the superego's acquiescence. Ostensibly the question might relate to embarking in some business enterprise, or to getting married, etc., but in the depths of these personalities there is a qualm of conscience as to whether these activities might not represent some hostility to the superego, or secretly gratify some defiance of the father. So authoritative reassurance becomes necessary. Furthermore, if the advice given should be opposed to the individuals' wishes, they by no means always follow it. They can always find rational ways of disposing of it, or can induce the adviser to change his mind. The latent hostility to authority may also be gratified by the trouble and time the adviser is necessarily put to. It must be remembered, however, that both the need for authority and regulation and the resistance to them are equally real, and are a manifestation of the ambivalence described above.

The reaction-formation against anal wishes may be seen in these persons' attitudes to cleanliness. In this respect they are very careful, with their person and with their belongings. Yet sometimes the cleansing process may be more formal than real, and in one or two ways allow some of the repressed pleasure in getting dirty to crop through. Thus, as Ferenczi (1916/1917a) has reported, a woman with strong cleaning compulsions spent most of her time cleaning—the water closet! A general insistance on cleanliness does not keep these people from heartily enjoying Rabelaisian jokes about excreta and defecation, even though they may frown severely on jokes dealing with genital sexuality.

Freud (1913a) has recognized that the compulsive's acute thinking capacity may be due to an early strengthening of the curiosity impulse (*Wisstrieb*), a modification of sadistic strivings. A reaction against anal strivings seems to give form to a certain type of thinking commonly met with in these persons, which might be called 'clean thinking'. It can be characterized as a preoccupation with abstract conceptions and problems of a philosophic or abstruse nature. What is truth ultimately? What assurance have we that we know things? What values are absolute? In arguing out these points, the thinking is divorced from the concrete, material, and worldly facts; it is kept 'clean' by isolation from the grime of data. That such thinking also serves to separate the intellectual processes from fantasy, and thus to encourage the development of doubt is apparent.

Thus certain scientists in a report will begin with broad metaphysical and a priori discussion, and having worked out their theory with no reference to empirical data, will suddenly plump down a vast quantity of material in which it is impossible to find any theoretical significance or orientation, evidently with the tacit assumption that this crass empirical mass somehow substantiates their theorizing. In point of fact here again the thinking is kept clean by divorcing it from the accumulated material.

Since their thinking evidently has some fantasy value for them, such persons tend either to dogmatism, or else take refuge from it in a sort of 'negative dogmatism', an exaggeratedly critical attitude toward all theorizing. Just as open-mindedness may degenerate into credulity, so such scepticism may become negativism. It is interesting that during analysis those very persons who are most attached to a priori principles and who most crave absolute certainty and guidance are the ones who will have the most to say about the 'dogmatism' of the analyst. Their arguments then usually show that their real grudge is against the analyst's inconsistencies; they crave a dogmatism against which they could rebel. The arguments are *ad hoc,* and like those of a good lawyer designed to win their case. Where such persons are not too personally involved, their ability to see both sides, their conscientiousness and capacity for detail may give them a valuable judicial temperament.

In these otherwise perhaps too rationalistic persons, there is usually to be found some banal superstitious belief or practice. Freud (1901) has explained the superstition of such persons as being dependent on their overpersonification of fate. Thus, through chance or coincidence they may frequently be led to some act at variance with their general way of life.

The compulsive personalities may be collectors, sublimating in this way the anal erotic pleasure in amassing. Other part-strivings may enter to determine the nature of the collections: with art collections, voyeur strivings, with cane collections, phallic strivings, with china, pewter collections, etc., a urethral element originating in an interest in chamber pots. On the other hand, a reaction-formation against amassing may lead to a Spartan simplicity in regard to possessions.

In the sex life in the narrower sense, there is extensive variety. In general, however, there is a relative impotency or lack of direct interest. Marriages for money or position are not uncommon. A splitting between sensual and tender aims is a common finding. But the sexual life cannot be thoroughly dealt with in a brief fashion. Among practices pointing to unconscious anal fantasies, coitus *a tergo* might be mentioned.

Compulsive personalities make up a large part of psychoanalytic practice. As a rule, they come for some extraneous difficulty, rarely for any symptoms. Analysis usually reveals that there was a compulsion neurosis in childhood, generally between the ages of five and twelve (the latency period). Abraham has pointed out that manic depressive patients frequently show a compulsive type of personality during the intervals between the psychotic periods. The general impression that such types of personality are very common, and indeed on the increase, leads us into questions that can only be answered by a study of modern civilization—the civilization to which these personalities are adaptations.

II. SMEARING OF FECES, MENSTRUATION, AND FEMALE SUPEREGO*

TRANSLATED BY WERNER NATHAN, M.D.

The Relationship between Cutaneous and Anal Erotism

Certain findings set forth in this paper led me to study the relationship between skin and anal erotism. These observations suggested that under certain circumstances the skin serves as a substitute organ for the satisfaction of passive anal impulses. They also led me to examine what role the fantasy of fecal smearing might play. In brief, fecal smearing seemed analogous to coprophagy. The urge to smear appeared to have the same motive as the one underlying coprophagy, namely, the wish to reintroject a lost object.

To demonstrate how these findings were arrived at, I will report first a fragment from a case history.

Patient A is a young man of weak genitality who achieves erotic satisfaction through the exhibition of his naked body. This is the indispensable precursor for pleasurable sexual intercourse and constitutes by far the most enjoyable component of the whole act. Exhibiting his penis per se holds little interest for him, in contrast to merely taking off his clothes which can lead to spontaneous orgasm. During puberty he did not masturbate at all, but experienced spontaneous orgasm when bathing, lying naked on the bed, and exercising without his clothes on. At this time he envied women, thought them beautiful, charming, alluring, etc., *because* they did not possess a penis. Indeed, he used to hide his own penis between his legs in order to admire his feminized image in the mirror. In his actual love life he is narcissistic according to female patterns: he desires to be loved and to seduce others into love proposals by means of his own personal charms.

* [No. 6 in Bibliography.]

This paper is published here for the first time in English.

This man has retained numerous infantile traits and engages in a series of secret anal perversions; for instance, he administers to himself a daily rectal douche with a small enema syringe. Earlier he had used a common candle; for future use he has bought a set of rectal dilators. The latter supposedly will aid his self-prescribed 'therapy' for an anal fissure. He is completely unaware and even indignantly rejects the idea that these procedures provide satisfaction for him. He rationalizes quite simply that he is forced to keep his stools soft and the fissure stretched so that it will heal properly. While describing his anal practices in the analysis and producing associations indicating passive-anal wishes toward his father, he dreamed:

> I attended a demonstration in the outpatient department of a dermatological clinic. Dr. X presented a Negro with an anular rash, and in the middle of each lesion there was some white fluid, probably pus. Dr. X said: 'Of course you see that this is a case of psoriasis. We will cut off only a small piece of his tongue; it squeezes the mucous membranes so that the skin heals.' Or he said: 'It squeezes the body. The disease will then move on to the rectum.'

I am not going into the associations related to the transference (a physician talking medical nonsense) but report only those pertinent to my topic: 'A rash is dirty like feces. The pus in the sore spots reminds me of semen. Anular—"anuli"—small anuses. Once Dr. X presented a Negro with anal chancre. The rash resembled an anular syphilitic eruption. Psoriasis—"sore asses"[1] the lesions were like sore asses. A woman I know squeezed her leg and got rid of her psoriasis after that. The squeezing of the leg reminds me of another dream I had a short time ago. In this dream my leg was squeezed. When I was five my governess once slapped me lightly on the leg, just where the squeeze was in the dream, and she said: "You are afraid that I see your genitals". The "clipping[2] of the tongue"—I think of excision of the tongue to prevent metastasis of a tumor; furthermore of some cutaneous tumor which was excised to avert metastasis.'

In the dream he obviously returns to his old idea that castration (clipping of the tongue, squeezing of the body) can

[1] A jocular *Klang* association, well known to medical students.

[2] *Translator's note:* In German, *Das Beschneiden der Zunge*. This means not only 'clipping' but conveys predominantly the idea of 'circumcision'.

bring about beautification (cure of psoriasis, prevention of metastasis). But he also equates the cutaneous lesions (anular, syphilitic, psoriatic) with anal ones (anal chancre, 'sore asses'). The skin becomes the equivalent of the anus, a passive organ (e.g., pus or semen in the anular sore, anal chancre), a collection of small anuses. The dream indicates too how the skin can become a substitute for the anus: the rash is dirty, fecal; the syphilitic eruption is subordinate to the anal chancre; tumors in the skin form by way of metastasis; metastasis is nothing more than the Greek word for *displacement.* The skin becomes an erotic organ through displacement from the anus, just like anal dirt (sores) becomes cutaneous. We might say that smearing transfers libidinous pleasure from the anus to the skin.

I cite another dream of the same patient with similar content and elaboration.

> I pull a clothes pole out of the soil and put it down. Then I lie down backwards on a balcony; many insects come and bite me all over my body.

Pulling out the pole reminds him of the loss of an erection, of uprooting, of the loss of the penis. The balcony of the dream had been the scene of an attempted rape that he knew about. It reminded him of a fantasy he had had a few days earlier in which he was anally raped by the analyst. The biting insects he associated with the rats in Freud's paper on the Rat Man. One insect was the size of the enema syringe he used for his daily rectal rinsing. We must add that one of the earliest memories of the patient deals with the fantasy of being eaten by the father.

Thus the dream is easily understood: it is a passive homosexual and masochistic one on three libidinal levels. He suffers castration; thereafter he seeks masochistic gratification on the anal level (to be penetrated or bitten in the anus). However, in renouncing the anal satisfaction he displaces libido to the surface of the body and receives bites all over. The relationship to the father remains passively masochistic throughout, but the libido is displaced from the genital by way of the anal level to the body surface.

A series of dreams at a later stage of the analysis had the same latent content. First he dreamed of being stung between the shoulder blades by a bee; later he was stung in the lumbar region. He also submitted to a lumbar puncture. Finally the insects were transformed into a serpent that tried to bite him in the anus.

One point seems worth stressing: in both dreams the skin lesions show a scattered distribution and much variety. The skin is not depicted as one organ, but as a multitude of organs. One is reminded of the schizophrenic Freud (1915a) described, who regarded the pores of his skin as so many vaginas. Our knowledge of polyphallic symbolism may help to provide an explanation. The head of the Medusa with its plethora of penis substitutes actually conveys the latent meaning of 'no penis' (Ferenczi, 1923a). It seems likely that we are dealing here with 'polyanal' symbolism; the many 'anuli' would constitute the polyanal compensation for giving up the erotic use of the anus.

To confirm the above interpretations I cite the dream of patient B, a young female medical student.

> I read a physician's report which asserts that I had examined a female patient with skin cancer without having detected the carcinoma. Then I go into another room where I see a black woman, and I think: 'Has she a tumor?'. I look closely and notice a big cauliflower-like mass coming out of her anus, a purulent tumor, and I see that the wall between her vagina and rectum is completely ulcerated. I say: 'She has an enormous carcinoma of the rectum'.

The rectal tumor reminded the patient of the mother of a close woman friend who is thus afflicted; then she remembered that her own mother had a miscarriage when the patient was ten years old. Rectal and cutaneous carcinoma brought to mind a case of syphilis which started as chancre *in ano* and developed a skin rash in addition. To the rash, she associated melanoma, then a brown spot (nevus) on her own skin, and finally, feces. Then there was an early childhood memory of her younger sister smearing herself with feces. 'No wall between vagina and rectum' led to associations about douches, enemas, etc., hence the equivalence of anus and vagina.

We are mainly interested in the fact that this patient too equates a rectal mass (chancre, tumor, feces) with spots on or in the skin (skin tumor, syphilitic eruption, smeared feces).

It is noteworthy that the anal mass means also the 'anal child', or rather the 'anal miscarriage'. Furthermore, the patient is aware of the erotic significance of the anus (no separation between anus and vagina). In short, here again the skin provides a substitute for the anus by means of smearing; matter on or in the skin replaces feces.

An observation concerning the same patient B: Some months after the above dream the patient, whose character showed many reaction-formations against anal drives, was asked by her sexual partner to permit anal intercourse. He attempted anal penetration with his penis but was unsuccessful because of her resistance. Two days later the patient fell ill with both impetigo and Vincent's angina. As she was most meticulous in the care of her body and mouth, she became very much annoyed and felt 'dirty'. Her associations revealed clearly that she regarded the impetiginous exudation as feces on her skin. Vincent's disease, by way of associations with Spirochaeta, syphilis, 'dirty' veneral disease, led to fantasies of coprophagy,—it was as if she had feces in her mouth, as if her breath smelled of feces, etc.

Analysis showed that the guilt for which she suffered these diseases was due to unconscious fantasies about being tempted to castrate the man during anal intercourse and to retain his penis in her anus. It also became clear that these wishes stemmed from the relationship with her father in early infancy.

Leaving aside the problems connected with the 'flight into somatization', it is obvious with regard to our topic that the patient erotized (and punished) her skin after she renounced the fantasied sexual-sadistic use of her anus. Through coprophagy and by smearing, she tried to regain what she had given up. Libido became displaced from the anus to the skin.

Menstruation=Excremental Incontinence: Compensatory Erotization of the Skin

Psychoanalysis discovered many years ago that the menstrual flow often consciously and sometimes unconsciously is viewed as a kind of excretion, and menstruation itself as a 'dirty' function. A direct consequence of such a view would be that women regard the menstrual flow as incontinence, as a failure of sphincter function. Some observations prove this to be actually the case.

Patient C, a young woman with a striking number of anal character traits, has the following habit: during menstruation she frequently goes to the toilet and tries by special movements of her perineal muscles to force the menstrual blood out of the vagina. In between these trips she believes herself capable of retaining the blood in the vagina by activating the vaginal muscles in a kind of sphincter-like movement. In the beginning of her analysis, she suffered from severe constipation which disappeared on the first day of her period. During menstruation diarrhea replaced the constipation, but the latter recurred as soon as menstruation stopped. Her usual stinginess yielded to compulsory buying, especially of clothes, while she was menstruating.

I cite these facts only to demonstrate the close connection this particular patient made between menstruation and excretion, to the extent, indeed, that she tried to exercise sphincter control over her menstrual flow. They may also serve to explain the following analytic observation.

Two days before one of her periods, her associations centered around her strongly positive transference; but on the first day of bleeding, associations connected with the castration complex came to the fore, particularly childhood memories of early admonitions concerning her behavior, screen memories of threats of castration which made it abundantly clear that for her menstruation meant 'losing a penis'. The following day she came to her session in a sullen mood, angry with her husband and other members of her family, and complained that life had nothing to offer her. Toward the end of the hour, which was mainly filled with the description of her depressed mood, she related the following fantasy.

> Yesterday I felt so dejected that I looked in the mirror and thought: there are only two things in this world that might give me satisfaction. Either I could buy myself a big box of chocolates—by no means ordinary ones, but really good, expensive chocolates—and then sit down and eat them all. Or I could take all my money out of the bank and blow it on clothes.[3] (With this remark she made an unmistakable gesture, brushing the palm of her hand over her whole body from her throat down to her knees.)

[3] 'To blow' conveys the impression of explosive expulsion and dispersion.

A comprehensive interpretation of her associations, which are characteristic of the patient's attitude, indicates that menstruation is regarded as castration, but as an anal one, as an unwished for and involuntary incontinence. To make up for the loss of the feces-penis she has two mechanisms at her disposal. The narcissistic loss (looking into the mirror) can be compensated for by coprophagy (eating expensive chocolate) or by smearing (her gesture of taking the money and rubbing it over her body in the form of clothes). If a lost object is equated with feces, then it can be regained by coprophagy, as we know from Abraham's work (1924a). We have here an illustration of this method of dealing with object loss; however we can observe too that there exists still another means, namely, the method of smearing.[4] The scene and the fantasy described seem to prove clearly that the menstrual flow is equated regressively with involuntary incontinence. To confirm this view we might add that the patient is always enraged when her period is too early but is very happy when it is delayed.

Patient B, whose dreams I mentioned earlier, has the same attitude even though for her the foremost feeling is one of humiliation rather than rage. Her explanation is that 'the idea that I am unable to control my own functions is repugnant to me'. She associates memories of early failures in sphincter control and the humiliation on the occasion of an involuntary excretion. It is noteworthy that her first menstruation occurred suddenly and unexpectedly, soiling her underwear. The intense feeling of humiliation was undoubtedly re-enforced by the involuntary soiling of her underwear with excretion in early childhood. Incidentally, with this patient memories of enuresis and involuntary micturition played a greater role than that of involuntary defecation. In the beginning of her analysis, while under the influence of the masculinity complex, she tried to deny that the menstrual fluid is blood. She brought many dreams repudiating the idea of blood and ascribing the flow to urine, even semen.[5] The following dream is an illustration.

[4] The same patient demonstrated in dreams that she equates blood and feces. In one dream the problem was whether to use iodine or mercurochrome (a red antiseptic fluid) on her skin. She decided on iodine. Moreover, she likes to eat chocolate syrup on ice cream, but cannot tolerate strawberry juice.

[5] It seems worth mentioning that toward the end of her analysis, which succeeded in removing much of her anal erotism, her menstrual cycle changed from 28 to 26 days.

> A house is surrounded by water and waves. The waves grow bigger and bigger, so that one could almost talk of a flood.

To flood she associated: 'I am flooding menstrually'. Furthermore, one of her friends became shipwrecked while menstruating. Blood soaked her clothes so that she appeared to have suffered a severe hemorrhage. Then the patient thought of the inundation of Johnstown, the eruption of Mount Etna, of lava flowing down a mountain and crushing houses, and of a town destroyed by an earthquake. A Ford car, whose radiator cover is blown off, occurred to her and then she said: 'It gives me pleasure to perceive the trickling of the menstrual flow; it seems to me like urine'.

Obviously she attempts to change the menstrual blood into urine and thereby to gain pleasure according to the infantile model of micturition (the flood). Moreover she tries to equate the menstrual flow with masculine (destructive, urinary) orgasm.

The material offered here leads me to conclude that menstruation can unconsciously mean the involuntary failure of the sphincters, among other things. In addition, I have presented evidence that smearing can represent the compensation for such failures, or rather for the loss of the feces (or their equivalents). This means the object can be preserved. What is lost in defecation can be returned to the self by way of anal-cutaneous displacement by means of smearing. Finally, if objects are equated with feces, an attempt may be made to perform such smearing in symbolic form.

The Role of Smearing in the Development of Female Narcissism and of the Superego

We have seen how easily menstrual bleeding can be viewed as involuntary incontinence and how the smearing of feces can then be used as compensatory consolation. Now the question arises: has this mechanism general significance? In one case we observed how the impulse to smear, derived from menstrual bleeding, was expressed ego-syntonically in a fantasy to spend money on clothes. In other cases, the same impulse appeared in the displacement of libido from the anus to the skin. Is there perhaps a time or an experience where the two mechanisms—

the regressive dealing with menstruation and the erotization of the skin by way of displacement—come together?

Our material demonstrates that the first menstrual bleeding can become tied in with regressive fantasies, which means that it can be regarded as involuntary incontinence. Certain analytic theories maintain that there exists a definite point in time during the libidinal development of women when a thrust of libido toward the whole surface of the body takes place, namely, puberty. Hárnik (1923) stressed the importance of the first menstrual bleeding in this process; the first period serves to trigger this thrust of libido. Therefore there are at least two reasons to direct our attention to female puberty and to the occurrence of the first menstruation.

Hárnik thinks, for good reasons, that the increase of body narcissism in young women during puberty is due to removal of libido away from the clitoris. According to his exposition, quantities of libido formerly connected with clitoris activity are then displaced to the body surface, where they increase the narcissism already present and are expressed as interest in beauty, charm, and other typically female ideals. 'Regarding the psychological motives for this process, analytic experience shows that the final push for the renunciation of clitoris masturbation is normally due to a decisive experience, the occurrence of the first menstrual bleeding.' Concurring with a remark by Rado to the effect that the leading libidinal zone of the fœtus is the whole body surface, Hárnik also points to the regressive significance of this thrust and he sees in the regression a revival of the intrauterine condition 'when the whole body is a genital'.

My findings agree with Hárnik's views. In addition, however, they seem to allow the supposition that there exists one more stage in between the renunciation of clitoris cathexis and the cathexis of the body surface which replaces it—an intermediate phase when the libido in question regresses to the anal level. The whole process started by the first period might be conceptualized as follows: the beginning of menstruation is unconsciously regarded as castration. At the same time, however, the castration is denied and the fantasy appears: 'this is not blood; it is feces (urine)'. In other words, an anal (or urethral) regression takes place. But the development does not rest there, because if this is an anal regression the psychic apparatus is able to easily master the situation: the loss can be undone by means of either smearing or coprophagy. One may assume, therefore, that in the growing girl the first menstruation leads to an impulse to smear. My observations demonstrate how this need is expressed because the unsublimated action would be taboo. In my cases, fecal smearing meant erotization of the skin, displacement of libido from the anus to the skin. Libido which at first is genital, becomes anal and is finally displaced to the skin. The impulses to smear, originating from the first menstrual bleeding, get their expression in the thrust of libido to the body surface.[6]

From a somewhat different point of view one might also say that just as the loss of feces constitutes a 'precursor of castration', so the smearing of feces is the 'precursor of the narcissistic compensation', and that this may play an important role in cases where the castration is represented regressively.

We find an intimation of the anal-cutaneous mechanism in the tattooing connected with primitive puberty rites. There too it serves as narcissistic compensation. The fundamental rite is a painful initiation to the tribe and the pain is often increased by mutilation of the foreskin or of the teeth. Simultaneously with this symbolic castration, however, the young man receives a narcissistic compensation: his skin is beautified by pigment (von Sydow, 1927). It seems likely that the basis for the use of pigment or for the right to paint oneself, etc., is an impulse to smear. In this connection it is interesting to compare the use of pigment by primitives with the habit of certain women to apply make-up only when menstruating. Their rationalizations that they are paler at such times, and similar excuses, do not conceal completely the underlying pleasure in smearing, nor the compensatory nature of the behavior.

The fact that my patients so frequently equate coprophagy and smearing as a way to make up for losses, combined with our knowledge about the meaning of oral rites of primitives during mourning (necrophagy, later funeral feast, etc.), suggests that the ceremony of smearing oneself with ashes as a

[6] Further discussion of the urethral regression is not attempted in this paper. The equation menstrual flow=urine, as in the 'flood dream' cited above, seems always to bring about an increase in the masculinity complex, as could be expected according to K. Horney's views.

sign of mourning may be interpreted as an attempt to reintroject the lost object by way of the skin, quite analogous to the cannibalistic (i.e., coprophagous) precedent.

I wish to introduce the following discussion by remarking that I can only provide hints and insufficient evidence to prove my points. However, it is tempting to inquire what role the compensatory impulse to smear, which we conceptualize as a displacement of libido, might play at the beginning of latency, i.e., at the time of the early formation of the superego. To begin with, we will have to make the very probable assumption that this procedure—the mechanism of smearing—is already constitutionally present in the psychic apparatus as *'anlage'*. It is probable because we have reason to believe that the mechanism originates at a time when the drive to retain feces and to restitute the lost body contents was paramount—namely, in the preceding anal-erotic phase of libido development. Obviously the impulse to smear in its crude form has been already repressed or transformed into some ego-syntonic mode in the postœdipal phase. Therefore, it is not contradictory to any psychoanalytic principles to assume that an impulse to smear is present in the early postœdipal phase. It arises as an attempt to repair the loss of anal values. In the early postœdipal phase, it appears in its later, modified form as an impulse to displace anal values onto the skin or surface of the body. We know too that the oral analogue of this anal-cutaneous displacement is also active at this time.

Let us look first at the characteristics of the girl's sexual organization in late infancy, when acceptance of castration as an accomplished, actual fact leads to renunciation of clitoris sexuality and to regressive revival of passive anal drives. These find their special expression in the wish for the 'anal child' (Freud, 1917, H. Deutsch, 1925). According to Deutsch, this represents the first thrust toward passivity which already anticipates the processes occurring during puberty. However, the wish for the child is never fulfilled and for this reason the œdipus complex is abandoned.

Now I propose to introduce a second assumption to the effect that the renunciation of the child (the 'anal child') is conceived of regressively and anal-symbolically as defecation. There is much evidence for the probability of this assumption (*cf.*, Freud, 1917). We must not forget that the interpretation of the menstrual function as castration is by no means exhaustive; menstruation means also the failure of the wish for the child. The rectal masses (anal chancre, carcinoma of the rectum) in the dreams of defecation and smearing by patients A and B represent anal children as well. Characteristically, B, like other female patients, felt menstruation to be not only an excretory function and a castration, but also a miscarriage. This is well known, of course, and I mention it only to strengthen my contention that the first important 'miscarriage', the renunciation of the wish for the child from the father, denotes defecation too. It demonstrates, moreover, that menstruation has the additional meaning of the loss of the anal child.

We would expect the girl to feel a need to undo the anal loss when she renounces the wish for an anal child and the desire for the father as love object. If my assumption proves correct, this need might find expression in two ways: 1, in coprophagous (or necrophagous) impulses, and 2, in impulses to smear.[7] Both of them are suitable to restore the object loss and it is conceivable that only one of these mechanisms operates or that both become effective in various proportions. We can assume the choice to be dependent on the strength of countercathexis against the various drives and, moreover, on how far they had become modified by ego-syntonic transformation. Constitutional preference for either mouth or skin may play its role in the choice too.

If the first (oral) compensatory tendency is prevalent, the result could be similar to that recently described by Sachs (1928). Oral wishes come to the fore and if there is complete renunciation of the father after the rejection, a true introjection with real superego formation takes place. If, however, the father is not given up as an object, a more primitive type of superego is formed. As depicted in Sachs's paper, the oral wishes then enter into the sexual act and a series of men become 'superegos' after having been 'incorporated via the vagina'. It is of interest, and seems to confirm my theory of the two possible directions, that Sachs's female patient, who had very powerful oral drives, showed an excessive lack of interest in

[7] I deliberately omit consideration of the 'masculinity complex'.

clothes and jewelry. Among other factors, this trait could have been conditioned by a preponderance of oral tendencies and a corresponding lack of compensatory needs with regard to skin or surface libido, in other words, a lack of the compensatory need to smear. I believe the oral wishes that arise out of the renunciation of anal œdipal desires are designed above all to compensate for this anal loss. In support of this idea, I cite the male masochist described by Sachs. Among other things he became actually coprophagous after analysis had removed his passive feminine position. I admit, of course, that oral regression can originate in other ways and can be due to other motives.

Let us take a close look at the second part of my contention: the anal loss after the passing of the œdipus complex is compensated for by smearing. A personality formed in this manner would correspond to the type described by Hárnik (1928). In another paper this author applied his theory concerning the vicissitudes of the libido during puberty to its fate in the postœdipal period. Renunciation of the penis leads to displacement of libido from the genital to the body surface. This finds ego-syntonic expression in overestimation of one's appearance. I readily agree with Hárnik on this point. Not only is it probable that events during puberty are repetitions of infantile precedents, but certain findings in three female patients confirm it.

All three of these patients passed through a period of infantile masturbation which ended because of castration fear. Their strong wish to receive an 'anal child' from the father likewise miscarried very early. All three experienced a latency period during which narcissistic fantasies predominated. One patient remembered her main fantasy vividly. She imagined herself in a beautifully starched, white dress, 'all clean and lovely'; then she went to see her father who praised her appearance. The second patient, who at an earlier stage had enjoyed smearing her dolls with mustard, had daydreams about beautiful clothes during latency. The third patient, even at the age of twenty-eight, showed an exaggerated interest in the most minute details of her person as well as her mind, and was excessively concerned with taking care of her body and appearance. Her narcissistic attitude began early in latency. At the time, the fantasy of being a 'small princess' who could enchant her whole environment through her 'personality' played an important role. With this fantasy she actually created her own private world.

These three cases seem to confirm Hárnik's view that displacement of libido from the genitals to the body can occur during the postphallic period. But in all three cases a phase of anal regression took place after the renunciation of the penis (clitoris masturbation, wish for the penis) and before the appearance of the narcissistic fantasies in latency. The anal regression was marked by the desire for an anal child. This wish was either given up or became burdened with strong guilt feelings. Whether the anal transitory stage is inevitably present during the process of displacement cannot be determined. It is most probable, however, that the thrust of libido derives its strength from the regressive fantasy of compensatory smearing. Furthermore, the concept of bodily beauty cannot be clearly separated from that of cleanliness—after all, wearing a nicely starched dress does increase beauty and cleanliness simultaneously. The high esteem in which this concept is held must derive in part at least from reaction-formation against anal soiling.

When the impulse to smear outweighs the one for oral incorporation—after the disappointment of the wish for the child—, then the complete or only partial renunciation of the father as love object may play a similar role, as does the oral regression in the patients described by Sachs. The three cases cited clearly demonstrate that object relationships may be given up in various degrees. Beautification (as in the first patient) obviously can aim at gaining the admiration of the father. This means that the libido does not necessarily become entirely narcissistic; it can still remain object-directed, at least in part. Be that as it may, a quantitative relation between body cathexis and that entering into the oral drives does seem to exist. The greater the one, the smaller the other. We know that the superego is formed by oral introjection. In cases where cathexis is mainly displaced to the body surface there will, therefore, be less oral libido available for the process of incorporation of objects. The result would be a less assimilated, less complete introjection and superego formation. Expressed in anal terms: what is smeared, does not need to be eaten. This factor together with the one mentioned by Sachs could be considered a second cause for the development of an incomplete superego.

III. ANAL EROTISM AND THE MECHANISM OF UNDOING*

A man of forty suffered from severe anxiety that he might cut off his penis while shaving, or injure this organ in some other way. His fears began after he had resorted to prostitutes during a period when his wife was suffering from a serious uterine illness. It was clear for many reasons that he regarded his intercourse with prostitutes as incestuous and unconsciously wished to harm himself by way of punishment. A curious manifestation of his self-punitive tendency was his preference for those prostitutes who worked as manicurists, that is, persons who might cut him. A second determinant for his self-castrative impulses was his identification through a sense of guilt with his wife, for whose illness he unconsciously accepted the blame. This brief sketch of the patient's psychic situation will furnish a background for an understanding of the following dream:

> I dreamed I had lost my penis, but in two segments, leaving the foreskin and the skin of the shaft hollow. I saw the two segments on the chair between my legs, but I felt no pain or fear. Then I went up on the roof of a tall building, and gleefully shouted, 'My penis is off.' A man on the street answered, 'You should worry! You can do that as often as you want.'

The patient associated the segmentary loss of the penis with defecation, and the hollow skin with vagina and anus. He commented on his going up to the roof, 'I guess I wanted to shout it from the house-tops'. The 'man in the street' he said was the proverbial representative of common sense. The latent content of the dream is clear: 'I wish my penis were a fecal mass. If I then lost my penis it would not be painful, I should have an anal vagina. I could shout from the house-tops that I am innocent and feel no guilt or anxiety; and common sense tells me that the loss would only be temporary, since in this

* [No. 10 in Bibliography.]

manner I can produce as many penises like that as I wish.' In the dream this man puts into effect his impulse to self-castration which is the source of his waking anxiety, but he does so without 'pain or fear'. His sense of guilt is satisfied by the castration, but the fear of permanently losing the penis is allayed by the reassuring thought that the castration is only temporary. We see then the economic value of his anal regression: for it is by virtue of equating penis with feces that he may expect new penises to replace the lost one. Hence the idea of castration, so painful at the genital level, loses its irreversibility.

The reversibility of the situation reminds us that the dream is constructed after the fashion of an obsessional symptom. The equation penis=feces permits the undoing (*Ungeschehenmachen*) of the castration. We have indeed two points of view from which to regard the same phenomenon: the id aspect of anal-sadistic satisfaction, and the ego aspect of defense. Waelder (1930) upheld the validity of considering psychic mechanisms from these standpoints, and maintained that the defense process of the ego may simultaneously serve as a vehicle of gratification for an id striving. Thus, he stated, the mechanism which, considered as a defensive function of the ego, we call 'identification' may be equally justifiably considered an oral gratification, if we think of it as a function of the id. The process called 'paranoid projection'—a defensive process of the ego—is also a process which gratifies a passive homosexual striving of the id.

Similarly in the dream, the defensive process, 'undoing', is seen to be itself a source of anal-sadistic gratification. Whereas the ego is concerned in undoing the castration, and the superego is gratified by the self-punishment, the id by the same process is indulging anal and sadistic impulses.

We have then a hint why *undoing* is a favorite defense mechanism in the compulsion neurosis, where an anal regression is cardinal. Freud (1917) tells us that the child's daily experience of parting with his feces may serve as a model for, or give content to, his fear of parting with his penis. This daily experience, however, is made less painful by the reassurance that tomorrow and the next day there will be more feces: that is to say, the loss will be 'undone'. This assurance is the forerunner of the one which our dreamer applied to genital castration, and which the compulsion neurotic applies to many other losses: they can be undone.

IV. THE BODY AS PHALLUS*

The knowledge that the whole body may serve as a symbol for the phallus dates back to Freud's discovery that in the manifest content of a dream, the penis may be represented by the dreamer's own body or by the body of another, frequently a child. In psychoanalysis, we are accustomed to a shorthand statement of this fact; we say, there is an unconscious equation of body and phallus, or of child and phallus.

The application of this finding to the psychology of the neuroses we owe primarily to Ferenczi (1916/1917b, 1927), who found that in hysteria the body as a whole, or nongenital parts of the body, may take over genital qualities. He was able to speak, for example, of organs other than the genital being 'in erection', and he invented the phrase 'the genitalization of the body'. In a case of schizophrenia, Tausk (1919) discovered that an 'influencing apparatus' described by the patient stood for the projected representation of her body and for her genital, and he epitomized the libidinal situation in the phrase: 'the whole body a genital'.

The equation, body=phallus, found other applications in psychoanalytic psychology. Hárnik (1923, 1928) discovered that a 'genitalization of the whole body' takes place normally in women at puberty and at the beginning of the latency period. Róheim (1932) found that primitive peoples regard the soul as a projected genitalized body—a symbol for both body and phallus; Sharpe (1930) emphasized the part played by the equation of body and phallus in the sublimation of dancing; and Hárnik (1932) and Flügel (1930) independently developed theories relating to clothes, which are in part based on the equation, body=phallus. Such works as Fuchs's *Sittengeschichte* contain numerous illustrations portraying a phallus clad as a little man.[1]

* [No. 17 in Bibliography.]

[1] *Cf.*, Fuchs (1909-1912) [Ed.].

The contributions referred to above applied the equation, body=phallus—or to use Tausk's expression, 'the whole body a genital'—in the fields of dream psychology, psychopathology, psychosexuality, ethnology, and the arts. The first attempt to explain how the entire body becomes unconsciously equated with the phallus, we owe to Abraham (1924a) who introduced the idea of the oral incorporation of a bodily part and the identification of one's entire body with this part. I shall return to a consideration of this important conception after I have reported certain manifestations of the equation, body=phallus, that are encountered in clinical psychoanalysis.

The Body a Phallus, the Mouth a Urethra

When the body is used to symbolize the phallus, the mouth may represent the urethra and the ejection of fluid from the mouth an ejaculation or urination. To illustrate this point I present the following striking dream:

> I am sitting with my little girl on my lap. I grasp her tightly by the shoulders and squeeze her. She vomits and the vomitus spurts straight out. I awaken and find I have had an emission.

The dreamer was a young man, who by way of the vomiting associatively identified himself with his wife during her pregnancy, and with the child. For my present purpose, I merely wish to point out the self-evident use of the child's body to represent the penis and vomiting to represent ejaculation.

A young woman patient reported a dream which in a sense is an antithetical companion piece of the one above.

> I was on board a small boat during a heavy storm. The boat pitched, and I slid back and forth in it and became seasick. I awoke vomiting.

Besides many associations dealing with pregnancy and prenatal existence, the patient associated the dream picture to a coitus. The motion of the boat suggested the motion of coitus; she herself was the penis sliding back and forth in the vagina. The vomiting she associated to earlier experiences of waking up and finding that she had had a liquid emission of a different sort—namely, urine. The waves, also, brought out associations relating to enuresis. Here again we find the body equated with a penis and the mouth with the urethra.

A very apt improper story illustrates exactly the idea that the mouth takes the place of the urethra when the body represents a phallus. The story is in the form of a conundrum. How, it is asked, can that little man sexually satisfy that big woman? The answer is: he puts his head and shoulders up her vagina, wiggles his ears, and vomits. This story neatly illustrates Freud's (1925a) and Ferenczi's (1927) contention that fantasies of 'returning to the mother' are 'coitus fantasies of the sexually inhibited'; it also illustrates the point that when the whole body stands for a phallus the mouth may stand for the urethra and vomiting for the orgasm.

The illustration from Frans Masereel's book of wood-cuts, *Das Werk* (Kurt Wolff, Munich), shows a gigantic figure, which—the preceding wood-cuts leave no doubt—symbolizes the phallus of a dreaming sculptor. 'Das Werk' is putting out a fire. Compare 'Das Werk's' technique with that of his gigantic colleagues, Gulliver (Ferenczi, 1927) and Gargantua. The ejection of water from the mouth is the analogue of the urination of the other two giants.

When the body represents the phallus, other bodily ejecta besides vomitus may represent a seminal ejaculation. More compactly than in any of my case material, this point is illustrated in a case which was presented by Lawrence S. Kubie at the Technical Seminar of the New York Psychoanalytic Society.[2]

This patient once stated that when he coughed he felt 'nauseated in his urethra'. The meaning of this statement became clear when the patient began to fantasy that his whole body was a penis. He wanted to be rubbed, and this, he said, was like having his penis rubbed; to rub another body with his body was like rubbing two penises together; to stand was to have an erection, to droop was to have a flaccid penis. Any excretion from his body, including vomitus, was like an ejaculation. In numerous ways he cross-equated semen, feces, and vomitus, and identified himself not only with a penis but also with a child and a fecal mass.

This identification with a so-called 'anal penis' will be discussed later.

[2] I wish to express my thanks to Dr. Kubie for the use of his notes and for permission to cite this material.

Other manifestations, besides vomiting, indicate the use of the mouth as a substitute for the urethra. A patient who was constantly expressing, in words, the fantasy that her whole body was a penis, reported her subjective feelings during a single day. She awoke lethargic, but gradually as the day wore on, she became more and more tense until she arrived at a plateau of tension. The tension consisted chiefly in an awareness of an increased sensitiveness of her skin and stiffness in her back. This state she compared *expressis verbis* to feelings in coitus interruptus. When she came to her analytic hour, in the afternoon, her back felt arched, as if it were about to raise her hips from the couch. Then, as she spoke during the hour, her tension disappeared in an 'outpour of words' which, she said, was her 'orgasm'.

Another patient equated her bodily sensations with those which might arise from an erect penis. As she lay in bed her body felt as if it were swelling and getting hot. It seemed to get longer; and as the tension and anxiety associated with this state increased, she felt an overwhelming urge to scream. Screaming she associated to a loss of sphincter control. The analysis showed that this tension repeated phallic sensations which she had had as a child when she was an unwilling passive witness to adult coitus. They were then frequently followed by enuresis; later by violent impulses to scream.

Since the work of Ferenczi (1924), it is well known that the flow of words is often unconsciously equated to a flow of urine, particularly in stammering. The topic of stammering will receive separate treatment in this paper. Here I shall merely refer to the fact that in stammerers whom I have analyzed, not only did the mouth stand for the urethra (and anus), but also the whole body was genitalized and represented the phallus.

The recognition of the fact that urethral qualities may be transposed to the mouth when the whole body represents a phallus may be useful in explaining a point in the origin of the character trait 'ambition'. Freud (1908a) first called attention to the fact that ambition is a trait of character frequently found in persons who in childhood had shown marked interest in the urinary function. Glover (1925) and Abraham (1924b), however, found that ambition is also an oral trait, fitting in with other traits to form what Abraham called an oral erotic character. The analysis of three very ambitious persons allows me to surmise how the oral erotism and the urethral erotism may be connected. All three of these patients had a great ambition to write; two were stammerers; all three constantly produced dreams and associations in which they represented their body as a penis and words as the flow from the penis which possessed magical qualities. The erect 'phallic' bearing of one of these individuals was very striking—in a transference fantasy he compared his body to a penis, the analytic room to a uterus, and his continual coming in and going out to coitus. Another of the patients dreamed that she was talking from a high mountain; as she spoke a cascade flowed from the mountain; when she ceased speaking it stopped. The dream represented the fulfilment of her wish to write a novel, for which she had already selected a title like 'The Cascade'.

It seems, therefore, that ambition may correctly be called a urethral character trait and an oral character trait; or in view of my material, a character trait depending on the displacement of urethral qualities to the mouth when the whole body represents a phallus.[3]

The role played by the fantasy of the whole body as a penis in early pregnancy and in fevers will receive separate treatment later in this paper.

The Body as Phallus, a Sign of a Postphallic Type of Libidinal Organization

So far I have described and discussed expressions in clinical psychoanalysis of the unconscious equation, body=phallus. I will now take up what might be called the deep psychology of this equation and discuss not by what signs the equation may be recognized, but by what mechanism it originates, and what its presence signifies in terms of libidinal organization.

Abraham (1924a) has answered the question, how does the equation originate? In his *Entwicklungsgeschichte der Libido,* he published two case reports in which the patients constantly identified their whole body with a penis. These patients unconsciously believed, and as the analysis progressed verbally fantasied, that they had become a penis because they had eaten one. Abraham worked out the unconscious mechanism in detail and found that the complete fantasy consisted in a biting off of the penis—that is, killing it—equating it thus to feces, then swallowing it, and by virtue of the swallowing and incor-

[3] In this paper so far, I have been dealing with vomiting as a representative of urethral (or anal) expulsion. At this point it is tangent to that of Hendrick (1931) and that of Hárnik (1931), who report cases in which vomiting, as an expulsion mechanism, is put to narcissistic use, to expel incorporated objects, or to prevent oral incorporation. The libidinal source of the vomiting in these cases could depend on a 'primary vomiting eroticism', yet especially in Hendrick's case, where the author emphasizes the 'phallic' bearing of the patient, the vomiting might well represent a displacement upward from excretory functions, according to the mechanisms to be described in this paper. Dr. Hendrick (in a personal communication) tells me that he regards the 'defense' as the primary motive in originating the vomiting and the erotic elements as due to secondary libidinization.

poration, making it one with the eater. The swallowing and incorporation produced the identification, which Abraham calls *partial,* that is to say, an identification with a bodily part of another person.

This process was neatly described by a patient of Ferenczi's (1927), cited in his paper, Gulliver Phantasies. The patient 'often dreamt of tiny little black men, and in one of her phantasies during free association she felt impelled to eat them. A quite spontaneous association to these thoughts was that of eating dark-colored fæces and then of biting and devouring a penis. By eating these up she felt that her whole body was in some way transformed into a male genital; in this guise she could in her unconscious phantasies have sexual intercourse with women.' In this same paper Ferenczi interprets fantasies of 'returning to the mother' as a coitus with the whole body instead of the penis.

A patient whom I analyzed frequently referred to his body when he meant his genital, and in dreams and fantasies constantly used his whole body for phallic purposes. Suddenly during the analysis he complained of a bad taste in his mouth, became nauseated, and began to utter a stream of obscene and scatologic words which he applied to all the persons and things in life that he held dear. He then frankly fantasied biting a penis and a breast. Analysis of his behavior showed that it was a way of expressing his early reaction to the sight of his father's penis. At that time he had eaten chalk and clay and drunk urine, and during the period succeeding, he had often fantasied biting off his father's penis and his mother's breast. The mechanism was that described by Abraham: the patient bit off the penis, equated it with feces, devoured it, and identified himself with it.

Frequently, as Fenichel (1932) states, the fantasy of fellatio in hysterias is a 'euphemistic expression for a more repulsive idea—to bite off the penis'. He gives as one of the four meanings of this fantasy, an identification with the man. In place of this identification, I have found more commonly that the fellatio fantasy—as cover for a biting fantasy—leads to an identification with the penis: the formula is then not 'I possess the penis I took from him' but rather 'I now am the penis I took from him'—and the male activities fantasied as ensuing from this identification make use of the whole body as the phallus.

We can now turn to the question, what is the sexual aim of the person who identifies his whole body with a penis? One aim was given above in discussing the views of Freud and Ferenczi on fantasies of 'returning to the mother': the idea may be used in the construction of a fantasy of coitus with the whole body as the penis. Other aims that have been referred to in this report, and in the contributions of the authors mentioned at the beginning of this paper, are urethral, anal, muscular, cutaneous, exhibitionistic, etc., covering most of the list of component erotisms. The question narrows then to a second question: what is the dominant sexual aim?

When the body represents a phallus, it means that a person has in fantasy eaten a phallus and identified himself with it; if he has become a phallus through identification, then it follows from what we know of identification that he has exchanged roles with the former object. A man who identifies himself with a woman takes over her role; similarly, the person who has identified himself with the penis takes over all the roles of a penis, but by virtue of the level at which the identification is made, the important role of the penis is—to be eaten. Logically, then, the sexual aim of a person who has in fantasy eaten the penis and become the penis is—to be eaten; and the fantasy is a sign of this unconscious wish.[4]

To leave logic and return to clinical facts, we must inquire whether there is empirical evidence for the thesis that the equation of one's body with a penis represents a wish to be devoured. To begin with the fantasy referred to several times in this paper, that of 'returning to the mother', sometimes erroneously referred to as 'intrauterine regression', I suggest that this is a genitally colored regressive variant of the Cronus myth: in place of an active penetration of the woman, the individual is swallowed *in toto*. Again this point seems related

[4] It might be objected that if this reasoning holds, then after every incorporation—not merely after an incorporation of the penis—the passive aim, to be eaten, should be dominant. But this is probably true in depressions (melancholia), too, for the ego, after incorporating the object orally, becomes passively masochistic to its superego and is 'gnawed', 'bitten' and 'stung' by conscience. The breast and the penis as partial objects and the total object in melancholia represent 'narcissistic object choice'. It remains to be learned whether the wish to be eaten follows an identification with less narcissistic antecedents.

to the well-known fantasy of the *vagina dentata.*

A young man, whose case was in part reported in another paper[5] had genitalized his whole body to a remarkable degree. His sexual life was disturbed by the fantasy that a set of teeth was concealed in the vagina of his sexual partner. This fantasy was a sign of his identification with the woman during coitus, for in his dreams he constantly represented himself as being bitten by snakes and rats, and these dreams of being bitten represented the gratification of passive homosexual wishes. Further analysis of this trend revealed that in early infancy he had enjoyed imagining that his father was eating him up. Curiously, then, in coitus with a woman he was disturbed by this infantile fantasy; her vagina became the father's mouth, and his penis, identified with his body, became the representative of himself in the infantile fantasy. His fear of castration was thus the equivalent of a fear of being eaten up by his father; and being eaten was a passive (feminine) fantasy.

In this case, as in several others where to bite and eat was the orally degraded representative of genital masculinity, to be eaten represented the corresponding feminine passive wish, and the fear of being eaten the fear of being made a woman (castrated).

This point was first touched on by Fenichel (1928a) in a brief paper entitled The Dread of Being Eaten. Two male patients of Fenichel's had the idea that to produce a girl baby, a boy must first go back into the mother, either by being 'stamped in' or 'swallowed'. In the mother he is deprived of his penis and then reborn a girl. Fenichel points out the obvious connection in these fantasies between the dread of being eaten and the fear of castration. He believes that the fantasy arises from an identification with a newborn child or fœtus, which analytically would also be a 'part' of the mother. He says that just as Freud has called the fantasy of returning to the mother 'the incest fantasy of the sexually inhibited', so the dread of being eaten is the corresponding 'fear of castration of the inhibited'.

I think Fenichel's and my own findings permit a bolder statement; namely, that the fantasy of one's whole body being a penis is symbolically a passive feminine fantasy, the equivalent of the phallic level fantasy of castration. The fantasy of

[5] See, *Smearing of Feces, Menstruation, and Female Superego,* pp. 12-25 [Ed.].

'returning to the mother' or of going into the mother with the whole body is a distortion of the idea of being eaten up. Fenichel's arguments on this score are particularly cogent. The specific anxiety connected with the idea of one's entire body being a penis is a fear of being eaten.[6]

Some details from the case history of a young woman patient will illustrate this point. This patient believed unconsciously in the existence of a penis in her mother and several other women. She often dreamed of overt sexual relations with her mother, in which her mother had a penis. Dreams of intercourse with phallic women were not accompanied by anxiety. Another type of dream was constantly accompanied by anxiety: in these she was represented as being in danger of falling over a precipice or into a canyon or lake. In childhood, the contents of such dreams had been falling off a bridge and drowning. In one dream, during her analysis, she was pursued by men and rescued herself by making her way hand over hand on a taut rope stretched across a deep chasm. She awoke with terror and a fear of falling. This dream occurred during a current situation with a man by whom she was figuratively being 'pursued', and her escape and fear of falling signified her attempt to avoid the situation. But interestingly, she depicted the danger of defloration (and castration) as a danger to her whole body, such as impending death from falling and the like, and her associations to herself dangling from the rope over the chasm were all to the effect that she was a phallus. The chasm, moreover, was described in strikingly oral terms: it 'yawned' beneath her, she feared she would be 'swallowed up', and the like. To fall, then, in genital terms meant to be castrated or deflorated, in oral terms to be swallowed.

The fear of being swallowed was related in this patient to a fear of pregnancy. For many months, with quite inadequate reason, she worried excessively when her menstruation was delayed, anxiously ruminating over the possibility of being pregnant. At such times she regularly had dreams of falling,

[6] To indicate how the child's animistic mode of thinking can endow inert objects with passive wishes and facilitate the child's identification with articles of diet, I report the following observation. A nurse was coaxing a four-year old to eat by saying: 'There's a little carrot wants to be eaten up. There's a little piece of bread wants to be eaten up' and so on—and succeeded in enormously interesting the child in the food.

such as the one referred to above, particularly of falling into water. The 'birth' symbolism in these dreams is of course well known; but the patient constantly referred to being 'swallowed' and 'sucked in' by the water. Numerous associations and symptoms showed that to become pregnant meant, for her, to eat a penis. In her fantasy of being pregnant, then, she had eaten a penis; she had, furthermore, identified herself with it and become a penis; and from this we might have deduced from our thesis that her aim (and fear) would be, to be eaten. Her manifest fear that she was pregnant, therefore, stood for an unconscious fear of being eaten. To be eaten, in this case, was an oral symbolic vehicle for the fear of castration—the feminine masochistic goal. This interpretation of the fear of being pregnant as equivalent to the fear of being eaten coincides with views expressed by Rado[7] on the basis of totally different material and working from a different point of view.

It might be asked at this point, why the *oral* phenomena connected with the fantasy that the body is a phallus should be emphasized; for it is evident that phallic, cutaneous, muscular, exhibitionistic, urethral, and anal strivings can be gratified through this fantasy. Abraham's contribution will support the statement that the identification of the body with the phallus is a special case of the more general mechanism of identifying the body with any bodily part; it represents the aim of a definite level of libidinal development; and so far as the cases which I have studied enable me to judge, we are dealing with a postphallic manifestation of this mechanism set into play by the influence of castration anxiety. To say, then, that the fantasy represents a regression to all the component strivings mentioned does not do justice to the relative importance of the oral factor. In the genital organization we also have component sexual strivings, but the nongenital ones are subordinated to the genital impulse; we speak of genital primacy and of nongenital forepleasures. Similarly and analogously, the non-oral impulses mentioned are subordinated under the dominance of the oral zone. We are dealing with a postphallic reorganization of the component impulses into an organization whose main aim is oral. The urethral, phallic, cutaneous, anal impulses and the rest should be regarded as subordinate or

[7] Rado, Sandor: personal communication.

accessory forepleasures in an organization in which there are two dominant erotic goals: (1) the active goal—to swallow a bodily part; (2) its passive counterpart—to be eaten up. It is a peculiarity of this organization and of the nature of the aims that the attainment of the active goal—the devouring of the part—produces an identification of the subject with the part and leads to the reversal of aim into the passive form.

That the favorite part chosen for incorporation at this stage should be the phallus is presumably due to the influence of the preceding early genital stage of development. All authors concur that the fantasy of being a phallus is characteristic of women rather than men; when it occurs in men it seems closely connected with their feminine identification. I suggest that the discovery of their 'castration' in little girls, with its emphasis on the importance of this *part* of the body, accounts for the greater distribution of this fantasy among women. That persons should insist that their whole body is a penis testifies to the persistence of the wish to have a penis, and fulfils this wish in an 'illusory' fashion (Rado, 1933a).

A postphallic regression to the oral level has been invoked by Freud (1923a) to explain superego formation. Sachs (1928) has explained certain types of female genitality by referring to a postphallic oral motivation (*Antrieb*). Hárnik (1928) has described a postphallic genitalization of the entire body. Helene Deutsch (1925, 1932), though emphasizing the anal aspect, has pointed out the importance of the postphallic *'Passivitätsschub'*.

The nature of my material unfortunately does not permit me to determine which elements in this postphallic reorganization arose from the prephallic organization recently described by Freud (1931). The primitive dread of being eaten up, referred to by Freud, may well have contributed to the genesis of the type described in the present paper. It may well be that the fear of being eaten up by the mother, after the 'shift to the male', may be covered by derivatives, such as a fear of pregnancy, a fear of infection, and the like, in which incorporation of the phallus enters into the construction.

Nosological Distribution of the Equation

The fantasy of the whole body as a phallus was discovered by Abraham in two cases, one a hysteria in which the presenting symptom was vomiting, the other a cleptomania. Of the patients whose material I am using in this paper, four were men, five were women. One of the women had typical anxiety hysteric symptoms; one woman and one man had outspoken compulsion neuroses; two men and three women showed a symptomatology which was predominantly hysterical, but which had many depressive features; one man had a 'character neurosis'.

Naming the formal 'diagnoses' of these cases is of no particular value so far as the understanding of the role played by the equation (and its unconscious sources) in the symptomatology is concerned. The possible exception to this statement is the group referred to with mixed hysteric and depressive symptomatology. Here the genitalization of the body and the orality were conspicuous. Such cases are doubtless often described as 'hysterical depressions' or as hysterias which show introjection (Feigenbaum, 1926; Fenichel, 1932). Here the equation and the organization in question may be intimately connected with the basic unconscious dynamics which give rise to the form of the neurosis. Otherwise, the finding explained or helped to explain individual features in the neuroses, rather than the nosogenesis.

Thus, in one compulsion neurotic, the genitalization of the body chiefly served to explain the gravidophobia which appeared from time to time, to which reference was made above. In the 'character disorder', it was related to a fear of being infected, which appeared as a transient complication during analysis. It seemed to throw light on stammering. Probably the genitalization of the body and its related oral mechanism plays a role in those phobias which have an oral coloring, such as gravidophobia or fear of infection, in a manner analogous to the anal element in agoraphobia, which Helene Deutsch (1928) first reported. The anxiety in such cases would mean among other things, the fear of being eaten.[8]

Stammering and the Body as Phallus

The role played by nongenital elements in the deep psychology of stammering has occupied the attention of several analytic writers. The displacement of the 'magical' value orig-

[8] For a discussion of the role of the pregenital components in anxiety hysteria, and the tendency to incorporation, see Fenichel (1932): *Outline of Clinical Psychoanalysis.*

inally attributed to the excretions onto speech has been given special emphasis by Ferenczi (1925). The flow of speech is equated with the flow of urine, the expulsion of feces, and the passing of flatus. The oral sadistic element in the neurosis has been emphasized by Coriat (1928).

My sole reason for introducing the topic of stammering in this paper is to record an impression of the interrelation of the pregenital aims which I obtained from two patients.

One of these was a sort of Demosthenes, who had been a stammerer in his youth and now prided himself on his oratorical ability and eloquence. He had many fetishistic traits, and in his unconscious, firmly believed in the existence of a female penis. Coitus with a woman was followed by a fear of infection, which was not only a representative of a fear of castration, but also included an identification with the woman by virtue of which he could think himself pregnant. In his dreams fellatio practiced on him figured largely and proved on analysis to represent an identification of his body with the maternal breast—his penis represented the nipple, his partner a child. His bearing was 'phallic', he constantly compared his whole body to the penis in fantasies of 'returning to the mother'; and in the analysis where the analyst played the transference role of a hated mother, he overtly fantasied having coitus with the analyst with his whole body as a penis. He constantly used his speech as a sadistic weapon and compared it to urine and flatus. His ambition has been referred to elsewhere in this paper.

The female patient had also stammered in her youth and overcame the defect by developing a 'self-curative' obsessional neurosis. She preserved a strong belief in the magical efficacy of words, which she had displaced from excrementitial functions. Her gravidophobia and its oral basis, as well as her identification of her body with a phallus, have been discussed in the preceding pages; and her ambition was referred to in the discussion of that topic. It will be recalled that she had extensively 'genitalized' her body and 'urethralized' her mouth. She constantly emphasized her oneness with her mother, closely pursued her mother's career, and reacted with anxiety to any effort to separate her from her mother. Her dreams showed that such a separation stood for (1) the mother's castration—this was manifested in dreams in which the mother was represented as losing a penis; (2) an ablation of the mother's breast—represented by a fear that her mother might have a cancer of the breast; and (3) a miscarriage by the mother—manifested in dreams of mother substitutes having miscarriages and accidents. In all three instances, she identified herself with the part of the mother which would be removed—penis, breast, fœtus.

In both patients the belief in the mother's phallus was unmistakable, as was their identification with it.

It seemed that the oral-sadistic aim was the chief or central aim in their stammering, the ideational content—to ablate the breast—being displaced by way of the equation, breast=penis, to the phallus; that the fantasied incorporation of the phallus led to an identification of themselves with it; that this in turn led to the 'urethralization' and 'analization' of the mouth, the 'excrementalization' of the flow of speech, and to stammering. In other words, I suggest that in these cases of stammering, the same situation occurred which I postulated for ambition: when the body becomes a phallus, the mouth becomes a urethra (and anus); and the stammering is a function of the reorganized libidinal arrangement.

The Body as Phallus in Fevers and Pregnancy

When a patient is stricken by a fever during analysis, he will usually report his associations relating to the fever. In these associations, it often happens that the fever is regarded as a pregnancy, or that the hot sensitive body is used to represent an erect penis. Not infrequently this idea is elaborated into a fantasy of 'returning to the mother'.

To one of my patients, who went through an infectious illness during her analysis, itching of her entire bodily surface—a symptom of the illness—was directly associated to genital itching which had occurred in infancy when, during an illness, her bed had been moved to the parents' room. Other patients have compared being sponged and bathed while ill to genital masturbation. It is not necessary to multiply examples of the genitalization of the body during a general infection: a reference to Ferenczi's (1916/1917b) discussion of inflammation and erotization will suffice. We are evidently dealing with a 'pathoneurosis' in which the entire body is the physically affected structure that is libidinized. The fantasy of the whole body as a penis is the psychological counterpart of the organically determined libido placement. Individual symptoms have correlated libidinal counterparts; body itching is aligned with genital itching; anorexia, nausea, vomiting, etc., with coprophagia or urinary fantasies.

If we take into consideration the libidinal changes that accompany an organic illness, there is little wonder that many hysterical symptoms are patterned on earlier organic illnesses; or that—as the Wolf-man's malaria reminds us—illnesses in infancy should have important psychological consequences. More obscure is the problem in which apparently organic, 'individual' features of an ordinary infectious illness are determined by the nature of earlier illnesses.

Can the genitalization of the body in fevers be an outcome of the same process which seems to lead to genitalization in the neuroses—namely, the oral incorporation of a penis? The question reminds us of the other associations to febrile illness, those relating to pregnancy. This pregnancy is thought of as originating orally—as is the infection.

This second interpretation of fevers, as a fantasied pregnancy, naturally leads us to consider the psychology of pregnancy, for the symptoms of pregnancy can also be thought of as arising on a 'pathoneurotic' basis. Helene Deutsch (1925) has ably dealt with this complicated subject. Here I should merely like to point out the operation in the early stages of pregnancy of the unconscious fantasy that the whole body is a phallus. The symptoms which seem to be manifestations of this equation are the vomiting and gustatory disturbances, which depend on fellatio and coprophagic fantasies (Deutsch), loss of appetite, the classical 'picas'—cravings for articles of food which are phallic symbols—and cutaneous sensitiveness.

When such symptoms appear during an analysis, transiently, we rightly suspect that the patient is reporting an unconscious fantasy of pregnancy and regard the oral symptoms as dependent on ideas of oral insemination and as manifestations of unconscious ideas of fellatio and coprophagia. Yet they are strikingly similar to those which arose, say, in the case of hysterical vomiting analyzed by Abraham, from which he arrived at the conception of partial incorporation. Hence, I am encouraged to offer the suggestion that the libidinal organization in the early stage of pregnancy is of the type so frequently mentioned in this paper: dominance of the aim of incorporating the penis (equated with feces) with resultant identification, so that the whole body becomes a phallus. The vomiting then would be not only a sign of unconscious coprophagia, but also of the unconscious aim to urinate like a penis.

The Specific Phallus and the Specific Body in the Equation, Body=Phallus

The statement that the whole body represents a penis is not sufficiently specific; for completeness of understanding we must know whose body and whose penis are referred to. Mathematically speaking, there are four possibilities:

(1) One's own body is one's own penis.
(2) One's own body is another's penis.
(3) Another's body is one's own penis.
(4) Another's body is another's penis.

(1) The equation, *one's own body=one's own penis,* is not, I believe, found in the neuroses. The penis referred to in the neuroses belongs to an object, even though superficial appearances may suggest that it is the subject's. The clearest example of one's own penis being one's own body is Tausk's case, in which the schizophrenic patient identified the 'influencing apparatus' with her own body and her own (imaginary) penis. Probably, this equation will be found in schizophrenia; it may, in that disorder, represent the unconscious content of certain fantasies of coprophagia and sadomasochistic auto-fellatio. By analogy, the schizophrenic content of the process of incorporating a bodily part of one's self should be: biting off one's own penis, equating it to feces, swallowing it, and thus becoming one's own penis.

Neurotic fantasies may deceptively give the impression of an identification of one's own body with one's own phallus. This is the case, for example, where the patient 'returns to mother' using his whole body as a penis; and in this paper I have referred to patients whose total bodily sensations were reminiscences and adult equivalents of infantile genital sensations. Yet these persons were identifying their body, not with their own penis, but with the penis of the father in an œdipal situation.

If the schizophrenic reincorporates his own phallus and identifies himself with it according to the hypothetical sequence of processes outlined above, it would throw light on Alexander's (1932, p. 143) idea that in schizophrenia self-castration serves a passive erotic rather than a punitive purpose.

(2) The second variant of the equation, *one's own body = another's penis,* is the one most frequently encountered in the analysis of the psychoneuroses. All the cases referred to in this paper, on which the discussion of vomiting, stammering, ambition, and the rest was based, demonstrate this form of the equation: the patient identified himself with a parental phallus. Usually this phallus was the father's—as in the two cases originally reported by Abraham—but in some instances the patient identified his body with the phallus of the mother.

The importance of the idea that there is a maternal penis has been made evident by Freud's (1927) paper on fetishism. It was with this fantasied phallus of the mother that two of the patients reported in the present paper constantly identified themselves, and the idea appeared transitorily in several other cases.

A patient who had transferred her hostility from her mother to men in the fashion recently described by Freud (1931) had the following dream: The analyst was in bed and she was lying at right angles to him at the level of the genitalia; she then said to him, 'I shall leave you'. Her associations dealt with her wish to leave the analysis, which she associated further with a wish to leave her mother; her position in bed she associated to the position of the analyst's penis, and she arrived at the idea, 'If I leave you it will be like removing your penis'. She had often fantasied overtly that her mother had a penis, and as her orientation to the analyst was the same as to her mother, her identification of her body with the analyst's penis seemed based on an identification with the removable penis of the mother.

The idea of one's body being the mother's penis is closely related to the idea of being a child at her breast, or a fœtus within her; and doubtless many 'birth dreams' are overdetermined and refer to the castration of the mother. Fenichel

(1928a) pointed out the identification with the newborn child or fœtus in the fantasy of being eaten up. A female patient reported a 'birth dream' which seems pertinent to this discussion. She was being born; as her head passed the vulva, her mouth and lips rubbed over the mother's clitoris and labia; the process went no further and she remained in this position. She associated first to early cunnilingal practices with her sister, then went on to ideas of suckling and remaining permanently at her mother's breast, 'hanging from it like a little opossum'. To hang from her mother's vulva, she thought, was like 'being a penis'.

Another patient, a man who believed firmly in the existence of a female penis, whose love choice was dependent on what for him were phallic qualities in a woman, and who had, indeed, frequented houses of prostitution where the women would strap on an artificial penis before cohabiting with him, began the practice of cunnilingus with his wife after she had had a miscarriage. He compared this act to penetrating her with his whole body and becoming her baby in the uterus, and one of its intentions was to make amends to her for the miscarriage for which he felt responsible. Deeper analysis showed that he unconsciously thought of the miscarriage as his wife's castration, and that the cunnilingus made him her penis and restored her to an uncastrated condition.

In many ways it is possible to think of cunnilingus as the perversion of which the fantasy of one's body being a penis (and its neurotic expression) is the negative.

(3) The third variant of the equation, *another's body = one's own penis,* is clearly seen in the common identification of one's penis with the whole body of a child. Several dreams cited in this paper will serve as examples, if they are necessary—for the narcissistic evaluation of the child as an 'anal penis' is too well known to warrant detailed discussion. The idea that a child's body is one's own penis also figures in the classical fantasy described by Freud (1919)—'a child is being beaten'.

(4) The fourth variant, *another's body = another's penis,* according to Freud, is an equation by virtue of which women normally proceed in their sexual development from the desire for a penis to the desire for a mate. The familiar equation, child=parent's penis, is also an example of this variant.

Summary

In summary, the following conclusions may be drawn from this consideration of the fantasy of the whole body being a penis:

1. The fantasy is a passive counterpart of the fantasy of eating the penis and represents an identification of the body with the penis.

2. The dominant sexual aim of the organization represented by the fantasy is to be eaten up, and this idea is an equivalent of the castration fantasy.

3. Other, subordinate aims are analogous to forepleasure. These are urethral, anal, muscular, cutaneous, phallic, etc. A table will help clarify some of the symbolic relations between the body and the phallus:

Body	*Phallus*
Hat, clothes, fur, hair, skin.	Prepuce, condom (Hárnik).
Mouth (other portals).	Urethra.
Vomitus and other ejecta (tears, saliva, etc.), voice, speech, screams, literary productions, etc.	Semen, urine.
Muscular and vascular tension, postural erectness.	Erection.
Rubbing (massage, baths, etc.).	Masturbation.
Relaxation (sleep, narcosis, death, etc.).	Detumescence.

To be Eaten	*Coitus*
'Return to mother's uterus' (body-uterus).	Vagina dentata (fellatio) (mouth-penis).

4. The fantasy is characteristically part of a postphallic reorganization of the libidinal components.

5. There are four variants of the fantasy according to whether one's own body or the body of another person is equated with one's own penis or the penis of another person.

V. CLAUSTROPHOBIA*

The technical term claustrophobia, introduced into medical literature by Raggi of Bologna in 1871, means literally a dread of being enclosed. There are several forms such a dread may take, and several fears that are akin to it, but current linguistic usage tends to limit the application of the term to a special type of fear dramatized for us by Poe in The Pit and the Pendulum—a fear of being caught or crushed by a gradual closing in of the space about one. This definition, which will be followed in the present essay, would exclude such fears as that of entering a closed space, which might, if one wishes, be considered 'claustrophoboid'; but the reason for this strict definition will become clear as we proceed.

Claustrophobia is a type of morbid fear, a form of anxiety hysteria, yet despite the numerous detailed studies of anxiety hysteria to be found in the psychoanalytic literature, there are nevertheless few references concerning this particular phobia. Jones (1912, p. 256) in one place remarks that dreams and fantasies concerning one's own birth are very common especially in childhood and that these fantasies constitute the basis of such phobias as being buried alive or being shut in an enclosed space (i.e., claustrophobia) and many others. Ferenczi (1922) too refers to the association between claustrophobia and the idea of being within one's mother: 'The psychoanalysis of numerous dreams and of neurotic claustrophobia explains the fear of being buried alive as the transformation into dread of the wish to return to the womb' (p. 357). Elsewhere Ferenczi (1909, pp. 50-51) states that claustrophobia and a fear of being alone in any closed room in one of his patients developed from an attempt to overcome masturbation.

These valuable comments establish for us a relationship

* [No. 23 in Bibliography.]

Read before the Thirteenth International Psychoanalytic Congress at Lucerne, 1934.

between manifest claustrophobia and latent fantasies of being within the mother's body, but so far no author (except Melanie Klein in passing) has considered the *specific* anxiety in claustrophobia, as this phrase is defined by Freud (1925a) in Inhibitions, Symptoms and Anxiety. The question—of what is the claustrophobic afraid?—has not been adequately answered. This essay will attempt to answer this question, in terms of specific anxiety and specific measures of defense.

A young woman of thirty had ordered her life in general so as to escape marriage and the male sex. A business woman, she affected masculine ways and consorted almost exclusively with women. For sexual pleasure she masturbated or, occasionally and casually, engaged in mutual masturbation with another woman. Men were often interested in her, for she was good-looking, clever, and wealthy, but with the remote approach of an intimate relationship they would find themselves baffled by alternations in her of tense moodiness and inept sudden aggressiveness; they would find her unaccountable and give her up as a bad job. Twice this patient had severe attacks of claustrophobia. One of these was in her berth on a sleeping car. She was on her way to spend some time with a married friend. This friend's husband had once caressed her, and it was while returning from the dressing room at the end of the car that the patient thought of this particular matter and felt a certain expectancy at seeing him again. Lying in her berth then she heard a man's footsteps as he passed by, and she was seized by fear. Subjectively this fear was marked by the feeling that the walls of the berth were closing in on her, by inability to catch her breath, by an intense warmth accompanied by sudden perspiration. She cut the attack short by jumping up and running into the dressing room. Her other claustrophobic attack occurred while she was spending some time at a friend's country place. Without her knowledge a young man had been invited there to meet her, and it was while in bed that she experienced the same fear as on the train.

The analysis of these two incidents was accompanied by several interesting 'transference phenomena' and transient symptoms. Thus she stated that she felt enveloped in an armor which the analyst's voice could not penetrate, then suddenly in terror exclaimed sharply, 'Don't touch me!'. While she was on the couch, the analyst was accidentally called out of the room and returning found her lying flexed on one side in the so-called fœtal posture. It was learned that she had rearranged the furnishings of her two-room apartment: all the things in the sitting room that possessed any emotional value for her, excepting her piano, which was too large,—her books, pictures, desk, and the rest, were crammed into her bedroom, and there she read or worked cozily in bed, with all her prized belongings crowded about her.

The terror of being touched appeared then in her dreams. In one of these a man identifiable as the analyst kicked a boat lying in drydock, which then plunged forward into the water. In another dream a long pole was violently pushed through a window pane into the room where she was lying; she grasped the pole in alarm and tried to pull it away from the man who was pushing it in. It became evident that the patient was imagining herself a fœtus in the maternal body—but this idea itself did not cause anxiety. Indeed, on the contrary, this was an idea of safety or defense. The anxiety arose when the defensive wall was threatened, that is to say, when the penis entered or threatened to touch her. This case therefore answers one aspect of the question posed above as to what it is that the claustrophobic fears. The intrauterine fantasy is one of defense (flight) and relief from anxiety; the anxiety arises with the idea of being disturbed or dislodged by the father or father's penis.

A second anxiety situation arises when the intracorporal status is interrupted by the fantasy of being born. The patient described above, after being comfortably settled in her bedroom and after becoming aware of her conflict and what it was she was fleeing, decided to come out. This she did symbolically by moving her belongings back into her sitting room, to the accompaniment of typical dreams of being born, needless to relate here, from which she would awake in anxiety; and at the level of the current situation, after this symbolical rearrangement, she was able to make a psychological rearrangement as well. She entered her first love affair and was deflorated at her next menstruation.

Briefly then this case showed that the idea of being a child within the mother is a defense fantasy, and that while this idea is sustained there is no anxiety. The anxiety appears linked to one of two contingencies. The first of these is of being dislodged or disturbed by parental coitus, by the father's penis or by his pressure on the mother's body (and it is this latter version that determines the central claustrophobic symptoms we would call classical); or of being born. This second idea—of birth—has numerous connotations and is sometimes reducible to the first situation according to the fantastic tocology: 'I am being forced out of mother by father's pushing on her abdomen'.

In the case under discussion, the birth process was supposed to be started by the father according to the enema principle: father in coitus urinates into mother's anus and the mother expelling the urine flushes the child out with it. (A variant of this idea has the mother bursting open from being overfilled with water.)

The infantile material in this patient concerned an observation of parental intercourse (reconstructed from screen memories) and memories of her mother's pregnancy and the birth of a sibling when the patient was three years old. Early masturbation was accompanied by ideas of parental coitus with herself in the uterus. Obviously, some information concerning coitus and pregnancy is needed to give rise to such fantasies. During her analysis then, the fear of a male approach reactivated the fears attaching to these early fantasies. Dr. Monroe A. Meyer has told me of a case of true claustrophobia in which it was found that as a child the patient had actually retired into enclosed spaces to masturbate; I should interpret this as probably an acting out of the ideas referred to above.

In another case a puberty claustrophobia was combined with a fear of going blind. This patient slept for many years in the parental bedroom, was constantly present at, and aware of, parental intercourse, and barely missed witnessing the birth of a younger child. Her anxiety attacks were especially marked by an attendant, almost asthmatic, difficulty in breathing, and it was from this patient that I learned an interesting theory of how a baby breathes while he is in the mother's body. The baby lies in the body immersed in water. When the mother urinates the water is partly drained off and its level sinks. The baby's head floats at the top, like the bell float in an old-fashioned water-closet tank. The water-closet tank, indeed, suggested the theory. The baby's head comes up as it were for air, the baby inhales, and as in the tank the water gradually rises and immerses the head again completely. Another patient came upon precisely the same idea, which played an important role in furnishing the latent content for early anxiety dreams. In these dreams the patient was under water rising to the surface, but her head always met the bottom of a boat or some structure that prevented its coming to the surface. The later neurosis of this patient, which unfortunately cannot be reported, affected chiefly the respiratory function.

The questions that arise in the child's mind concerning the embryo, its origin and physiology, its life in the uterus, and the cause of its ultimate birth, with the infantile and childhood theories designed to answer these questions, leave their mark in fantasy, dream, and symptom. In the illustrations given above I have pointed out the prominence of skin and respiratory phenomena attending the fantasy of being a fœtus. Skin and chest sensations are particularly prominent in claustrophobic anxiety. Several analytic observers have been struck by the erotic skin and respiratory phenomena of early infancy and some have speculated on intrauterine libido organizations dominated by the skin or by the apnœic respiratory tract. Aside from this, however, there is no doubt about the prominence of these two fields in connection with the *fantasy* of being in the mother, and they are bound up with ideas concerning the tactile sensations and the breathing of the fœtus.

The process which initiates the fantasy of being in the mother's body is the familiar one of partial identification through oral incorporation. In several instances the fantasy was preceded by active oral aggression. This was true historically in the case reported at the beginning of this paper, where the mother's pregnancy led the three-year-old girl to bite everything and everybody in tantrum-like rages. The latent wish is to bite or destroy the fœtus by an oral attack. The fantasy gratification of this wish leads to an identification with the fœtus, thought of as a quasi-part of the mother's body. In some instances of this identification process, a checking of the oral-sadistic wish led to its reversal into the opposite,—that is, a wish to be eaten by the mother, but with the same consequences, for after being ingested the wisher found himself in the mother's body in place of the fœtus. In one case this reversal was indicated in a series of dreams, in the first of which coitus with the pregnant woman was undertaken with a 'biting penis', a snake, later with a rat; finally after the reversal, by means of a cucumber, which disappeared for good. In an interesting footnote in her book The Psychoanalysis of Children, Melanie Klein (1932, p. 329) remarks that claustrophobic anxiety, in some forms, appears to be connected with the idea of being shut up within the mother, which may be then deflected and limited to the genital, so that it consists in a fear of being unable to disengage the penis. She relates this to the infantile fear of both parents united in coitus and of being castrated by the father's penis in the mother's body. This finding would not be at variance with the ideas put forward in my account, namely, that the entrance into the mother is conceived as an eating or a being eaten. Indeed fantasies of entering the mother through some other portal than the mouth are quite probably distortions of this one.

The central claustrophobic fantasy according to the definition we are using is the fear of being expelled from the mother's body by the crushing, flushing, or other activity of the father. From this would radiate certain other combinations of ideas concerning coitus and the mother's body that would give rise to related fears. Thus, the fear of entering an enclosed space, as in the case reported by Oberndorf (1915), has among its latent ideas the one that the enclosure is the mother's body; however, the person who fears to enter does not identify himself with a fœtus but with a phallus. Yet the underlying dynamics are very similar, for the identification with the fœtus or with the penis is of the same sort,—an identification of the person's body with a part (or quasi-part) of another person through a fantasied oral ingestion of this part.

The identification of one's self with the penis may instructively be compared with the identification with a fœtus. Both originate through an oral incorporation of the 'part' and the ensuing identification with it.[1] But the penis and its functions are well known, whereas the fœtus and its behavior, how it lives

[1] See *The Body as Phallus*, pp. 28-47 [Ed.].

and breathes, are in the main unknown and only to be guessed at by the inquisitive child. Thus it is that in contrast with the almost uniform ideas concerning the penis and what it can do, the ideas as to what the fœtus is like and what the fœtus can do are very diverse.

Claustrophobic anxiety, to summarize, is correlated with the idea of being disturbed while an embryo in the mother's body, especially by parental coitus. The antecedent of the fantasy of being a fœtus is an oral aggression against a real fœtus, which leads to an incorporation of and identification with the fœtus, the incorporation and identification being of the type known as 'partial'; and the fantasy takes its form and ideational content from early childhood theories of gestation, embryology, and birth.

THE PSYCHOLOGY OF MANIA

Lewin's papers on the psychology of hypomania form a logical bridge between the clinical studies centering around re-incorporation into the claustrum of the mother's body and the oral triad of wishes which grew out of his study of the dream screen. By analyzing meticulously the details his patients reported about their hypomanic attacks, Lewin was able to demonstrate not only the multiple identifications which take place during hypomania, but also derivatives of a fantasy of incorporating and being incorporated. This observation corroborated Freud's assertion that mania is a fusion of the ego with the superego, and Rado's comment that this fusion is an accurate intrapsychic repetition of the union with the mother while nursing at the breast.

J. A. A.

I. ANALYSIS AND STRUCTURE OF A TRANSIENT HYPOMANIA*

It was my good fortune to observe a definite hypomanic attack of seven days' duration, which arose, developed and subsided during the analysis of a person with predominantly hysterical symptoms. The initial presenting symptoms of the hysteria were marked photophobia and sensitiveness to noises. The hypomanic attack occurred one month after she had been in analysis. To provide a background for the understanding of this episode I shall give a very brief account of the pertinent facts in her history.

The patient was an unmarried woman in the early thirties, reared in a puritanical home. Her father, a gentle ineffectual dreamer; her mother a rigid conventional person, with whom the patient had for a long while been on openly hostile terms; and a brother six years her junior, toward whom she was affectionate but 'bossy', made up the household. Of her infantile sexual life, the important facts will appear in the discussion of her transient hypomania. Masturbation was never abandoned, and her prepubertal period and puberty were filled with overt sexual games and fantasies. The latter included rape and prostitution fantasies, frank fantasies of coitus with her brother, and a dream of overt sex relations with her father. In this dream, she and the father faced each other, kneeling, his penis touching her vulva. They remained perfectly immobile, and he urinated on her genital. This procedure corresponded to her theory of adult sexual intercourse. A game played with another little girl depicts a somewhat different theory of coitus. Each would alternately be the 'man' or the 'woman'; the 'man' would expose the 'woman'. The daydream in common was that they were in a crowded public place such as a market square. The game ended by both parties

* [No. 11 in Bibliography.]

urinating. The patient suggested that they suck each other's breasts, but the other child was not willing. Dreams of women with a penis and open envy of her brother's penis attest to her bisexual interest. At college she was unhappy, and an attack of photophobia, headaches, and 'mucous colitis' associated with fears of syphilitic and tuberculous infection interrupted her studies and forced her to return home. The free sexual language of her fellow students had stimulated her sexual fantasies and 'shocked' her. She deflorated herself at twenty with a candle, tearing the hymen slightly, and with the pain experienced an intense vaginal orgasm. True to her conception of adult intercourse, she kneeled and held perfectly still during the act.

Two years before her analysis her grandmother's death precipitated a depression, in which she accused herself 'of all the things in grandmother I didn't like'. Following this she felt peculiarly well and free and entered her first love affair.

Her choice was narcissistic according to the formula: I love what I should like to be. She identified herself intensely with her lover in his interests. The affair was very sensual and very stormy. It ended by her own unconscious but evident contrivance. Actually the precipitating event was an act of fellatio. While the penis was in her mouth she imagined that a baby must have the same sensation when his mouth is filled by a nipple; for a baby, the nipple must have the same relative proportion to the mouth as the penis had for her as an adult.[1]

By the time the transient hypomanic attack began the patient's initial symptoms had gradually disappeared. The attack was precipitated by a very definite incident. Arriving in my office a quarter of an hour earlier than usual she heard me conversing with a woman. That hour she lay morosely on the couch refusing to speak, rushing to the bathroom at the end of the hour where she vigorously washed her hands. The next day she told me that she had fantasied that I was having sexual relations with the woman, and that she had been sexually excited and angry. Her associations then dealt with persons being surprised in the act of coitus, attempts she had made to spy on her former lover and the mistress who succeeded her, and stories of analysts seducing patients.

[1] Compare this fantasy with the dream analyzed by Abraham (1924a, p. 436).

Three days after the traumatic eavesdropping, she entered the room in marked good humor. She lay down, but was on her feet several times to get her handkerchief, close her purse, and the like. She pounded the pillow and rearranged the cloth covering it. She spoke with push, allowed no interruption, and chuckled as she related apparently banal stories of how much she had enjoyed this or that conversation, and how well she had accomplished her tasks. The next day her push and restlessness continued, and she was chuckling now because of a funny dream. She had dreamt: 'I was in church or at a class, and the preacher or teacher was reading from the Bible in French. It was responsive reading: first he read a line, then the congregation the next one, and so on. Then all except a Miss Z quit reading.' She commented, 'I have to laugh when I think of this dream.'

The *church* she disliked as a child, attended to please her mother, but had to be allowed to take her dolls and playthings with her. *French*: erotic literature, loose sex habits. Her photophobia at school had arisen while she was studying languages. *Reading the Bible in French*: sneaking in the erotic surreptitiously, something clandestine. *Preacher or teacher* suggest the analyst and indirectly her former lover. *Responsive reading* means something mutual that goes back and forth, the fitting of two parts to make sense. Miss Z is a paranoid spinster who believes that a certain conspicuously proper physician is having affairs with his patients. Miss Z has been spying on him. The patient is indignant over Miss Z's attitude. At this point she related a dream which had preceded the one given above: 'I was hastily dressing to go to church where I had been asked to take the minister's place. I had trouble packing my bag with an exhibit I was to show there.' The *bag* was the one she had used on clandestine journeys with her lover.

The dreams were evidently precipitated by her analytic situation, as her associations show. In the first dream she surreptitiously gains sexual pleasure from what she hears (sexual sounds in a 'foreign' language). The playthings and her packing indicate her masturbational impulses; the responsive reading is a coitus. Miss Z is her repudiated 'unconscious insight'. She herself appears in a passive role as one of the responsive congregation. In the second dream she expresses her wish to take the place of the man.

An unavoidable absence of two days intervened. Returning, the patient continued euphoric and overactive for three more days. She related during these days how in adolescence she had joined a circle for religious discussion, and how at this circle she had felt an ecstatic striving for oneness with God, or for mystical unity with some higher entity, whether divine or mundane, such as the church. The proximity of attractive young men at the meetings may have been a factor in her sense of well-being. The fact that her lover was religious had been a big factor in her choice. During these three days her distractibility prevented any deep dream interpretation, but two dream fragments are worth citing for their superficial content. In one of these dreams she puts on a Jersey sweater, a man's sweater, but resembling one of her mother's. The neck is low, V-shaped, and at the point of the V is a long pendant. Her associations dealt with adolescent fantasies in which she imagined the breasts uniting to form a penis. The dream seems to say that she wishes to have on her chest that which mother has, namely, breasts, but also a penis. In the other dream, at an art lecture where the men (analysts) are standing and the women (patients) are seated, a man urinates. Her association to this was to an art class in which someone vomited. Apparently this suggests a wish for coitus, depicted as an act in which the man urinates into the woman's mouth. The vomiting may be a male act, since she equates it with male urination.

After these excited seven days, her behavior returned to its more normal level, but with this return she complained that her old symptoms were back in full force. She found herself yelling at people, and conversely she found even ordinary conversation 'ear-splitting'. She was squinting and felt that people were looking at her. She wished that she were in some dark peaceful place, in fact, laughing a little, 'the way Rank says everybody wants to be in the uterus'. She then related a dream: 'I had lost my big trunk traveling, and thought I had lost my jewels, but I found them in my little bag.' Her associations showed that *traveling* stood for sexual pleasure; the *big trunk* (elephant's trunk, big nose) meant penis; the *bag*, used for clandestine sexual journeys, the vagina; and the *jewels*, virginity, the hymen, or the clitoris. From ideas concerning virginity came the equation: hymen=membrane=eardrum or eyelid. She accepted the interpretation of her pleasure in finding the clitoris, but when the interpretation of her ear and eye as passive organs was pointed out to her she felt nauseated, and began to think of foamy candy which had nauseated her when she was twelve, and of a boy who had played the flute.

Here she was told that her symptoms showed both passive and active sexual wishes: she split ears, and her ears were split; she squinted to keep from looking, and she felt she was looked at; she thought of candy in her mouth and of a flute in her admirer's. She was told that she must have been a witness to a coitus, and have wished to play both roles.

She was silent a moment, then took up her associations. She had been told, she said, that when she was six weeks old a feather on her mother's hat had tickled her, and that she had 'nearly had a fit'; and that when she was six months old her mother had played a game like 'pat-a-cake', and that she had imitated the movements with her hands. That is, her associations were confirmatory.[2] To interpret: 'when I was very little I was easily excited, and I tried to repeat motions I saw'.

She then related a fantasy which she had had the previous evening while masturbating: First she had intercourse lying on her lover with his legs spread, then behind him with her vulva touching his anal region—this she explained is as near as she can approach being a man in coitus—and finally he was behind her with his penis introduced into her vagina. She described her subjective feelings during orgasm: 'At orgasm I melt into the other person. It is hard to describe, but there is a certain oneness, a loss of my body in the other person, as if I were part of him without my individual identity, yet in him part of a larger whole. At other times I am the dominant individual and he the lost one, so that I become the perfect whole. It is something like aligning one's self in a great cause like Christianity[3] or woman's suffrage, a complete

[2] I am aware of the 'precocious baby' resistance, but the tell-tale number *six* will soon be explained.

[3] 'God establishes himself in the interior of the soul in such a way, that when she returns to herself, it is wholly impossible for her to doubt that she has been in God, and God in her.' Saint Theresa, quoted by William James (1902) in *The Varieties of Religious Experience* (1928 ed., p. 406).

loss of the self in them. When he seemed to enter me I gained his attributes; for example, his æsthetic taste, which was better than mine. It seemed as if I had absorbed the beauty he made me aware of. It was a substitute for having it. For a man to take a woman's breast in his mouth at orgasm makes the sexual act mutual and simultaneous.' Here she complained of headache and nausea.

So far it is apparent that the patient reacted to her eavesdropping on the analyst and the woman as if she had overheard sexual relations; and that her reaction was a transient hypomania in which she was acting out a coitus from the standpoint of both sexes, culminating in a fantasy of taking both roles in the sex act at practically the same time. During the period following, the infantile situation of which this episode was a repetition became clear. Chance, which is so kind to neuroses and analyses, or perhaps only apparent chance, threw the patient into contact with a man a few years her junior, who had just recovered from a manic attack and been paroled from a hospital. She identified with this young man, would say, 'I'm a manic too', took up the cudgels for him in his struggles with his mother, and produced little symptomatic acts in the analytic hour that were seen to be imitations of him. During this period she developed transitory itches on various regions of her body. It turned out that she identified this young man with her brother, who was born when she was six, when, as a neighbor said to her, 'her nose was broken'. She had slept up to the birth of her brother in a little bed in the parents' room. Now she was removed to the room adjoining. The little brother occupied her place near the parents, and it is interesting that along with the more usual penis envy and oral envy, her big grudge against the brother was visual and auditory; that is, he was able to hear and see more than she.

The situations before and after her removal to the next room could be reconstructed. The itch was a reminiscence of an attack of measles in her fifth year, before the removal. The measles had been characterized by photophobia and itching, and she had scratched, been ashamed of scratching, and had hidden her hands under the covers. She remembered having warts at the age of three from 'touching a nasty toad', she had been told. Sometime during this early period she had played with pictures called *legerdemain*. She remembered, very early, lying cramped in bed turned away from the parents, and she remembered, very early, her father opening a steam pipe and water flooding the floor. She remembered how at the age of one and a half she had straddled her grandfather's foot, playing 'horsey', and her keen pleasure in this game.

During this period of her analysis, the patient developed an interesting symptom: she began biting her finger. There seemed no doubt that these memories referred to phallic masturbation in the parents' room, under the stimulus of parental behavior.

In the next room where she slept from six till fourteen, her symptoms really began. As early as the age of eight her vision was disturbed, so that notes blurred when she tried to play music. She could not sleep if there was the slightest ray of light in the room. Her auditory acuity dates back to this period, as does her theory of sexual relations in the standing or kneeling position with the participants completely immobile. The position is of course that of a man urinating. In this connection, it is to be noted that in the analysis, her eye and ear symptoms returned *after* the transient hypomania while she was working through her identification with the observing brother, just as they arose after she was removed from the parents' room. But the content of the hypomania itself represented the situation before the removal: stimulation and vicarious participation in the sexual act as if she were both parties at the same time—an identification with both parents in the sexual act.

Inevitably a theoretical discussion of a case of hypomania must begin with a study of the superego. In this patient the situation is apparent. She had what Sachs (1928) has referred to as an incomplete superego; she was one of those women who have included a large amount of oral libido in the vaginal cathexis, and for whom coitus means not only a relation with an object but also a vaginal incorporation of the partner, who transitorily becomes 'a superego'. In her introspective account of coitus, the patient describes this role of the sexual partner very well. Interestingly enough she goes further and openly identifies attempts at mystical union with God, the church, or woman's suffrage with the sexual act, and these ideals with her sexual object. That she identifies her lover not only with her superego but also with her mother's breast is clear from her fantasy during fellatio—that his penis was a mother's nipple and she a babe. We have, consequently, an equation of several terms: fusion with superego=fusion with ideals (God) in religious transport=fusion with man in coitus=fusion with mother's breast. That her religious experiences, her love affair, and her transient episode during the analysis were structurally fusions of ego and superego and 'clinically' hypomanic states merely goes to corroborate Freud's (1921) assertion that mania is a fusion (*Verschmelzung*) of the ego with its superego. The equation also thoroughly substantiates Rado's (1927) commentary on Freud's statement: 'this . . . is the faithful intrapsychic repetition . . . of that fusing with the mother [while] drinking at her breast' (p. 428).

Physical sexual relations with a superego figure to represent a mystical union have brought scandal upon many present-day religious bodies, and they have figured largely in the so-called pathological religious cults of paranoid leaders (Rorschach, 1927). The sexual act with 'the dwellers in the castle', who represent the superego, is Franz Kafka's mystical symbolic way of representing the attainment of spiritual grace in his novel, *Das Schloss.* The patient's sense of erotic mystical unity was indeed in the best tradition of the female mystics; for example, the 'orisons' of Saint Theresa. That the oral aspect of the union has not been recognized more often is rather surprising in view of a statement by William James, which curiously enough he includes in an attempted *reductio ad absurdum* of the arguments for the sexual basis of religious experience. In The Varieties of Religious Experience, he says, 'But then, why not equally call religion an aberration of the digestive function, and prove one's point by the worship of Bacchus and Ceres, or by the ecstatic feelings of some other saints about the Eucharist? . . . Language drawn from eating and drinking is probably as common in religious literature as is language drawn from the sexual life. We "hunger and thirst" after righteousness; we "find the Lord a sweet savor"; we "taste and see that He is good". "Spiritual milk for American babes, drawn from the breasts of both testaments", is a sub-title of the once famous New England Primer, and Christian devotional literature indeed quite floats in milk, thought of from the point of view, not of the mother, but of the greedy babe' (p. 11, n.).

James wrote this argument some three years before the appearance of the *Drei Abhandlungen,* so in a way his objection to what we should call a genital theory of religious experience is not unfounded; but as fate and research would have it, in so far as he considered his argument from the 'digestive function' a *reductio ad absurdum,* we can only say, psychoanalytically, not patristically, *credo quia absurdum!*

But to return to the patient. She spoke, in her hypomanic episode, now as if she were the incorporating party, now as if the incorporated. From this we see that her hypomanic ego included both elements of the combination, so that she could speak either as if she were the original ego or the superego. I refer to her description of coitus and orgasm in which she was both active and passive, incorporating and being incorporated, as an example. Her new ego was ego plus superego.

If a hypomanic state is structurally the same as an identification with both parties in coitus, is it possible to derive the formal, general, and characteristic elements of the neurosis from the elements present in the coitus observation, taking into account the 'translation' necessitated by the double identification? Dora's nervous asthma (Freud, 1905[1901]) and the Wolf-man's afternoon depression (Freud, 1918[1914]) could be traced back to two elements in coitus scenes; namely, the dyspnoea of Dora's father and the choice of an afternoon for coitus by the Wolf-man's parents. That is to say, specific elements in a neurosis corresponded to specific or accidental elements in an observation of coitus. But can the grosser, more general features which are differentially diagnostic in psychiatric nosology be thus derived? This is problematic, but I am encouraged to make an attempt because of the material in my case, and because Abraham (1924a) proved that a coitus scene and the reaction to it was an infantile *'Vorbild einer melancholischen Depression'.* As Abraham speaks of a primal mood disturbance (*Urverstimmung*) referring to a depressive mood, let me postulate a primal enjoyable excitement, an *Urerregung,* as seems plausible in my case, as well. I can only present what seem to be analogous elements in the coitus observation and in the hypomanic attack:

Coitus Observation.	*Hypomanic Attack.*
Two active participants.	Bisexual productions.
Motion of adults. Immobility of child.	Motor overactivity.
Sounds from adults.	Talkativeness, noisiness.
Sexual excitement.	Sexual excitement.
Adults' orgasm. Child's orgastic equivalent.	'Expulsions' (Abraham).
A 'celebration'.	A celebration (Freud).
Stimulation of fantasy in child.	Flight of ideas.
'Violence' of adults.	Aggressive symptoms (?).

I am aware of the weakness inherent in analogical reasoning; yet Abraham's observation that there is an increase in sexual desire and in sublimated activity following normal grief, an 'acting out', so to speak, of the primal scene in a normal way, and his conclusion that this state is the normal analogue of mania, encourages me to hope that the comparison is not entirely superficial.

Here we encounter a very obvious question. Even if it is true that in this case a transient hypomania was a repetition of an infantile observation of coitus, need it be true that this finding is of general validity? Naturally I cannot answer this question for lack of sufficient data. However, I saw one young man for several hours during a short manic attack—I did not analyze him—and obtained the following impressions. His manic state had begun while he was under great pressure to start his overt sex life, either heterosexually or homosexually. In his illness, he spoke of having discovered the sexual significance of eating and the bisexual nature of the individual. He was enthusiastically listing his talents and capacities according to their origin from father or from mother, and emphasized their synthesis in him according to a formula he had discovered for bisexuality not unlike Weininger's.[4] Unfortunately this case could give only a superficial impression, but fortunately I am able to refer to two case reports of transient hypomanias in patients under analysis.

[4] Was the book of this young genius with its hostility to women and its preoccupation with the synthesis of bisexuality a 'hypomanic' production?

Nunberg (1926) described a young man with a compulsion neurosis who had 'Saturday depressions' preceded by Friday night hypomanic moods. They were reactions to the fact that his parents engaged in sexual relations regularly every Friday evening. Nunberg states: 'Identifying with his mother and the Sabbath, he formed oral sexual fantasies, in which he not only desired the father, but identified with him also'.

Brill (1928a) also has reported a transient hypomania which interrupted a compulsion neurosis. The patient had been under treatment for about a year. She became absorbed in the details of the Snyder-Gray murder case, in which a man named Gray and a woman named Snyder, his mistress, had murdered the woman's husband. 'On the day they were executed', says Brill, 'she was much depressed and cried. The next day she told me she was perfectly well. Her symptoms had disappeared . . . By living through and identifying with the criminals . . .' she had been able to develop a transient hypomania. Dr. Brill had the kindness to discuss this case with me at greater length than the printed report, and agreed that the double identification with the two who 'died together' was present, and he added that the patient resembled mine in her intense overt hostility to her mother.

So, I am able to say that at least two transient hypomanias have been studied in which double identifications were present, and which were reactions to an adult coitus, in Nunberg's case a real one, in Brill's case a symbolic one of a man and woman 'dying together'. Cases reported by other writers have not been of assistance to me, for although they note bisexual productions, the specific points mentioned were not reported.

The next problem presented in the case I have been discussing is the nature of the new 'hypomanic' ego resulting from the fusion of the ego and superego. I have already shown that it contains sexualized identifications with the father and mother. There has, indeed, been a reversal of the process which leads to superego formation. It is possible to describe this in a formula almost directly contrary to Freud's formulation of the origin of the superego[5] and say: the superego

[5] 'The superego . . . came into being through the introjection into the ego of the first objects of the id's libidinal impulses—namely, the two parents. In this process the relation to those objects was desexualized; it was diverted from its direct sexual aims' (Freud, 1924a, p. 167).

Standard Edition has been used for all Freud quotations [Ed.].

disappeared and the relationship with the first libidinal objects for the id, the parents, represented in the ego by identifications, was resexualized. But the nature of the new ego may best be ascertained by considering the typical mode of defense used by the patient; namely, *denial* (*Verneinung*). In the first dream during her hypomanic attack, she put the interpretation of her behavior into the mouth of Miss Z, of whom she could say 'She is paranoid. I cannot believe her.' Similarly she rebutted unwelcome interpretations by saying, 'That's what you analysts think!'. Or she would make the organic gesture of being nauseated. She was furious with her mother for harboring well-founded suspicions concerning her love affair; to the patient this maternal insight merely proved how 'evil-minded' her mother was. She denied or repudiated painful critique from the environment or from her reality testing apparatus, and altered to this extent her contact with the real world. The patient's 'hypomanic' ego then was essentially a purified pleasure-ego (*purifiziertes Lust-Ich*) introjecting the sources of pleasure, and rejecting the sources of pain, saying, as Freud (1925b) puts it, in the language of the earliest oral instincts: 'I should like to eat this' or 'I should like to spit it out' (p. 237).[6] In so far as the representations of the parents in the premanic ego and superego were pleasurable they were accepted and incorporated; in so far as they were painful, they were expelled by the new 'hypomanic pleasure-ego'.

During the hypomanic episode the patient's sublimated activities were efficient, easy, and pleasant. Since the patient's work represented a sublimation of an aggressive bisexual trend, and her work inhibitions at other times represented hostility against the father and mother identifications in her, we may conclude that the sublimations were essentially manifestations of the more whole-hearted identification with the parents.

In summary, I shall give an abstract description of the personality structure as seen in this transient hypomanic attack. The ego fused with the superego by an oral mechanism. The resultant 'hypomanic ego' was a purified pleasure-ego, ingesting the sources of pleasure, ejecting the sources of pain by

[6] See also, Freud (1915b).

denying. The new ego contained the parental identifications previously in the superego. These identifications were sexualized, and the sadism previously emanating from the superego, but now in the ego, was turned against the environment, partly in sublimations, partly in denial of parts of reality or the intrapsychic representatives of reality which might cause pain. The content of the hypomanic attack was an identification with both parents in coitus.

The discussion of this paper at a meeting of the New York Psychoanalytic Society in 1931 brought out several interesting points. These were (1) the immediate antecedents of the transient hypomania, particularly in regard to the presence or absence of signs of depression; (2) the actual time in infancy when the 'primal excitement' occurred; and (3) related to this, the meaning of the euphoria.

Gregory Zilboorg and Dorian Feigenbaum were sceptical of the absence of an antecedent depression. Zilboorg particularly, appealing to Abraham's and Rado's work on this point, questioned whether depression had not been evident in some extra analytic situation. Rado believed that the psychological equivalent of a depression was to be found in the anger and the hand-washing which immediately followed the traumatic analytic experience and that the hypomanic state constituted an attempt to escape from the more painful depressive state. Brill commented that in the case which he had studied hand-washing had definitely been a reaction against sadistic wishes involving the mother, and he believed the same interpretation was valid here. Unfortunately, the facts observed are not as unambiguous as might be desired, although my opinion coincides with Rado's and Brill's. The patient was distinctly in an angry mood; the hand-washing could not be analyzed at the time, and this was the only occasion during the eighteen months of analysis that there was any hand-washing. No signs of depression were observed, but the patient's silence may well have covered any traces present. It might be mentioned that although in Brill's case the hypomania was preceded by depression, in Nunberg's case the order seems to have been reversed.

Zilboorg, referring to the idea of an infantile 'primal excitement', pointed out that this state would not be a direct contrast to the *Urverstimmung* described by Abraham. This is true; the concept is analogous, not opposite. As I understand Abraham's case, the *Urverstimmung* also was not an immediate reaction to the primal scene, but subsequent painful anticipations of its recurrence. The two theories advanced during the discussion of the primal excitement were: (1) that it occurred directly during the coitus observation, and (2) that it occurred after the removal to the next room. Brill and Hendrick supported the first point of view, basing their argument on the status of the ego during the original coitus observations. The ego was then presumably a 'pleasure ego' unhampered by a superego, which indeed could not at the time have been very well developed. Brill added that from his experience he was inclined to think the 'pleasure ego' organization very persistent in cyclothymics throughout life, so that the superego was always of the incomplete type. Rado advanced the theory that the patient's experiences in the parents' room had been painful, but that subsequently in the next room, she had identified with the observing brother, with the parents in coitus, with the fantasy 'I am making a baby for myself just as the parents did', and that this was the primal excitement—an identification with the pregnant mother and the unborn child, the true basis for religious conceptions of *unio mystica.* Here the delusional pleasure overweighed the pain. For Rado's idea is the fact that at the patient's first self-induced orgasm she thought 'I must be having a baby'; and later in the analysis it became clear that she had 'adopted' her brother and wished for a child; but definite associations which might connect the hypomania with ideas of pregnancy and intrauterine existence were few and ambiguous. I think Rado's suggestion very plausible; the depressive-manic sequence begins with oral incorporation and ends with anal expulsion, and this 'psychic metabolism' coincides with that of the fertilization-pregnancy-birth sequence in infantile thinking. The synthetic function of the ego may well utilize the same series of processes simultaneously for two purposes.

This leads us to the third question, also raised by Zilboorg, the meaning of the euphoria, which Rado interprets as a euphoria of pregnancy, a narcissistic pleasure in being pregnant. No other theory was offered. Zilboorg questioned the advisability of using the term 'hypomania' in speaking of this episode; he preferred 'euphoria', in order to avoid an implied acceptance of Kraepelinian nosology. Feigenbaum thought, 'hypomanic reaction' would be the right term. My use of 'hypomania' does not commit me to any nosology. I entirely agree with Zilboorg in considering 'hypomania', 'manic-depressive', etc., as reaction types of greater or less typical purity, in accordance with the well-known views of Adolf Meyer.

II. A TYPE OF NEUROTIC HYPOMANIC REACTION*

In an issue of the Archives of Neurology and Psychiatry which does honor to Adolf Meyer it is not necessary to apologize for, or explain, the apparently loose and unorthodox term that appears in the title of this essay or to assure the reader that there is no intention in it to postulate a new 'disease'. Rather, the title is intended to call attention to a picture encountered not infrequently, especially in psychoanalytic practice, and it was chosen by analogy with similarly loose current terms, such as 'neurotic', 'psychogenic', and 'hysterical' depression. Dr. Meyer (1917) wrote:

> I do not share the holy horror of the *Ding an sich* or *noumenon* entertained by some people; it is well that we should have concepts and words for the totalities even if they never can be realized as wholly indisputable entities. For both scientific and practical purposes, it is, however, wisest . . . to choose one's noumena or ideal entities and bedside terms as closely as possible to where one can actually work and not to sacrifice our progress to the old notion of unitary one-name 'diseases' where many facts call for consideration.

It is in this spirit that I describe the type of reaction I have in mind.

Cases of transient elevations of mood with the accompanying motor and verbal push, which last from minutes to days, are not rare in psychoanalytic practice. Besides these petit attacks, there are also to be discerned by the experienced eye certain hypomanic equivalents: ambitious enterprises, artistic or scientific 'inspirations', sexual celebrations, fights, alcoholic sprees or more diffuse states of being generally 'keyed up'. The state to be considered in this essay is a more chronic and subtle one, which may have prevailed for years before the

* [No. 27 in Bibliography.]

analysis is begun and may then persist for an indefinite period. The patients come to analysis for various reasons. They are generally unsettled in life and dissatisfied with their sexual adjustment and the way they are getting along in their work, or there is a crisis in marriage or in their business career. Some one of these reasons brings them to an acute realization of the precariousness of their adjustment. Usually, in addition, they tend to center their complaints on an obvious presenting symptom, such as sleeplessness or indigestion.

The patients start analysis and have hardly begun to give an account of themselves before the analyst is struck by their immense enterprise in daily affairs. Their lives consist in an endless series of appointments, parties, social activities and activities that lie outside their calling. These activities are in the main such as might ordinarily be pursued as hobbies or for some special interest, but here they are chosen as if haphazardly; the patient enters on them abruptly, becomes involved as if in his lifework and as abruptly drops them. While these activities are in the foreground, they absorb a remarkable amount of passionate interest and energy, day and night. Similarly, a vast number of persons figure in the patient's daily life, with all of whom he has dramatically intense but extremely short-lived relationships. In the analytic hour the patient devotes little attention to introspection but is absorbed in relating little dramas of the day, with their ever-changing cast of characters, which enable him to 'act out' the chief tendencies of his instinctual make-up.

The attitude to the analyst varies from respect to flippancy and, in spite of intelligence and a sufficient understanding of the general purpose of the analysis, it seems as if there is little interest in getting at the motives underlying the material. A dream is related, a few casual associations are given, and the patient returns to his dramatic recital. Moreover, such insight as may be gained from the study of a given event may be accepted as an intellectual 'treat' or with the gleeful expectancy of using the knowledge 'practically' in some trivial fashion for the immediate furtherance of some, often fantastic, design. The analysis of a conversion symptom, a compulsion or an anxiety is welcomed for the relief it brings, but there is no incentive to pursue the lead into the depths. The pertinent analytic material comes out almost incidentally, chiefly in relation to certain persons of importance in the patient's life.

In overt sexual behavior, the patients may be completely abstinent, or they may be inhibited or conditioned by neurosis. However, when the overt sexual behavior is relatively free from neurosis, it tends to be promiscuous, but not casual, in the sense that there is an immense glorification of each new sexual partner, often with allegations of great sensual gratification and intense ephemeral jealousy. However, the marvelous mistress or lover is quickly and painlessly abandoned, heedlessly and with no sense of responsibility or conflict. There is surprisingly little sense of guilt. Usually there is more guilt and conflict about masturbation, but these, too, are ordinarily quickly dispelled by a few reassuring words from a physician or an authoritative person. Masturbation is usually performed without individual fantasies, aided by pornographic reading or pictures. The love affairs referred to are noteworthy for the fact that in them the sexual pleasure and the emotional elements are of secondary importance; each affair is a caricature of a *mariage de convenance*. The other party is by no means a prostitute or gigolo but someone who would be a 'good match' in the worldly sense, a person of social, professional or financial importance, and the Casanovanic quality is a camouflage for the distorted worldly ambition. Sometimes the patient is aware of his ultimate ambition to marry 'well' and seeks his cure in such a marriage. The marriage then does not work well, for the relation is disturbed by an overestimation of the mate, to whom are attributed all the virtues but who is at the same time envied and quarreled with in a most childish way—who is, in short, treated as an incomparable, totally responsible arbiter of the patient's destiny.

More obviously than the sexual life, the activities that lie outside the work proper are all in the direction of winning prominence and fame. The activities chosen are not so frivolous as to give the impression of pure play, as in manic psychosis; rather, the patients appear as irresponsible dilettanti, or when the activities are more readily rationalized as legitimate side interests, they take them up with all the eagerness of new toys, later to relinquish them as easily, so that they appear fantastically inconstant. Yet each of these games, too, sounds like a 'success story'. In brief, the general impression obtained from the mass of activities, sexual, social and quasiprofessional, is that the patients are sacrificing their time, energy, health and the possibility of establishing firm, satisfying relationships in order to obtain a travesty fulfilment of ambition.

Why these patients are so impetuously insistent on the immediate attainment of popularity, success and prestige becomes clear in the light of their life histories. As children they led their classes and shone in athletics. Before this they were intensely competitive with siblings, when there were any, and as most of the patients were only children or the oldest of their generation, they found little difficulty in establishing their supremacy. As to the relation to the parents, one finding is of great importance: there is an almost complete amnesia for all events involving one of the parents and for all that parent's characteristics. Uniformly, this parent is of the same sex as the patient and, in all cases under consideration, either died when the patient was between five and ten years of age or was otherwise removed from the family life, through divorce, separation or illness. The few memories that are retained from infancy concerning this parent are of being spanked, punished or mistreated. In spite of this and in spite of information from relatives or friends that hints at the parent's egoism, worldliness or eccentricity, the patient endows this parent, often consciously but certainly emotionally, with all the attributes of greatness. The deceased father becomes in the patient's imagination a brilliant man, a genius; the mother, a perfect housewife, with great social and artistic talents. Owing to accidental circumstances in particular cases, my first impression was that there might be a real basis for the overestimation, but this impression was not to be confirmed. In other cases it was shown that the ideal of the absent parent was definitely due to the child's imagination and that the parent's real merits merely served as an aid to the fantastic idealization—a process which came to full bloom only after the death or separation.

With this anamnesis the patients' behavior becomes more intelligible. They appear to be trying to compete with or live up to an imaginary ideal of perfection, ability or success, which they attribute to an absent parent. As an initial formulation, it might be said that they are in their behavior fantastically fulfilling ambitions which the absent parent had for them; but as an explanation this is insufficient. The hectic desire for fame and renown is soon readily interpreted as a wish for some sort of immortality. It is an attempt to pattern after an absent parent, one who is not dead but immortal. The dream life constantly reveals the unconscious belief that the parent did not die (or leave the family). The absent parent lives on, as it were, in the patient, and it is as though the patient led not his own life but one that is a grandiose idealization and travesty.

Before this state is reached, other processes are utilized to annul the absence of the parent. Before puberty (after the death or departure of the parent), a violent effort is made to transfer the relationship to the remaining parent, who must then, as it is popularly stated, be both father and mother to the child. If this parent spoils the child and can, to a great degree, fulfil this double role, the child is satisfied for a time and forms an intense attachment to the remaining parent, forgetting (i.e., repressing or covering with incertitude) at that time the whole relationship with the absent one. Later in life a marriage may be patterned on this relationship to the surviving parent, so that the mate is given the same double role, which accounts for the overestimation of the mate and the subsequent disappointment in him. The ephemeral sexual affairs are travesties of this relationship. To a certain extent, too, the child takes the absent parent's place at that time, playing the little wife and mother, in the case of the girl, or engaging in the absent father's activities, in the case of the boy.

The factor which disturbs the pleasant relationship to the parent who plays two roles and which starts the 'neurotic hypomanic' mechanisms is puberty. The intense attachment to the sole parent accentuates the incestuous resurgence of that period. Uniformly among my patients at puberty came conscious, overt, incestuous feelings for the surviving or remaining parent. In several cases they appeared in frank dreams of sexual intercourse. The patients were frightened by the eruption of incestuous sexuality, which seemed to 'come from the blue', and there developed neurotic symptoms. These varied in type. Often, after a brief period of homosexual relations or intense love for a person of the same sex, there began a period in which all sexual feeling was repressed and was manifested only in hysterical conversion symptoms. In other cases the same end was attained through protective compulsions, which followed the typical course of such phenomena. Compulsive praying at bedtime, originally that there might not be an erotic dream, later seemed to lose this content and became simply compulsive praying. Compulsive masturbation was intended as a prophylactic against the same type of dreams. Sleeplessness was essentially a vigil, undertaken as in the days of knighthood, to ward off 'impure feelings' and incestuous dreams. Compulsive overwork served the same function by day. At the same time, the relationship to the remaining parent, which had been so satisfactorily placid, was disturbed and superseded by intense hostility and rebellion—part of an attempt at avoidance.

With this turning from the parent arose the necessity for dealing with the relationship to the absent parent. No longer could the remaining parent be both parents in one. Yet it was important that the unconscious relationship to the absent one be maintained. It then happened that the adolescent permitted the role of the absent parent to hypertrophy in him: the boy burdened himself with the role of the absent father; the girl, with that of the absent mother. They turned sharply from home to school, to athletics and to parties and later to professional and quasiprofessional enterprises, distracting themselves thereby from the sexual-incestuous environment. At the same time, in the new fields they strove to fulfil the identification with the idealized absent parent. The result ultimately was the picture presented at the beginning of this paper.

In the preceding discussion the person who is well read in psychoanalysis will note ideas put forth by Freud and Abraham in regard to manic-depressive states, such as the importance of identifications, formation of ideals and the loss of a beloved object. In a recent paper on hypomanic chronic states, Helene Deutsch (1933) stressed the importance of identifications in determining hypomanic behavior, as well as the extensive use of the mechanism of denial. A probable difference between the outspoken hypomanic state and the neurotic hypomanic reaction I have described in this paper may lie in the fact that the latter does not use the mechanism of denial. Instead of this, the patient represses or uses one of the obsessive mechanisms to deal with unwelcome psychologic facts. On the other hand, the use of identifications is common to both types. A relevant discussion of 'postponed mourning' will be found in a paper by Deutsch, which has not yet been published.[1] The present essay must remain a preliminary sketch of a broader undertaking that might determine the essential differences between the various pathologic pictures in this field.

In conclusion, it is fitting that I express my debt to Dr. Meyer, who saw clearly that there is an unsolved problem in the states 'allied to manic-depressive psychosis'.

[1] *Editor's note:* (Deutsch, 1937).

III. COMMENTS ON HYPOMANIC AND RELATED STATES*

Psychoanalysis has had less to say of states of elation and euphoria than of states of depression. Whether this is so because elated persons more rarely come to analysis, or whether it is because they prove relatively inaccessible to our methods when they do, it remains true that our knowledge of the psychology and dynamics of elation in its finer details lags considerably behind our understanding of the depressions. We have, to be sure, many sidelights on the problem of elation, due mainly to the work of Freud (1915c) and Abraham (1911, 1924a), especially in regard to the role of narcissism and oral regression, and Rado (1927) has given us an excellent formulation of the narcissistic economy of this state. But these contributions have been in a sense incidental to the main focus of interest, which was on the depressive state.

Some years ago I was able to report on a very transient hypomania[1] which intervened during the analysis of a case of hysteria, and in understanding this case was much aided by a report by Brill (1928a) of an analogous hypomania, or rather of a 'miniature manic-depressive attack' which interrupted the analysis of a compulsion neurosis. Brill's case, my own, and one reported by Nunberg (1926) had much in common in the way of provocative antecedents: the transient affective disturbance in each case was a reaction to a coitus observation and its content represented a reliving of this scene. In each case the patient identified himself simultaneously with both of the sexual partners.

It was possible to show that my patient's ego had regressed to the stage designated by Freud, the 'purified pleasure-ego' (*purifiziertes Lust-Ich*), and that it was making extensive use of the defense mechanism which Freud called denial (*Ver-*

* [No. 30 in Bibliography.]

[1] See, *Analysis and Structure of a Transient Hypomania*, pp. 57-70 [Ed.].

neinung). The patient was denying a part of her own experience, certain facts or events perfectly well known to her, the acknowledgment of which would commit her to the recognition of her own anxiety, guilt, or aggression. About the same time there appeared a paper by Helene Deutsch (1933) which quite independently reported a similar defense process at work in states of more prolonged elation or excitement, a process which the author called *Verleugnung,* that is, repudiation or disavowal. Deutsch recognized a period in her analyses where this was the predominant defense and another in which projection played the main role in handling aggression. Anna Freud (1936) has subsequently commented on the use of this mechanism as a defense in general.

Later in a separate paper I described a type of neurotic hypomanic reaction[2] which might with equal justice have been called a neurotic hypomanic personality. The paper dealt with a group of patients in whom the excitement was at the same time less intense and more persistent. In these more extensive and subtle reactions, denial did not play the predominant role, as in the acute attacks; instead the mechanisms to be found in the neuroses—repression, undoing, reaction-formation and the rest—were more conspicuous. In all my cases and in those reported by Deutsch, identifications were most important.[3]

The present paper is an attempt to assess in the light of newer and greater experience some of the statements and views of the previous essays. This newer experience has been with 'true' mild manias, transient elations, and more prolonged overactive states.

For *transient* elations, in my own work, and in that reported to me during the course of my teaching, the content of importance still seems to be the double identification with the parents in the sexual act. It was possible correctly to predict, several times, that an unusual elevation of mood was the harbinger of material referring to such an event. I should say this is true if I am permitted one proviso: namely, that this elevation should occur concomitantly with, or immediately

[2] See, *A Type of Neurotic Hypomanic Reaction,* pp. 71-77 [Ed.].

[3] The reader is referred to an excellent summary of the literature dealing with the psychology of the manic states by Blalock (1936). An article by Mittelmann (1940) is somewhat off the present line of interest.

subsequent to the successful resolution by analysis of neurotic symptoms which had been used as a defense; or alternatively, that some actual event should have provided the stimulation for the repetition. This is in keeping with the transient cases reported by Brill, Nunberg and myself. I have recently been able to analyze an airplane phobia of an unusual type. The fear in this case was not connected with any idea of falling or heights, but was brought out simply by riding in a plane. Through several dreams it became clear that the airplane reminded the patient, unconsciously, of the upstairs glass-enclosed sleeping porch which she had shared as a child with her parents, and the excitement of the ride repeated for her the excitement she had experienced on that porch. Clinically of importance here is the fact that when this fear was analyzed she showed in the analytic situation a very definite elevation in mood and a restlessness quite out of keeping with her previous rather depressed and quiet behavior. I present this as an example to serve for several other comparable experiences. I shall merely state without presenting the evidence that in this case too there was the above-mentioned identification with both parents.

It is worthy of remark that such 'primal scene' elations, which appear in conjunction with hysteric or obsessive symptoms, are always very brief and transient. Apparently these states mark the release often on the basis of identification, of erotic-aggressive admixtures previously restrained and inferrable only from the anxiety and the neurotic defenses.

As to the more diffuse states, I should like to single out for descriptive purposes one especial type which deserves some such title as *hypomanic obsessional neurosis*. Briefly, the patients of this type are persons with a predominantly typical obsessional symptomatology, but who in addition display a prevailing mood of cheerfulness, with a tendency to be very enterprising in their daily life (though this is not an indispensable feature), who are optimistic, and continually a little 'plus' in affectivity. This cheerfulness they maintain in the face of their most masochistic manifestations. This attitude comes out not only in life but more clearly even in their reactions in the analytic situation. They constantly say or indicate to the analyst that everything is all right, they are pleased with very little improvement indeed, they bring scant dream material and fail to associate to it adequately but instead go off on dissertations and elaborations based on one element of the dream or some one word suggested by it, as if they had been given a title to which they were supposed to write a theme. Their response to interpretations similarly is to pay attention to the word, often to the sound, rather than to the sense, and to enjoy the use of puns and rhymes. These puns and rhymes are interesting, for unlike the wordplays of the textbook manic these are not silly ones or necessarily very original, but often stem from the comic weekly or the book of humorous verse, so that the 'manic' quality is much tempered by the secondary elaboration, and is only very sub-sub-manic indeed. Similarly snatches of song may appear, and as in the manic these are apt to be hymns or popular ditties, yet invariably as if to entertain the analyst rather than to express pleasure. In this description I am trying to indicate a diffuse 'subliminal' manic type of production, never purely playful but on the whole rather jolly. I describe this type for comparison with the more usual type of obsessional neurotic, who is apt to be more tense or depressed. It is also noteworthy that in times of stress, these persons do not tend to get depressed, but overactive. As a contrast to the cases which Abraham mentions, one might think of this type as being a transition to cases of periodic mania, with intervals of compulsion neurosis. This type shares with mania the flight into the superficial and verbal.

The primal scene does not seem to play the striking role which it plays in the acute transient attacks. The manic-like tricks of resistance here seem to be usable against committing one's self to any recognition of various rejected tendencies. The superficial picture is that of a clever and on the whole agreeable child. The identifications here are not particularly connected with any specific content so far as my experience goes. In some cases there was strong identification with a younger sibling, but this was not a universal element.

Among the more prolonged excited states, of the type one sees in the *manic-depressive* group, the psychological situation seems more obscure than in the other types. In spite of an argument which I presented in an earlier paper, it is not evident that the form of the mania or hypomania represents in content a repetition of the primal scene, although with many reservations, I still think this plausible as one special case, even in the extreme conditions. More obvious usually are the better known elements of the content, the reaction to a loss, and the fantastic assertion of narcissistic autarchy.

Something may be said, however, of the defenses employed by the definitely disturbed patient. In spite of the speed of production and the apparent jumping from subject to subject, the striking thing in regard to the patient's associations is the monotony of the manifest content, both emotional and intellectual. Whole months may pass without the addition of a really novel element to the material, which is hashed over and rehashed. If for example during the attack there should be an involvement with a person of the other sex, this situation is endlessly elaborated and exploited. The affair furnishes a convenient rationalization for everything that happens; all events in and out of the analysis are referred to it, so that it may become systematized, in a way reminiscent of a paranoid erotomania.

For a greater or lesser period of time, sometimes all through the attack, whatever the analyst has to say, no matter how much it would ordinarily be expected to provoke contradiction, is greeted by the patient with a hearty 'Yes!'. But then the remark will be taken up, played with, paraphrased, and subjected to punning, and then let drop as if forever. What this suggests is that the patient makes a rapid identification with the analyst, seizes aggressively upon his words, quickly to destroy their sense. The patient is an antisemanticist, who busies himself with the verbal representations. Again in other phases of the work, the patient will simply shout 'No!' to the analyst's remarks.

As to the spontaneous production, speech is used primarily to distract and conceal, and only in the occasional calm moments or after the attack, will there be associations that can give insight of the sort we find in the analysis of the neuroses. Of dreams, infantile material, or material relating to the transference, other than that in keeping with the gross affect, there will be little said, or nothing. When the patient's words threaten to reveal too much, recourse is taken to humor, poetry, even to singing; and as an analogy in the graphic field, excessive typewriting may be replaced by piano playing. One prime purpose of the flight is to shut out other people, even to the exclusion of all sounds from without.

The foregoing represents the manner in which the process of denial operates. Besides this process, there is a secondary reassertion of reality or of a certain sort of reality. This is revealed in the patient's need to bolster his ideal of being 'all right'. It comes out in the first place in the transference, and to a certain extent underlies his initial agreement with the analyst, when he assents vigorously though only ephemerally to what the analyst has to say. Such an agreement produces an illusion of objectivity, a pseudo sense of reality that comes from a belief held in common, whether this belief be well founded or not. It is the same urge that impels the elated or overactive to join vigorously in religious or quasi-religious activities, political or mystic. A certain plausibility arises from agreement. The same process of refinding reality comes out in the occasional dreams, where a repudiated figure may utter the patient's unconscious insight. In the same way, too, the activity is directed into what often looks like a sublimation, which has the same social plausibility.

The manic state is evidently an unstable one, difficult to perpetuate without auxiliary modes of defense besides denial. Denial constantly meets the counterassertion of the outer world and part of this counterassertion is congenial to the patient. So that in contradistinction to schizophrenia, what corresponds to the secondary attempt at cure is always in the making and always at cross purposes with the initial defense.

THE DREAM SCREEN

In many respects, the introduction of the concept of the dream screen may be regarded as the turning point in Lewin's work. With very few exceptions, almost everything he wrote thereafter reflected in some way Lewin's ideas about the psychology of wakefulness and sleep. These were expressed in concrete terms in the triad of oral wishes, i.e., to eat, to be eaten, and to sleep. Subsequent contributions considered the implications and derivatives of these wishes as elaborated and transformed by the defensive needs of the ego. Lewin's insight into the dream screen demonstrated more than a logical progression of his ideas about incorporation and hypomania. It derived from his thorough knowledge of the psychology of dreaming, as his analysis of the famous dream about 'the two tumblers' demonstrates. What is perhaps most striking was Lewin's ability to free himself of the strictures of applying the methods of analysis rigorously only to the dream. He applied the same method of analysis to the 'manifest content' of the symptomatology of elation, depression, and phobias, thereby clarifying many problems of clinical interpretation which hitherto had remained elusive. Thus, for example, problems of affect as in the case of elation, and problems of creativity as in the case of poetic and scientific work, could be examined through the same method of approach—the method of differentiating the pictorially expressed experience from the screen onto which it is projected.

J. A. A.

I. SLEEP, THE MOUTH, AND THE DREAM SCREEN*

In this paper I make use of an old familiar conception of Freud's—the oral libido—to elucidate certain manifestations associated with sleep; and I apply ideas gained thereby to other observations of psychoanalytic practice and to psychoanalytic theory.

Freud (1900-1901), in The Interpretation of Dreams, assumes a wish to sleep, which he makes the prime reason for all dreaming, the dream being the great guardian of sleep (pp. 233-234). Of this wish he has little to say. In A Metapsychological Supplement to the Theory of Dreams (1915d), he makes his famous, humorous statement about what we do when we go to sleep. He tells us that we strip off most of our ego with our clothes, glasses, false teeth, and other removables, and assimilate ourselves to the babe newborn, or the babe *in utero* (p. 222). This comparison struck M. J. Eisler (1921) forcibly, and he reported several cases of sleep disturbance (not entirely lucid ones perhaps), which were intended to show that sleep was a regressive phenomenon, a return to a hypothetical preoral or apnœic stage, such as might be imagined for the unborn child. Incidentally, however, Eisler made the important remark that the first going to sleep we know of takes place when the nursling has drunk its fill at the breast. Recently in the concluding remarks of a valuable symposium on sleep disturbances, Simmel (1942) saw fit to call attention to Eisler's old statement, thinking it worthy of note even today.[1] Another author, Isakower (1936), in an important paper, turns to the same familiar idea to explain certain hypnagogic phenomena that precede sleep and sleeplike states.

There is nothing new, therefore, in the idea that sleep, even

* [No. 66 in Bibliography.]

[1] *Cf.* also Windholz (1942), Maenchen (1942), and Fenichel (1942) in the same symposium.

in adults, repeats an orally determined infantile situation, and is consciously or unconsciously associated with the idea of being a satiated nursling; and the idea has found some limited application in psychoanalytic literature. I should like to present a few new findings relevant to this idea and to exploit it more fully. To begin with, let me introduce a term, the *dream screen*. The dream screen, as I define it, is the surface onto which a dream appears to be projected. It is the blank background, present in the dream though not necessarily seen, and the visually perceived action in ordinary manifest dream contents takes place on it or before it. Theoretically it may be part of the latent or the manifest content, but this distinction is academic. The dream screen is not often noted or mentioned by the analytic patient, and in the practical business of dream interpretation, the analyst is not concerned with it.

The dream screen came to my notice when a young woman patient reported as follows: 'I had my dream all ready for you; but while I was lying here looking at it, it turned over away from me, rolled up, and rolled away from me—over and over like two tumblers'. She repeated the description several times at my request, so that I could substantiate the gist of her experience, namely, that the dream screen with the dream on it bent over backwards away from her, and then like a carpet or canvas rolled up and off into the distance with the rotary motion of machine tumblers. The idea occurred that the patient was describing hypnagogic phenomena of the type reported by Isakower, who also mentions their occurrence on waking up, though he interprets those at the beginning of sleep.

Forgetting dreams, as we know, is like no other forgetting. Like a patient's comments on awaking or when telling a dream ('This is an important dream', or 'a stupid dream' and the like), forgetting or remembering a dream belongs to the dream content itself, and may be analyzed as a manifest dream element. Hence, when my patient's dream rolled away from her while she was on my couch, she was putting the final element into the dream. Theoretically, under pressure of her resistances, she was taking the last step in waking up (forgetting the dream) which was several hours after she had awakened in the conventional sense of returning to consciousness in bed. The dream screen rolling away was the final event in her complete awakening. As long as she remembered the dream, it might be said, she was partly asleep. Partial sleep, an idea suggested by posthypnotic and other phenomena, is coming to be employed in the explanation of certain apparently waking states (Kubie, 1948).[2]

Isakower interprets the large masses, that approach beginning sleepers, as breasts. As they approach the sleeper, the breast seems to grow; its convex surface flattens out and finally merges with the sleeper, often to the accompaniment of mouth sensations. My patient's belated waking up was the reverse experience. The flat dream screen curved over into a convex surface and went away. This appears to end the process that begins with going to sleep. When one falls asleep, the breast is taken into one's perceptual world: it flattens out or approaches flatness, and when one wakes up it disappears, reversing the events of its entrance. A dream appears to be projected on this flattened breast—the dream screen—provided, that is, that the dream is visual; for if there is no visual content the dream screen would be blank, and the manifest content would consist solely of impressions from other fields of perception. I shall try in this paper to show that there are such visually blank dreams, and shall also suggest their meaning.

Another dream of the patient referred to appears to give us another glimpse of the dream screen. She dreamed of a large iron lattice work, which stood between her and the landscape. On analysis, this lattice was found to represent the metal frame pad which her mother had worn after an ablation of the breasts. The operation took place when the patient was seven, and a good part of her analysis revolved about the three-year interval that began with the breast operation and ended with her mother's death. For these three years the patient had an unusually refractory amnesia to everything that touched upon her mother. In contrast, her dream life dealt almost exclusively with this stretch of time; so, when she forgot her dream—when it rolled away—her wish to avoid and to forget the topics, mother and breast, was being realized.

The dream screen appears to represent the breast during sleep, but it is ordinarily obscured by the various derivatives of the preconscious and unconscious that locate themselves

[2] *Cf.* also Grotjahn and French, 1938; Grotjahn, 1942; and the 1942 *Symposium.*

before it or upon it. These derivatives, according to Freud (1900-1901, 573, ff.), are the intruders in sleep. They threaten to wake us up, and it is they in disguise that we see as the visual contents of the dream. On the other hand, the dream screen is sleep itself; it is not only the breast, but is as well that content of sleep or the dream which fulfils the wish to sleep, the wish that Freud assumes to enter into all dreaming. The dream screen is the representative of the wish to sleep. The visual contents represent its opponents, the wakers. The blank dream screen is the copy of primary infantile sleep.

Accordingly, there should be dreams without visual content in which the dream screen appears by itself. Such dreams are obviously rare. They would be pure fulfilment, and under the circumstances the sleeper might not note that he had dreamed. The statement that a given night passed without a dream is always received sceptically by analysts, for dreams are readily forgotten and often come to mind later, when the dreamer, in analysis or by chance, has overcome a resistance. However, I suggest that in a special sense there are dreams without content, the special sense being one which the Russians, who call dreaming 'seeing in sleep', might find hard to phrase. I refer to the visually blank dream, accompanied by lower level, so-called organic sensations. Such a dream, we may suppose, is what hungry babies are having when they smack their lips before awakening to cry for nourishment.

Confirmation that the visually blank dream does occur, and that it represents the breast situation in a nearly pure state, came from the dream life of a schizophrenic patient. This young woman, most clearly of all my patients, was fixed preœdipally on her mother. Her apparent heterosexuality was spurious, at times delusional; her true sexual interest was bound up exclusively (though entirely unconsciously) with mother surrogates. The dream I refer to was dreamed four times during her analysis, in each instance after a day spent shopping and lunching with a mother figure. Due to the pleasurable stimulation of such a day, she would enter an excited, blissful, erotic abstraction. That night she would have 'no dream', as she said, but a sexual orgasm. This blank sexual dream each time heralded a hypomanic attack of varying duration, with grandiose and erotomanic content.

Orgasm during sleep without a remembered dream is, of course, familiar enough. Ferenczi (1916/1917c) states that 'pollutions' without a dream are incestuous, which is true but not illuminating. Some compulsive patients must masturbate before going to sleep to prevent sexual feeling from entering their frankly incestuous, but emotionally empty, dreams. But in the case I am speaking of, in spite of alternatives of slight probability, I am inclined to trust the patient's introspection that she had no visual dream, and to assume that she was stating a fact.

Certain other facts may be adduced in support. Her psychosis began with a stupor lasting several days, of which she could tell nothing. Efforts to pierce the amnesia surrounding those days brought out nothing but obvious confabulations, mixed with false 'memories' of her infancy. The patient's orality in general was intense and pervasive. The elated delusional states that followed directly upon the herald dream may be considered a belated part of the dream. The heterosexual delusions of the manic state correspond to the content that was lacking in the blank dream. They are the secondary elaboration and the denial of the wish fulfilled simply and purely in the dream: union with the mother in visually blank sleep. Her delusions were erotomanic reversals of content, such as we encounter frequently in the secondary elaboration of dreams. They resembled dream more than waking consciousness; for she thoroughly believed in the truth of her erotic fantasies as a sleeper believes in what he dreams. The same oral wishes dominated the dream and the manic attacks.

That manics may banish their sexual life completely into the realm of sleep was stated as far back as Abraham's (1911) first paper on manic-depressive states. In the terminology of the time, Abraham attributes this to increased withdrawal into 'autoerotism'. Abraham's manic patient had ordinary erotic dreams, not blank ones followed by erotic delusions. It would harmonize with Abraham's (1924a) later views on the role of orality in manic states to say that the sleep manifestations in mania are oral in origin, even when in adults they culminate in genital orgasm. The blank dream of genital satisfaction, which follows an intense oral stimulation and heralds or initiates an elation, fulfils the requirements of the hypothetical primal dream. In the primal dream, the ego takes no part and does not exert its distorting influence. In short, this dream repeats the very young infant's dream after nursing—the dream which is pure breast or dream screen, and which fulfils the wish to sleep.

The dreams which Grotjahn (1938) reports of a baby two years and four months old, are structurally far in advance of the blank dream screen. Grotjahn says: 'Sleep, to which the child in very early infancy devotes most of its time, seems to be much more important and preferable to waking life during the first year. . . . During early childhood the waking state seems to be a continuation of getting the same pleasure as in sleep by similar means.' Like my patient of the blank dream, the very young ego carries dream wishes and dream mechanisms into waking life, with less distortion to be sure. The young ego does not separate dreams from waking. The taste hallucinations of the very young baby's first dream have everything any other taste sensation has, except the real chemical basis. Yet in the dream they have the spurious psychological reality that sleep provides the dreamer; and if in waking life the baby recaptures this sense of dream reality, it is foreshadowing what may happen later in a psychosis. As in my patient's case, the sense of reality may be carried over from the dream onto the secondarily elaborated delusions that serve as a cover, a defense and an attempt at recovery.

Piaget's (1926) questioning of small children about 'where they dream' furnishes us no useful information. Usually the children (older than the ones we have in mind) told him that their dream was in the room or in their eyes, although one little boy said, inexplicably in terms of Piaget's method, that he dreamed in his mouth. To have followed this up would have gone beyond Piaget's fixed questionnaire and spoiled the tabulations.

I return at this point to an element in Isakower's description of falling asleep—the flattening of the world, equated or reduced to a breast, as it is taken into the mouth. This flattening brings to mind the same process in the case of Natalija A's influencing machine, described by Tausk (1919). It will be recalled that with the appearance of new areas of depersonalization in Natalija A's own body, a smoothing out took place in the corresponding areas of the machine, which was a sarcophagal replica of her own body. When she lost her capacity for genital feeling, the genital knobbiness on the machine disappeared, and similarly the other organs and parts that were alienated from her body ego lost their roundness on the machine and flattened out. By a clever piece of psychoanalytic algebra, Tausk equated the machine to the genital (invoking dream symbolism), and since the machine was also her body, he equated the body with the genital. Tausk's paper, which professes to treat of the most primitive ego states, omits all reference to the breast and orality. Influenced by his equation, Tausk assumes that the libido is still genital, and the formulations he applies are accordingly derived from the psychology of genital sexuality, as his terminology and analogies prove. For example, he speaks of 'body finding' when the infant is learning to know his own body and is investing its parts with libido; and this term he invents by analogy with the term 'object finding', which belongs to later object libidinal psychology. Following consistently the scheme of genital development, Tausk uses only the conception of object regression to explain the changes in Natalija A's symptoms and libido distribution, skips over the early oral phenomena and the breast, and lands at a hypothetical intrauterine stage of elementary narcissism. Tausk thinks of the bodily part as if it were a love object, and interprets the withdrawal of libido from it as if this were a regression from object love to narcissism, which gets him into difficulties not satisfactorily solved by his ideas about two kinds of narcissism. Though he defines the object of the libido (or its absence) in Natalija A, Tausk ignores the other attribute ascribed by Freud to an erotic impulse, namely, its aim.

The time that has passed since Tausk's paper was published in 1919, and the discoveries and literature of the intervening years warrant a revaluation of his findings. There will be some gain, especially, if we invoke early oral rather than genital conceptions, and libidinal aim rather than object relationship to explain some of the changes that took place in Natalija A's influencing machine. The smoothing out of the machine suggests the flattening of the breast in the hypnagogic hallucination. A third part, therefore, might be added to Tausk's classic equation of body and genital, so that it would read: body equals genital equals breast.[3] According to this line of thought, the breakdown of Natalija A's body ego boundaries would be due to an oral ingestion of the parts, a partial autocannibalism (to follow Abraham's [1924a] terminology), and the disappearance of each part of her body would mean that she had in fantasy swallowed that part. The particular piece of the world represented by the organ-representation is subjected to a (partial) world destruction.

It will be recalled that Spring (1939) in his study of world destruction fantasies (Freud, 1911a) came to the conclusion that world destruction was an oral act, an ingestion of the world. Spring's schizophrenic patients and Dr. Schreber (as Spring's reworking of the Autobiography proved) identified themselves with the world, then destroyed it by swallowing it. World destruction and the abolition of bodily boundaries follow the same course. Indeed, the idea that bodily boundaries are lost because of oral action is already familiar to us in many other connections. The baby does not distinguish between his body and the breast, and Isakower makes use of this idea to explain the hypnagogic events preceding sleep. Ego boundaries are lost when there is a fusion with the breast; the absence of ego boundaries implies an antecedent oral event.

That the ego boundaries are lost in sleep and dreams we know, due to Federn's (1932) classic paper. I should like to utilize Federn's discovery to support my contention that the dreamer, or sleeper, remains in unified contact with the breast and that this determines constant characteristics of the dream, such as the dream screen, which are not always readily noted. Federn's finding that the body ego disappears in sleep is to be aligned with the analogous loss of Natalija A's boundaries and interpreted in the same way. The sleeper has identified himself with the breast and has eaten and retained all the parts of himself which do not appear outlined or symbolized in the manifest dream content. The sleeper has eaten himself up, completely or partially, like Natalija A or Dr. Schreber, and become divested of his body—which then is lost, merged in its identification with the vastly enlarged and flattened breast, the dream screen. In short, the sleeper has lost his ego boundaries

[3] See, *Body as Phallus*, pp. 38, ff. and 44, ff., for a discussion of this point [Ed.].

because when he went to sleep he became united with the breast. Representations of the body or its parts in the visual content of the dream then mean that the body or the part is awake. It is an intruder and disturber of sleep. Symbols of the phallus, for example, appearing in the dream, represent the unconscious or preconscious waking of that part and signify a tendency to wake up, which opposes the tendency expressed by the dream screen—that is, pure fulfilment of the wish to sleep. The visual content of the dream in general represents the wakers; the dream screen, primary infantile sleep.

Beyond the witty remarks alluded to, in which he compares it with undressing, Freud has little to say of the process of falling asleep. In The Interpretation of Dreams he assumes the wish to sleep as the great motive for all dream-making, but of this wish as such he offers no explanation. So, in order that Freud's almost casual remarks about the sleeper's return to the uterus may not be thought to offset what I have brought forward about the oral meaning of sleep, it should be noted that what we know of so-called intrauterine regression is in fact our acquaintance with fantasies of returning to the womb (Freud, 1925a; Ferenczi, 1927; Simmel, 1942). So far as they have been studied, such fantasies appear to be based on oral ideas. Thus, in claustrophobia,[4] where the retreat to the uterus is used as a defense, and the fantasy represents a going into hiding, the mother's body is always pictured as being entered orally, either actively or passively. Either one bites one's way in or one is swallowed by the mother. To rejoin the mother, whether inside or out, appears to rest on the oral pattern and to get its basic mold from the earliest oral experiences. The fœtus with which the claustrophobe identifies himself is a retro-projected neonate and is supposed to be either eating or sleeping. The fantasy of returning to the mother's body is a secondary fantasy, combining the idea of union with the mother at the breast and later impressions.

I referred above to the two polar ideas of eating and being eaten and their interchangeability. This interchangeability is intrinsic in oral psychology. The effect of eating is an identification with the thing eaten. As Isakower and others have stated, there is primarily no appreciation in the baby of the

[4] See, *Claustrophobia*, pp. 48-54 [Ed.].

distinction between himself—that is, his skin and mouth—and the surface of the mother's breast. The baby does not know what he is eating: he may be eating something on the breast or in the breast, or something that belongs to himself. Perhaps for this reason, the psychology of the skin is closely bound up with oral erotism (*cf.*, Fenichel, 1942). Certainly in many cases, patients equate skin lesions with bites. From their dreams I learned that two depressed patients believed that their skin symptoms were due to worms eating their dead body. They thereby identified themselves with dead mothers. Another version says that the skin is a mouth, and when there are multiple lesions, many mouths. Healing and treatment are regarded as 'skin-feeding'. It is tempting to wonder, in passing, whether the mouth may not originally have been felt as a wound, so that the first healing attempt (to use the schizophrenic term) coincides with eating. The possibility of this interpretation is indicated by the fantasies reported in Nunberg's (1920) paper on schizophrenic attempts at cure.

The dream screen may partake of cutaneous qualities; the original fusion of breast and the sleeper's skin in babyhood may enable the skin to register itself on the dream screen. This point is still obscure. One of the depressed patients referred to above dreamed of being in a small bed under a bassinet, which was protecting her from swarms of mosquitos that were trying to bite through the netting. She awoke scratching. The bassinet represented her skin, but a skin without sensation projected from her body against the dream background. The other depressed patient, during an attack of poison ivy, in a dream projected her very much awake and rather disfiguring lesions not onto a screen or neutral surface but onto the round arms of her children's nurse, in the form of beautiful tattooed pictures. This is more in line with Natalija A's projections; tattooing does not itch, and some of the poison ivy lesions were on the patient's genital which, along with other 'pictures', her children at the time were very much interested in seeing. But the nurse's tattooing did not represent only the patient's body and genital; it also referred to the tattooing of her mother's chest after the breast ablation. The patient's awakened skin was projected onto an unusual representative of the breast, to put it into the region of sleep.

The appearance of sleep at the end of the oral series—hunger, nursing, satiety—prompts us to find a place for it in the psychology and symptomatology of the disorders which repeat this sequence in pathological form. We should expect sleep to be represented in the psychology of manic-depressive and allied conditions, and in pharmacothymia. The frequent finding that death and sleep are equated psychologically suggests itself as a proper point of departure, especially since the interesting metapsychological treatment given this topic by Jekels and Bergler (1940) and by Jekels (1945) independently. My own approach does not involve metapsychology or the dual theory of instincts but proceeds from a consideration of the meaning of the stubborn insomnia of certain depressions.

The neurotic depression of the woman who dreamed of the bassinet will serve for illustration. A persistent insomnia, her presenting symptom, which had been present for eleven years, began shortly after the death of her mother. The first analytic material showed that the patient feared going to sleep, and that the devices she used ostensibly to put herself to sleep, such as reading, in fact had the contrary effect; furthermore, that she feared going to sleep because she was afraid of dreaming. When she overcame this fear and began to dream, it turned out that all her dreams dealt with her dead mother. Once she dreamed of the Heaven which, when she was a child, her pious mother had depicted to her, and of which the mother herself had dreamed in her last illness. The patient's dreams were fulfilments of the wish to be a passive, submissive child, although she was an aggressive person in waking life. About the time of the bassinet dream, for example, she dreamed of being wheeled in a baby carriage by her nurse. In many dreams she rejoined her mother, and it was clear that beneath the more superficial fear of dreaming was a fear of dying. This fear could be analyzed: it concealed the corresponding wish to die, and this wish in turn meant an infantile wish to sleep with her mother. The idea of sleeping with her mother had several implications; but at the age of three, she remembered, she had waked up in bed next to her sleeping mother, and wondered whether her mother was asleep or dead. In short, her conflict was whether to sleep with her mother and be dead, or to stay awake and live. The sleep she feared was not the pure sleep of the satiated infant—this she desired—but the complex, dreaming sleep, from which she could not trust her censorship to delete the wish to die. Her vigil was designed to frustrate the entrance of her wish to die (perceived with anxiety) into the visual manifest content of her sleep.

To recapitulate, the neurotic fear of sleeping was based on a fear of death, which warded off a wish to die. The wish to die represented the infantile wish to sleep in union with the mother. The prototype of this wish for death is the wish for the undisturbed, blank sleep that is the probable state of mind of the satiated sleeping infant. This was the death yearned for in the depression. This blank sleep would be the fulfilment of Freud's assumed wish to sleep. Many neurotic wishes for death are basically the desire for oral satisfaction and the ensuing sleep. Death fears are the anxious equivalent of this wish. Suicide and suicidal fantasies represent a breaking through in a distorted form of the primitive wish for infantile sleep.

Strict analytic logic compels us to see in the wish to sleep a wish to be eaten up. Falling asleep coincides with the baby's ingestion of the breast; the result is an identification with what was eaten. Hence, the wish to fall asleep means an assumption of the qualities of what was eaten, including, in accord with animistic mentality, the wish to be eaten. The ramifications of this wish in psychoanalytic theory and practice require fuller discussion; but as we meet it in the neurotic depressions with insomnia, it coincides completely with the wish to sleep. In some of the dreams cited above, there are indications of its appearance as such, notably where the skin is the recipient organ for the biting.

Infantile sleep that follows nursing has not received adequate attention in formulations of the narcissistic neuroses. It has not been included in the chain of oral phenomena that underlie the events of manic-depressive and pharmacothymic disorders. Yet there should be no difficulty in fitting it into the sequences which Rado (1926, 1927, 1933b) formulated. For in the intoxications, most of the drugs produce not only elation but a subsequent sleep as well, and the wish for sleep may rank more or less with the wish for elation, or be considered as part of the same wish. In the pharmacothymic's fantasy, elation would include or be followed by the same effect that the baby gets from drinking—namely, sleep. Rado's category, 'bliss' after oral satisfaction, need only be broadened to include the sleep of early infancy.

Similarly, in the affective disorders, the primary infantile wish to sleep should play a role in fantastic or real suicide. Without some such hypothesis, we must fall back on the assumption of a primary impulse to kill one's self, and equate this with the primary, inwardly directed death impulse, a metapsychological proposition, which, to be sure, in no way conflicts with the clinical, oral hypothesis (*cf.*, Zilboorg, 1937). Or, if we fall back upon the tested idea that suicide is symbolic murder, we cannot rest analytically with this statement as if it were a primary premise. For the statement implies an identification with the object and this in turn an antecedent oral event. Therefore, it does not controvert the idea that the wish to die that motivates suicidal fantasies repeats the earliest wish to sleep. In the affective disorders, Rado's sequence would need a slight expansion. Again we should add the provision that the bliss sought and obtained at the mother's breast includes the sleep that follows. Perhaps it is in sleep or while going to sleep that the hypothetical 'alimentary orgasm' takes place. In the pharmacothymic series, we have only to add the sleep that comes from the drug; and among the pharmacothymic sequelæ, we find symbolic infantile sleep represented when, as Rado puts it, the pharmacothymic regime breaks down and the addict turns to fantasies of suicide—to infantile sleep at any cost. Thus, sleep, mania, suicide, and world destruction complete and partial, are all the very different results of the same simple, primary, oral wish.

Rado has correctly stated that the person who kills himself does not believe he is entering death, but immortality, the *paradis artificiel* of the addict's imagining. But there is another, an unwelcome immortality, as we know from the deathlessness, or extreme longevity, of the Wandering Jew, to whom it was a curse and a doom. Because he did not permit Christ bearing the Cross to rest in his shop, this character had a rare penalty inflicted upon him: long life. I suspect that this extraordinary sentence represents the 'immortality' of the sleepless, a bad case of insomnia. The poor Wandering Jew, for his sin against the weary Christ, may not sleep until the Second Coming, a prospect that still appears remote.

In conclusion, I recapitulate the main points made in this paper. The baby's first sleep is without visual dream content. It follows oral satiety. Later hypnagogic events preceding sleep represent an incorporation of the breast (Isakower); those that follow occasionally may show the breast departing. The breast is represented in sleep by the dream screen. The dream screen also represents the fulfilment of the wish to sleep. The intruding preconscious or unconscious wishes that threaten to wake the sleeper form the visual contents, and lose their place in the sleeper's ego by being projected onto or before the dream screen. The visual contents fulfil wishes other than the wish to sleep, and are the mental life during sleep to which Aristotle refers in his definition of the dream. The pure infantile dream without visual content, which repeats the infantile situation, was found heralding states of elation. The flattening out of the breast into the dream screen is analogous to the smoothing of Natalija A's influencing machine, and the unreal figures of Dr. Schreber's *Weltuntergang*. Finally, the blank sleep of oral satiety is seen to fit readily into the sequences which underlie the psychology of the narcissistic neuroses, to be one of the oral desiderata of the drug addictions, and the prototype of the death implied in the fantasy of suicide.

II. INFERENCES FROM THE DREAM SCREEN*

In a previous communication,[1] a special structure, the dream screen, was distinguished from the rest of the dream and defined as the blank background upon which the dream picture appears to be projected. The term was suggested by the motion pictures; because, like its analogue in the cinema, the dream screen is either not noted by the dreaming spectator, or it is ignored due to the interest in the pictures and action that appear on it. However, under certain circumstances, the screen plays a role of its own and becomes perceptible. Then it enters to alter what is called the form of the dream.

As we know from Freud's (1900-1901) discussion, peculiarities in the manifest form of the dream are apt to have their origin in the latent content. The dream screen is no exception to this rule. It has a definite meaning in itself, and in view of its assumed ubiquity it is not surprising that the meaning should be general. The dream screen represents the idea of 'sleep'; it is the element of the dream that betokens the fulfilment of the cardinal wish to sleep, which Freud considered responsible for all dreaming. Also, it represents the maternal breast, usually flattened out, as the infant might perceive it while falling asleep. It appears to be the equivalent or the continuation, in sleep, of the breast hallucinated in certain predormescent states, occasionally observed in adults (Isakower, 1936).

In M. J. Eisler's (1921) view, each falling asleep psychologically repeats the events that take place in the baby when he falls asleep after nursing. Accordingly, the blank dream screen would approximate the baby's state of mind in sleep. The prototypic dream would be visually blank; it would consist only of the dream screen, that is to say, of the flattened surface of

* [No. 71 in Bibliography.]

[1] See, *Sleep, the Mouth, and the Dream Screen,* pp. 87-100 [Ed.].

the recently suckled breast (or its equivalent), plus whatever elementary disturbing sensations might enter from other external or internal fields of perception. Dreams with precisely this content do occur, even in adults, and on analysis are found to be complete fulfilments of the wish to sleep at the maternal breast after nursing. Examples were given in my previous paper, and their occurrence has been confirmed by Nunberg and Atkin.[2] Ferenczi (1931), I have since found, has reported visually blank dreams with 'lower segment' sensations; because the dreams were repeated, he interpreted them, to support his later theory of the neuroses, as the result of early trauma. In my view, the element of repetition represents the latent thought of repeated feeding experiences, a topic to be dealt with below.

Schematically, I have summarized the essential ideas about the meaning of the dream screen that were contained in my earlier paper. I must err further in the way of repetition in order to remind my reader of the relation between the dream screen and the act of forgetting the dream. I shall quote a paragraph [from the preceding paper] for this purpose.

> The dream screen came to my notice when a young patient reported as follows: 'I had my dream all ready for you; but while I was lying here looking at it, it turned over away from me, rolled up, and rolled away from me—over and over like two tumblers'. She repeated the description several times at my request, so that I could substantiate the gist of her experience, namely, that the dream screen with the dream on it bent over backwards away from her, and then like a carpet or a canvas rolled up and off into the distance with the rotary motion of two machine tumblers. The idea naturally occurred that the patient was describing hypnagogic phenomena of the type reported by Isakower (1936), who also mentions their occurrence on waking up, though he interprets those at the beginning of sleep. Forgetting dreams, as we know, is like no other forgetting. Like a patient's comments on awaking or when telling a dream ('This is an important dream' or 'a stupid dream' and the like), forgetting or remembering a dream belongs to the dream content itself, and may be analyzed as a manifest dream element. . . . The dream screen rolling away was the final event in [my patient's] complete awakening.

[2] Discussion at the New York Psychoanalytic Society, October 15, 1946.

Subsequently the analysis of other dreams permitted me to show that the rolling away of the dream screen represented the dreamer's successful resistance against her wish to be asleep, and against recalling ideas concerning her mother and her mother's breast.

Without further comment on the data presented in my other paper, I should like to continue a consideration of the topic, dream screen and dream forgetting, on the basis of new clinical material. A fresh example came from a young woman, whose analysis at the time was being slowed down by a conflict centering about seduction fantasies. She found it hard to recall her dreams, they were remembered vaguely, and partly preserved only by the futile device of note-taking. Usually, she said, when she woke up her dreams 'receded' from her, or perhaps she from them; she could not be sure which was in apparent motion. This was not interpreted to her. Finally after several days of conflict, she reported one dream, which in receding was 'shattered' and which burst 'like a pane of glass'; and she had a sense of picking up the pieces. My remark that such an occurrence in a dream often stood for an orgasm did not immediately lead to fresh associations, but the next day the patient took up the matter. The dream's bursting did represent an orgasm, she now knew, but not her own. It recalled the man's orgasm at her seduction, which had been into her mouth, with much the same sense of an 'explosion' that she had noted in the dream. Although she had related this event earlier in the analysis, she realized that she had not got over it completely. From this point on the patient was able to recall her dreams for a considerable period with no more than average resistance.

The act of forgetting dreams, their receding, is to be interpreted as a repetition of the withdrawal of the breast. By an overdetermination in the above case, breast was fused with penis, with which the patient was psychologically in contact during sleep. Another patient, commenting on forgotten dreams, said that they 'slid from her head'; like jelly, she added, when asked for associations, and continued, comparing jelly to quivering breasts.

Waking up has often been interpreted as a rebirth, a reconstruction of the ego from the beginning; such an implication is alluded to by Federn (1934) in his conception of orthriogenesis. But as a libidinal phenomenon, the repetition resembles the hungry awakening of the small child, who has gone to sleep remembering the taste of the breast or the milk, and who misses the presence of the solid object which is sliding away, receding, or slipping from the mouth.

It may be appropriate here to define what is meant by the breast, as the word is used in this exposition and in most psychoanalytic literature. Both patients cited above were bottle babies, but to see special significance in this circumstance is analytically unsophisticated. The 'breast' refers to perceptions in the infant: it is whatever the infant experiences at the lips or mouth. Bottle babies later learn what breasts are; the breast-fed sooner or later have supplementary bottle feedings; both presumably suck their fingers, perhaps their toes, their clothing, and so on. Whether the pane of glass mentioned above has anything to do with a bottle is unknown to me. Possibly it has; the dream screen of other patients sometimes appeared as a glass, and references to magic lantern slides, food *sous cloche,* and other glass breasts and screens are no rarity. But breast, bottle, and finger are all viewed from the perspective of the greedy baby, and in terms of his satisfactions and frustrations.

To summarize the problem of forgetting and orality, it may be said that the pattern suggested by the above material, if not universal, at least represents a common type. It demonstrates that forgetting or remembering dreams is not solely a matter of 'form' but of 'content' as well. The act of forgetting a dream reflects the dreamer's attitude toward his wish to sleep and more generally toward his oral wishes. Furthermore, when the oral nature of the forgetting is made conscious, resistances are diminished, which suggests a useful technical method for dealing with the resistance to remembering dreams.

An interesting example of the dream screen and its relation to forgetting was furnished me by Isakower and one of his analysands, to whom my thanks are due. The dreamer records his dream as follows, entitling it, 'The Dream of the Bit of Film'.

> As I recall it, the dream occurred while I was in the process of waking up. I believe I was aware of having had a dream while still fully asleep, and that there was some thought about

forgetting it—perhaps even a desire to push it aside, but this is quite uncertain. The actual visual content of the dream was as follows: I seemed to have a strip of some dark, rather soft (almost gelatinous) material wrapped around one of my fingers. I put my hand under a running spigot and the strip of material washed away. My present recollection is that the strip had the shape of a piece of Scotch tape which is torn off the roll in an irregular way, so that one end tapers irregularly. An hour or so after getting up, I was riding on the 'el' when I suddenly had the thought that the strip in the dream was like a bit of photographic film, and it was either then or later in the day that it occurred to me quite spontaneously that the film was really the dream and that washing it away was really a representation of the process of forgetting it. (I am not sure that the latter idea did not come up during my analytic hour.)

The doubts expressed by the dreamer as to the correctness of his memory of the dream text remind one of Freud's comment on such uncertainties, that they are 'incomplete erasures', a fitting phrase here. The conflict between the wish to preserve the dream and the wish to forget it is vividly portrayed in the next part of the report, where the dreamer projects the ego-alien wish to forget onto the environment.

The gelatinous quality of the strip recalled to me an experience I once had in trying to develop color film with a home-developing kit. I was in a hot climate and had meagre temperature-control facilities; as a result, during the repeated washings which were called for in the procedure, I noticed bits of dark, gelatinous material coming out in the wash water. I was concerned over this and feared something was going wrong with the whole elaborate procedure, but I was at a loss to explain what it was that was washing away. Finally I realized that little sheets of the photographic emulsion were washing off the film. As a result I ended with a picture in only one color—a sickly blue.

During the analytic hour (I think it was) the idea came up that the dream image was also something similar to a bit of string tied about the finger to aid in remembering something one has to do, and this was seen to be related to the whole idea of forgetting the preceding dream.

The dreamer added a note to the effect that he learned only after these thoughts of 'Dr. Lewin's idea that the dream content is imposed on a screen'.

Noting the dreamer's fantasy of using photography as a mnemonic aid, I should like to refer back to the dream of the shattered pane of glass, where the analysand had a sense of picking up the pieces of the dream. Literally, she picked up the pieces by immediately setting down a few key words on a scrap of paper. As in the chain of associations about the bit of film, the conflict about remembering the dream came to expression in terms of preserving a record. Freud (1911b) clearly explained the futility of writing down dreams, so far as the progress of the analysis is concerned. He warned against it, stating that it presaged an intense resistance to the latent dream thoughts which would prevent the work of interpretation. A written dream goes uninterpreted. So far as its latent content is concerned it might as well not be written. The paper is an ideational void, which might serve as the representation of a blank dream; the dream is literally worth only the paper on which it is written. Yet, the impulse to preserve something and to bring it to the analyst is obviously included in the procedure.

Abraham (1913a) confirmed Freud's remark as to the futility of trying to analyze recorded dreams, and gave several examples that showed the resistance attacking the act of recording. He observed instances in which persons consciously eager to preserve the text of their dreams in graphic form, nevertheless brought him illegible jottings and scrawls, or notations unintelligible to the dreamer himself. One man set up his dictaphone handily at his bedside, and when he awoke in the middle of the night, hastily dictated his dream into it, contentedly going back to sleep. The next morning, having forgotten his dream, he found that he had also forgotten another fact well known to him, namely, that the machine had been out of order for several days, so that he ended up with no memory of the dream and a blank phonographic cylinder. Abraham regards recorded dreams as manifestations of the transference, as anal gifts to the analyst. They may well be, yet the distinction between what is destroyed and what preserved in the process of recording suggests further possibilities of interpretation.

Monroe A. Meyer (1933) has indicated the effectiveness of another motive, the wish to sleep. He reports a dream of his own, dreamed while he was not being analyzed, so that gift and transference motives were absent. He writes:

> I tried the futile experiment of wrenching myself out of my sleep to make an instantaneous transcription of my dreams. My mind was, therefore, a battleground of two opposing wishes—the wish to sleep, which regularly participates in all dream formation, and the wish to terminate sleep in order to record my dreams. One night, I had a dream and jotted it down. On awakening the next morning, I was surprised to find the writing tablet that I had kept at my bedside bare of any notation. I then realized that I had only dreamed the recording of the dream.

Since, after all, dreams are remembered, forgotten, and even recorded outside of the transference setting, it appears unwise to overestimate the special significance of the transference, and more profitable to view the problem generally. From this standpoint, what Freud, Abraham, Meyer, and Isakower's analysands are apparently saying is that a dreamer may distinguish the dream text from that on which it is recorded, so that paper, film, or phonograph record, all representatives of the dream screen, may be preserved, while the content is subjected to further distortion and more or less effaced. The dreamer who mars or effaces the record has two motives: he wishes to destroy or censor the dream content, [or] he wishes to preserve the dream screen. The wish to preserve the dream screen is the same wish that under other conditions produces the blank dream. The blank page, like the blank dream, contains no representatives of the unconscious and preconscious disturbers and wakers. It represents solely the wish to sleep predicated by Freud as entering into all dream formation, so that Meyer's account as it stands is as if an experimental representation of the wish to sleep. To use Freud's terminology, the progressive wish to put the dream into words, into the *psi* (ψ) system *Pcs*, backfires; the dream thoughts are distorted further by a new passage through the memory systems near *Pcpt* and given a new visual form. The graphic record is a new, 'redreamed', manifest text.

Some of the above discussion applies to a dream brought me by a patient, intellectually very coöperative, who had been traditionally enjoined not to write down her dreams. Although she heeded my advice, her wish persisted. As a substitute gratification she dreamed of presenting me with a book printed in Braille characters, and that her breasts were bare while she was doing so. The book, of course, was the record of her dreams. Freud's hint that a gift from a patient is a demand on the analyst, clarified the rest of the dream. She wished the analyst to play the role of a mother and offer her the breast. In the transference, this wish appeared as fantasies of borrowing or stealing my books to read at night before going to sleep. It will be noted that the dream screen gets separate representation in the dream, as a visually blank book; it is recognizable as the dream screen only by inference, from the fact of its being a blank 'record' of dreams.

In addition to the screen, other formal elements of the dream are determined by the wish to sleep. One of my patients, a man with an intense mother fixation, once stated his chief neurotic problem as a continuous struggle against a wish to remain asleep. He sought in dreaming a substitute for most real satisfactions, and during occasional mild elations would bring as many as twenty unanalyzable dreams into one analytic hour, enjoying in an overdone, anxious way the mere relation of all the manifest content. Telling his dreams was pure acting out: he was literally repeating his sleep of the previous night. But his prolix account had the same meaning as a blank dream or unintelligibly written record. He was as if redreaming the dreams. The manifest content was getting a resubmersion into the system *Ucs* and was being re-utilized in the interest of the pleasure principle. The wish to sleep was triumphing in a new distortion. Once, combining the idea of dream screen and eternity, the patient dreamed of looking through a window at a long, decorated canvas that rolled off one large drum onto another continuously, showing an endless panorama.

The patient realized that his dreams were manifestations of resistance. Empirically, psychoanalysts have been aware that a dream overflow is a maneuver of the censorship. Eder (1930), who made a special study of this point, remarks that the use of dreams as resistance is not limited to any particular type of person or neurosis, holding that spite furnishes the chief motive. However, the best technical point I have discovered is to make the patient aware of the persistence of his wish to sleep. The patient referred to above found this out for himself.

Angel Garma, in a personal communication, corroborates the idea that a profusion of manifest content signifies a wish to sleep, and states that he has noted a complementary counter-transference effect among the Institute students attending his course on dreams. They became so somnolent in classes where much manifest dream material was presented that Garma used pictures of dreams instead. The sleepiness did not become evident in classes dealing with other analytic topics.

Near the beginning of this paper, alluding to Ferenczi's theory about blank, repetitive dreams, I suggested that the formal element 'repetition' was not necessarily as Ferenczi thought an oneiric compulsive repetition of a traumatic event. Instead, a content interpretation was given; namely, that this 'repetition' signified multiple feedings. This was deduced from my belief that the visually blank dream repeats the baby's state of mind after a satisfactory nursing; so that, as a corollary, several repetitions of a dream, or in a dream, would be the result of multiple feedings or an interrupted feeding.

As though bearing unwitting testimony in favor of this reasoning is a brief communication (published only in German) by Monroe A. Meyer (1922), The Form of the Dream as Representation of Content. The title refers to Freud's (1900-1901) statement that '*the form of a dream or the form in which it is dreamt is used with quite surprising frequency for representing its concealed subject-matter*' (p. 332). Indeed, a 'feeding problem' is enacted in the manifest content of the dream that Meyer reports. The dream reads:

> During an afternoon sleep, the analysand dreamed repeatedly, four, five, six times, the following dream: He was about to eat a steak and had put too large a piece of it into his mouth, so that he choked. Reaching into his mouth, he pulled out the meat. In the dream he experienced a sense of pressure and distressed breathing, as well as a feeling of anxiety, with which he awoke after the sixth repetition.

The occasion for the dream was a much desired additional analytic hour, the sixth hour of the week, which the analyst was able to give him because one of the dreamer's friends, also in analysis, had fallen ill. The number 'five' referred to the fact that the dreamer had five friends in analysis; the dream gratified a latent transference wish that his five rivals might die, leaving the dreamer an analytic 'only child'; it also reflected an infantile wish for oral impregnation by the father. Meyer indicates as especially noteworthy the fact that the dream occurred during an 'extra hour' of sleep, for the analysand was not accustomed to taking daytime naps. The dreamer not only represented the additional analytic hour as an extra feeding, but reacted to the extra feeding with an extra hour of sleep. The reader is referred to the original account of this unusual dream for further interpretation.

A subtler oral reference is contained in the following dream of my patient who presented the dreams with profuse manifest content.

> I am walking upstairs in a tall building with many floors. All the floors, as I pass them, seem to have the same lay-out and the same furniture and decoration. After climbing many flights I come out into a sort of clubroom or restaurant. There I see my friend, N, kissing Mr. Q, who is disguised, dressed like a girl.

N, some years back, was the dreamer's best friend and stands for the dreamer, Mr. Q for the dreamer's father. The disguise is to fool the dreamer's father, for Mr. Q's name resembles that of a girl in whom the patient was interested at the time N was his close friend, and Mr. Q's race is the same as the girl's. The patient's father disapproved of the girl as a companion for his son because of the name and race. Repeating the historical situation, the father appears to win out over the girl in the contest for the son's affections. The kissing, however, is also historical and refers to the dreamer's having kissed the same girl (similar floors) many times (as the many flights of stairs indicate). He wishes that he had 'climbed the stairs to the top' then, that is, that he had had intercourse with her many times.

The patient had never mentioned in the analysis that he had kissed this girl repeatedly, giving the impression that there had been only a hasty kiss or two; and at the beginning of the analysis the relationship was hidden under the symptom of nausea. Not only was 'repeated kissing' the main new element, but in associating, the dreamer gave an unusual number of examples of buildings all of which had restaurants on the top floor, a long list of 'repetitions'. The restaurant and the repeated kissing allude to the repeated early oral pleasures.

So far the wish to sleep has been invoked to explain formal elements of the dream, such as the screen and its actions, forgetting, remembering, inflating the manifest dream text, and repetitions, the latter indirectly because the wish to sleep is closely tied up with the gratification of oral wishes. In short, as Freud stated, formal manifest elements signify concealed latent content; in the present instances, oral wishes or the wish to sleep.

The wish to sleep, one would expect, should be a conspicuous factor in one type of dream, that referring to a primal scene or coitus observation. In this type of dream, sleep serves a special purpose, that of defense, due to a psychological repetition; for the child often attempts to avoid the scene by making strenuous efforts to sleep. The study of neurotic sleeplessness and of pathological, erotized, sleep has provided numerous examples of compromises that arise from a conflict-ridden effort to sleep through the primal scene (Abraham, 1924a; B. Lewin, 1945a; Symposium, 1942). In primal scene dreams the wish to sleep has a double purpose; it is overcathected because of its accessory, defensive use.

Evidence of this peculiarity should appear either in the form or in the content of primal scene dreams. Clinical facts bear out this surmise. A classical example is one element of the Wolf-man's dream (Freud, 1918 [1914], p. 34), in which the opening of a window is interpreted, 'I woke up'. Before this moment, the window was of course closed—of which the obvious interpretation would be, 'I was asleep'. The closed window was a dream screen and stood for the wish to sleep undisturbed.[3] The conflict between the wish to sleep and the disturbing latent thoughts may account for the frequently noted predominance of oral imagery in dreams of coitus observation (Abraham, 1924a; Brunswick, 1929; Federn, 1913). Discussing the primal scene dream of the Wolf-man, Freud speaks of a special fear of death connected with the oral organization of the libido, a fear of being devoured, also conceived in a later paper

[3] Garma, in a personal communication, remarks that certain dreams begin by an image or a figure emerging from 'somewhere', especially from a 'dark place', which he interprets as referring to sleep or the dream screen. In one dream (Garma, 1947, p. 51) the dark place is characterized 'as if a theatre'. Garma comments that the dark place (the dream screen, sleep) becomes 'a theatre' when it acquires the manifest content, and would be no more thought worthy of mention by the dreamer, ordinarily, than would the motion picture screen by someone narrating the action in the film.

as a wish to be devoured (Freud, 1925a). Going to sleep is an orally bipolar action. In the hypnagogic hallucinations of the breast, the sleeper not only swallows but is swallowed, that is, he is enveloped by the expanding breast, recalled later in many dreams of sinking into soft yielding substances; and in their origin and in many clinical manifestations swallowing and being swallowed are conceived as the same process (Nunberg, 1932, p. 63).[4] In short, oral imagery and oral dream thoughts, common to so many primal scene dreams appear to arise from the exceptional, defensively oriented, augmentation of the wish to sleep. In his sleep, the dreamer becomes aware of his wish to sleep and the oral events that preceded sleep in the nursing situation.

Freud preferred when it was possible to attribute content significance to the formal features of a dream.[5] The present essay follows his lead in this respect. One formal feature of the dream has so far resisted all efforts to reduce it to content, namely, visual representation. Freud is consistently aware of the fundamental importance of this common characteristic of dreams, for the requirement that dream thoughts be expressed chiefly in pictures explains many qualities of dream distortion. Indeed, objecting as he does to Silberer's (1911) attempts to reverse his working principle and to turn content into form interpretations, Freud nevertheless has taken several occasions to refer to Silberer's observations of abstract, verbally expressed thoughts being given concrete visual form when the thinker becomes drowsy.

Several analysts appear to believe that Freud's commendation extends beyond this to a blanket approval of Silberer's views on functional phenomena, threshold symbolism, and even anagogical interpretation. Freud (1900-1901, 1915d) of course explicitly states the contrary several times. My rereading of Silberer leaves me with an enhanced appreciation of Freud's good judgment, and of the profundity of Jones's (1916) critique of Silberer. Because of the special relevance of some of Silberer's contentions about 'waking phenomena', it might be

[4] See also, *Sleep, the Mouth, and the Dream Screen*, pp. 87-100 [Ed.].

[5] Freud's general preference for content as opposed to form was noted by Karl Bühler in *Die Krise der Psychologie*, a reference for which I am indebted to Dr. Robert Waelder. Bühler calls Freud, *der Stoffdenker*. Fritz Wittels (1931) comments at length on this point in his book, *Freud and His Time*.

well to show by an appeal to his writings how far short he comes of translating content into form, and how little he succeeds in establishing the presence in dreams of special 'symbols' that specifically mean the approach of the waking state.

To take an example, Silberer (1911, p. 641) reports a dream in which he is walking with a female companion referred to by the letter H. The dream ends with the sentence: '. . . There I lost H.; one of the horses (in the dream) came at me and threatened me, showing its teeth, so that I shrank back in fright.' From this Silberer concluded that 'shrinking back' was a 'waking phenomenon', and he dealt with the content as follows: 'Furthermore, it is quite possible that the baring of the teeth is related to the thought of being devoured, which has the same place among threshold symbols as diving or sinking into a fluid, entering a room, etc.'. He mentions other figurative devourings, such as being swallowed up by a forest, and swallowed up by water. Then he extols the courage of Schiller's 'Diver' (*der Taucher*) who successfully defied the perils of death from the waters. But he quite obviously misses the fear of death and castration contained in the associations.

His interpretation of another dream (p. 636) goes even further astray. In the dream he parted from companions to traverse a field where snow lay in puddles, then began to sink into a sheet of snow that lay over soggy, yielding terrain.

> At first, I was seized by a nameless anxiety and made desperate attempts to save myself, but in vain. As I continued to sink, comforting thoughts about the nature of death came to me, and calm and composed, I gave myself up to fate. The anxiety was immediately dispelled, the sinking no longer distressed me. I no longer struggled to be free.

Against this dream of dying, Silberer marshals the anagogic rationalization: 'Waking up, in its relation to sleep, is a death, a departure from a temporary form of existence. Hence, death, in whatever form it may be imagined, is a suitable "threshold" symbol. It is all the more suitable if a form of dying is selected which already signifies a threshold, as, for example, sinking into a liquid (drowning) or into a chasm (falling); both of these are found in previous examples.'

Certainly these elaborations are resistances to the content of the dream. Indeed, the selection of symbols of awakening is based on an extraordinary assumption—that the dream element connected with anxiety is a symbol of 'waking up'. Another terminal element, the appearance of flight in a dream, is also taken to signify the approach of awakening, an equally untenable assumption.

Ernest Jones has made a comment in regard to the 'autosymbolic phenomena' which Silberer produced while in a drowsy state—that these differed from dreams because Silberer was trying to remain awake. This penetrating remark has an application more extensive than Jones gave it. It illuminates the fight against the wish to sleep that appears in such dreams as those just cited and explains many of Silberer's comments on his dreams, which show the same ambivalence toward being asleep. But more importantly, the comment suggests the possibility of finding a content interpretation for the formal fact of visual representation itself.

As the dream screen represents the wish to sleep in a pure state, so visual representation would express a general wish to be awake. This is not the special, overdetermined, often defensive wish to be awake, such as accompanies a fear of sleeping, but the general wish that goes with the lack of fulfilment of wishes—the Joshuan wish that the day shall not end till the wish be fulfilled, or that a new day shall dawn. A visual dream repeats the infant's early impression of being awake: his eyes are open and he sees. To see represents being awake. If there is no unitary wish to be awake, simply for the sake of being awake, at work in the dream, it is still true that each unconscious and preconscious cathected element is as if awake or potentially awake.

Freud explains the predominance of visual elements in dreams by the remark that the latent dream thoughts are partly shaped by early unconscious memory traces which existed only in visual form, and that the regression to these traces imposes the visual form on dream thoughts. This explains the visual form as a repetition of a formal element in primary experiences, but does not contradict the possibility of the content interpretation. It is hard to say whether the idea of a wish to be awake is new, or whether it is not a mere restatement of an assumption implicit in the theory of the dream as the 'mental life during sleep'.

III. MANIA AND SLEEP*

Metapsychological Analogy of Mania and Sleep

In mania, to cite Rado (1927), the ego fuses with its superego in an intrapsychic reproduction of that fusion with the breast which takes place at nursing. In going to sleep, as many have remarked (since M. J. Eisler's [1921] original exposition), the ego repeats a process like the first infantile falling asleep, a fusion with the breast at nursing. Except for the topography and the two mental end states, these remarks are identical: an intrapsychic fusion repeats the baby's psychic procedure at the breast and leads in one case to mania, in the other to sleep. In Group Psychology and the Analysis of the Ego, Freud (1921) compares sleep and mania because of the disappearance in both of a part of the personality. In sleep the ego disappears, rejoining the id, and comparably in mania the superego disappears, rejoining the ego. Referring to the Saturnalia, carnivals, and other feasts, Freud thinks of a possible periodic biological necessity for both types of psychological dedifferentiation.

Superficially, certainly, it is hard to see what this common feature of the two states could mean, for the manic patient appears supremely awake. Our phenomenologist friends, who try through *Einfühlung* and *Nacherleben* to grasp the subjective *Erlebnis* of a mental state, would hardly find themselves intuiting or re-experiencing anything that suggested the subjective experience of sleep. The introspective method, and common sense, too, would say at this point: 'Go no further'. But once we leave the introspective surface, many paths lead to a truer comprehension of the mania-sleep relationship.

Sleep, basically, comes from oral satisfaction. The baby after nursing falls into a presumably dreamless sleep. Theoretically, it may be more correct to speak of the baby's having a 'blank dream', a vision of uniform blankness which is a persistent

* [No. 83 in Bibliography; also Chapter 4 from No. 89 in Bibliography.]

after-image of the breast. Later in life, this blank picture of the flattened breast, preserved in dreams as a sort of backdrop or projection screen, like its analogue in the cinema, comes to have projected upon it the picture that we call the visual manifest content of the dream. The fulfilment of the wish to sleep produces only sound sleep and the dream screen. So far as falling asleep reproduces the infant's first sleep after nursing, it reproduces the fusion of the ego and the breast. The primitive sleeping ego is id, except for the dream screen—the erstwhile breast, sole and first representative of the environment.

Into sleep and into the hypnagogic moments that precede it, intrude other representatives of the environment, past and present. An early one is hunger, and the first dream 'picture' might well be a hallucination of milk, if we are entitled to infer this from the sucking motions of the soon-to-be-awakened babe. Not much later, besides such immediate 'organic' intruders into sleep as hunger, cold, and pain, daytime recollections participate as visual elements on or before the dream screen. We do not have the data to follow unbrokenly the growing complexity of the sleeping consciousness, or manifest dream life. But as the child has more and more contact with the world, and the waking life becomes longer, more filled with meaning, more complex, and more varied, daytime wishes and ideas increasingly penetrate the nighttime world. The wish to sleep is opposed then by other wishes, the unconscious and preconscious wakers and disturbers, which with greater or less distortion generate the manifest content of later dreams.

That there is a development in the dream life from the simple to the complex, with an increased participation of the growing ego, is proved not only by the potential richness of adult dream life, but by the dreams of children as well. Those who observe regressions in adults, where they are intricate and show the effect of subsequent stages of development, may need to be reminded that the original infantile phenomena which are copied and travestied in the regressions may have been very simple. Many adult dreams, owing to the censorship of the riper ego, are complex, but the dreams of the very young are not. Freud's (1900-1901, pp. 130-131) example of little Hermann, who with much reluctance gave his uncle a basket of cherries as a birthday present, was quite direct and simple. The twenty-two-month-old child dreamt: 'Hermann eaten up all the chewwies'. Thus the unfulfilled disturbers of sleep, residuals of more and more days of waking life, add gradually to the complexity of the state of consciousness during sleep by instigating increasingly intricate dreams.

The above discussion of the basic facts of consciousness and lack of consciousness during sleep was written to indicate that there are different states called 'sleep'. As Kubie (1948) said: 'We are never totally awake or totally asleep. These are relative and not absolute terms. Parts of us are asleep in our waking moments, and parts of us are awake in our sleeping moments; and in between lie all gradations of states of activity and inactivity.' Rado (1925), too, has argued that we should not be misled by the etymology of the word *hypnosis,* as our forefathers were by the derivation of *hysteria* from ὑστέρα ('the uterus'). Hypnosis, from ὕπνος ('sleep'), he remarks, should not be thought of as a simple artificial sleep, but more properly as an artificial dream state.

Continuation of Mania-Sleep Comparison

Mania, then, may be compared with sleep if we specify the kind of sleep we mean, and if we take into account that dreams of different degrees of complexity and with a variable amount of censorship are also parts of sleep as we know it. Mania thus could be a kind of sleep even if it is not a deep sopor. So considered, a typical elation or mania is seen to resemble the dream of a small child, with its playful fantasy wish fulfilments. Basically, it would be the dream life of the narcissistic pleasure ego, if it were possible to grant a dream life to an ideal construction of this sort. It would also, ideally, be free from anxiety and any affect other than good spirits.

Nowadays no one will be deceived by the idea that children's playful fantasy is the conflict-free affair it was once thought to be. A reference to Anna Freud's discussion of 'denial through fantasy' should dispel any doubt on this account. The simple dreams of children which Freud relates in The Interpretation of Dreams closely resemble the simple denying fantasies recorded by Anna Freud and the child analysts. (Anna Freud, 1936; Berta Bornstein, 1936, 1949.) We may, indeed, have been hampered in our past study of elations by an old familiar resistance; unconsciously, we may have equated the fun and play of mania with children's happiness and thus fulfilled our own fantasy of that Age of Innocent Play. The similarity of manic activity and children's play is an ancient psychiatric idea; the understanding of children's play is as new as psychoanalysis.

The comparison of mania and the child's dream was possibly somewhat obscured in the paragraph above by the reference to the child's wish-fulfilling fantasies and games. It should be stated that in the elations, the fantasies, words, and deeds are used mainly for denial and that they resemble the denying secondary elaborations that come after the distortion of the latent dream thoughts. The content of the elations is a direct denial of a fact, is believed unreservedly and gladly, and so resembles in mode of operation the believed dreams of the child rather than the playfully held fantasy.

Illustrative Material

The case of a young woman whose oral attachment to her mother was extreme may illustrate the relation of mania and dream psychology. She had intellectual insight into her passive erotic, oral needs, but she denied that they affected her in any way. During her analysis, she had four hypomanic attacks, all of them set off by the same circumstances. After a day spent with a certain mother surrogate, in shopping and lunching, she would come to her analytic hour in a blissful mood of rapt, erotic absorption. Carrying this over into the night, she would have a visually blank dream with sexual orgasm. Then, next day a hypomanic excitement would begin, which denied the meaning and importance of what had happened. It was filled completely with heterosexuality and independence. She would tell of numerous fiancés, various prominent young men in political and artistic circles, and with them, she alleged, she was engaged in various coöperative enterprises, combining love with art and business. Previous to her hypomania, dreams had occurred that were simple to interpret; for example, she found herself in bed with a young man she admired and he turned into her mother. In the hypomania, she hotly resented any dream interpretation which suggested that the men represented any person but themselves. If a dream exactly reproduced a fact which was familiar to her from childhood and obviously referred to her mother, but which manifestly pictured as the mother one of her erotomanically loved objects, she would confabulate about her childhood. This man, she said, had been her nurse or baby sitter, he had sung her to sleep, taught her to walk, etc. The patient regarded the dreams exactly as a child might regard a dream of simple, undistorted wish fulfilment. The analyst was knocking vainly on a closed door in her ego, which had been open before the attack. Beyond that door lay her reality testing.

The blank dream with orgasm, stimulated directly by the contact with a mother figure, reproduced for her a union with the mother at nursing. The elated delusional state that followed was like a belated part of the blank dream; in fact, it was the belated manifest content, which denied the wish that was simply and directly fulfilled in it. In this sense the patient was partly asleep while awake, for a large part of her waking consciousness was busy performing a function ordinarily, or better, classically, performed by the dream work through distortion and secondary elaboration. Her sense of reality when awake was a manifest-dream reality, made up of a thoroughgoing denial of the source of the excitement in the dream.

Toward the beginning of her attacks the patient was nearly sleepless, despite medication. She dreamed little or forgot her dreams. Later, she remembered some at great length: they were involved, dealt much with the day's doings, and included connected narratives of pleasant activities with her fantasied heterosexual pseudo objects. The repudiative daydreams thus altered the content of her nighttime dreams, which she tried to take as literal wish fulfilments that simply meant what they said. Like the dreams of children, they overdid the use of day residuals. She avoided free associations by flighty evasion or by a downright refusal to give them as soon as they neared the denied facts. The analyst's intervention in favor of reality led to angry and stubborn contradiction.

Structurally, manic dreams do not differ markedly from the general pattern. The blank dream is an exception; it is to be interpreted not only as a dream of oral satisfaction, of fusion with the mother at the breast, but as picturing in pure culture the fulfilment of the wish to sleep, which Freud considers the main reason for all dreaming. Excluded from the dream picture is all but the dream screen and the 'organic' sexual stimulus.

Paradoxically, the very elaborate dreams that often appear in milder transient elations, such as those which accompany denials during therapy, also represent the wish to sleep. For by repeating a dream for the better part of an analytic hour, the patient is 'acting out', i.e., reproducing and reliving, the sleep of the night before; so that for analytic purposes, he might as well have had a blank dream. Usually, however, in these 'analytic' states of denial and elation, the denial comes to expression in the dream content itself.

The patient's hypomanic attacks were like manifest dreams which denied the latent dream thoughts that came from day residuals. By a rough analogy with little Hermann's dream, her hypomanic attack stated: 'I didn't want the cherries. I have all the other fruit I need and always did have'. The hypomanic attack resembles the dreams of children more closely than their games in one important respect: children's dreams have a sense of reality and complete credibility, and mania includes these too. Put a bit differently, the sleeping child's ego is more nearly a pure pleasure ego than that of the child at fantasy or play.

The patient was surer of herself awake than asleep, and as we have seen, her dream life only gradually regained its capacity for excluding unwanted stimuli. As guardians of sleep, those dreams were most successful which took over directly the imaginations of daytime life, as when the patient introduced her imaginary lovers into her dreams. These dreams, however, had to stand on the single leg of these very specially selected day residuals, and they had to continue the accepted falsification. The analysis of this patient's dreams and those of others, some of which I have reported, reveal the mechanisms of defense described for the ego of manics. These defenses are used against the unwelcome residuals of the day, including analytic interpretations, in the form of denials, or they express appropriate fantasies in the form of identifications, and show reversals of role and affect. Their use is quite intelligible: they are part of the ego's contribution to the dream structure. Manic sleep is notoriously poor, owing doubtless to the great defensive cathexis on the ego. The possibility of a special defense against sleep needs further discussion and will receive it later.

Manic Phenomena Interpreted as Manifest Dream Content

To deal more directly with the question of the extent to which manic states resemble dreams, we may inquire what classic symptoms of mania are capable of interpretation as if they were dream elements. This would mean an attempt to give 'dream meanings' to the common features of manic verbal and psychomotor production.

The most striking of these manic features is of course the elated mood. Dreams with a manifest elated mood are well known; dreams which contain laughter or which palm themselves off as 'happy dreams' mean the reverse of what they seem to say. They contain latent death wishes or thoughts of one's own death. (See, Freud, 1900-1901; Ferenczi, 1916; Grotjahn, 1945.) The elation in such dreams is like manic elation or the elation that comes with denial during analytic treatment. Again, much motion is a well-recognized feature of the elations. The manic moves a great deal, romps, plays, and is impatient of any postponement. If we turn to Freud's The Interpretation of Dreams, we find that he records dreams of romping and playing, which depict the 'innocent' fun of childhood and hide and deny other fun that has come to be considered less innocent. Several dreams of children which Freud selects are called *dreams of impatience.* Many manic attacks are bursting with innocent games and impatience. Some, precipitated by a stroke of evil fortune or great real trouble, are exactly like the boisterous, impatient dreams.

Another common feature of the elation is the variety of content and the apparent speed of thought known as *flight of ideas.* Dreams filled to the guards with manifest content, to which there is no end of the telling, are no novelty in analytic practice. They are resistant dreams that do not get analyzed; their plenitude and variety distract the dreamer from the latent content. Mania, with its plethora of manifest action and its speed, resembles that type of dream.

The blank dream, which initiated each of the four hypomanic attacks of the patient discussed above, at first sight appears to stand apart from manic symptomatology, especially because of its presumed rarity. It signifies a pure fulfilment of the wish to sleep and might be considered as something not reflected in the psychoses. Yet, it has its exact counterpart in the nosology of the manic-depressive states—not, it is true, in the schematic ups and downs of mood, or excitements and inhibitions, of the circular psychoses, but in the benign stupor.

Sleep and Stupor

The benign stupor, first defined by Kirby (1913) and then studied extensively by Hoch (1921) and later by MacCurdy (1925), consists in a recoverable stupor with no conscious mental content. Before the stupor, the patient often expresses a wish that he were dead, and the stupor is frequently followed by an attack of elation, or 'post-stuporous hypomania' (Hoch, 1921). The anamnesis shows that there have been previous depressions, manic attacks, or similar stupors. When Hoch first described benign stupors, he thought of them not as 'empty' of meaning, because of their lack of conscious content, but as a living-out of the fantasy of being dead. My own feeling is that this is not the deepest interpretation, but that like blank dreams, they repeat early infantile, visually contentless sleep. To borrow Kubie's neat paradoxical formulation, benign stupors are somnambulic representations of sleep.

The patient who reported her four blank dreams with orgasms and subsequent hypomanic elaborations had, in late adolescence, lived through what in all probability was a benign stupor of several days' duration. For these days, she had absolutely no memory, as if she had slept through them; and later attempts to pierce her amnesia led to nothing but screen-memory-like imaginings patently fabricated on the spot. There is some evidence that the stupor was precipitated by a relationship not unlike those that preceded the blank dreams. Later, I shall have more to say of ideas of sleep and death. Here it will suffice to say that a wish to sleep is obviously ontogenetically older than a wish to die, and that the idea of death is a modification of the idea of sleep.

Viewed as a problem in sleep psychology, the difference between the artificial excitements of drug intoxication and the natural manic and elated states becomes more evident. The manic does not follow through in his approach to sleep; the pharmacothymic patient does. Hence, taking the transition from waking awareness to sleep as a gradually descending slope rather than a discontinuous set of steps, the manic gets only so far in his descent, the pharmacothymic ultimately all the way in his drug stupor. In the drug addict's stuporous sleep, the union with the breast is more complete, less avoided, than is the case in mania. Suicide in both types, which psychologically also may represent a fusion of ego and superego, or a return to the mother, perhaps reproduces in its most extreme form the fantasy of sleep at the breast. Because in German the addict's drugs are called *Rauschgifte,* and *Rausch* means 'spree', we may again have been partly misled by language, and we may not have given due consideration to the artificial stupor the drugs usually produce. Rado (1933b) has remarked on both stupor and suicide as sequelae of drug addiction, and because of the value of his account, symbolized by his fresh term for the illness, *pharmacothymia,* I prefer and use this designation.

In Abraham's (1924a) discussion of regression in the depressions and manias, he noted, without precisely clarifying his idea, that there was a regressive pull toward the early oral stage, antecedent to the biting, cannibal stage where he postulated the main point of libidinal fixation. The early oral wish to be nursed at the breast would be completed or fulfilled by a falling asleep, if the fantasy is carried consistently to the end. Such a fantasy we recognize in the blank dream, the benign stupor, and the suicide. The psychological identity of predormescent and prestuporous phenomena was shown in the descriptions given in Zilboorg's (1933) paper of states of consciousness that precede stupors, catatonic and benign.

Mania and Children's Dreams

We began with the question, in what sense mania could be called a form of sleep, since both states reproduce psychologically the fusion with the breast at nursing. Having expanded the idea of sleep to include dream states, we found that for all its appearance of vigil, mania repeats a fusion with the breast at nursing and a falling asleep. The ego's fusion with the superego in mania repeats a falling asleep, but it is not a direct duplicate of the original model of infancy. Mania lacks the blank-dream quality of the baby's sound sleep, which would be repeated by a stupor. It reproduces a reproduction—namely, the later sleep of a somewhat older child, with his dreams of relatively simple manifest structure, with denials, identifications, and happy wish fulfilments. Hence, mania is an altered copy of a child's sleep, which itself is an altered and developed copy of the first sleep at the breast.[1]

The Nature of the Ego in Different Dreams

Mania, it was shown, splits off a fact-denying part of the ego from the rest. Before the elated ego has successfully influenced the dream life, there may be a period in which nighttime dreaming gives more evidence of reality testing than does the daytime elated fantasy state. This situation was noted by Freud (1938) in a case of paranoid jealousy, where the dreams were perfectly 'sane', and by Ruth Mack Brunswick (1928a) in her paranoid patient. The split in the ego was demarcated by the sleep-waking boundary. In early infancy, apparently, this boundary is not so sharp as it later becomes. Grotjahn (1938), reporting the dreams of a child, two years and four months old, stated that going to sleep and waking had not the abrupt effect which they have for adults; the child carried over manifest dream thoughts into waking life. This particular direction of influence, from the sleeping to the waking state, must come to be blocked very early in life. There are few dream residuals in ordinary waking life, or they pass unnoticed. Sterba (1946), it is true, has reported on analytic patients who acted out the dream content of the previous night, and this direction was noted in an early paper of Ernest Jones (1911). But ordinarily the action is one-way and valvular; thoughts from the

[1] Here a few words may clarify my difference with Melanie Klein (1935) as to more or less normal infantile forerunners of mania. For Klein, the earliest antecedent of elation is the 'manic position' about the end of the first year of life. This manic position is a defense against a preceding 'depressive position', and generally against the danger to which the baby's ego is exposed from within, by the death instinct emanating from his id and introjected bad objects. In my construction, I specify two points, or rather planes or levels, in the child's chronological development, one earlier and one later than Klein's manic position. One of these is the very earliest nursing period, with emphasis on falling asleep at the breast. This level, of smaller area in absolute terms though greater perhaps proportionately, I take to be a relatively uniform, physiologically grounded, reflex-like experience, quite regardless of ego structure; consequently, any idea of the baby's defending himself is irrelevant. The second level is a later cross section of larger area in the development of the function of sleep, and one that is clearly dependent on an ego of some complexity. The young child that dreams away his daytime privations is of course employing a defense mechanism, denial.

day enter into dream formations, but night thoughts, except pathologically or sporadically, do not enter into waking formations. Going to sleep and waking up become the obvious initial splits in mental life.

Insight, Denial, Censorship

I expanded, above, Freud's idea of the determinants of the analytic defensive response, negation, and assumed that the condition which evokes a denial during analysis, namely, intellectual insight without emotional self-commitment, is also provocative of elation or depression, especially the former, and that similar insight or near insight in ordinary life might have the same effect. In ordinary life, it is true, insight is relatively easily avoided through the usual defenses, such as repression, but it is less avoidable at night. Then we may be given insight we do not wish, accompanied by vivid emotions and organic reactions that cannot be escaped, if the dream censorship fails in its sleep-guarding function.

The dream censorship fends off the instincts, usually, but it sometimes gives the impression of needing education and practice to perform its duties efficiently. In the absence of any definitive work on the maturation of the censorship from childhood on, we must assume that there is an evolution that more or less keeps pace with the growth of the child—an assumption borne out by all that we know of ego development and of childhood dreams. The superego and the reality-testing function, the two other great ego 'institutions', alter and develop with time; so we may plausibly believe that the censorship too undergoes a ripening and is influenced by the individual's history, in other words, that it probably does profit from 'education and practice'. The adaptability and modifiability of the censorship in one or another sense is implicit in our general theory of analytic therapy, as French (1937) has made clear.

When the censorship is circumvented by a sufficiently disguised wish, the sleep-waking boundary is secure; but occasionally, as though it were inept or taken by surprise, it permits the passage into consciousness of deeply dreaded erotic and aggressive wishes, sometimes with their full emotional charge. In puberty especially, the dream censorship is often unprepared for the new biological re-enforcement of the instincts, and it is taken off guard by direct incestuous thoughts with intense feelings, which appear starkly in the manifest content of dreams. Despite Jocasta's remark that 'many ere now have dreamt of things like this, But who cares least about them bears life best', a thought and feeling of this sort is not easy to set aside. It acts like a premature or ill-timed analytic insight into the unconscious and provokes a reaction in waking life.

It will be recalled that the young woman with the blank dreams, in her clear periods, had dreams in which young men in bed with her turned into her mother, and that in the hypomanic attacks that followed the blank dreams, the men played a great role in her imaginations, while all reference to the mother was taboo. Her prehypomanic dream censorship was inadequate to its task of sheltering her from recognizing the stimulating effect of her relations with women, and in the blank dream failed completely to protect her by a denying hallucinatory dream. This task was accomplished by her waking ego through the repudiative erotomanic fantasies of her elation. A new sleep-guarding mechanism was then built up during the later days of her elation, when the daytime imaginings had gained sufficient strength to deceive her ego.

Innocent surely of any psychoanalytic thinking, Reiss (1910) reported the following 'psychogenic depression'. A woman brooded over the approaching marriage of her son. The night after the wedding ceremony, she dreamed that lightning flashed through the church window and struck the bride as she was standing at the altar, tearing off the veil. The patient became sleepless, depressed, anxious, and, a Swabian Jocasta, hanged herself. The failure of her dream censorship brought unwelcome insight and affected her waking life.

In my own practice, a girl who lost her mother just before puberty slept, through her teens, in close proximity to her father and brother, sometimes sharing a room or a bed with one or the other. She was troubled by overt dreams of sexual relations with these two men. Going to sleep was an agony for her, and when she awoke after a dream, she would thank God that it was only a dream after all. In her later character neurosis, which followed a depressive pattern, she took to homosexuality and—the escape that led back to the beginning—to bouts of alcoholic self-stupefaction, which signified for her the erotic sleep of her teens and about which collected the guilt she had felt at that time. From these stupors she would awaken, alarmed at what might have happened, particularly that she might have masturbated while she was unconscious, and resolved never to repeat the performance. In her analysis, her outspoken dread was that she might have a frank sexual dream about the analyst.

In two cases of neurotic hypomanic personality, frank dreams at adolescence of incestuous relations with the surviving parent of the opposite sex precipitated both the neurosis and the vast career of denial on which these persons embarked. One of the patients had lost her mother at about the age of eight; the other, a young man, had lost his father at nine. Both were upset by the incestuous dream and defended themselves against its recurrence, at first by rituals and hysterical symptoms, but finally by altering their personalities into overactive, overcheerful, but dissatisfied types, with an inflated identification with the lost parent. They were not homosexual, save for brief adolescent experiences, nor alcoholic, but relied on an excess of action (including much sexual behavior) to distract them from any repetition of incestuous thoughts and dreams.

These patients were menaced by insight that came to them in dreams, and they sought escape from instinct and anxiety in alcoholic stupor or hypomania. The older, natural sleep had become unreliable, because of the weakness of the censorship; the stupor and the hypomania were the new equivalents of sleep, where the censorship, ego defense, and the wish to sleep prevailed, in the case of stupor because of the complete absence of consciousness, in the hypomania because of the alertness and possibility of acting out a denial. The psychological equivalents of biological sleep—the stupor and hypomania—were dependent on the same mechanism of fusion with the breast or its later successors. As if the adolescent breach in the sleep-waking boundary needed a healing, other forms of sleep with different, well-guarded boundaries were established. The failure of the adolescent dream censorship set up compensatory oral mechanisms that represented new and pathological fulfilments of the wish to sleep.

To return to the problem of mania and sleep, enlarged by our consideration of certain stupors and by an expansion of the idea of sleep to include various types of dreaming, we may summarize our equation. Both sleep and mania are the result of an intrapsychic fusion with the breast at nursing, but only a stupor reproduces the infant's sound sleep. Elation repeats a repetition and a development of this primal sleep—the wish-fulfilling, dreaming sleep of a somewhat older child; it is a substitute sleep, or a sleep equivalent, guarded by a type of censorship that is created particularly to employ the defense mechanism, denial, and to prevent emotional acceptance.

IV. ADDENDA TO THE THEORY OF ORAL EROTISM*

The Oral Triad of Wishes

Among Freud's contributions to the theory of sexuality and neurosis, none is better established than the conception of oral erotism. A relatively superficial observer can be convinced of the dominant role of the mouth in early childhood. Very young children exercise their mouths most extensively for hedonistic ends, and adults retain a greater or lesser interest in the use of this organ for purely pleasurable purposes. By now everyone recognizes the importance of the baby's oral needs and frustrations, and their later consequences. In the adult's unconscious, oral needs and patterns persist; the language of dreams, neuroses, and psychoses offers an inexhaustible supply of variegated fantasies centering about the mouth. Abraham (1916), to whom we owe so many original observations on the psychology of the mouth, established the regressive nature of the 'melancholic depressions' (p. 278), formulating them as reactivations of oral sadism. The preponderance of cannibal fantasies in the depressions has been confirmed countless times by observations on psychoanalytic patients and in the hospitals. And with this mass of data, the idea of an active, sadistic, cannibal wish has become a matter of everyday familiarity.

The fact that these fantasies are technically known as 'cannibal' has promoted an attention to the mouth as an active organ. Yet, active fantasies of devouring by no means exhaust the range of oral fantasies. There exist fantasies of being devoured, and psychoanalytic students of sleep have seen the necessity of including the process of going to sleep among the data of oral erotism. For completeness, the idea of active orality —the wish to devour—must be studied in conjunction with its passive counterpart, that is, the wish to be devoured, and with

* [Chapter 5 from No. 89 in Bibliography.]

the wish to go to sleep, and for convenience I shall refer to these three wishes together as the 'oral triad'. The wishes originate in the nursing situation. For at least two of the wishes this statement is obvious: the nursing baby certainly wishes to eat, and for many of his first months of life he falls asleep rapidly after his nourishment. Soon the physiological needs become psychological wishes.

The Wish To Be Devoured

The middle element of the triad, the wish to be devoured, is not superficially evident in the nursing situation. It is not, like its companions, an inevitable observation, but a heuristic fiction—a construction, in the psychoanalytic sense, based on inference. That the nursling 'wishes to be eaten' means merely that toward the end of the act of suckling, and with the gradual approach of sleep, the infant has certain perceptions and experiences of yielding, relaxing, and falling that leave a strong mnemonic impression, and that later on these memories and experiences serve as a nucleus for the cluster of ideas of being eaten, in various forms. The assumption that the three wishes—to eat, to be eaten, and to go to sleep—are closely linked because of their common origin has a heuristic value in the study of neurotic and psychotic manifestations that repeat and revive the nursing situation. Stress will be laid on the second and third wishes, not because they are more important than the first, but because they have not received sufficient consideration in the psychoanalytic literature.

The idea of being devoured was first noted in the form of a fear, as a phobia, and the first part of this chapter will treat mainly of what has been learned by the psychoanalytic study of certain phobias. In childhood phobias, the fear of being bitten or eaten was seen to stand for a fear of castration. It expressed in regressive oral terms a fear of retributive castration for sexual wishes toward the mother and castrative wishes toward the father, as in Freud's (1909a) case of Little Hans with his horse phobia; or, as in the Wolf-man (Freud, 1918 [1914]), it arose from a wish to play a feminine part in coitus with the father, with its presumptive castrative effect or precondition. In the analysis of adults, comparable fears are found, and as in children, they usually signify a fear of castration or its equivalent, a fear of taking a female role. Often they are seen to be fears of retribution for wishes to bite, eat, or attack with the mouth—a talion punishment of the form, the biter bit. Unconscious sadistic intentions of this sort are commonly attended by their appropriate passive counterparts. And the wish to play a female role, as a mother, may be expressed through a fear of being eaten not only in men but in many women as well. In adults, the symbolism of dreams and neuroses may conceal the direct fear of being swallowed and eaten, so that the content of the phobia shows only a figurative devouring, as a phobia of 'being eaten' by cancer or other diseases, or in other elaborations to be mentioned later.

Any anxiety of childhood may serve as a substitute for a fear of castration. However, the idea of being devoured is not always attended by fear. It may be a wish, as Freud (1918 [1914]) pointed out when he discussed the regressive meaning of being eaten up. Children are often told that they are sweet enough to eat, and they are dubbed with the names of comestibles, such as Lamb Chop, Honey, Cookie, and the rest, and to their obvious delight they are playfully threatened by adults: 'I am going to eat you up!'. In Inhibitions, Symptoms and Anxiety, by way of contrast to Little Hans and the Wolf-man, with their fears, Freud (1925a) tells of a masturbation fantasy in which being devoured was conceived as a pleasure. A boy imagined that he was John Dough, the Gingerbread Man, who was pursued by an Arab chieftain with ravenous intent. Children evidently can attribute to food a pleasurable wish to be eaten; they are able phenomenologists and seem readily to appreciate how the cookie and sugar-pie feel.

The wish to be eaten arises in the nursing situation, where it is adumbrated by the sensation of being engulfed or surrounded by the mother's breast, or of being supported by the mother during the relaxation that precedes sleep. In the predormescent phenomena reported by Isakower (1936), the sleeper feels large masses being stuffed into his mouth as he falls asleep; at the same time he has a sense of being enveloped or wrapped into the breast symbol, as if he were being swallowed by it. In dreams, sinking into soft yielding masses, such as snow or bodies of water, or more figuratively into dense forests or into a crowd, repeats this sense of being swallowed and put to sleep.

Our English idiom, 'to fall asleep', has its justifiable origin in these moments of predormescent fulfilment. The baby's muscles become more and more relaxed, so that he would in fact fall if he were not supported by the mother or her later substitute (and a well-known symbol for her), the bed. I should therefore differ with Silberer (1911), who interprets sensations and pictures of falling in dreams as premonitions of waking up. They are such only incidentally, I believe, for they much more plausibly stand for falling asleep, even in the dreams he records. Fenichel (1945), following Oberndorf (1929), interprets the difficulty of breathing that appears in certain dreams—of being drowned, for example—as repetitions of the feeling of being smothered when a baby's nose is pushed into the breast. More generally, it repeats the difficulty a baby has in managing his breath while nursing. In their later development, all such sinking and smothering sensations, along with the losing of consciousness, are included in fantasies of being devoured.

At least a trace of the original 'being eaten' idea appears to accompany all fantasies of oral incorporation. This may be, as Nunberg (1932) suggests, because the baby originally does not distinguish the breast as a foreign body but treats it as he does his own fingers, big toe, and other parts, when he stuffs them into his mouth and gnaws them. One may say, with license, that he indulges thereby in an act of autocannibalism. Hence, theoretically, any object that is eaten up becomes treated as the subject. The subject identifies himself with it and takes over the fantasy potentiality of being eaten.

Application of Oral Triad to Claustrophobia

The fantasy of being eaten up, along with that of devouring and of going to sleep, is readily studied in a form of claustrophobia, where, as in Poe's tale, The Pit and the Pendulum, anxiety arises from the imputed danger of having one's rest in a closed space disturbed by an intrusion or by the closing in of the walls of the space. The content of the phobia comes from childhood fantasies about the prenatal state. The enclosure stands for the mother's body, the intruding object (the pendulum, in the story) for the father's penis, and the closing in of the pit walls for the threat of extrusion at birth. The idea of being within the closed space is not an anxiety fantasy, but one of safety, of being in hiding. The anxiety arises from the threat of interruption. The fantasy of being within the mother is regularly accompanied by ideas as to how one got in, and the imagination recognizes two modes of entry. The child either imagines himself gnawing his way in or being swallowed. In either case, it takes the place of a foetus, and the foetus with which the claustrophobe identifies himself in imagination is patterned on some real, newborn baby. Accordingly the foetus is supposed to be engaged in one of two activities: it is either eating or sleeping—for the most part, the latter.

Displacement Downward and Inward—The Erect Gait

Despite earlier naïve views that a primary wish to return to the uterus was operating here, it can be shown that the oral triad of wishes suffices to explain the claustrophobic fantasy, and it is not necessary to postulate any memories of blissful intrauterine feelings. The 'intrauterine' fantasy, in which the child identifies himself with a nursling, is taken into the abdomen, and in that location continues his feeding or comes to rest in a sound sleep, is a nursing fantasy with a shift downward from the breast to the abdomen. It is the fantasy of a baby that stands, which Bateson and Mead (1942) call the *knee baby,* as distinguished from the younger *lap baby,* terms which the authors adopted from the Southern mountain people. Freud's and others' remark that the erect gait is most decisive in human evolution has its ontogenetic as well as its phylogenetic reference. For the knee baby's view of the world is lower than the lap baby's. He has factually been displaced downward, and he contemplates, instead of the mother's breast and arms, her lap and abdomen—but not necessarily with any new thoughts or intentions. In his wishful fantasy he nurses himself into the abdomen as he did into the breast, or perhaps he fortifies the nursing by biting or other improvements, and then accordingly goes to sleep. He does in fantasy what the lap baby is doing in reality, but at a lower altitude.

The same displacement downward leads to the well-known fantasies of nursing at the father's penis, and indeed at the mother's penis too in certain fantasies of the phallic mother.[1] The main point is that upper or lower level, inside or outside

[1] See *The Body as Phallus,* pp. 28-47 [Ed.].

the mother, no matter what the locale of the fantasy, the mechanisms and the wishes are oral. Along with the idea of devouring goes the idea of being devoured and of going to sleep. Prenatal psychology has been a field for rich psychoanalytic speculation and few facts, whereas the sleep of infants that follows nursing is an assured fact and the speculations about it have not been numerous.

Undeniably the care of small babies seeks to reproduce the physical conditions within the uterus, and there is no objection to this sensible and biologically sound idea; but there is nothing besides our imagination that says the baby is happy in the mother's body. Offhand, one would suppose that the pleasure principle was not established and that prepsychological organic agencies ruled the field *jenseits*—beyond the pleasure principle. With all allowance for the traumatic effects of the birth process, inspection of the newly born fails to show evidence of bliss or pleasure. On the other hand, in the mother's lap some months later, the baby is obviously happy when he is fed, cuddled, and put to sleep. It takes several months for the physical care to change from biological necessity into psychological pleasure. The known pleasure of the baby's sleep should make us wary of immediately invoking the prenatal state to explain the 'intrauterine' ideas as repetitions of the real sojourn in the mother, and should turn our attention to the sleeping phenomena of the nursing babe.

Needless to say, the claustrophobic fantasies are secondary in the neurosis and represent a flight from sexual, internally originating dangers. The uterus is the great haven in which the patient hides. The fantasy of being swallowed logically precedes the idea of being asleep within the mother, as the passive sense of yielding and being 'engulfed' precedes the baby's sleep at the breast.[2]

Other Phobias

The moment before falling asleep (when the sense of being engulfed is strongest) is unconsciously remembered most prom-

[2] Recently Melitta Schmideberg (1948) has reported an interesting variant of the 'Pit and Pendulum' type of claustrophobia, in which the patient's fantasy carried him no further than the mouth on his way into his mother's body, so that the pendulum represented the tongue, the narrowing walls the chewing mouth. To go into the mother's body only as far as the floor of the mouth is a very curtailed flight to alleged safety.

inently in connection with so-called 'feminine' fantasies, particularly those of masochistic coloring. Although the idea of impregnation *via* the mouth, by eating, is an old, familiar analytic finding which explains hysterical nausea, vomiting, and other eating and digestive difficulties, it has not been sufficiently recognized, or commented upon, how much the fantasy of being eaten and falling asleep contributes to the content of anxieties with 'feminine' meaning. The common fear of falling from a height into a chasm or onto the street, long recognized as expressing a wish for a child, and of which Freud (1925a) remarked that it had an independent masochistic element, is a portrayal of falling asleep. In several cases, I have found that the patient dreams of clinging to a rock or cliff, which represents the mother, while the place below is described in strikingly oral terms: there is a pool or lake which will 'swallow her up', or there is a 'yawning' or 'gaping' chasm or canyon. More elaborately, the dreamer may be threatened by the jaws of death (like Henry V, for whom 'this hungry war opened its vasty jaws') or by the mouth of Hell, or may be sucked into whirlpools.

In such phobias, the idea of death and dying represents sleeping and falling asleep. The anxiety is attached to the two parts of the oral triad that mean being swallowed and falling asleep; that is, it becomes tied to the early sensations that follow satisfaction and is perceived, when it 'returns from repression', as a fear of dying or death. In short, the fear of death is an anxious transmutation of the original pleasure of falling asleep. The idea of oral impregnation includes not only the active eating process, but the passive 'being eaten' as well. Dreams of drowning have been explained as reversals of the common fantasy of a baby's coming from out of the water, familiar to us from the legends of Moses and the birth of Venus. But the reversal should not be ignored, as if of no importance or further unanalyzable. (See Freud, 1900-1901, pp. 312, ff.) In the nursing situation the reversal of aim comes when the baby has approached the end of his active suckling, when his face is wet with milk and he feels himself falling asleep.

Oral Triad in Female Genitality

In pregnancy, it is known, the idea of being eaten occurs as a pleasant daydream to some expectant mothers. They think of the baby within them as a cunning little animal, nibbling at them, or 'tugging' within them, foreshadowing in a way the pleasure of giving the breast. Rado (1933a) has remarked on the oral implication of the German popular word for placenta, *Mutterkuchen* ('mother-cake'); inferentially, the embryo is eating. Such ideas predominate in the early part of pregnancy, at the very time that somnolence is a prominent symptom. Free of anxiety, the oral triad finds representation in early pregnancy in three manifestations: in the bulimic cravings for symbolic articles of food (the classical 'picas'), in the fantasies of being nibbled, and in contented somnolence.

Morbid fears of cancer and other diseases have long been known to conceal wishes for a child. Here the idea of being eaten up by something within is usually evident, with its logical ending in the sleep of death. In the neuroses, generally speaking, the infantile pleasure of falling asleep is not so conspicuous as its derivative, the fear of death. Indeed, sleep itself may be feared, as in the neurotic insomnias, which are often unrecognized phobias of falling asleep. The patient, consciously desiring nothing so much as a good night's rest, will ostensibly try to put himself to sleep by measures, such as reading, which in fact tend to keep him awake. The paradox lies in the fact that 'sleep' has two meanings. The sleep the patient desires is the blank sleep that he knew in early infancy. But the 'other' sleep, erotized, has come to be associated with anxiety and the fear of being eaten and of dying. These ideas threaten to enter his dream life, and the phobia signifies a fear of meeting in dreams the ideas of death and destruction.

Two patients of this type in their dreams pictured itching skin, which disturbed their sleep, as being due to the bites of graveworms, by which they identified themselves with dead mothers (and incidentally with pregnant mothers). Another patient dreamed of being devoured by flames, literally, being cooked preparatory to being eaten, and thus identified herself with her dead, cremated father.[3] In each case the fantasy was

[3] The patient identified kitchen middens, those archeological garbage heaps, with the barrows, or graves. Those unfamiliar with the idea of cremation as cooking should look at the pictures of Balinese cremations in Bateson and Mead's (1942) book and note the garnishing of the corpse, the 'barbecue' atmosphere, and the ambivalence about finally disposing of the body—i.e., the reluctance to let it go without being eaten. A comic drawing that appeared recently in

traced to experiences with the deceased parent, and to an early infantile wish to sleep with the parent in question. Instead of sleep bringing the fulfilment of the wish to be devoured, the wish appeared in the dream life as an anxiety. As these ideas indicate, the mechanism of incorporation and identification is not necessarily purely active; identification also may follow the passive method of being eaten. (See Graber, 1937.)

Being put to sleep is often unconsciously equated to childbirth, usually through the superficial association of general anesthesia. Fears emphasize the danger of this substitute for the original, primal-chemical, lactic somnifacient. Several patients, who brought about pharmacothymic sleep or stupors, unconsciously expected to wake up with a child. An interesting variant of this idea, through the notion of 'child-wife' and the Bible story of Adam's sleep, came from a male alcoholic, who woke up to find that he had nearly acquired a wife.

In one extraordinary case, the pangs of childbirth were unconsciously equated with hunger pangs, vaginal motions and sensations during delivery to those of nursing, while the child's head stood for the breast and his birth for a painful withdrawal of the breast. This patient in general identified vaginal with oral activity—a process frequently commented upon in psychoanalytic literature (H. Deutsch, 1925; Sachs, 1928). Not impossibly, the sexual orgasms which have been noted as occasional accompaniments of childbirth, usually in an elated setting, are orally patterned phenomena, like the orgasm in otherwise blank dreams. The fantasied nursing is displaced downward, so that the contractions of labor simulate or reactivate the process of suckling, with the baby's head substituting for the breast. The elation or sleep which follows reproduces the pleasure and sleep of the nursing situation. Shortly thereafter, the same pattern, reversed, may be seen when giving the breast to the child produces sexual excitement.

This survey of oral phenomena in phobias and in genital

---

a newspaper showed a surprised 'G.I. Joe' being ejected violently from a building labeled 'Crematory' by a group of indignant mourners. 'I don't know what's the matter', he answered his inquiring buddies. 'All I did was go in there and ask, "What's cooking?" '.

Prometheus, the fire bringer, is devoured by the carrion bird; carrion birds and fire serve the same post-mortem function—this by way of a note on the overdetermination of the firebird legends.

processes, particularly those connected with female sexuality, appears to strengthen the assumption, made earlier, that it is profitable to consider orality not exclusively from the standpoint of active devouring fantasies, but to include as well the two immediate consequences of satiation at the breast, even in the realm of later oral sadism: namely, the predormescent relaxation that is later reflected in the ideas of being swallowed up, yielding, and falling, and finally the falling asleep. In this interpretation, the idea of being bitten or devoured is not simply a reversal of the active aim, a self-punishment for oral aggression. It reproduces a process that is inherent in oral activity, an experience of the nursing baby after he has had his fill. The sinking, falling, yielding, passive giving way that is expressed in the phobias as a fear of death and of being devoured is a replica of the passive erotic relaxation that follows upon nursing.

To see this yielding as an element in the nursing situation would aid our understanding of masochism, especially of that variety which Freud (1924a) called feminine. For it would indicate that we need not choose between a primary sadism and a primary masochism as the original psychological representative of the death instinct. In the nursing situation, sadism finds its foreshadowing in the first active stage, masochism in the ensuing yielding and sleep. The second stage of passive pleasure could be taken, speculatively, as the prototype of later types of passivity, and sleep as the model for later, erotically colored wishes to die. Thus, in its three attitudes at the breast, potentially, the baby would be, in succession or in overlap, a cannibal, a masochist, and a suicide.

Pregenital Origin of Oral Wishes and Fears—The Primal Scene

In the above, the oral triad of wishes was discussed in relation to genitality and its corollaries, castration anxiety and the genitally determined neuroses. Yet, as it was said, the idea of being devoured is not completely explained as a defensive maneuver or as a reversal of the active wish to devour. Owing to immediate castration anxiety or to fears connected with feminine wishes, in the phobias the formula that the biter fears being bitten often applies. There is, however, no logical necessity to assume that the fear of being devoured, or the wish to be, can arise only in connection with genital wishes and fears, and that it must always represent a defense and a reversal of aim. Indeed, even the reversal of aim from active eating to passive being eaten is not a late pattern, born of an emergency need for defense. It exists from the start in the act of nursing, when active eating is followed by the passive relaxation which later comes to be conceived as a being swallowed and which ultimately merges into sleep.

Indeed, Freud (1918 [1914]) remarked on the pregenital determination of the fear of dying and of being devoured in his discussion of the Wolf-man's primal scene and the fear on that occasion. Oral fears, Freud thought, might be due to events in early infancy that were unrelated in any way originally with genitality or ideas of castration. The Wolf-man's fear of death might have been determined in the first instance by a disturbance in the oral stage of libidinal development and then reactivated by the primal scene. An oral reaction to a primal scene is not uncommon. The adult's genital excitement communicated to the child often gets expressed in the language of the child's oral experiences, so that even where the adult coitus is not pictured as an act of reciprocal cannibalism, the unconscious formulation portrays it as reciprocal suckling (Federn, 1913; Abraham, 1924a; Brunswick, 1929).[4] One may safely assume that the frequent conjunction of primal scene and oral 'analytic material' is not purely accidental, and one may attempt some explanation.

Further illumination of the oral reaction to the primal scene is especially welcome in a study of the elations or of the affective disorders in general, for the primal scene is often the event that gets reproduced in adult depressions and elations (Abraham, 1924a; Nunberg, 1926; Brill, 1928b; French, 1929; B. Lewin, 1932; M. Klein, 1935; Jacobson, 1943). It would be helpful to know what there is about a primal scene that could reactivate the oral triad of wishes.

A theory lies at hand in the nature of this oral triad, which consists not only of the two directly oral wishes to eat and to be eaten, but includes as well the wish to go to sleep. The intimate genetic linkage of these three wishes in the nursing situation suggests that they may be reactivated together, en

[4] See also, *Analysis and Structure of a Transient Hypomania*, pp. 57-70 [Ed.].

masse, so to say—that the reactivation of one would mean the reactivation of all three. To apply this conjecture to the primal scene situation, we should evidently begin with the third wish, for at the primal scene the child's sleep is disturbed. When children are present during an adult coitus, they are either awakened or partly awakened, or the stimuli penetrate in greater or less degree the sleep barrier and affect them in their rest. In any of these cases, the child is stimulated, his wish to sleep frustrated or antagonized. In defense, he will try to get back to sleep, to stay asleep, or to deepen sleep, perhaps by dreaming, which Freud tells us is the great guardian of sleep. We assume, in other words, that the initial defense against the sights and sounds of the disturbing event is a mobilization of the wish to continue sleep.

Adult utilization of going to sleep as a form of defense has been reported in such diverse situations as battle (H. Winterstein, 1932); concentration camps (Friedman, 1949); a new environment or an unpleasant predicament, such as a trial for theft, among the Balinese (Bateson and Mead, 1942); the analytic couch (Stone, 1947); and in various neurotic, perverse, and psychotic situations (Davison, 1945). The wish to sleep or to stay asleep is a defense, but it is connected in the unconscious with memories of the earliest falling asleep at the breast. The little witness to the coitus, awake in some degree, thus calls on the fantasy of nursing to preserve and intensify his sleep.

Besides the 'inherently oral' ideas of being devoured, to which Freud refers, the Wolf-man's dream demonstrates the presence of the wish to stay asleep. When the dream starts, the Wolf-man is in bed looking at a closed window. The window opens, which Freud interprets to mean 'I wake up'. The closed window should then mean 'I am asleep'. It should in fact represent the dream screen,[5] that is, a visual representation of the wish for an empty, blank, unstimulated sleep. And since the dream screen stands at the same time for the breast, it would repeat the fulfilment of the wish to sleep in its full form: to fall into a sound sleep after being nursed. Assuming this re-enforced wish to sleep, we have a clue to

[5] See *Sleep, the Mouth, and the Dream Screen,* pp. 87-100, and *Inferences from the Dream Screen,* pp. 101-114 [Ed.].

the Wolf-man's associations about being eaten. The re-awakened fantasy of being eaten, on which Freud comments that it stems from the previous oral period of development, is a reproduction of the 'being swallowed' that arises in the nursing situation before the baby falls asleep. The wish to be devoured, so far as it is not substitutive for the Wolf-man's wish to play his mother's role, is the inherently oral wish to be 'devoured into sleep'—in other words, the intimate companion of the wish to sleep. Charged with anxiety, the wish to sleep becomes transmuted into a fear of death, an easy intellectual alteration of 'good' sleep into 'bad' death.

In the discussion of claustrophobia, it was noted that the fantasy of being within the mother's body, there to eat and sleep, is a displacement downward and inward of the wish to eat and sleep at the breast. A very frequent version of the primal scene dream includes this idea, in what is called a fantasy of intrauterine coitus observation. This dream or fantasy has several motives, among them the gratification of spying from a hidden observation post, and from the standpoint of defense, the idea of being concealed and unnoticed. I propose an additional, perhaps essential factor, namely, the wish to sleep is a repetition of nursing and a defense against the disturbance of the primal scene. In general, it is my present view that the fantasy of being within the mother is tantamount to the wish to be nursed and to go to sleep.

Because the primal scene interferes with the course of sleep, it reactivates the whole oral triad. This may be studied in certain insomnias. The sleeplessness can be traced back to the primal scene experiences, but the problem of going to sleep is expressed in oral terms. The patient manifests a continual hunger of one sort or another, the devices hit upon to induce sleep have a direct or symbolic oral significance (drinking milk, using sedatives, reading, even masturbating without conscious fantasy, i.e., at the breast), and the insomnia of the primal scene is equated unconsciously to the sleeplessness of an unfed baby. The patient wishes to eat so that he may sleep, and the insomnia of the primal scene gets put into the terminology of the nursing process. These cases, descriptively designable as neurotic depressions, reveal the intrinsic oral factor to which Freud alluded, for their sleeplessness turns out to be a fear of sleep, which they equate with dying and being devoured.

The first line of defense against the primal scene stimuli at their origin is sound sleep, a complete repetitive success of the oral procedure of nursing. The secondary defense, after some penetration of the stimuli, would be a dream, a guarding of sleep by the oneiric neutralization of the intruders. Analytic experience indicates that many dreams of young children deal with the primal scene, particularly those that are disagreeable and inadequate to prevent waking up (Freud, 1900-1901; Federn, 1913). Since the affective disorders depend on an oral regression, the primal scene, with its demands on the sleep mechanism and hence on orality, seems made to order to enter into the early history of the future elated or depressive patient.

Penis Envy

Besides the primal scene a prominent feature in the case histories of the elated is penis envy (H. Deutsch, 1933; A. Katan, 1934). In their hypomania, Deutsch's patients were denying their phallic deficiency; confrontation with this fact provoked denial, contradiction, and elation. In a manic phase, one of Deutsch's patients dreamed that her son had two pipes and gave her one of them—a dream that made up for her shortcoming—and Deutsch comments that this dream epitomizes the meaning of the patient's hypomanic reaction. Deutsch does not imply that the penis envy itself is responsible for the form of the reaction, stating that hypomania is part of the psychology of 'melancholia', i.e., that it is due to pregenital determinants—a statement which M. Klein (1935) does not sufficiently weigh in her criticism of Deutsch's views. Katan's chronic optimists looked forward to the happy days when everything would be all right and they would have a penis. Such denials as these resemble the 'denials through wish fulfilment' of small children. Rado (1933a) tells us that the little girl, made aware of her phallic deficiency by a view of the male organ, turns to her mother to have the deficiency made good, and that this demand is couched in oral terms, such as an attack on the mother's breast or body. According to the same author, the fulfilment may come in a dream wherein the girl possesses a penis and denies her castration. It would confirm my views on elations as repetitions of childhood dreams if such a girl, having become a woman, repeated this dream with appropriate and suitably up-to-date elaborations in the form of a denying elation. As in Deutsch's case, a mania which denied the lack of a penis by a fantastic assertion of its possession would reproduce the little girl's dreaming sleep.

A related fantasy, sometimes accompanied by elation or 'good humor' during analysis, is the idea of the whole body being a penis, which is a denial of castration and at the same time a knee baby's downwardly displaced identification with the breast.

Oral Triad in Stupors

Before proceeding to the further study of the more general effect of the oral triad in the elated states, it will be profitable to consider stupors, pharmacothymic and affective, since these may be taken to represent the complete 'logical' outcome of the triad, with its ultimate aim of sleep. Preceding the pharmacothymic stupors, the wish to be eaten sometimes makes its appearance starkly in the delirious hallucinations of menacing animals, large and small. Bromberg and Schilder (1933) reported a less obvious version of the fantasy of being eaten, the dismemberment fantasy of some drug deliria. The patient sees his limbs, genitalia, and other parts of his body separated from the rest of him, he feels them being detached, or he represents himself in one way or another as falling to pieces in segments. This dissolution of bodily ego is the same as that reported by Federn (1926, 1934) in the process of falling asleep, as shown by the study of certain dreams and hypnagogic fantasies. Malcove (1933) reported quite similar fantasies that were told her by neurotic children, and she supplied elements that were not included in the adult deliria. The children imagined that they were being cut up and chewed, and they included in their accounts the homely means of being dismembered, namely, by the teeth and the table silver. Malcove found that the fantasy of being cut up occurred in both anxious and pleasurable versions. In most pharmacothymias, the wish to sleep, as brought out in a previous discussion, is obviously fulfilled in the stupefaction produced by the various drugs. When the drugs do not cause a deep, blank sleep, they permit happy dreamlike states.

In the affective stupors, the oral yielding is more subtly expressed. Hoch's (1921) 'benign stupor' patients, before the onset of the sleeplike state, spoke much of death and dying, and several attempted to commit suicide. Outside of this constant idea, their elated and depressed productions in other phases of their psychosis, differed little from the usual run of affective disorders. Hoch accepted Kirby's original theory that the stupor psychologically represented an escape into a feigned death. He remarked, however, that we knew little about feigned death and that there was an evident parallel between the stupor reaction and sleep. He recognized drowsy states of partial stupor, and he hoped that the future might show some physiological parallels as well.

'Sleep reactions', Hoch commented, 'do not occur in bed alone. Weariness produces indifference, physical sluggishness, inattention, and a mild thinking disorder such as are seen in partial stupors. The phenomena of the midday nap are strikingly like those of stupor. The individual who enjoys this faculty has a facility for retiring from the world psychologically and as a result of this psychic release is capable of renewed activity (analogous to post-stuporous hypomania) that cannot be the result of physiological repair, since the whole affair may last for only a few minutes.'

In this train of thought, Hoch was looking for the 'normal analogue' of the stupor to serve as his guide, and he missed it only barely because of the adultomorphic prejudice common to the psychiatric thinking of his era. Genetically considered, the normal analogue of the stupor is the dreamless sleep of the baby; the poststuporous hypomania has its analogue in the simple dreams of children. On the other hand, his comparison with the midday nap is a very happy intuition. I have had several opportunities to analyze the nap, when it appeared as a compulsive symptom in neurotic characters. The postprandial nap is a vestige of a childhood habit, which begins of course in infancy and is directly connected genetically with the infantile sleep after meals that starts with the nursing situation. In fact, the idea of the stupor as an 'after-dinner' nap is essentially the point of the present discussion. In the analyzed cases I refer to, the naps were miniature stupors, though not always dreamless, and the dreams were not infrequently denials of the problems that were being dealt with at the time in the analysis. In one case, during certain conflict-filled periods, the napper would be awakened from a dream in which he would find himself pulling disagreeable stringy or sticky substances from his mouth (like Freud's pleasure ego), to which one association was the navel cord, and another the 'nasty stuff' in the analysis, but which stood in general for the smothering breast. The nap, if not the normal 'analogue' of the benign stupor, is certainly its analogue in the analysis of persons with oral fixations and depressive and elated tendencies. Such minor happenings as naps during the analytic hour may be as fruitful for a study of stupors as the little elations and depressions that appear among the resistances. (See Stone, 1947.) The very striking analogy, and probable identity, of the benign stupors and the blank dreams which preceded the elations of the young woman mentioned several times in these pages is also worthy of remark.

Simmel (1944) appears to have anticipated some of the ideas presented here in his discussion of the state of rest that follows instinctual gratification. If we follow his suggestions, we should see in sleep, or what he calls more generally *nirvana* or the state of rest, a turning inward of the interest directed previously to objects and primarily to food. This interest, as I understand his theoretical explanation, follows the food down the digestive tract which supplies a kind of topographical indication, like a road map, of the locus of libidinal and aggressive internal action. The organism attacks the food internally as it had externally. Many remarks of Melanie Klein (1935) contain allusions to a comparable assumption. I cite these authors to show that it is theoretically possible to envision a material substrate for the idea of a turning inward of instinctual activity, but in my own thinking I do not go beyond the relatively observable events of the nursing situation. In accord with Simmel's theory especially, the eaten food becomes part of the baby's ego, it is not only in the body but of it, and the baby might thus be considered as eating himself. The metaphysics here is a little difficult; yet clinically there is no gainsaying the occurrence of fantasies of identification with food, combined with ideas of being eaten and 'coming to rest'. The interpretation is the only issue. Simmel's and Klein's ideas link up the notion of being eaten to an original instinctual experience. It is Klein's theory that the idea of being devoured and destroyed is originally a fear which the baby has during his first year of life, and that it is even then a projection of the baby's aggressive wish to destroy. Thus, the idea of being devoured appears as a fear, and for her, in opposition to Freud's idea, an original fear of death.

Jekels' (1945) theory that sleep is due to the persistent action throughout life of the death instinct is a biological, not a psychological, theory. True or false, it can furnish no answer as to whether the psychological experience, sleep, precedes or succeeds the psychologically understood idea, death. It furnishes no answer either way as to the priority of a wish to sleep over a wish to die. Contrariwise the genetic psychological study neither affirms nor invalidates Jekels' idea.

Following Freud's implications in Inhibitions, Symptoms and Anxiety, I am inclined to assume a libidinal rather than an aggressive or anxious primary form and to say that a wish to die or be devoured precedes the fears. The wish would be an expression and formulation of the desire for the relaxation and sleep that originally followed upon uninterrupted nursing. This wish for sleep and rest would be the bedrock of the idea, and the aggressive and anxious versions would represent later deposits.

V. REFLECTIONS ON DEPRESSION*

In previous centuries, psychiatry did not use freely the term *depression,* as it does now, to indicate a pathological complex of symptoms. The old literature was apt to speak of *melancholia* instead, and the history of the melancholia concept from Hippocrates to Kraepelin constitutes a large part of the history of psychiatry. That the word *depression* has replaced it so extensively may be due to the authority of Kraepelin and his use of its cognate adjective in the diagnostic label, *manic-depressive.* In one application, *involutional melancholia,* the older word survives, and it was current at the time of Freud's early writings. We find Freud and Abraham writing of *melancholische Depression,* implying thereby that they meant one form of depression—a structured complex of symptoms.

Present-day psychiatry has not completely rejected the concepts which Kraepelin used in regard to manic-depressive psychoses, but it has let them lie fallow. Not much, for example, is done operationally with Kraepelin's organic assumptions, and indeed the idea of symptom, in its nineteenth-century meaning of sign of a disease process, has fallen into desuetude. The word symptom remains, but it has a new meaning. In manic-depressive psychoses, in other psychoses and in the neuroses, symptom has come to mean a psychological structure, as Freud (1925a) defines it in Inhibitions, Symptoms and Anxiety. Psychiatrists are gradually getting away from the word's original denotative implication.

Certainly, in psychoanalytically pervaded thinking, there has been an inevitable, insidious change of meaning not only in the concept of symptom, but also in the concept of depression. Although depression is still the diagnostic label of a psychosis, it is predominantly the label of a definite set of mechanisms. These mechanisms, which include as elements aggression turned inwards, identification, tension between ego and super-

* [No. 114 in Bibliography.]

ego, narcissistic and oral regression, are familiar to us all. In our thinking, depression has come to mean this complex of mechanisms rather than a disease process; the metapsychological concept has largely replaced the psychiatric-diagnostic one. A third meaning of the word depression creeps into our writing and thinking, and in a way too this is due to our background of Kraepelin's psychological assumptions. I refer to the everyday idea of depression as an elementary feeling. As the song puts it, 'The blues ain't nothing but a good man feeling bad'. Beneath all the Kraepelinian nosological system lies a faculty psychology which assumes that an affect is something elemental and unstructured, pure and pristine. If this has come to seem a matter of common sense and something obvious, we must remind ourselves again of the philosopher's remark that what we regard as common sense is apt to be the residue of habit and that today's common sense was yesterday's bias.

Let us therefore look more closely at the idea of depression as a sad feeling. Psychoanalysts have many opportunities for observation and assessment of this feeling. Gero[1] has remarked that it appears, along with anxiety, in any analysis, even in the analysis of persons called normal, that is, those who have no specific neurotic and psychotic symptoms—students in analytic training, for example. The emergence of feelings of anxiety and depression during an analysis is indeed a corollary of what we believe to be a feature of the analytic process, namely, the uncovering of conflict. During analysis, conflicts previously latent become manifest. Those between ego and id are attended by the evolution of anxiety, those between ego and superego by depression. We think of these technically as feelings indicative of the conflicts, and we are attentive to their presence as signs and signals. Such transient anxieties and depressions, we also believe, are not unlike those which could appear in anybody, and they are of an intensity usually which one would say was within the range of the normal. Particularly is this true if the person who experiences the feeling is able to account for it rationally or through rationalization. Also, offhand, we are apt to think of the feeling as a pure and elementary process in the sense of faculty psychology, as an elementary affect. We conceptualize signal anxiety especially

[1] Personal communication.

and do not usually attend to cognitive elements nor to questions of special genesis and structure.

Yet the simplicity we predicate, on second thought, is purely conceptual. On the couch, we see that the anxiety is a sign of id-ego tension, but we also observe that it occurs in various forms and in different settings. The same anxiety that shows us the presence of open conflict tends to have more or less of a structure. We even approximate a sort of classification, for we note that sometimes the anxiety makes its appearance in the form of a mild phobia, that is, it includes or is linked with displacement. Or in other instances, where there is projection, we may speak of a paranoid anxiety. When we think in this way, we already imply that there is a possible diagnostic and metapsychological aspect even in the case of signal anxiety. Genetically too, since the publication of Inhibitions, Symptoms and Anxiety, we know that we may be dealing repetitively in the analytic situation with anxieties that are formed at various stages of development, and we speak accordingly of separation anxiety, castration anxiety, social anxiety, and the rest. Though we know that anxiety on the couch has its genetic history and structure, conceptually and in the context of analytic technique, we neglect this in favor of its major meaning of a signal or sign of conflict.

On the couch, the more or less passing depressive affects, which could be characterized as blue feelings, unhappiness, etc., can be subjected to the same considerations that were introduced concerning anxiety. Depression, like anxiety, is a sign of conflict within the personality; and the forms we meet on the couch range from what may present themselves as nearly pure affect, in the old-fashioned sense, through the various forms known to us from psychiatry. Thus we speak of anxious depression and paranoid depression, and we have even designated one familiar form by a label originating in psychoanalytic technique. I refer to the negative therapeutic reaction. Gero (1936) has stated that this is a common occurrence in the analysis of cases diagnosed as depressions. The negative therapeutic reaction may not show itself starkly as a depression. But when it does, it is possible to recognize in it various structures.

I do not wish to suggest an exhaustive classification of the forms of negative therapeutic reaction, and I particularly wish to leave any list of depressive forms entirely open-end, but it might be useful to mention examples. One example would be a young woman whose every analytic step that gave promise of possible instinct satisfaction was regularly followed by a guilty depression. The superego here was a lineal descendant of a really very jealous mother and older sister, and her guilt had originally been displayed in real appeasing gestures, designed to curry their benevolence and ward off their jealousy. Internalized, this became visible during the analysis in fantasy. We speak in such a case of moral masochism and a fear of object loss. But it is noteworthy that so far as the patient's introspections were concerned, all of this was for a long time unknown, and even the precipitating actual event for the reaction was not connected in her mind with the ensuing depression. If she had been examined for diagnosis during one of the episodes, she might have been called a case of anxious depression, though the diagnosis would have been qualified by some such term as 'subliminal' or 'mild'.

I have not carefully distinguished in my language between guilt and depression, leaving it to my audience to understand the level of exposition. Theoretically, of course, I follow our usual terminology in this respect. The main point here is that when a transient depressed mood appears during the analytic hour—even if it is 'reasonable' or rationalized—we can usually find in it one or more of the familiar features of the depressive mechanism, such as turning of aggression against the self, reaction to an object loss, etc. Under the microscopic scrutiny of analytic procedure, we do not find examples of simple affective elements.

I should like to pursue this somewhat further. The studied cases of momentary sadness show a mechanism and are not pure affects in the old faculty-psychology sense. Let us therefore make a radical assumption, somewhat as follows: that in the depressed moods and momentary sadnesses of everyday life, in adults at least, such a pure affect never occurs and that sadnesses, 'blues', and the like all are complicated reactions involving instinct and ego psychology. To make this idea more concrete through a hypothetical example: I hear of a friend's illness and I become sad. Faculty psychology would predicate two elements—a stimulus (the bad news) and the response (sadness). Such two-term stimulus and response would be considered the elemental model for the origin and appearance of an affect. According to the idea presented above, which is suggested by experience with transient moods in the analytic hour and their analysis, the model would be as follows. Bad news such as the friend's illness is a stimulus, but it is what psychiatry calls a *precipitating* event. The reaction is not a pure simple feeling, harmonious and appropriate (as common sense would say) to a bad situation. The bad news has the form of a threatened object loss, hence in psychological reality is *as if* an object loss and the response is a form of grief, which under scrutiny could be empirically analyzed into aggression turned inward, identification, and more or fewer of the classical elements of the depressive symptom complex. I realize that this hypothesis implies a kind of psychiatrization of psychology and would surely meet with many academic objections. What we have been naïvely calling a normal emotion turns out to be a minor neurosis. Yet I should like to point out that psychology has benefited many times from the introduction of this point of view. My model is Freud's attack on the genesis of anxiety. In considering the hysteric attack, he said that this might be considered an artificial emotion, and turning the matter around, that the original modeling of anxiety on the trauma of birth would mean that the emotion repeated an original 'attack'.

I shall not speculate further about the genesis of emotions in general, but instead call attention to a clinical difficulty encountered in the study of elation. For many years, elation of low intensity passed relatively unobserved in clinical psychoanalysis. The subject was joyful, one supposed, because things were coming his way. Only when elation did not fit our common-sense preconceptions of when it was to be expected did we give it more intensive study and develop psychological models and explanations. Yet the mild elations encountered during an analysis proved a fruitful field of study. They revealed mechanisms, now well recognized. They could be understood in terms of denial, of coalescence of ego and superego, of identification, and the rest. It is possibly the case that everyday joys too are structured. They are probably not simple responses to simple stimuli, like a reflex, but can be shown to have a structure as complicated as a pathological elation. The organic analogy would not be a reflex, but the firing of some of the complex structures called to our attention by modern neurophysiology.

In the light of our assumption of the individual specificity of affective responses, we may attempt a kind of shorthand metapsychological restatement of some of the above. As an example, we may take the transient depression of individuals in whom, as we say, there is a paranoid coloring. We would assume here the bad news of a friend's illness leads not only to a sad response but to a suspicion that this illness was caused by mistreatment this friend may have been subjected to by his wife or employers or physicians. Such transient suspicions would perhaps disappear with the friend's recovery but might be revived under later stresses. Plainly, we should have a bringing into play of ego defenses other than those classically present in the Freud-Abraham model for depression, notably projection designed to shift an unconscious sense of guilt. Or the sadness could take on a secondary exhibitionistic quality, seeking an outlet for unconscious aggression—if the occasion was used to nag the environment, the friend's family, for example. Such forms would, I think, still come under the head of intelligible reaction and on the whole not be thought particularly pathological.

I have no wish to get involved in an attempt to define normality as opposed to pathology. My standpoint here would be approximately that expressed by Freud (1937a) in the following quotation in regard to the ego in analysis:

> The ego, if we are to be able to make [a compact] with it, must be a normal one. But a normal ego of this sort is, like normality in general, an ideal fiction. The abnormal ego, which is unserviceable for our purposes, is unfortunately no fiction. Every normal person, in fact, is only normal on the average. His ego approximates to that of the psychotic in some part or other and to a greater or lesser extent . . . (p. 235).

This is a profound statement, and I should like to use a partial paraphrase for the sake of exposition to comment on the emotions. The normal emotion is an ideal fiction; emotions we encounter are no fiction. Every one of them is only approximately normal in the sense of faculty psychology. They resemble a psychosis in one point or another, in a greater or lesser degree.

Such a point of view, which admits more factors than are accounted for by faculty psychology and its corollary, Kraepelinian nosology, appears more adaptable to that state of affairs which led Kraepelin to formulate mixed manic-depressive states and the other dubious syndromes in his classifications. It would also, I believe, shed some light on the matter called 'the prognosis of the attack'. The guiding principle in psychiatry has been roughly that the more pronounced the affect in a psychotic attack, the better the prognosis. More accurately one would wish to have stated not whether an attack is temporary but which elements in the attack will probably persist into the so-called period of recovery, and which will not be present. Notably there are variations here, and we still need a study of what particular mechanisms tend to be tied together in different individuals.

As examples of the approach for which I have outlined a sketchy methodology might be mentioned studies by Fenichel (1934) on boredom and by Greenson (1949) on apathy, which are contributions from pathology to the psychology of affective states.

Up to this point in our exposition, the main effort has been to see what Freud's idea as to the genesis of an affect, as elaborated in Inhibitions, Symptoms and Anxiety, might contribute to our conception of the affect, depression. Now, using the same text, we may apply other ideas of Freud's to the concept of depression as a combination of neurotic mechanisms. In the main and in principle this has already been done, so what appears here are truly reflections. During years of teaching, I have noted that when the matter of symptom formation is under discussion, we all make many references to Little Hans and the Wolf-man. The references, however, are not often to the original case histories but are more apt to be to the formulations given by Freud in Inhibitions, Symptoms and Anxiety, where the infantile phobias of these two patients are used to illustrate Freud's concept of phobia formation and the role of anxiety and the ego in this process. Indeed, in this context, Little Hans and the Wolf-man come to stand for simple phobia formation. This has become evident from the follow-up work done on the Wolf-man, first by Ruth Mack Brunswick (1928b), now by Muriel Gardiner (1953, 1958), and other material gathered for the Freud Archives. This new material has had to do somewhat with the Wolf-man's famous dream and with his phobia, but it has illuminated other parts of his personality and other features. The more we consider Freud's statements in Inhibitions, Symptoms and Anxiety, the more we realize that so far as Little Hans and the Wolf-man are concerned, he has given us there not a bit of case history but an abstract model for the formation of a simple phobia. The model gains in sharpness by the abstraction, that is, by Freud's cutting to the psychological core of the matter. We can say that in general conflict of id and ego are shown by signal anxiety; and that in the simple phobia, repression and displacement appear in response to the anxiety.

But even in these simple phobias, the anxiety (except for conceptualizing) is not a simple one-element process. In the case of the Wolf-man, after attributing the anxiety in the main to a fear of castration, Freud adds that it also contains an oral component which arises from a previous period of development and contributes to the manifest fear of being eaten. In Little Hans the fear of being bitten implies a similar oral component. However, we are left with the idea that this is an adventitious rather than a constant matter. The phobia, we are to understand, is a genital neurosis, and the anxiety is typically castration anxiety, while the oral coloration is an individual peculiarity of the two little patients. Some years ago,[2] I gathered material which showed that the façade of other, especially adult phobias (claustrophobia and agoraphobia) also showed traces of oral components, and I thought I could demonstrate in them elements that sprang from the nursing situation. My method in that study was based on Freud's comparison of the façade of a phobia with the manifest content of a dream.

I should like here to take some of the thoughts presented above and transpose them to a similar frame of reference, to

[2] See *Phobic Symptoms and Dream Interpretation*, pp. 187-212 [Ed.].

speak now of the façade of a depression, and to invoke for the depression a state of affairs such as we find in phobias. The variety in the manifest picture of the phobia led to the invention of a variety of neologistic combinations with the Greek root *phobia:* claustrophobia, agoraphobia, aleurophobia, gephyrophobia, and the rest. That the façade of a depression may show variety was, I believe, adumbrated by the psychiatrists before Kraepelin; for example, when Kahlbaum invented the name *cyclothymia.* But on the whole, these psychiatrists were concerned not with the façade nor the manifest content. They emphasized the course and the form, as the name just mentioned illustrates. The namers of phobias impressed us with their manifest variety; contrariwise Kraepelin and his predecessors and successors ignored variety. In the depressions and elations, they stressed a presumptive unity and sameness. Traditional psychiatry has alerted us to variety in the phobias and to uniformity in the depressions. There is no general terminological agreement concerning the variety of depressions. In different official classifications, subheadings designed to indicate varieties of depression differ widely.

Here, I think, the psychoanalysts are beginning to make their contribution. However, they are not following the tradition of the phobia-namers, nor yet that of the descriptive psychiatrists who spoke of *folie circulaire,* simple depression, simple mania, etc. Analysts have instead seen variety in the psychological sense; for example, in the types of identification that can be demonstrated in different patients (Annie Reich, 1954), and in other specific features of the ego (Jacobson, 1954). This type of clinical approach is very different from the one of naming and descriptive classification, and we hope will ultimately replace it. Ultimately, too, such replacement may go far to extend the psychoanalyzation of psychiatry and to substitute for an outworn psychology, based on faculty psychology, a true dynamic model.

I have elsewhere[3] stated my conviction that all psychoanalytic statements concerning the neuroses must be tested by sleep and dream psychology. This conviction is based on Freud's crucial finding of the sameness in essence of the dream and neurosis psychology, and on the empirically successful ap-

[3] See *Sleep, Narcissistic Neurosis and the Analytic Situation,* pp. 227-247 [Ed.].

plication of this idea. I should therefore like to repeat here briefly a comparison I once drew between the depression and a certain type of dream, in which I continue an idea Freud introduced by comparing the phobic façade and manifest dream content. As a frequent manifest façade of the depression, I select the standardized picture used by Freud and Abraham.

Our first approach to treating the melancholia picture as if it were a manifest dream façade assumes that *narcissistic* has the same meaning when it is used in connection with the regression in melancholia and with the regression during sleep, where it implies a dreamless state. Hence, what appears in the manifest picture of melancholia is an analogue of the manifest dream picture, the result of intruding impulses from id and superego which are the analogues of stimuli that threaten to waken the sleeper. In other words, the manifestations of the classical picture of melancholia are the façade ultimately derived from the distorted expression of such impulses.

In this respect we may say further, the depression is manifestly an unpleasant dream, in which the latent narcissistic wish for sleep at the breast is disturbed in its fulfilment by an opposite intruding tendency, that is, by weaners and wakeners. Like the narcissism of sleep, the narcissism of the depressive regression is subject to disturbance by impulses and memories, and these get analogous representation. As in the well-known dream of the burning child in Chapter VII of The Interpretation of Dreams, dreams are represented in a way which is influenced by the need to preserve the narcissistic regression. In the example mentioned, you will recall, a father dreams that his dead child, whose body is laid out in a nearby room, comes to him, shakes him by the arm and whispers, 'Father, don't you see I'm burning?' The father wakens and finds that one of the candles has started a real fire. Freud uses this dream to show the operation of the wish to sleep, for the dreaming provides the father with a moment more of sleep (Freud, 1900-1901, pp. 509-510, 533-534).

The well-known superego commands, if they are considered as wakers and weaners, are demands that the depressed patient give up the breast; they are analogues of the real fire which disturbed the father's sleep. The handling of these by the depressed patient is analogous to the dream distortion and serves the same purpose, namely, to preserve the narcissistic regression. In the dream example, the real arouser, the fire, becomes a dream sentence. In the depression, the superego injunctions are distorted expressions of commands to waken. Their form tends to guard the analogous narcissistic regression of the depressions. The narcissistic sleep analogue of the depressed person is constantly being intruded upon and told, 'Get away from your mother's breast! Wake up!'. But the demand is not obeyed. The persistence with which this command is repeated over and over shows that it is heard but not heeded. As long as the depressed patient is thus admonished, he is evidently secretly or unconsciously still maintaining his regressive place at the breast. The admonition is treated in the way a dreamer treats a stimulus from within or without—it is given attention and registered, but the narcissistic regression is preserved.

I have chosen a very simple type of dream, that of the burning child, as the analogue of a frequent simple form of depression, in which prominent symptoms are due to guilt and oral regression. Freud commented on the contrast between the conscious sense of unworthiness and the unconscious narcissistic grandiosity in such cases. There is a similar paradox in the conscious pain of this disagreeable melancholic picture and the unconscious pleasurable wish fulfilment of sleep at the breast.

To return now to the point made above in regard to the forms and classification of the depressions, we could take the variety of the means used to preserve the narcissistic regression, and the different defense mechanisms of the ego that are invoked to preserve it, as the source of the individual coloring and varying mechanisms found in different depressions. We have type dreams which, like that of the burning child, are relatively simple and can be used to demonstrate a basic mechanism. In fact, Freud used the dream of the burning child in this very way, as a type to indicate a feature of all dreaming. So, in the analogies drawn above, we have been dealing with a type, and as in the case of the dream, with something which in one way or another may enter all depressions, while the façade presents an analogous variety.

VI. REFLECTIONS ON AFFECT*

Drives, Affects, Behavior, our 1953 tribute to Marie Bonaparte, in which she took great pleasure, was a notable collection of essays, some of them lasting contributions. In one chapter, Edith Jacobson (1953) points out that Freud's first theory of neurosis, an 'affect theory', developed into an 'instinct theory', which in the minds of many superseded it. This she believes halted efforts to clarify the concept of affects and their relation to drives. 'In fact, we are in need of a consistent affect theory, which psychoanalysis so far has failed to develop' (p. 38). Jacobson's essay summarized critically the thoughts of other authors. In general, however, it must be conceded that in this book and in psychoanalytic writings since its appearance, drives have continued to receive more attention. Much that Freud formulated originally in terms of emotions has been shifted and rephrased into instinct theory, but pieces of affect theory have not been well absorbed and persist as isolated fragments. 'We do not yet have an adequate theory of affects in general', writes Benjamin (1961, p. 665), 'and of anxiety in particular, in spite of the significant contributions of Rapaport and others. If it is possible to achieve such a theory on the psychological level alone, this would demand a considerable refinement and elaboration of drive theory also.'

Some of the unabsorbed areas and other difficulties arise from history. The first of these is the fundamental matter of definition. Customarily writers evade the issue by appealing to the aphorism that definitions come last in the history of science. The evasion is venial, the trouble ancient. Most terms used in talking about the central idea of affect have confusing histories. The word *affect* itself has been used over and over not only by recent nosologists but by the ancients too (*vide infra*). Philosophers' attempts to classify mental processes, including the old academic or *faculty psychology,* which anato-

* [No. 124 in Bibliography.]

mizes the mind into the so-called faculties (perception, cognition, emotion, volition, etc.), have interplayed with the nosologies. Zilboorg (1941), referring to nineteenth-century psychiatric classification, was alluding to faculty psychology when he spoke of the 'unreal psychology' lying behind the psychiatric dogma. But till well in the nineteenth century, doctors in all branches of medicine did not distinguish between symptom and 'disease process' in Kahlbaum's and Kraepelin's sense, and there was equal confusion in definition and in characterizing the relation of emotion and illness. *Melancholia* seemed both a mood and a disease; so did *nostalgia* and other *passions* (de Sauvages, 1768). Galen's four body fluids had each their separate emotion, temperament, and illness. As for the classical philosophers, a glance into Baldwin's (1940) dictionary will show the mix-up in their writings, where *affect, emotion,* and kindred words were used with numerous denotations and connotations, sometimes as equivalent to impulse or drive.

The word *affect* itself is old, antedating Saint Augustine, who says: 'Those mental states which the Greeks call *pathe* and Cicero *perturbationes* are by some called *affectus,* or *affectiones* by others, keeping to the literal meaning of the Greek *passiones*' (Baldwin, 1940). The divisions of the mind and corresponding classifications of mental illness persisted down through Kahlbaum and Kraepelin and appear even today disguised in the terms *affective psychosis* and *emotional disorder.* A massive tradition behind the use of these terms still comes in to bother us. Psychoanalytic efforts to think about affects are colored by it, and in part our efforts at clarification will be a struggle with our presumed need for some kind of faculty psychology.

Faculty psychology was a sophisticated development. The early Greeks, newer philological studies show, did not clearly distinguish semantically between perception, knowledge, feeling, and action. The word that later meant *to fear* originally (perhaps also) meant 'to be put to flight'; the word for *I know* originally meant 'I have seen'—or rather, there was no differentiation between flight and fear, sight and knowledge. The distinction between idea, emotion, and action many think is the result of human culture and social development and, in the individual, of education. Commenting in this connection on the words used by Homer's heroes to refer to what we should consider their ideas and feelings, Onians (1951) has this to say:

'Greeks like Aristotle and we today have apparently attained to greater "detachment", power of thinking in cold blood without bodily movement, as we have to a sharper discrimination and definition of the aspects and phases of the mind's activity. It is with the consciousness, the knowing self, the spectator aware of what happens within and without (emotions, sensations, etc.) that a man would tend to identify himself. As the spectator became more "detached", the purely intellectual, the cognitive bearing of such words as *oida* would naturally prevail.' And referring to Lévy-Bruhl's analysis of 'primitive thought' and 'collective representations', Onians comments: 'There is, perhaps, no such thing as *"un phénomène intellectuel ou cognitif pur"* for us either. It is rather a difference of degree in the impurity.'

From these and similar comments, particularly if we give words to implications, it appears that the subjective experiences of early life become split up only with the development and education of the ego. Then, the holistic mass-event becomes conceptually differentiated into cognitive, affective, and motor elements. Before this, when in waking life the seeing person became detached from the scene, and in the dream the seeing 'eye' (system *Cs*) from the dream picture, the massed impression was split into the Cartesian *res cogitans* and *res extensa*. And as there are hallucinations and mirages that trick the *res cogitans* and require correction by education, so finally intellection, feeling, and action become separated through comparable corrective education. Of Homer's heroes it suffices us to say that *I know* means 'I have seen' and *I fear* means 'I am fleeing'. But Aristotle, Onians, and 'we today' can be more precisely differential as to which faculty is involved when we say 'I know' or 'I feel'.

If there were no concept of the independent observing cognitive self, we should have no corresponding concept of the independent feeling or the independent action. The growing, intellectually developing ego recapitulates the history of philosophy. We have an intellectualist bias, and so we find it more intelligible that events should be purified into concepts with an elimination of feeling tone than that there should be a purification in the opposite direction—that is, the exclusion of the cognitive and the identification of the self with 'pure feeling'. William James (1909) characterizes concepts as 'dead', hence by implication more amenable to visual inspection; for example, in the following: 'To understand life by concepts is to arrest its movement, cutting it up into bits as if with scissors, and immobilizing these in our logical herbarium where, comparing them as dried specimens, we can ascertain which of them statically includes which other. This treatment supposes life to have already accomplished itself, for the concepts being so many views taken after the fact, are retrospective and post mortem' (p. 244).

Onians and James and those who taught them can think of pure thinking, provided they can eliminate motility and emotion. They put the living event to sleep or kill it before they see the concept plain. For James, indeed, emotion was a secondary result of motion, if one wishes thus aphoristically to boil down the James-Lange theory. The thinking *I* is the motionless and ultimately the emotionless *I*. Language does much to turn events into 'pure' cognition. For if I must name my feelings I inevitably select from the total mass of what I know or feel or do. Words single out the bits that are to be scissored; the labels characterize the empirical bits. To introduce here a figure from dream psychology, we 'de condense' or decompress the subjective event: the event has come to us massively as if it were a 'condensation' in terms of the dream processes. The word does 'cut', in James's sense, by attracting and thus subtracting from the total experience some of the cathexis. This formula also brings 'instinct theory' to bear on the matter of pure and impure affect. The system *Cs* after the de-condensation can separate idea and feeling.

Feelings may vitiate the efficiency of action as well as of thinking. To illustrate this point, I once suggested that perhaps Milo, the athletic tyrant of Syracuse, was responsible for the whole stoic philosophy. In this home-made myth, Milo is supposed to point out to Pythagoras that a boxer is not angry with his opponent and that his efficiency suffers if he reacts with rage or fear instead of following the rules learned during training. Pythagoras, then, is supposed to have passed on this knowledge somehow to Zeno the Stoic, who in turn applied it to the more subtle athletics of argument and then to abstract thinking in general. This non-Plutarchan story assumes that the separation and elimination of feeling, as a source of inefficiency, is an almost self-evident corollary of conscious, trained functioning.

As to whether what is felt comes from an 'instinct', another moot question in academic psychology, the faculty psychology which has continued to permeate even pragmatism and behaviorism is responsible for such statements as the following, by William James (1890, Vol. II): *'Instinctive reactions and emotional expressions thus shade imperceptibly into each other. Every object that excites an instinct excites an emotion as well'* (p. 442). And Watson (1919), closely following James, says that 'there is no sharp line of separation between emotion and instinct' (p. 231). For Watson, the two are 'hereditary modes of response'; his behavioristic reductionalism abolishes the emoting self's *res cogitans.* In the quotations given above, the *'instincts'* are, of course, not Freud's *Triebe,* but they show some of the difficulties attached to the problem of the relationship, which militate against a conceptual separation.

The idea of an affect discharging itself goes back to cathartic days in analytic history, is perhaps influenced by neurological concepts relating to convulsions, and certainly has overtones of the 'attack', the acute emotional action. The 'affect charge' (translating *Affektbetrag*) is an evident vestige of faculty psychology in which an atomic affect representation is separable from a cognitive one. Superficially, this appears to save faculty-psychology thinking and to predicate the atomicity of affect and idea. It is not easily assimilated into the newer theory, but it would be difficult to replace or discard. It is too convenient as a near descriptive theory—a sort of 'auxiliary construction'—of displacements seen in dreams, jokes, neuroses, and in the psychopathology of everyday life, regardless of any theory of discharge. We shall return to this matter later on.

Here, the definition of an emotion needs more comment. Watson (1919) apologizes for the tautology in his definition. He frankly admits that his statements could be boiled down to 'an emotion occurs when there is an emotion-provoking situation'. This admission is helpful. Most definitions of emotion (when the matter is not deferred till 'the end') are given in terms of some scientific theory. This would apply, for example, to the James-Lange theory, which is essentially neurological, as well as to those which take off from Cannon's findings. But there are at least two sorts of definitions. To use the word *green* as an example, one dictionary definition depends on the wave theory of light and states that green is the color seen when the light used ranges from 495 to 515 millimus in wave length. But the dictionary also gives a common-sense or demonstrative definition; namely, that green is the color of grass, emeralds, etc., which is tantamount to pointing and saying 'That color is called *green*'. For *emotion,* we still lack an analogue of the wave theory of light. We say of our own or of our neighbors' affects, when they appear, 'That is anger, that is anxiety', etc. The list of affective states that we draw up is arbitrary and the naming pragmatic, determined by our purposes. We may, for good reasons, decide to name only what James calls the 'gross emotions', which could correspond to the VIBGYOR spectrum of our analogy, or like a paint dealer we may wish to distinguish the analogues of tints and mixed colors, such as coral, Nile green, mauve, magenta, etc. It is noteworthy that under the common-sense or demonstrative definition we could not name infrared or ultraviolet.

This all seems very commonplace, but the comparison may nevertheless be illuminating. No theory of affect has ever permitted the assumption of such an emotion as infra-anxiety or ultra-rage. As Freud puts it, an affect is always conscious. Our affect-naming has been strictly pragmatically psychiatric and psychoanalytic: we use such words as anxiety, depression, elation, love, rage, etc., because we need them. Our definition is still demonstration, despite efforts of Federn (1936) and others to define some affects in terms of a theory. For a bibliography containing other references than those given here, the reader is referred to sources used by Rapaport (1942) in his book, Emotions and Memory.

However, it seems to me that when we evade giving a scientific definition and postpone this until some undetermined late stage in our development, we have appealed not only to the conventional justification but have made a tacit demonstrative definition just the same, by default as it were, pointing to some specific affect each time we use the word. If, for example, we consider the idea of affect discharge, we immediately see that we are appealing to common sense. We assume that everyone knows that a rage 'discharges' itself in certain actions, joy in others, anxiety in still others. At this common-sense demonstrative level or tacit definition we are not much better off than Onians's Homeric Greeks, or the 'primitives' of Lévy-Bruhl. We are still asserting that an emotion includes motion in its terminal state, and we are raising the inevitable question attending all demonstrative definition—the 'white crow' exception—as to whether this is true of all sorts of emotion. The answer must come from observation and again depend on empirical common sense, and it remains doubtful whether physiological accompaniments or motor ingredients in an event are properly to be called 'discharge'. Freud (1925a) in fact asserts the opposite when he writes: 'The last two points [attributes of the anxiety states, i.e., (2) acts of discharge and (3) perceptions of those acts] indicate at once a difference between states of anxiety and other similar states, like those of mourning and pain. The latter do not have any motor manifestation; or if they have, the manifestation is not an integral part of the whole state but is distinct from it as being a result of it or a reaction to it' (p. 133).

To this remark, I call the attention of those who would generalize Freud's analysis of anxiety and apply it to all affects. If grief and sorrow lack essential motor manifestations, the idea of 'affect-discharge channels' is inapplicable (Rapaport, 1953). Indeed, if one arbitrarily assumes discharge, one has not made the conceptual separation of motion and emotion and one has still in mind some total experience, such as fear-flight, joy-orgasm, rage-fight; these are all regressions to the undifferentiated Homeric experience. If we follow this thought consistently, what we know empirically as an emotional discharge could be regarded as a regression from the de-condensed separate-element situation to the original collective representation, where feeling and action were inseparable.

I referred above to the possible retention of an atomistic faculty psychology in Freud's statement concerning affect. The reason for this seemed to be the existence of the phenomena of displacement: in dreams, in neurotic formations, in jokes, in everyday life, etc. The retention of the concept of affect charge is also empirically useful in explaining the phenomena noted that are due to repression and isolation; that is, the cognitive aspect of an event or series of events may make its conscious appearance separated from the affect with which it was presumably originally connected, as in certain obsessions. Affect charge as a term may have unfortunate connotations for present-day theory. Thus, it is certainly purely conceptual and has no affective or any other conscious quality. It is also not the equivalent of the 'free-floating' affect of the early theories; *a fortiori*, not the floating affect in the anxiety neurosis of toxic frustration.

The finding that an 'appropriate affect' can be inhibited or isolated from its idea or from its original motor expression, sets up a new background for an old question: can there be a 'pure affect', one without intellectual content or idea? To this question, experience permits a qualified affirmative answer. Animal experimentation recognizes 'sham rage', 'sham fear', 'sham love' in animals after ablation of higher nervous centers. Birth anxiety, too, is of this order physiologically, since the cortex and other brain parts are functionally inert. Presumably also a pure affect could be a baby's experience before the prison walls of cognition and semantics close in about his psyche. Epileptic rage attacks and certain toxic states may show affects that are 'pure' or nearly so.

Less out of the way from psychoanalytic observation and study are certain adult and nonexperimental, spontaneous mental states. There are ecstasy and related states of inner absorption of contentless quality, the kind of which the subject tells us that no words or thoughts can describe the immediate ineffable feeling experience, which can be told only later by means of comparisons and metaphors. The ecstatic trances are described as being 'pure feeling', 'rapture', and the like. Comparable 'darknesses' with depressive quality are described in Evelyn Underhill's (1948) book on mysticism. Finally, if we include 'apathy' among the affects, as many do, we can locate certain contentless mystic states of absorption in the same class of mental states. These conditions fit empirically among the 'pure' affects, but they are far from elementary states; they have a complex structure in the sense of psychoanalytic symptom theory. They employ or appear along with one or more of the ego defenses, and some of them can be attained through special education and training. In this way, the isolation or detachment with the purpose of retaining pure feeling forms a counterpart of the acquired detachment by which, in abstract thinking, we isolate and retain pure cognitions, and in athletic and manipulative functioning pure action.

More common than the daytime mystic experiences are certain blank dreams of pure affect. In such nonvisual dreams the sleeper 'sees' no dream and has 'no ideas' but feels a strong emotion. All such dreams have two characteristics: the emotion in them is intense, whether it be bliss or terror, and there is no projection of dream picture or dream action onto a screen, so that the dreamer and dream are as if one. No Cartesian visual *res cogitans* is there to look at the *res extensa* of a dream picture, and the sense of ego boundaries is lost. The dreamer is 'bathed' in the contentless dream. The dream observer (system *Cs*) is not detached from an 'objectified' dream.

This latter circumstance aligns such phenomena as the blank mystic state and the blank dream of an emotion with the special neurological and experimental conditions mentioned before. For one or another reason, all of these lack the independent *Cs* system, the subjective observer, whether this was due to immaturity or disease or accomplished through surgery, or whether it was a product of regression and a complex set of ego processes that resemble symptom formation.

A sexual orgasm may accompany the mystic state and the blank dream, simulating the 'purely physiological' action. But these speciously simple phenomena are possible only when the dreamer or the mystic has made extensive use of regression and other ego mechanisms such as denial and identification—in brief, they are not simple and elemental but highly structured. The physical state of orgasm (and comparably that of any intense feeling) draws the attention from the rest of the ego functions.

The above discussion suggests two statements about 'pure emotion' and two points of view or frames of assumption. Pure emotion can occur under certain pathological immature or experimental somatic circumstances and be recognized by introspection or intuited by observation. Emotion can be 'pure' according to the subject's introspective, immediate, observation and can appear to be elemental; yet when the point of view is psychoanalytic, its 'purity' becomes simply one formal element of a manifest picture which yields to further interpretation, so that it enters into a structure such as a dream or a mystic state.

We cannot address ourselves to a psychological problem as psychoanalysts unless we take along, overtly or implicitly, all the implications of psychoanalytic observation. Therefore, we should have to go beyond introspection, tacitly assume the existence of unconscious content, and ultimately decide that although with introspective methods, the question of the existence of pure emotion yields an affirmative answer, with psychoanalytic scrutiny the answer would have to be 'Yes, as manifest content and after regression'. The pure emotional states then are seen to be of two kinds—grossly, the structured (i.e., part of a structure) and the unstructured. It seems logical to expand the application of this division to the less pure emotions, with the burden of proof resting on those who assert that an emotional state is unstructured.

The concept of structuring implies the Cartesian split as well as the processes of maturation and development, implicit in present-day psychoanalytic writings. It includes also such considerations as Rapaport (1953) and others give to 'taming' and development, especially in discussions of anxiety.

The capacity to detach feeling from idea is observable early in life, as infantile phobias testify. Another mark of growth of this capacity would be the appearance of projected dreams, which would indicate the beginnings of the Cartesian split in the collective representation. Federn (1936) may have been near to this notion when he spoke of emotions taking their origin at the boundaries of the ego-parts. The trained capacity to form the split could be reflected in two ways: in the development of the 'purely intellectual', and the 'purely emotional'. As to the first of these, though surely structured as we observe it in the psychoanalytic setting, on introspection it too seems simple. Through such defenses as regression, repression, isolation, denial, etc., what are subjectively 'purely rational' matters are made to seem pure. Computers and robotic machines are projections of such detached functioning. *Mutatis mutandis,* the purity of the 'purely emotional' is preserved by the same mechanisms. Here belongs probably the set of emotions observed with 'thought-free' sexual orgasm, studied by Jacobson (1953), which, still linked to action, has been compared with other organic 'attacks' and narcissistic states. Again what is simple to introspection may be complex in total structure.

To follow and extend Freud's method of locating the representation of the dreamer in a dream, we could say that, in the three pure states considered above, the ego involved comes to be defined and 'located' according to the three main topics. It is respectively a feeling ego, a thinking ego, or an acting ego. Its perceptive apparatus in each case is narrowed to focus on the thoughts, the feelings, or the actions. To paraphrase Descartes, in one case the ego says with him 'I think therefore I am', in the second case 'I feel therefore I am' and in the third 'I act therefore I am'. Descartes's remark coincides with the state of the observing, motionless, system *Cs* in the dream. The reality sense of the 'feeling ego' is known to us from psychoanalysis as one of the states involved in working through. This too is the æsthetic sense of reality that characterizes creative artists when they test reality by how they 'feel'. The feeling ego may also be the character in the projected dream picture that represents the dreamer, according to Freud's (1900-1901) remark in The Interpretation of Dreams. As a character trait, the coalescence of ego reality and motility is found in athletes, dancers, and in general in those who feel their life in every limb. The skilled musical virtuoso, like Milo the boxer, is an example of the (secondary autonomous in Hartmann's sense) acting ego. The purely acting ego is the behaviorist's model of the individual, since an ultimately acting *res—*a *res agens—* takes the central position assigned by Descartes to *res cogitans.*

Having used extreme examples to bring out the need for a distinction between affect and idea and the usefulness of some such concept as *Affektbetrag,* I should like to proceed with the matter of introspective versus psychoanalytic psychologies. Psychoanalytic method, procedure, and theory begin with introspection, but with a very special kind. The analysand is pledged to verbalize all free associations; in 'self-analysis' he pledges this to himself. Action is relatively eliminated by an arbitrary rule. Emotions that arise during this procedure are verbalized. They are, of course, not 'pure', nor do they seem pure very long. They emerge in a structured formation which a psychoanalyst would call a *symptom.* I am referring to the emotions called 'normal' or 'appropriate' as well as those obviously inappropriate or pathological. Cautiously and empirically, it would be well to sharpen our statement and say that this is true for the 'gross' feelings with which psychoanalysts deal practically—in particular, for the three about which there has been the most discussion, namely, anxiety, depression, and elation. The word *symptom* as used here should not mislead us because of its origin in somatic medicine. Since Inhibitions, Symptoms and Anxiety (Freud, 1925a), to psychoanalysts the word no longer is used in its old diagnostic sense of a subjective indication of an underlying disease process. It now means a structure built up by the interaction of the three agencies of the total personality—id, ego, and superego—that depends on the interaction of the 'instincts' and the ego's defense mechanisms.

Anxiety, in the abstract, is often spoken of as if it appeared pure and idea-free in consciousness. This must be rare, and if it does the matter needs special treatment; perhaps it received it in the older literature, where 'free-floating' anxiety was thought to arise as if toxically. But when we encounter what we call 'signal anxiety' during free association and when we have perceived the id-ego conflict that it signals, we note that this anxiety and this conflict make their manifest appearance as a structure. What we see is a mild phobia when there is displacement, or with projections, a paranoid formation. We know that anxiety is a response to danger. Genetically we know that phenomenal anxiety and the underlying danger have a history, and we have learned to distinguish in the general setting of a phobic, depressive, elated or paranoid structure the various types of anxiety in response to a hierarchy of danger situations, such as separation anxiety, castration anxiety, social anxiety, and the rest (Schur, 1953).[1] The distinction between the normal and the neurotic is no sharper here than

[1] See also, *Phobic Symptoms and Dream Interpretation,* pp. 187-212 [Ed.].

in many other areas. Reality is individual, and one person's reality may be another's phobia. To judge by the fears during free association, despite the practical necessity of distinguishing the neurotic from the normal, nothing in the structure of the fearful experience will distinguish them. Only common sense will serve this purpose.

On the couch, momentary sadness, a transient symptom, is also not unstructured. If we permit ourselves to extend this observation to apply to the same experiences off the couch, we may say that after a certain age in early childhood, all are structured and complex reactions of id-ego psychology. I once gave a hypothetical example (B. Lewin, 1959)[2] : A friend's illness saddens us. This by common sense would be called an 'appropriate' reaction. But, regardless of appropriateness, if we apply psychiatric ideas, the news of this illness becomes a 'precipitating circumstance'. It threatens us with an object loss; in terms of psychic reality, it is as if one. Our sadness then is a form of grief, analyzable if scrutinized through the method of free association into aggression turned inward, identification, and possibly other recognized elements of depressive mechanisms. Our common-sense idea of appropriateness is a kind of convention or general assumption. On the couch, judged analytically, the sadness would be viewed as having intrapsychic structure; off the couch, and judged by a pragmatic rule of thumb, the sadness is not analyzed and is taken to be immediately intelligible.

The resistances to diagnosing little hypomanic attacks during psychoanalysis, on the part of patient and physician alike, led to a certain neglect of this topic for many years. Presumably, everybody wishes an elation to be an appropriate emotion. Ella Wheeler Wilcox's 'Laugh and the world laughs with you' is an excellent public defense against 'Laugh, Clown, laugh!'. Pleasure is 'body-ego syntonic' (as Royden Astley has phrased it), and we do not try to explain good moods with near the assiduity we use for bad ones. But the thoughts applied in the paragraphs above concerning depression and its normality or appropriateness apply here also. As a matter of fact, Freud gave us a lead to the analysis of the feeling of elation when he interpreted the delight in certain jokes as a

[2] See also, *Reflections on Depression*, pp. 147-157 [Ed.].

release of aggression; and the context and setting of the good feeling, on or off the couch, often reveal the structure of the event. Pleasure too seems never to be 'pure', psychoanalytically.

Anxiety, sadness, and elation can in many cases apparently be analyzed, regardless of their common-sense appropriateness; whether *always* is the familiar objection that only new findings can confirm or deny. Other objections come to mind. Thus, if the model for an affective experience is a symptom formation, would we not have a 'conflict theory' of emotions, so that all emotions would arise only as symptoms do, when there is a conflict between the 'instincts' and the ego? There are ways of getting around this objection. Conceivably, one might undertake the difficult task of finding evidence to support the assumption and try to prove the existence of such conflict. Or one could recognize secondary nonconflictual structure, following Hartmann, and assume that what we call, conventionally and according to common sense, normality itself has a 'symptomatic' structure. The roads fork here. Assuming with Hartmann (1939) that general psychology can be given a general psychoanalyzation, we should want the affects to yield to this type of analysis; or with Waelder (1960), we could opt for the probability that psychoanalytic theory will not entirely invade and conquer common-sense ego psychology in this instance too. There may be no dilemma in regard to 'normal' emotions and we may be able to emulate Solomon's judgment. Empirically, we may find it possible for psychoanalysis and psychiatry to invade this particular matter of the affective states in regard to other feelings in the way it seems to have invaded an appreciable area of the special emotional states of anxiety, depression, and elation. In their proper contexts, we may have to follow both common-sense and psychoanalytic psychology, each according to its basic set of definitions and assumptions. At present, we are forced to admit a practical syncretism.

To take another look at the affects as seen on the couch, we find that here psychoanalysis is attached to the idea that they are ultimately as if direct memories or the indirect products of memories. In the analytic situation and in dreams, these two possibilities are recognized. The affect brought to light may appear to be a direct ecphoriation, like a cathartic discharge of an *Affektbetrag,* which 'should have happened' in some older, more appropriate setting. Or it could be what I once called *screen affect,* when in place of an intuitively expected affect appropriate to the remembered or near-remembered situation, another inappropriate one appears. Without naming this concept, Freud introduced it when he interpreted the 'happiness' of certain dreams as covering ideas of dying and again when he saw the latent 'ugliness' of beautiful dreams. The same phenomenon is recognized in the analytic situation when hypomanic moods and episodes appear instead of more appropriate anxiety (B. Lewin, 1950).

The formulations just cited show the present inevitability of following both roads. In interpreting the happy dream and the hypomanic mood we used psychoanalytic ideas about the affects (denial, 'reversal', defense against anxiety, etc.), but when we used the word *appropriate* we were in the position of all common-sense psychologists and psychiatrists: compelled to accept the tautology of the common-sense definition. This I think is also consistent with Freud's final statement that an affect is always a conscious manifestation. This entails the acceptance of its common-sense demonstrative definition, whatever other theory may be brought to bear.

To attempt some sort of summary of the statements above, I should say: 1. Affects are conscious phenomena and subject to common-sense, demonstrative definition and pragmatic classification. 2. Abstractly, some such idea as *Affektbetrag* is unavoidable because of the empirical findings of repression, displacement, and isolation where the emotional representation has a fate different from the ideational one. 3. Empirically, 'pure emotions' are of two sorts, the one 'neurological' in experimental ablations, etc., while the second kind of purity is a highly developed conscious state with much psychological structural organization (e.g., ecstasies). The first could be called unstructured, the second structured 'pure' affect. 4. Structured 'pure' emotion, like 'pure thought' or 'pure action', depends on the position of the ego's perceptive organ vis-à-vis the function in question. 5. Developmental specialization determines our need for a common-sense remnant of faculty psychology.

VII. REMARKS ON CREATIVITY, IMAGERY, AND THE DREAM*

The dream in its day has been called many things, sometimes poetically, sometimes scientifically, but I believe one aphoristic *quasi* definition is both forthright and at the same time suggestive. I refer to a phrase of Lawrence S. Kubie's, (1958) '. . . that form of creative art which is the most universal of all, the Dream' (p. 3). Besides its striking epigrammatism, this phrase seems a reflexive transformation of the usual direction of such statements, which, from Freud and his contemporaries on, have put the matter the other way: the creative product is 'as if' a dream. Artists have responded to this and other applications of psychoanalytic ideas to the creative process in various ways. Some did not at all approve, often for reasons which Kubie had already made clear. Thus, on learning of Kubie's psychoanalytic literary criticism, Ernest Hemingway is said to have commented very belligerently.

But other artists and authors have shown more sympathy to the psychoanalytic efforts. Thornton Wilder is one of these and, replying to a letter of inquiry about the sources of The Bridge of San Luis Rey, he wrote to Dr. Paul Friedman (1952), 'First let me say how justified I feel it to be that psychoanalysts read imaginative literature as they do dreams'. Not only in this letter but also in private and public statements, Mr. Wilder has demonstrated his conviction and his understanding of dream analysis and the manner in which one should examine the manifest elements of a story. Thus, he has written that the dinosaur in The Skin of Our Teeth came from the Olsen-Johnson show, Hellzapoppin; that, in The Ides of March he 'lifted' from Dostoevski 'Caesar's' description of the aura that preceded the 'Dream of the Void'; and, in the letter to Dr. Friedman, he hinted at the origin of some of the 'dream thoughts' about the bridge from his own experiences and circumstances.

* [No. 136 in Bibliography.]

But writers with less knowledge of Freud than Mr. Wilder (or with none) have understood the analogy intuitively, and here we come to the obvious ambiguity in the word and the concept 'dream' and 'dreaming', clearly enough, one hopes, for the sophisticated who can distinguish manifest dream picture, latent dream thoughts, the dream work, etc. Among the prepsychoanalytic observers (or perhaps nonpsychoanalytic ones), what seems to have suggested the equation of dream and imaginative product is the 'vision', the visual quality of most manifest dreams. Thus, there is Keats's dictum that 'only the poem can record the dream'. We should have to differ with the poet in one detail, in regard to the word 'only'. Kekulé notably recorded two of his dreams as chains and rings of atoms, directly in the drawings of linked atoms. Perhaps Kekulé's recordings are a kind of scientific poetry.

If we must take exception to 'only', we can agree to the importance of the word and idea, 'record'. There are permanent records (we vainly hope) and transient ones, and visions that flow by and others that get caught. I should also like to extend and paraphrase Keats: the poetic or creative product (and this includes many varieties of creation along with certain neurotic and psychotic phenomena and certain varieties of free association) can give rise to *recordable* visions. Sometimes we can almost catch a glimpse of the processes that intervene between the incipient visions and the records. Often these look very familiar to the student of the dream; at least they can be given familiar names, which is always comforting.

In the aphoristic accounts given and to be given, the word 'vision' is ambiguous, yet it implies the unconscious or preconscious fantasy which exists either *under* or *with* the manifest production. The reader is free to use other possible prepositions, metaphorically naturally, to indicate potentiality or latency.

F. García Lorca (1955) apparently strives for some such formulation in his essay, The Poetic Image in Don Luis Góngora. He writes, 'Metaphor is always ordered by vision—the faculty of sight (sometimes a sublimated vision). It is vision that delimits it and renders it actual.' Then he quotes Keats's remark and continues, 'Sight will not suffer what is obscure to distort the image's contour, once it has taken form.

The congenitally blind cannot be plastic poets of the objective image because they have no knowledge of Nature's proportions. The blind are happiest in the realm of the mystical, where light can be infinite, a landscape without real objects, open to the cross-winds of wisdom. But images unfold in the visual field. From the sense of touch we learn the quality of their lyric materiality, their quality—almost the picture itself. The images which the other senses compose are subordinate to the first two' (p. 172).

The poet's opinions are not as clear as some of his images themselves, but they are based on his introspections. He appears to have in mind the clear *Gestalten* of adult visual imagery, either that of the manifest dream picture or of waking imagination. At least, his limitations on the congenitally blind suggest this. But if this means that a poet must necessarily agree with García Lorca in attaining pictorially sharp imagery, then García Lorca, as do many of us when we introspect, has been narrow and solipsistic in his formulations.

I say this, thinking of poems where the image is purposely not sharp, where the manifest text depicts quite another visual situation. Such a poem can perhaps be said to arise from 'vision' but not from a vision. The poem which I think substantiates this idea and which comes from the same Spanish language evidently seeks to record what we know as an Isakower phenomenon. The poet is Gustavo Adolfo Bécquer (1836-1870).[1]

No dormía; vagaba en ese limbo
en que cambian de forma los objetos,
misteriosos espacios que separan
la vigilia del sueño.

Las ideas, que en ronda silenciosa
daban vueltas en torno a mi cerebro,
poco a poco en su danza se movían
con un compás mas lento.

De la luz que entra al alma por los ojos
los párpados velaban el reflejo;
mas otra luz el mundo de visiones
alumbraba por dentro.

1 The text of Bécquer's poem is reprinted from *The Penguin Book of Spanish Verse,* with the permission of Penguin Books, Baltimore, 1956.

En este punto resonó en mi oído
un rumor semejante al que en el templo
vaga confuso, al terminar los fieles
con un amén sus rezos.

Y oí como una voz delgada y triste
que por mi nombre me llamó a lo lejos,
y sentí olor de cirios apagados,
de humidad y de incienso.

Entró en la noche y, del olvido en brazos,
caí, cual piedra, en su profundo seno:
dormí, y al despertar exclamé: '¡Alguno
que yo quería ha muerto!'

I did not sleep but wandered in that limbo where objects change shape, the mysterious tracts that separate waking from sleep. Thoughts that revolved on their silent circuit about my brain gradually moved in their dance to slower time. My lids veiled the reflection of the light that enters through the eyes; but another light lit the world of visions from within. At this point there echoed in my ears a sound like that which wavers confusedly in a church when the faithful are concluding their prayers with an amen. And I seemed to hear a delicate and sad voice calling me from afar by name, and I smelled the odor of snuffed candles, of dampness and incense. Night came on, and in the arms of oblivion I fell into her deep breast like a stone; I slept and when I awoke I cried out: 'Someone whom I loved has died!'

Other poems of Bécquer make use of the same going-to-sleep phenomena, though with more definite imagery, imagery which nevertheless remains in the hypnagogic area. Thus one of them begins:

Olas gigantes que os rompéis bramando
en las playas desiertas y remotas,
revuelto entre la sábana de espumas
¡llevadme con vosotras!

Giant waves that break roaring on deserted and remote shores, carry me with you, wrapped in a sheet of foam.

Surely being wrapped in a sheet (of whatever kind) might have served directly for one of Silberer's autosymbolic 'threshold' expressions of falling asleep.

Bécquer in a letter refers to his poetry as 'confused images that pass singing a song without rhythm or words, which only the spirit can perceive and comprehend'. This is cited in editorial comments by Chandler and Schwartz (1967) who comment further, 'He [Bécquer] despaired in his attempt to translate into words the untranslatable "extravagant children of his fancy huddled in the dark corners of his brain".' And they cite from one of his letters, 'If you only knew how the greatest ideas dwindle when they are enclosed in the circle of words; if you only knew how diaphanous, light and impalpable is the gossamer of gold that floats in the imagination, to enclose the mysterious figures that are born, of which one can successfully reproduce only the bared skeleton; if you only knew how imperceptible is the thread of light that ties together the most absurd thoughts that swim in this chaos' (p. 328).

I have quoted García Lorca and Bécquer for more than one reason. First, I wished to bring their poetic creativeness and their introspections and interpretations to the attention of psychoanalysts, and I wished to utilize them for psychoanalytic comments. To contrast the two poets: García Lorca extols the clear picture and the clear sensation, of which he is evidently capable, perhaps as a *type visuel,* and which he utilizes in poetry. It is no accident that he quotes Keats; every high school student hears of Keats's 'sensuousness', illustrated by the legend that he filled his mouth with pepper to experience 'sensation' in the raw. When García Lorca lays stress on the modalities of sight and touch, he implies that from them come the (pre-)conscious images that furnish the 'ultra-clarity' (in Freud's expression) of his poetic figures. He invokes, one is tempted to say, the type of consciousness in which pictorial images predominate. This is the form of thinking that characterizes what I have called 'the pictorial past' (B. Lewin, 1968),[2] the years that come after the very earliest in childhood, whose visual form recurs dominantly in ordinary dreams.

On the other hand, Bécquer seems to be striving to *find* visual images and visual forms in which he can then clothe the indefinite feelings and vague images of a state of consciousness which characterizes an even earlier stage than the pictorial

2 See *The Pictorial Past,* pp. 385-399 [Ed.].

past—a stage which recurs later in life in certain dreams without visual content, dreams of 'pure feeling', or dreams which are nearly imageless and focus on a background, and also in certain hypnagogic states such as the one he tries to express in his poem. The person who has had such experiences in later life also finds them difficult to put into words or even into images, and when he does use images, often declares them to be metaphoric. The psychoanalytic literature contains several studies of this state of consciousness.[3]

It is not unusual that memories, or if one prefers for these vague impressions, *mnemic traces,* of the early infantile period before sensations and feelings are tied into visual images to recur in hypnagogic states, and Bécquer's poem is an excellent example of the way such experiences and memories can be portrayed. It is not rare that states of this kind, when they recur later in life, should be given mystical interpretations and regarded as inspired or even supernatural. Again, if the feelings are disagreeable, sometimes when they are ecstatic, such experiences may be evaluated as 'sick', reversing what Kubie (1958) gives as the title of his book; they are as if creative distortions of the neurotic process. I have in mind, for instance, ecstatic blank dreams, which the dreamer himself interprets as revelations but which are then followed by a psychotic-manic attack. An interesting analogue to such subjectively judged creativity appears in manic symptomatology, when the patient fills reams of paper with figures and scrawls, on which he sets high value as possible 'masterpieces' but which make no sense. The pictures and the writing can be completely discounted. They mean nothing, so that the background, the paper, is in a sense blank; the situation can be summarized as 'feeling and blankness'.

The dreamer who re-creates his prepictorial past in this way tries to find visual images to use metaphorically. In a very different but comparable way, images play a role in the dreams and half-sleep states of persons who solve an intellectual problem while in the sleeping or dormescent state. A classic example of an intellectual problem solved in a doze is given in Kekulé's invention of the benzene ring. As is well known, while he dozed before an open fire, he saw snakes, which represented

[3] *Cf.* especially Rycroft (1951).

atoms, form a mouth-to-tail chain. The front snake took the hind snake's tail in its mouth, and Kekulé awoke, knowing that he had solved the linkage of carbon atoms in the benzene ring. In this dream and other 'creative' ones like it, verbal and abstract thoughts were put into pictures.

A striking example of such thinking was recorded by William A. Lamberton and reported in a letter written to William Romaine Newbold (1897). The event was not a dream but a hypnopompic fantasy which preserved the visual modality of a dream after Lamberton awoke. Lamberton does not tell us whether there was a dream in the sleep that preceded the experience. To judge from his careful style, either there was none or he did not recall it when he wrote the letter. Lamberton begins by telling of his hobby, solving 'original' mathematical problems. He states expressly that his formal mathematical training, except for a course in descriptive geometry, was 'entirely algebraic and analytic'. He had set himself a problem: 'Given an ellipse, to find the locus of the foot of the perpendicular let fall from either focus upon a tangent to this ellipse at any point'. He tried unsuccessfully to use analytic equations to solve this problem for about two weeks; he became 'bogged' and resolved to dismiss the problem completely from his thoughts.

This he did for perhaps a week, but one morning on awakening, he unexpectedly and suddenly found himself in possession of the desired solution,

> under circumstances to me strange and interesting. . . . First, the solution was entirely geometrical, whereas I had been laboring for it analytically without ever drawing or attempting to draw a single figure. Second, it presented itself by means of a figure objectively pictured at a considerable distance from me on the opposite wall. Now although I have been able, and have been so for years, to picture to myself a geometrical figure—even moderately complicated—and use it for the solution of a geometrical problem without external lines being drawn, such figures sensationally for me have a distinct locus in myself; viz., in the eye itself; they are never, so far as I know, externally presented. This, however, was distinctly external.

He describes the room where this figure appeared. It was a made-over classroom, and the wall in question was a painted-over blackboard. This, of course, raises the question whether such a locale induced some kind of regression to being a student again. In that case, the blackboard-wall, serving as a kind of day residue, could conceivably have 'suggested' his early plane geometry instruction and figures. He continues,

> On opening my eyes on the morning in question, I saw projected upon this blackboard surface a complete figure, containing not only the lines given by the problem but also a number of auxiliary lines and just such lines as without further thought solved the problem at once. Both foci were joined with the point of contact of the tangent; the perpendicular was prolonged beyond its point of intersection with the tangent till it met the line from the other focus through the point of contact with the ellipse; a line was drawn from the center of the ellipse to the foot of the perpendicular, and, lastly, the locus, a circle on the major axis of the ellipse as diameter, was drawn. I sprang from bed and drew the figure on paper; needless to say, perhaps, that the geometrical solution being thus given, only a few minutes were needed to get the analytical one.

I quoted this account at length for several reasons besides the wish to 'retrieve' this admirable introspective observation from the aging literature of the late nineteenth century. When I read Newbold's article and others in this old volume of the *Proceedings of the Society for Psychical Research,* I found many treatments of comparable phenomena, well investigated, and I could understand why Freud consistently preserved his interest in this publication and in the Society. A more important reason for my quotation was the observation itself. The hypnopompic fantasy was visual. It was well processed secondarily (in our terminology); it was sensible and orderly; and it was a direct perception of a preconscious formation become conscious. It was unexpected, presenting itself in a state of conscious inattention. Unless we insist that 'creativity' must refer to some very important problem, like the structure of the benzene ring, we can arbitrarily call this experience 'creative'.[4] In a different modality, it bears great resemblance to the auditory 'after thought' in undistorted words, reported by Isakower (1939, 1954); and it offers an interesting contrast to Bécquer's poem.

[4] I wish to avoid the controversy about this word, 'creativity', and its various shades of meaning. *Cf.*, the articles in *Creativity and Learning* (Kagan, 1968).

Lamberton at the end of sleep found that he had solved a conscious problem (French, 1952, pp. 71, ff.). His final attention was to an objective fact—a *Gegenstand*. Bécquer's focus was on his own subjective state—his *Zustand*, which he transformed into metaphorical images, to produce voluntarily perhaps something like the hypnagogic images that Silberer (1911) described. In both Lamberton and Bécquer, the function called 'intention' played a role; respectively, to solve a problem, to write a poem. Similarly Silberer was moved by his intention to produce his crystal-ball image for scientific purposes and studies. Lamberton recorded a finished product directly and studied it rationally; Bécquer sounds in his letter as if he were groping for such a product; Silberer obtained his images artificially and interpreted them.

My dwelling on the examples may be a bringing of coals to Newcastle. The phenomena are well known. Yet I think they well illustrate one point: the role of visual imagery in certain chosen instances. Lamberton's case speaks for itself; his forgotten lessons in plane geometry came back to his aid in the vision-compatible hypnopompic state of consciousness. On the other hand, Bécquer was subjected to a different, although related, process. His search for visual images to describe an emotional, confused 'previsual' state or set of experiences has several analogues in states known to psychoanalysis. One such analogue is what I have described as the 'pedomorphic' way (B. Lewin, 1968, p. 43) a child of say three or four tries to imagine or formulate the presumed mind of a new infant; that is, he uses language and visual fantasies that are appropriate to the later development to formulate prespeech and previsual mentation. Such projection and translation brings nonvisual phenomena into the pictorial and linguistic range of one who speaks and visualizes.

In either case, something was set in motion or, better, bestirred itself, taking on the attributes of motility and life. Lamberton's plane geometry, we say, was 'revived'. Bécquer's feelings, already awhirl—his already alive confused consciousness—combined their existence with whatever life and motion resided in the visual metaphors. As I stated, the word 'creative' has several shades of meaning; one connotation is certainly *to create,* in the sense of bring to life. Certain writers, and readers vicariously, say that characters in books 'come alive', quite often because their images become clear and in motion. Bernard Shaw has said that once he imagines his characters, they take over and act the play for him. Since Abraham's (1913b) paper on scopophilia, too, we have been aware that the wish to revive old memories is derived from a wish to see the old events, to animate them. A telling clinical observation of such animation appeared in the case of Abraham's scopophilic patient who wished to see ghosts.

Later writers have added to our knowledge of the visual image in the psychoanalytic situation. Max Warren (1961) brought to our attention, and in a way retrieved, the passages in the Breuer-Freud essays, where the 'concentration technique' led to vivid visual memories and indeed was intended to do just that. He quotes a telling paragraph on this score (Breuer and Freud, 1893-1895, pp. 280–281). The same passages caught the attention of Martin Stein (1965) in connection with his studies on states of consciousness in the analytic situation. Also relevant to the topic is the paper by Mark Kanzer (1958) on image formation during free association. When, in catharsis, old memories were 'revived', came alive, they came in visual imagery often nearly hallucinatory in intensity. As late as his paper on construction, Freud (1937b) refers to such imagery as being ultra clear and even 'as if hallucinatory' and regards the form as testimony to the reality of a past event. Analogies between the psychoanalytic process and the 'creative' have been recorded by Beres (1957).

It is interesting that Professor Lamberton wished to report to the Society for Psychical Research the revival of his 'dead' or dormant plane goemetry. The Society was interested in receiving communications from the dead and in possible *revenants.* Freud spoke of visual imagery as being 'nearer to unconscious processes'. In a similar epigrammatic way, I should say that it is 'alive', linked with the sense of living reality that held sway in childhood's fantasy, in the 'pictorial past'. Whether in the analytic session or in a dream, or intercurrent with artistic or scientific work, the pictorial form is a true revival.

The above seems to lay stress on the actual perceiving of the image, but I do not wish to be understood as precisely doing this. Hence, I shall clarify my meaning with the aid of a metaphor which was used by Freud (1915-1917, pp. 295, ff). I refer to his model of the psychical apparatus. There are two rooms connected by a door. The first and larger room is the unconscious, the smaller one is the preconscious, and the way through the door from the first to the second room is guarded by a watchman, the censor. Those ideas that have somehow been able to get past the censor and through the door and are now in the 'preconscious' room are not in 'consciousness' until they have been perceived by a permanent denizen of the room, an 'inner eye', the perceptive organ. This inner eye functions best during sleep. But Lamberton's 'eye' that saw the ellipse (which was projected onto the wall) behaved as if it were an 'outer eye'. The inner eye seemed to become condensed with the real organ of vision and saw the preconscious construction. There had been a 'revival'. The hallucination, for all its strangeness, was a preconscious construct that got into a strangely processed inner eye. In this it differed from solutions of problems that simply 'come to mind' after a person has slept on them, as one says, but do not appear in a projected vision. We have here an unusual structural position for the organs of perception.[5]

For me, therefore, the creativeness that is a bringing to life is tied up with the psychology of visual imagery, which is my commentary on Kubie's remark that the commonest creative act is to dream. Such imagery, whether it occurs as such in the dream or the hallucination, or whether it is just 'off-stage' in Freud's preconscious room and needs the final action of *Cs,* is fed from two directions. As in certain examples, very much *von oben,* like Lamberton's ellipse it is fed by conscious verbal and abstract thinking. But the material is fed so it may come from below (*von unten*) too, from the strange region of Bécquer's previsual consciousness.

Written for Lawrence S. Kubie's *Festschrift,* this paper is a belated reaction to the stimulus of his work.

[5] *Cf.* the views expressed by Isakower in the papers cited and in his 1936 paper.

CLINICAL APPLICATIONS OF DREAM PSYCHOLOGY

Throughout the 1950's, with only one or two exceptions, in all his papers Lewin used the ideas of dream psychology and the dream screen to deepen insight into problems of clinical interpretation and to shed new light on the principles underlying psychoanalytic technique. The papers in this section belong to this period and illustrate this trend.

Lewin noted that as a technique of treatment, psychoanalysis originated from an induced sleep—that is to say, hypnosis. In comparing the analytic situation with sleep and hypnosis, Lewin suggested that the therapeutic activity of the analyst may be seen as reflecting how the analyst functions at times to induce and preserve sleep, and at other times to interrupt sleep and arouse the analysand. For example, interpretation of defense may be likened to fostering sleep in a patient, while interpretation of content may be compared to the process of arousing a sleeper—alerting the ego to look at unwelcome intrusions into the state of sleep.

In the same way, the mechanism of dream formation may be applied to the origin of depression. In *Sleep, Narcissistic Neurosis, and the Analytic Situation,* Lewin writes: 'the latent unconscious wish in the depressive picture is to remain in the nursing situation, narcissistically; the latent thought includes the idea of being wakened and weaned; the manifest text pictures the unsuccessful weaning and waking injunctions, disguised and revised. Since the manifest content consists largely of painful feelings and auditory impressions, the analogue of the visual text of ordinary dreams is to be found precisely in these two fields. We have a painful and auditory text rather than a visual one. The manifest picture is painful weaning and waking; the latent wish fulfilment is pleasure and sleep at the breast.'

The concepts elaborated by Lewin in this section have become the central issues in much of current psychoanalytic writing. Three themes in particular should be mentioned: the idea of fusion, the concept of levels of consciousness, and, finally, the detailing of the stages of narcissistic regression.

J. A. A.

I. PHOBIC SYMPTOMS AND DREAM INTERPRETATION*

Early in the history of psychoanalysis, Freud discovered that the interpretation of dreams and the interpretation of neurotic and psychotic symptoms were merely two applications of the same depth psychology. Properly translated, dreams and symptoms often said the same thing, and the processes that led to symptom formation were in part identical with those that formed dreams. In Some General Remarks on Hysterical Attacks, Freud (1908b, p. 229) stated this explicitly: the unconscious fantasies of hysterical patients were 'of the same nature as the phantasies which can be observed directly in day-dreams or which can be elicited by interpretation from dreams at night'. He added that 'as a rule . . . the pantomimic portrayal of the phantasy [in the hysterical attack] has undergone distortions which are completely analogous to the hallucinatory distortions of a dream', and he indicated many distortions (such as condensation, multiple identifications, representation by opposites, reversal of the sequence of events) common to both mental structures. The equivalence of dream and psychosis or neurosis has been accepted in analytic practice and theory, and there has been a constant reciprocal enrichment by borrowings and exchanges between the two fields of study. Among others, Alexander (1927b) showed the essential dynamic and topologic similarity of certain paired dreams and the paired symptoms of obsessional neurosis. Recently, I have tried to demonstrate the value of applying the methods of dream interpretation in the study of the elations.

Although the seeds of present-day ego psychology are contained in Chapter VII of The Interpretation of Dreams, Freud (1900-1901) adopted a different set of terms in later publications, especially in Inhibitions, Symptoms and Anxiety (Freud, 1925a), to describe the intrapsychic processes. Nowadays most

* [No. 93 in Bibliography.]

writers use both terminologies, the older when discussing dreams, the newer when writing about the neuroses. This cleavage is not deep-seated. It is due in the main to convenience and tradition, just as in mathematics certain formulations (the algebraic, geometric, trigonometric, etc.) are more convenient and more wieldy for one or another problem. Ordinarily such considerations offset any disadvantages arising from a double terminology. Many terms, such as *displacement* and *repression,* are in fact used in both fields; but others, such as *conversion,* are not used in connection with dreams, and still others, such as *censorship,* only rarely find a place in a discussion of the neuroses. Freud built up his new terminology by resurrecting words used in some of his earliest formulations of neuroses (particularly the word *defense*), yet he had successfully formulated certain mental states, for instance, the acute hallucinatory psychoses, in 'metapsychology' that used the terms of Chapter VII.

Both terminologies have demonstrated their particular merits, and the thought arises that it might be worth while to crisscross, to put dreams into the terminology of Inhibitions, Symptoms and Anxiety and neurotic structures into that of The Interpretation of Dreams; for it is conceivable that this maneuver might demonstrate new relationships, or bring out some new thoughts. At least the mathematical precedent is valid, as we know from the Cartesian application of algebra to geometry, Euler's application of trigonometry to complex variables, etc. Where the newer vocabulary excels in the description of conflict, psychic topology, and ego functions, the older, dream-based concepts are superior in utility when conscious manifestations are to be interpreted as derivatives of latent unconscious thoughts.

A familiar and suitable object for this approach is that group of morbid fears called the phobias. Freud (1915-1917, p. 411), indeed, began the comparison of phobias and dreams in the Introductory Lectures when he said that the phobic façade was analogous to the manifest content of a dream; but later in Inhibitions, Symptoms and Anxiety he dropped the comparison and used the phobias particularly to demonstrate the relation of symptom and neurotic anxiety. Neurotic anxiety is a signal, and this is most sharply visible in the phobias. Here the central role of anxiety is more evident than in other neuroses, and the phobia (or *anxiety hysteria*) becomes a sort of dynamic paradigm of all other neuroses where the anxiety may not be an evident part of the manifest picture. Phobias were taken as the simplest demonstrations of how symptoms arise. Yet the newer, and very illuminating, formulation of the phobias did not exhaustively explain many elements of individual phobic syndromes.

During the nineteenth century, many morbid fears had been described, and many names were coined to designate them. Usually to the suffix, *-phobia,* the namers prefixed Latin and Greek forms, such as *claustro-* and *agora-*, in the first instance mixing the Chian and the Falernian wines.[1] At different times Freud has indicated how many clues to psychological truth may come from popular etymology and folk wisdom, and from the simple lore of such naïve persons as midwives and children's nurses. The name-givers of the phobias[2] were academic and erudite, and their intentions sophisticated, yet we may permit them to serve us in the same way. For the names imply that there are at least two problems in a phobia: one an anxiety problem (the *-phobia*), the other a claustrum or an agora problem. That is to say, phobias present a need for a theory of anxiety and for an interpretation of the many situations and objects that give their special name and special quality to the various phobias. Another etymological remark concerns the tacit connective between the two parts of the name. It is easy to assume offhand that in all cases this should be the preposition *of*,[3] for this is the preposition so often used or tacitly understood. There are morbid fears *of* dogs, *of* thunder, *of* trains, and so on; nevertheless the generalization would be inexact, as we readily see by considering two types of claustrophobia. In one of these, anxiety arises when the patient is about to go through an entrance—the specific fear of going into a closed space. In the second type, the situation is precisely the reverse: the patient enters the space readily, feels comfortable and secure in it, and is attacked by anxiety only when he is disturbed in the claustrum by an intrusion, or when he is threatened by expulsion from it. Evidently, in the second case there is no fear *of* the

1 Horace: *Satires* I, x, 20-24.

2 Among them, Westphal, Legrand du Saulle, Raggi, Beard, Verga.

3 As in the definition given in Hack Tuke's *Dictionary*.

claustrum in any sense, and no tacit simple connective such as *of* will suffice. The connection between anxiety and claustrum differs in the two types enough to compel a somewhat complex explanation of the connective, which, as we shall see, is itself an element in the manifest content of the phobia.

In the Introductory Lectures, Freud (1915-1917, p. 411) expounded the similarity of phobias and dreams. He said that the manifest content of the phobias, or the object or situation which appears to provoke the fear is comparable to the manifest content of a dream, that it is a façade behind which are concealed the latent thoughts that truly call forth the anxiety. Thus phobias are like dreams which fail in their sleep-guarding function and terminate with anxiety. Freud also cited G. Stanley Hall, who suggested that the contents of many phobias were influenced by racial memories, as if they reflected a phylogenetically realistic fear. Thus a fire phobia might be the ontogenetic vestige of a dread such as wild animals have of fire, a falling phobia might reproduce our ancestral primate's fear of falling out of a tree, and so on. In these remarks, Freud saw a bearing on the relation of phobic content and manifest dream content, for he believed that dream symbolism has a similar atavistic origin. There would, accordingly, be something like a biogenetic homology between these elements of phobia and dream.

Here Freud is referring to the universal symbolism to be found in dreams, and several students of the neuroses have profitably followed this lead, the most recent being Paul Friedman (1952) in his erudite study of the bridge as symbol. Friedman's analyses of persons with different types of bridge phobia demonstrated that the anxiety in each case was castration anxiety or one of its feminine equivalents or later derivatives. But to show the more general and, as it were, universal meaning of the bridge, Friedman turned to the dream, to folklore, religion, and belles-lettres, where the significance of the bridge as an independent symbol, for example, as a road to death or to life eternal, appears more clearly. Regardless of the applicability of the biogenetic law (and its Lamarckian extensions) in psychology,[4] the constant dream symbols have

[4] See the criticism of Freud's evolutionist views by Hartmann, Kris, and Loewenstein (1951) with which I am in agreement.

aided us in understanding the neuroses, for many of them appear in the manifest text of the phobias.

Freud's hint to interpret the overt content of the phobia as the psychological equivalent of a manifest dream text has also influenced Fenichel (1944, 1945), who has paid attention to certain manifest details of frequent occurrence in the common phobias, for example, in the street phobias, the quality of narrowness or width of the street. He interprets these details according to the rules for dream interpretation, and I shall take up his discussion later.

Though the procedure seems obvious, its rationale warrants explicit statement. The phobic façade is built up like the manifest content of a dream. There are of course simple dreams with little or no distortion, and comparable anxieties that may or may not justify the appellation, phobia (Freud 1925a). But the regular predominance of displacement as a source of distortion in phobias indicates that, as in dream formation, the conscious and preconscious ideas that instigate the anxiety are linked with unconscious libidinal and aggressive impulses, and that the latent thoughts of the phobia, those that determined the façade, were subjected to the primary process.[5] Evidently the manifest text of the phobias, influenced by this dip into the unconscious and the primary process, shows not only the effect of displacement but of other id processes as well, such as condensation, disregard of time and consistency, etc. In addition, as I shall try to illustrate, like the dream text, the phobic façade may also include traces of very early memories, which persist in the system *Ucs*, in particular those that betray orality and are encountered in connection with the wish to sleep; for example, the dream screen. The possibility of a tendency to visual portrayal should also be considered here. Briefly, the manifest phobic façade should reveal, at least to some extent and in its variations, the same sort of overdetermination and the same qualities that we know from dreams. The manifest anxiety itself could be overdetermined and fed by more than one latent source, so that besides castration anxiety, it would contain contributions from the anxieties of pregenital and preœdipal times.

We may in this connection consider the bearing on the psy-

[5] *Cf.* Gero's (1951) discussion of this point.

chology of neurosis of what are called typical dreams, like those of flying or of being nude in company without embarrassment. According to Freud such dreams have nothing to do with the history of the race though they are of universal occurrence. They permit of a standard interpretation because they reflect typical, standard situations of childhood—being tossed in the air in the first instance, and being naked in the presence of adults in the second. Due to Freud and others, we are able to utilize what we have learned about typical dreams to explain phenomena in fields other than dream psychology proper, and we can apply our knowledge to the interpretation of certain typical phobias. The guiding principle here is an application of relatively constant interpretations learned from the analysis of dreams.

The dream's most general attribute is its sleep-guarding function. It serves the ego by preserving sleep. If the wish for sleep alone were served, fulfilment would consist in blank sleep, or the nearly blank sleep that is represented by the dream screen. Dreaming in sleep is a compromise, which fulfils mainly through visual and motor hallucinations other wishes besides the wish to sleep, subject to more or less distortion and censorship. In going to sleep we turn away from conscious and preconscious day thoughts and their potential associations with unconscious matters. We forget what is on our mind. But the push of forgotten matters, and particularly our not using words to think about them, seems of itself to promote the use of visual forms of thinking. Such at any rate I take to be the bearing of a remark which Freud (1901) published in The Psychopathology of Everyday Life. I refer to his discussion of forgetting a name. Freud had forgotten the name of the artist, Signorelli, and his mind might have shown a blank after this repression, for as he said elsewhere (Freud, 1937a, p. 236) and more generally, . . . 'repression has the same relation to the other methods of defence as omission [of words and passages] has to distortion of the text', and in connection with the dream he spoke of repression as 'an erasure' or 'blacking out'. However, in this particular instance the push of the repressed filled the blankness with a visual equivalent of the name. Freud's (1901, p. 13, n.) note reads: 'For example, in the *Signorelli* case, so long as the painter's name remained inaccessible, the visual memory that I had of the series of frescoes and of the self-portrait which is introduced into the corner of one of the pictures was *ultra-clear*—at any rate much more intense than visual memory-traces normally appear to me'. This disappeared when the name was recalled.

Some of this 'more intense . . . visual memory' may appear in childhood phobias, less often than in those of adults, especially so if the phobic façade deals with ghosts and bogies that come during the night. Even in children the bugaboos are not often clearly hallucinated, although this happens occasionally. There is more commonly a fear that the specter will suddenly materialize and become visible in the dark, in the way that a sudden manifest dream picture intrudes upon the *tabula rasa* of the sleeping mind. Fear of the ogre resembles the fear of having a bad dream. One is of course helpless to prevent monsters and ogres from becoming visible in dreams, but the phenomenon seems to be due to a general tendency of the repressed to return in visual representations, as in the Signorelli example. The disturber of slumber, the 'waker', is projected outward in dreams, as the source of the anxiety or 'disturber' is similarly projected outward in many phobias. Later in this paper I shall indicate certain reasons for this that are based in preœdipal psychology. Here I may anticipate my exposition and say that there are intrinsic reasons why the ogres, monsters, ghosts, and bugaboos in childhood and, later on, burglars and savages and in general all such wakers and disturbers of sleep should represent the father. Night terrors and many infantile anxiety dreams lie in a segment where phobia and dream overlap. The waker, i.e., the manifest element in the dream that apparently frightens the child, is identical or nearly identical with the 'frightener' in the simple quasi-hallucinatory phobia. In both anxiety dream and phobia the true disturber, that is, the repressed impulse, breaks through as a displacement or projection. Waking up itself has the character of a flight from the object upon which the anxiety was displaced. We could without much difficulty formulate the simple anxiety dreams of childhood in the same terms as the childhood phobias (Freud, 1900-1901; Federn, 1913; Mittelmann, 1949).

In general the anxiety in phobias, which at all ages serves as a signal and a warning to the ego, is currently considered to represent castration anxiety or analogous fears which are involved in female sexual functioning (Freud, 1925a; H. Deutsch, 1930; Fenichel, 1945). Even in the simple phobias of children the anxiety is intercalated differently in the different phobic structures, so that it may be attached to active or passive libidinal wishes, or to aggressive elements in the œdipal situation, a matter thoroughly discussed by Freud in Inhibitions, Symptoms and Anxiety.

In this same discussion Freud tends to slight a point which he made in his original explanation of the Wolf-man's infantile fears. The Wolf-man, like Little Hans and many other children, expressed his fears in oral terms: he feared that he would be eaten up and die. Freud stated that besides the anxiety which arose from the latent thought of castration, there was amalgamated into the Wolf-man's total manifest emotion another more primitive anxiety which arose from disturbances in the oral pregenital stage of development. He suggested that the fear might be an anxious version of a primitive libidinal wish to be devoured, such as is represented in games where adults pretend that they are wolves or other carnivora and tell the child that they are going to eat him up. In my second paper on the dream screen,[6] I referred to Freud's statement and suggested a reason for the emergence of this pregenital element. I advanced the idea that the Wolf-man's wish to be devoured was activated during the primal scene because of its intimate genetic linkage with the wish to sleep in the triad of early oral wishes, and that the wish to sleep had been a defensive response to the wakening disturbance of the primal scene. Be that as it may, Freud's formulation indicates that anxieties which characterize the years before genital development may find a place even in the simpler childhood phobias where they may distort, regressively, the manifest façade.

It is worth our while to examine the manifest content of the common phobias for evidence of such pregenitality and preœdipality, particularly for remnants of the oral triad. A good point of departure is the problem, the meaning of the *claustrum* in claustrophobia. The claustrum, as Jones (1912) and Ferenczi (1922) discovered, represents the uterus, or more exactly the interior of the mother's body. It may, of course,

[6] See, *Inferences from the Dream Screen*, pp. 101-114 [Ed.].

also have secondary or derivative meanings, such as the bed, the bath, or other symbolic substitutes. In the different types of claustrophobia, this significance of the claustrum is invariant, but its functions vary in different contexts, much as one and the same dream symbol may be used in the expression of different latent thoughts. That is to say, the claustrum is the interior of the mother's body, but the emotions and ideas concerning this body are varied. Thus, there is a form of claustrophobia in which the claustrum gives the patient a feeling of safety, and anxiety attacks him only when his stay is threatened (B. Lewin, 1950).[7] The claustrum, symbol of his intramaternal situation, here is a refuge and a haven, and in it the patient finds protection and defense. As in Poe's tale, The Pit and the Pendulum,[8] anxiety comes from one of two interruptions: the intrusion of the father's penis, represented by the pendulum in the story, or the gradual closing in of the claustral walls. This particular form of claustrophobia is much colored by the oral triad. The fantasy of being a baby in the safe haven of the uterus depends on an identification with an infant, one that was in reality seen eating and sleeping at the breast, and it is this infant that is projected back in time and thought of as a fœtus, to continue his eating and sleeping in the uterus. This baby too is unconsciously identified with the breast, and the identification includes his being a part of the mother. In fantasy, the entrance to the mother is effected actively, by gnawing, or passively, by being swallowed (Fenichel, 1928a).

As in the case of the Wolf-man, I consider that this being swallowed had its point of origin in those moments of relaxation that intervene between the infant's satiation at the breast and the subsequent falling asleep, memory traces of which lend content to the second wish of the oral triad. The same element makes its appearance in other forms of claustrophobia. As an illustration we may take the fear that arises when the patient is about to enter a claustrum, such as the common fear of going through the door of a subway station or through the entrance of a tunnel. In a case of this type, reported by Oberndorf (1915), it was evident that the patient equated himself with

7 See also, *Claustrophobia*, pp. 48-54 [Ed.].

8 For a fuller interpretation of this tale see Bonaparte (1933).

his penis (or rather with his father's penis), the station entrance with his mother's genital portal, and the underground claustrum with her dangerous interior. Evidently too, the anxiety was a version of castration anxiety. I should like to point out, however, that the fantasy of the body's being a penis in itself connotes a concomitant oral mechanism. The patient has in fantasy swallowed a penis, and he has an anxiety that he will be eaten, so that along with castration anxiety here too there is a trace of this oral fear. Finally, the idea of death, attached to the danger spot of the manifest content, refers to the third element of the oral triad, namely, sleep.

Fenichel (1945) reminds us that such fears of entering a claustrum are to be found in persons who suffer also from a fear of the female genitalia, which they unconsciously equip with teeth in the fantasy known as the *vagina dentata.* The same author, following Oberndorf (1929), interprets the feeling that one will be smothered or suffocated in the claustrum as a repetition of the experience of having the nose pushed into the breast during nursing, or more generally as a reproduction of the infant's difficulty in managing his breathing while he is at the breast. In a converse interpretation, Melanie Klein (1932, p. 329, n.) interprets the fear of having the penis caught by a clamping vagina as a 'narrowing down' and displacement to the genitals of an originally claustrophobic fear of the whole person's being shut up in the mother's body.

Another, somewhat different version of the dangerous claustrum is present in that type of phobia where the anxiety appears when the person is shut in by the closing of a door. Often this is combined with a fear of being smothered and of being in the dark. The choice of this moment of incipient enclosure and sudden separation from the outer world I take to indicate a fear of losing contact with the world of waking life and of being engulfed in the breast or the intramaternal world of sleep. It repeats childhood fears of going to sleep or being put to sleep. This fear of being sealed in resembles or coincides with the familiar fear of being buried alive to which Jones and Ferenczi have referred. It is noteworthy that in this fantasy the fear is not a fear of being dead, but of being alive. The impossibility of imagining one's self really dead does not by itself account for this idea. Being alive means being conscious or awake, and this same fantasy is to be found playing a role in certain neurotic insomnias, where the patient unconsciously fears that his sleep will bring on bad dreams—that he will be awake during sleep. The idea of being awake is also linked with that of being hungry and of being unsatisfied in respect of the second wish of the oral triad, for which we lack a convenient simple word. I refer to the passive analogue of hunger, the craving to be eaten. Briefly, in this form of claustrophobia, the claustrum is a place of deprivation and unpleasure; fear of being shut in the claustrum coincides with fear of disturbed sleep, anticipation of unpleasant effects when the world is shut out. Neither sleep nor death nor the grave as such provokes the anxiety, nor the claustrum itself, but the thought of what happens *after* falling asleep, after death or after being buried. Thus, one of my patients imagined herself alive in the grave, starving and being eaten by worms. She had imagined this fate in her childhood, after the birth of a sibling, at which time it was a self-punitive identification with her pregnant mother and the fœtus. Later, in adolescence after the mother's death, the same fantasy entered her mourning and expressed the wish for union with her mother in the grave. Being awake and alive in the grave and a lack of satisfaction of oral wishes summarizes the meaning of the fantasy.

The fear of being alive after burial is a variant of an idea which occurs in many forms; it is a special form of the fear of a living death, immortality, or survival. The Wandering Jew legend classically portrays the disadvantages of such unwanted survival; the latent meaning of the curse put upon him is that he shall not sleep. It is sometimes difficult for us to remember that our ancestors were very ambivalent about immortality, which for them was not only credible but inevitable, and that fear of Hell offset the hope of Heaven. Nevertheless, we still encounter many neurotic fears of the afterlife. The thought of being cremated, a defense against being buried alive, when it does not succeed in checking the fear, turns into fears of being caught in a conflagration or of the eternal fires of Hell. One disagreeable picture of the afterlife takes the child in the uterus or at the breast as the prototype of our mental state after death, but a hungry child that cannot rest undisturbed. An analysis of a patient with a fear of this sort, at first called vaguely 'a fear of dying', showed that it depended on a wish to rejoin her dead mother in the other world. The patient had a symptomatic habit of haunting museums of all kinds, from waxworks to the Metropolitan, which indicated her desire to dwell in the 'house of the dead' and of the immortals. It was significant that her dreams placed her mother in Heaven or in Hell, according to the phase of the ambivalence that was temporarily in the ascendance. Her reunion was correspondingly feared and desired.

A young man, complaining of a compulsion to drink, combined his neurotic alcoholism with the type of claustrophobia in which the closing of the door to a subway car or an airplane precipitated the anxiety attack. In other words, the patient became panicky when he found himself caught by the formation of a new claustrum. At the age of four he had really been caught after the closing of a door, namely, the door of a surgical operating room, where he had been chased around the room by his relatives and the hospital staff, caught, held down, and anesthetized. He woke up from this relieved of his tonsils, as he had anticipated, but unexpectedly of his prepuce as well. This event served as a screen memory employed against passive homosexual fantasies, and his phobia was precipitated by his father's death, after which he also began to overdo his drinking. An accessory determinant of the drinking was his mother's alcoholism, for which she had been hospitalized. In the newly formed claustrum, he feared death by suffocation, which reproduced the anesthesia, and he feared alcoholism because of his mother's fate. But the quasi castration in the traumatic event did not figure in the manifest text of his phobias or of his worries. The significance of his fear of being smothered came out in the analysis of his use of alcohol, which held for him the masochistic temptation of being put to sleep. Alcohol represented his father's semen, for his primal scene fantasy depicted his father as poisoning his mother through fellatio, which put her to sleep or killed her, all after a door had shut the two parents in. The phobia and the use of alcohol arose in related latent fantasies. The alcohol gratified his suicidal feminine wish for sleep; the phobia treated it as a danger.

These various illustrations show that the claustrum functions in many ways within the structure of the phobic symptoms. Preœdipal relationships play an important role in determining these functions. The intraclaustral situation may be a place of wakefulness and starvation; but if the claustrum is affectively toned by the associated idea of a quiet uterus, a good breast, or peaceful sleep, it is a haven and a place that can be used in the construction of defense mechanisms, so that it becomes a natural refuge. The claustrum in this case is not the projection of a danger; the danger is projected elsewhere, and to the claustrum is projected the warding-off function, i.e., a part of the ego's defensive function. The projection in this form of claustrophobia is not limited to id representations, nor to the extrojection of wishful ideas. It also functions to send forth part of the ego's fantasy of defense. The ego sees its safety as well as the danger in certain external situations, just as in a dream one may see one's self hiding in a safe place from some frightening figure. Both danger and safety are projected.

We may now return to The Pit and the Pendulum and, since we have to a large extent dealt with the pit, inquire into the significance of the pendulum. If the story were a dream, the pendulum would certainly be a disturber. In the manifest text of dreams, the wakening stimulus, the strongest disturber, is ordinarily pictured as some external figure or situation and not as something that arises from within. Similarly in most true phobias, the disturbance is supposed to come from the outside. This is particularly true of one disturber of the peaceful rest in the safe claustrum. The intruder into this peaceful, or at any rate safe, place, the pendulum in Poe's story, is a stock figure, like the 'companion' in Deutsch's (1928) interpretation of agoraphobia. Primarily here the intruder is the father's penis. But this phallic interpretation is not sufficient. The pendulum (and the penis) is also the 'waker' and the disturber of infantile sleep and orality; and for this reason it appears suitably in fantasies of the primal scene and intrauterine observation of coitus, where the father's sexual purpose arouses the unwilling witness of the sexual act. In the psychology of dreams, too, the father or his representative appears very often as the arouser. A classic example in the psychoanalytic literature is Silberer's (1911) dream of walking with a certain female figure and then being awakened by a horse who menaces him by drawing back its lips and baring its teeth. Indeed, Silberer could have included among his 'wakening symbols' representations of the father. For when 'sleep' means union with the mother or at the breast, 'being awakened' means by the father, and in accord with oral psychology, as in the above example, by the orally jealous and hungry father. In many dreams and phobias, the biting or ravenous animal has this connotation: it is the greedy and jealous father, intruding with his claims, as the child thinks, for his full share of the oral enjoyment. To those persons who depend on sleep for libidinal gratification, the father is waker and weaner, for in the unconscious *qui dort mange* is a literal truth. Thus the preœdipal, intrusive function of the father contributes an element to such symbols as the pendulum, and finds its place in dreams and phobias.

More subtly than in Silberer's example, one of my patients expressed the idea of the father as waker and weaner very clearly. Of this young man it could be stated with some justification that he had a 'sleep addiction', for he obtained most of his emotional satisfaction from sleep and dreams. He was awakened from an œdipal dream of taking a ride with a young woman by the sound of the bugle playing reveille. But before he recognized the bugle call for what it was he thought it was the mess call.[9] Where sleep is concerned specifically, the time to wake up is the intruder upon a state that retains some of the timelessness and hence the immortality of the primary process. Like so many early demands of the reality principle, the demands of time are originally understood as demands of the upbringers, for the measurement of time is impressed upon the child from without. Particularly the idea of *time* comes to represent the father, and the realistic demand to be awake is joined to this in the conception that it is time to be awake. The demands of time, as part of reality, conflict with the pleasure principle. As there is a general tendency to give to the father attributes of the reality principle in unconscious thinking, so to the mother are given those of the primary process, pleasure principle, and timelessness. Poets and artists

[9] Evidently Irving Berlin's well-known lines represent an orally conceived œdipal drama: 'Some day I'm going to murder the bugler./ Some day you're going to find him dead./ I'm going to put my gun away and move to Philadelphiay,/ And spend the rest of my life in bed.'

depict time as a father figure,[10] but they see immortality in the sense of timelessness which is a gift of the mother, who in the beginning made us immortal by magical potions of sleep-bringing nourishment. Immortality or timelessness is an oral gift. Goethe's Faust depended for it on *'das ewig weibliche'*, Marlowe's on Helen's kiss. Thus time as the father is the intruder into the timeless relation with the mother, and in the fantasy of being buried alive we have a version of being immortal in the mother or at the mother's breast, where timelessness and immortality reign.

It may seem to the reader that I have generalized rashly as to the 'waker', for there surely are many wishes that intrude into sleep and wake one up, such as the simple wish to urinate, and in the dream text such wakers are represented by well-known elements that may have nothing to do with the father. This is certainly true, but it will be noted that in the examples given above, the father intruded himself into dreams of œdipal fulfilment. I hold that the representations of the waking impulse differ from dream to dream according to the nature of the wishes which the dream is supposed to fulfil. And it is quite in accord with our conception of the phobias that such a simple dream as Silberer's, quoted above, should so nearly resemble an infantile zoophobia. For the simpler anxiety dreams and the simpler phobias both refer to various latent elements of the œdipus complex, and their attempted fantasy or hallucinatory satisfaction in both forms brings forth castration anxiety. To set up a parallel series between

[10] See Erwin Panofsky's (1939) *Studies in Iconography,* Chapter 3: Father Time. In early antiquity, time was not represented by the familiar old man with the scythe. This was a later, philosophically elaborated condensation of two concepts, Chronos (time) and Kronos (Saturn). 'The learned writers of the fourth and fifth centuries A.D. began to provide Kronos-Saturn with new attributes . . . which were meant to emphasize his temporal significance. Also, they re-interpreted the original features of his image as symbols of time. His sickle, traditionally explained either as an agricultural implement or as the instrument of castration [of domesticated animals], came to be interpreted as a symbol of *tempora quae sicut falx in se recurrunt;* and the mythical tale that he had devoured his own children was said to signify that Time, who had already been termed "sharp-toothed" by Simonides and *edax rerum* by Ovid, devours whatever he has created.' The Middle Ages added other elements to the picture borrowed from the astrologic ideas of the 'saturnine' and from the conception of Satan. When I showed the late Fritz Wittels the above passage, he succinctly remarked: 'So Freud was right; death means castration'.

the dreams and the phobias we have been considering, we may equate: 1, undisturbed sleep and successful repression; 2, return of the repressed in both cases in a 'distorted' latent fantasy; 3, attempted hallucinatory fulfilment in the dream (walking or riding with the sexual object, etc.), and attempted active symbolic fulfilment in the phobias (going out on the street, entering the subway, etc.); 4, the warning to awaken (reveille or the menacing horse) in the one case, and in the other the warning to desist (anxiety).

As to the claustrum, to return to this specific symbol, it appears that we may formulate an empirical rule. Contentment in or acceptance of the claustrum as a place of safety implies the ability to find solace or gratification in sleep as a satisfactory substitute for the protective and preœdipal mother. This may be and often is connected with a corresponding denial of dissatisfaction with her. On the other hand, anxiety over being within the claustrum implies that this fantasy of rest is not attainable because of a disturbance in the relation to the mother and sleep cannot serve as an equivalent of good mother or good breast. Accepting Freud's statement that the events of the œdipus complex and the phallic stage determine the anxiety of the phobias, we may nevertheless recognize the alterations in the façade that are introduced by the admixture of pregenital motives, and we may note many instances where the anxiety is overdetermined and fed by pregenital fears. The anxiety that arises with the latent thought of castration or its derivatives may contain a large ingredient from the pregenital relationship.

For anxiety, though a signal, is not merely a signal. It has a content and it is a sort of 'memory'. That is, anxiety attacks not only serve as warnings; they also reproduce earlier life events. Freud's theory that anxiety is a 'reliving' and a memory of birth illustrates this idea. I therefore see no difficulty or contradiction in the idea that a given access of anxiety, even though it be a signal and a warning of a danger of presumed impending castration, should also repeat and simultaneously signify some other anxiety, such as a fear of being separated from the mother, or of 'being eaten', or of any fear that might be appropriate somewhere between birth and the œdipal stage.

The topic of the claustrum has not been exhausted, but this discussion has illustrated the approach implicit in the dictum that the phobic façade is the psychological equivalent of the manifest text of a dream. To continue our application of dream theory to familiar elements of the phobias, we may turn to the agoraphobias. As originally named and described by Westphal in 1872, *agora* in this word retained the literal meaning of the Greek root, namely, a market place or open square since it translated the German *Platz* in *Platzangst*.[11] Westphal's patient was attacked by anxiety on open places, especially when he attempted to cross a public square. This topophobia then was characterized by the wide-openness of the space in the 'phobic façade'. As to the *phobia* part of the word, it again is certain that the anxiety is genital. The danger implied is that of encountering sexual temptation (Freud, 1925a; Alexander, 1927b; Deutsch, 1928; Weiss, 1935, 1936; A. Katan, 1937).

In an interesting train of thought relating to the special interpretation of certain qualities of the *topos* in the topophobias, Fenichel (1944) suggested that these might be due to a projection to the external world of conditions having their origin in the patient's own body. Thus the illusion in certain cases that the street was becoming narrow or that the walls were coming together would be in fact a projection of the feeling of constriction which the anxious person feels in his own chest because of the physiological changes during the emotion. Phobics then would displace outward not only the presumed source of danger (and part of the defensive fantasy, as the 'haven'), but part of the anxiety reaction as well, so that the pressure felt in the walls of the thorax is displaced and projected to the walls of the enclosure or street. This explanation is credible when it is applied to forms of claustro-

[11] See Edoardo Weiss (1936, p. 8) 'Nonpsychoanalytic authors described as *agoraphobia* only the phobia connected with squares, wide streets, spacious and empty places, e.g., the interior of a church, etc. (Westphal, Legrand du Saulle). In the psychoanalytic literature the term *agoraphobia* (German, *Platzangst*) is often extended to all forms of phobia that refer to streets, which might seem an improper usage; at other times, however, they speak more accurately of "street fear" (*Strassenangst*).'

Beard's term *topophobia* originally was synonymous with agoraphobia, but has come to be the general term for all phobias referring to locations, whether wide places, streets, narrow places, claustra, etc.

phobia and street phobia in which narrowing is a conspicuous element, but its validity is not immediately plausible in the case of agoraphobia of the Westphal type. Here the patient consciously fears the space because it is wide. To meet this difficulty, Fenichel transposed from dream interpretation the idea of 'displacement through reversal', which Freud used when he interpreted the manifest dream element 'to be in a crowd' as meaning the opposite latent idea, 'to be alone'. Accordingly, Fenichel supposed that the agoraphobic person manifestly fears the wide space, the agora, but that he is unconsciously referring 'by opposites' to the same thoracic narrowing. Fenichel's method is proper, but the resort to 'reversal' is uncertain and, given the oral triad, not entirely necessary in the case of the large open spaces.

Instead of the idea of reversal, we may choose another idea that comes from dream interpretation. If we take the fear of being in a crowd, the neurotic homologue of the dream element that Freud uses in his example, we find another possible explanation. This fear is usually grouped with the agoraphobias, since it is an out-of-doors symptom, yet it could as plausibly be considered a claustrophobia, if one thinks of the crowd as a sort of enclosure; and as Weiss (1936) justly observes, for dynamic purposes any such strictness of classification is valueless hairsplitting. In many dreams, the idea of a crowd, like that of a forest or the sea, stands for a place where one can be lost, and here 'lost' means to lose one's identity and be merged in a larger whole. In anxiety dreams with this content, the dreamer fears that he will be swallowed by the crowd, join it inseparably, and perish as an individual absorbed by the larger unit. In this dream the crowd stands for what I have called loosely 'the devouring breast', and sinking and merging with it repeats the feeling of sinking, relaxing, and losing the sense of one's individuality which characterizes going to sleep. The corresponding anxiety represents the orally based fear of being devoured into sleep.

On the open space, the agoraphobe misses the protecting presence of his mother; there is a sense of being abandoned, which may be compensated if the patient has a companion of a certain type (Deutsch, 1928). Often this companion is not needed if the patient remains within sight of his home or, by extension, within sight of houses in general. (Janet's agoraphobic patient Hnu said: *'Je vois le vide de chaque côté; quand je vois des maisons cela ne me fait plus le même effet'.*) The companion stands for the mother in many cases, and the homes or houses have a similar symbolic meaning. Again one hears that the agoraphobe feels safe if he is in a place that feels familiar; yet paradoxically in some new situations the anxiety is accompanied by a sense of *déjà vu,* interpretable as a reproduction of something familiar, that is, a reminiscence of childhood; and, as Freud says, of no place so surely as of the mother's body can one say, 'I have been here before'.

Many agoraphobes give other subjective details of their anxiety; they feel their legs giving way, they fear they will fall or lose their minds, etc. Weiss (1936) records 'sensations in them which they find hard to describe; for instance, they say they feel as if the ground were giving way under their feet or as if they were walking on the verge of a precipice or on an uneven surface, etc.' (p. 64). He also speaks of fears of fainting, and of traumatic dreamlike states of 'coming to'. The words *uneven surface* in the Italian version are *un piano ricurvo,* which suggests a curving of the ground surface; I remark on this to indicate that this agoral plane has many characteristics of the dream screen. And in many of Weiss's interpretations the open space refers anatomically to the mother: in a dream, the analyst has an open space, *un vuoto,* where his penis should have been, and he represents the castrated mother; or for another patient walking on the ground meant 'trampling on her mother's body and killing the unborn child', and Weiss also records many oral fantasies that accompany the attacks—birth through the mouth, attempts at fellatio, etc. Weiss states that when patients speak of a 'fear of fear' this is inexact: they dread painful changes in consciousness, depersonalizations, half-dream states that overcome them rather than the emotion itself. To such changes in ego feeling (or other hysteric manifestations) in the initial attack, Weiss attributes an etiological traumatic significance.

The feelings relating to the legs led Abraham (1913c) to speak of the locomotor anxiety of these patients. He pointed out the genital significance of the legs, which are hypererоtized and become the site of many displaced fantasies, so that their 'loss' is psychologically tantamount to castration. Besides this interpretation, another meaning suggests itself to account for the special importance of the legs. At least, in cases where the *topos* of the topophobia is a wide expanse, the total picture is of losing one's self into it. Besides Fenichel's interpretation of a 'reversal' of an anxious sense of constriction, a direct interpretation is possible, namely, that the width itself is the frightening element. The wide agora is like the dream screen and all those expanses which stand for the surface of the mother. In one version of agoraphobic anxiety the patient fears that he will spread out and merge with this screen, lose himself in a reproduction of the merging and being merged that takes place when the infant falls asleep. The agora is a mother symbol; the fear is of bad sleep or its equivalent, bad death. Thus it is a version, but an anxious one, of the oceanic feeling of which Romain Rolland wrote to Freud.

In the past six years many colleagues have sent me records of dreams in which a 'dream screen' is discernible. It is striking that the screen is frequently represented precisely as something inedible, tasteless or even disagreeable to the mouth, such as a marble cliff with blue veins in it, a desert, or other wastes and barren tracts.[12] To merge with this sort of dream screen suggests destruction, and it appears that this is the type of expanse to which these particular agoraphobes are referring. Here a collapse of the legs would be a reminiscence of the flaccidity that precedes sleep and of the union with the breast at nursing.

This interpretation of the agoraphobic sense of losing the legs is analogous to that given by Lorand (1948) for the loss of teeth in dreams—that the dreamer wishes to return to the toothless stage when he was being nursed. We are indebted to Gero (1939) and ultimately to Abraham (1913c) and Sadger (1911) for the knowledge that a tooth and a leg are mutually replaceable symbols. Both may represent the genitalia or sadistic weapons and they may both be organs with muscular-

[12] *Cf.* Weiss (1935) for the resemblance of certain painful elements in the anxiety to states of half-sleep and half-awakening. See Isakower (1936) for unpleasant hypnagogic sensations.

erotic function. Their loss consequently implies castration or passive masochistic gratification. However, in addition, teeth and legs both may be lost in dreams to fulfil a wish to be nursed and carried, passive feeding and passive locomotion taking the dreamer back to the same stage of infancy. Not to go out is a mild form of not walking at all, and this is probably the main idea behind the remark that Abraham (1913d) quotes of his five-year-old incipient agoraphobic: *'Ich will kein Spazierkind sein, ich will ein Mutterkind sein'*. If the ego drastically eliminates those of its organs that make for independent existence, it is ultimately thrown back on the mother and the helplessness that precedes sleep. When Freud (1915d, p. 222) described how a person prepares for sleep by shedding his clothes, his false teeth and other prosthetic equipment, he indicated that this procedure was followed by the psychological shedding of the organs of independent action. In fact, except for the rare phenomenon of sleepwalking, the legs in particular are eliminated in the sleeping state. Finally, like Tausk's (1919) Miss Natalija A, the dormescent ego loses itself and becomes a blank (Federn, 1926; Isakower, 1936). It is this process which is subtly reflected in agoraphobic sensations of 'loss' and of the self widening out as if to become congruent with the agora.

Morbid fears of being on the street are usually listed among the agoraphobias, yet they may show differences in several details of the façade. The manifest elements are painted on the same canvas as the agoral picture, but in a different genre. Sometimes, as Fenichel (1944) stated, the houses lining the street seem to approach each other, or the street seems to get narrow, and Fenichel believed this to be due to the anxiety, the *angustia* or constriction felt in the person's own thorax. Here again, despite plausibility, the interpretation is not exhaustive and may conceal deeper possibilities of interpretation. I refer to the possibility that such elements are 'repetitions' of latent fantasies of joining the mother in sleep, and of hypnagogic or hypnopompic sensations.

The manifest content of the street phobias shows considerable variation, yet certain topics crop up with some regularity. In many well-studied cases, there is a good deal of reference to prostitutes and prostitution, and several observers have been struck by the frequent appearance of a sister in the latent pathogenetic thoughts (Cohn, 1928; A. Katan, 1937). The topics, sister and prostitute, figured largely in the analysis of a young man in my practice, who spent several weeks unable to go out on the street unless his family doctor went along. The patient, an obsessional neurotic, began his analysis by reporting a dream of intercourse with his sister, in which he had no emotion either pleasant or unpleasant, upon which he commented somewhat contemptuously, 'So what?'. Much of his ensuing analysis was a mixed attempt to give and to prevent an answer to this question. The street phobia followed a break with his mistress, who was a prostitute and a surrogate for his sister. He needed his physician's constant attendance because he was afraid that he might suddenly go into labor and give birth unaided, a frightening event in his sister's history. From this young man and from others it was possible to learn some of the deeper meaning of street, sister, and prostitute, all mutually replaceable conceptions in his unconscious thinking.

Many persons, not only those with a street phobia or a prostitution complex, use nuns, prostitutes, and streets in their dreams to refer to a sister. As to the nuns, they are of course 'sisters' by profession and may by reversal ironically stand for prostitutes. A patient told me of a brothel in which the parlor was furnished like a chapel, where the girls were dressed as nuns, and the madam was called Mother Superior. In the split between sacred and profane love in individual development, a sister comes easily to be equated with a prostitute; she is less respected than the mother and more available as a sexual playmate. As a displacement from the mother in the œdipus complex, the sister tends to be a debased object, cognate with the debased mother representation, while the mother herself retains the purity. As to the street, the prostitute may be identified with it, as in the French colloquialism, *la rue*. Indeed, my patient's fantasy of his sister's giving birth on the street is of interest linguistically. The etymology of such family names as La Rue, La Place, La Porte, etc., may be based on the same idea, for these names originated in French orphanages where foundlings were named *the street, the place,* etc., that is, for the place where they were found.[13] Most illegitimate children of known mothers received their names; hence the procedure may reflect the unconscious idea that the street or the market place is the prostitute-mother who has borne a fatherless child, in a sort of Black Mass version of the virgin birth.

In the case of the sister there is considerably more identification, as compared with the degree of object love, than in the relation to the mother. The sister may appear in strange symbolic guise in dreams and fantasies, and as the member of strange symbolic equations. I am indebted to Dr. Gregory Zilboorg for telling me years ago that a river in the manifest dream text often stands for a sister, in contrast to the maternal ocean or large body of water, and I have met with examples that confirm this interpretation. Whether there is some kinship between the ideas of street and river I cannot say. But there are stranger equivalents for the sister. One of them is the penis, as Fenichel (1936) discovered. Certainly this is a narcissistic aspect of the sister relationship; but that the sister may represent a true *alter ego,* indeed a former part of one's self, is best demonstrated in Nunberg's (1949) analysis of circumcision. Nunberg's patient not only equated his sister with his lost foreskin, but also approximated in a fantasy Plato's well-known account of the origin of love; namely, that a human being was to begin with a double individual, and that the gods severed this individual, making two, a male and a female, two males, or two females, whereupon love arose as a reciprocal desire for reunion. The knowledge that sister and brother began life in the same mother leads to a theory that they were originally joined in a unity. The nature of this union needs interpretation not available in Nunberg's analysis. Brother and sister were in fact 'separated', but not from each other; both were one, but with the mother, not only *in utero* but also at the breast, and they were both in a union with the breast while nursing. In fact Plato's drinking-party story denies the fact that a man was originally attached to his mother. In her place Plato puts a narcissistically conceived sister or brother; for the breast

[13] Thus *Jean le Rond,* the real name of the philosopher D'Alembert, was given him because he was found on the steps of a church of that name.

he substitutes a Siamese-twin commissure; and for weaning he puts severing. This is a version of the anaclitic basis of love which omits mother and the breast.

For more instruction as to the meaning of *sister,* we may appeal directly to dream psychology in Freud's The Interpretation of Dreams. There he states that 'sisters' in the manifest text are symbols for the breasts, and in the Introductory Lectures, he illustrates this by an example. This use of sisters is one instance, of which there are several, where persons in dreams may stand for bodily parts. Therefore one is encouraged to ascribe to the *sister* of the street phobias this same meaning of a narcissistically invested object, genetically related to the breast; for it is an identification with a sister, or a defense against such an identification, which appears in the manifest text of the phobia. Accordingly, the unconscious equation of sister and breast, both as parts (or quasi parts) of the mother, should contribute to an impulse to a 'reunion', to an identification, or to the correlated anxiety. It must be noted that there are agoraphobias which contain no reference to a sister (Alexander, 1927b; Deutsch, 1928; Weiss, 1935). Some of these, however, leave no doubt of a strong oral factor. In one of Deutsch's cases where the symptoms were intermediate between phobia and perversion, the patient at twenty-two years of age 'still slept with her mother, and when going to sleep would suck at her mother's breast or finger'.

In certain respects the fear of crossing a bridge is related to the street phobias (A. Katan, 1937), but this fear too possesses intrinsic peculiarities. Friedman (1952), in his clinical study of the role of the bridge, revealed the dominance of genital conflicts, for the anxiety ordinarily referred to a sexual danger, œdipal in origin, which was represented manifestly as the collapse of the bridge, at other times as a peril to be encountered on the other shore. The more general study brought out nongenital components of the anxiety, especially those that related to death and destruction. Friedman writes: 'The neurotic fear of bridges and of the opposite shore, which is so pathognomonic of some patients with sexual disturbances, was perhaps best described in the free associations of a patient who suffered from a true gephyrophobia. He defined it as *a fear that he would cross into an unknown, dangerous country, where he might be ripped apart or devoured by prehistoric animals.* One might speculate whether this oral connotation of the intrauterine fantasy may not be an underlying motivation of the neurotic fear of bridges. Perhaps further clinical study will substantiate this idea and contribute to our understanding of the symbolic contents of such phobias and dreams' (pp. 60-61).

My experience does not permit me to add to Friedman's cautious comments. However, the oral danger to which he refers was evident in a young woman cited in my paper, The Body as Phallus.[14] In adolescence she had had a bridge phobia, and in a dream she found herself pursued by a man and tried to escape from him by pulling herself hand over hand across a chasm or canyon on a taut rope. Her associations showed that her body represented a phallus, but her fear of falling was expressed in oral terms. She referred to being swallowed and sucked in by the waters beneath; the chasm yawned and gaped for her. Thus she demonstrated that her fear of being deflorated (and impregnated) was condensed with a fear of dying and being eaten up. Two anxieties were fused, one of them genital, the other oral. Yet the presumed safety of the opposite shore must be the safety of the protective mother, and the passage across the canyon a transition to a renewed peaceful sleep. Chasms and canyons are splits, and the first split that is thoroughly perceived by the young child is the split between waking and sleep.

This primal split reminds us that the present application of dream psychology concepts to the neuroses is far from complete. The phobias offered themselves for study because of their key position in our theory of anxiety and symptom-formation, but we have necessarily omitted more than a passing mention of the mechanism of repression. Is it too soon to suspect that more consideration of sleep and the dream will bring illumination to this topic? The dream is a return from repression, and the earliest defense may well be not denial, as some have suggested, but the forerunner of denial, namely, going to sleep; for sleep and repression bring *tabulae rasae* to the mind. A comparison of sleep and the dream with the

[14] See pp. 28-47 [Ed.].

manifestations of conversion hysteria and hypnosis, in line with the method illustrated in this paper, might be useful. It would unite one of the oldest of Freud's findings (the essential similarity of dream and neurosis) with one of our latest ego-psychological intentions, the discovering of early forerunners of the mechanisms of defense.

II. THE FORGETTING OF DREAMS*

The forgetting of dreams, Freud (1900-1901, p. 517) tells us, is inexplicable until we seek to explain it by the power of the dream censorship. All forgetting of dreams or dream elements, all blurring of the picture, all of the dreamer's doubts about the contents, are signs of resistance to the dream or to dream elements. And during analysis, when a resistance is overcome, it often happens that the forgotten dream or dream-part is recalled. There are many motives for the forgetting of dreams during analysis, since resistance may affect a large variety of ideas and impulses, including many kinds of transference wishes. Thus, the forgetting of a dream may be due to such ego attitudes as shame, hostility, spite, or revenge; and the whole dream may be treated as if it were something substantial, as an object for barter between the dreamer and the analyst, or as a gift or coin that may be given or withheld or used for purchases. On the whole, the remembering of a dream betokens less resistance, for this promotes the analysis, but even the remembering of dreams can exceptionally and paradoxically be perverted into a resistance, a fact first pointed out by Eder (1930). The patient may remember too much of a dream or too many dreams and may thus sabotage an analytic hour, filling it with a long exposition of elaborate unanalyzable material. My interpretation[1] of this resistant remembering is that the patient is acting out his sleep of the night before and is repeating it in the analytic hour; in other words, the wish to sleep is the motive for an excessive and futile remembering, a finding strikingly confirmed by a patient of Jacob Arlow.[2]

Thus, the motives for forgetting a dream are the same as the motives for repressing in general—not different from the motives for forgetting a name or a word—as Freud (1901) has ex-

*[No. 95 in Bibliography.]

1 See, *Inferences from the Dream Screen*, pp. 101-114 [Ed.].

2 Personal communication.

plained in The Psychopathology of Everyday Life. I call your attention to the fact that the word *forgetting* is a gerund, a verbal noun, and that it implies both action and substance. When we spoke above of the motives for forgetting, we were implying action and were thinking more of the verb *to forget,* the process of forgetting as a movement or a dynamic fact. But we may stress the substantival nature of the word, and thereby treat the forgetting statically as a piece of the manifest dream itself, as the last piece in the dream text. Then we can interpret a forgetting as if it were a symptom or any manifest conscious content, and thus determine its latent meaning. Concretely what I mean is this: if the dreamer associates to his forgetting a dream, he will be led, as by any other free association, to the latent or unconscious meaning of the forgetting. This is true whether the associations are prompted by the analyst or if they spontaneously accompany the dreamer's efforts to recall the dream. In the process, the dream will sometimes be remembered, but by no means always, for the resistant motives may well maintain the upper hand.

Now a good many of the associations to anything that is forgotten are of the sort we call *regressive* in the topographic sense. In a famous example, Freud's (1901) attempt to recall the name of the artist Signorelli, we find an exact statement of how Freud introspectively experienced this regressive process. For he tells us:

> . . . so long as the painter's name remained inaccessible, the visual memory that I had of the series of frescoes and of the self-portrait which is introduced into the corner of one of the pictures was *ultra-clear*—at any rate much more intense than visual memory-traces normally appear to me. In another case, also described in my 1898 paper, which concerned a visit which I was very reluctant to pay to an address in a strange town, I had forgotten the name of the street beyond all hope of recovery, but my memory of the house number, as if in derision, was ultra-clear, whereas normally I have the greatest difficulty in remembering numbers (p. 13, n.).

The regression is from the later form of remembering, that is, from verbal memory traces of the name *Signorelli* or the name of the street to the associated visually remembered mental pictures. And the regression of latent dream thoughts during dream formation follows this same course as a rule: from verbal thoughts to visual images.

Since the forgotten dream is usually a picture to begin with and not verbal predominantly, the question arises as to what regressive substitute formation is to be expected, analogous to the visual pictures when a word is forgotten. There should be memory traces older than the formed pictures that are the substitutes for words. There should be regressive substitutes for formed pictures, memory traces further back and nearer the perception system (P) in Freud's scheme of the psychic apparatus. To our introspective efforts, the results of forgetting a dream picture is to wipe it out, to erase it or blur it and reduce it to an amorphous state. Sometimes we catch this process *in statu nascendi* while a dream is going on, or when the dreamer turns his attention to the dream after waking; and I shall give later on an instance in which the forgetting is represented in the manifest dream itself and the dream picture is turned into an amorphous one.

I was led to think about the special nature of dream forgetting by an observation which I used to show what I meant by the *dream screen*.[3] I had an opportunity, as it were, to watch a dream being forgotten. For, while one of my patients was on the couch, ready to tell me her dream, she 'saw it' suddenly curve over backwards away from her and then like a canvas or a carpet roll up and away into the distance. The process of forgetting the dream was dramatized: the dream was like a painting, which was then rolled up and rolled away from her. This was the final element in her waking process and in her dream; it was a sort of hypnopompic phenomenon, and the action could be analyzed. For the patient, it was a weaning experience. On going to sleep she had joined herself in fantasy to the breast, in the manner described by Isakower (1936), and when she awoke she lost this breast.

In previous communications, I have given reasons for assuming that the visual manifest dream picture is as if painted on or projected like a motion picture onto a screen, and I tried to show why this screen is the dream representative of the breast—the continuance in sleep and dreaming of the baby's first background when he falls asleep. In a recent criticism of

[3] See, *Sleep, the Mouth and the Dream Screen*, pp. 87-100 [Ed.].

the idea of the dream screen, Fliess (1953) has raised the question whether the dream screen has empirical existence or whether it is a model, an explanatory construction. I believe that it exists; however, for my present purposes there is no need for a final answer to this question.

Let us consider the manifest dream as a picture, as a 'technicolor' motion picture if necessary, projected onto the dream screen. The screen would not show through from under a perfect or ideally remembered dream picture. But when a dream is remembered only in part, blanks (erasures, Freud calls them) may appear in the manifest picture; and when the whole dream is forgotten, it is as if the picture was wiped off, leaving a blankish, amorphous background. Now, properly considered, this background too is made up of memory traces. It is composed of the very earliest ones laid down in infancy during nursing and dormescent experiences. Perhaps the background is a reminiscence of the 'primal dream' of the smallest infant, before the various sensations have been arranged and combined in significant and consistent, formed perceptions. When the process that leads from formed vision to amorphous blur or to complete forgetting is gradual, or when it takes place in stages, we may get a view of the details in the blanking-out or fading-out procedure, as in the example mentioned above and as in some to follow. When we do, we are in a position to analyze and interpret the latent meaning of the manifest forgetting.

This picture of the dream as a painting or as a stage or moving picture performance is a simplification, but for me a useful one as a model or diagram into which one can fit many details of clinical observation on the forgetting and remembering of dreams. I am aware that it leaves out the matter of nonvisual dreams and dream elements, with their at present unsolved problems, such as the auditory phenomena for which Isakower (1939) has given us an explanation. Along with the visually blank dreams, moreover, we find many nonvisual, so-called organic, qualities, such as touch, taste, warmth, sexual excitement and the rest, as Rycroft (1951) has confirmed. However, the breast experience too is not purely visual, but tactile, gustatory and thermally exciting; and many other sensory qualities may arise indirectly during nursing. With all these reservations and conditions, there still remains the fact that the large majority of dreams are visual, and that it is perfectly proper to investigate as a special problem the forgetting of this prevalent form of the dream.

My general thesis is that the forgetting or remembering of dreams, considered as if a dream element, or as I have phrased it, as the noun part of the gerund, may be interpreted as an oral phenomenon by means of the method of free association. Now, I should like to present examples of this general thesis. The first example will explain what I mean by the statement that dream-forgetting stands for weaning. It is the case of a young woman, early in her analysis, who said that she had forgotten her dream. Casually I asked her what occurred to her in connection with forgetting it, and she replied, 'I think of the dog I had when I was a child, with a tennis ball in his mouth'. This was a memory of something that had really occurred, and it turned out to be a screen memory, for she went on to relate that she had never been breast-fed, and that this, more than any other circumstance, had made her envious of her sister, who had been. The association about the dog appeared to portray her own intense need to sink her teeth into the breast and to cling to it stubbornly, a wish that was evident enough in her life story and in her subsequent analytic behavior.

Listening carefully, one hears many oral ideas arise spontaneously after the statement, 'I forgot my dream'. Sometimes they appear to portray a search, as if the dreamer were looking for it. Thus one patient reported, 'My dream slipped away from me while I was brushing my teeth', and there are comparable oral hints in many other efforts to find the dream. On another occasion the same patient said of a forgotten dream, 'It was uninteresting'. Whereupon her stomach rumbled and (so to say) began to associate for her, and she continued: She had dined out with her husband and parents at a restaurant, and the slice of lamb she had got was 'uninteresting', whereas her husband and her father had both commented on the excellence of their portion. Often the same patient, having forgotten a dream and trying to recall it, would speak of her lunch and of her lunching companion. In her particular case, the motive for her resistant forgetting was usually a wish to avoid speaking of her current unsatisfactory and uninteresting sexual life. But her attempts to recall her dreams led invariably to thoughts of drinking, eating, pleasant table companionship; there was an obvious desire to think of the pleasures of the table rather than to recall the privations of the bed. To give an example, one day trying to recall her dream, she spoke of having had lunch with an aunt, then through some superficial associations about her aunt's proposed vacation journey, she recalled that she had had a dream of packing the night before. This led to her admission of having masturbated before going to sleep, and of an unsatisfactory coitus before the masturbation.

That the forgotten dream is a concrete object, which has been as if physically lost or misplaced, is implied in many remarks, as in those above to the effect that it was brushed off the teeth or swallowed. One of my friends, a colleague, tells me that when she tries to remember a dream, she has the feeling of its being somewhere in her mouth or throat, as if she were trying to find it there. Such spatial ideas are very common. The lost dream is sometimes thought of as being somewhere in the body, sometimes outside somewhere. One patient of mine began her analysis by saying that she ought to pray to Saint Anthony, to help her find her lost memories. And William James (1890, Vol. I) has this charming description of looking for a forgotten idea:

> . . . we make search in our memory for a forgotten idea, just as we rummage our house for a lost object. In both cases we visit what seems to us the probable *neighborhood* of that which we miss. We turn over the things under which, or within which, or alongside of which, it may possibly be; and if it lies near them, it soon comes to view. But these matters, in the case of a mental object sought, are nothing but its *associates* (p. 654).

Since in this allegory the house we live in must be a symbol for our body, there is an interesting hint here for the future study of where we think memories go when they are forgotten. So far as my experience goes, the forgotten dream seems to take one of two paths; either it goes inward, that is, stomachward, or it goes away carried along by the illusively departing breast.

Freud has remarked that a very small fragment of a dream will often be sufficient to yield on association a large part, perhaps all, of the latent dream thoughts. Sometimes the statement, 'I forgot my dream', will serve as such a fragment and lead to latent thoughts of great importance, even though the dreamer may not recall the forgotten manifest dream text. Thus the word *uninteresting* in the above example, which seemed to be a comment on the dream text, was in fact such a fragment. The other patient's initial association to her dog and the tennis ball was not a fragment or a comment; it was an association, spontaneous and not immediately comprehensible, captured in her effort to remember the dream. It was a real screen memory, formed in the way described by Fenichel (1928b) after an 'injunction to make a mental note'. Her wish to remember the dream re-enforced by my request, brought forth this screen memory, which stood not only for the forgotten dream but also for the underlying latent memories of oral sibling rivalry. Fenichel (1927) has explained how screen memories arise from a comparable conflict of a wish to remember and a wish to forget, as compromises, a theorem which Greenacre (1949) has developed and elaborated. It is interesting that Fenichel calls the intense need to remember something a hunger for screen events, *ein Deckerlebnishunger,* a conception which Greenacre also finds useful. In the effort to remember a dream and the immediate associations that accompany this effort, this is certainly a happy term, for the dreamer very often turns to thoughts of food or oral satisfactions. I am indebted to Dr. David Rubinfine[4] for the following interesting example. His patient reported: 'I had a long dream last night. I kept forgetting it, but then I remembered a code word: *Marzipan*'. The dream that followed confirmed the idea that the manifest subjective length of the dream indicated the fulfilment of intense oral wishes—that it was so to say a long drink or a long repast.

I present two contrasting examples: in one an external stimulus led a young man to remember some of his forgotten dream, in the other the external stimulus drove a remembered dream from a young woman's mind. The stimulus for remembering was food. A conscientious patient was sitting in the drug store across the street from my office, wondering why he had

[4] Personal communication.

forgotten his dream, when the soda-counter attendant came in with a plate of chopped eggs. He thereupon remembered that he had dreamed of steamed spaghetti. His associations led to food poisoning, due to rat dirt, and to other negative oral topics. In contrast, the stimulus that chased the other patient's dream away was a waker, a bell. She was engaged in remembering her dream while she was still in bed, when her telephone bell rang and she lost it completely. The bell reminded her of the rising bell at school and the bugle at summer camp, which was a signal to get up and put on her swimming suit. This was at an age when she was comparing her growing breasts to those of other girls. The dream text was not recalled.[5] To make the meaning of these events clear, I must explain that for both patients sleep was a highly libidinal matter, unconsciously equated with being loved and fed. The man relied on sedatives to secure a good night's sleep; the woman was 'irritable' and 'not herself' till after breakfast. From this one may infer why the sight of food induced the first patient to remember his dream, and why the bell sent the other's dream to oblivion. The food, particularly drugstore food with its pharmaco-toxicological connotations, suggested sleep, or that food mixed with drugs or poison would put one to sleep. It put the patient in the mood for dreaming again and probably too for freely associating, which as Freud (1900-1901) says, is 'a psychical state which, in its distribution of psychical energy (that is, of mobile attention), bears some analogy to the state before falling asleep—and no doubt also to hypnosis' (p. 102). The symbolic sleep-inducer led to a partial recall of the dream.

The bell, on the other hand, was a waker and a symbol of school and camp discipline. Its admonition: sleep no more, was obeyed. The dream, remnant and successor after waking of the oral satisfaction of sleep, was hastily put aside. In my recent paper, Phobic Symptoms and Dream Interpretation,[6] I pointed out that in preœdipal psychology, to sleep and to dream mean to repeat being at the breast, while to be awakened means the disturbing of that situation, usually by the father,

[5] To spell out the message of the rising bell, it said: Leave the mother (the bed); establish your separateness by an ego boundary (clothes); be active (swim), not orally passive and quiet for you are too old (note *your* breasts).

[6] See pp. 187-212 [Ed.].

though in the example just given evidently by the superego, which is a possible confirmation of Isakower's views on the relation of superego and auditory sphere. I should like to add here that not only are sleeping and dreaming possible symbols for being nursed, but that to *remember* the dream is a quasi prolongation of sleep and stands for sleep, while *forgetting* the dream repeats and stands for waking up and is a step in the weaning process.

The male patient just mentioned once forgot *two* dreams. The fact that there were two reminded him of one of them; it was a dream of watching a partly undressed woman in a window of the opposite house. She had on her brassiere, and as a day residue he remarked that on the evening before the dream, friends he had visited had shown him home movies of a baby nursing at the breast. Another patient surprised me by saying, 'I can't remember my dream. No! No!' I asked her why two such emphatic 'noes'. 'Oh', she said, 'that's because I had two dreams'. Association through 'double zero' led to her mother's double mastectomy.

Dr. Sylvan Keiser wrote me about a patient who told him, 'I feel I had two dreams that I can't remember'. Asked for associations to that, she expanded: it was as if something were just beyond her reach, as if she were reaching for food, just as in recurrent dreams of adolescence, she seemed to run after a ball without reaching it. Then her associations took up fellatio, her feeling that her mother loved her children only when they were being nursed. Finally, the patient remarked that the two dreams seemed extraordinary, since forgotten material followed the removal of resistance, but that there was nothing else in the dreams except that something was moving away.

The dream fragment, or dream token (to distinguish a 'solid' form of condensed dream residue), is often highly charged with transference meaning. One of my patients said to her husband that she had no dream for her analytic hour. He teased her, 'Why don't you take him a chocolate bar?' As a matter of fact, a patient of Dr. Charles Fisher (1953), under very interesting circumstances, did in fact bring him a chocolate Easter egg about six inches long—an anal gift-baby. Dr. Fisher was experimentally testing what the effect would be on patients in analysis of a direct 'suggestion' to them that they bring in a dream. This patient brought the gift, saying, 'I couldn't bring you a dream, so I brought you an Easter egg instead'. During analysis, we are reminded, dreams are often dreamed and remembered as something *for* the analyst. Yet as in the examples given, even in the choice of the gift which is substituted for the dream and stands for it, an oral mechanism is to be divined. A gift of food is a demand for a return gift in kind.

Among the 'gifts' for the analyst that stand very directly for dreams, Abraham (1913a) described a special variety, the dream which the patient writes down or tries to write down or to record in order to bring it to the analytic hour. Such dreams, as Freud, Abraham, and others have shown, are usually unanalyzable; the writing indicates great resistance to the content. In a previous paper,[7] I pointed out that such a purely transference interpretation as Abraham gave—that the written dream is a gift to the analyst—sets limitations for any general theory of the impulse to write down a dream. I thought that the writing showed a wish to continue sleep, particularly where the aim was not accomplished and produced only blank records or jumbled notations (Abraham, 1913a) or even simply a dream of having written down the dream (M. Meyer, 1933). The blank page, like the blank dictaphone record in one of Abraham's cases, represented the blank dream screen and (more deeply) blank, undisturbed, infantile sleep; the recorded dream is the equivalent of a new version of the dream, which, since it proves unanalyzable is equal to 'no dream at all' or only to the paper on which it is written. That is to say, the paper itself is the main addition to the new manifest version, and it stands for the 'background' of the dream, that is, the dream screen or the breast, as an indicator of the wish for more, uninterrupted sleep. Furthermore, the written dream shows exquisitely the mechanism which Fenichel predicated for screen-memory formations, in the other sense of 'screen', a *Deckerinnerung,* for it is an evident compromise between the wish to remember and the wish to forget.

The patients whose material I have been citing here have all at one time or another had a desire, sometimes almost a

[7] See, *Inferences from the Dream Screen,* pp. 101-114 [Ed.].

compulsion, to write down their dreams, and many of them have made waking notes. Since I have discussed this impulse and its interpretation at some length in my second paper on the dream, and there given several examples, I shall present only one more example of dream notation, or rather of its miscarriage. A patient reacted to a long weekend's absence of the analyst by producing a great many long dreams. This is a well-known reaction; weekend dreams frequently try to make up for the frustrating absence. But the interesting fact here is a slip which the patient made after telling me two long dreams and starting to tell me a third. She said, 'I am afraid I am forgetting some of the details. I had better look at some notes I made.' She took a scrap of paper from her purse; but the notes were not on that paper. 'Why!' she said in surprise, 'This is a list of restaurants I made for my father.'

Some patients become more or less obsessional about recalling their dreams and feel guilt for not remembering them better. Their conflict then may be portrayed in the manifest text of the dream. Thus, one patient dreamed that he was trying to take a camera shot of a beautiful, spired cathedral, which stood on the crest of a hill, terraced ornately like Mont Saint-Michel in the travel advertisements. The cathedral shone in brilliant colors, but while he was aiming his camera, the scene darkened and clouded up and the view was obscured behind a bank of clouds. There was no more possibility of taking the picture and even less of any color photography. Obviously the patient's wish to remember the dream, which he really fulfilled, was indicated by his dream wish to take the photograph. He had in fact shown me color photographs after he returned from previous summer vacations. By his effort to record the scene in all its colors on a film, he was complying with his analytic 'duty' and with his wish to show me the dream—a procedure which brings to mind dreams reported by Blitzsten and the Eisslers (1950), where the patient exhibited her dreams to the analyst, at the same time repudiating any responsibility for their contents. But my patient clouded up his dream even while he was dreaming it, to indicate his counterwish; i.e., the wish not to see it and not to be able to show it to me. In other words, the 'clouding up' was an unsuccessful attempt to 'forget' the dream picture. I shall not enumerate the topics the patient wished to conceal and exhibit. Instead I shall turn to an interpretation of the *cloud.*

This cloud I take to be the dream screen, wandering around from behind the view and then covering it. I should like, for general confirmation, to refer to the papers of Rycroft (1951) and Kepecs (1952). In the latter's case, the dream screen appeared as a hallucination, which came between the patient's eyes and the world and obscured his vision. As always, I consider that the dream screen is a symbol for the breast, and that in the dream above the patient was finally seeing and showing nothing but the breast. Due to the kindness of Dr. Kubie,[8] I am able to give an illustrative dream. This dream was recurrent and first dreamed early in childhood; now it became less vivid and less compelling, a dream 'hard to describe, because', in the patient's words, 'it was almost pure emotion'. He continues, 'The contents of the dream were of something pure white, like an endless wall that you don't see—perhaps as though your eyes were closed and you just felt it, or as though you just knew it was there without any senses; almost like gazing through a window *into a milky substance,* or you were pressed up so close to the wall that it was all-enveloping and endless and you were *both in it and at the same time against it.*' I owe to Dr. Zilboorg[9] the account of a comparable dream: 'The patient, a man, dreamed of a big slab of marble—white, smooth. There was nothing else seen; nothing was happening except this: the piece of marble seemed to come closer and closer to the dreamer's eye (it was coming *to* the dreamer; the dreamer was not moving toward it) and the dreamer began to discern bluish veins which "one clearly sees in marble stones".' Dr. Zilboorg added, 'I explained to the doctor (in supervision) on the basis of associations, which I don't remember (it was almost twenty years ago) though I do remember they were scanty, that that slab was the breast.'

I return to the dream of the camera and the cathedral to outline a theory of dream-forgetting in terms of Freud's dream psychology, as this is stated in Chapter VII of The Interpretation of Dreams. The patient's preconscious wish to remember the dream was in fact fulfilled, but only after it was modified by

[8] Personal communication.
[9] Personal communication.

his unconscious wish to forget it. These two ideas are expressed respectively by the camera, which is a memory aid, and the clouds. The action in the dream shows the formed, colored, visual memory traces giving way before older, dull, amorphous, colorless ones. In terms of the psychic apparatus and Freud's ideas of dream formation, at the moment that the clouds appear there is a regressive movement. Early amorphous memory traces, which stand very near to the system P are activated in place of the colored and formed memories, and they gradually fill the major part of the picture. Indeed, the clouds stand for the earliest of all memory traces—those of the breast. In other dreams, even such early amorphous visual traces are lacking, the memory traces are elusive, vague, 'more like pure emotion'; that is, they are made up of deeper tactile, thermal, and dimly protopathic qualities not readily localizable or namable, which are in their way 'memory traces' of early dim consciousness of the breast or of the half-asleep state.

Hence, the reduction of a dream to this relatively blank state, to the state of a dream screen, is a near approach to forgetting. All its visual contents except representatives of the very earliest memories have been eliminated. To forget a dream, then, may be given the following interpretation in terms of psychic functioning: The dream thoughts regress to the memory traces that stand near the P entrance to the psychic apparatus, and in particular to those laid down during the nursing period. Theoretically it is hard to say whether the process might not go on to cathect 'no memory traces'; this would represent the abstraction of absolute sleep. I suspect that such an absolute might be very difficult to attain, and I tend to believe empirically that there is always some *Wachbereitschaft,* some trace of the disposition to awaken.

Finally, two questions arise naturally from the above descriptions and interpretations. The first is, must the forgetting of dreams *always* be interpreted in oral terms, as a 'losing of the breast'? So far as I am concerned, I must say 'Yes', but I have to concede that some day some additional interpretation may be discovered and empirically substantiated. The more cautious statement that this is the case *sometimes* would not be correct for me until such a demonstration, for it implies that some other process of dream forgetting is now known. In other words, *always* means 'so far as I know'. The other question relates to repression in general. Since dreams are forgotten through an act of repression, can we extend our results to cover all repressions, not merely the forgetting of dreams, and can we then assume that the same interpretation of oral loss and regressive reduction to the blankness of the breast applies here also? This is very hard to answer. Repression is said to be a differentiated form of the more primitive *denial,* and the earliest manifestation of denial according to Freud is a spitting out. But the dream always contains the wish to sleep, linked from the start to oral satisfaction, and the forgetting of dreams comes readily into union with this wish. Hence, there is certainly the possibility that we have found orality here because we are in a predominantly oral region of the mind, and we need many broader studies before we can make a positive assertion about repression in general.

III. SLEEP, NARCISSISTIC NEUROSIS, AND THE ANALYTIC SITUATION*

In the first part of this paper I continue a previous train of thought, comparing dreams and the narcissistic neuroses; in the second part I follow a different path and comment upon sleep and its relation to analysis as a technique and therapy.

Dreams and Narcissistic Neuroses

I begin with a reference to two papers of Freud (1915d, 1915c), published in the same volume of the *Zeitschrift* (IV). One is The Metapsychological Supplement to the Theory of Dreams, the other, Mourning and Melancholia, both of which powerfully affected psychoanalytic thought. To unify theory and combine the work on dreams with that on the neuroses, in the Supplement Freud formally introduced into dream theory the concept of narcissism. The dream was treated in theory as if it were a variety of psychosis: sleep was an expression of primary narcissism to which the libido had regressed, while in dreaming the ego expressed itself regressively in hallucinations. The purpose of dreaming was to rechannel leftover disturbers and impulses, so that they should not waken the sleeper but, instead, come to hallucinatory wish fulfilment. The dream, accordingly, was a psychosis due to the wish to sleep. In the fact of the dream, Freud (1915d) takes pains to point out, there is evidence that the narcissistic regression is not complete, or, as he puts it, 'the narcissism of sleep has . . . to admit an exception . . .' (p. 224). The dream is evoked by and attests to the fact that there is a certain amount of leftover waking libidinal or ego interest.

Presumably, therefore, the less there is to a manifest dream and the nearer it comes to being blank, so much the nearer is the sleeper to a state of consciousness expressive of primary narcissism; that is to say, the blanker the dream, the fewer

* [No. 101 in Bibliography.]

impurities are there in the narcissism of sleep. Therefore, I call attention to an unusual class of dreams, described in previous publications of my own and of others, where there is relatively little or no visual content, which if present is amorphous and is called *misty* or *vague,* and in which the optical projection effect is imperfect because the dream screen is not sharply externalized. Sometimes the whole dream remains unprojected and feels to the dreamer as if it took place within him or inseparably from him rather than somewhere before him in his visual field. Such dreams come very near representing what Freud means by narcissism in this particular paper, for they approximate concretely his idea of narcissistic sleep, with very little of the 'exception' indicated by the text of ordinary dreams. This was immediately recognized by Rycroft (1951), who calls them *sleep dreams,* and by Scott (1951), who speaks in this connection of *narcissistic dreams,* both of which designations apply very accurately. Hoffer (1952), explicitly aligning himself with me, writes, 'I should exemplify primary narcissism . . . by the infant's state of deep sleep'.

In the other, contemporaneous, essay, Mourning and Melancholia, Freud (1915c) brought the same concept, narcissism, to bear on depression and elation, which he interprets by two assumptions, namely, that they operate like the process of grief, and that there is regression from object relationship to narcissism. Most of Freud's exposition in this and later papers stems from the grief-melancholia comparison; nevertheless, he apparently believed the regression to be more central, perhaps crucial, for he wonders whether a 'loss in the ego irrespectively of the object—a purely narcissistic blow to the ego—may not suffice to produce the picture of melancholia and whether an impoverishment of ego-libido directly due to toxins may not be able to produce certain forms of the disease' (p. 253).[1] He thus distinguishes two sets of factors in melancholia, one related to object loss and grief, the other to narcissism. His tentative formulation of mania as a sort of recovery from depression also arises from the comparison with grief.

All in all, the essay on Mourning and Melancholia, devoted to instinct and ego psychology, diverges from the line taken in

[1] *Cf.* also Edward Bibring (1953).

the series of metapsychological papers that Freud had just published and from the Metapsychological Supplement, which was still to appear, for in Mourning and Melancholia Freud dropped the explicit comparison of dream and neurosis. Subsequent studies were to continue the new direction, so that dream psychology and clinical psychopathology developed as two separate interests with two separate literatures. The two fields that Freud was eager to unite in the Metapsychological Supplement were divorced. Dream interpretation became subordinated to technique—'*gehandhabt*'. Freud's (1932) statement in The New Introductory Lectures, that analysts in the main were neglecting the dream, is true enough so far as it refers to this particular point—the bringing together of neurosis and dream. Analysts had followed the direction that Freud took in Mourning and Melancholia, and later in Inhibitions, Symptoms and Anxiety (Freud, 1925a), rather than the direction of the Metapsychological Supplement. An exception, noted by Freud, was Alexander's (1925) study of dream pairs. More recently, some of my use of dream psychology in studies of elation and the phobias returns to the older path (B. Lewin, 1950).[2]

There were, to be sure, obvious reasons for not beginning the study of melancholia by comparing it to a dream. Unlike Meynert's amentia or schizophrenic visual hallucinosis, there was no immediately evident point of similarity, no regression to hallucinatory wish-fulfilment or to a dreamlike state, whereas the comparison to grief and the new instinct and ego concepts were very clarifying. However, I believe that other reasons participated in the general trend away from the combination of neurosis and dream, including certain historic ones which I shall indicate later.

The first formulation of depressions and elations contained several obscurities. Thus, ordinarily neurosis and psychosis are based on conflict, but mania was stated to depend on an absence of conflict between the ego and the superego. It is not clear offhand why this should not represent mental health; at any rate, no distinction is made between the two.[3] Again, the theory seems to call upon us to assume that mania is al-

[2] See also, *Phobic Symptoms and Dream Interpretations,* pp. 187-212 [Ed.].
[3] *Cf.* Maurits Katan (1953).

ways preceded by depression, which is contrary to fact; and a theory that explains among the elations only those that follow a depression does not cover the field, which includes 'simple' manias and 'simple' depressions with no signs of the opposite state. Then, the cardinal idea, due to Rado (1927), that mania is a state of satiated oral bliss, although it has support in clinical observation and is latently correct, does not suffice to explain many findings collected by analytic observers. Complete satisfaction in the nursing situation leads to sleep, and the elations of the drug addictions, from which Rado transferred the idea, are much nearer to this end-state, whereas manic and hypomanic are manifestly very much awake; hence, it was necessary to say a good deal more about the state of affairs in mania and in the nursing situation before the relationship of the two became intelligible.

Newer clinical observations came to our assistance here, for there are two types of elated states, and what we see clinically may be one or the other or a combination of the two. The same observations forced us to introduce dream psychology into the study of the elations. To economize I shall be somewhat diagrammatic, referring my readers to my other publications for detailed descriptions. I saw a young woman go through four elations. In each of them, first came the state of *ecstasy,* an absorbed, rapt, blissful state, quite similar to what religious mystics have described, which culminated in a blank dream with orgasm, and was then followed by the second state, *hypomania proper,* the typical overactive, jocose, ebullient textbook picture. Ecstasy is indeed a state of bliss, and its interpretation as a union with the breast and the superego is very evident empirically. Rado, I suppose, was influenced by his experiences with the drug-*Rausch* when he wrote of the bliss that attends the fantasied union with the breast, following upon the hungry craving of the depression. Abraham (1924a) and others, including Helene Deutsch (1933), were looking more at hypomania proper, which shows the active cannibalism and the defensive devices of denial and projection more violently at work.

My later study gave me a forceful impression of the relationship between dream life and the clinical waking picture. For the erotized blank dream—the 'sleep dream' or 'narcissistic dream'—was so much part of the ecstasy, and the ecstasy and ensuing hypomania were so much a part of the dream (if one cared to look at it that way), that neither of them could be interpreted fully without the other. Both ecstasy and blank dream had to be formulated in terms of sleep; the mover of both of them was a special variety of a wish to sleep—that is, the wish to enjoy the narcissistically blissful sleep of the satiated nursling. This wish persisted into the distractible, overactive, overvigilant hypomania that followed the dream, where it was denied and disguised. The hypomania was like that part of a manifest dream text which denies the latent thought, and here it neatly denied not only the meaning of the waking ecstatic state, but of the blank dream as well.

A few words may be said of the sequence: ecstasy (or blank dream) and hypomania. It appears that blank dreams need not be followed by clinical hypomania according to Rycroft's (1951) observation, although in the case he reported a blank dream was followed by 'manic defense'. On the other hand, it seems plausible to me that, conversely, an ecstasy or its equivalent may be a constant forerunner of a hypomanic state (B. Lewin 1950, 1953), and I shall assume at least this potentiality in the following discussion.

After this clarification, it is easy to formulate the structure of the two elated reactions in the terminology of the dream. The dream formula for the *ecstasy* is the same as that for the blissful blank dream: the latent thought in the ecstasy, as in the blank narcissistic dream, is the satisfaction of the nursing triad of wishes, culminating in erotic sleep at the breast. Typically this is expressed not in visual, formed images; instead, the thoughts regress to amorphous feeling memories, so that the typical ecstatic patient and the dreamer say that they cannot put in words what they feel and know, and that the pictures and verbal descriptions which come to mind when they try to communicate are to be understood only as allegories or metaphorical approximations. In the ecstasy, the person relives and reproduces affective qualities—the thrill or the 'kick', to put it colloquially—and not primarily pictorial or verbal memories. The memory traces to which the latent thoughts regress and which then come to consciousness are those that were perceptions in very early infancy during the nursing situation on the way to satiated sleep, and they are the vague, deep, feeling sensations that enter into emotional states—in this particular instance, those of intense pleasure.

The sense of reality that comes with them is quite in line with that which enters a dream. Freud (1915d) remarks that we accept the hallucinations of ordinary dreaming as real because they come before our eyes in manifest pictures with visual impressions that originated in real experiences, intensified in the dream by the characteristic energic shift to them. The same holds true for the nonvisual or unformed impressions of pleasure and excitement in the ecstatic state, for they too reproduce sensations and qualities, intensified by condensation, that once really existed, and they too have the convincingness of immediate presentation. I think the situation in ordinary dreams may be more complex than Freud's statement of it, since the oldest oral elements may contribute here too to the sense of reality; yet, in the ecstasy it might be said that a person relives an intensified hypnagogic, partly asleep, or dreaming state that was suffused with pleasure, and the dream formula for ecstasy is that of a blank dream or near-blank dream, in which the return to the blissful nursing sensation is accomplished.

Hypomania proper is a somewhat more complicated formation in terms of the dream. Its basic latent wish to return to the nursing situation and to enjoy narcissistic bliss and sleep is the same as in the ecstasy, but the expression of this wish is distorted. The wish does not come to consciousness directly, for its fantasied fulfilment is barred by anxiety or attended by terror. The wish is therefore fulfilled only in the way a dream wish which cannot be faced starkly is fulfilled, i.e., in disguise. Hypomania proper is all activity, eating, and independence in its manifest text. To consider the hypomanic manifest picture as if it were the second member of a dream pair, of which ecstasy was the first member, we should say that in ecstasy the wish was fulfilled with little or no disguise, in hypomania with very much. The hypomania displaces and rationalizes the pleasure that comes from the repetition of the breast situation, at the same time denying its true source. Euphoria is attributed to a quite false or, at any rate, irrelevant motor or mental efficacy. The latent dream thought or its analogue extracts cathexis from the same memory traces that figure in the ecstasy; the cathexis is displaced to later, mainly motor memory traces, and after the distortion and the revision (elaboration) that it receives from the later traces, it is accepted by consciousness. Consciousness believes that other wishes, erotic or ambitious, are being fulfilled, whereas the secret fulfilment is still of the wishes of the oral triad. Thus, hypomania too yields to the terminology of dream interpretation. The unconscious wish is for the nursing situation; the preconscious wishes (many of them from the actual situation and analogues of 'day residues') are intensified and come to consciousness in the various enterprises, and the regression is disguised in the manifest picture. If it were not for the disguises and revisions, the manic too would be acknowledging his wish for the breast and for sleep and would be yielding to the bliss or the anxiety that attends the wish.

At the beginning of this paper, in connection with my discussion of the Metapsychological Supplement, I referred to the dream as a psychosis originating in a wish to sleep. I have presented ecstasy and hypomania proper as dependent on a wish to which the same name was applied, a wish to sleep. The ordinary wish to sleep is not represented in the ordinary visually projected dream text, except for that usually invisible or unnoticed part which I have called the dream screen, an undynamic element on the whole. Contrary to this common situation, in the infrequent dreams to which I have been referring, this is not the case. The wish to sleep is important and it is expressed in the sensations of the dream which are hallucinations of nursing and of sleep at the breast. This is why Rycroft could refer to such dreams as 'sleep-dreams'. The wish to sleep that appears in the ecstasy and as the latent wish in hypomania proper is the same that produces the 'sleep-dream'. The desired sleep is the blissful narcissistic sleep which repeats that of the nursing situation. The wish for this sleep is fulfilled directly in the blissful dream or the ecstasy and in a distorted form in hypomania proper.[4]

[4] In Robert Fliess's (1953) valuable survey *(The Revival of Interest in the Dream)*, the author criticizes me for not accepting Freud's early statement that the wish to sleep is 'biological' and letting it go at that. I should not think however that Freud meant the term *biological* to exclude psychology, for sexuality too is biological, and later Freud calls sleep a state of narcissism, which introduces a

In referring to Mourning and Melancholia, I mentioned that it was not easy to see immediately where the wish to sleep, the state of sleep, or dreaming, made any logical contact with the symptomatology of depressions or with the formulations given by Freud in this and later papers. We are so accustomed to think of the ego and the superego and of the two classes of instincts in this context that the use of other terminologies seems strange. It seems artificial to ignore the standardized, familiar terms and formulas that have dominated the literature, where certainly they have often been debased and oversimplified. Let us, however, begin with Freud's conception of depression as a regression to narcissism, which, he speculates, might in itself be a sufficient cause. I should like to use the blank dream, which represents the nursing situation, as the concrete indicator of such a regression, and I shall take up first of all Freud's idea that toxins might produce a depression regardless of object loss and the grief processes. Many toxic depressions are encountered clinically, due to drugs or to the presence of known infectious agents. In such cases, familiar to us from many psychiatric studies (e.g., Bonhoeffer, 1910), the patient is obviously in a state that approaches or resembles sleep, half-sleep, or a dream; hence, to say that the 'toxin' has acted to cause a narcissistic regression is correct in the very sense that Freud uses the phrase in the Metapsychological Supplement, when he calls sleep a state of primary narcissism. The true toxic depression (or elation) is narcissistic in the same sense as sleep, and the psychological content is the same kind of 'exception' that Freud recognizes in the case of the dream.

But this simple situation does not test the general validity of putting the depression into dream terminology. We must turn to the more complicated picture, always remembering that the first step remains the narcissistic regression. The basic unconscious wish in the depression, therefore, is the same as in the other narcissistic neuroses, to wit, the wish for the breast, including narcissistic sleep. Since the direct fulfilment of the

---

psychological interpretation. Fliess also questions the existence of the dream screen and by implication that of the blank dream too. It is not known whether Freud was acquainted with the type of dreams that I have reported. They do, however, exist, as many colleagues have become aware.

triad would result in the 'sleep-dream' or ecstasy, we must take into account that the clinical picture of depression is a manifest picture, like a dream text, which distorts and conceals the fulfilment of the latent wish. Our theoretical problem then is reduced to the following task: to construct a manifest picture of depression, beginning with the unconscious wish for the breast, which becomes distorted and revised according to the processes of dream formation outlined in Chapter VII.[5]

Our task of diagraming the depression will be easier if we fit the superego into the scheme of Chapter VII by determining the location of its memory traces. The superego is an arouser; it is an opponent of blissful sleep at the breast. External wakers that arouse the dreamer are often in the final moment of the dream translated into superego injunctions (*cf.*, Freud, 1900-1901; Isakower, 1939, 1954). Isakower, commenting on the meaning of words in dreams, pointed out that they often give the superego's opinion of the latent dream wish, which is exemplified in Freud's paradigm of the dream, that of 'the burning child', where the child whispers reproaches and seems to wake the father through them, although the real arouser is a real fire. The superego in dreams may also be represented by significant sounds, which serve as signals, as I indicated in my article, The Forgetting of Dreams. Thus, a patient who forgot her dream (i.e., awoke completely) when her telephone bell rang, associated this bell to the rising bell at school, to the bugle at camp, etc., and in general to disciplinary signals and injunctions. In the interest of guarding sleep, its chief concern, the dream may for a time depict and hallucinate an external arousing stimulus as a superego command.

However, many stimuli, coming from the external or internal environment, may disturb sleep. Many of them are present from near the beginning of life.[6] These are loud noises, bright lights, cold, pain, hunger,—to mention the more conspicuous. The iconography of dreams and myths readily combines them with superego action. Thus noises and lights figure as thunder and lightning and the wrath of God. The waking brightness of a new day figures as the sun and God's all-seeing eye. The watery cold of an enuresis is depicted as God's puni-

[5] Freud (1900-1901): *The Interpretation of Dreams.*

[6] *Cf.* Zetzel (1953).

tive Deluge. Hunger pangs become the punitive bird that gnaws at Prometheus's vitals. The earliest arousers form ready alliance with the superego when it tries to waken or wean the sleeper from his sleep at the breast. Between the preœdipal arousers and the superego injunctions and punishments, somewhere along the line is the father in the œdipal situation, who is a waker and in the full fantasy a weaner too; for it is the hungry, jealous father that becomes the wolf or the animal that takes over the mother's breast and prevents the infant's contented sleep.[7]

The superego's punishments have preœdipal roots in the earliest weaners and wakeners; the superego is the heir of the jealous, devouring, sleep-disturbing father. The memory traces of these superego precursors persist in the unconscious. Later memory traces that enter into the superego are verbal, according to Freud, a point emphasized in Isakower's (1939) studies of the 'auditory sphere' in dreams; hence the *mem* traces of the superego are to be found in at least two locations in the diagram of the psychic apparatus. One set of *mem* traces is very near those revived in the ecstasy, but this is a set of unpleasant memories of being awakened and weaned, such as hunger, pain, etc. The other superego *mem* traces are further to the right in the diagram, among the early verbal impressions, and in line with certain analytic suppositions and certain observations, the words would be in the imperative mood. For our present theoretical purposes, it suffices to assume that the latter set belongs to the unconscious system of the ego or superego. If some of them are preconscious, the scheme needs no alteration.

If then we approach the depressive picture as though it were a manifest dream text and if we inquire how well it preserves the narcissistic state (as the dream preserves sleep), we see first of all that it is an unpleasant dream, in which the latent unconscious wish for sleep at the breast is disturbed in its fulfilment by an opposite intruding tendency, that is, by weaning and wakening. As in the dream of the burning child, the representation of this tendency to a certain extent serves the regression. As the real, arousing fire became a superego command and in this form operated to preserve sleep, so the

[7] See, *Phobic Symptoms and Dream Interpretation*, pp. 187-212 [Ed.].

verbal forms of the superego injunctions tend to guard the analogous regression in the depressions. The narcissistic sleep analogue in the depressive person is constantly beset by the admonition, 'Get away from your mother's breast! Wake up!'. The persistence and repetition of the injunction over a considerable period shows that it is heard but not obeyed. The depressed ego listens but it does not move. Like the Cornish Constabulary in The Pirates of Penzance, the depressed hear the commands and repeat, 'Yes, yes, we go!', on which the irritated General Stanley in the operetta comments, 'But you *don't* go!'. As long as the depressed patient is being admonished, he is evidently secretly or unconsciously still regressively at the breast. This statement, I believe, simply amplifies Freud's thought that the depression is a narcissistic state, and the pleasure premium is hidden while the unpleasure is blatantly manifest.

The dream-formation scheme, then, can be applied somewhat as follows: the latent unconscious wish in the depressive picture is to remain in the nursing situation, narcissistically; the latent thought includes the idea of being wakened and weaned; the manifest text pictures the unsuccessful weaning and waking injunctions, disguised and revised. Since the manifest content consists largely of painful feelings and auditory impressions, the analogue of the visual text of ordinary dreams is to be found precisely in these two fields. We have a painful and auditory text rather than a visual one. The manifest picture is painful weaning and waking; the latent wish-fulfilment is pleasure and sleep at the breast.

The depressive picture presented here is didactically oversimplified. The 'father-superego' figure who wakens the infant from the breast may be called upon to supplant the mother and the breast as soother and provider. And suicide may serve symbolically as a return to sleep at the breast. But such complications deserve more complicated treatment. (See B. Lewin, 1950, discussion of suicide.)

If we compare the three narcissistic neuroses (ecstasy, hypomania proper, and depression) with the dream, we may say that ecstasy is like a blank or nearly blank, narcissistic, satisfying dream. Hypomania is like a dream in which the same regression is effected but unconsciously and is covered by denials and other disguising defenses, especially displacement to action. Depression also unconsciously maintains the regression, but consciously uses the auditory and painful impressions as manifest cover. In both hypomania proper and depression, the cathexis of the breast is maintained; in the first picture it is revealed consciously by the pleasure qualities, in the second by qualities of unpleasure that go back to the same situation.

I should like to take exception to occasional misunderstandings of my views on elations and depressions. I do not subscribe to the idea that 'elation covers depression', or that when a person is elated there is an 'underlying' depression. This seems to me too gross a formula to fit the deep psychological situation. I do not think that interval obsessional neuroses, as described by Abraham (1924a), 'cover' the depression between attacks; surely a more accurate statement would be that different defenses are brought into play, e.g., reaction-formation instead of identification. As to the narcissistic neuroses, the idea of 'cover' is extremely loose. Genetically and topographically, ecstasy is in all probability the earliest state, hypomania and depression later ones, for ecstasy is 'purer' in its narcissism, so that even the father-superego becomes a feeder and provider, and rapturous saints imbibe directly from the breast of God. But hypomania is rarely pure ecstasy; when it alternates with depression it is hard to say which state 'covers' which. Empirically, there are cases where a prolonged oral indulgence is followed by a difficult and resented weaning, so that pleasure elements in later hypomanias are older for the most part than the painful elements that appear in the depressions. A 'manic defense' after such a weaning would, I believe, be a regression. The earliest factors cannot be treated in such an isolated fashion, however, for the relation of the preœdipal and œdipal events provides opportunities for several possible combinations. In the main, from the genetic and topographical points of view inherent in the diagram of the psychic apparatus, ecstasy would be the probable primal state that contained the earliest memories, and both hypomania and depression, in a very loose sense, would be the 'covers'. Certainly one of these does not cover the other; different memory traces from many age levels are revived in the two states.

This exposition does not seek to elevate dream psychology

into a sole mode of formulating the narcissistic neuroses. I wished to demonstrate again the essential identity of dream and neurosis as wish-fulfilments, and particularly the role of the wish to sleep as a narcissistic aim, thus picking up the thread relinquished after the publication of the Metapsychological Supplement.

Sleep and Technique

I have mentioned without comment that there may be historic reasons for our having abandoned some of our interest in sleep and the dream. In daily practice, our analytic activity deals with neurosis, and when we formulate it, we speak naturally of the transference *neurosis,* and of transference *symptoms,* indicating thereby our preference for the theory of the neuroses. We do not primarily think of the patient as a dreamer, and we do not use the terminology of dream psychology in formulating the psychological events on the couch. Only occasionally, for didactic purposes or as a play of virtuosity, do we find in the literature attempts to interpret the transference in terms of what goes on in the three psychic systems. It is then often incidental to other matters, as in Nunberg's (1951) paper, but even this variety of treatment is unusual, and it rather looks as though we may have some resistance to the idea that analytic therapy and technique are related to sleep. As analysts know better than most, the human tendency is to put away childish things and to belie our infantile past once we have reached maturity, and since psychoanalysis, as a science, has come of age and wishes to appear mature, we may be denying or ignoring the fact that when it was still growing up, its technique consisted in putting the patient into a sleep-like state, and that it encouraged the dreamlike productions of the talking cure.

Freud (1888-1892) in his preface to Bernheim's book on hypnotism and suggestion tried to overcome the resistances of the medical profession and of the public to the therapeutic use of hypnosis, a method he was then using to uncover repressed memories. In perspective, his arguments are still interesting, for the resistances he dealt with are not limited to hypnosis, and they were to be repeated many times in reference to psychoanalytic therapy. Freud had to assure his readers that the hypnotist did not create symptoms nor put ideas into his patient's head, but his arguments furnish deeper insight into the resistances Freud was combating. He states that the fear of harm from being hypnotized is unfounded, as much so as the fear of being harmed by chloroform anesthesia. Hypnosis and anesthesia are both comparable to natural sleep, he argues, and as the resistance to chloroform was overcome by familiarity and reason, so, one might expect, would the resistance to hypnotism be overcome. He emphasizes the naturalness of hypnosis, adducing the fact that persons not necessarily neurotic have been known to fall asleep accidentally when a bright light was thrown into their eyes during a medical examination of their eyes or throats. (Such persons were to be called 'suggestible', but dynamically and more simply, they had a wish to be put to sleep.)

It is instructive that in defending hypnotic sleep, Freud used the same arguments and comparisons as the early anesthetists. Anesthetists and hypnotists alike assuaged the anxieties of prospective patients and members of the medical profession by calling their method a way of inducing sleep. Since psychoanalysts no longer regard their method as dependent on sleep, it is interesting to note the resistances of those who were opposed to anesthesia and hypnosis. Certainly, many of these resistances have been heard in regard to analysis too. Patients dreaded what they might say when they were relaxed by hypnosis or the anesthetic, and what they might do if they abandoned voluntary control. The erotic danger was alluded to. Tales were rife of nuns unexpectedly breaking out into vulgar language when they were given chloroform, and in France the illustrious and neurotic Magendie, often called the Father of Physiology, told a medical audience that he would never permit his wife or daughter to be given chloroform because, he said, certain surgeons might be tempted to take advantage of an anesthetized female patient.[8] His assertion is all the more interesting because Magendie did not have a daughter, and his remarks caused embarrassed laughter; but not so many years ago a distinguished American neurologist and a professed fellow student of Freud expressed the opinion

[8] *Cf.*, Olmsted (1944); see also, *Countertransference in the Technique of Medical Practice*, pp. 449-458 [Ed.].

that analytic patients should be treated by a therapist of the same sex, presumably to obviate the same danger.

Thus, so far as the resistances go, we find anesthesia, hypnosis, and psychoanalysis lumped together, the public and even doctors projecting to the practitioners of a new technique the Svengali and Dr. Caligari fantasies of the œdipus complex. It is indeed true that therapies are invented from time to time which combine two or more of these methods. Many analysts have turned again to experiment with hypnosis in connection with psychoanalysis, while others, especially during the recent war, combined catharsis or hypnosis with partial anesthesia by means of drugs. In the general field of psychotherapy, broadly speaking, we evidently have a choice as to the extent to which we may put our patients to sleep. Some patients, like the 'suggestible' ones Freud mentioned, appear to have a wish to be put to sleep; others (perhaps 'Miss Anna O') fear this or have a strong resistance.

Psychoanalytic therapy, as it evolved, came more and more to prefer the patient awake. One indication of this is the increasing interest in ego psychology; another, perhaps, the neglect of the dream to which Freud referred. In practice, the unconscious must certainly be presented properly to the patients' waking ego, so that they may, when awake, recognize what they are like when they are asleep or partly asleep. But gradually, since the beginnings of analysis in hypnotism, we got away more and more from the sleeping or partly asleep patient, and we rejected a good deal of the technique that depended on the patient's partial sleep. It is worth examining whether, along with this rational development, we may not have erected an unconscious defense as well, so as to live down our suspect history as hypnotists and our mythical prehistory as anesthetists. If we have, we may not be aware of all the traces of hypnotism and anesthesia we have unwittingly carried along with us.

Traditionally, we state that the recumbent position is an atavism, a reminder to medical historians that psychoanalysis had its origin in hypnotism. But if we ask why the hypnotist used the couch, we come upon the obvious reason: to accommodate the patient hypnotically asleep. Many of our patients remark on, or indicate, the suggestive effect of lying down. I do not refer to those who go to sleep. Many others take the couch as a bed for sleeping, for dreaming, or for dormescent fantasy; they loosen their clothing, take off their glasses and ornaments, perhaps kick off their shoes, or they make other trivial and abortive preparations for sleep. They complain or comment pleasantly on the pillow and the mattress, and sometimes bring a bed into their initial transference dreams. On the psychological level, our patients assume with us that what they say on the couch is not to be taken as a sworn statement of a fully aroused and critical person, but more like what they are apt to think of when they are alone and relaxed, as when they are in bed; this point is the basis of one of Freud's (1900-1901) comments on the nature of free associations in The Interpretation of Dreams. He writes:

> What is in question, evidently, is the establishment of a psychical state, which in its distribution of psychical energy (that is, of mobile attention), bears some analogy to the state before falling asleep—and no doubt also to hypnosis. As we fall asleep, 'involuntary ideas' emerge, owing to the relaxation of a certain deliberate (and no doubt also critical) activity which we allow to influence the course of our ideas when we are awake. (We usually attribute this relaxation to 'fatigue'.) As the involuntary ideas emerge they change into visual and acoustic images. . . . In the state used for the analysis of dreams and pathological ideas, the patient purposely and deliberately abandons this activity and employs the psychical energy thus saved (or a portion of it) in attentively following the involuntary thoughts which now emerge, and which—and here the situation differs from that of falling asleep—retain the character of ideas. *In this way the 'involuntary' ideas are transformed into 'voluntary' ones* (p. 102).

Many associations refer to the similarity of bed and couch, and some patients reproduce the process of going to sleep, occasionally including the characteristic Isakower phenomena (*cf.*, Rycroft, 1951; Heilbrunn, 1953).[9] Again with many patients the couch as bed and hence an early substitute and symbol for the mother, enters into the transference situation, for the analyst's remarks become the equivalent of the noises and wakers, and are equated with the father's or superego's

[9] See also *Claustrophobia*, pp. 48-51 [Ed.]

wakening and weaning injunctions (Stone, 1947). Thus it happens that patients with oral problems may automatically react to the analyst as a disturber or even a noise they must ignore.

One sometimes encounters a fear of being asleep on the couch, which is related to a fear of dreaming. A patient brought a dream the first day of her analysis, in which she entered a motion picture theater where she saw the most terrifying things on the screen (she did not know what), and she rushed out to keep from seeing them. She immediately recognized that this was her reaction to beginning her analysis, and that the screen showed her her 'unconscious'. The screen did not show her her 'unconscious' really; it was her dream screen and it showed her fear of dreaming, a matter which came up almost immediately. This is the more exact interpretation, but it is noteworthy that the uninstructed patient naïvely used the words 'my unconscious' to mean *my dreams*. In most patients' experience, the nearest thing to what they are asked to do on the couch is what they have sometimes done in bed, when, with a fluctuating state of consciousness somewhat influenced by the anticipation of sleep, they have let idle thoughts run through their mind, with whatever consequence.

The equation of the analytic work to being in bed is very evident in some patients. Years ago, a patient made a remark which I have always remembered but apparently did not fully understand at the time. Toward the end of her analysis she went to her physician for a physical examination. To his surprise he found that a gastric ulcer of some years' standing had healed, and he asked her what she had been doing for it. 'Oh', she said, 'I have been lying down for an hour every afternoon'. This was a joke; it was long before the term *psychosomatic* had gained popularity, and I was amused. Retrospectively, I see that she was stating a deep analytic verity, one particularly clear to me since Stone's (1947) report of the duodenal ulcer patient who fell asleep on the couch. My patient is the one I referred to in my paper on claustrophobia, who assumed the 'fœtal posture' on the couch and anxiously blurted out, 'Don't touch me!'. Her conflict was between her genital wishes and her attachment to her mother, and she was saying to me (ambivalently), 'Don't wean or waken me!'. But her joke was psychologically penetrating: her ulcer had been cured by 'lying down', by a form of therapy which enabled her to relive and understand infantile sleep.

A male patient could not lie down for several months at the beginning of his analysis. Finally, he lay down with marked pleasure, rationalized as a realistic triumph, but which was certainly also a libidinal repetition, for, as he told me many times, his life and his analysis involved a constant struggle against spending all his time in sleep. The ability to assume the recumbent posture was not the brilliant technical achievement it might seem; for long after he was settled on the couch, he came to realize that he automatically 'closed his ears' to what I said to him, as if to guard against being disturbed in his sleep, and after an upsetting analytic session he would often react by taking a nap.

Patients have some inkling of the historic secrets of psychoanalysis when they ask to be hypnotized or to be given drugs. Aside from the various transference implications of the request for passive indulgence, the patient senses in himself a resistance and a conflict that would be solved in one way if he were asleep and could forget, or which could be solved perhaps in a disguised form if he dreamed. At this point, the waking ego can admit the repressed impulse only with the reservations that a dream censorship might impose or that a half-sleep might excuse. If the analyst accedes to the patient's request for a drug, the action could be interpreted from the standpoint of psychoanalytic history as a return of the repressed.

It has been said that the effectiveness of psychoanalytic therapy depends on a split. The patient on the couch is as if aware of two realities, and we speak loosely of psychological and objective reality. Since ordinarily the patient has not been indoctrinated in psychological theory and is not much affected if he has been, how is it that he comes to distinguish between the two during his analytic work? Elsewhere I have remarked that the first split which all of us know from experience is that which comes with going to sleep or waking up, the more or less sharp division between the 'me' as a waking person and the 'me' as a sleeper or dreamer. This is a normal, persistent discontinuity throughout life. All of us in a way are Peter Ibbetsons who lead two parallel, though often interacting, lives and we assume that this duality is based on an evolution from an originally undifferentiated state. Freud has taught us how the reality principle enters human development to separate for us what goes on in our head from what goes on in the world about us. Part of our life continues to go on only within us, and one very early result of the functioning of the sense of reality is our appreciation of the fact that we are awake, or, in retrospect, that we have been asleep and dreaming. The most obvious and palpable outcome of 'reality testing' is everyone's normal, reasonably assured knowledge of this split.

It is this split which the analytic patient understands from experience and which he repeats when he works through analytic material. Naïvely the patient differentiates not between the 'real' and the 'unreal' in what he says and feels, but between that which can stand the light of day and that which is real only in sleep. As the recumbent posture is an adumbration of being in bed, so the patient comes to judge his ideas not in the old Aristotelian categories of *true* and *false,* but metalogically in the noncontradictive categories: (a) 'true (or false) when I am awake', and (b) 'true when I am asleep'. Freud (1925b) recognized this in the example he used in his paper on negation where the patient says, 'I do not know who the person was in the dream; surely, it was not my mother'. Whereupon, Freud says, we emend this: 'So it was his mother!'. The patient in the dialogue means 'false when I am awake', Freud means, 'true when you are asleep', and there is no contradiction. 'Many a man ere now in dreams hath lain/ With her who bare him. He hath least annoy/ Who with such omens troubleth not his mind',[10] says Jocasta, displaying a perfect comprehension of the two realities.

As a sort of mental experiment, let us look aside from the content of the analyst's interpretative remarks and regard them solely as some patients have done from, so to speak, a musical standpoint, as tending to soothe or to arouse. It sometimes happens that a patient strips the analyst's words of logical sense and treats them as if they were simply pleasant or unpleasant perceptions. At this primitive level, the patient simulates the baby that either smiles happily or cries with displeasure according to whether the adult is cooing or making

[10] Lewis Campbell's translation in the Standard Edition, IV, p. 264.

an unpleasant noise. But since the analyst is articulate, an affective response to the content of what he says is also registered and regressively put into the category of pleasant or unpleasant, and in the context we are considering here, treated as either arousing or producing sleep.

Patients differ in a wide range and with great fluctuation in their degree of awakeness, from the extreme of going to sleep on the couch to the other extreme of complete vigilance. Ordinarily their state is an intermediate one, or they would not be analyzable. In a sense, the wish to be awake and the wish to be asleep are both present at the same time, and the interpretations given by the analyst play on one or the other. From this narrow angle, interpretations can be classified as those which induce the patient to favor one or the other side of the analytic split. Some induce him to be more awake, others to be more asleep; they shift the 'quantities' of energy from one to the other side. To give what Anna Freud (1936) calls an 'id interpretation' would produce a shift in the direction of wakening. It would be the equivalent of stripping the disguise off a manifest association and revealing that the latent idea is of the kind that holds only in sleep. One implicitly has said to the patient, 'This is true of you when you are asleep', and his waking part tends to become more alert. On the other hand, an 'ego' or 'defense' interpretation tells the patient that he is being unduly vigilant and on the *qui vive* against the sleep-suitable class of ideas. It says in effect, 'Relax your attention', and the quantities are shifted toward the sleep side. Here, of course, one notably operates with small quantities, and this fact further differentiates psychoanalysis from hypnotism and the drug psychotherapies, where massive quantities are shifted in this direction. Leaving aside the important quantitative difference and the other differences implicit in the various methods, all three methods at some point agree in favoring the switch toward the sleeping side.

In psychoanalytic technique the wish to sleep plays a role which bears an interesting similarity to its role in dream formation. In both cases, it is a silent *sine qua non,* for there is no dream formation without a wish to sleep and no analysis without its weaker counterpart, the wish to associate freely. In ordinary dreams and dream interpretation, the wish to sleep rarely needs explicit interpretation, or at any rate is rarely given it, and the extent to which he is asleep is not often brought to the attention of the analytic patient. Yet, in dream analysis and in the analysis of the analytic situation, there are occasions (and these not only the dramatic ones referred to) when the wish to sleep becomes represented in the manifest content of the dream or of the analytic communications and when its meaning must be brought home to the patient. In other words, the background 'couch' of the analytic situation, ordinarily as inconspicuous and as subordinate practically as the background dream screen, may dominate the manifest picture. As there are the rare blank 'sleep dreams' so there may be the blank 'analytic couch' of the transference sleep during the analytic session.

This may be more than an analogy. The earliest memory trace that can be represented as a manifest element in the dream is the screen, especially in its purest form when it appears as a blank unprojected dream. Similarly, the earliest memory that can appear as a manifest element or 'symptom' in the analytic situation is the sleep on the couch. Both repeat the nursing situation and both indicate a wish for narcissistic sleep. The analytic situation, therefore, can be diagramed too according to Chapter VII. The analysand is in a quasi dream, making accessible to consciousness (which is the manifest analytic picture) memory traces from all parts of the psychic apparatus, even those near its topographical and chronological beginning.

IV. CLINICAL HINTS FROM DREAM STUDIES*

In ancient times, mankind held the dreamer and the psychotic to be inspired. Dreams came mysteriously to the sleeper through the gates of horn and ivory, bearing to him the true or deceptive messages of the gods, and the madman spoke an arcane language. It seems to us now that those who believed in the second sight of the madman and the dreamer were themselves near to prophetic insight, for they apparently realized, as we do today, that the dream is like a psychosis. To give folk-wisdom more credit than it probably deserves, we may add another old belief, embodied in the saying that out of the mouths of babes and sucklings shall come forth truth. In this we may read, if we wish, an inkling of a third pillar of present-day psychiatry, for we too are interested in what may be learned from the mind of the infant. Thus, most venerable adages and magical traditions agree with modern scientific beliefs. We know that the ill, the dreamer, and the child, all three have much to teach us.

Many pre-Freudian psychiatrists saw that dreams had much in common with psychoses, and Hughlings Jackson was responsible for the statement: 'Find out all about dreams, and you will have found out all about insanity' (Freud, 1900-1901, p. 569, n.). But it remained for Freud to teach us the surprising fact that from both dreams and symptoms we should learn about the small child. In dreams and symptoms, we found the expression of infantile thoughts and wishes such as those of the famous œdipus complex. It was not difficult to appreciate that psychotic and neurotic symptoms are distorted wish-fulfilments. Many years before Freud, Griesinger (1867) made the observation that 'ideas in dreams and in psychoses have in common the characteristic of being wish-fulfilments'. Since 1900, when The Interpretation of Dreams

* [No. 102 in Bibliography.]

was published, it has become clear that dreams fulfil the same infantile wishes that we encounter in the psychoses and neuroses.

But the statement that the dream is a wish-fulfilment does not exhaust its significance. It resembles psychoses in other respects too, some of them quite evident. Griesinger, again, remarked that many persons who have recovered from an acute psychosis say that the attack appears in retrospect as if it were a dream, sometimes a painful dream, sometimes a happy one. Nunberg's (1920) catatonic patient consistently referred back to his attack as 'my dream', and stated that he wished to forget it. It has been noted that many recovered patients repudiate their illness by forgetting it, and it is quite beyond their ability to bring back to mind the forgotten events. This type of forgetting differs from ordinary, everyday forgetting, but it resembles closely the forgetting of dreams, which often cannot be brought back to mind by direct, conscious effort. The memories of such psychotic attacks and the memories of such dreams are, as we say, repressed; and in this again, psychosis and dream agree with infancy, for we are familiar with a similar amnesia in regard to infantile events. The study of individual cases has shown that there is a close connection between psychotic experiences and the dream life, for in many recovered persons, the delusions of the illness continue to appear in their dreams; and conversely, it has been noted that the delusional ideas appeared in dreams before the onset of the illness. There are indeed many reasons, besides wish-fulfilment, for studying the two states in parallel.

But the full impact of the relation between dream and psychosis was not felt until Freud (1915d) wrote his essay, A Metapsychological Supplement to the Theory of Dreams. In The Interpretation of Dreams, Freud (1900-1901) had already made clear that the central purpose of the dream was to preserve sleep. The wishes that arose during sleep were considered intruders and disturbers, which threatened to awaken the sleeper, and the dream represented them as fulfilled, so that the sleeper might continue in the fulfilment of his real, dominant wish, namely, the wish to sleep. The wish to sleep is therefore the ultimate reason for all dreaming. In the Metapsychological

Supplement, Freud brings this out more sharply, and he no longer says that a dream is like a psychosis, but that it *is* one. It is declared to be a hallucinatory wish-fulfilment psychosis, due to the wish to sleep.

The new implication in Freud's statement is a profound one. It shows that Hughlings Jackson's dictum, 'Find out all about dreams, and you will have found out all about insanity', has a new dimension—a dimension which may be expressed: 'And to find out all about dreams, you must find out all you can about sleep.' In the same essay, Freud brings sleep into the realm of psychological theory. He is no longer content to leave sleep a purely physiological problem without psychological interpretation; for he now states that sleep is a manifestation of *narcissism,* which is a conception originally introduced into psychoanalytic theory to explain certain findings in the psychoses and in infantile development. This narcissism is only indirectly evident in the dream psychosis, however, for the dream text is an 'exception' to the narcissism of sleep. The dream is made up of remnants from waking life of various wishes and interests, which, as it were, did not go to sleep with the rest of the person. Therefore, at first glance, it seems as if the study of the dream could not lead to any understanding of sleep and narcissism. If, as Freud puts it, what we know about the psychology of sleep is only the psychology of the nonsleeping part of it, how can dream studies take us beyond the barrier? If the dream is only an impurity in sleep, how shall we ever know about sleep? Yet, if we take seriously the dictum that the dream is a psychosis, and that sleep is a regression to narcissism, must we not be eager to understand sleep itself?

Fortunately, the situation is not quite so baffling as it was. We are indeed far from understanding all about sleep or all about the psychoses and neuroses, but in recent years certain new observations have been made on dreams and on hypnagogic states which, along with parallel studies of symptoms and of the child, appear to hold promise of a profitable attack on the problem.

The ordinary dream is a visual projection. That is to say, the hallucinated action and the story appear to take place somewhere in front of the dreamer, as if in his visual field.

It now seems probable that this imagined action is projected on an imaginary screen, like a motion picture; at least, such a *dream-screen* has been detected many times and the assumption that it exists in all dreams has been a useful one. The dream-screen first came to my attention when a young woman patient reported to me as follows:

> I had my dream all ready for you, but while I was lying here looking at it, it turned over away from me, rolled up, and rolled away from me—over and over like two tumblers.

That is, she saw her dream, as if it were a picture on canvas or a screen, and in the act of forgetting it, she saw it become convex, roll up and then roll away. I was in the fortunate position of being able to analyze the meaning of the screen. It stood for her mother's breasts, which had figured tragically in her life. Her mother had undergone a mastectomy when the patient was seven years old and had died three years later, and although the patient had an almost complete amnesia for all the events dealing with her mother's illness and death, the topic of mother and breast figured constantly and extensively in her dream life. Her successful wish to forget the dream was a corollary of her wish to repress the idea of the breast.

My patient's experience brought to mind certain phenomena reported by Isakower (1936), a particular fantasy which appeared under certain circumstances while his patients were falling asleep. In this hypnagogic phenomenon, the beginning sleeper has a sudden hallucination of approaching large masses, which seem to grow larger and larger as they get near and finally merge with the sleeper, to the accompaniment of skin and mouth sensations. These Isakower phenomena were interpreted as repetitions of the earliest nursing experiences of the infant falling asleep at the breast. I shall have more to say of them later on. Here I should like to point out their relationship to the dream screen.

I reasoned that my patient had included the breast in her dream as a background screen, and that the ordinary events of the dream and the manifest story had been projected on to it like a motion picture play. What she reported of the process of forgetting was the flattening out and disappearance on to the screen of the dream story, which then took breast shape and was removed from her. The manner in which the breast-screen rolled away was similar to the way other large objects mysteriously move in dreams, for which there is a recognized interpretation. Such objects moving about in the air of themselves are often based on early memories of things being moved about by adults, equally mysteriously so far as the baby is concerned, and indeed in dreams we often feel ourselves floating about, a repetition of our experience of being tossed or carried by adults.

The breast interpretation of the screen or background has now been confirmed by my further experience and by that of others. Thus, the patient in question later dreamed of a large iron trellis which came between her and the background of the dream, which on interpretation turned out to represent the prosthetic iron frame her mother had worn after the breast ablation.

When we think how many times in the life of a small baby the act of going to sleep follows a meal, it cannot surprise us that there should survive many associations between sleep and the mouth, and that this connection should include the dream too. Thus, when my patient's dream rolled away from her and she portrayed this as the removal of the breast, she gave us a clue to the meaning of dream-forgetting. To forget a dream means to wake up completely, and it means to give up oral pleasure. This finding has been confirmed many times. For example, one of my colleagues tells me that when she tries to recall a dream, she always has a feeling as if she had it somewhere in the back of her mouth, as if she could somehow find it there. Patients in analysis, trying to remember their dreams, often bring up instead associations dealing with food or the mouth.

The discovery of the dream screen led naturally to a consideration of visually blank dreams, and in fact I had previously studied a case where the blank dream had come to my attention in a very impressive way, four times in the same patient. This was a young schizophrenic woman who went through four hypomanic attacks while she was under my care. Each time the attack appeared when, after a rather long abstinence from contact with women, she had spent a happy, exciting day, shopping and lunching with an affectionate, maternal woman. Such a day always sent her into a rapturous state, which culminated that night in a blank dream with orgasm. After this dream, each time, the patient had a hypomanic attack that was full of independence and delusional heterosexuality, and which was an obvious flight from the passivity and homosexuality that was directly expressed, so far as her feelings were concerned, in the erotic blank dream. From the clinical standpoint, the dream belonged to the story of the psychotic upset; or conversely, one could say from the standpoint of dream study, that the ensuing attack was like a belated, defensive, denying part of the dream state.

There is not *a* blank dream, but a whole class of blank and nearly blank dreams, and the assumed 'screen dream' is merely a possible variety or subclass. That there are such varieties pointed up the fact that the analogy of the dream and the motion picture play is inexact. When we go into the motion picture theater, the screen is already hung; a dreamer, however, projects not only the story but the screen too, so that the screen, even if it should make up the whole of the dreaming experience, is still a dream projection. What really led to a reconsideration of the whole blank dream idea was the realization that all dreams are not projected. Many blank and nearly blank dreams are not located in front of the dreamer in his apparent visual field; instead, dream and dreamer may feel and seem as if they occupied the same segment of space, so that the dream and dreamer are not separate.

At this point, I should like to return to Freud's statement that the ordinary visual elements in a dream represent an impurity in the primal narcissism of sleep. For in the dreams I have been presenting there is a minimum of such elements. They would therefore be very special dreams, with little manifestation of the intruding and disturbing wishes from the day. The interest is indeed centered on the sleep itself, and the dreams come very close to being concrete expressions and examples of what Freud means by the narcissism of sleep. This was immediately recognized by Rycroft (1951), who calls them 'sleep dreams', and by Scott (1951), who speaks in this connection of 'narcissistic dreams'. Hoffer (1952), too, explicitly aligning himself with me, writes: 'I should exemplify primary narcissism . . . by the infant's state of deep sleep' (p. 33).

In all the comparable blank and nearly blank dreams which have been collected so far, there are certain constant findings. There is a surprising consistency about the way they are told. All the dreamers say that the dream is hard to describe, that it was an experience for which they cannot readily find words, or they refer to it as an immanent experience, like an emotion, and they explain that their efforts to communicate are metaphorical or allegorical. In the unprojected type of dream, the position of the dreamer is unspecifiable, and they speak of being in, or on, or against some vague, indefinite, nebulous object or substance. In related dreams, where there is some projection, the dreamer sees large, looming masses, with which then he unites or merges to become one. The dreams are apt to be repetitive, either over a stretch of time or during the course of the night, and most interesting fact of all perhaps, they are always intense emotional experiences. Either the dreamer finds that he has had a sexual orgasm, or an intense blissful sleep, or on the other hand, that he was severely anxious, sometimes to the point of nightmare terror. The dream work in no way tries to provide anything pictorial which might rationalize such feelings, but leaves them as pure, intense, and immediate feelings. The dreamer either enjoys his sleep and his dream, or fears them.

Of interest in connection with the blank dreams are certain hypnagogic fantasies, which have become known as the Isakower phenomena, so-called because of Otto Isakower's (1936) original, classic description. The Isakower phenomena appear under certain circumstances in certain persons while they are dropping off to sleep. Typically, a large mass, usually round and dark, appears to approach the beginning sleeper; it envelops him and at the same time enters him through the mouth, producing a rough, doughy, corrugated sensation in the buccal mucous membranes and the skin. The dormescent person loses his sense of ego boundary, and he cannot tell where the division is between his own body and the mass. He feels that the mass is corrugated or that he is, or that he and it are having the same experience. All this is a reproduction of the little baby's sensations on falling asleep. The mass is a reproduction of the breast or the food, and the changes in body feelings and in the orientation of the body presumably repeat comparable feelings in the dormescent baby.

The study of the Isakower phenomena and of blank dreams thus holds promise of a lead to the study of beginning psychoses. For if dream and psychosis are of the same order of things, to find out what going to sleep may mean should ultimately illuminate the problem of going into a psychosis. This idea has in fact been recognized, and I may refer to a paper of Zilboorg (1933), Anxiety Without Affect, in which the author describes prestuporous states and beginning stupors, where the Isakower phenomena, as we should now call them, are prominent, and where there are also strange ego states and feelings of bodily alteration that appear while we are going to sleep. In this connection, too, we should think of the studies of Paul Federn (1952), who studied these alterations in ego feelings not only in psychoses and neurotic conditions but also as they appeared in dreams and hypnagogic states.

It will profit us some day to study the relationship of waking up fantasies, those called hypnopompic, and the ideas that accompany recovery from a psychosis. It may turn out that the common fantasy of rebirth that often attends recovery is based on early experiences of waking up.

To return to the blank, narcissistic dream and its place in a clinical picture. In discussing the blank, orgastic dreams of my young patient, I mentioned that they definitely belonged in the anamnesis of the hypomanic attack. These blank dreams were followed by the flighty denial of the hypomania proper. The sequence in all four attacks was the same; a happy, rapturous day spent with a maternal friend, a blank dream with orgasm that night, then a typical jubilant elation with delusional heterosexual and independence fantasies. The distracted, euphoric, overtalkative manifestations denied the meaning of her blissful dream and of the passive, narcissistic pleasure it contained. It seems possible to me that a dream of this sort, or its psychological equivalent, may be a constant precursor of the hypomanic state proper. We do not yet possess the experience which would tell us what a 'psychological equivalent' would be, but it might take the form of a dreamlike or cloudy state.

On the other hand, the ecstatic or blank dream need not be followed by a clearcut manic state, even though there is a strong suggestion that it may always be followed by a manic equivalent. Further experience is necessary to clarify this problem. In my practice, I have noted that when a patient has made a special point of commenting on how satisfying his sleep has been, the following day may show a certain amount of hypomanic behavior.

If we considered the blissful dreams as psychoses, we should class them as ecstasies; which then, under certain circumstances, become filled with anxiety and lead to the defensive flight of the exuberant, overactive hypomanic or manic state proper. Let us try to see this situation in simple terms. A person, due to a fantasy of an extremely regressive quality, finds in a dream of ecstatic bliss an intense satisfaction and happiness, such as he cannot attain in his actual, waking situation. In his dream, he was as happy and irresponsible as the satiated nursling, and the sight of such a possibility is most attractive to him. However, to preserve this ecstasy, he must remain asleep or stuporous, and when he awakens, his ego with its defensive powers and its waking claims, is aroused to withstand the dangers of such a fantastic temptation. The ego may feel anxiety or it may still feel the euphoria of the dream situation. In the latter case, it is compelled to explain the euphoria. This it does, and in the overactive hypomania there is an assertion of vast activity and effectiveness, the happiness is attributed to fantastic successes and accomplishments, and all passivity and dependence are repudiated in the distortions of the manic or hypomanic attack.

The manic state, no less than a paranoid delusion, is like a piece of dream thinking, and it is an attempt at restitution of the relationship with the real world. Where the paranoid patient tries to form a compromise world through his false intellectual constructions, the manic tries to find in the world about him and in his doing a justification for his false euphoria. The overactive manic state is a flight from the passive ecstasy, the narcissism of the blank dream.

Experience does not yet permit us to correlate the ecstatic narcissistic dream with the manifestations of depression. It is not that we lack a plausible theory, for it seems assured that the same regression takes place in the depression as in the elation. Moreover, as Freud pointed out, under the blatant and painful complaints of the depression, there is an unconscious groundwork of narcissistic pleasure. We are certain too that the relationship between sleep and symptoms must be of great importance in the depressions, for insomnia is a prominent and characteristic symptom. Gregory Rochlin (1953), by a close study of the transition period between elation and depression, or vice versa, has demonstrated that the difference in the two states lies not in the fundamental libidinal situation but in the ego defenses and attitudes. Our uncertainty comes from lack of adequate observations of the dream life of depressive cases in statu nascendi, such observations as have become available in the case of hypomania.

A hopeful approach to one aspect of the depressive problem may be opened for us by Isakower's (1954) work on the meaning of words in dreams. Isakower has shown that words in dreams give the superego's opinion of the latent thoughts that the dreams express. Sometimes at the end of a dream, a final remark of this sort, which comes too late to be distorted by the dream work, appears to waken the dreamer. A typical example is to be found in Freud's (1900-1901) account of the dream of the burning child, where the child appears to the father in the dream and reproachfully whispers, *'Father, don't you see I'm burning?'* (p. 509). The father wakes up and finds that a candle burning by the child's bier has fallen over and threatened to set fire to it. Here the superego makes its appearance in the reproachful words of the child, and it appears as a waker. In fact, the real arouser, that is, the real fire, is for a moment given the dream disguise of a superego utterance. In the depression too, the voice of the superego may also be considered as a wakener and a weaner, telling the person who is unconsciously clinging to the narcissistic situation that it is time to awaken and leave this state. What characterizes the depression and accounts for the persistence of the superego's voice, is the tenacity with which the patient clings to his state. He remains in fantasy fixed in the nursing situation, struggling to preserve his position, despite all conscience and pain.

In my above description, I have attempted to present as a good example of primitive narcissistic states of consciousness, the blank dream, and particularly the blank dream in what is perhaps its most primitive form: the unprojected, emotionally highly charged variety or subclass. I have also tried to point out where such phenomena as the blank dream and the dream screen fit into our clinical theory of the narcissistic neuroses and psychoses. I have omitted examples of the narcissistic picture that may be found in the psychoneuroses, for in these milder states they are not so conspicuous, and the only systematic study of them in this field has been limited to the phobias. In the field of analytic technique, we have been able to deduce certain useful principles and practical guidance to interpretation, but so far, too, there has been no systematic application, although I plan one. As I indicated in passing, we have got some aid in the understanding of the process of the forgetting of dreams, and papers by Stone (1947) and Scott (1951) have pointed the way to an understanding of what has been called 'transference sleep', that is, neurotic sleep on the analytic couch. It is possible that further study of the appearance of blank dreams and screen phenomena in the neuroses and on the couch will help us to a more profound understanding of neuroses and analytic technique, but a systematic treatment of these fields lies in the future.

What requires more discussion now is the genetic aspect of these narcissistic phenomena. A mental datum of such regressive quality is not considered to be understood analytically until we have discovered the infantile state in which it appeared originally, and which it repeats later in life, and we are particularly interested in determining which instincts are involved in its production. Here several theories present themselves, unavoidably containing conjectures and assumptions, and we must select from among those which have been suggested. For simplicity we may refer here solely to an unprojected blank dream, for among the manifestations that appear in this field such a dream is probably at the core, and whatever applies to it can easily be translated to apply to the dream screen, the Isakower phenomena, and related states.

Some thirty years ago, it would have seemed quite proper in the analytic world to say that the blank dream repeated the state of consciousness of an unborn child, and that it was a representation of intrauterine regression due to a universal, inborn instinctual wish to return to the womb. Because the state of sleep bears a marked resemblance to the prenatal state, it seemed plausible to consider that such a manifestation of narcissism would depend on such a wish. Ferenczi (1924) and Rank (1924a) are two of the names associated with the exploitation of this idea; in fact, the latter instituted a method of analytic therapy which was based on the assumption that to lie on the couch was a repetition of going into the mother's body, and that the end of the treatment necessarily meant to be born again. Nowadays such ideas seem to us to be unanalyzed fantasies rather than true repetitions. There is no doubt that many patients have fantasies about having been in the uterus and about being born, but we doubt that these are direct memories and for an excellent reason.

For we have all learned from an early mistake of Freud. If you recall Freud's account or if you have read Ernest Jones's (1953-1957, Vol. I, pp. 265-267) brilliant book, you will probably remember that Freud was initially deceived by his hysterical female patients into thinking that they had really been seduced by their father or some other near male relative in infancy. He therefore originally proposed a theory of infantile seduction to account for the symptoms of hysteria. To his surprise he later found out that his patients had not been seduced, and that they had been telling him memories of infantile fantasies rather than of facts. This clarified the situation, so that Freud could then formulate a correct theory of hysteria and of infantile sexuality. We find ourselves in a comparable position in relation to the ideas presented by patients concerning their gestation and birth. Certainly they were in the uterus and they were also born, but even if we should some day be sure that real memory traces persist from these early days, we may well disbelieve that they recall very much about it, and certainly we must not credit their elaborate imaginations about these matters. For we know that the ideas presented to us about the insides of the mother's body and about birth are fantasies. They are infantile sexual theories which arise not from personally lived experiences, but in the days when the child becomes aware of the facts of life and puzzles out his own theoretical explanations.

Having rejected the fœtus as an assured basis of reference, we may consider an alternative assumption about the narcissistic dream; namely, that it repeats a state of mind which arises in early postnatal life. We should then have to assume that the very small baby's state of consciousness is repeated in the unprojected dream, that the dreamer who is immersed and inseparable from the environment of his dream is reproducing an infantile state of consciousness, and that the strong affects often contained in the dream are also repetitions from the earliest months of life. From analytic studies and direct observation, certain notions are now held concerning the early state of mind of the baby. They have been well formulated, simply and plastically, in a recent paper of Anna Freud (1953), from which I should like to introduce a relevant excerpt:

> While the observer sees the infant as a separate entity, he has to realize that the infant himself has as yet no correct conception of where he himself ends and the environment begins. . . . The observer, watching the infant on the mother's lap, will notice that he makes no distinction between his own body and hers; he plays with the mother's breast, or her hair, or nose, or eyes, as he plays with his own fingers, or feet, or explores his own cavities. He is surprised and indignant when his mother walks away from him as if he were suddenly left by part of his own body. Only through the painful experience of losing his mother periodically does the child learn very gradually in the course of the first year that the big pleasure-self he has constructed in his mind is not all his own. Parts of it walk away from him and become his environment, while other parts remain with him forever. . . . While adults think in terms of a 'self', infants think, or rather feel, in terms of a body (p. 14).

I think it is this 'preverbal' and 'preconceptualizing' lap baby, as yet unextricated from the mother as an independent self, that we should think of when we try to work out what the blank dream may reproduce. Especially we should think of this new baby in the nursing situation, drinking, relaxing, his bodily feelings becoming more and more blurred until he finally falls asleep. It is not so much that we must deny categorically any mentation to the embryo, as that we do not at present need any ideas about the embryo's state of mind to explain our findings. Assumptions about the embryo's mental life do not matter; in present parlance, they are not 'operational'. Biologically, it may be the case that sleep is a restoration of an intrauterine state, but psychologically, deep sleep is a basic fact, a datum. It may occur in the embryo, but it certainly occurs in the child and in the adult of all ages.

When we compare the blank unprojected dream with the description given by Anna Freud, we see how consistent such a dream is with the mental state of the baby. Miss Freud's construction, it should be understood, was made without any consideration of these dreams but on the basis of much other material of many varieties. Again, compare Anna Freud's statement of how the child and mother periodically become one and then separate, with the Isakower phenomena, where the large mass approaches the beginning sleeper, grows larger and larger and comes nearer and nearer until it finally merges with the beginning sleeper through his whole body, so that he loses all sense of separateness.

The periodic and repeated union with the mother, suggested in the periodic and recurrent nature of the dream is doubtless felt through many modalities of sensation, but our clinical findings come to us predominantly in the form of oral fantasies. The mouth and the act of incorporation seem to have attracted most of the interest and feeling with which the idea of union is charged. To be sure, the oral libido has for long been a well-recognized psychoanalytic concept, designating as it does the pleasure aspect of the mouth's functions. Its central model has always been the nursing situation, and a working concept of this situation is clinically and theoretically useful.

For many years it has been known that the wish to devour represents a large part of this early instinctual activity. There is no trouble in inferring from a baby's behavior that he wants to eat, and the importance of this part of the oral striving is now common knowledge. But this function and this wish do not cover the totality of the nursing situation, and to explain the phenomena centering around the blank dreams, as well as the clinical picture in the elations, I saw fit to include two other instinctual wishes in the nursing situation, which I called, perhaps too adultomorphically, the wish to be eaten and the wish to sleep, and I spoke of these three wishes together as the oral triad of wishes. With the baby's wish to eat and the wish to go to sleep, there is no difficulty in empathizing. Everyone can put himself in the baby's place and can imagine the baby enjoying the fulfilment of these two wishes. But the middle wish of the triad, the wish to be eaten, is more difficult. Its name may suggest a conscious impulse in the baby which of course should not be assumed; strictly speaking we also should not assume a conscious wish to eat and sleep until later.

By inserting in the nursing situation what I call the wish to be eaten, I am actually referring to a pleasurable state, which I assume arises near the end of the oral satiation and before the baby drops off to sleep, when he relaxes and experiences some of those stages of union which intervene between eating and complete rest. The strange appellation was chosen for a special reason. From the memories and revived feelings of this state, later in life, in dreams and in psychopathological states, there are constructed pleasurable as well as anxious fantasies which center about being eaten, and these fantasies are closely linked with ideas of being put to sleep. By assuming that the equivalent or precursor of this wish is present in the nursing situation, I act not as an empathizer, but more the way a mathematician does when he postulates an ideal point at infinity—because it is an aid in thinking.

Thus, to consider from this point of view the Isakower phenomena, when the mass enters the beginning sleeper's mouth and he feels himself merge with it, the experience includes not only the idea of engulfing the mass but also of being engulfed, that is, being eaten by it. If we contemplate Anna Freud's description and try to understand the baby's frame of mind, we can readily see that the uncertain position of the actor and the acted upon, and the inability to distinguish self from environment, must operate in the nursing situation too. Breast, mother, and mouth are all included in the large pleasure-self. But the pragmatic reason for speaking of a wish to be eaten comes from the manifestations of later years, when it is possible to distinguish the wishes, which have taken on relative independence and formed separate connections.

As an example of this later relative independence of the elements in the oral triad, I may refer again to the case of the young woman with the orgastic blank dreams and the ensuing hypomania. Her blissful sleep was a fulfilment of the two latter elements of the triad: in this sleep she gratified the wish to be engulfed by the mother not only at the breast but within her too as if she were part of a larger unity. In her subsequent flight from this tempting narcissistic state, the patient turned to the first of the wishes in the oral triad, always remaining within the domain of the triad, but choosing the active fulfilment of the first wish. That is, instead of reliving a deep narcissistic sleep, she became all activity, all independence, gratifying only her wish to devour. By this defensive turn to the active first wish, she was able to deny her wish to be eaten and put to sleep.

In this essay, it has been my purpose to present certain unusual dream states and phenomena related to them, and to demonstrate their clinical application, as well as to give a theory of their genesis and their instinctual basis. More generally, I wish to show the profundity of the idea that the dream is a psychosis, an idea capable today of ever-new application. In fact, I should like to close my remarks by quoting for the third time Hughlings Jackson's statement: 'Find out all about dreams, and you will have found out all about insanity'.

V. DREAM PSYCHOLOGY AND THE ANALYTIC SITUATION*

This paper will try to apply some of our knowledge and theory about sleep and the dream to an understanding of the analytic situation, which is here defined, empirically, as the familiar standard hour, or loosely, as 'what happens on the couch'; and sometimes the word 'couch' will be used metaphorically as synonymous with 'analytic situation'. Included in the idea of analytic situation are the phenomena of free association, resistance, transference, repetition, and others well known and generally admitted as working concepts.

Genetically, the analytic situation is an altered hypnotic situation, as the analytic hour is an altered hypnotic session. The analytic patient takes his origin from the hypnotic patient, for originally Freud's patients were attracted to therapy by their knowledge of cures due to hypnosis. The development of analysis from hypnosis has been studied and told with much detail and perspicacity by Ernest Jones (1953-1957, Vol. I). It seems that some patients could not be hypnotized, or they 'countersuggested' too vigorously; that is, they had a resistance to being hypnotized or, more likely, a fear of being put to sleep. The refractory patient made the following *as if* proposal that the treatment be modified: 'Although I cannot, for reasons of my own, let myself be put to sleep,[1] or into a state resembling sleep, nevertheless, I promise to relax as if I were in bed and to tell everything that comes to me in this quasi-hypnotic or quasi-hypnagogic state. In return for this concession, I accept more responsibility for what I say.'

* [No. 103 in Bibliography.]

[1] The wording of the 'patient's proposal' does not mean that hypnosis is necessarily sleep, any more than 'to be put to sleep by ether' means that drug anesthesia is absolutely the same thing as natural sleep. No assumption of the sort is necessary. The assumption merely is that the patient regards being hypnotized, as he might regard being anesthetized, as such an action, and that he has the same attitude toward being hypnotized as he might have toward going to sleep. See Freud (1888-1892).

We may put it that a resistance appeared in therapy even before psychoanalysis was properly born and was of major importance in its subsequent development. It changed the hypnotic situation into an analytic situation. It should be noted that the time of this change coincides with the time in the embryology of psychoanalysis, when hypnosis was being used not to produce suggestive, irrational cures, but to uncover traumatic, repressed memories; so that this purpose is tacitly assumed in the above-stated bargain.

With this modification of the hypnotic session into the analytic hour, the therapist's theoretical interest was diverted from the problems centering about sleeplike states and became more and more focused on the contents of the patient's remarks and behavior. The study of the patient as a quasi-sleeper or quasi-dreamer was completely subordinated to the therapeutic and theoretical study of his symptoms. The theory of the neuroses was developed, and it seems in retrospect inevitable that the writings on technique should have been couched largely in terms of this theory. The patient on the couch was prima facie a neurotic person and only incidentally a dreamer. It is well, however, to question the complete inevitability of this particular choice of formulation and terminology. We may plausibly speculate whether an alternative path could not have been chosen; namely, to regard the analytic material and 'what happens on the couch' not as something like a neurosis, but instead, something like a dream, and to introduce dream concepts and dream psychology terminology. If this path had been taken, quite possibly we would have developed a poorer and less useful terminology than we have now, but that is not the issue. We are not raising the question of better or worse, merely of difference.

The relationship between neurosis theory and dream theory seems to have been a slippery one for analysts to hang on to. Thus, Freud (1887-1902) confessed that he discovered the essential unity of the two, then forgot, and had to rediscover it. Perhaps it is necessary for all of us to repeat this rediscovery. So much of our analytic phylogeny recapitulates Freud's scientific ontogeny that we may not have, even now, thoroughly 'worked through' this insight and taken in all its implications. We have no doubt that the dream is the royal road to the unconscious and that dream analysis is an indispensable instrument in therapeutic practice. We know that the dream is a wish-fulfilment and a communication, and we bank heavily on this knowledge. But we have paid little attention to the chief function of dreaming, its guardianship of sleep. Attention to the interpretation of contents and to the dream work has distracted us, here too, from the problem of sleep and from a consideration of the analytic subject as a fractional dreamer or sleeper. Again in retrospect, Freud's rejection of Breuer's ideas of hypnoidal states appears consistent with the general turning from an interest in the sleeper as such.

We all know the psychoanalytic dictum that whatever is rejected in the course of conflict-solving may return and find a disguised place in that which is accepted. So, sleep, excluded by agreement from the analytic situation, gained access to it in another form—the method of free association. I developed this idea in a recent paper[2] where I pointed out that the wish to be put to sleep, which the patient brought to the hypnotic situation, has been supplanted by the wish to associate freely in the analytic situation. The patient lies down, not to sleep, but to associate. The interpretation of free association as the substitute for sleep in the therapeutic situation was based not only on the tacit bargain cited above, but also on one of Freud's (1900-1901) definitions of free association, given in The Interpretation of Dreams (p. 102), where it is likened to the state of mind that precedes sleep (also to the hypnotic state).

For our present purposes, then, we shall project the metapsychology of sleep and the dream onto the analytic situation. We readily note certain coincidences. Thus the narcissism of sleep, an element assumed in dream psychology, coincides with narcissism on the couch, and the rare blank 'sleep dreams' are analogous to the rare transient falling asleep on the couch, both phenomena being the unusual near zeros of their respective domains. The manifest dream text coincides with the manifest analytic material, expressing, in processed form, latent thoughts that become preconscious. Dream formation is to be compared with 'analytic-situation formation'; it is the 'exception', to use Freud's word, to the basic narcissism. Other analogies suggest themselves, but be-

[2] See, *Sleep, Narcissistic Neurosis and the Analytic Situation,* pp. 227-247 [Ed.].

cause there are so many differences of detail and elaboration, due to the opposite paths taken in the psychic apparatus by the dream process and the analytic-situation process (one terminating mainly in visual hallucinations, the other mainly in words), it is well to consider at first only the broader coincidences.

Narcissism

Since we mentioned the concept of *narcissism* as an element of the psychoanalytic theory of sleep and the dream, and suggested its application in the analytic situation, it would be well to come to terms with this word and its meaning. To ignore its origin in sexology, *narcissism* was introduced into psychoanalysis as a definition of an erotic relationship in which the self was the object, that is to say, self-love; but the youth gazing at his image in the fountain always had a more abstract and symbolical quality, as a representation of a form of love, than did, for example, the picture conjured up by the word, *libido,* with its etymology of sexual desire and its implication of the excited genital and sexual congress as the representation of object relationship. Narcissism has always seemed to be more conceptual, to be something behind the phenomena, and as far as factual existence is concerned, it has some of the shadowy and absent quality of its mythological eponym's forlorn sweetheart, the nymph Echo.

I mean that narcissism is an abstraction, with visible correlates in childhood psychology, in neurosis, in sleep, and in the love life. Narcissism, as a concept, is behind the dream, behind the depression and elation, behind somatic symptoms, etc. We must carefully distinguish between narcissism the concept and narcissistic phenomena as we distinguish the conceptual points and lines of pure mathematics from the ink dots and strokes that we see and measure (*cf.,* Hartmann, Kris, and Loewenstein's [1953] discussion of theory). But as the dot is the *approximate* concrete representative of the abstract point, so, I believe, we may take a certain type of blank dream as a sort of concrete, approximate, 'inkspot' picture of the abstract 'point' narcissism. This blank dream (Lewin, 1953) though concrete, approximates the narcissism of sleep, and as a manifestation, epitomizes what *narcissism* can mean not only in dream and sleep psychology but also in the phrase *narcissistic neurosis,* its content signifying an intense, primitive, direct experience of the baby in the nursing situation, inclusive of sleep at the breast.

The relevance of this discussion of narcissism to the theme, the application of dream psychology to the analytic situation, depends on a rather subtle point. Despite our theory, in ordinary dream interpretation, narcissism is left to one side, and to a certain extent this is also true in our ordinary interpretation of the standard analytic situation. However, certain narcissistic phenomena that appear on the couch (some of them related to sleep) will help us to understand the nature and psychology of the standard situation, as the 'narcissistic dream' throws light on the psychology of sleep and ordinary dreaming.

Toxic Technique

Before entering into an investigation of the standard analytic hour, it will be profitable to take up another, simpler modification of the older hypnotist's seance. I refer to what might be called the *toxic therapeutic situation,* where one or another drug is used as an adjuvant or an initiator of something like a cathartic situation. Here it is easy to apply dream psychology to interpret the situation, for the drug produces something like a sleep or a half-sleep state, and the fantasies that appear are readily compared to dream formations. For theoretical purposes, however, let us approach the matter indirectly, and treat the situation as a toxic neurosis.

In Mourning and Melancholia, Freud (1915c) states that a 'toxic' condition might of itself lead to narcissistic regression and depression (and presumably also elation) without the intervention of any object loss. But toxins may initiate many other types of mental states. In psychiatry, it has long been known that the psychological contents of a drug psychosis may include not only manifestations of direct impairment of the cerebral cortex (disorientation, torpor, intellectual inhibition, etc.), but also others called 'psychogenic' and due to individual mental factors, such as significant life experiences. In other words, a drug delirium has somewhat the structure of a dream, the drug being the incentive to a kind of sleep or 'state of narcissism', the psychogenic symptoms being cast in a form resembling a dream.

When 'narco' drugs are used in combined sleep- and psychotherapy, they produce a comparable state, where the narcissistic regression of anesthesia, like the narcissism of natural sleep, is made imperfect by an 'exception', which is like a dream. Excluding such heavy methods as the *Dauerschlaf,* which would be dreamless, the desideratum in the therapies I have in mind is not deep sleep nor hallucinosis, but a state nearer 'muttering delirium with sense in it'; that is, something not too far from intelligible or interpretable hypnagogic free association and catharsis.

From our present standpoint of historical reconstruction, we may say that the therapist acts here to supply a different answer to the problem raised by the Anna O type of patient, the type who resists and 'cannot be hypnotized'. The primitive resistance to being put to sleep is overcome by pharmacological aid. The drug promotes the relaxation and submission which is undertaken voluntarily in the hypnotic or standard analytic situation.

Fear of Sleep and Death

The wish for a soothing drug, or the fear of it, often comes up in associations during an analytic hour, among other reasons because of conflicts centering about sleep. The interpretation of this wish or fear throws light on the resistance of patients to hypnotism, which was not interpreted when historically the bargain of free association was struck. Some of the ambivalence about sleep and anesthesia was discussed in a previous paper[3] where I recounted some of the fantasies of seduction, or of being disgracefully uninhibited in language and action, and the moral objections that were raised to the introduction of the use of chloroform. In Papers on Hypnotism and Suggestion, Freud (1888-1892) tried to allay some of the public's and the medical profession's fear of harm coming from hypnotism by reminding his readers that anesthesia had been feared in the same way, but that this fear had gradually been dispelled through familiarity and reason.

It is true, as Freud says, that common sense and familiarity

[3] See, *Sleep, Narcissistic Neurosis and the Analytic Situation,* pp. 227-247 [Ed.].

have overcome some of the irrational alarm over being put to sleep by chloroform, and its social sanctioning (*accouchement à la reine*) has caused some of the anxiety to be ignored. Nevertheless, there still remain certain fears of being anesthetized, and the commonest one is not the fear of being uninhibited and losing self-control but the fear of dying. There is no need here to repeat arguments or furnish evidence for the idea that this fear is symptomatic and covers other latent ones. I shall merely name some of the pregenital varieties of the fear of death, or the fear of being put to sleep which is the same. These are: the fear of being devoured, of being poisoned, of being suffocated; and finally, a variety which is not so much a fear of dying in the sense of losing consciousness (sleeping) as a fear of the afterlife (and bad dreams), a fear rather ignored in our materialistic era. The equivalence of sleep and death and its clinical applicability is demonstrated in the following account, kindly placed at my disposal some years ago by Dr. Maxwell Gitelson.[4]

> The patient was a fifty-six-year-old man, seen in consultation, who had had a coronary attack, and who after recovery from this was suffering from an aversion to food, from a feeling that food did not go down, and from breathing difficulties, subjectively experienced as 'inability to get enough of what I need'. After much emotional distress and subjective torture, at one point he burst out to his wife and daughter, who were standing by, 'I am going to stop fighting this thing. I am going to let myself die.' Thereupon he collapsed on the pillow, fully believing that he was going to die, and instead dropped into the first peaceful sleep that he had had in many months.

Dr. Gitelson comments: 'This resignation to death really represented in his critical emotional state the development of a capacity to accept a profound oral regression with which death and sleep were equated'. A not irrelevant illness in this patient was a peptic ulcer of many years' standing. (*Cf.*, Stone [1947], who describes sleep on the analytic couch in a duodenal ulcer patient.)

It would not be difficult to imagine that Dr. Gitelson's patient might have shown the same behavior if he had tried to accommodate himself to the analytic couch. The resistance to analysis, like the resistance to sleep or to anesthesia, may, par-

[4] Personal communication.

ticularly at the beginning, be due to a fear of death or its corollaries. Being hypnotized, anesthetized, killed, put to sleep, are equivalents, and all may be represented by lying down on the analytic couch. Many patients have dreamed of their analysis as a surgical operation, the table (the surgical one this time, not the dining table) representing the bed or couch. By extension, and for other reasons that come from medical education, physicians often think of themselves being dissected when they dream of their analysis, and sometimes they even turn the autopsy into a cannibal procedure. In the literature we have a record of a famous dream in which a young physician with strong scientific curiosity sees himself as a cadaver undergoing dissection. The analysand was of course Freud (1900-1901), and since it was a self-analysis, appropriately he is also the anatomist. The dream begins:

> '*Old Brücke must have set me some task;* strangely enough, *it related to a dissection of the lower part of my own body, my pelvis and legs, which I saw before me as though in the dissecting-room, but without noticing their absence in myself and also without a trace of any gruesome feeling. . . . The pelvis had been eviscerated . . .*' (p. 452).

It is significant historically that the founder of psychoanalysis could see himself as a prosector and at the same time as the anatomical preparation, and later we shall have more to say about the identification of an analysand with a physically ill patient or a cadaver.

At this point, however, I should merely like to emphasize once more the natural unconscious equivalence of sleep and death, both of them states of narcissism, psychologically. Also that the exception to the narcissism of sleep, to wit, the dream, is the same as the exception to the narcissism of death, to wit, the afterlife. But more to the present purpose, I wish to indicate by these examples the sort of resistances there might be to lying down on the analytic couch, and how the couch and the analytic situation itself need interpretation. In all its variety, the most obvious interpretation, not necessarily the deepest, is that the couch is a place for sleeping.

Rank's Fallacy

In the above exposition I have tried to tie up some loose ends, many of them historical, which are related to the main theme of this paper, and to offer some justification for applying sleep metapsychology to the analytic situation. I should like now briefly to discuss an important error, which has a position in the history of psychoanalysis, and which involved both the theory of the analytic situation and the matter of sleep. I refer to the theory propounded by Otto Rank, and by him embodied in a technique, that in analysis patients relive their stay in the uterus and with its termination, their birth.

Rank, I believe, always had an unconscious feeling that the analytic situation was somehow a sleep and that the associative material was the equivalent of manifest dreaming. This I infer from an article of his called *Eine Neurosenanalyse in Träumen* (Rank, 1924b), a tour de force, based on the tacit assumption that an entire analysis and the whole process of the analytic situation could be understood as if it were a dream. A reading of this paper clarifies some of Rank's later erroneous views.

Rank's (1924a) argument that the analytic situation represents an intrauterine state and its termination a rebirth begins with the observation, correct enough, that rebirth fantasies accompany the resolution of the analytic situation, that patients dream of leaving the analyst as a being born. In this Rank saw not a metaphorical expression of separation, but a 'so to speak biological' repetition of the act of birth, '*meist in allen seinen Einzelheiten getreu*' (for the most part accurate in all details), so that the time spent on the couch is a true and immediate replica and reliving of that spent in the uterus. This idea Rank got directly from his patients, and he says, '*psychologisch hat also der Patient recht*', a quotation which conceals evident special pleading. It seems that Rank fell into the same sort of error which so distressed Freud when, at a critical moment in psychoanalytic history, he found that he had been misled by hysterical women's fantasies during analysis into believing that they had really been seduced in early childhood by their father or a near male relative. Freud took the hard step, then, of recognizing his error and realizing that he was dealing with the memory of an infantile fantasy. Rank was not aware that he had been deceived in the same way. He did not take into account the comparable alternative to his interpretation of the rebirth fantasy, namely, that it was a fantasy of waking up. For, among the fantastic elaborations of the fact of pleasurable sleep is the idea that one is *in utero,* or rather, within the mother's body, and this intramaternal fantasy is a later, more complicated and more highly processed fantasy of the œdipal period, which contains later knowledge and impressions about gestation.

In other words, Rank could equally well have thought that the fœtal postures adopted by patients on the couch and other signs and symptoms of the 'intramaternal situation' were fantasy attempts to fulfil the wish to sleep; similarly he could have interpreted the 'birth trauma' manifestations as the correlated resistance to waking up from the analytic bed. The insight that really resides in Rank's theory, if one analyzes his elaborations and misunderstandings, is expressed in his statement that '. . . *die eigentliche Übertragungsliebe, die wir bei beiden Geschlechtern analytisch aufzulösen haben, die mütterliche ist* . . .', which is blurry and an overstatement, but nevertheless contains an intuition of the whole preœdipal development and approximates in a way an interpretation of the position on the couch as a relationship to the mother. This it is, though hardly so directly and 'biologically' (whatever that implies) as Rank states. The couch is reminiscent of *sleep* and therefore an important element of the nursing situation. Rank felt the importance of the fact that the patient was lying down, and that somehow this was connected with the preœdipal relationship to the mother, but in his qualification of the statement quoted above, he himself fell into a fantasy in the clause, '. . . *wie sie in der pränatalen physiologischen Bindung zwischen Mutter und Kind gegeben war*'. Here he was believing a fantasy to be a literal statement of genetic facts.

To Rank, in fact, as to Jung, the story of Œdipus seemed only a myth, not a genetic fact. However, the point here is that Rank's analysis of the analytic situation and his failure to see that he was observing symptoms of sleeping and waking, led him to theorize falsely and, along with Ferenczi for a while, to regress in his technique to a quasi catharsis, where the patient relived fantasies on the couch and acted out the script suggested, and this acting out Rank identified with the therapeutic process. His active injunction, the setting of a definite terminal date, provoked the patient into a regressive protest to having his stay on the couch cut short, and the patient then portrayed being 'untimely ripp'd' from the analytic couch as an anxious, painful awakening, the traumatic 'birth'. In the œdipal setting, the regressively expressed formula for this would read: the father is waking and weaning me betimes from my sleep with the mother.

Rank was not saved from his fallacy by his knowledge of the theory of the neuroses, which indeed was shattered when he applied it to the analytic situation; but he might have been saved from his mistake if he had followed and analyzed thoroughly his perception about the 'prenatal state', which meant that the analytic situation was some kind of sleep and the associative material some kind of dreamlike production; that is, if he had consistently applied the metapsychology of the dream. Instead, he built his theory of the analytic situation on unanalyzed infantile fantasies about the unborn child and childbirth.

The reason I have dealt here so extensively with Rank's theory may not be immediately evident. But I regard it as an attempt, thwarted by a mistake, to do what I am attempting now, that is, to project upon the couch and the analytic situation the idea that the patient is as if somewhat asleep.

Free Association

From such general expositions of the analytic situation in terms of sleep and dream psychology, we may turn to individual elements in it, and to begin with, the very important one of free association. It is often profitable and instructive to see a familiar fact in a different context—to see the dream, for instance, as something that occurs in nature as well as in an analytic procedure, which as a matter of fact Freud's own dreams gave us a chance to do. We must, in other words, remind ourselves occasionally that God could not care less whether a dream is reported to an analyst or not; and we may well look for the phenomenal elements of the analytic situation in their natural habitats.

Let us, therefore, consider a solitary individual who is contemplating his own thoughts, feelings, memories and impulses. Let him approximate Freud's idea of free association by having him limit action to a minimum and by letting him put his mental processes into words with no care for style or form. That he should report these words to anyone is, for the time being, irrelevant. In any event, we have as yet no 'analysis', not even a self-analysis, for many persons have used very much this method of introspection for many purposes.

Freud (1920a) tells us that he came upon this method of giving free rein to the contents of consciousness in the writings of the German author, Boerne. In an essay written in 1827, The Art of Becoming an Original Writer in Three Days, Boerne concludes his exposition with the following words: 'Take a sheet of paper and for three days in succession write down, without any falsification or hypocrisy, everything that comes into your head. Write what you think of yourself, of your women, of the Turkish War, of Goethe, of the Funk criminal case, of the Last Judgment, of those senior to you in authority—and when the three days are over, you will be amazed at what novel and startling thoughts have welled up in you. This is the art of becoming a writer in three days.'[5] Boerne evidently intended to use the scribbling as the raw material for his literary work. He had as his purpose the liberation of the imagination, or as we might prefer to say, the exploration of the preconscious system, for the advancement of literary composition. In The Interpretation of Dreams, Freud (1900-1901, pp. 102-103) calls attention to Schiller's use of a method very like free association for the same purpose. We see, therefore, that from the start analysts have known that there was involved not merely a way of thinking, but also purposes and intentions that determined its use.

These intentions may be various. If we consider the works of Herbert Silberer (1909, 1911), another solitary associator, we see two evident motives for his recording freely arising ideas and feelings. One of these motives was psychological investigation in the narrower sense; he was interested in examining the why and how of this variety of thinking. His second purpose might be called, loosely, philosophical or mystical. Pursuing his first intention, Silberer noted his associations and the contents of his dreams and hypnagogic reveries, making scientific inferences and assumptions concerning the representation of waking up, the nature of symbols, and the way certain

[5] Ernest Jones (1953-1957, Vol. I, pp. 246-247); Zilboorg (1952).

states of the dreamer enter the manifest dream text. His scientific psychological interest lay not in dream interpretation in Freud's sense of unearthing unconscious contents and wishes, but in establishing the nature of certain formal properties in the manifest contents. In addition to this interest, Silberer had another which he called 'anagogic'. He used the dream thoughts and associations as incentives and directives for philosophic and theologic speculation, and possibly for the evocation of moods and feelings that went with them. In both endeavors, there was of course nothing like the 'analytic situation' or a 'therapeutic intention'. Silberer was led from verbal associations—a cardinal requirement in Freud's definition of free association—into visual and symbolic representation, and in reveries, during states of fatigue, he came very near to dreaming.

Jung (1916) was much influenced by Silberer, and it is fair to assume that he was describing his own variant of free association when he spoke of 'undirected thinking', which, he says, starts in words but is later replaced by visual images and after that by dreamlike fantasies. The latter he came to regard as the basic or elemental contents of the unconscious, and he held them in a certain awe, much as the ancients had for dreams that emerged through the gates of horn and ivory to bring to mortals the messages of the gods. They suggested to him ethical and religious beliefs and goals, and reminded him of parallels in myth and fable. As Boerne took notes for literary composition, so Jung (and in part, Silberer) used associations and reveries for metaphysical and mythological constructions. In fact, as Glover (1950) noted, Jung's psychological constructions resemble an Olympus, and his allegedly basic concepts are themselves the complex condensations, distortions, and symbols of a sort of manifest dream text.

Given any fantasy which arises during free and solitary ruminations, such as Silberer's while he gazed into his crystal globe, it is clear that one or another feature will be more likely to impress the observer when he retrospectively assesses them, and that he will be guided by his purposes, special interests, and education. One observer will be struck by the similarity of the given fantasy to ideas he held as a child or which possibly he has heard expressed by children. Another person, with little empathy for children but well versed in cultural history or anthropology, will be more aware that the fantasy resembles a certain series of myths. Consequently, the first observer would ultimately try to construct a psychology of the child, while the second might contribute to anthropology or the history of culture. A third observer, departing from the principle of putting the fantasy into words and running into complex reveries and unusual absorbed states, might come to accept these manifest, processed ideas and qualities as the final desiderata of the method. Still another observer could ignore all the frames of reference mentioned; in fact from Zilboorg's (1952) account of Francis Galton's use of the method, an academic psychologist of the old school, interested in the study of the mind according to the old canons of the science, might view the associations simply as novel, static 'enlargements of consciousness'. Clearly, all such observers have brought to the field their own measures and coördinates.

Freud's self-analytic intentions and purposes can be indicated in a few words. He approached his own associations as he did those of his patients, and he was guided by the same medical and analytic intentions, little concerned, to begin with, as to their nonmedical application. However, when one uses the word *medical* in connection with Freud, it must be in a very broad and enlightened sense, not synonymous with *therapy,* and including all the connotations and implications of science and research. Free association for him was calm self-observation and the verbal reporting or recording of the associations, which rules out of the method some of the 'inexpressibles' to which Jung refers, or at least insists on attempting to verbalize. This verbalization is by no means impossible; witness the brilliant descriptions of mystical experiences by many saints and poets.

We might use as an instance of Freud's attitude toward nonverbalization his pursuit through indirect associations of the forgotten name, *Signorelli,* when he could bring to mind only the visual images of the artist's frescoes. Under the same circumstances, it is conceivable that some other person, say an artist, not particularly interested in the problem of forgetting, might have been sidetracked into æsthetic moods, and he might have lost his interest in the painter's name. Freud's special interest in remembering and forgetting outweighed any tendency toward pleasurable æsthetic memories. From the purely psychoanalytic point of view or according to Freud's rules, many of the reveries and states of mind in question represent resistances to putting thoughts into words and to the hidden implications and associative links to these same thoughts. In his reference to quiet self-observation, as well as in the account of resistance and transference which immediately follows this in the Introductory Lectures, Freud leaves aside the problem of the relative awakeness of the person who is freely associating.

There are doubtless many other purposes that free association might be made to serve. Those mentioned are: 1, literary creation; 2, psychological science; 3, mystical experience; 4, ethical and philosophical guidance or inspiration; 5, therapy. As a drug is only *materia medica* in itself and variously utilizable for experiment or therapy or pleasure, so are free associations capable of varied employment. They can be elaborated, superseded, used 'anagogically' for moral illumination, or permitted to lead to buried memories, according to the interests and intentions, conscious or unconscious, of the self-observer. The thoughts and reveries of the relaxed, solitary person may lead off in many directions, guided by the pleasure principle, by impulses to action (Hartmann, 1947), or by intellectual and secondary intentions. Actions may include gestures or fugues or 'rational behavior'. The spontaneous ideas of the solitary self-observer can belong to various parts of his personality: different ego interests and pleasure strivings can seize upon the newly arisen ideas and feelings, progressively or regressively (E. Kris, 1950a). They may be turned into practical channels, such as literary production or problem solving, go over into æsthetic or athletic action, or be passively enjoyed or tolerated.

For the purposes of this discussion, it will be noted that the conception of free association is given a very loose construction. But at its core, again for our purposes, stands Freud's (1915-1917) special, tight definition of 'a state of quiet, unreflecting self-observation . . .' (p. 287), something which is quite different from reflection without precluding it, an attention to what is on the conscious surface of the mind, with a relinquishing of all objections to what might appear there, no matter from what source, or what the form or content. Around this nuclear, strictly defined norm, radiate the states of consciousness of all degrees of awakeness and sleepiness, including the artificial 'toxic' states; and there are insensible transitions toward reveries and dreams in one direction, and, in the other, toward directed, secondarily processed, structured mental work.

Indeed, what William James (1890, Vol. II) has to say about primitive reasoning may be interesting in this context.

> . . . it is by no means easy to decide just what is meant by reason, or how the peculiar thinking process called reasoning differs from other thought-sequences which may lead to similar results.
>
> Much of our thinking consists of trains of images suggested one by another, of a sort of spontaneous reverie of which it seems likely enough that the higher brutes should be capable. This sort of thinking leads nevertheless to rational conclusions, both practical and theoretical. . . . As a rule, in this sort of irresponsible thinking, the terms which fall to be coupled together are empirical concretes, not abstractions. A sunset may call up the vessel's deck from which I saw one last summer, the companions of my voyage, my arrival into port, etc.; or it may make me think of solar myths, of Hercules' and Hector's funeral pyres, of Homer and whether he could write, of the Greek alphabet, etc. If habitual contiguities predominate, we have a prosaic mind; if rare contiguities, or similarities, have free play, we call the person fanciful, poetic, or witty. . . . The upshot of it may be that we are reminded of some practical duty: we may write a letter to a friend abroad, or we may take down the lexicon and study our Greek lesson (pp. 325-326).[6]

Evidently, James was associating pretty freely himself, and he goes on to say that such actions as he mentioned, although 'rational', are not performed as the result of reasoning. (*Cf.*, Hartmann, 1947.) Later under the rubric of *resistance,* we shall refer to a special sort of action that may issue under such circumstances. Here it will suffice to call attention to James's quietly inspired differentiation of the prosaic and the poetic

[6] William James said that if you have a noble emotion such as you might get from going to The Symphony, you should do something about it, act on it, even go and pay a call on your great-aunt.

I wish to thank Dr. Carl Binger for this reference, which he rightly calls 'the apotheosis of the pragmatic'.

mind in free association, which contains *in nuce* premonitions of psychoanalytic formulations. Writing in 1889, James often astonishes us by what he might have called 'poetic' prophecy; for after trying to sum up thinking, he says, 'If we could say in English "it thinks," as we say "it rains" or "it blows," we should be stating the fact most simply and with the minimum of assumption. As we cannot, we must simply say that *thought goes on*' (James, 1890, Vol. I, pp. 224-225).

I might of course have omitted James's remarks and simply referred to Kris's (1950b) exposition of preconscious thinking, which covers this field; yet, James's words seemed worth quoting for themselves.

We must now ask how this big, loose process of solitary thinking or associating differs from the association desirable on the analytic couch. We may say, first of all, that there is probably no transference situation; we say *probably*, for there may be an occult one, such as we believe existed in Freud's thinking in relation to Wilhelm Fliess, and we cannot be too sure whether some of the accounts of self-analysis are entirely accurate when their reporter assumes that there was no analyst. I have in mind Pickworth Farrow's (1945) account and Freud's comments thereon in the Introduction. Certainly, if one has been in an analytic situation, subsequent self-analytic procedures will contain elements of the original transference. However, in nature, there would probably be no analyst in a self-analysis in the narrower sense.

On the other hand, there would certainly be resistances, in the freudian sense. These Freud observed in his own self-analysis, and he constantly alludes to them in his work with his own dreams. Nor is it hard to make them out in Silberer's or in Jung's writings. Indeed, the recognition that there are resistances to free thought ranks as one of Freud's great technical discoveries. Although some of the persons mentioned near the beginning of this discussion, like Boerne and Schiller, had an inkling that they were overcoming some sort of impediment to thinking, and although some mystics write of the 'darkness' when no ineffable experiences can be reached, yet it remained for Freud to note that certain paths of thought 'led nowhere', or to a halt, or *ins Unendliche* (into the endless, as he says in one place), and in general certainly away from the place that Freud was interested in—from repressed material which is not ego-syntonic. In short, in free solitary association, there may be no transference but there is surely resistance. If, for terminological reasons, one wishes to reserve the word *resistance* for the situation on the couch,[7] then one would still have to say *repression* or *defense.*

Resistance, Sleep, and the Dream

The analytic resistance is a pragmatic concept. After hypnotism was abandoned, Freud found that the patient would or could not live up completely to his promise to associate freely in a useful way; and it is well to emphasize the word *useful* and to specify the use. Freud had a therapeutic and scientific intention, and the resistance was directed against the instrument of this intention. I follow Freud in calling free association an instrument, for he compares analytic resistance to the resistance a person might offer to the use of dental forceps. The resistance was discovered in the analytic situation; but in his self analysis also, Freud felt his resistances as he felt those of his neurotic patients. They felt like a counterforce that reminded him of the countersuggestion he knew from his prepsychoanalytic work, which recalcitrants used against being hypnotized. Resistance, therefore, is something that exists in self-analysis too, but, be it noted, in self-analysis which coincides with freudian intentions. It also exists in free association and rumination that resembles free association, but if this occurs without freudian intentions, it may not be noted or, if it is, not considered to be of practical importance.

There is no need here to repeat the insight into resistances which came from further experience with the neuroses. I shall merely mention the addenda to Freud's (1925a) Inhibitions, Symptoms and Anxiety, Anna Freud's (1936) classic account in The Ego and the Mechanisms of Defense, and call attention to Loewenstein's (1954) recent paper, Defenses, Autonomous Ego, and Technique, and to its bibliography.

I wish to go back to nature and the more general field of solitary association outside the analytic situation. Solitary

[7] One should not take the phrase *on the couch* too physically and literally. Free association, and an analytic situation too, occur with a person sitting up or in other positions. But this alters only a few obvious details; the person can also daydream, doze, and even sleep in the sitting position, and he can 'associate'.

meditators, or whatever we may choose to call them, who do not have the specific freudian intent have no objection to the appearance of resistances. When they encounter what we call resistances, they do not face them as Freud had to, for they are swayed by other motives. They are not co-signers of the contract with Anna O. They elaborate the resistances, act them out, enjoy them, or use them in some other way, but they do not recognize them. The intentions and the point of view are crucial. Freudians must call such manifestations *resistance,* but others may be content with manifest, processed material not to be further analyzed. Boerne and Silberer and William James arrive at ends different from Freud.

On the couch, however, the resistance to being hypnotized or put to sleep shown by Anna O has been replaced by the resistance to free association, its substitute. In the resistance to free association, the old agreement about being put to sleep may be placed on the agenda for reconsideration. The patient, in conflict about free association, may suggest that he be hypnotized or be given a drug. Or he may depart from the basic contract by getting into a mystic state of mind, or into some of the sleepy states described by Silberer. I have indicated in a previous paper that the resistive patient may become either too sleepy or too alert for useful free association. His behavior may come to resemble that of the solitary associator with no freudian intentions.

If you recall William James's hypothetical case of associations to a sunset, one outcome of the undirected thinking was action: the person was led by his associations to take down a Greek lexicon and study his Greek lesson. Such an action, from our standpoint, would not be an end, though it might have been for James's nonfreudian; we should consider it, even in self-analysis, an evasion of the fundamental rule. We should say: This man has quit associating. In a discussion, Rado once compared a certain resistive acting out to sleepwalking, thus correlating phenomena of resistance with those of the dream, and R. Sterba (1946) reported instances where persons have acted out the dream contents of the previous night. More often action in place of association should be considered a waking-up analogue. But Rado's reference to sleepwalking, perhaps the least 'rational' of actions, brings out hyperbolically the fact that, to a freudian, motion is not in itself an end. It may be as disturbing to free association as to sleep. Aphoristically, one might say that the dream is the guardian of sleep, but the analyst is the guardian of free association.

In the cathartic cure and in early psychoanalysis, did the listening doctor relinquish the use of sleep? Perhaps not entirely, on close inspection, for when the patient found communication impeded, he was encouraged to associate freely (even by the laying on of hands), and in effect he was set to work to produce more or less dreamlike fantasies, to approach therefore in quality the mentation of sleep. At the point of resistance, to put it strongly, the patient was soothed a little, encouraged to be 'more asleep'. In this context, resistance meant too much alertness which thwarted the doctor's intentions. Other resistances were soon encountered, in which, contrariwise, the patient let himself be in too much of a dream and eliminated too much responsibility and reality testing. With the years, after much study of the neuroses and psychoses, a good deal of this behavior was clarified, and the knowledge that accumulated was formulated in terms of a theory, and finally organized in Inhibitions, Symptoms and Anxiety and the literature that stems from this work.

Affects

Affects on the couch or arising during solitary association are like those that appear in dreams. They are part of the manifest content. The freudian intention is to analyze them, and as in dream analysis determine whether a 'happy mood' may not conceal a fear of death, or whether an anxiety is a signal and a repetition. The solitary meditator may take the affect at its face manifest value and go on from there, taking the elated and depressed feelings especially as warranted.

The Analyst

We may approach the matter of the analyst and where he fits into the metapsychology of the dream by a preliminary consideration of the solitary associator. If he is following Freud's rules, i.e., if he is a self-analyst, there may be a kind of occult analyst, or at least an occult transference figure, as we learn from the role which Wilhelm Fliess played in Freud's self-analysis. Let us assume, however, for the general situation of self-analysis, that it is possible to do what Freud did in his self-study without someone else (real or ideal), therefore, without a transference.

As to the unanalytic free associator, for his unanalytic purposes he may wish to confide, so that we may speak of a possible confidant for such solitary meditations who would be the recipient of the ideas that go through his mind. It is needless to list here the possibilities of such a relationship, which might include any kind of human communication from the most primitive to the most sophisticated, nor do I wish to document them. We again encounter the matter of purpose. Hanns Sachs (1924) has described one variety of such communication in his article, Daydreams in Common, where the common ground was originally the sharing of masturbation fantasies, later of more elaborate stories. Supposing Boerne or Schiller had sought a confidant; then the other person could have been called an editor or a collaborator. Silberer might simply have considered such a person an intruder.

It was during the transition from hypnotic treatment to catharsis and analysis that the neurotic patient changed from being a hypnotic subject to being a confider, and the therapist *pari passu* became a psychoanalyst. Freud's and Breuer's first subjects came to them with the stated purpose of relief from symptoms, and to the end persons continued to go to Freud either to be cured or to learn, by sampling the cure, a therapeutic method. But before there was an official psychoanalysis, patients had come to be put under hypnosis, which they knew of as a sort of magical sleep. The idea that sleep is a magical healing method must be very ancient, more ancient than the sleep of the Æsculapian temple; and the general prevalence of this idea in the unconscious may well have attracted patients to hypnotists. 'And God put Adam into a deep sleep', the early anesthetists reminded their theologically oriented opponents and their reluctant patients, and certainly sleep has its rational place in therapy even today. In its origins, however, the therapeutic use of sleep quite possibly depended on fantasy, and the original hypnotic patients may have asked for it with the idea that after sleep should come a better waking, one into a new world, a dream world or heaven, in short, into a wish-fulfilling world where the blind see, the mute speak, the lame walk and are whole. Baudelaire called the drug addict's goal an artificial paradise, and this it was that the seeker after hypnotic sleep desired. The hysterical person, having been hypnotized, acted out many fantasies and miracles of therapy, and we still see often enough flights into health of the same shaky order.

The magical sleep-maker became a confidant, and the analytic situation arrived in history. But the confidant listening to associations as they appear is a very special kind of listener. Sometimes the person on the couch is hardly aware of his presence and is even surprised by it at the end of an analytic session; at other times, the patient can think of nothing but the analyst's person. We speak of the transference, thinking of the building up of fantasies about the analyst which are new editions of older ones in the patient's history. Evidently the analyst is not a unitary element that can be directly mapped to a unitary spot in the diagram of the psychic apparatus and into the psychology of sleep and the dream. In fact, in what follows it will become clear that the analyst belongs in several places in the diagram, also 'around' the diagram, and that he can be mapped in terms of dream psychology as a day residue, as an external excitant, and as an external or 'border' soother.

As the focus for infantile transference fantasies, the analyst was compared by Otto Rank, with Freud's (1915d, pp. 228-229, n.) approval, to a day residue, a recent stimulus of the immediate environment which is processed into manifest material by the addition of unconscious ideas. In this sense, the analyst is a perception; he is recent material. Rank's point was made in refuting some of Silberer's views of 'anagogy' and in reference to dreams about the analyst, but the waking fantasies on the couch use him in the same way in this context. That the analyst is a sleep-maker or a waker needs more elaboration, and will receive it in the discussion that follows. Also, it will be necessary to analyze in dream metapsychology the superego role often attributed to him.

Let us leave the patient aside for a moment and consider the analyst as an interpreter, where his wishes and actions are central. Is the patient still clothed for him in traces of the sleep or part-sleep from his phylogenetic history as a hypnotic and cathartic subject? Or has the concept of the recumbent sleeper and dreamer been repressed? In the latter case we might look for some return of the repressed, and possibly see it when analysts turn to drugs as an adjuvant to cathartic or analytic therapy. However, let us consider two psychoanalytic aphorisms which epitomize the aim of analysis. The first is: 'Where id was, there let ego be!'. Let us combine this with another familiar remark, that the ego rejoins the id in deep sleep. The inference is that the analyst is a waker. To confirm this inference, we have another aphoristic statement, much quoted, *'Ich verstand, dass ich von jetzt ab zu denen gehörte, die "am Schlaf der Welt gerührt" haben, nach Hebbels Ausdruck'*. ['I understood that from now onwards I was one of those who have "disturbed the sleep of the world", as Hebbel says . . .' (Freud, 1914a, p. 21).] Inescapably the analyst is an arouser, as well as a day residue. As an external neutral fact, regardless of his intentions, he may become part of the subject's analytic situation manifest content, and he is in the structure of the analytic situation as if a dream day residue. But when the analyst's intentions come into play, and he interprets and analyzes, he is often not in the structure but an external waker or disturber of the situation. We shall see later that he may also at times play the role of a soother.

I suggested in a previous paper[8] that coincidental with all other effects of the analyst's remarks or perhaps even of his presence, there is a deep effect, which I likened to the musical: the analyst continuously operates either to wake the patient somewhat or to put him to sleep a little, to soothe or to arouse; and this effect may be quite unconscious both for subject and analyst.

There are apparently some simple therapeutic situations, comparable to the standard analytic but different nevertheless, in which the aim is more nearly the simple one of arousing or wakening the patient. The idea that a psychosis is a kind of dream is ancient, and many maneuvers used in the treatment of schizophrenia have a rousing intention, as those most experienced in the field have stated or indicated. Zilboorg (1930), for example, as a preliminary to using the classical technique, put his schizophrenic patient through a course of training in

[8] See, *Sleep, Narcissistic Neurosis and The Analytic Situation*, pp. 227-247 [Ed.].

reality discrimination, as if to insert into a dream some of the functions of the waking state. K. R. Eissler (1951) insists on dealing directly with 'the primary process', which is a concept of dream psychology, so that the maneuver is a concession to the patient's dreaming. In a somewhat different context, Eissler (1943, 1951) states that at one stage of the treatment, the intellectual content of what is told the patient is not as important as the therapist's voice or manner—that one could influence the patient perhaps even by mumbling, surely a 'musical' remark. John Rosen (1953) says explicitly and generally, 'What is the psychosis but an interminable nightmare in which the wishes are so well disguised that the psychotic does not awaken? Why not then awaken him by unmasking the real content of his psychosis? Once the psychosis is stripped of its disguises, will not this dreamer awaken too?'

Other, less clearly understood, methods of dealing with schizophrenia put the patient to 'sleep' by more or less drastic means. Empirically they often wake up different, and often they speak of the experience as a 'rebirth'. The 'rebirth' fantasy is the counterpart of the 'intrauterine fantasy'; the latter is an infantile fantasy which takes the child asleep as its model for life before birth; the 'birth' fantasy uses the child's waking up, or perhaps his 'waking up' into a dream. In any case, the therapist appears to have the intention of fulfilling the sleeper's wish for a healthy paradise, as I suggested in discussing the use of hypnotic sleep as an implementation of this idea in neurotics. We can gain some insight into the sleep-making intention of the physician by considering the ambivalence of physicians toward patients, their vacillation between a preference for a live or a dead patient, which I partly analyzed as due to their double experience in medical school, where they dealt with cadavers as their first patients and later had to transfer some of their conception of the patient as cadaver to live persons.[9] But as the sleep therapies of schizophrenia are organized, the doctor's wish to put the patient to sleep is subordinated to his wish to waken him and to cure him. As in surgery, the physician's sleep-making enters the larger therapeutic activity with its arousing intention, as a 'feed-back' and regulator or subordinate action.

[9] See, *Countertransference in Medical Practice*, pp. 449-458 [Ed.].

To return to the topic of arousing, and the analyst's excitant role in this direction, we may again consider a schizophrenic case. I refer to Nunberg's (1920) classic analysis of the patient who had had a catatonic attack. He constantly referred to the attack as 'my dream', and he called his desire for recovery a wish to forget this dream completely. Elsewhere I have shown how the wish to forget a dream is equivalent to a wish to be completely awake,[10] and in Nunberg's patient the way this was expressed is worth noting. For he set the physician up as a father and ego ideal, endowed him with tremendous power, expressed deep submission, and stated that he wished to be cured by the 'power' of this father's words. That is, as I interpret it, he wished the father to awaken him through powerful loud noises. In infancy, words and noises are powerful excitants and arousers, and apparently the same holds in the case of the dream.

Here I rely on Isakower's (1939, 1954) studies, according to which manifest words that appear just at the end of dreams during wakening moments represent wakener-superego, and because they have not been caught by the full dream work, they retain their verbal and environmental sense. Reasoning further, to be wakened is to be weaned, and as a variant, to be brought back to this world, which returns us to Rank and his fallacy. It also reminds us of Rank's insight into the preœdipal transference situation, and of his attempted analysis of the 'couch' and of the analytic situation *per se*. The 'couch' means sleep, with its maternal implications; and the spoor of the preœdipal father, who is not a dream element but a wakener, is sublimated in the therapy into the analyst who is not an element of the 'couch situation' but one who disturbs the sleep of the world and its inhabitants. The 'auditory sphere', which borders on the atmosphere where the sound waves travel, catches most of the stimuli (though surely not all) that awaken the child, the dreamer, and the analysand.

That the analyst is on the border of the dream becomes evident, by contrast, in those dreams where he is represented as a soother, and where there is no border. I am referring to those unprojected, blank, 'sleep', or 'narcissistic' dreams in which the analyst is represented. For example, in the dream

[10] See, *The Forgetting of Dreams*, pp. 213-226 [Ed.].

reported by Rycroft (1951), where the border of the dreamer is vague, and the dream is not visually projected but is 'pure feeling', the analyst is a soothing atmosphere and the homologue of the breast or dream screen. In Rycroft's report, the patient said he felt as if he were being taken under the analyst's wing, but that there was no visual content, and that it was an allegorical way of expressing a feeling which was more like an emotion. I have encountered comparable 'transference remarks' in patients who expressed their preœdipal wish to sleep at the breast by fantasies of occupying the same space as the analyst, as if they could walk right into or through him. This is an unusual mapping of the analyst; it puts him in the place of sleep itself.

Nunberg's patient wished to be thoroughly awake and to forget his catatonic 'dream'. Rycroft's patient, not psychotic, in dreaming portrayed his analyst as the bland 'spirit of sleep' and enjoyed the best night's sleep he had ever had. Both patients centered their relationship about the fact of *sleep*, reminding us again of Freud's bargain with Anna O, and suggesting that both of these patients sensed the relationship *as if* in terms of the old prepsychoanalytic days, when the hypnotist put his patient to sleep and awakened him. Their manifest thoughts referred to this latent doctor-patient relationship.

Other clinical examples might be given, but they are readily available in analytic practice. Therefore, I shall be content to summarize some of the results of our mapping of the elements of dream psychology to the couch situation. With ingenuity, it is possible to find the couch situation's counterparts in The Interpretation of Dreams. In the sense of 'transference figure', the analyst is to be paired with what seemed in dream interpretation a very minor piece of material: he is the opposite number of indifferent precipitates or day residues to which unconscious ideas lend their cathexis. As interpreter, he stands for another minor element—a current external stimulus, which may threaten to arouse the dreamer, like the real fire in Freud's (1900-1901) paradigm of the dream in Chapter VII, that of the burning child. He is also the opposite number of certain external stimuli which did not interest Freud in connection with the dream—the stimuli which promote sleep. These were taken for granted and did not need to be counteracted by the guardianship function of the dream, for they too assisted the maintenance of sleep and ordinarily were not registered in the dream. We know a great many of these, differing at different ages: lulling and crooning, the full meal, and other satisfactions, all in a way wish-fulfilments too. There are also soporific drugs, and as an interesting psychological example, the memory of the nursing situation, which, when it appears, often coincides with sound and happy sleep. In this context, the analyst's position is that of peripheral stimulus.

It will be noted that the analyst is at both ends and around the diagram of the psychic apparatus; that he is 'around' the couch as the external world is around the dream.

The rest of the mapping on to the couch of dream psychology is not difficult, for 'analysis-formation' is like dream formation and involves the same memory traces and psychic systems, though usually in different proportions. Blank dreams are approximated by the 'blank couch', that is, sleep on the couch where the narcissism of sleep which is 'under' the dream comes out into the open as 'couch narcissism'. I omit what the analyst does besides lulling and rousing from the present statement; that is, I omit most of analytic technique, the contents of the specific interpretations and other operations, which of course matter very much. To fall back on Freud's old comparison of hypnosis and chloroform anesthesia, it is what one does after the patient is chloroformed that matters most, and this is what we call technique and not situation. As the surgeon cannot always ignore or completely forget the basic situation of anesthesia, so we cannot always ignore the ratio between sleep and waking in the analytic patient.

VI. THE ANALYTIC SITUATION: TOPOGRAPHIC CONSIDERATIONS*

For psychoanalysts there are three ways of formulating a psychological event: the dynamic, the economic (quantitative), and the topographic. The dynamic point of view, which considers motives, is the one most familiar. Psychoanalysis is called a 'dynamic psychology', and semantically tempered and slightly vitiated psychoanalysis is sometimes called dynamic psychology. Yet, even simple courses in dynamic psychology do not stick to a purely dynamic point of view, for they introduce ideas of intensity and cathexis, that is, energy and quantity. Topography usually comes rather short in such treatment. Topography, etymology shows, is a matter of place and whereabouts. The word comes from the Greek *topos,* which means place, which itself is compounded of two words *to pos,* 'the where'. In psychoanalytic explanations at different stages of development of the science, the 'places' that came into consideration were: 1, in older theory, the systems conscious, preconscious, and unconscious; later 2, the id, the ego, and the superego. If then in a so-called dynamic psychology we introduce the idea of cathexis and of systems graded according to accessibility to consciousness, and if we use the id-ego-superego terminology, 'dynamic' psychology actually becomes economic and topographic psychology too.

By topographic consideration, we mean that we are answering the question, Where?. Is an idea 'in' the conscious system or in the unconscious? Does an impulse 'arise' in the id, the ego, or the superego? And so on. If something is 'in' something else we are thinking spatially and can draw a diagram. Two familiar diagrams exist: the id-ego one, and the 'psychic apparatus' diagram in Chapter VII of The Interpretation of Dreams. Despite their simplicity, they have been used to demonstrate rather complex situations. It has long

* [No. 110 in Bibliography.]

been evident that the id-ego diagram was modeled on those used in studies on aphasia. Freud's comparisons of the cerebral cortex and consciousness, of the little upside-down man along the fissure of Rolando and the bodily ego, etc., bring this home to readers. The picture of the superego in the diagram is like the *Hörkappe* in the aphasia scheme.

Freud tells us that the 'psychic apparatus' is modeled on an optical instrument—logically, for it is supposed to produce a 'dream picture'. A wish travels like a ray of light through a medium of memory traces. A moment's reflection tells us that a dream is necessarily made up completely of memory traces, even though some may be very recent and all immediate external stimuli or perceptions get turned into dream thoughts and dream images made up of memories.

Dreams can therefore be represented by another, simpler, diagram which would disregard some of the considerations detailed in Chapter VII. A dream can be represented, if one wishes, by a circle in which every point or element represents a *memory trace*. This corresponds to the familiar mathematical idea of a *set;* in this simple representation the dream is a *set,* the individual memory an *element.*

Mathematics defines a set M as 'a collection into a whole of definite well-distinguished objects, called the elements of M, of our perception or of our thoughts. . . . For example, the prime numbers between 1 and 100 constitute a set of 25 elements; the vertices of a square, a set of four elements; the points of a circle, a set of infinitely many elements. For a set, the order of succession of its elements shall not matter, provided that nothing is said to the contrary' (Kramke, 1950).

In an analogous way we may, if we wish, disregard the structural lines in the id-ego diagram and arrive at a simpler (circular) diagram, the elements of which have already been given the name in German of *Triebrepräsentanzen,* that is, 'instinct representations'. These are ideas which represent instinct activities, and the simplified diagram is again a set of such elements. This leaves out much that is useful to us, but it is theoretically possible. It becomes static rather than dynamic.

The few propositions from set-theory to be introduced here are very simple. Let us consider now the analytic situation. This can be defined loosely but adequately enough as what goes on 'on the couch', and its elements are well known. They are called, whether verbal or not, 'free associations'. Without realizing it, Ferenczi and Rank (1924) have put us in the way of diagraming the analytic situation. They classify the ideas that arise on the couch into three categories, speaking of the corresponding situations: 1, the actual situation, 2, the transference situation, and 3, the infantile situation. At any given moment the analysand, directly or by interpretative inference, is thinking about what is going on currently in his environment, or about the psychoanalyst and their relationship, or about something in the past, especially in his infancy.

These terms are useful and widely employed. Apparently they are derived from The Interpretation of Dreams, not from Chapter VII but from preceding chapters where Freud lists the sources of dream thoughts: recent material including the 'day residues'—that is, the 'actual situation'—, ideas that come from the past, and, during the psychoanalytic procedure, to these would naturally be added the ideas specifically referring to the transference situation.

In accord with this, the total analytic situation shown in Figure 1 is represented by three intersecting circles: A the actual situation, T the transference situation, and I the infantile situation. These are not 'deep' terms theoretically, nor is this a deep theoretical diagram. The terms were introduced pragmatically; they arose from everyday psychoanalytic practice because they conveniently describe and classify the associations and events on the couch. At this level, classification is not 'depth psychology'.

Despite my use of their terminology I dissociate myself, through the 'intersections', from Rank's assumptions concerning the three classes of associations. Rank assumed that every element in an hour's associations without exception contained three references, one to each of the three categories, and he rather strained himself to prove that the Wolf-man's infantile dream included references to Freud's consultation room—that the arrangement of the animals on the tree was derived from the arrangement of photographs hanging on the wall, that the window in the dream was the window in Freud's

Figure 1. The Analytic Situation

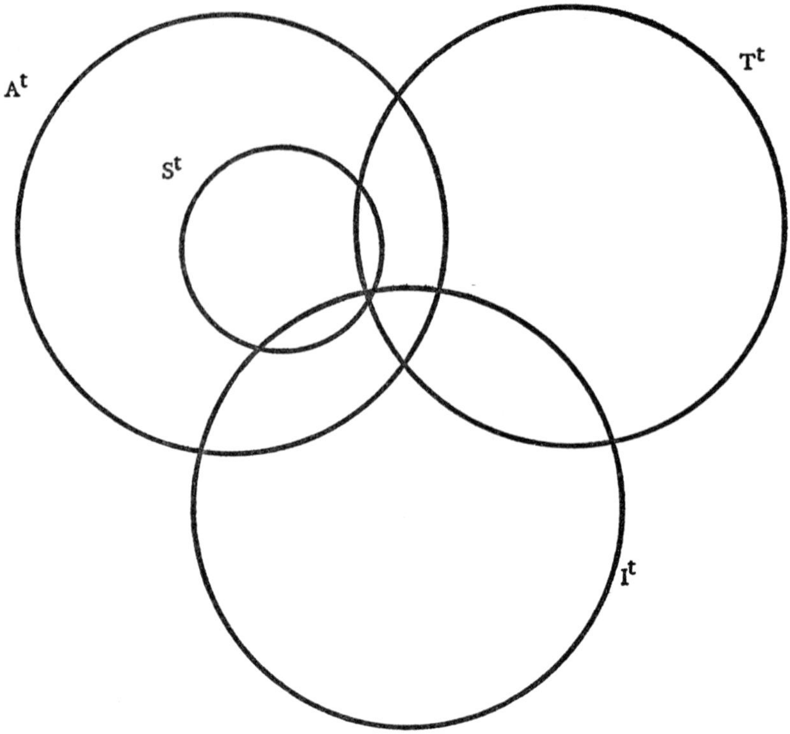

Legend: A, actual situation. T, transference situation.
I, infantile situation. S, school situation.

The superscript 't' indicates that there is also a time-dimension, and that the diagram is a 'cross-section' in time.

office, etc. Hence I suppose Rank would insist that there were not intersecting circles but that the three coincided. This seems too extreme and dubious to me and to most readers of Rank, but in diagraming we may make whichever assumption we find most useful. The assumption of intersecting circles enables us to make more useful diagrams.

To show how one may use the diagram of Figure 1, I choose a familiar situation, namely, the school situation of the student in a psychoanalytic institute, represented in Figure 1 by the small broken circle marked S. The school situation is certainly part of the student-analysand's current or actual situation, as much so, say, as his domestic situation is part of his everyday life. In the present context then we represent by the small circle S, entirely within the larger circle A, that part of the actual situation which is the school situation and we call this the 'subset S in A'. Though entirely within A, it is shown in the figure as located in a part of A which cuts the other two sets, T and I, the transference and infantile situations, and for an obvious reason. For all ideas and associations and behavior refer to the fact that the student *is* a student and that he is in a school, or that he is in a student-teacher relation with his personal analyst, or that he was a schoolboy, and the like belong together.

There is a mathematical analogue to the singling out of the school situation in this way and differentiating it within the larger model. What we do here is called in set theory 'systematic definition', of which the simplest example would be the subset of even numbers within the larger set of all the ordinary natural numbers or integers. The systematic definition here is 'divisible by two', and this systematically defined subset of even integers would itself intersect other systematically defined subsets, such as the square numbers, which include some even numbers. The subset S would quite analogously intersect with other subsets of its own kind.

For example (Figure 2), let another circle or subset in the actual situation be called—that is, systematically defined as—M, the money situation. The element 'paying for institute courses' would then be located in both S and M, and the intersection of S and M would contain this elemental event. I may use this simple example to demonstrate the meaning of the superscript 't' in the diagram. The 't' means there is a time dimension, which in turn means the following: as time goes on, the diagram and the intersectional and general positional relationships change. As given, the diagram is general. The 't' is a variable, and if you drew a diagram for the first hour of treatment, another for the second, and so on to the 'nth' or last hour, you could indicate this by writing t_0, t_1, t_2, . . . t_n in the consecutive diagrams and you could build up a sort of three-dimensional snakelike figure. Or if you wished and thought it expedient, the 't' series could stand for the minutes in the same hour and you could build up a similar snake out of the fifty cross-sections. Here we shall consider that 't' refers to hours.

Figure 2. The Analytic Situation

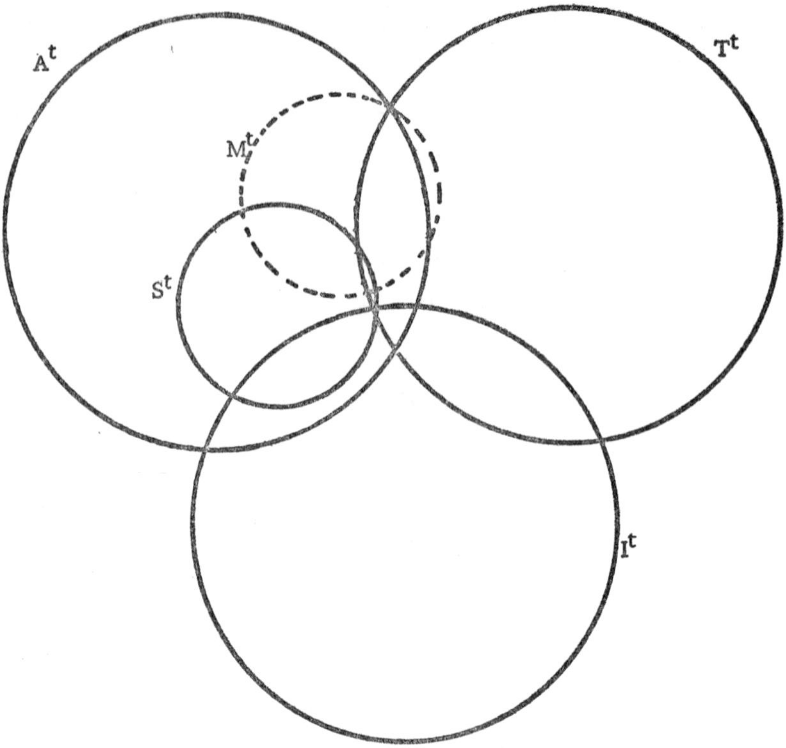

Legends as before and M, money situation.

Suppose it is October 2 and that on October 1 the student received his first bill for the sessions. If October 2 is his 15th session, the proper designations on the diagram are: $A^{t_{15}}$, $T^{t_{15}}$, $I^{t_{15}}$, and, because of the bill, $M^{t_{15}}$ could be the locus of many associations and probably $M^{t_{15}}$ would have a large intersection with $T^{t_{15}}$. Many associations concerning the matter of paying the analyst should create this overlap. A week or so later M might conceivably not cut the T set; that is, on $t = t_{22}$ the money associations might relate predominantly to domestic expenses or to other actual topics. Some other day, perhaps through constipation and the like, the money subset M would intersect more with the set I, the infantile situation.

All these pictures and parodies have a point only if they clarify the student or the money problem. The most important idea in all this is the 'systematic definition' of the subsituation, which implies that there is good reason for supplying it with a name and that this reason is a pragmatic one. The idea of a defined system is like the old analytic idea of a 'complex', which presupposed a valid reason for combining certain ideas as elements. It is a heuristic construction (not a 'deep' one!) which helps the analyst organize his thoughts about analytic material. Freud's difference with Jung concerning the Electra complex was not over the existence of infantile femininity, but about the usefulness of the naming—more precisely, whether the name need be introduced as an *auxiliary* construction, like the dotted lines in a geometry problem. The terms œdipus complex and castration complex have survived as denotations for auxiliary conceptual theorems when they are used in the solution of clinical or dream problems.

Figures 3 and 4 are diagrams of the analytic situation that show the position of such an unconscious complex. It is located by definition completely in I, the infantile situation; that is, OE is a subset of I. It is known too that associations connected with, say, the œdipus complex are also found which are at the same time elements of the actual or the transference situations. Hence in drawing in the subset OE in I, on some days it will be placed in the part of I which intersects one or both of the other sets A and T. From a geometrical point of view, the œdipus complex OE is represented by the same sort of circle as the student situation S, and for the same reason. It can be systematically defined as a subset, every one of its elements referring to this particular infantile situation.

The same applies to the other infantile situation that we term the castration complex. It too is mapped as lying entirely within the set I but with some elements in T and A, that is, in the intersections. Like the subsets S and M, it also may be given a superscript 't' to indicate a time dimension, and its position in the total analytic situation (the three circles of the diagram) will differ from hour to hour, from minute to minute perhaps, etc. In one hour, presumably an early one in the analysis, say $t = t_1$, it will lie entirely in I. Later, at say $t = t_{101}$, it could lie entirely in the intersection of I and T. Worthy of remark is that just as the school situation can never completely leave A until graduation, and

Figure 3. Analytic Situation and Œdipus Complex

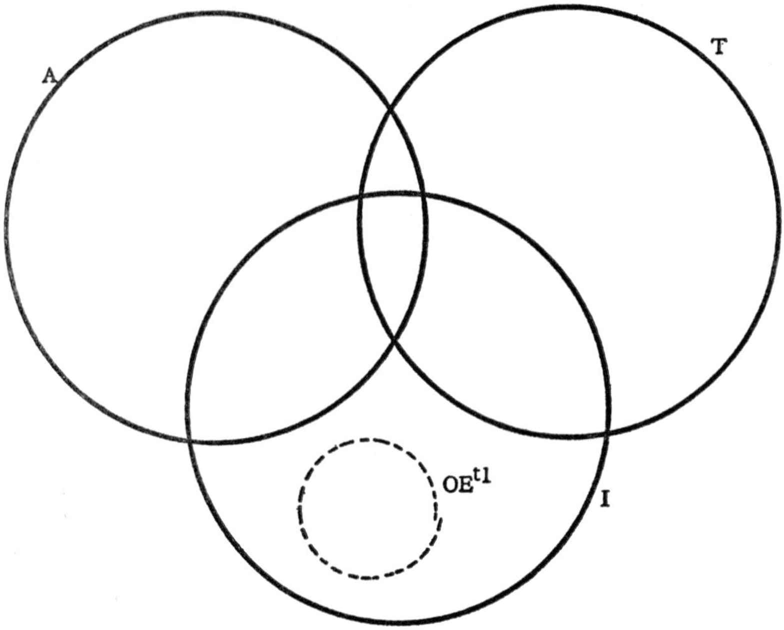

Legend as before, and OE, œdipus complex. $t = t_1$ indicates the first analytic hour.

even when S is in T, it must still lie in the intersection, so the œdipus complex must always be located in I, and when it is 'in the transference' it too must be located in the intersection of I and T.

The phrase '*in* the transference' is such a natural and everyday phrase that it may not have struck one as a topographic formulation. The diagraming of the subsets within the three large sets points up this fact, for if we say something is in the transference now, whether it has entered from A or from I, we are giving an answer to the question, Where?, that is, a place or *topos*.

The term, 'dynamic interpretation', means that the motives behind a set of associations can be stated and the wishes or instincts specified. The statement that someone has incestuous intentions is such a dynamic interpretation. Now, it is generally appreciated, even when the designation is not

Figure 4. Analytic Situation and Œdipus Complex

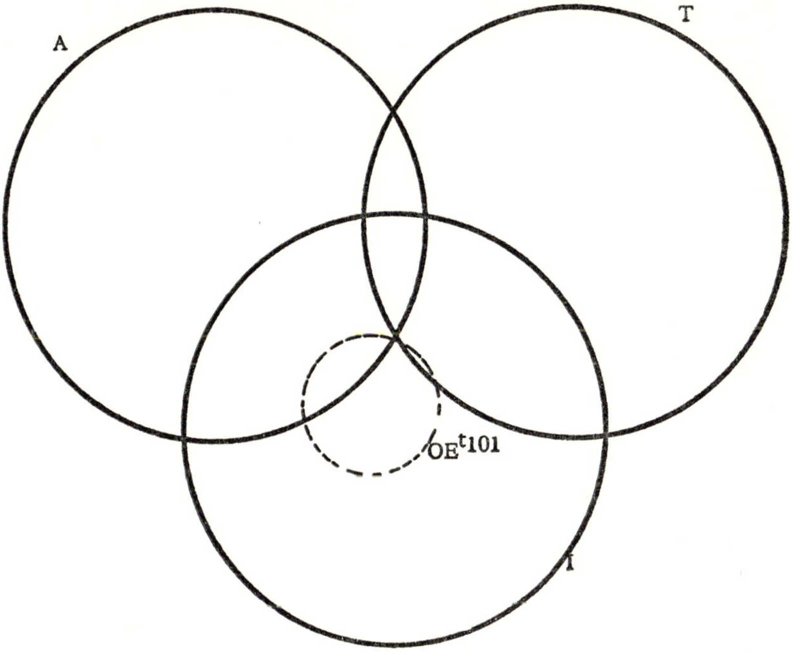

Legends as before. t_{101} indicates the 101st hour of the analysis.

used, that for such an interpretation to hit the mark it must also be topographically correct. A story which was told by the late Géza Róheim will bring this out.

In a remote island, a famous anthropologist sat reading a copy of Totem and Taboo, just sent him from Europe, learning to his amazement that 'every man wants to have sexual intercourse with his mother'. An exciting idea that demanded validation! So, clapping his hands he shouted to the nearest tribesman saying (in approximate translation), 'Hey boy! Do you want to consummate the sexual act with your mother?' The man's face broke into a grin and he laughed and answered, 'Oh no! She's too old.' Here we have a dynamic interpretation that somehow missed fire because of a mistake about topography. Freud had placed the œdipus complex in the set I; the anthropologist unwittingly and the Pacific islander wittingly had placed it in set A, and so the interpretation failed. Though it was dynamically correct, as understood and given it was topographically wrong. The story illustrates how false topography, falling in the general category of displacement, may be used as a defense and a resistance.

The practicing analyst knows many comparable situations from experience. The sophisticated student-psychiatrist is not shocked any more by the idea of unconscious incestuous and parricidal wishes, but he may blanch and tremble when he knocks over his analyst's ash tray, for that little 'transference acting-out' has intensity and a correlated sense of reality. Many persons thus discover in their analysis the proper topography of their unconscious wishes.

To return to the S subset, that of the student and school, let us suppose a resistance arises in the course of a training analysis. A student-analysand, with no previous difficulty of this kind, one day finds himself unable to understand any interpretation his analyst gives him. To enter for the moment the territory of clinical nosological terminology, he has developed a pseudo imbecility. The infantile roots for this are discovered and so are the transference purposes. Still, nothing changes. Then somehow he comes upon the idea that he has just started his first course of lectures in the psychoanalytic institute and that he is repeating some of his early experiences in elementary school—in other words, he has a school problem. He has made a topographic discovery. He has located the symptom. The 'associations' represented by it are, he sees, in the subset S and in the part of A that is intersected by the sets I and T.

Suppose that the analyst had not understood the resistance and had come up with the idea that this was simply a stupid fellow, and suppose that the same idea occurred to the student's supervisors and other teachers. They would then have misplaced the phenomena topographically. The stupidity would have been located in A, not specifically in S, and perhaps only after the analysand had ceased to be a student would he find that his intellectual inhibition was a result of its location. A subsequent analysis undertaken outside the school environment would be free of the annoying resistance. Experiences of this sort have been reported by Gitelson (1954). An analysand's statement was that his first analysis was used

Figure 5. Types of Dream Associations.

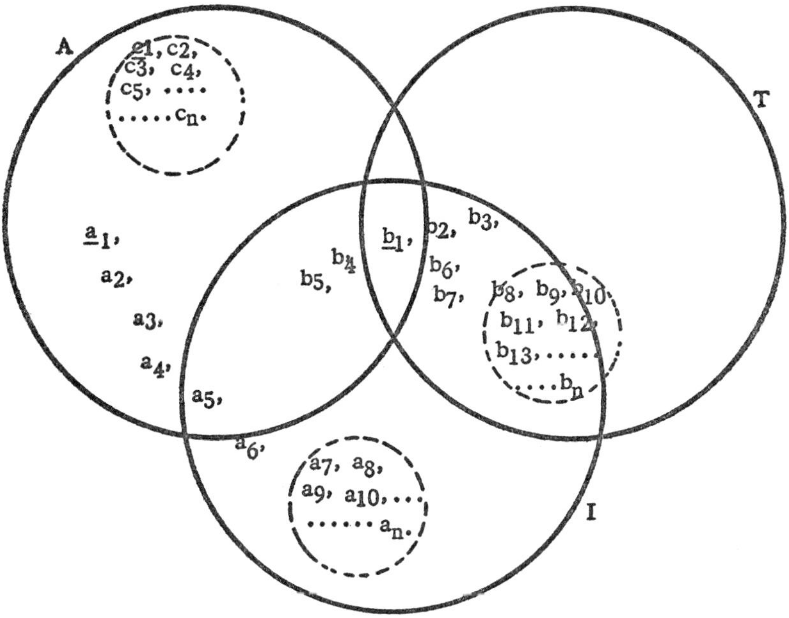

Elements of all three subsets are associations. In subset a, associations start from a recent element, in b from an 'intense' element, in c the associations remain in the 'from above' category.

Small broken circles at the end of the train of associations represent (. . . a_n) an infantile complex, (. . . b_n) a transference fantasy, (. . . c_n) a theme near waking thoughts, like Kekulé's dream and the benzene-ring associations.

to 'get him through school', while the postgraduate analysis was for himself.

The circumscription of one part of the analytic situation as subset S, school situation, has a suggestive value, for it reminds us of many constant and particular things that we know about schools and school problems: reaction to school routines, to classrooms and classmates, to tests and examinations, etc. A particular feature of the psychoanalytic school situation is the heaping onto it of all blame for the long educational careers of present-day students.

The diagram also suggests that there may be other standard subset situations which can be systematically defined and studied intensively. Dr. Isakower, examining the diagrams, remarked that the situation of the low-fee clinic patient, which includes relatively specific features, would also be representable by a subset. It is indeed well known that Freud's advice concerning certain arrangements between analyst and patient referred to private practice and are difficult to establish when patients come through a clinic. The knowledge that they are low-fee patients, that their analysts are students and are 'being supervised', and the various effects of this social and economic position are relatively constant elements. Not recognized as such topographically, they can be misunderstood.

Figure 5 uses the three-circle or so-called Venn's diagram not for the analytic situation but for the representation of dream interpretation. During analysis, dream associations too arise either from A, T, or I. Indeed, as I remarked, it is probable that Rank and Ferenczi divided the analytic situation as they did by analogy with the dream.

Let us then call the diagram dream associations (not the manifest content!) and use it to illustrate Freud's advice concerning the analysis of dreams during analysis (Figure 5). He tells us one way to start is to select an element in the manifest content which is clearly connected with an event of the previous day or to ask the analysand to choose one of this sort as a starting point for his associations. In this case we should obtain the series $\underline{a}$ in Figure 5. The first association $\underline{a}_1$ is chosen because it is in the actual situation. Those that follow in the diagram, a_2, a_3, . . . , a_n, are (arbitrarily) shown as leading to an infantile 'complex', where there should be many related associations. The $\underline{a}$'s form a subset, since they can be systematically defined as the 'associations that begin with $\underline{a}_1$'.

Another piece of advice given by Freud is to start the train of free associations from an element in the manifest content which is intense or striking, such as the most vivid element in the dream. This intensity is regarded as a sign of an accumulation of cathexis on the element; in other words, one may assume that the (manifest-dream) element is a condensation linked with memory traces from various parts of the psychic apparatus. In the diagram, this is shown as a series of associations leading off from $\underline{b}_1$. Here in a way, 'Rank's assumption' comes into its own in a special application, for it is assumed for the elements in the conjoint intersection of all three sets, A, T, and I, that they have acquired the cathexis from all three situations. Hence, each element, like $\underline{b}_1$, of the three-way intersection are 'Rankian' and stand for ideas in three sets. The diagram therefore shows the subsequent associations, $b_2, b_3, \ldots, b_n$, as radiating from the first manifest element $\underline{b}_1$ in three directions. After the train of thought goes out a certain way, the original $\underline{b}_1$ is picked up again and a new train is started.

The $\underline{c}$ associations belong to the thoughts which occur when one is associating in a way Freud characterized by the words *'von oben'*. The starting point c_1 is an element in the manifest dream content, but all the associations $c_2, c_3, \ldots, c_n$, are of the kind which have been called anagogic. The associations do not go deeply into the individual's life; they use the dream text as if it were a fable from which to draw a lesson. In this ancient tradition dreams are treated as messages or revelations. Freud has remarked that when dreams make this kind of sense they consist of ideas which the dreamer might just as well have entertained while he was awake for they are very near to consciousness. The dreams of Descartes, Kekulé, and Otto Loewi are also in this category.[1]

A more experienced mathematician might, I think, make more profound use of the diagrammatic method of presentation, might for example see other inferences to be made from the representation of other empirically grounded phenomena and procedures. A diagram can often be applied unexpectedly to phenomena for which it was not specifically constructed.

I should like to say a good word for the idea of 'systematic definition'. For me, this places such concepts as the student situation or the clinic-patient situation at a certain level of abstraction, one very near the empirical and pragmatic, and suggests that others of a like nature will be found that are worth systematizing and defining. It is also interesting that just as these can be considered subsets of the actual situation, with important technical intersections, so the obsoles-

[1] See, *Dreams and the Uses of Regression,* pp. 329-352 [Ed.].

cent idea of 'complex' may be represented as a subset of the infantile situation. Again, it is possible that the idea of intensity, so far as this depends on displacement and condensation (topographic ideas), may be representable graphically in terms of intersections common to several sets. Chains of associations such as those represented in the series a, b, c of Figure 5 suggest that other phenomena in the analytic process or analytic theory may yield to ideas concerning ordered sets. Though such diagrams as these are static, once 'time' is taken into account a number of time-ordered serial sections come to approximate a dynamic continuum.

Meanwhile, this sort of mathematical presentation seems to me to have, besides entertainment, considerable value as a teaching device and as a semantic and conceptual clarifier.

THE PURSUIT OF KNOWLEDGE AND THE NATURE OF THE MIND

It is noteworthy that this section, dedicated to the pursuit of knowledge and the nature of the mind, contains contributions from every decade of Lewin's professional career. This was perhaps his basic interest. However, one thing remains clear: Lewin was always an analyst first and a philosopher second. His philosophical observations were made primarily from the vantage point of psychoanalysis. This is explicit in the first four papers which comprise this section: the observations are clinical, tentative, and circumscribed. The last contributions in this section probably reflect the finest examples of Lewin's thought. In these papers he is at his imaginative best, integrating his vast erudition from many fields and synthesizing all these elements with what he learned from years of clinical investigation.

That Lewin should be attracted to Descartes was natural and predictable. Many analysts have been attracted to Descartes's introspective ruminations, particularly because of Descartes's fascination with dreams and altered states of consciousness. It would seem however, that there was an additional factor in Descartes's writings which aroused sympathetic resonance in Lewin's mind. Descartes's *res cogitans,* an internalized observer residing in the pineal body and passing judgment on the passing scene, is a philosophical concretization of Lewin's 'erudite nursling' retrotransposed to become the homunculus in the claustrum. The idea of the homunculus in the claustrum appears not only in *Dreams and the Uses of Regression* but in all the subsequent papers which deal with models of memory or the mind: memories are stored within the cavern of the mind like pictures on the walls of a claustrum which an internalized observer may study at his leisure. And in the paper, *Metaphor, Mind, and Manikin,* Lewin comments on several theories of the mind, organizing his observations on how the metaphors used in philosophy and science are based on the fantasy of a minuscule homunculus busily fulfilling the intellectual purposes of its creator in some variant of the claustrum.

J. A. A.

I. CONSCIENCE AND CONSCIOUSNESS IN MEDICAL PSYCHOLOGY—A HISTORICAL STUDY*

In twelfth century French one finds the word *conscience* used in its ethical sense: conscience, consciousness of guilt. This word was introduced into middle English where it completely superseded the older Anglo-Saxon *inwit* (*cf.*, German *'Innewissen'*). What *inwit* signified is not entirely clear. It is generally thought that the word stood for both 'conscience' and 'consciousness'. It is certain that little distinction was made between these two ideas. According to Harzfeld and Darmsteter, the French word *conscience* originally signified only conscience in the present-day English sense of the term, and in the other sense *'la connaissance immédiate et directe que l'âme a d'elle-même'*, is only to be found since Malebranche (d. 1715). In English, too, we find this same ambiguity up to the time of John Locke. It was he who in 1678 first defined *consciousness* as the 'perception of what passes in a Man's own mind', and who in 1690 first used the form *conscious,* stating that it meant 'having internal perceptions of one's own sensations, feelings, thoughts, etc.'. Since this time, that is, about the end of the seventeenth century, the two concepts, conscience and consciousness, have been quite distinctly separate. In German, the word *Bewusstsein* has had a not dissimilar history. It is to be found in Luther's translation of the Bible, where it means consciousness of guilt, or conscience. In its present meaning (consciousness), according to the philologist Weigandt, it was first used by Christian Wolff in the year 1720. Grimm in his dictionary merely states: *'Erst im achtzehnten Jahrhundert gebildet und häufig gebraucht'*. ('First invented and frequently used in the eighteenth century.')

* [No. 4 in Bibliography.]
Read before the Berlin Psychoanalytic Society, January 4, 1927.

From this etymological discussion one point emerges clearly: the concept of consciousness evolved from the concept of conscience. Consciousness was at first a sort of secularized conscience. Up to about 1700, introspection was employed to examine the state of one's conscience, only later the state of one's consciousness. The germ of the rationalistic concept of consciousness was the moral theological concept of conscience. It was not accidental that the words *consciousness* and *Bewusstsein* appeared just when they did. For their appearance coincided with the flourishing of the great rationalizing French and English thinkers who were trying to liberate human thought from scholasticism and ancient authority. To put the matter briefly, in order that the psyche should be studied at all, the soul had, in part at least, to be taken from the clerics; as one should judge from Descartes's and Hobbes's difficulties when they were suspected of insufficient faith in Bible stories; and for that matter, the events in Dayton, Tennessee, in 1926, point the same moral. Therefore, 'conscience' was left to the priests and the moral philosophers; science took over 'consciousness', and relinquished its interest in conscience and the soul. Whereas in French and German, *l'âme* and *die Seele* still mean both soul *and* mind, our English usage shows quite clearly the effect of the division of territory between science and theology. Theology is concerned with the *soul,* science with the *mind,* indeed perhaps more usually with *consciousness.*

The physicians of the late seventeenth and of the eighteenth centuries, whose training took place in this atmosphere, could not remain impervious to it. It is interesting to note its manifestations in the medical, especially the psychiatric, literature of the period. One finds there that this 'consciousness epoch' is one with virile points of view. The ordinary component impulses are not mentioned. The sexual aberrations which the physicians wish to discuss are satyriasis and nymphomania, the 'popular' abnormalities, one might say, in the literary discussion of these two centuries. Onanism was regarded by all simply as a sin and as the source of all manner of disabilities ranging from anorexia to *tabes dorsalis* and epilepsy. Perhaps the most extreme views ever put forth on this subject are to be found in a book belonging to this period, Tissot's

De l'onanisme (1750). De Sauvages (1768) hardly ever uses the word *mastupratio* without adding '*Infamum vitium*'. Impotence, on the other hand, is treated very painstakingly, indeed sympathetically, by the same authors.

I should like to suggest that there is a relation between the ruling psychology and this attitude toward sexuality. A rationalistic consciousness psychology, as we well know, leads those who uphold it to deny in themselves all that is unconscious, and to emphasize and overvalue the importance of that which can be found in consciousness. In these rationalizing years we have been discussing, the genital impulses were found in consciousness, and overemphasized. This can be seen not only in the field of medical literature. It is also true of general literature. This was the time of Casanova, Restif de la Bretonne, and Tom Jones. It was not the time of Rabelais or Proust.

Until about the end of the eighteenth century, it is hardly possible to speak of psychiatry as an independent branch of medicine. Mental diseases or disease symptoms, for little distinction was made between disease and symptom, were regarded by physicians from the same point of view as any other disease or symptom and usually treated with the same *materia medica,* although particularly in England there were to be found a few good psychologically minded physicians. In Germany the mentally ill were generally turned over to clergymen. Kant indeed went so far as to deny that physicians were in a position to pass judgment on mental disorder. He maintained that this was the province of the philosophy faculty. (The problem of lay therapy is not so new as it might appear.)

About the beginning of the nineteenth century there arose an independent psychiatry. It teetered then, as it still does, between medicine and philosophy. Arnold classified mental disorders according to Locke's 'faculties'; and Pinel named his book *Traité médico-philosophique,* etc., and quoted extensively from Locke and Condorcet. In general it might be said, there were three standpoints: first, the *practical* standpoint of institutional care, represented chiefly by English physicians; second, the *somatic* standpoint of the French (Pinel, Bayle, Esquirol); and third, the *moral-psychological* standpoint. This latter flourished among the adherents of an important German school. These three standpoints were, to be sure, not sharply limited each to one nation, for in all countries there were representatives of all three tendencies. In Germany there were not only the '*Psychiker*' as they called themselves, but also the '*Somatiker*'.

Members of the German somatic school, Nasse, Jacobi, Friedreich, and others, sought for the cause of all mental illness in the body. Jacobi, indeed, found definite causes in definite organs, and spoke, for example, of a special stomach-psychosis, liver-psychosis, etc. In opposition to this school stood the '*Psychiker*' ('the psychological physicians'), Beneke, Heinroth, Ideler and others. The most important of these was Heinroth. As we have seen, the concept of consciousness had originally been derived from the concepts of conscience. It had been found, so to speak, in moral philosophy (ethics), borrowed, secularized, and rationalized. Now the '*Psychiker*' returned to the original source once again: they reintroduced into psychological medicine the old concept of conscience in its original form.

To elaborate the different views of the various members of this school would not be fruitful. It is, however, worth while going into the psychological and etiological theories held by Heinroth in some detail; particularly because of numerous unmistakable analogies and similarities between them and recent psychoanalytic doctrines.

These theories are set forth in Heinroth's *Lehrbuch der Störungen des Seelenliebens* published in 1818, and written during his professorship at Leipzig. He begins with a psychological presentation: he constructs a theory of the ego. Consciousness is peculiar to man; it distinguishes him from plants and animals. But consciousness is not ultimate and unanalyzable; there are three levels of consciousness. To quote: 'On the lowest level of consciousness, and consequently of humanity, stands the child, savage man, savage peoples. This consciousness is one of externals alone—world consciousness. Man on this level is himself still merely world, merely external, merely an object. He is entirely sense and sensory being; his feelings, sentiments, and impulses still belong to the outer world, which according to whether it meets man in the making as a friend or an enemy, fills him with pleasure or pain.

Enjoyment is his aim, chance his ruling destiny.' It is hardly necessary to point out the similarity of this description with the usual psychoanalytic account of infantile development (the rule of the pleasure principle).

'Man attains the second level of consciousness as soon as the general development and manifold activities of the senses awaken the intelligence, and impressions become clarified into concepts. . . . In opposition to the world consciousness there is formed a self-consciousness . . . and this single indivisible whole [is] the ego. Thus is man an *Individual.*' So, at this level the reality principle makes its appearance, and the ego becomes more tightly organized and unified.

'Only in a few does consciousness reach its last highest level. . . . Just as the self-consciousness arose from an opposition (*Entgegensetzung*) of the inward and the outward, similarly the highest consciousness arises through an inner opposition in the self-consciousness.' Note here the similarity in the idea of *Entgegensetzung* and the freudian *Gegenbesetzung*. Note also how Heinroth assumes that conflict within the ego is the source of a splitting with the production of an inhibitory '*entgegengesetzte*' part.

'All of us experience this opposition quite early in our childhood. Against the ego and its strivings there arises within the boundaries of the self-conscious being a resistance (*Widerspruch*), which though in the ego is yet not of the ego, but comes from a higher activity which enters the ego, and which we usually call conscience.' This conscience appears as an opponent of our 'world life and our self life'. It demands that the ego make sacrifices. But the sacrifices are only 'a stake used to bring in a higher return', and if we are once 'inclined to the higher, the lower means nothing to us. . . . This higher, however, which we do not find outside us in the world, nor yet within us in our own self-ego (*selbstisches Ich*), is of necessity a *super-us* (*ein Ueberuns*) which makes itself known to us in conscience and through the conscience, so that this . . . finally occupies this consciousness completely, and in this way repressing (*verdrängend*) all lower consciousness, becomes a new especial consciousness, and no longer appears in us as something alien, as conscience. . . .' This highest consciousness is reason (*Vernunft*). 'Through our reason we apprehend the higher, the super-us.'

The striking comparison need not be elaborated: Heinroth's third level, the 'super-us', is that consciousness which represses the lower ones; it is something introjected, and represents the standpoint of training and morality. Heinroth then describes a faculty which has much in common, even in terminology, with the analytic ego ideal or superego.

To say that Heinroth had constructed a libido theory also would be exaggerating. Yet there were analogies to a libido theory in his ideas as to the origin of mental disorders. He does not, to be sure, speak of the libido, but he asserts that mental disorders arise from sin and vice, from a surrender of the soul to evil. The soul (or mind, if one wishes—*die Seele*) is originally free; only through sin does it lose its freedom. The word *Unfreyheit* (lack of freedom) he uses quite freely as a synonym for *Insania* or *Vecordia,* that is, mental illness. Now if we read instead of 'sin', 'forbidden desires', and for 'lack of freedom', 'control by repressed tendencies', we should not perhaps be very far from his meaning. That a 'super-us' through overseverity might also bring about 'lack of freedom' remained far from Heinroth's moralistic mind.

Heinroth finds confirmatory evidence of his idea that 'with a falling away from God, there can be only mental disorder' everywhere. In all his cases he sees the result of crime and vice. Even though admitting that in some few cases external factors, such as fright, worry, etc., may have produced a mental disorder, he nevertheless sticks to his theory: these individuals were 'already morally corrupt'. The sole prophylaxis against mental disease is the Christian faith.

For several reasons this school of psychiatry declined, and temporarily at any rate the victory went to the '*Somatiker*'. In the first place, the psychologic attitude was too moralistic, too stern for a sinful world—it was overdone. Secondly, as we have noted, psychiatry was vacillating between philosophy and medicine, and the new medical developments of the nineteenth century (with men like Louis, Laennec, and others) were so fruitful that psychiatry naturally turned for aid in this direction; more and more mental disorders came to be regarded as of the same order as infectious diseases, or any other disease in internal medicine. Only recently have we seen the beginning of a decline of the pure 'somatic' school.

II. SOME OBSERVATIONS ON KNOWLEDGE, BELIEF AND THE IMPULSE TO KNOW*

The problem of knowledge and belief, which has exercised so many philosophical minds, comes to our psychoanalytical attention in a very homely way. For we find that some of our patients know without believing or believe without knowing, and the task devolves upon us of eliminating the tension between these two processes. Fortunately, we are not limited in our attack on the problem to abstract considerations, but have several points of support well known to us from daily clinical practice. For one, we know that a sense of omniscience is to be considered in general as part of the native endowment of every baby, a part of his narcissistic birthright. For another starting point, we have the investigatory impulse, which, particularly in its sexual manifestations, has been much studied and which can be traced back to an early age. The extraordinary proliferation which manifestations of this impulse attain in certain obsessional cases is well known. Less attention has been paid to its manifestations in other types of neurosis, though they have been noted.

A certain aspect of the impulse to learn and its relationship to repression was particularly lucid in a hysterical case. The patient, a woman in her middle thirties, the only child of a Western ranch owner, spent her early childhood playing with the children of her father's laborers, learning a great many things about sexuality, adult and infantile. She was early aware of her father's anatomical make-up and was able to draw inferences as to coitus from certain impressions acquired on the sleeping porch she shared with her parents. For the first six years of her life her investigations into sex were unhampered and her conclusions on the whole correct. In this

* [No. 28 in Bibliography.]

investigation she was naïve, natural, and unconcerned. One fact came to be shut off from her, and that through a traumatic event—the structure of her genitalia. Her natural bent for research suggested to her that she should find out for herself what her vulva was like and to that end she inserted a finger between her labia. At this point her father walked in and told her sternly that she must never 'do that' again. It is literally true that she obeyed him for over thirty years. She turned her curiosity into a field approved of by her parents; they had told her about the sex life of flowers and birds in the conventional way, and she seriously followed this cue, becoming unusually well informed as to wild life. She began botanical and zoological collections and took great pleasure in tramping through the woods. But in spite of these interests and satisfactions, she was in the position of a hearty eater put on a bulky reducing diet; she was not finding out the right thing in the right way. Sexuality and knowledge remained linked, and in her teens she appropriately turned to a teacher to remove her father's injunction, or as she thought, to be enlightened. This man understood her, and to enlighten her, along with his explanations, produced an orgasm by manipulating her genitalia. She chose a calling which would bring her into contact with human sexual facts, and on several occasions tried to 'find out' by going to bed with a man, but, with great anxiety, stopped the sexual proceedings at the point of penetration.

Her type of resistance was correlated with the structure of her neurosis. Consciously very amiable and amenable, she responded readily to interpretations of her sexual wishes, participating intellectually in the interpretative work; but then to her astonishment she would bring in a dream full of botany and birdlore which completely took back statements of the day before on which the sexual interpretation was based.

Another young woman, also a hysteric, came to analysis under the impression that in a week or so a very knotty current problem would be thoroughly solved. She believed herself a very conscious person, who understood people very well, and that a simple explanation of one or two incompletely understood points would clear everything up. Her reaction to an interpretation was essentially that now her self-knowledge was perfect and that she need not come any more. Her first shock came when she was told that she was not a good psychologist with respect to a certain person. Her subjective sense of knowing practically all about herself and other people did not in fact correspond with the objective situation, for she misunderstood her parents, her brothers and sisters, her husband and children, and particularly her relationship to them. It was as though she lived in an epistemological enclosure, where everything was known and understood, and a novel idea simply meant a slight enlargement of the fence.

This subjective sense of psychological omniscience was linked to her analytical resistance to knowing. Her sexual experiences in fact went back to her third year. Yet, when she began her analysis, she dated her first sexual information from some instructional talks given her in her thirteenth year by her mother. She had indeed repressed her infantile knowledge and with the repression had felt a lack, a gap. To offset this feeling she became a voracious reader of girls' books and modeled herself on the good girls she read of there. Somewhat older, she turned to romantic novels. Blocked by repression in her epistemology, she developed as it were successively an ethic, and then a psychology, as a guide to life. For she formulated her psychology in terms of the heroine of a romantic novel, and opposed the analyst's interpretations with formulations derived from this source. She was a most insistent questioner, posing questions in the main that were unanswerable and which were designed to divert the analyst. She wanted an answer but was satisfied with any kind at all, as a child is satisfied with a nominal answer: 'What makes the sky blue?' 'It's the blueness.' On the analyst's refusal to give her an immediate answer to every question her pain was intense. For, it became evident, these 'answers' were really not answers but magical material to repair the fence where she felt a threatened breach in her omniscience. The analyst, she thought, like the philosopher in the poem, '*stopft die Lücken des Himmelblaus*' ('fills up the holes in the sky'). That our discussions of knowledge, ignorance, intactness, and defect showed that knowledge was phallic, ignorance a symbol of castration, was not in itself unusual. If knowledge is power, she jokingly remarked once, ignorance is bliss. But apart from the castration complex aspect, it was evident that, in this patient, repression had produced a sense of limitation of knowledge, which was perceived as a narcissistic weakness, which in turn had to be compensated for and reduced more or less magically. Her reading and naïve philosophizing as well as her questioning were magical methods of recovering her sense of narcissistic unity and omniscience.

Other artifices devised to overcome a painful sense of ignorance will occur to analytic readers. As in many other fields, Ernest Jones here too is a pioneer. Under the title, Simulated Foolishness in Hysteria, Jones (1910) vividly describes the child's behavior when he is disturbed by an imperfection in his knowledge. 'When a mother chats with her intimate friends over various private topics, frequently the child will resort to the strangest devices in order to stay in the room and listen to the conversation. Then when someone remarks him, and by her look insinuates a doubt as to the propriety of conversing in his presence, he will interrupt his innocent crooning over his toys and indulge in exaggeratedly foolish antics, to disarm, as it were, the suspicions of the company by convincing them of his thorough simple-mindedness and innocence.'

A young man of the obsessive type strove to recapture his sense of omniscience in a different way. His mother's pregnancy and the events centering around the subsequent birth of a sister were early subjected to profound repression. To offset the ignorance which in this case he definitely enjoined on himself, he decreed himself a fantastic omniscience. This affected his work in school and his later career, to the extent that he found it hard to accept the fact that others might be superior to him in knowledge. A good memory enabled him to comply with the demands of his educators, but he was contemptuous of them and preserved a sense of secret superiority, believing them only when he could reformulate their teachings. He became a typical hypochondriac with more medical information than a doctor, a theoretical economist unable to cope with his simple accounts. In his analysis, he would ostensibly ignore an interpretation, or 'improve' it, assuming an air of having learned something, adding his comments and corrections and remaining unconvinced. Though he was in no way averse to theorizing, he often charged the analyst with doing so. This charge was simply enough analyzed: theories of other persons were to him their fantastic inventions, and quite specifically the sort of fantasies he had heard from his elders in regard to sexual matters. The structure of this case was typical and of no importance here; the point to be made here again is the narcissistic defect, the offense taken by the patient at his self-imposed ignorance, and the magical devices he introduced to reinstate a sense of omniscience.

It often happens that a patient divides the world of information roughly into two spheres: a sphere of that which he believes because he has always believed it (i.e., from the child's standpoint, 'what I know'), and a sphere of knowledge that is imparted to him and which he can take or leave (again from the child's standpoint, 'what they tell me'). Patients who are the children of physicians, and who may themselves be physicians, often illustrate this dichotomy by bringing up old-fashioned medical theories in explanation of their neurotic symptoms. One patient of this group, railing against psychoanalysis at home, led his wife to say, 'You sound exactly like your father', which was the correct interpretation.

To summarize what has been presented so far: in many persons a repression is perceived narcissistically as a blow to their omniscience, which they try to repair through real or magical means. It also happens that later any insult to narcissism, whether in the field of knowledge or in other fields, evokes as a response an assertion of omniscience or a setting into play of the investigatory impulse in an attempt to recapture the sense of omniscient perfection. The magical methods used vary; several examples have been given as types.

To leave the topic of knowledge and its relation to learning and omniscience and to consider the topic of belief, we may state immediately that in a certain sense, belief *is* a partial omniscience—a statement we must hasten to clarify. When knowledge obtained from the person's own perceptions or from others failed to produce the conviction of its validity, in the cases studied something was added: a magical approval or amendment, a magical comment, or a magical act, a narcissistic sanction which then endowed the fact with trustworthiness and made it worthy of belief. What was striven for in these mechanisms was obviously a repetition of the sense of narcissistic perfection and omniscience. Even when the father's opinion was brought in to produce the same sense of security, the same essential device was at work, with the familiar shift of originally narcissistic omniscience to the all-knowing parent.

There are certain phenomena known to us from analysis which will tend to clarify the notion that belief is a partial omniscience. Besides the examples of belief, given above, which stood in relation to facts or learned ideas, there is another type which does not depend on learning or evidence, but which is immediate. Of this type is the phenomenon of *déjà vu*. This is a sense of familiarity with an event which takes the subjective form, 'I have seen or done this before', which, as is well known, Freud explains by saying that the person has in some sense really seen or done this, that he is repeating an element of some earlier situation. From this, it should follow that the element of belief which appears in the experience is itself a repetition: viz., a repetition of an early confidence in one's perceptions, a justification of an original sense of omniscience. Another example of immediate belief is to be found in analytic work when the patient recaptures an infantile memory. His conviction when this occurs is striking. Whether he is surprised or whether he alleges he must always have known the fact in question, his certainty as to its reality is always beyond question or need of evidence: he believes. This belief itself would represent the repetition of an element in the original situation, for clearly if a memory is regained, repression has been lifted, the damage done to the sense of omniscience has been repaired. The belief, then, which is an accompaniment to or part of the memory is a repetition of the feeling of conviction or belief that was an element in the original sense of omniscience which was present before the repression. With the remembered infantile experience the patient regains a part of his infantile omniscience, and this is registered as 'belief'.

Apart from analytic experience, it is quite probable that such phrases as 'all men hold these truths to be self-evident', or philosophical systems of knowledge which begin with an appeal to the self-evident, or those which predicate a surer and higher nonempirical knowledge, owe their emotional appeal to their harmony with the unconscious trust in the original narcissistically orientated conviction that everything is known and that what is true is self-evident. Somewhat differently, an 'intuition' brings with it an indisputable and immediate belief. It is known that such intuitions can often be traced to unconscious mentation and that their emergence is the equivalent of an instinctual release. In fact, intuitions, inspirations, and the like are not infrequently attributed to a 'daemon', a 'genius', and in this sense the feeling of their evidential value rests on a repetitive omniscience.

III. THE NATURE OF REALITY, THE MEANING OF NOTHING, WITH AN ADDENDUM ON CONCENTRATION*

Reality

Freud (1900-1901, pp. 372-373) states that if a sense of reality accompanies a dream, analysis will show that one or more latent thoughts in it do in fact refer to something real. As an example, he cites a dream accompanied by a sense of reality, in which two pears that the dreamer is given represent the maternal breasts, which the dreamer had once indeed received. The quality of realness in the dream indicates the reality present in the original situation.

One of my patients had a strong castration complex which prevented him from looking at a nude woman. Discussing reality, not in a dream but more abstractly, he lamented that he had never been able to see it starkly. 'I have never faced reality', he said sadly, 'I haven't faced reality since the day I was born'. This equation of reality with the mother's genital differs from the one cited by Freud. However, there are many attitudes to reality, according to whether it is faced optimistically or pessimistically. Proverbially, the optimist sees the doughnut, the pessimist sees the hole.

So far as I have noted, the idea 'reality', as it appears in free associations, stands for the female genitalia. I have been correct in anticipating remarks about the female genital following a patient's expression of thoughts about reality. It occurred to me to check up on some of the literature and see what others have recorded. The Wolf-man's famous dream (Freud, 1918 [1914]) left him with a strong sense of reality. Among the real things referred to was the real aspect of the vagina. In Ruth Mack Brunswick's (1928a) paper on paranoid

* [No. 72 in Bibliography.]

jealousy two pages are devoted to two dreams that had an intense sense of reality. The first dream depicts the patient, a woman, in bed with a woman; the patient is instructed to hold the woman's labia open with one hand and rub the clitoris with the other. The patient has an intense orgasm in the dream and awakes with a feeling of absolute reality; in fact, she examines her own genital with her hand, finds that she is menstruating and wearing a napkin, and only this convinces her that she was dreaming. The second dream, in which reality also appears, is only slightly different: the patient is masturbating her sister, who has an orgasm, and the patient awakes to find her husband's penis in her hand.

As the free association, 'reality', usually refers to the real female genital, so remarks about 'illusion' signify latent ideas about the imaginary one which, as is well known, Rado (1933a) has called the 'illusory' penis. The words, 'vagueness' and 'confusion' have the same reference; for reasons sufficient to the patient, the female genital is a vagueness, a confusion. 'In my confusion', said one, 'I found something concrete', referring to the clitoris.

I do not know to what extent unconscious associations of this sort have affected philosophers' ideas on the nature of reality. I note in one instance, however, that a philosopher chides authorities he has read for giving him a false impression, as if anatomic charts had led him to false anticipations. He says: 'They have substituted economical and orderly conceptions for the first sensible tangle; and whether they were morally or only intellectually neat, they were at any rate always æsthetically pure and definite, and aimed at ascribing to the world something clean and intellectual in the way of inner structure'. The view he professes 'offers but a sorry appearance'. 'It is a turbid, muddled, Gothic sort of affair, without a sweeping outline, and with little pictorial solidity. Those of you who are accustomed to the classical construction of reality may be excused if your first reaction upon it be absolute contempt. . . . But one must have lived some time with a system to appreciate its merits. Perhaps a little more familiarity may mitigate your first surprise at such a programme as I offer.'

Nothing

For the association 'I am thinking of nothing', the interpretation is the same. The phrase is soon followed by allusions to the female genital. One of my patients was pleased with this interpretation, which struck his sense of humor. One day he began his analytic hour by telling me, 'Well, doctor, I've been thinking of nothing all day'.

Concentration

The common remark, 'I cannot concentrate', refers not to the stream of thought, but to the urinary flow, which in women (and in male incontinence) is not concentrated. After numerous instances of this reference in my practice, I ventured to guess at a Technical Seminar that a girl complaining of lack of concentration had a urethral story to tell. The student confirmed this by informing us that she had enuresis.

IV. A PSYCHOANALYTIC NOTATION ON THE ROOT *GN, KN, CN**

WITH HENRY ALDEN BUNKER, M.D.

In an unpublished paper on the Feast of Tantalus, one of us[1] has recounted a tale of the Modoc Indians of western Oregon with reference to its rather striking resemblance to the well-known Greek myth of the (second) birth of Dionysus from the thigh of Zeus[2]—each of these tales, along with its more recondite version in the form of the myth retailed by Pindar of the Feast of Tantalus, representing the narrative form of that which is acted out in innumerable puberty rites or initiation ceremonies,[3] namely, the *second* birth of the child from the *father*—symbolizing the severance of even more the preœdipal[4] than the œdipal ties to the mother, and the 'rebirth' of the neophyte into equality with and the fellowship of the men of the tribe.[5]

Now, in the Modoc myth this rebirth of the child from the father takes place not from the belly of Durumulun, not from the thigh of Zeus, but from the knee of the god Kumush. But if in this Modoc myth it is the knee which is the 'male womb', the question arises, when the facts are taken into account, whether this equation which is directly verbalized in the Indian tale does not find its implied but precise counterpart in the philology of the Indogermanic group of languages. In other words, can it be mere coincidence, rife though this is in the deceptive field of language, that the word for *knee* in a number of members of this language group—Greek γόνυ, Latin *genu,*

* [No. 92 in Bibliography.]

1 *See,* Bunker, Henry Alden: *The Feast of Tantalus.* Psa. Quart., XXI, 1952, pp. 355-372 [Ed.].

2 H. J. Rose (*Dionysiaca,* in Aberystwyth Studies, IV:19, 1922) was the first to call attention to this similarity.

3 See Jane Ellen Harrison (*Themis,* 2nd ed.; Cambridge, 1927, p. 328): 'The myth . . . is the spoken correlative of the acted rite; the thing done; it is Τὸ λεγόμενον as contrasted with or rather as related to Τὸ δρώμενον.'

4 *Cf.,* Róheim (1942), *Transition Rites.*

5 See in particular Theodor Reik (1931), *Ritual: Psychoanalytic Studies.*

Sanskrit *jānu;* and, for that matter, by a slight and familiar change, the English *knee,* German *Knie,* Anglo-Saxon *cneō,* Gothic *Kniv*—should seem to contain the same root, GN (KN), as occurs in *generation,* begetting, the same root as is found in the Sanskrit *jan,* to beget, the Greek γένος, race, γίγνομαι, I am born; the Latin *gi-gn-ere,* to beget, *gnascor,* I am born, *genus,* kin; Gothic *kun-i,* kin? Though we expose ourselves to the scorn of professional philologists, we are beguiled by the notion that the (unconscious) concept of the knee as a 'begetter', as a womb, which appears in the manifest content of the Modoc myth, is strikingly paralleled in the latent content, as it were, of the philology of the Indogermanic languages, in that the root GN (KN) appears both in the various words for 'knee' and in the various words having to do with begetting, generating, creating. This might still be coincidence, and professional philologists might still call it so; but, to us, it seems once and for all to be removed from that category by the Modoc myth, in which the knee *is* the womb. (Purely by the way, there is a Greek phrase which might be thought of as referring, if ever so indirectly, to such an equating of 'knee' with 'womb': a development or outcome in the unknown future is said to 'lie in the knees of the gods' [θεῶν ἐν γούνασι κεῖται, *Iliad,* XVII:514], as we sometimes say 'in the womb of Time' or 'in the bosom of the gods' or even 'in the lap of the gods'. Equally parenthetically might be mentioned the male analysand who, in a dream of an obvious sexual attack upon him, was shot in the knee.)

As far as the womb, indeed, is concerned, this same root GN (KN) is found, in a number of languages, in the word for the possessor of the womb. Most familiar of these words for 'woman' is of course the Greek γυνή. There is also the Sanskrit (in compounds)—*jāni,* wife (*cf.,* the Sanskirt *jan,* to beget, and, if you like, the Sanskrit *jānu,* knee). There is the Anglo-Saxon *cwēn,* and the cognate Icelandic *kvān,* a wife (and modern Swedish *kvinna,* woman); whence Middle English *queen* or *queene,* modern *queen.* But there is also, with a short *e,* the Anglo-Saxon *cwene,* a woman, and the cognate Old High German *quena,* and the Gothic *kwinō,* a woman; whence, the short *e* lengthening in Tudor English into *ea,* the word *quean,* a contemptible woman, a hussy—a word very closely related, if in an opposite direction, so to speak, to *queen,* the original sense being in both cases 'woman'. (Skeat quotes the author of *Piers Plowman* [C. IX:46] as saying that in the grave all are alike; you cannot there tell a knight from a knave, or a *queen* from a *quean.*) As not too remote from the Greek γυνή should perhaps be added the Russian *zhena,* a wife, and the Persian *zan,* a woman.

What follows may perhaps be a digression from our theme, which is, in a word, that the mythological evidence is unequivocal of an (unconscious) equating of the knee with the womb (or at any rate with the 'male womb' of the 'second birth' which at puberty every male child must undergo), but that, besides, this same unconscious concept is implicitly present in the 'structure' of the Indogermanic group of languages, such that the root GN (KN), common to innumerable words denoting or connoting generation or begetting, is also present in various words in these languages meaning 'knee'.

Skeat, in his List of Indogermanic Roots,[6] cites twice over, successively, the root GEN (KEN); between them he does not distinguish in any way except with regard to the philological material which follows each of the two citations. Thus:

> 'GEN (KEN), to generate, produce. Skt. *jan,* to beget; Gk. γέν-ος, race, γίγνομαι, I am born, L. *gi-gn-ere,* to beget, *gen-itor,* father, *gn-ascor,* I am born, *gen-us,* kin; Goth. *kun-i,* kin. Ex. *genesis, endogenous, cosmogony; genus, genius, gentile, benign, cognate, indigenous, natal, native, nature; kin, kind, kindred, kith'*—to which examples might be added, among numerous others, such words as *general, gender, genitive, genital, genuine, ingenious, ingenuous, progeny, gentle, genteel, hydrogen, oxygen, nitrogen,* and so on.
>
> 'GEN (KEN), to know; also gnā, gnō (knā). Skt. *jnā,* to know; Gk. γιγνώσκειν, to know [and note the reduplication, for a reason not known to the present writers, common to γίγνομαι, I am born, and γιγνώσκω, I know], γνω-τός, known; L. *gnō-scere, nō-scere,* to know, *i-gnō-rāre,* not to know, *gnā-rus,* knowing (whence *narrāre,* to tell); Goth. *kann,* I know; AS. *cnā-wan,* to know. Ex. *gnostic, gnomic; ignorant, narrate, noble; can, ken, know, cunning, keen, uncouth.'*

In spite or because of our technical inexperience in this field, we are naïve enough to believe that although they

6 W. W. Skeat, *An Etymological Dictionary of the English Language,* new and revised ed., Oxford, 1910, p. 751. To this monumental and still reasonably definitive work we are indebted for most of the derivations above.

lead in semantically quite different directions (and thus are necessarily listed separately by Skeat), the two roots GN (KN) or GEN (KEN) just noted must fundamentally be the same root. In other words, it seems to us unlikely to be merely a coincidence that the root GEN (KEN), to know, is or appears to be identical with the root GEN (KEN), to generate, to produce, to beget. Is there any evidence, acceptable or not to the philologist, which could be said to throw light on this question?

Our word *know* is the Anglo-Saxon *cnāwan* (Middle English *knowen*), which is cognate with the Icelandic *knā,* I know how to; and these, along with the also cognate Sanskrit *jnā,* the Greek γιγνώσκειν, the Latin *nōscere* (for *gnōscere*), Russian *znate,* to know, are all, according to Skeat, secondary forms from the Indogermanic root GEN, to know; whence also *can, ken, keen,* among others.

Our word *can,* I am able, is the Anglo-Saxon *cunnan,* to know, to know how to do, to be able—cognate with Icelandic *kunna,* to know, to be able; Danish *kunde,* to know, to be able (*cf.,* the German *Heilkunde);* Middle High German *kunnen,* German *können,* to be able (*cf.,* German *kennen,* to know). Thus, in the last analysis, no real distinction exists between to *know* and *to be able;* to know, particularly in the practical and workaday sense of knowing how to, *is* to be able.[7] 'Knowledge is Power', as it were.

If *I know* and *I can* are ultimately indistinguishable, both etymologically and semantically, light from a different direction —a semantic one only—is thrown by Latin. For in Latin the word for *I can, I am able,* is *possum;* and *possum* is a contraction of *potissum,* formed from *potis,* powerful, properly 'lord' or 'master', cognate with Sanskrit *pati-,* a master, owner, governor, lord, husband; the *-pod* in Russian *gospod* (lord) and the *-pot* in *despot;* Lithuanian *patis,* a husband.[8]

[7] It may be appropriate to mention here the familiar fact that *to know* in the more purely intellectual sense is often designated by words referring primarily to the visual—as by our words *see, perceive, discern,* although here the shade of meaning is more immediately of *understanding* than of *knowing.* But in Greek the present tense meaning *I know* is οἶδα, but this is the aorist tense of εἴδω, I see; thus *I know* means *I saw;* 'seeing is believing'. *Kenn-ing* means the range of sight, as far as one can see; and this derives from *ken,* to know (Scandinavian and Scots), Icelandic *kenna,* to know; cognate with the German *kennen,* to know.

[8] Skeat, *op. cit.,* p. 466.

In the foregoing we have made certain assumptions which may on their face appear to be quite arbitrary and without sufficient foundation; we have nevertheless believed them not unjustified in the light of certain facts. In sum: we found the fact that in a certain Indian myth a (second) birth of a male child takes place from the knee of a god, which is thus the 'male womb' of the father (as in other versions of this familiar story). This fact we found arresting when taken in conjunction with the unquestionable fact that in the word *knee* and in a number of its Indogermanic equivalents (e.g., *jānu*, γόνυ, *genu*, and others) there occurs the same pair of consonants (GN, KN, CN) as occurs not only in a number of Indogermanic words meaning or relating to 'woman' (e.g., *-jani*, γυνή, *cwēn*, *kvān*, *queen*, etc.[9]), who is after all possessor of the womb,[10] but also and even more significantly in a large number of words having directly or indirectly to do with begetting, creating, producing, and the like, common to all of which is the Indogermanic root GEN (KEN), to beget, to GENerate. These two facts, the anthropological and the philological, we have taken as complementing each other to mean that unconsciously the knee is somehow thought of as having the same generative capacities, at least under certain circumstances, as the womb.[11]

[9] Why do we slangily refer sometimes to a girl as a 'Jane', instead of using for this slightly derogatory purpose any of the dozens of other girls' names?

[10] We mean this purely literally, and not of course in accordance with the popular fancy that connects *woman* with *womb*, as if the former were really *womb-man*. Actually, *woman* is the Anglo-Saxon *wifman*, literally wife-man, *man* being used, like the Latin *homo*, of both sexes; the successive spellings are *wifman, wimman, wumman, womman, woman* (Skeat, *op. cit.*, p. 721). *Wife*—for those interested in gynæco-etymology—is the Anglo-Saxon *wif*, a woman, a married woman—neuter, like *das Weib* in German; according to Skeat (*op. cit.*, p. 715), its Indogermanic root is WEIP, 'in accordance with which we find OHG. *weibōn, weipōn,* to waver, be irresolute [*"varium et mutabile semper femina"*, shall we say?], L. *vibrare,* to quiver, Skt. *vep,* to tremble; but the real origin of the word remains obscure.'

[11] The question of the choice of unconsciously determined anatomical locus perhaps defies solution; one of us has shown, for example, that in two completely independent myths (Greek and Magyar) the shoulder blade unquestionably represents in each the phallus.

Or, we may discern possible genetic importance in the term 'knee baby', which Bateson and Mead (1942) introduced in their *Balinese Character*. The expression was borrowed by these authors from the mountaineers of the southeastern United States, who use it to refer to the toddler that stands at the mother's knee, while the younger infant is appropriately, from his position, called the 'lap baby'. The suggestion we receive from this designation is that of considering the level, i.e., the altitude, at which these children view the world:

It seemed to us to transcend the intended modesty of these mere *obiter dicta* to attempt any discussion of that large group of words having reference either to *knowing* or to *being able* or to both, to which is common the same pair of consonants (GN, KN, CN) already dwelt upon—underlying which, that is, is the seemingly identical Indogermanic root, separately listed by Skeat, GEN (KEN), to know. Yet when we considered the Latin of *to be able,* which has nothing etymologically to do with *knowing* (in Latin) or with the great group of Indogermanic words just referred to, it was at once clear that *to be able* (*posse*) has still to do with begetting and the like, in that *possum,* I am able, I can = *potissum* = I am powerful, I am the master, I am the husband.

Herewith, then, perhaps the circle of begetting, or creating, of generating, of procreating, is complete—that circle which, semantically when it does not do so philologically, includes the prolific root GN, KN, CN.

---

more specifically, how they view the bodies of adults. For it is the lower part that now comprises their vista and occupies their attention—a part that taken *in toto* constitutes a specific *Gestalt* compounded of belly, thigh, genitalia and knees. If ignorance of function is assumed, then it might make sense to conceive this lower part *sub specie* a 'total' GN, later to be differentiated into separate words as the separate topographical units become themselves differentiated as unitary, individualized perceptions.

V. DREAMS AND THE USES OF REGRESSION*[1]

AROUND the year 500 B.C., natural science began with a repudiation of the dream. Heraclitus of Ephesus issued a scientific manifesto in the two sentences: 'We must not act and speak like sleepers, for in our sleep too we act and speak', and, 'The waking have one world in common, but the sleeping turn aside each into a world of his own'. Professor Schrödinger (1956), from whose chapter, On the Peculiarity of the Scientific World View, I am quoting these fragments, explains their importance. People were accustomed, then, he says, to treat what we now call the manifest content of dreams as valid perceptions; that is, they believed that the persons and things they saw in dreams were real. They thought, for example, that gods must exist because they appeared in one's dreams. When therefore Heraclitus referred to the world that is common to all men, he meant the world of waking life; and in another fragment he specifically stated that whosoever does not recognize the world in common is not of sound mind but insane, and that he acts and speaks like a sleeper. We as psychiatrists and students of the dream thus have an ancient reason for great pride—at least a great negative reason. For at the very dawn of science, the dream and the psychologic symptom were such nuisances that science could not begin until they were explicitly expelled from scientific consideration.

Leaving Heraclitus, let us leap from 500 B.C. to 1952 A.D. and to Professor W. Ross Ashby. In Design for a Brain, Ashby (1952) gives a clear and careful statement of what must be excluded from physical science—which is, generally speaking, consciousness. When we exclude consciousness from science, and in his context, from the observable functions of the brain, we do not, he says, deny its existence. 'The truth is quite other-

* [No. 107 in Bibliography.]

[1] The title is phrased thus to recall Ernst Kris.

wise, for the fact of consciousness is prior to all facts.' Here Ashby is referring to consciousness in the sense of subjective experience; for he continues: 'If I perceive, am aware of, a chair, I may later be persuaded by other evidence that the appearance was produced by a trick of lighting; I may be persuaded that it occurred in a dream or even that it was a hallucination; but there is no evidence in existence that could persuade me that my awareness itself was mistaken—that I had not really been aware at all. This knowledge of personal awareness, therefore, is prior to all knowledge.'

Why then must one exclude not only the dream consciousness but also the waking consciousness from one's thinking if one is to design a brain? Ashby echoes Heraclitus: 'The answer, in my opinion, is that Science deals, and can deal, only with what one man can demonstrate to another. Vivid though consciousness may be to its possessor, there is as yet no method known by which he can demonstrate his experience to another. And until such a method, or its equivalent is found, the facts of consciousness cannot be used in scientific method.'

The metaphysical assumptions of Heraclitus and Ashby are related but different. The Greek philosopher warns us against trusting our perceptions, especially those that come in sleep. The English scientist throws out all qualities of self-observation, even the raw stuff of waking common sense, as well as mirages, hallucinations, and dreams. I think we must recognize the propriety of Ashby's working assumptions; however, it is difficult not to be wistful in regard to one matter: because of his adherence to the rules of scientific method, Professor Ashby will be prevented from telling us whether the brain he has designed can dream. Heraclitus, apparently, was content to say that the manifest dream content does not mirror an objective reality, that *Träume sind Schäume*. Ashby, for the sake of preserving scientific method, must not mention dreams as objects of investigation. I do not know precisely what metaphysical complications would arise if the designed brain, built by some science-fiction super-engineers and given a chance to talk, should begin to tell its dreams. I presume we should rule them out from science too, though I can think of other science-fiction possibilities. Nevertheless, as the physical sciences stand, or stood yesterday, the only function of consciousness is to observe and to perceive; the observer as a dreamer or self-observer is out of the scientific world picture.

Professor Schrödinger (1956) is authority for the statement, that this retreat of the observer from the world picture is one of the basic metaphysical principles of the scientific view of the world. He calls it 'the hypothesis of the real world around us' or 'objectivation'. He defines *objectivation* as the 'exclusion of or dispensing with the cognizing subject (from the understandable world-picture aspired to), who steps back into the role of an external spectator'. I, my ego, am supposed to be there as if I were totally detached, a spectator. This philosophic point of view is called dualism; there is perceiving mind and objective matter, or, in Descartes's original statement, two kinds of things or substances: the thing that knows (*res cogitans*) and the thing that has extension in time and space (*res extensa*).

Schrödinger elaborates: 'The scientist, almost inadvertently, simplifies his problem of understanding Nature by disregarding or cutting out of the picture to be constructed, himself, his own personality, the subject of cognizance. Inadvertently, the thinker steps back into the role of an external observer.' Elsewhere the same author repeats that the scientific point of view is 'cutting out oneself', 'stepping back into the position of an observer who has nothing to do with the whole performance'. The idea of the scientist as a purely observing, almost a purely looking, ego is to be found in all serious discussions of the metaphysics of science. Thus Professor Burtt (1954), in The Metaphysical Foundations of Modern Physical Science: 'Man is but a puny and local spectator' in the Newtonian picture of the world, and elsewhere he uses the phrase, 'irrelevant spectator'. These quotations and many others that could be adduced indicate that somewhere during the 2500 years between Heraclitus and Ashby, a great deal more was eliminated from science than the mere delusive testimony of manifest dream contents. The three great names associated with the scientific world view that made the spectator irrelevant are Galileo, Newton, and Descartes; and Descartes was its formulating philosopher.

Descartes explicitly stated that the mind has 'no relation to extension or dimensions' and that 'we cannot conceive of its occupying space', but it is important to note Professor Burtt's remark that in popularizations, and more particularly in those based on Hobbes's writings, the mind came to be thought of in space. In nonmetaphysical circles, it somehow gravitated to a location in the head, so that by Newton's time, 'it is safe to say . . . the soul was conceived as occupying a seat, or a small portion of extension, within the brain, which place had come to be known as the sensorium'. Like the little upside-down man along the fissure of Rolando that we learned of in school, who became in modern parlance our 'body image', a little observing homunculus inhabited the pineal gland, floated in the fourth ventricle, or sat near the crossing of the optic nerves, a weightless creature, kinsman of Descartes's other homunculus, the Cartesian diver. This *res cogitans* had only one function, that of the sensorium—to take in all impressions that came in from the organs of perception, one supposes mainly from the eyes.

In this somewhat sketchy version of the Cartesian view of mind and matter, or mind and body, the mind is a small purely cognitive *res*; it is reduced to spectatorship; even the body to which it is somehow related becomes a part of the outer world, for it can be seen 'out there' in extension. Descartes thus separated observing mind and extended matter. We are told of precursors for this point of view among the early Greek philosophers. Descartes was soundly grounded in their writings, and they may have impressed him very much, but his own opinion as to the event most influential, indeed, portentous in shaping his thoughts was the dreaming of three dreams on the night of November 10, 1619. If his opinion is correct and to be taken seriously, we come upon a strange situation. The dream, rigorously excluded from the natural science world, for different reasons, by scientists from Heraclitus to Ashby, would be the very source of the world view from which it was excluded. One aim of the present essay is to muster the possible evidence for this idea, and to suggest that what began as a dream experience may have determined the Cartesian scientific view of the whole world. The stone the builders rejected may have become the cornerstone.

To be perfectly direct about the matter, I shall try to show that Descartes's dualistic view of the world is the view that we commonly find in an ordinary well-projected visual dream, where the dreamer is exactly what the observer is supposed to be and tries to be in the Cartesian system, that is, *res cogitans,* the pure and irrelevant spectator, the external observer. In such a dream, the dreamer is all observer, and he does not directly feel himself as body in the dream picture, where he is represented only by projected images. In dreams of a different character and in certain going-to-sleep visual imaginations, the body may itself be felt in the dream picture; in these dreams that include body sensations, sleep is lighter, the disturbers of sleep more effective in waking the sleeper completely or partly; and in this sense, dreams with much body in them are not satisfactory as guardians of sleep. However, in those dreams which successfully exclude stimuli from the body, the dreamer is there only with what Federn calls 'mental ego feeling'.

In fact, the psychoanalytic literature contains a very Cartesian discussion of the relation of the dreamer as the dreaming spectator to himself as a bodily participant, in Federn's (1926) study, Some Variations of Ego Feeling. Federn there distinguishes what he calls 'mental ego feeling' from 'bodily ego feeling', according to where and what the dreamer feels himself to be. I think it would be possible to simplify Federn's terminology for our present purpose and to speak in the context of this lecture of mind and body. Indeed, to explain what he meant by mental ego feeling, Federn said that it was the observer in the dream, and he added, 'The phrase, *cogito ergo sum,* is a rational formulation of mental ego feeling'. I think that with this phrase, Federn is returning the Cartesian idea to its place of origin, namely, the dream. My existence *qua* dreamer has in the dream the same validity as my existence in waking life *qua* cogitator. *Somnio ergo sum.* Most dreams are, in the optical sense, projected and appear as if before us in our visual field, so that we readily understand the idea of spectator and dream picture. We are observers only and remain without bodily feelings, which disappear as we go to sleep.

In certain less frequent dreams, however, the body is felt intensely. These are dreams of flying, swimming and the like, certain anxiety dreams, and dreams of inhibited movement; and they are signs of physically disturbed sleep. Dreams vary in their capacity to overcome such intrusions from the body and differ in the extent to which they can delude the sleeper into believing either that he is not feeling or that he is feeling something else.

A few examples will clarify this statement. Freud (1900-1901, pp. 229-230) records a dream where a poultice between the legs of a sleeper, who was suffering from an abscess in that region, became in the dream picture a saddle and the dreamer an equestrian. Scherner (Freud, *ibid,* p. 227) reports a dream which represented dental irritation by two rows of fair-haired boys attacking each other. I may refer to a comparable dream of dental irritation from my own practice: the dreamer found himself in the House of Lords. The Lords were seated not in rows but in a semicircle, the dreamer was at the center of the circle. Suddenly a very large rubber ax blade chopped down between two of the Lords on the right, and the dreamer awoke to find an irritating fragment of food between two teeth of his lower jaw in an exactly corresponding position. While the dream lasted, the teeth had been projected out into the dream world as Lords and had not 'belonged' to him.

The following dream illustrates variations in the representations of different parts of the body. The dreamer fell asleep sitting upright in bed and holding a book in his left hand. In the beginning of the dream, from which he woke immediately, he felt his shoulder and neck muscles under great strain, as he heavily tried to pull himself up a steeply inclined sidewalk. He was intensely aware of the weight of his head and shoulders, less so of his chest, and not at all aware of any part of him from the waist down. He was thus perceiving the actual state of the musculature used to maintain his sitting-up position. As to his left arm: on the left in the dream, the middle of the street was full of lively, rapid horse-and-buggy traffic. Awaking, he found in place of the street, his left arm shaking in a clonic effort to keep the book in its raised position.

Such dreams are relevant in illustrating the way the body is represented in dreams under such special circumstances. They show that parts of the body which are as if still awake may appear in such a dream, and that they may be felt then exactly as they would be if the dreamer were awake, or the visual images may delude him into believing that something else and not his body is responsible. Since the dream's main function is to preserve the dreamer's sleep, we may assume that the part of the dream related above, in which the tingling of the left arm is transmuted to street traffic on the left and in which the dreamer has no direct experience of his arm, is guarding sleep better than the part that permitted the dreamer to feel the painful tensions of his neck and shoulders directly. In the terminology of Descartes, the preservation of sleep is best accomplished in those dreams where the dreamer is only *res cogitans,* that is, mind, and not also *res extensa,* that is, body; unless of course there is too much cogitation.

We are now ready to get back to Descartes himself, for the philosopher had an unusual dream, one into which his body entered in a very spectacular way. The dream and two that followed on the same night made a deep impression on him. He was convinced that they were a revelation from God, and later he told them often and always spoke of them as marking the decisive point in his career (Burtt, 1954, p. 106). He said that they had brought him illumination and the complete conviction that mathematics was the sole key needed to unlock the secrets of nature. If we find a way to understand Descartes's profound conviction, we may possibly learn how he came to set up his dualistic world, a world, moreover, in which all that was physical was reduced to the three fundamentals of time, space, and matter.

The three dreams of November 10, 1619, have been published twice in the psychoanalytic literature, once in French as a footnote to a letter of Freud,[2] and once in an essay of Professor J. O. Wisdom (1947) which appeared in the International Journal of Psycho-Analysis, titled, Three Dreams of Descartes. Descartes was twenty-three years old at the time of the dreaming, and the surviving account is due to his first biographer, Baillet. The text used here is from the translation by Professor Norman Kemp Smith (1952) in his book, New Studies in the Philosophy of Descartes.

> Descartes tells us that, on November 10, 1619, having returned to rest full of enthusiasm and entirely taken up with the thought of having discovered the foundations of a science so marvelous, he had in a single night three consecutive dreams which he imagined could only have come from on high. After he had fallen asleep his imagination was strongly impressed

[2] For English translation see, Freud (1929a), Editor's Note, pp. 200-201 [Ed.].

> with certain phantoms which appeared before him and terrified him in such wise that, while walking, as he fancied, through the streets, he was obliged to turn himself over to his left side so as to be able to advance to the place where he wished to go, feeling, as he did, a great weakness in his right side which disabled him from leaning on it. Ashamed of walking in that manner he made an effort to straighten himself, but felt an impetuous wind which, catching him up in a kind of whirlwind, made him revolve three or four times on his left foot. But what really frightened him was something more; the difficulty he had in dragging himself along made him think he was falling at every step.

So far, we interrupt to note, this is an unusual dream. There is a great deal of bodily feeling in it, and Descartes is painfully aware of part of his own body's *res extensa* or matter. It corroborates Federn's assertion that the body is felt intensely in dreams of motion and inhibition of motion. Since this part of the text is the beginning of the dream, we may surmise that the dream work has not proceeded far from the waking state or the transition between waking and sleep where bodily sensations are still registered directly, of which the 'tingling arm' dream above would be a good example. Descartes notes that when he awoke, he found himself lying on his left side, the side to which he felt himself turn in the dream. As a guardian of sleep, this part of the dream is not satisfactory; it may be contrasted with the one recounted above where the representation of the teeth as the Lords, seen but not felt, had successfully eliminated from consciousness the concomitant dental irritation. This is in accord with the general rule: the more the dream thoughts can be turned into purely visual representations, the more satisfactory and uninterrupted the dream.

To return to the dream:

> [He finally] perceived on his path a college with open gate [and he] entered, seeking there a refuge and a remedy for his trouble.

We recognize this type of dream element; it is a 'threshold phenomenon' like those first described and so named by Silberer (1911). In a dream, going into another room and the like are signs, according to Silberer, of a change in the dream thoughts. My own alternative or additional interpretation of these elements is that they indicate the appearance in the dream text of the wish to sleep and a second try at forming a dream that would eliminate its disturbers by a new representation. Descartes's dream appears on the face of it to permit this interpretation, although, as we shall see immediately, the attempt was a failure. Whatever new thought may have arisen was one of defense—to get out of danger and distress.

The dream continues:

> He tried to reach the church of the college, his thought being to go there for prayer, but perceiving that he had passed a man of his acquaintance without saluting him, he tried to return on his steps to make due acknowledgment and was flung violently against the church by the wind. At the same moment, he saw in the middle of the college court another person who called him by name in very civil and obliging terms, and told him that if he cared to go in search of Monsieur N., the latter had something to give him. M. Descartes imagined that it was a melon that had been brought from some foreign country. But what surprised him still more was to see that those who together with this person were gathering round him for conversations stood on their feet straight and steady, whereas he himself on this same ground was still bowed and staggering, and that the wind which more than once had been on the point of upsetting him had become less strong. With these imaginations in mind, he awoke . . .

Thus ends the second scene of the first dream, with the realization that his body was in distress and not the body or bodies of everyone. These terminal details of the dream demonstrate the reason for its failure to preserve sleep. Descartes found out that he was not able to project his sensations from himself—or perhaps his self from his sensations (Hartmann, 1950). The attempt at projection failed and he awakened.

As to the meaning of the dream so far, we shall later learn Freud's few comments concerning certain elements, such as the gentlemen and the melon. On general principles of universal symbolism, Wisdom (1947) has proffered more conventional suggestions in terms of sexuality. He thought that Descartes's body in the dream represented his phallus, that his struggle to stand up straight represented an effort to overcome impotence, that the violent wind was a castration threat, and that the retreat to the college church signified a flight to a protective mother. This interpretation at the infantile level may of course be correct, despite its generality. Yet it seems incongruous to attach so commonplace an interpretation to so unusual a dream.

We left the text of the dream at the words, 'With these imaginations in mind, he awoke . . .'

> . . . he awoke and, as he did so, felt a pain that caused him to fear that all this was the work of some evil genius bent on seducing him. He turned at once to his right side, for it was on his left side that he had gone to sleep and had his dream. He addressed a prayer to God begging to be protected from the evil effect of his dream and to be preserved from any misfortunes that might menace him in punishment for his sins, which, so he recognized, might be grievous enough to draw upon his head the bolts of divine vengeance—however irreproachable his life might hitherto have been in the eyes of men. In this situation, after an interval of nearly two hours passed in thoughts of various kinds on all the good and evil in this world, he fell asleep again . . .

In short, as he himself was to say later, he spent the two waking hours in a moral conflict. Descartes, Freud, and Wisdom all agree that here *right* and *left* are used in the moral sense, as so often in dreams and symptoms. It is nevertheless worth considering whether Descartes's turning in bed was not also intended to relieve the tensions of his left side, which had felt so heavy in the dream.

To continue: After he had fallen asleep,

> immediately there came to him a new dream, in which he believed he heard a sharp and piercing noise which he took for a clap of thunder, and opening his eyes, he perceived a large number of fiery sparks all around him in the room. This had often happened at other times; it was nothing very extraordinary for him to wake in the middle of the night and find his eyes sparkling to such a degree as to give him glimpses of the objects nearest him. But on this occasion, he chose to have recourse to reasons from philosophy; and after having observed by alternately opening and closing his eyes, the quality of the objects thus brought before him, he drew from it conclusions favorable to his understanding. Thus his fear was dissipated, and it was in a reasonably tranquil condition that he fell asleep again.

Descartes suggests later on in this account that his fright was remorse of conscience, and that the thunderbolt was a sign or portent, indicating that the Angel of Truth had come down to possess him. As for the lights, which he recognized as familiar, recurrent manifestations, I shall venture a plausible suggestion; namely, that they were flicker symptoms of an attack of some sort related to migraine or a convulsive condition. In support of this snap diagnosis, I suggest that the one-sided paralysis and the spinning felt in the first dream were experiences of the same attack. I have no idea why Descartes thought his flicker lit up the room. This may have represented an effort on his part to bring the phenomenon into line with the thunderbolt idea, as if the room had been filled by a flash of lightning; or Descartes may have been influenced by the pre-Newtonian theory of vision as a function that proceeded from the eyes onto objects; or it may simply be an attempt at projection; but the issue cannot be decided.

Another detail in Baillet's record also speaks for my hypothetical diagnosis, since it can be interpreted as indicating a prodromal intimation. When Descartes's friends wondered whether he had not drunk too much wine that evening, since it was Martinmas when heavy drinking was customary, he replied that he had not had a drop of wine for three months before the night of the dream, and 'that the Genius which had been exciting in him the enthusiasm, with which, as he felt, his brain had been inflamed for several days, had predicted these dreams to him prior to his retiral to rest, and that the human mind had had no share in them'.

Now, a premonition that one is to have a certain dream is something extraordinarily rare, if not completely unheard of. On the other hand, a premonition of migraine or a convulsive attack even several days before the event is relatively common. The statement therefore lends force to the idea that the dream was a psychic equivalent or accompaniment of such an experience, and that Descartes, during his sleep and on awaking from his second dream, had symptoms that we now believe are due to autonomous closed electrical circuits in the brain. The presence of such circuits was predicated many years ago, because of the paths taken by scintillations that accompany migraine headaches (Kubie, 1930).

To interpret the two dreams from the standpoint of the body sensations alone, we need only to repeat Freud's cardinal statement, that the purpose of the dream is to preserve sleep. To stay asleep, Descartes processed his physical symptoms into a struggle against the 'impetuous wind'. His use of the word *wind* reminds us that the word *aura* entered the language of medicine when a boy told Galen that before his convulsions, he felt an *aura,* that is, a breeze, mount his body upward from his feet. Apart from any other determinations, we may postulate one meaning of the action of the dream, and one basic wish: Descartes wished to rid himself of his alarming bodily sensations in order to continue his sleep. He wished to sleep, and if he had to dream to do so, he wished to retain, as he might have put it, only his *res cogitans* and his position as a 'detached and irrelevant observer'. As to his painful *res extensa* and his bodily feelings, these he would be glad to banish and to project entirely to the insentient world picture of the dream.

To turn again to the account of this extraordinary night, we find that the third dream was mild and agreeable. A moment after falling asleep, he began his final dream,

> which unlike the two earlier dreams, had nothing terrifying in it. In this third dream, he found a book on his table, without knowing who had put it there. He opened it, and seeing that it was a dictionary, he was delighted, hoping that he might find it useful. At the same instant, he happened on another book, no less of a surprise to him than the first, not knowing how it had come to be there. He found it to be the collection of poems entitled *Corpus Poetarum,* etc. Curiosity made him wish to read a little in it, and on opening the volume, he chanced to fall on the line *Quod vitae sectabor iter?,* etc. [Which path in life shall I pursue?] At the same moment, he perceived a man he did not know, who presented him with some verses beginning with the words, *Est et Non.*[3] These he recommended highly, insisting on the excellence of the poem. M. Descartes told him that he knew what the piece was, and that it was among the *Idylls* of Ausonius, one of the authors in the bulky poetical anthology on the table. Wishing to show it to the man, he began to turn over the leaves of the

[3] Smith (1952, p. 35) states that these two poems are on the same page of the 1603 edition of the *Corpus,* and that they are face to face on two pages of the 1611 edition. In both they come under the eyes simultaneously.

> volume, quite certain of being perfectly acquainted with the order and general arrangement of the work. As he was thus searching for the place, the man asked him where he had got the book. M. Descartes replied that he was unable to say how he had come by it, but that the moment before he had been handling another, which had now disappeared, and all this without his knowing either who had brought it to him or who had taken it from him again. No sooner had he finished saying so, than he saw the book reappearing at the other end of the table. But he found that this Dictionary was somewhat different from what he had seen it to be the first time. Meantime he came upon the poems of Ausonius in the collection of poems he was handling and being unable to find the piece beginning with the words, *Est et Non,* he said to the man that he knew another passage of the same poet even finer, and that it began with the words, *Quod vitae sectabor iter?*

Because of the length and circumstantiality, I shall, for a moment, interrupt the story of the third dream. Psychoanalysts will be reminded by it of many they have heard, usually introduced by the dreamer's statement that he had an interesting dream. It will be of interest to you to learn, later on, Freud's opinion of this type of dream, for a psychoanalyst's tendency to be impatient during the telling of such dreams depends on a difference in aim between himself and the dreamer, which Freud points out.

However, to continue the story about the books and the book-lovers,

> The person asked to have [the poem] shown to him, and M. Descartes was proceeding to look for it, when he came upon several small portrait engravings, and this caused him to remark that the volume was very handsome, but that the edition was not the one he was acquainted with. He was at this point in his dreams, when both the man and the books disappeared, vanishing from his fantasy, without his yet awaking. What especially calls for remark is that, in doubt whether what he had just seen was dream or actual vision, not merely did he decide in his sleep that it was a dream, but he proceeded to interpret the dream prior to his awaking.

Before taking up Descartes's interpretation, it may be remarked that several others have commented on the dream. The suggestion of its alcoholic etiology, made by Descartes's friends, was refuted immediately by the dreamer himself; he had not drunk too much but had been completely abstinent. Other interpretations have come from Professor Wisdom, quoted above in passing, and from Freud. But since Descartes's priority of interpretation is so well established, we must first give his.

His account of the interpretation shows that he was not interested in the analysis of the dream in Freud's sense; his interest was entirely anagogic, so that he may be regarded as a precursor of Silberer rather than Freud. He wished, in other words, to get away from his unconscious and to get into the field of moral and philosophical speculations, and to make an allegory of the dream. Thus, he said that the Dictionary in the third dream stood for all of the sciences, the anthology of poems for a union of philosophy and wisdom—for poets, due to the divine nature of inspiration, were often wiser than professional philosophers. The verse about the choice of a path in life represented a sage's advice, or possibly, moral theology. These ideas came to him while he was still asleep.

He awoke and, still meditating, interpreted the poets in the anthology as signifying 'revelation and inspiration'. *Est et Non* were the Yes and No of Pythagoras and referred to truth and error in human knowledge and the sciences. Descartes was so pleased by his success in fitting the pieces of the dream together, that he was convinced it was the Angel of Truth who had descended from Heaven to reveal to him the treasures of all the sciences. He could not find an explanation for the little copperplate portraits in the second book, but after an Italian artist visited him next day, he was satisfied and decided to look for no further explanation.

So much for Descartes's associations to the third dream, which was pleasant and which, he believed, bore on the future. The other two dreams, he believed, bore on the past, and they were admonitions from God. The melon he linked up, strangely, with the charms of solitude. The wind that thrust him toward the college and the church, he thought, was an evil genius trying to force him into a place he would have gone of his own accord, but which God did not permit. It was God, however, that made him take his first step toward the church. The terror of his second dream marked his remorse of conscience for sins he might have committed, and the thunder was the sign that the Angel of Truth had entered into him. After this, he prayed again to the Virgin, vowing to make a pilgrimage to her shrine at Loreto, part of the way on foot and clad in lowly garb. This vow was fulfilled only four years later. His enthusiasm left in a few days.

Descartes's work on the dream may be anagogic and in the mode of Silberer, but let us not from our twentieth-century vantage point brush off his comments as banal moralizings. It is not unimportant that this great scientist was struck by a dream, that he quite naturally associated to the elements in it, and that he communicated his associations to his friends; and we should take seriously the judgment he made on the dream, that it had a prospective tendency and was a major event in his life, from which he was to incubate his later convictions.

This brings us to Freud's (1929a) opinion of the dream, which was expressed in a letter of a few hundred words. A French author, Maxim Leroy, sent him the text and asked for his comments. Freud gently explained that one prefers to have the dreamer's associations if one must analyze a dream. He remarked, however, that the dream was of a familiar type, called a dream 'from above' (*von oben*), that is, one consisting of ideas that might just as easily have arisen during the waking state. Such dreams, Freud continues, most often express abstract, poetic, or symbolic ideas—a remark which suggests that he too was reminded of Silberer. He states further that psychoanalysts hearing such a dream would not be able to interpret it, but that, on the other hand, the dreamer would know how to translate it immediately, since the ideas in it are very near to his conscious thoughts. Nevertheless, certain elements in such dreams remain unintelligible to the dreamer and are to be got at only through free associations from them. 'From a certain point of view', he adds, meaning of course the point of view of psychoanalytic theory and genesis, 'these are the most interesting details'.[4]

Freud, therefore, is willing to accept Descartes's comments as relevant to the interpretation of this dream 'from above', and he agrees that it portrays a moral conflict, quite on the

[4] B. Lewin's translation from *Brief an Maxim Leroy über einen Traum des Cartesius* (in French). In: *Gesammelte Schriften,* Vol. XII, pp. 403-405. See also, Freud (1929a), p. 203 [Ed.].

surface. The left side stands for sin and the wind is literally an ill wind. Descartes, he is sure, could have identified the persons in the dream, etc. But without more associations to such bizarre elements as the melon from a foreign country and the engravings, one could not get at the deeper unconscious meaning. Descartes's unexpected idea that the melon had to do with the 'charms of solitude in a human sense' would make one surmise that it signified sexual material. Freud obviously felt it unwise to be more specific than this, and the letter is written in a restrained style, appropriate to the serious but unsophisticated request. Professor Wisdom, writing in the International Journal of Psycho-Analysis, naturally was surer of his readers' critical understanding.

I shall now try to bring together more systematically the ideas which were suggested by the formal aspects of the dream, omitting those that referred to the sexual and moral contents and focusing upon its function as a guardian of sleep. I have assumed that the dream took place during a period of ill health, and I made up a hypothesis of a disturbance in the brain such as usually produces migrainous or convulsive symptoms. The evidence for this assumption was the following: (1) The prodromal intimations, which Descartes reports as present for some days before the dream. (2) The strange sensory and motor images that appeared in the dream; namely, his one-sided paralysis, his spinning around three or four times on his left foot, the feeling of staggering and being bent over, the sensations he interpreted as a high wind, and possibly the 'phantoms' he saw at the beginning of the first dream. (3) The sparkling lights in the second dream, inaugurated by the thunderclap and continuing into the waking state, which Descartes states he had experienced many times previously. Although Descartes felt himself to be in violent motion in the first dream and turned from his left to his right side after he awoke from it, it need not follow that he had actually been moving while he was asleep, in the pattern indicated in the dream. Even if the motor phenomena were in fact absent, the symptoms would be intelligible as a so-called 'psychic equivalent' of a convulsive or migrainous attack. As to the anamnesis, Descartes's mother died when he was five days old, and his health was the constant worry of his solicitous father and later, from his tenth year on, of the Jesuit teachers to whom his upbringing was entrusted. He spent a large part of his childhood in bed, where his teachers permitted him to stay whenever he wished.

Using the hypothesis just stated, namely, that Descartes was suffering from a physical illness while he was dreaming on the night of November 10, 1619, I shall attempt to interpret certain elements in the dream from the standpoint of its sleep-guarding function and to show how these were used by the dreamer in his effort to preserve sleep. Later I shall try to show that the philosopher's efforts to solve the problem, how may one preserve sleep in the face of intrusive bodily pain and discomfort, have a relationship to his later dualistic picture of the world.

Descartes went to sleep on Martinmas eve, he tells us, quite sober so far as wine was concerned but filled with enthusiasm—inspired excitement—because of his recent intellectual discoveries. But the first dream tries to deal not so much with the wakening effects of thinking; rather it tries to rid him of physical stimuli by the usual dream process of projecting them as hallucinations. It presents the visual 'phantoms' to delude him about any optic impressions and it puts the responsibility for feelings in his body onto a wind. Even so, Descartes's sleep is still threatened. He feels his body very acutely, the hallucinated 'wind' makes him stagger, nearly fall; it spins him round, and so the hallucination does not succeed in letting him rest. At this point appears the 'threshold phenomenon': he wishes to get away from the wind, that is, his bodily feelings, by taking refuge within the college chapel, where he would be protected and would not feel a wind. The reason he cannot complete this intention in the dream is not clear: the rationalization he gives is that he must turn back to speak to an acquaintance who has greeted him, and whose greeting he has not acknowledged. However, this alternative action and the ensuing conversations with another person and with several others who gather round him, include an attempt to ignore his bodily feelings—an unsuccessful one again, for he is surprised to note suddenly that all these people are standing up perfectly straight and that he alone is reeling and bowed. This surprise we interpret as a new failure of the dream work;

for if Descartes is to be deluded into thinking that his disturbing sensations are not internal, the dream must see to it that the wind also affects the others. Descartes was philosopher and Bible scholar enough to know that the empirical reality of a wind depends on its blowing on everyone, the just and the unjust alike, and he had to face the fact that it was his body alone that was affected. The dream was unable to project the staggering, painful sensations away from him and onto other persons or onto the physical world. At this point the sleep-preserving mechanisms failed completely and Descartes awoke, discovering the factual nature of his physical discomforts. The failure of the dream to guard his sleep lay in its inability to maintain the delusion that his body was an insentient, non-motile part of the projected dream picture. A successful dream would, perhaps, have shown him all kinds of phantasms and motions, but it would have permitted him to be present solely with 'mental ego feeling', that is, as a detached observer, as an irrelevant spectator.

When through prayer he was able to sleep again, the second dream was an even less effective guardian of sleep. The best it could do by way of hallucination was to depict an internal bodily event as a crash of thunder. Like the waking dream about the 'burning child', its illusion lasted a brief moment and Descartes awoke already conscious of the optical phenomena, the sparkles and illumination which he tried to attribute to reflections from objects in the room.

It is too bad that we have no complete record of what went on during this period of wakefulness. We know that there were intense, excited thoughts about what Descartes had just dreamed, by means of which he tried to account for the disturbing events. His thoughts were of sin, of divine illumination, and the like, and they included the moral interpretation; but his thinking must have proceeded in a rapid and complicated fashion and covered many topics. By the time he fell asleep for the third time and began his third dream, as Freud points out, and as Descartes realized, his dreaming intellect carried on the complicated, 'abstract, poetic, and symbolic' mentation, which he might just as well have experienced in a waking state, and indeed, which he may well have been experiencing during the waking hours between the dreams, for at the end of the third dream he resumed this style of thinking in what he called his interpretation.

It seems to me that during the intervening waking hours, the physical processes had subsided, the electrical circuits in his brain had ceased, and Descartes had brought his body to relative rest by the device of diffuse thinking, that took as its content the moral and intellectual problems that he enjoyed. To express this in more psychoanalytic language, though perhaps not very precisely, Descartes had succeeded in becoming much less body ego and much more observing and thinking mental ego.

This he certainly was in his third dream, which was filled with interesting conversation about science, philosophy, inspiration, and poetry, and even about popular books, for according to Professor Smith, the anthology of Latin poets, first published in 1603, appeared in a second edition in 1611. In this dream, Descartes could identify himself with a looking spectator. Professor Wisdom has remarked on the scopophilic quality of the dream, with all its looking at poems and engravings. But if we think of a person as being conveniently and arbitrarily divisible into various parts and functions—such as arms, legs, sensorium, intellect, and the like—then in this dream we could say, Descartes's body is at rest, but his observing and thinking faculties are pleasantly awake.

Now in his interpretation of the dreams, which began while he was still asleep, Descartes continues in an allegorical and anagogical vein. He is not interested in analyzing the dream, in our sense; he is not interested in finding repressed memories or conflicts. He is quite content to let his resistances triumph when he considers the copperplate engravings, for resistances are interesting only to us freudians who wish to get at the repressed. Instead, Descartes took the manifest contents of the dream as a starting point for the sort of poetic, abstract, and symbolic thoughts that interested him. In his third dream, his main preoccupation was in this direction, but the usual dream device of hallucinatory projection and visual representation successfully protected his sleep.

Long, long before Silberer's idea of using manifest dream elements to give the start for allegorical trains of thought, men had realized this possibility. If there were delusive dreams that came to us through the gate of ivory, there were also true dreams that came through the gate of horn. Possibly it had been noted too that some of the thinking done in dreams made sense and was valid when it was checked by later empirical tests. Yet, with Heraclitus's imprecation loud in their ears throughout the centuries, most men have been ashamed of what they think while they are asleep, and if by chance their dream does come through the gate of horn, they are apt to be startled. If they dream rationally, sober men experience an eerie feeling, as if they had been singled out for some rare dispensation. Poets are accustomed to the idea of their irrationality and sometimes vaunt it, our fifth Freud Lecturer, Lionel Trilling (1950), has told us. Perhaps because of this old tradition, Coleridge was ready to tell that he had dreamed the Kubla Khan fragment in its final, highly wrought, prosodic form. Now, from the standpoint of essential dream theory, which has always taken into account 'day thoughts' and secondary elaboration, it hardly matters whether Coleridge put the poem into its final and æsthetically acceptable form while he was asleep, or whether he did so after he woke up, while ruminating over a dream.

The same holds true for scientific inventions that come while scientists are dreaming. The story of Kekulé's hexagonal model of the benzene ring is to the effect that the configuration came to him during a doze:

> I sat writing at my textbook, but the writing did not go at all well, my mind was on other things. I turned my chair to face the fireplace and sank into a half-sleep. Again atoms fluttered before my eyes. Smaller groups remained modestly in the background. My mind's eye, made acute by previous repeated visions of this sort, now distinguished large arrangements of complex structure. Long rows much more densely put together, all in motion, twisting and squirming like snakes. And, lo! What was that? Why, one of the snakes has taken hold of its own tail, and the configuration whirls arrogantly before my eyes. As if lightning had struck, I awoke, and this time I spent the rest of the night working out the consequences of my hypothesis.

Kekulé's rather flowery account was given in a lecture to celebrate the twenty-fifth anniversary of the discovery of the benzene ring, and it is somewhat dressed up to suit the occasion. But it tells us that he suddenly realized that he had the proper structural formula for the benzene ring; and the idea which came from the dream or near-dream stood the empirical tests of science. However, given Kekulé's preoccupation with atoms and benzene, the interesting point is not so much that the model came to him along with the snaky images of his doze, but that it had not come to him during his study hours directly. Like Archimedes's bath, the hearth fire promoted a useful regression.[5]

Similarly, in a dream of Professor Hilprecht, of the Department of Assyrian Studies at the University of Pennsylvania (Woods, 1947, p. 525), there came a High Priest of ancient Nippur to bring him a message. The message was not, as one might be prepared to think, of divine import. The priest quite practically told Professor Hilprecht that if he put together three fragments that belonged to the University collection, he would find that the characters on them made an intelligible inscription. It does seem that Hilprecht might have given himself this advice directly; in truth he was doing so in his dream, but he needed the hallucination of the priest to stay asleep. The point I am making is one quite familiar to you, namely, that mentation may take place in words, in pictures, and even without either words or pictures so far as one is aware, and that the thinking part of the ego can be quite active and in that sense, awake, during a dream.

Because Descartes led us away anagogically into the poetic and mystical, I purposely shifted the attention of this essay to the matter of intellectual and scientific creation. For when one learns from Descartes that he believed this dream revealed to him that the physical world can be completely formulated in mathematical terms, and when one compares this remarkable assertion to the dilettante *Deuterei* that followed the dream, one cannot suppress astonishment. I intend to take the assertion seriously. It seems to me plausible that Descartes reworked or re-edited the events of the first dream many times; he repeated it frequently to his friends, he recorded it in the lost manuscript that Baillet used to write his account. Gen-

5 More of Kekulé's address is quoted by Winterstein (1929) and by Robitsek (1912). Comments on Descartes are to be found in another article by Winterstein (1913). I am indebted to Dr. Alfred Winterstein of Vienna for these helpful references and for other comments.

erally, from the great importance he attributed to it, it is not difficult to assume that the dream and the problems it set him should often occupy his unconscious, preconscious, and conscious mentation. Now, whether Descartes knew it or not, one of the dream's problems was how to maintain sleep—specifically what to do about the body in a dream, or how to keep in a dream only 'mental ego feeling' and have oneself remain a detached, external, excluded, irrelevant spectator or observer.

I think that at some time or other Descartes came upon the correct solution: the body must be projected out into the 'not-I' of the dream world, leaving only the observing and thinking self to have the dream. Naturally, there is no way of knowing when such a solution came to him, or whether he ever consciously applied it to the problem of sleep. But if one should guess at the time of this occurrence, the best assumption would be that it came to him some time within the ten years that intervened between the dreaming of his famous dream and the writing of his famous Discourse on Method. The best dream world, so far as the sleep of Descartes on that night was concerned, was a world in which all matter, including the matter of the dreamer's body was 'out there', and where the perceiving dreamer was nothing but that little weightless, immaterial being, vaguely located behind the eyes. This is the state of affairs in most untroubled dreams; there is only mind or 'mental ego feeling' and the body is insentient and thoroughly projected out into the rest of the dream picture before us.

In short, I should like to hazard a hypothesis: when Descartes came to formulate his scientific picture of the world, he made it conform with the state of affairs in an ordinary successful dream. The picture of the dream world that succeeds best in preserving sleep—the solution of Descartes's sleep problem as of November 10, 1619—came to be the picture of the waking world that succeeded best in explaining it scientifically. The relation of the observer to the observed in a dream was set up as the metaphysically proper relation of the scientific observer to the scientifically observed and observable in waking life. Mental ego feeling in the dream became Cartesian mind, *res cogitans*; the dream picture became

Cartesian matter, *res extensa*. It is desirable in a dream to separate mind and matter; this helps preserve sleep. It was desirable for Descartes also in his philosophy to separate mind and matter, as a preliminary assumption for the understanding of the real world. Whereas we often use the principle that 'reality' must correct fantasy, here we find the great philosopher using fantasy to correct common-sense reality.

In formulating his physical science, Descartes proposed the long-abandoned theory of 'vortices'. Matter, he thought, filled all of space in the form of infinitely divisible particles, and the particles were packed so tightly that one of them could not move without communicating the motion to the rest. To quote Professor Butterfield (1949): 'This matter formed whirlpools in the skies, and it was because the planets were caught each in its own whirlpool that they were carried around like pieces of straw. . . . Gravity itself was the result of these whirlpools of invisible matter, which had the effect of sucking things down towards their own center' (p. 132). In other words, the whole universe was spinning, and I hazard the conjecture that it was spinning like himself in the dream when the 'impetuous wind' spun him around three or four times on his left foot. The projected world of physical science was a windy world, isomorphic with the world in his dream, but Descartes as *res cogitans* and with him all cogitating mankind could come to rest.

The real importance of Descartes's dreaming, then, would not—could not—have been the banal moralizing and mystical fantasies, nor his pilgrimage to the shrine of Our Lady of Loreto. Such thoughts and such a ritual were excursions away from the understanding of the message of his dream. They were absurdly incommensurate with the importance he attributed to it. The real consequences of Descartes's dreaming were in precise harmony with his statement that the Angel of Truth had come to illuminate him, to reveal to him the mathematical nature of the world, for which, as Schrödinger has told us, the separation of mind from matter is the first postulate.

The psychoanalytic literature contains several studies comparing some of Freud's ideas with those of philosophers: Plato, Hobbes, Spinoza, Schopenhauer, Nietzsche, and others listed by Ernst Kris (1952), come to mind. The question, to what extent Freud is a Cartesian, in this general form makes no sense, but we may specifically ask whether the Cartesian split-off, detached observer appears in freudian theory. I believe, at least twice. Once we find him as the ideal free-associator, metaphorically sitting in a railroad carriage and passively watching the scenery of ideas go by. This free-associator, as I tried to show several years ago, has always partaken of the role of a dreamer, and the relationship with Descartes's metaphysics here is indeed dubious; certainly, it could be plausibly maintained that Freud's relationship to dreams was as intimate as Descartes's. The second time the Cartesian observer seems to appear in Freud's theories is in a more abstract situation, in Chapter VII of The Interpretation of Dreams (Freud, 1900-1901). There he appears as the abbreviation *Cs* for the system Consciousness, which in the psychology of the dream has assigned to it as a role, *'only that of a sense-organ for the perception of psychical qualities'* (p. 615), analogous to the role which *Pcpt,* the perceptive systems, play in regard to external reality. It is, therefore, the viewer of or spectator at the dream that was processed through the psychic apparatus diagram. It is idle, however, to speculate to what extent Freud was influenced indirectly by Descartes's thinking.

It would be interesting to inquire whether dreams other than those of the ordinary visually depicted type may have led to other and non-Cartesian views on mind and matter. One would like to know what Einstein dreamed, or Leibnitz, or Lao-Tse. We know more about such matters in the nonscientific world, where many saints have been ready to equate the experiences of intensely affective unprojected, nonvisual, blank dreams with direct knowledge of God and the supernatural. In such dreams, the Cartesian observer himself is lost as such. The dreamer does not separate himself as a spectator, but merges himself with the pure feelings of the dream.

However, any such inquiry would take us quite far from the field where the use of regression and of dreams has here interested us, that is, the metaphysics of science. Science began with Heraclitus's banishment of the dream. But with Descartes the dream returned to science in disguise, like Œdipus to Thebes, or the repressed to consciousness—and incidentally, to demonstrate to us the uses of regression.

VI. KNOWLEDGE AND DREAMS*

Three years ago I published an interpretation of the long tripartite dream on the night of November 10, 1619 of the then twenty-three-year-old Descartes, to which he attributed great significance. The dream, he said, was not natural but divinely inspired; it betokened a visit by the Angel of Truth to reveal to him the certainty of his new philosophic and mathematic discoveries and to assure him of their truth. There was no visual representation of an angel in the manifest dream. This was his own interpretation. The dream was long and reported by him discursively, and since it was published by Smith (1952), Wisdom (1947) and Lewin,[1] I shall give only a summary of its action here. In the first of the three parts of the dream, Descartes is in pain, limping, dragging one foot, impeded in his gait by what he calls an 'impetuous wind' which whirls him about several times on one foot and prevents him from standing erect. In the second part of the dream, he is in bed when a sudden flash of scintillations, radiating forth from his eyes, lights up the room so that he can distinguish objects clearly. (This flash is what he interprets as the supernatural epiphany.) The third part of the dream is calm; he is at his table examining books and discussing poetry and philosophy with some invisible person, fluently and anagogically, chiefly in terms of ethics and directives for his future life: '*Quod vitae sectabor iter?*'. Divine or not, the truths formulated were applied to mundane matters.

I tried to show how this dream might be as significant as Descartes thought it to be, but in a way more personal to him—in the sense that it presented him with the problem of how to stay asleep. The pain, the motion, and the light flashes, I thought, were indications of somatic disturbances, and the dream failed for some time in its function as a

* [No. 118 in Bibliography.]

[1] See, *Dreams and the Uses of Regression*, pp. 329-352 [Ed.].

guardian of sleep. Sleep is protected most effectively when the dreaming ego is not a body ego, certainly not a restless body ego in pain. In sleep and in the dream, there should be no painful or sensorimotor body ego, but only Federn's (1926) detached, dreaming 'mental ego', the purely observant recipient of the dream picture. Federn said of this mental ego that in its rational version it would be the Cartesian *res cogitans,* but in the actual Cartesian dream the body itself was receiving nonvisual, painful sensations and did not behave like a truly Cartesian body or *res extensa.*

I came upon the idea that the usual dream—a picture projected on a sort of screen, with totally insentient representatives of the dreamer's body—would correspond exactly with Descartes's dualistic division of the world into mind and matter. The dream was significant and inspirational, though not precisely in Descartes's terms. It seemed as if Descartes in his theory of knowledge fashioned the real world to copy the sleeping world in which dreamer and thing dreamt are entirely separate. The sleeping world of the philosopher's dreams was best served by complete separation, so that his pain and restlessness were relieved. Similarly, the waking world too seemed best served if thinker and the world of extension were considered separately and dualistically. The mechanism at work in Descartes was described many years ago by Robert Waelder (1926), as the principle of *hypergnosis,* the making over of the external world, literally the 'seeing in it' the shape of a subjective experience, a process demonstrated by Waelder in paranoia as well as in creative thinking.

I shall not repeat the details used in my previous paper to support this conception of the origin of Descartes's world views. I shall use his dream experiences and those of other philosophers and writers for a different purpose; namely, to compare the feeling of revelation in a dream with comparable experiences and with other 'inspired' dreams, and to introduce some words about dreams and knowledge in general, with some comment on dream theory.

I will first discuss the sense of absolute certainty which Descartes found so remarkable and remind you of Freud's insight into the feeling of reality that is intense in some dreams. In the dream which Freud (1900-1901, p. 372) reports in this connection, his patient had dreamed that in his childhood he was given two pears and that this act was accompanied by a feeling that was *absolutely real.* Freud found that the dreamer was displacing his feeling from what was indeed an absolute reality, namely, that he had been fed from both breasts. There was no special manifest element to which Descartes attached his sense of absolute truth and revelation. He attached it to what we call the 'day residues', to his mathematical and philosophic speculations of the preceding period, when, as he put it, he was filled with enthusiasm and inspiration. Descartes's interpretation of his dream was by no means original or unique. It furnished putative evidence of acquaintance with older writings on dreams. As far as the manifest elements of the dream were concerned, he was content with an entirely anagogic, almost Jungian interpretation, taking each manifest element as a direct symbol for one or another abstract notion and was convinced generally that the dream was teaching him a moral lesson.

I do not know how many philosophers can turn their dormescent thoughts into direct dream pictures, which then proceed in a sort of allegorical charade. As Freud remarked, such dreams *von oben* are much conditioned by day residues and habits of thought. This certainly is borne out by a dream of the philosopher, Dilthey, brought to my attention by the kindness of Professor Paul Lazarsfeld. The following account is quoted from The Philosophy of Wilhelm Dilthey, by H. A. Hodges (1952).

> For hundreds of years we have lived in the faith that there are unconditional principles which we can know and by which we must live. The impulse to seek such principles is as lively today as it ever was. If philosophy and history combine to show that the search is vain, must they not do something to allay the resulting bewilderment?
>
> Dilthey accepts the responsibility; but the clearest account of how he tried to meet it is not in the *Kritik.* It is found in two unfinished sketches which he wrote in 1903-4, ostensibly describing a dream which he had and a conversation in which he took part some ten years before, while visiting his friend, von Wartenburg, at his castle in Silesia.

In the first, Dilthey tells how one night, after a long philosophical discussion, he went to sleep in a room which contained a copy of Raphael's School of Athens, and he had a dream in which the picture came to life. The philosophers of post-Renaissance times came in and joined the ancients and medievals who were already there, and then the whole company began to sort themselves into homogeneous groups. First, the naturalistic and positivistic thinkers came together around Archimedes and Ptolemy; then the philosophers of freedom around Socrates and Plato; and the objective idealists formed a group around Pythagoras and Heraclitus. Descartes and Kant, who were at first among the mathematicians and scientists, left that group to join the idealists of freedom. When the three groups began to recede from each other, great fissures appeared in the groups between them. 'A dreadful hostile alienation seemed to separate them. I was seized by a strange anxiety, that philosophy seemed to exist in three or possibly more different forms. The unity of my own being seemed to be rent, as I was longingly drawn now to this group, now to that, and I struggled to retain it.'

Here the dream ends and Dilthey continues his reflections on it. 'Every *Weltanschauung* is historically conditioned, and therefore limited relatively. A dreadful anarchy of thought results from this. But the same historical consciousness, which has given rise to this absolute doubt, can also set limits to it. First of all, the *Weltanschauungen* have separated from one another according to an inner law. . . . These types of *Weltanschauung* maintain themselves side by side in the course of centuries. And then the second, the liberating thought: the *Weltanschauungen* are grounded in the nature of the universe and the relation of the finite knowing mind to it. So each of them expresses one side of the universe within limits of our thought. Each is herein true, but each is one-sided' (pp. 311-314).

Dilthey's second sketch relates his conversation on the evening after the day of the dream in which, as it were, he re-elaborates the nocturnal residue. Von Wartenburg, a painter, and a neurologist support some of the views represented by the different groups in the dream. Finally Dilthey is consoled by the thought of a friend who died nobly in the Christian faith and 'became a proof of that which breaks through nature and her necessity'. But the sketch does not give his final conclusions.

Here, certainly, is a dream *von oben*. Dilthey carried his thoughts into sleep and back again into waking life. At his disposal was a ready-made dream screen that hung on the wall, the painted scenery of the School of Athens. I usually heed Freud's warning that we need the dreamer's free associations and not our own to interpret a dream properly. Yet I shall emulate Artemidorus and Scherner and countless others and make an informal guess. Dilthey's loyalties are split at least three ways. Dreams with historic periods in them often refer to the dreamer's own history: the archeologic and paleontologic events refer to what Freud has called the individual's prehistory, the Dark Ages are the latency period, the Renaissance adolescence, etc. Since Dilthey pictures various schools, I think his loyalties refer to different schoolmasters. The antique figures may be his earliest teachers and the mingling of eras suggests again that the unconscious knows no time. However, secondary elaboration does know time, and Dilthey seems to be split three ways and to seek a difficult integration. I suppose we could diagnose tentatively a problem of identity and for the rest turn the matter over to a specialist in adolescence.

Dilthey claimed no especial significance for this dream and got from it no sense of revelation. It fitted into his waking life without being crucial or critical. Nor did it bring the solution to a concrete problem, like Kekulé's dream (Robitsek, 1912) of the twisting snake which was to form a model for the benzene ring. In this rather simple dream or half-asleep reverie, Kekulé, dozing before a fire, thinking visually of atom combinations, suddenly finds them turned into snakes and sees one of them take its own tail into its mouth, so that a chain becomes a ring. Kekulé did not think this a supernatural experience. With common sense and reverence, he ascribed his success to his father. Kekulé's father wanted him to be an architect and had insisted on his studying mechanical drawing and drafting, and to this experience Kekulé attributed his capacity for visual imagination and formulation. To strain a point, Kekulé owed his inspiration ultimately to his father. Yet, even this statement sounds a little conventional and reminds one of the formal acknowledgments one often reads that 'this paper could not have been written without the constant encouragement and advice of Professor Head-of-the-Department'.

If Kekulé specified a real father as the bringer of the dream, a father figure is portrayed in the comparable dream of Professor Hilprecht, the Philadelphia Assyriologist (*cf.*, Woods, 1947). A priest of ancient Nippur visits his dream and tells him, quite practically, that if he will put together three fragments in the museum collection, he will find that they present an inscription. The next day he carried out the suggestion with good results. The inscription read: 'To the god, Ninib, son of Bel, his lord, has Kurigalzu, pontifex of Bel, presented this'. Since the dream priest was ostensibly wiser than the dreamer and a professional besides, I think he represented a teacher.

I know that the late Professor Otto Loewi had a kind of eerie feeling about the dream which led to his discovery of the role of acetylcholine. His feeling contained a certain awe, and I have always thought his interest in psychoanalysis and his proposing of Freud for the Nobel Prize were as if in gratitude for the dream.

Whatever the manifest symbols or elaboration in the dream which brings a practical solution of concrete problems, the knowledge seems entirely the same in quality as that received by Poincaré getting on the bus in Caen or by Archimedes in his bath. Whether in the more relaxed state of bath, fireside, bed, or, as with another of Kekulé's experiences, in the jogging of a bus ride, inspiration has the same quality of revelation. The content of the dreams and Kekulé's filial piety tend to confirm Kris's (1952, pp. 281-302) idea of the father as the source of inspiration. Light sleep or reverie in a hypnagogic state fosters the passive recipience of the thinker and the proneness to visual fantasy in this state may be important. For the rest, Kris's exposition of inspiration and its apparent external provenance apply rigorously to this situation. Here I leave my identification with Artemidorus, the interpreter from out of his own associations, and join Heraclitus and Xenophanes by taking an essentially naturalistic attitude toward the informative dream.

The great sense of truth and certainty, such as Descartes experienced, can occur without much intellectual content. After a dream which seems exceptionally revealing, a dreamer retains a sense of its great importance and is seized with an impulse to write it down. This not infrequently occurs with the induction stage of general anesthesia. A feeling of great illumination not unlike Descartes's sense of direct supernatural inspiration often arises; Saint Theresa of Ávila, when she tried to describe one of her orisons, exclaimed: '*Ojalá pudiera tener diez manos para escribirlos*' ('If I only had ten hands to write this down with'). But the records are no more illuminating than those of other dreams, and indeed often there is no record at all.

An instance of this sense of pure inspiration is preserved by a diary entry of the poet, Stephen Spender (1956). It relates to his inspiration under gas anesthesia.

> Having had teeth extracted under gas five or six times, I am puzzled and fascinated by the dream I always have under gas, which I know to be as formal as some special figure of speech. I remember it right up to the moment of regaining consciousness. Part of the dream is my determination, while I am dreaming, to remember it. The elements that go into the dream are as follows: I am conscious of the mask being placed over my face, and I start thinking, 'Now I am going under'. Then this thought changes to its opposite—that I am not under, that I wish the operation had taken place, and I know it has done so. This idea repeats over and over again, until finally it is interrupted by a click (which is the tooth being extracted) and I recover consciousness. Recently when I had this experience, the dream was particularly vivid, and I was very conscious of dreaming it. I thought I would recall every detail and then (as it also seemed extremely funny) I would make an article for Punch out of my always having the same dream under gas. At the moment of regaining consciousness, I remembered to tell the dentist that I would be able to pay him his fee out of my Punch article. I then tried to explain to him the dream and I said (really very aptly) 'It is like a trill'. At the same time I could no longer understand what 'It' was, although even now it still leaves me with the feeling of something classically clear and extremely vivid, which nevertheless I cannot recapture. The dream under gas brought up into consciousness is like bringing up to the ocean surface one of those enormous, strange-shaped fish which (we are told) dwell on the deepest ocean floor and then, as soon as they reach the surface, explode.

I imagine Mr. Spender could have supplied associations to his final metaphor that would have given insight into the experience, but I present the text here to show the existence of what might by an analogy be called 'blank inspiration'.

A comparable dream experience comes from a work of fiction, Thornton Wilder's (1948) *Ides of March.* Julius Caesar is writing to an old friend:

> You asked me, laughingly, whether I had experienced the dream of the void. I told you I had and I have dreamed it since.
>
> It is perhaps occasioned by a chance posture of the sleeping body or by some indigestion or derangement within us, but the terror in the mind is no less real for that. It is not, as I once thought, the image of death and the grin of the skull. It is the state in which one divines the end of all things. This nothingness, however, does not present itself to us as a blank and quiet, but as a total evil unmasked. It is at once laughter and menace. It turns into ridicule all delights and sears and shrivels all endeavor. The dream is the counterpart of that other vision which comes to me in the paroxysm of my illness. Then I seem to grasp the fair harmony of the world. I am filled with unspeakable happiness and confidence. I wish to cry out to all the living and all the dead that there is no part of the universe that is untouched by bliss.
>
> [The entry continues in Greek.] Both states arise from vapors in the body, yet of both of them the mind says: henceforth I know. They cannot be dismissed as illusions. To each our memory brings many a radiant and many a woeful corroboration. We cannot disown one without disowning the other, nor would I—like a village peacemaker reconciling the differences of two contending parties—accord to each a shrunken measure of the right (p. 231).

The above specimens of dream cognition and dream inspiration show great qualitative differences in manifest content. They range from pure rhapsodic feeling with no contribution to ordinary knowledge and great symbolic sense of discovery (Descartes) to the nearly matter-of-fact dream statement about such things as the benzene ring. The ecstatic sense of knowing without sensory evidence resembles one of the types of knowledge described by Freud, but there is a difference. For example, the certainty that a recovered memory refers to a real event, which Kris (1952, pp. 281-302) aligns with *recognition,* does not have the grandiose quality of ecstatic knowledge and is subject to reason. The superego seems to have yielded and has not re-enforced the archaic omniscience of the ego. It is the same difference we imply when we contrast strength to omnipotence.

Knowledge obtained from dreams has figured constantly in philosophic discussions since the fifth century B.C., when Heraclitus and Xenophanes stated that the dreamer lives in a private world and that science must deal only with what men know in common. Obviously, dream in this definition means manifest picture. E. R. Dodds (1951) tells us that the Greeks distinguished between ordinary dreams, which were considered valid and quasi-factual, and supernatural divine dreams, which were brought to the sleeper by the gods. Descartes's dream as well as Professor Hilprecht's fall into the latter category, though they differ from each other; Descartes believes his dream to be supernatural, while Hilprecht only alleges this as manifest dream content. Both may have been influenced by the ideas of antiquity. Regardless of form, dreams that come through the gates of horn are troublesome to mortals, and only since 1900 have they lost their uncanny aura.

When Descartes wrote his Principles of Philosophy[2] and came to the discussions of dreams, he appears to take an entirely naturalistic position about the validity of dreams. He concurs with Heraclitus in regarding dreams invalid as statements of fact. He begins his statement of Principles by immediately taking for granted Heraclitus's point of view and by using the invalidity of dream sensations to question the validity of waking sense evidence. The first reason for doubting our senses, he tells us, is because we know from experience that they may deceive us. But in the second place, we must doubt them 'because in sleep we continually seem to feel or imagine innumerable things which have no existence'. He comes back to this uncertainty later in a famous passage in his Meditations:

> I am in this place, seated by the fire, clothed in a winter dressing-gown . . . but I nevertheless consider that I am a man, and that consequently I am in the habit of sleeping and rep-

[2] See *The Philosophical Works of Descartes*. New York: Dover Publications, 1955 [Ed.].

> resenting to myself in dreams those same things, or sometimes others less probable, which the insane think are presented to them in their waking moments. How often have I dreamt that I was in these familiar circumstances—that I was dressed and occupied this place by the fire, when I was lying undressed in bed? . . . I cannot forget that at other times I have been deceived in sleep by similar illusions; and attentively considering these cases, I perceive so clearly that there exist no certain marks by which the state of waking can ever be distinguished from sleep that I feel greatly astonished, and in amazement I almost persuade myself that I am now dreaming (Vol. I, pp. 145-146).

Again in the Principle numbered IX, he says: 'If by seeing and walking I mean the action of my eyes and legs, which is the work of my body, my conclusion is not absolutely certain; because it may be that, as often happens in sleep, I think I see or walk, although I never open my eyes or move from my place, and the same things perhaps might occur if I had not a body at all.' (Descartes's wish that he had no body at all, I think, is derived from that old dream where he had too much body.) Elsewhere Descartes's thoughts revert to the difference between dreaming and waking states and also to the question, 'Where is my body?'. To take his strict statement of uncertainty with its implication of the illusiveness of all dreams, and then to compare it with his belief in the divine intervention in his dream of 1619, some twenty years before, shows a strange split in the philosopher's beliefs. He trusts the divine dream, he distrusts the ordinary dream, like a not entirely rational Greek. What he has to say in his writings about the quality of *clarity* as a criterion of reliability of knowledge reminds one forcibly of the 'clarity' he experienced in the illuminated section of his old dream. The brightening of his room permitted him to understand in the usual French way of expressing it—'*voir clair*'.

Let us turn now to dreams which have a kind of objective epistemological validity, which Heraclitus himself might not have ridiculed, and use as an example the dreams of the chemist, Kekulé (Robitsek, 1912). His first dream or half-sleeping reverie, dreamt on a long ride on top of a London bus, brought him a picture of the allophatic chain of carbon atoms. In his second dream, which appeared while he was nodding before his fireplace in Ghent, hypnagogic atoms became snakes and then the benzene ring. Both sleeps were brief and light; the sleeper awoke almost immediately. Motility was limited, disturbers of concentration reduced. Kekulé on the Clapham bus has always reminded me of Freud's (1913b, p. 135) hypothetical or paradigmatic psychoanalyst on his imaginary train ride. In this metaphor, the psychoanalyst sits quietly, letting his patient's free associations pass by outside the window. The difference is a matter of psychological optics. Freud's train windows are transparent, the light and the images shine onto them from without. Kekulé, and any dreamer, illuminates from within the screen on which play the visualized incarnations of his own thoughts. In this statement I have barely touched the models which we know as the 'dreaming' psychic apparatus and the 'analyzing instrument' (Isakower, 1939).

Kekulé's dreams were limited to pictures, to snakes and atoms in motion, and he himself supplied the rationalized interpretation. Other dreams contain the 'objective' comment, spoken or tacit. This is best illustrated by the dream in which Professor Hilprecht was visited by the oracular priest of Nippur, who admonished him to put together the three pottery fragments and to note the resulting text. Such a dream resembles closely that type described by Isakower (1954) in which verbal remarks at the end of a dream express the superego's opinion of the dream content or the dreamer. In the example used by Isakower, there was no visually represented superego-figure; a voice, while the sleeper was waking up, said: 'Your swinish lovelife [*deine Liebesschweinereien*] shall yet come into the open'. Professor Hilprecht on the surface had no bad conscience. What he needed to preserve sleep was to exclude from his mind further thinking about the museum specimens, and he let the priest in the dream do his thinking for him. This dream form is the same as the one used by Freud (1900-1901, p. 510) as a paradigm in Chapter VII of The Interpretation of Dreams to illustrate the sleep-guarding function of the dream; namely, the dream of the burning child.

However, a priest is certainly an authoritative superego or

father figure and this should differentiate even his most objective remarks from a pure copy of the dreamer's rationalizing. The priest seems to represent a projection of rational thought condensed with that authority which belongs to an initiate or master of a craft. The priest is not only thinker but authority and knowledge bringer. The dream allocation reminds us of Freud's two different statements about the location of the sense of reality and rational critique, which at one time he placed in the superego (1923a), at another in the ego (1923b). In Hilprecht's dream, the dreamer reverts to a time and stage where not only all ethical knowledge but rational knowledge too is the province of parents and teachers, the stage of the ego to which Descartes also may be regressing when he says that omniscient God would not deceive us. The Assyriologist may have needed such a quasi-divine reassurance concerning his new knowledge; the priest, as a father-teacher figure, not only permits new knowledge but even reveals it to him. Many thinkers appear to have difficulty in passing beyond this state of development, perhaps unconsciously, and must somehow deal with scientific and allegedly objective ideas of their teachers as if they were dogma. In this sense, the priest's knowledge was 'divine', with the compelling quality of early childhood instruction concerning nature.

Descartes too seems to have been insecure not so much about the evidence of his senses (for all his ruminations) as about his right to think originally.[3] He had been restless and filled by 'enthusiasm' concerning his discoveries for many days before his dream. His dream resolved whatever conflict he had about their validity. For if, as he knew, the Angel of Truth had come to inspire him with certainty and the dream was divinely inspired, he then had the Greatest Teacher in agreement with him, one surely superior to the professional theologians of the University of Paris, who were later on to disagree with his philosophy. In many passages, Descartes is at pains to show that confidence in his Principles does not depend ultimately on him and on his thinking. In the discourse in which he outlines the reasons for his philosophic doubt, he asserts the inevitable knowledge of God's existence and perfec-

[3] See, *Aristotelian Society Symposia.* London: Harrison & Sons, 1956.

tion; not too far away from his statement 'I think, therefore I am' he makes his often-quoted remarks that God would not deceive us, echoed in our day by Einstein's 'The good Lord does not play games'.

Conceivably, in the sense outlined above, the new is always tainted with the impious since it goes against what has been learned. New knowledge struggles not only against error and imperfection in the old, but also against its veneration. When a psychoanalytic patient asks the analyst to tell him what is 'the truth', we have a mild example of this conflict. In the transference, teachers figure more than many realize, certainly when the patient is also a learner. All of us, including Descartes, are still somewhat afraid of teachers and endow them unconsciously with omniscience even while we are doubting them. The authority of teachers as an element in the transference has been recognized at least since Freud's (1918[1914]) account of the Wolf-man, who gave Freud the confidence he had in childhood given to his German tutor.

As a tentative classification of informative dreams we can distinguish: 1, the dream of direct instruction, such as Professor Hilprecht's; 2, the dream of visual thinking, such as Kekulé's; and 3, the dream of symbolic inspiration such as Descartes's.

Our attempt to classify dreams makes appropriate a reference to the chapter called Dream Pattern and Culture in Dodds' book referred to previously. Dodds thinks that the early Greeks may have had dreams of a different form from those we have nowadays. Homer's characters had their dreams brought to them, whether these were prophetic, ordinary, or oracular experiences. The ordinary dream was called an *oneiros,* and the word meant not only dream but also the presumed figure that brought it, whether god, ghost, absent friend, or other messenger. This *oneiros* came into the bedroom through the keyhole, stood over the sleeper and announced directly: 'You are asleep, son of Atreus', or in the form of Patroclus: 'You are asleep, Achilles', or as a shadowy figure: 'You are asleep, Penelope'. It then stated the message and departed again through the keyhole. The second form of dream was called the *horama,* described by Professor Dodds as 'a straightforward enactment of a future event, like those dreams described in the book of the ingenious J. W. Dunne'. The third type of Homeric dream was named the *chrematismos* or oracle; 'when the dreamer's parent, or some other respected or impressive personage, perhaps a priest or even a god, reveals without symbolism what will or will not happen, or should or should not be done'. For this reason our Assyriologist's dream noted earlier in this paper would be oracular, a *chrematismos*.

I do not know that Dodds is correct in assuming that Homeric culture determined that the Greeks should have this form of dream and did really dream this way. It seems rather stylized and literary. Nevertheless, their irrational attitude concerning the message of manifest dream contents and their wish to find in them divine or superior knowledge, particularly in the *chrematismos,* deserves some attention. A wish for such oneirogenic or chrematistogenic knowledge is at the bottom of Silberer's and Jung's special interpretations, while more rational interpreters such as Kekulé attribute such knowledge to the father. The Assyriologist invented a dream-teacher and Dilthey summoned the great teachers of all time to enter the picture of the School of Athens to instruct him.

I once noted that a dreamer attributes his awakening to his father of the pre-œdipal nursing period who comes to disturb him in his sleep at the maternal breast. In such circumstances the message is either a simple or a more complex 'Get up!'. The father-figures visualized or latent in the dreams discussed here do not seem to bring such a message; in fact, they carry on the dreamer's thinking for him. They and not the dreamer seem to carry on the waking functions. The *res cogitans* in such a dream, so far as the self-perception is of intellectual workings, is not merged with the *res cogitans* that is simply viewing the dream. Thought is external and projectible, as Isakower has explained. Nevertheless, it seems to me that the dreams of information and knowledge are 'waking dreams' in one sense of that phrase, i.e., dreams which occur near waking up and include some reference to the process, not unlike Freud's paradigmatic dream of the burning child. Homeric messengers and gods, standing over the sleeper, are the arouser-figures transmuted into the dream content by the device of visualization; their assurance 'you are asleep' is the denial of their more usual wakening function, somewhat as if they were using hypnotic suggestion. When rational thoughts and intellectual solutions disturb our sleep, we can identify them with the original pre-œdipal waker, the father, and we can use the dream work to mingle with the arouser-figure attributes of later father-figures. Arousing in this way is turned into instruction, and the sleep-guarding triumphs for its brief moment.

The dreams of pure rhapsodic revelation, such as Mr. Spender's at the dentist, are not dreams of instruction nor are they dreams of the near awake period. They resemble the knowledge that one is said to imbibe with one's mother's milk. When they are without any visual content or action, that is, when they are blank ecstatic dreams, they do indeed repeat that situation and are the fantasy guarantee of good sleep, uncompromised by the disturbing presence of father, thought, and everyday reality. Their sense of reality corresponds to the sense of reality of Freud's dreamer who received the two pears.

Somewhere between this early learning experience and the formal instruction of priests and teachers, mostly verbally transmitted, comes the mixed type of learning by seeing for one's self. There may be some comment and demonstration that helps show us how to see, resembling perhaps in lucky circumstances the instruction Minnie Abercrombie (1960) gives her class. This genetically intermediate type of experience promotes our originally unshakable belief in our eyes, to which Descartes also refers, in our a priori synthetic judgments, if it is appropriate to introduce this term here. Our early naïve experiences, like the visual contents of dreams, had a direct certainty in them and Descartes appeals to this certainty in the passage quoted earlier in this paper. Later the certainty of our early perceptions is also attacked, and when we awaken the same thing happens that we saw in dreams. But for all that, with greater or less pretext and rationalization, there apparently persists in all of us, consciously or unconsciously, a certain faith in dream experiences or in some dream experiences and a reluctance to dismiss them, as well as a corresponding reluctance to credit them. It may be that latent confidence in the truth of dreams stands us in good stead as psychoanalysts. Freud's reliance on his dream discoveries was, as we know, heroic.

We all seem primitive enough to have somewhere in us the same belief as the Greeks in the messages that come through the gates of horn and ivory. And we may consider Professor Dodds' wise remarks as substantive:

> It is not surprising that man was slow to confine the attribute of reality to one of his two worlds and to dismiss the other as pure illusion. The stage was reached in antiquity only by a small number of intellectuals, and there are still today many primitive peoples who attribute to a certain type of dream experience a validity equal to that of waking life, though of a different kind.

Frazer called the development of superstition into science Psyche's task. Psyche's task for the psychoanalyst has been with dreams; Freud's accomplishment is an appropriate subject to celebrate on the occasion of this Freud Memorial Lecture.

VII. THE TRAIN RIDE: A STUDY OF ONE OF FREUD'S FIGURES OF SPEECH*

In an apt analogy, Freud (1913b) compares the psychoanalytic situation to a train ride and the emergent free associations to the passing scenery. This appears in his paper, On Beginning the Treatment, one in a series of papers on technique written to counsel his younger colleagues. Freud writes as a friendly mentor, taking the less experienced into his confidence and letting them have a look over his shoulder while he handles the various concrete details of psychoanalytic treatment. His matter-of-fact, didactic but undogmatic style is consistently that of an adviser who assumes implicitly that his readers are journeymen and professionals with skill and experience, capable of making intelligent comparison of the master's way and their own.

The passage that includes the train-ride figure is written in direct discourse, as if Freud were addressing a beginning patient and explaining to him the requirements of the analytic situation:

> So say whatever goes through your mind. Act as though, for instance, you were a traveller sitting next to the window of a railway carriage and describing to someone inside the carriage the changing views which you see outside (p. 135).

This figure is now so familiar that the reference is rarely given, and it is sometimes attributed to the Introductory Lectures.

I have made this mistake, and I am grateful to Lottie M. Newman for setting me right and also for referring me to another train-ride comparison which I shall quote from the letters to Fliess. Such a mistake seems trivial, but it conceals or ignores the difference between the audiences addressed. The

* [No. 137 in Bibliography.]

recipients of Freud's messages—Fliess, younger colleagues, a more general public—differ in readiness to understand. The messages differ accordingly.

To search for antecedents of a trope is in the psychoanalytic tradition. To cite Arlow's (1969) neat sentence, 'Metaphor constitutes an outcropping into conscious expression of a fragment of unconscious fantasy' (p. 7). And he quotes Ella Freeman Sharpe's (1940) remark: 'When dynamic thought and emotional experiences of the forgotten past find the appropriate verbal image in the preconscious, language is as predetermined as a slip of the tongue or trick of behavior'.

As to the train ride, the ostensibly common-sense comparison has antecedents. A train window appears much earlier in Freud's (1887-1902) thoughts, in a different setting and written down for a different order of reader.

> . . . I am living only for 'inner' work. It gets hold of me and hauls me through the past in rapid association of ideas; and my mood changes like the landscape seen by a traveller from a train; and, as the great poet [Goethe], using his privilege to ennoble (sublimate) things, puts it:—
>
> *Und manche liebe Schatten steigen auf;*
> *Gleich einer alten, halbverklungnen Sage,*
> *Kommt erste Lieb' und Freundschaft mit herauf.*
>
> ['And the shades of loved ones appear, and with them, like an old, half-forgotten myth, first love and friendship.'] (p. 225).

This quotation is from a letter to Wilhelm Fliess (No. 72), written on October 27, 1897; that is, fifteen to seventeen years before Freud's papers on technique. The train-ride figure is already implicit in the clause that begins 'It gets hold of me and hauls me'. The original German reads '*Es packt und zerrt mich durch alte Zeiten*' and the word *es* does not have as its antecedent 'inner work' (*innere Arbeit*), which the word *it* seems to have in English.[1] '*Es*' here has no antecedent noun, but as in *es freut mich* or *es träumt mir,* etc., is the kind of *es* which was itself to become substantified as *das Es,* the id. The German *packt* is more vigorous than 'gets hold of'; its

[1] See, *Aus den Anfängen der Psychoanalyse; Briefe an Wilhelm Fliess, Abhandlungen und Notizen aus den Jahren 1887-1902.* London: Imago Publishing Co., 1950, p. 240 [Ed.].

phonetic effect is *grab* or *grapple.* In the context of what follows immediately, i.e., the comparison with the traveler, the image produced in a reader is something like a locomotive latching on to cars and hauling them to wherever it is headed.

The letters to Fliess, a man of Freud's own generation and a close friend, naturally have no didactic intention. They continue and supplement intimate conversations. The passage just quoted describes moods and daydreams lyrically. They might have taken form in a poem if Goethe's lines had not been at hand, ready to serve vicariously.[2] Taking Fliess's understanding for granted, Freud is alluding to the progress of his self-analysis, conveying the feeling of it and alluding to its cognitive contents and to intellectual insights.

The day that Letter No. 72 was written, October 27, 1897, the train-ride idea may have been fresh in Freud's mind; for in another letter, No. 70, written twenty-four days earlier on October 3, Freud (1887-1902) tells Fliess of very early train rides.

> . . . later (between the ages of two and two-and-a-half) libido towards *matrem* was aroused; the occasion must have been the journey with her from Leipzig to Vienna, during which we spent a night together and I must have had the opportunity of seeing her *nudam* (you have long since drawn the conclusions from this for your own son, as a remark of yours revealed) . . . (p. 219).

Dr. Otto Isakower has pointed out to me that this letter was written just four days after Freud returned from a visit with Fliess in Berlin (p. 217, n.), so that he could have been affected by the events of the recent ride too.[3]

Freud's ideas about the early train ride were constructions. This is evident from his way of phrasing his account ('I *must*

[2] Following K. R. Eissler (1963), one could also put it that Goethe when he wrote the poem had a 'proto-psychoanalytic' experience. Eissler writes that Goethe undertook a proto-psychoanalysis with a lady at the court of Weimar, and he indicates many parallels between Goethe and Freud.

[3] Dr. Isakower interprets the events on the September 29 train ride as follows: 'Freud was sitting in the railway car, looking *out* of the window and *into* himself. He paid no attention to the view at all but was "talking" to Fliess what he then wrote to him four days later.' He suggests: 'The return journey, modulating the Cs.-Pcs. into a predormescent "railwaying" state, could be seen as a catalyst facilitating a merging of Fliess's remark about his son (probably during this visit) with the early Leipzig-Vienna journey and its *matrem-nudam* glimpse'.

have had the opportunity . . .') and more directly because of his statement after he had listed the putative early events: 'I still have not got to the scenes which lie at the bottom of all this'. He hopes to get at them, and

> If they emerge, and I succeed in resolving my hysteria, I shall have to thank the memory of the old woman [his nurse] who provided me at such an early age with the means for living and surviving (pp. 219-220).

That 'scenes' would emerge suggests that Freud expected his early memories would appear to him in pictorial form.

Another remark in the later of the two letters (Letter No. 72) equates psychoanalysis with a railroad journey:

> An idea about resistance has enabled me to put back on the rails all the cases of mine which looked like breaking down . . . (p. 226).

Two years then passed and on December 21, 1899, Freud again alludes to a railroad in quite a different unmetaphorical context. Apropos a scene remembered by a patient, Freud writes to Fliess (Letter No. 126):

> Buried deep beneath all his phantasies we found a scene from his primal period (before twenty-two months) which meets all requirements and into which all the surviving puzzles flow. . . . I can hardly bring myself to believe it yet. It is as if Schliemann had dug up another Troy which had hitherto been believed to be mythical . . . . with a surprising turn [in his analysis] he provided me with the solution of my own railway phobia (which I had overlooked) (pp. 305-306).

Fliess may have had further information, but from the letter alone it is hard to say whether Freud meant that he had recalled an equivalent scene in his own infancy, that an unexpected 'scene' had emerged, or whether the patient provided him with a new fragment in his construction. One would infer the emergence of a memory, but his later remarks on the therapeutic efficacy of some constructions without recall permit a doubt (Freud, 1937b).

An overview of Freud's early travel is given by Ernest Jones (1953-1957, Vol. I). When Freud was three years old, the family moved from Freiberg to Leipzig, and

> He remembered the long ride in the horse-drawn vehicle and his first sight of a railway. This took him from his beautifully

> rolling country with its meadows, hills, and forests to the town of Leipzig.
>
> . . . On the way to Leipzig the train passed through Breslau, where Freud saw gas jets for the first time; they made him think of souls burning in hell! From this journey also dated the beginning of a 'phobia' of traveling by train, from which he suffered a good deal for about a dozen years (1887-1899), before he was able to dispel it by analysis. It turned out to be connected with the fear of losing his home (and ultimately his mother's breast)—a panic of starvation which must have been in its turn a reaction to some infantile greed. Traces of it remained in later life in the form of slightly undue anxiety about catching trains.
>
> On the journey from Leipzig to Vienna, a year later, Freud had occasion to see his mother naked; an awesome fact which forty years later he related in a letter to Fliess—but in Latin! Curiously enough he gives his age then as between two and two and a half, whereas he was in fact four years old on that journey. One must surmise that the memories of two such experiences had got telescoped (p. 13).

For the sake of exposition, I have omitted the references that Jones gives to support his statements, but one of them does not bear him out; considering Jones's knowledge of his subject, I think he made a slip. Freud (1899) does not say he remembered the early train and carriage ride. In fact,

> I have no knowledge of the birth of a sister, who is two and a half years younger than I am; my departure, my first sight of the railway and the long carriage-drive before it—none of these has left a trace in my memory. On the other hand, I can remember two small occurrences during the railway-journey; these, as you will recollect, came up in the analysis of my phobia (p. 310).

This is a quotation from the paper on screen memories which is known to be a disguised piece of autobiography. The fictitious patient writes to his doctor very much as Freud wrote to Fliess. In this paper, Freud was considering precisely the difference between genuine, significant early memories and the screen or cover memories of 'small occurrences' which themselves needed further analysis. His statement indicates that he was aware that the events 'must have happened' but that he had no pictorial memories to report.

It is of course impossible to say for sure whether Freud, in 1899, definitely expected to recapture vivid pictures from his earliest years. Nevertheless, a good deal of collateral information, contained in the Studies on Hysteria (Breuer and Freud, 1893-1895) suggests such an expectation. The patients responsible for the case reports were treated by methods transitional from hypnosis through catharsis to near-psychoanalysis,[4] and they provided Breuer and Freud with vivid pictures.

Near the beginning of the Studies, Breuer speaks of 'another patient' (other than Anna O), who 'partly under hypnosis and partly during spontaneous attacks, re-lived with hallucinatory clarity all the events of a hysterical psychosis which she had passed through ten years earlier' (p. 9). Hallucinatory clarity impressed Freud too. His patient, Emmy von N, recalling and describing certain scenes, 'saw them before her, in a plastic form and in their natural colors . . . with all the vividness of reality' (p. 53). Another patient, Lucy R, according to Freud, was of the 'visual type' (p. 115) and with therapy switched the sensory modality in which an important event was remembered. The smell of burnt pudding, which plagued her as a symptom, disappeared when she replaced it by a picture of the occasion when the pudding was burnt. Freud asked her, 'Do you see this scene clearly before your eyes?' And she responded, 'As large as life, just as I experienced it' (p. 114).

With another patient, Elisabeth von R, Freud, exerting 'pressure' on her head, instructed her 'to report to me faithfully whatever appeared before her inner eye or passed through her memory at the moment of the pressure' (p. 145). 'Throughout the analysis I made use of the technique of bringing out pictures and ideas by means of pressing on the patient's head . . .' (p. 153). Shortly after this remark, we come upon a precursor of the railroad-window analogy, this time with no railroad but with the same visual reference: 'It was as though she were reading a lengthy book of pictures, whose pages were being turned over before her eyes' (p. 153).[5]

[4] For a justification of these designations, see James Strachey's Editor's Introduction to the Studies on Hysteria (pp. ix-xxviii).

[5] Dr. Otto Isakower writes me concerning this 'precursor of the railroad-window analogy':

'Your statement received a stunning super-confirmation. Reading your quotation from p. 153, I suddenly saw what Freud must have meant to describe in his analogy, because—yes, because—I felt curiously irritated by the wording of the

Other patients also 'saw' and reported to Freud what they were seeing. A patient not named and referred to as 'a mourner'

> Every day . . . would go through each impression once more . . . a work of reproduction which once more brought up before her eyes the scenes of the illness and death (p. 162) [and] . . . her vivid visual reproduction and expressions of feeling kept to the date [of anniversaries] precisely (p. 163).

The patients were all in treatment between 1889 and 1892, before Freud began his self-analysis and wrote to Fliess about his moods and the passing scenery.[6]

With this as a background, we can hazard an 'informed guess' as to what Freud expected to happen in his self-analysis. For if, in 1897 or 1899, the self-analysis was to resemble in its own way those of his patients, he would expect free associations to bring back before his inner eye the important scenes of his early life. Tacitly, like Schliemann, with whom he identified himself, he would wish to see the past with his own eyes, certainly with the inner eye of which he spoke to his patients.

To continue the 'informed guess', it is conceivable that Freud's experience with hypnosis, catharsis, and near-analysis would initially make him take for granted that the store of memories was not exhausted until pictures of forgotten early events stood plastically before his eyes, as they did before

---

text (the translator evidently did not see the image suggested by Freud). In the German original (*Gesammelte Werke,* 1, 218): *"Es war, als läse sie in einem* langen *Bilderbuche, dessen Seiten vor ihren Augen* vorübergezogen *würden"* ['pulled along before her eyes'].

'This undoubtedly refers to a type of picture-book (called "Leporello book") for very young children, the pictures mounted on strong cardboard, hinged together like an accordion; the pictures, often "running scenes", forming one long frieze.'

[6] In a footnote added to the case history of Emmy von N in 1924, Freud (Breuer and Freud, 1893-1895) writes, 'I am aware that no analyst can read this case history to-day without a smile of pity. But it should be borne in mind that this was the first case in which I employed the cathartic procedure to a large extent' (p. 105, n.). In 1969, however, one reads with admiration and instruction. The smile comes when the stage and cinema portray 'psychoanalysis' and 'Sigmund Freud'. Then Lucy R or one of her fellow patients is presented so that the medium can show the dramatic 'hallucinatory clarity' of her memories and can flash back to earlier scenes. The media have to settle for the pictorial simplicity of hypnotism or catharsis.

the inner eye of his patients. His discovery of the nature of screen memories, fantasies, and false memories—which also usually present themselves as pictures—and his beginning insight into the defenses indicated other possibilities. Yet, significantly, hallucinatory clarity (and ultra-clarity) were to occupy him many times, from the Studies on Hysteria through his late paper on construction (Freud, 1937b). The same phenomena interested other psychoanalysts as well, particularly Abraham (1913b). Some of the old expectation may have lurked behind Freud's (1918[1914]) discussion of the reality of the Wolf-man's primal scene.

To return to Freud's account of the eventful early train rides and to Ernest Jones's comment on the *matrem nudam* episode, Jones calls the sight of the nude mother 'an awesome fact which forty years later he related in a letter to Fliess—but in Latin!'. The exclamation point is of course purposely ambiguous, a sign perhaps that Jones appreciated the mock-medical-history humor in Freud's style. However, even without certainty as to Jones's intentions, the exclamation point can be used as what was at one time called a 'complex indicator', a signal that more can be said about the reasons for using Latin.

Why Jones chose the word *awesome* is not clear. As Jones (1953-1957, Vol. I, p. 8) faithfully reports, in the letter Freud speaks not of being awed but bluntly of his aroused libido. *Awe* is best known to psychoanalysts as phallic awe,[7] such as Jones (1933) elsewhere tells us is inspired by contemplation of the decorations on certain South Asian temples—having to do, that is, more with *patrem nudum* than with *matrem nudam*.

As to the Latin words in the letter to Fliess, Latin of this sort is doctors' and medical students' argot. Its use implies confidentiality and confraternity, and among confreres such Latin remarks are part of a professional or guild dialect, stemming from the universities and the Middle Ages.[8] To put the

[7] *Cf.*, Greenacre (1953b): *Penis Awe and Penis Envy.*

[8] 'European works of learning were normally written in Latin until the late seventeenth century. Latin continued to be used for degree disputations at Cambridge until about the middle of the nineteenth century; and it was not until 1845 that an Oxonian Master of Arts, when arraigned before the authorities of the University, was given permission to defend himself in English rather than in Latin' (Brittain, 1962, p. 1).

matter a bit reductively, students' Latin furnishes an ideal language for the colloquial transmission of private information between brothers. In the social microcosm of the family and in the original 'peer group' (an 'ennobling' term for a community of brothers), or more simply, from 'the boys', Freud had found out a good deal.[9] Paradoxically, then, the use of Latin, because it is Latin, testifies to Freud's forthrightness, as I hope to show below after I have brought to bear other events and statements.

The first of such statements is an appeal to Freud's (1905 [1901]) readers and especially to doctors for understanding: he defends his right to use plain language in dealing with sexual matters.

> Now in this case history . . . sexual questions will be discussed with all possible frankness, the organs and functions of sexual life will be called by their proper names, and the pure-minded reader can convince himself from my description that I have not hesitated to converse upon such subjects in such language even with a young woman. Am I, then, to defend myself upon this score as well? I will simply claim for myself the rights of the gynaecologist—or rather, much more modest ones–and add that it would be the mark of a singular and perverse prurience to suppose that conversations of this kind are a good means of exciting or of gratifying sexual desires (p. 9).[10]

I quote the above passage not to demonstrate Freud's candor but to inquire into his choice of 'the gynaecologist' as a pertinent model. Quite rationally of course, gynecologists must speak openly about sexual matters with their patients and in their writings. Since Freud specifically disclaims any gynecological rights beyond these, and since what he does claim seems nothing more than any responsible physician would be entitled to, there appears to be a problem here: why a gynecologist? The answer may lie in another excerpt from

[9] 'One would remark on the coincidence (?) that the boy from whom Freud derived early sexual knowledge in the Freiberg period was also called Philipp. It seems odd that he should have remembered, and also troubled to record, this name, but it was from his brother Philipp that he had learned something about pregnancy' (Jones, 1953-1957, Vol. I, p. 9, n.).

[10] Actually in this paper I found only six instances of Latin: *Tussis nervosa; 'inter urinas et faeces nascimur'; tu quoque; Psychopathia sexualis* (book title); *ipso facto;* and *deus ex machina.*

Freud's writings, oddly enough one in which doctors' Latin again appears.

The *matrem nudam* episode was recorded at a time (1897) when his practice and professional life had provided Freud a highly valued contact with an eminent gynecologist, Rudolf Chrobak, mentioned several times in the letters to Fliess (Freud, 1887-1902, pp. 54, 139);[11] and later in On the History of the Psychoanalytic Movement, Freud (1914a) ranked him with Charcot and Breuer as an important guide to the sexual theory of hysteria. As Freud tells the story, the occasion was a consultation on a patient whom Chrobak wished to turn over to Freud for treatment.

> When Chrobak arrived he took me aside and told me that the patient's anxiety was due to the fact that although she had been married for eighteen years she was still *virgo intacta.* The husband was absolutely impotent. . . . The sole prescription for such a malady, he added, is familiar enough to us, but we cannot order it. It runs:
>
> 'ꝶ Penis normalis
> dosim
> repetatur!'
>
> I had never heard of such a prescription, and felt inclined to shake my head over my kind friend's cynicism (pp. 14-15).

Yet despite the negation implied in the head-shake and the judgment of cynicism, Freud came to 'espouse the idea', and as he says this was a genuine espousal and no mere flirtation. Chrobak later on could not remember the incident (*ibid.,* p. 13), nor did Freud until he came to write the History (*cf.,* Freud, 1887-1902, p. 54, n.). Freud admired Chrobak, called him 'perhaps the most eminent of all our Vienna physicians', and said that his 'opinions commanded my deepest respect'.

That Chrobak's off-the-record prescription (like the comparable remark of Breuer about the *secrets d'alcôve* and Charcot's *c'est toujours la chose génitale*) gave Freud a right start is hardly the whole story. What Freud admired was the forthrightness of Chrobak and the other two, and this forthrightness of 'the gynaecologist' seems to enter into his claim

[11] In a consultation with Chrobak early in 1888, Freud spoke 'very strongly in the patient's presence, and not without intention, about the harmfulness of *coitus reservatus*'. (Surely not in Latin!) Such an occasion was good training for psychoanalytic frankness.

to use plain language. 'The gynaecologist' as such may have a special meaning; certainly psychoanalysts recently have shown a willingness to learn from him many more *secrets d'alcôve*.[12]

The Chrobak story returns us to the papers on technique, unexpectedly, though not to the train ride. These papers, as I said, were pedagogical in style, didactic though undogmatic, directed to less experienced colleagues. From the quality of the practical wisdom in them, there forms a picture of Freud's playing the same role of friendly mentor that Chrobak played during the consultation, and that Breuer played on other occasions—of Freud imparting as they did empirical knowledge to a junior confrere. It is difficult to say how much the example of his masters and their willingness to share with him the secrets of the bed chamber and of the consulting room may have been in Freud's mind when he wrote the technical papers. But the papers were written from 1912 to 1914, and the Chrobak story was recalled and written down in the latter year.

After these extensive quotations and side excursions, it is time, as Freud said, to get back on the rails; that is, to the train compartment and specifically to the analytic situation described in the 1913 instructions—to the figure of the two passengers and the landscape. The figure, we assumed, had its roots in the train rides of early infancy. The viewing passenger at that time was certainly Freud, and the scenes of importance were within the compartment, if one makes the interpretative reversal and gives landscape its standard dream-symbolic feminine meaning (Freud, 1915-1917, pp. 158, 162, 193). This frequent displacement from (latent) inside to (manifest) outside is perhaps best exemplified by another window, familiar to Freud's readers, the one in the Wolf-man's dream. There the sights depicted in the dream as being outside the window referred to what went on inside a room.

The early train ride, not as a scene but in disguise, broke through into consciousness as a trope in the letter to Fliess.

[12] In a discussion of Mary Jane Sherfey's (1966) paper, *The Evolution and Nature of Female Sexuality in Relation to Psychoanalytic Theory,* the writers agree, in Benedek's words, that 'the method of direct observation . . . reveals phenomena which are not accessible to psychoanalysts'. Vice versa, of course, the method of psychoanalysis reveals phenomena which are not accessible to direct observation.

It was, as Arlow (1969) put it, 'an outcropping into conscious expression of a fragment of unconscious fantasy', invested with the lyrical emotion of Goethe's poem. Freud was borrowing the privilege which he assigned to Goethe of 'ennobling (sublimating)' into poetry his impressions and feelings. Both primary and secondary processes had conspired to alter the infantile experiences into verse and poetic imagery.

A comparison of the text in the 1897 letter with the advice given to younger colleagues in 1913 demonstrates the aptness of Strachey's word *revision* and of Isakower's suggested *redaction* in place of Brill's *elaboration* to translate Freud's *Bearbeitung* (Isakower, 1954).[13] For it seems really as if Freud had started with a rough draft of the train-ride metaphor (not available to us) based on unconscious note-taking in a childhood diary, which was later mislaid and only much later retrieved when the metaphor came to mind 'somehow'. Letter No. 70 resembled Boerne's way of gathering material; Freud permitted himself to record whatever came to mind, not only facts but speculations and partially organized texts still not for publication. Letter No. 72, where the train-ride image appears in connection with a mood-description and the lines from Goethe, is organized. The original notes, some of them still not retrieved, but sufficiently recalled to be adequate for mood-description when combined with other impressions of a railroad journey, enter into a quasi-poetic statement. The train ride appears as image, kinesthetic and visual, in the form of a poetic trope.

Then the same material, whether in draft or partly organized, gets utilized for a new version. It gets revised and redacted, certainly; whether elaborated depends on the definition of this word. The final redaction came when the material was organized for publication in 1913. The comparison is rid of the affective connections of its precursors and of their subjectivity. The beginning analysand is told in direct and matter-of-fact new words to proceed as though he were a passenger looking through the train window and reporting on the sights to an inside passenger. By 1913, much had been secondarily revised and redacted since the early train rides, and the new

[13] Brill's and Strachey's words appear respectively in their translations of *The Interpretation of Dreams*.

text was in truth in form for the printer. Specifically the originally visual impressions had been so winnowed, so much of the personal had been eliminated, that the residue of visual imagery was relatively slight and well subordinated to the verbal, cognitive message. The metaphor had become 'practical'.

The final train-ride figure is excellently adapted for the purposes of psychoanalytic instruction and therapy. A beginning analysand has surely ridden in a train and has probably sat by the window watching the passing scenery. He has (less surely) been exposed to scenes like the intra-compartmental ones of early childhood. But to speak of the window and the train ride is a *lege artis* maneuver. It is an example of what is meant by 'starting with the surface', that is, with the consciously familiar. The rest is initially left up to the beginner, who hopefully will be 'hauled along' when he gets down to real 'inner work' and comes to find and make up his own particular metaphors and similes for the pictures and moods and 'the shadows of old loves', which still have their place in the most modern and sophisticated theories of psychoanalytic technique.

The sequence of events in outline form would run:

1. October 3, 1897 (Letter No. 70): Associations and partial constructions of early events, including train rides. Written with humor, mock-medical style in the 'Latin' part.

2. October 21, 1897 (Letter No. 72): Emergence in lyrical language of a railroad figure of speech, motor and visual. Train ride = analysis. It is interesting that the editors of the Origins chose as the extended title, 'letters, drafts, and notes'.

3. December 21, 1899 (Letter No. 126): Possible emergence of the original scene. Insight into origin of railway phobia and resolution. New material requires new and perhaps extensive conscious redaction; more likely, from the editorial standpoint, to be reserved for a new and different publication.

4. 1913 (On Beginning the Analysis): Matter-of-fact use of train analogy in exposition of psychoanalytic technique, aligning free association with a visual analogue. A relatively small, still visual but unsubjective 'outcropping' of the originally visual.

Freud was well aware that he gathered material for his theories, often without knowing at the time what use he might put such 'mental notes' to. In On the History of the Psychoanalytic Movement, he introduces the anecdotes about Breuer, Charcot, and Chrobak with the following reflection:

> . . . one day, certain memories gathered in my mind which disturbed this pleasing notion [of autochthonous originality of the sexual theory of hysteria], but which gave me in exchange a valuable insight into the processes of human creative activity and the nature of human knowledge. The idea for which I was being made responsible had by no means originated with me. It had been imparted to me by three people whose opinion had commanded my deepest respect . . . (Freud, 1914a, p. 13).

Interestingly, until Freud came to write this essay, he had forgotten one of the incidents, the one which Chrobak too had forgot; Breuer had forgotten the incident that Freud remembered; and Freud felt sure that Charcot too would not have recalled his remarks.

Freud's discovery of such figurative inseminations in the creative process was to receive a general formulation in the works of Ernst Kris (1952, Chapters 13 and 14). In the above passage, Freud disclaims parthenogenesis, finds fathers to his ideas in his three masters, and details the seminal events, which, in themselves ostensibly ephemeral and trivial, were important as inspirations for subsequent unconscious incubation. In much the same way, Freud found the germinal antecedent of his invention of the method of free association in a brief passage in Boerne's writings, which he had read when he was about fourteen.[14]

But the train ride comparison was unfathered. No Breuer and no Chrobak voiced any observations on train journeys;

[14] *Cf.*, Jones (1953-1957, Vol. I): 'When Freud put his trust in the validity of free associations he said he was "following an obscure intuition". We have now a clue to the source of this interesting intuition.' Jones then gives Boerne's 'practical prescription' for becoming 'an original writer in three days', which was to set down everything on paper that came to mind, no matter what. Jones continues: 'He recollected half a century later many passages from the volume in which the essay in question is to be found, though not the actual lines quoted above. Still we may be sure that Börne's startling proposal had sunk into Freud's mind and played its part twenty years later in stimulating him to give his patients' thoughts free play' (pp. 245-246).

nor had he, so far as we know, been alerted to watching scenery by Boerne or any other author. The figure arose from out of his store of personal, private memories. It falls into the general category of sublimation, in accord with Freud's (1914a) rapid definition in the same History, where he speaks of 'the sublimation of erotic instinctual forces and of their transformation into trends which can no longer be called erotic' (p. 61).

Such de-erotizing and increased control by the ego can be demonstrated by considering the different forms assumed by 'train ride'. Three forms can be distinguished definitely in this history: 1, erotic, 2, lyrical, and 3, technical. Historically, the first infantile form is not figurative at all. It is visual, libidinal, experienced personally, suited to take part in the formation of sexual fantasies under the pleasure principle, also susceptible, therefore, to repression and to subsequent vicissitudes. When one of these vicissitudes leads to the outcropping of the lyrical passage in the letter, we have the second form where the figure is close to a daydream. It is emotionally charged but certainly ego controlled, striving for and perhaps attaining sublimation in lyric form, resembling Goethe's 'ennobling' of his shadows. The third form of the figure, which I loosely called technical, is devoid of erotic interest or lyrical emotion. It is part of a sober, didactic exposition, ego-syntonic, socially acceptable, and publishable.

In terms of communicability, the infantile form is something not shared, not told readily even to one's self. It is censored or repressed. The second form can be communicated in friendly intimacy or in the intimate convention of poetic lyricism. The third form is highly publishable.

For all its very different quality, the second, lyrical form of the figure shares its 'intimate' character with the three private foreign-language anecdotes, in that these stories could be told to friends and would be understood in a fraternal setting. The letters to Fliess and the anecdotes were not originally intended for publication; they were finally printed but for exceptional reasons. The lyrical form was not edited into the final technical form. At least it seems to me that both were separate elaborations—this word seems acceptable here—of a common origin.

From the first to the second and third forms there is a steady diminution not only in affective charge but also in degree of conflict. Conflict led to the repression of the original train rides. Conflict was attenuated in the friendly and intimate setting of the letters. (A certain amount is suggested when Freud calls Chrobak's remark cynical but kindly, and when he shakes his head. There was a vestige of conflict at the hearing but not later in the telling.) Finally came the conflict-free exposition in the paper on technique. The story of the comparison from its unmetaphorical origins through its publication maps for us the path from the pleasure principle to the ego-controlled sublimation.

So far in this essay, attention has been directed mainly to the man in the window seat with apparent neglect of the person inside who cannot see the landscape directly. Freud's advice is addressed to this person and there is much to say about the history of his mental processes and evolution, even in terms of the metaphor. He had his own infancy and conflicts and his own store of visual memories, some of them reactivated in the professional setting. Of the many possible things that might be said about him in terms of the analogy, I shall only point out that there are two sides to a train, therefore a second window and corresponding landscape. The passenger at the window in the original figure, concentrating on his side of the road, would not perceive the second window. The inside passenger, passively attentive to the verbal messages, would be inattentive to this window too—but not unaffected. He would be subject to an 'internal' Pötzl (1917) phenomenon, and he would register images received from the window through the corner of his eye; that is, by 'indirect [peripheral] vision', which, then, he might or might not combine with the messages from the other passenger on the train, while they are traveling companions on the terminable or interminable journey.

VIII. THE PICTORIAL PAST*

There is a period in childhood when much of our thinking and imagining is predominantly visual. An old-fashioned terminology speaks of the faculty for vivid visual imagery. This faculty originates very early in life, comes to predominate in childhood over other modalities of sensory imagination, determines thus the sensory quality of early memories and fantasies, and usually declines, perhaps comes to an end, though its fate in adult life is variable. Most of our adult recollections of this important period of childhood come to us as pictures or scenes. 'Even in those whose memory is not normally of a visual type, the earliest recollections of childhood retain far into life the quality of sensory vividness' (Freud, 1900-1901, p. 546). Persistence of memories in visual form appears to be one reason why dream pictures are predominantly visual—a result, in Freud's words, of the '*attraction* exercised by the visually recollected scenes touched upon by the dream-thoughts' and thus brought into dream consciousness (p. 548). Freud uses the fact that the manifest dream picture is visual (or otherwise sensory) to illustrate what he means by regression to a childhood form of mentation.

For convenience I shall refer to the childhood period of visual thinking and imagery as the *pictorial past,* realizing of course that this is an adultomorph and retrospective way of speaking and one that comes from psychoanalytic practice, where gaps in an adult's memory of his past are often filled out. Psychoanalytic technique has various ways of assisting an analysand to recall forgotten events. One of these has been singled out for special consideration and given the name *construction,* which Strachey uses and which I shall use to translate the German *Konstruktion.* Other translators and authors writing in English use the form *reconstruction* instead.

* [Chapter I of No. 130 in Bibliography.]

Current usage leaves us a bit uncertain whether the word, as used in psychoanalysis, is a strictly defined technical term. I shall use it as Freud (1937b) does in his main essay, Constructions in Analysis, narrowly, to mean the inference and formulation of forgotten events in an analysand's life. Conjectures are made of early or later events, but in Freud's essay and a fortiori in his account of how he constructed the Wolf-man's primal scene (Freud, 1918 [1914])—an observation of parental intercourse at the age of eighteen months—the word does refer importantly to the infant's prehistory (pp. 50, ff.).

Freud (1937b) differentiates explicitly between a construction and an ordinary analytic interpretation. The latter 'applies to something that one does to some single element of the material, such as an association or a parapraxis' (p. 261); that is, the analyst puts into conscious form and words the analysand's unconscious meaning. In contrast, a construction is like detective work. It is a statement of forgotten events and is a 'conjecture which awaits examination, confirmation or rejection' (p. 265). It is a vicarious memory. The psychoanalyst as if remembers for the analysand and fills his memory gap with a properly ordered picture or story about something now forgotten. In this strict sense of the word, the construction is something thought up mainly by the analyst, and its subsequent communication to the analysand and his subsequent reactions are not inherent in the conception of construction.

Freud compares the analyst's part in this effort at recovery with the work of an archeologist. Guided by surface indications, both dig up the past and put together unearthed fragments that belong together, even though the fragments are found at different chronological levels. Both organize the pieces to make a thing or perhaps a thing presentation: an urn or a primal scene or, less concretely, a map of an ancient settlement or a series of infantile events. The most obvious difference is in what follows this work. The archeologist cannot check his constructions with a surviving Trojan or Babylonian or submit to him maps and monographs, even if this is one of his dreams.

It is not surprising that an archeologist, the Assyriologist H. V. Hilprecht, did dream of this. Having put together certain fragments in the museum of the University of Pennsylvania and having written them up as finger rings, Hilprecht was visited in a dream, while his monograph was in page proof, by a priest of ancient Nippur, who spoke:

> The two fragments thou hast described on pages 22 and 26 do indeed belong together, but they are not finger rings. [The priest then told him they were earrings cut from a cylinder and gave him the history of the cylinder and the cutting.] The fragments that have so troubled thee are the fragments of this cylinder. Put them together and thou shalt find this to be true.

The priest's advice proved reliable. Hilprecht adopted his interpretation and noted the correction in the introduction of the monograph.[1]

Freud has described the different ways that patients respond to a construction that is imparted to them (1937b, pp. 261, ff.). The communication may provoke an immediate recall of the event in question; or further contributions to the construction via dreams and free association—i.e., more fragments—or emendations; or a sense of conviction without recall; or disbelief; or a feeling of strangeness; or various other detectable conscious and unconscious evidences of acceptance or of denial and negation. It is often as if the analysand were trying to match the proposed construction with an unconscious picture of his own. Sometimes, whether the event is recalled or not, the construction may be supported independently by other persons, a kinsman, servant, or the like, who consciously recalls the incident.

Thus a young man who had attended one of Freud's (1900-1901, pp. 189, ff.) lectures dreamed without distortion of seeing a former tutor in bed with his nurse and recognized the details of the setting but could not recall any such inci-

[1] The original account of the dream is in a letter from Professor Hilprecht to William Romaine Newbold (1897), published in the latter's article entitled, *Subconscious Reasoning,* along with the results of Newbold's further investigation of the circumstances of the dream. The above version is adapted from W. von Siebenthal (1953, p. 134).

dent. His older brother, however, who had been about six years old at the time, did remember the incident very well.[2]

The most general and interesting effect of the communication is that in any case it incites the patient to investigate. It stimulates him to *look* for something. With sharpened vision he starts a research. Consequently he reports 'lively recollections', which are 'ultra-clear' or of 'abnormal sharpness',[3] and particularly visual images of objects remembered, even though these may be of the apparently 'irrelevant' and 'meaningless' sort that we also know from vivid screen memories or from dreams that leave a feeling of reality. This psychological process of searching and looking reminds us of the part of dream formation where the sleeper as if scans his past for old pictures in which to express his dream thoughts.

Freud (1913b) elsewhere compares free association to a report of sights viewed from a moving railroad-car window by a relaxed passenger. Having heard the construction, the passenger is alerted and tries to *see* his past concretely and to reify Freud's figurative statement. Or he takes, as more than a metaphor, William James's (1890, Vol. I) account of the search for forgotten memories, which compares it to rummaging 'our house for a lost object'. In both cases 'we visit what seems to us the probable *neighborhood* of that which we miss. We turn over the things under, or within which, or alongside of which, it may possibly be' (p. 654).

As if concretizing and acting out James's metaphor, patients of Samuel Novey (1966) started looking for memories. They explored old diaries and papers, returned to childhood milieus, 'accidentally' parked their car in front of their old home, tried to find things they had dreamed of, and the like.[4] In my comparison of the analytic couch with the bed of a not very deep sleeper, these people would be sleepwalkers engaged in retrieval.

[2] A similar independent outside confirmation of a similar scene was obtained from a participant in the act. See Marie Bonaparte (1945). Also see Victor H. Rosen (1955). In Rosen's case, the forgotten event was the witnessing of the mother's suicide attempt.

[3] See Freud (1937b, p. 266), and Strachey's footnote there.

[4] See also, Novey (1968).

Freud (1937b) was impressed by the ultraclarity (*Überdeutlichkeit*) of the mental pictures and by the sense of reality they inspired. Some he found 'might have been described as hallucinations if a belief in their actual presence had been added to their clearness' (p. 266). He used this observation to 'widen the perspective' of his remarks on constructions: 'Perhaps it may be a general characteristic of hallucinations to which sufficient attention has not hitherto been paid that in them something that has been experienced in infancy and then forgotten returns—something that the child has seen or heard at a time when he could still hardly speak and that now forces its way into consciousness, probably distorted and displaced owing to the operation of forces that are opposed to this return' (p. 267). He adds: 'The delusions of patients appear to me to be the equivalents of the constructions which we build up in the course of an analytic treatment—attempts at explanation and cure . . .' (p. 268).

I do not know how well this statement has been attended to in modern psychiatry. It says that the hallucinated vision or voice is basically a memory of infancy and that the delusional thinking is basically a retrospective falsification and at the same time an attempt to get at such a memory or memories. This comparison of hallucination with repressed memory and delusional thinking with 'construction' seems to me to have been foreshadowed in Freud's remarks about the pictorial past (and 'present') in The Interpretation of Dreams (1900-1901, p. 546): '. . . one of the facts arrived at in the *Studies on Hysteria* [Breuer and Freud, 1893-1895—e.g., in Breuer's first case history] was that when it was possible to bring infantile scenes (whether they were memories or phantasies) into consciousness, they were seen like hallucinations and lost that characteristic only in the process of being reported. It is moreover a familiar observation that, even in those whose memory is not normally of a visual type, the earliest recollections of childhood retain far into life the quality of sensory vividness.'

The visual images recalled during therapy, like the pictures of Signorelli's frescoes which were recalled when Freud (1901, p. 13, n.) tried to think of the artist's forgotten name through free associations (a sort of 'therapy of everyday life'), were visual way stations to words and verbal thinking. They became dim then as they might normally in the course of an individual's life and development from childhood to adulthood, which can be rephrased and formulated to the effect that a regression was canceled by a process that normally occurs with the growth and experience of the individual. The lifting of repression included the canceling of regression. 'Recall' then, in itself, combined with associations, may lead to real attempts at cure or to the distorted attempts known as delusions, in either case to constructions in a wider sense.

Since the psychoanalyst as constructor attempts to have the patient recall or figuratively recalls for the patient in the interest of explanation and cure, his psychology too is a valid ingredient in the total process. In the train-window comparison, he too would like a look; indeed, he too is looking for something he can recognize in the passing scenery. His visual curiosity also is stimulated.

This leads directly to Karl Abraham's (1913b) study of scopophilia, the drive that impels pleasurable looking, *Schaulust,* as it is called in German. Among the neurotic manifestations of this impulse, Abraham records turnings of visual attention inward, to mental pictures and to 'the products of the mind'. A. Winterstein (1913) had applied the libido theory to explain differences in systems of philosophy, mainly in terms of inner- and outer-directedness of the libido and had remarked that certain inward-looking philosophers were governed by 'the impossible desire of an individual of the *type visuel* to look at his own unconscious, at the secret and forbidden'.[5]

Abraham (1913b) was struck by the clinical applicability of Winterstein's idea, for he had in treatment a young philosopher who 'was not content with brooding and with abstract forms of thinking alone, but used to endeavor to get a visual image of how thoughts arose in the brain and how they "come out" of it. He desired actually to *see* this process' (p. 211). Another of Abraham's patients astounded him by an

[5] Remarkably, Winterstein knew, and in 1913, that such an impulse might lead to a coalescence *(Ineinanderfallen)* of the subjective and objective 'which in ecstasies like those of Plotinus terminated in a concrete, blissful grasp of the Absolute' (p. 182).

elaborate recital of recollections from between the ages of four and seven, especially of two brief summer vacations at the ages of three and six. The patient recalled 'a great number of names . . . , described minutely the appearance of his playfellows, remembered what this or that person had said, and recollected each piece of furniture in the house in which he lived. His memories were so vivid and gave such an impression of freshness that one could rightly speak of a regular hypermnesia. . . . His statements had nothing of the phantastic about them, for they dealt with the most ordinary matters of everyday life.' Abraham calls the recollections 'a mass of uninteresting details . . . [with] no strongly affective impressions and no memories that might have flattered a desire for greatness either in the child or in the adult' (pp. 195-196). The hypermnesia turned out to be protective; it selected meaningless elements for remembering and covered the amnesias of the same period.

What Abraham's scopophilic patients produced spontaneously, and what Freud's patients produced as the result of hearing a construction, show astonishing similarity. Abraham's patients seem to be steadily searching and trying to see more, with much visual material, and the same applies to Freud's. Both sets of patients are comparable to the analyst with his 'neutralized' wish to see more and to cure.

The extent to which the visual is stressed in constructions is impressive. Most constructed memories and most recovered, sometimes attested, memories are of scenes, notably of course of the primal scene and of the difference between the sexes. Notable too is the frequent immobility of the processed mental picture, whether screen memory, dream element, or fantasy. They are 'still', whereas the events from which they stem are often full of motion. They are as if immobilized for better viewing.

With obvious differences, the psychoanalyst tries to fulfil the scopophilic philosopher's wish to see thoughts—in this context, those of his analysand. In his conjoint looking with the analysand, he too is hypermnestic, vicariously, when he constructs. And he shares Leonard Woolley's (1930, p. 25) 'green jealousy' that the worker on other archeological sites feels when he visits Pompeii and *sees* the past preserved in all its details. The comparison of psychoanalytic science to archeology may lead to misinterpretations of the nature of psychoanalytic science, as Hartmann (1964, p. 324) remarks. But among the similarities, both types of diggers-up of the past have a strong wish to see it. This paraphrases the familiar statement that one of the psychoanalyst's professional motives, his wish to investigate, is fed by sublimated scopophilia.

The analyst's capacity for visual imagery is rarely discussed. Because of his statement in connection with the forgetting of the name *Signorelli,* Freud (1901, p. 13, n.) is generally supposed not ordinarily to have used his visual imagination. While he could not recall the name, the artist's frescoes stood out '*ultra-clear*[ly]—at any rate much more *intense*[ly] than visual memory-traces normally appear to me', and then disappeared when he found the name.[6]

Because of my own weak adult capacity for waking visual imagery and propensity for 'imageless thinking'[7], I assumed that while listening to a patient, an analyst necessarily 'blanks out' and does not think or associate consciously until an idea forces its way into his mind. But this assumption has been challenged by colleagues who have visual images under such circumstances, particularly when patients describe pictures, such as a dream. There may be type variations, as in hearing instrumental music, which some simply listen to without images, while others have visual images or a 'program'. Apropos of the dream screen, Martin Grotjahn wrote me in a letter (January 24, 1950), 'As a rule I have to write dreams down in order to follow them. If I do not, I actually see the patient's words projected into pictures on the wall of my office.'

[6] See K. R. Eissler's discussion of Freud's thinking in his *Medical Orthodoxy and the Future of Psychoanalysis* (1965, Appendix I). Eissler cites Freud's designating Charcot a *type visuel* as another probable disclaimer that he was himself of this type. 'This particular endowment which . . . seems to me was so strongly developed in Freud was the ability of rendering concrete something that is essentially abstract' (p. 396). The four-dimensional picture of Rome (in *Civilization and Its Discontents* [Freud, 1929b, pp. 69, ff.]) immediately comes to mind as an excellent example.

[7] That is, 'cognitive processes in which no [introspective] evidence of imagery could be secured', which would include answers to puzzles and problems that come as if by a flash, etc. See the article, *Thinking—The Field,* by W. Edgar Vinacke (1968).

Grotjahn's remark reminds us of the futile question whether an analysand is telling us what he 'really' dreamed, whether he is 'showing' us what he saw, directly and concretely, as 'true' *Ding-* or *Sachvorstellungen.*

A direct study of the analyst's visual images is to be found in the experiments of Ross and Kapp (1962). Serota (1964) approximated conjoint looking at the past by viewing home movies of the analysand's childhood with him, an experiment he found useful in corroborating constructions of infantile events.

Conscious visual mentation and its varieties are well known, and I am not referring specifically to this functioning when I speak of the psychoanalyst's scopophilia. I concur with Abraham (1913b) that the capacity to induce visions 'seems to exist in every one in childhood, but disappears in many as they grow older' and that it is erroneous to conclude that a man 'does not belong to the "visual" type if he does not have such pictorial accompaniments of his thought' (pp. 220-221). To his remark that such a lack comes from an inhibition of scopophilia, I should add: and possibly from maturation, disuse, and type of education.[8]

The analyst's sublimated scopophilia for me is not so much a matter of conscious imagery as it is of a certain visual undertone beneath his consciousness as he attends to analytic material. His consciousness may include visual images or may be imageless. This I take to be part of Isakower's analyzing instrument, though not all.[9] This undertone produces subtonic visual constructions, either with contents familiar to the analyst because of his self-study, training, and experience;

[8] *Cf.* William James (1890, Vol. I): 'the older men are and the more effective as thinkers, the more, as a rule, they have lost their visualizing power. . . . This was ascertained by Mr. Galton to be the case with members of the Royal Society. The present writer [aged then forty-eight] observes it in his own person distinctly' (p. 266).

The same author says that words are more efficient and more rapidly revived than other items in one's experience. James was, of course, a great verbal communicator of his ideas as writer and lecturer, and he does not note that his career trained him and necessitated him 'pragmatically' to use words rather than simply to form visual images of things.

[9] Minutes of Faculty Meeting, New York Psychoanalytic Institute, November 20, 1963, and personal communications.

or they may be 'discoveries'. As vicarious memories for his analysand (or for himself), scenes are the analytic products best suited for independent verification.

Recently, therapeutic sessions of different kinds have been taped for sight and sound and studied intensively. The question is frequently asked, 'But what is going on in the therapist's head?' This is not a simple question. Books have been written that treat of the philosophic problem—How can one know another's mind? How is it that we are not all solipsists? (Chappell, 1962). Regrettably, we also lack a calculus for quantifying the probable accuracy of constructions and must depend on empirical rules such as those evolved by Freud. Many of us react to such lacks with a sense of frustration and doubt. Some of this feeling arises from our not attaining the satisfied feeling of reality that comes from ocular proof.[10] We often get the equivalent of a defendant's confession, but then, like a conscientious prosecutor, we treat it with methodical doubt until we are as if assured of eyewitness testimony.

In his essay, Sophocles' Œdipus, Bernard Knox (1960)[11] has described such an 'undertone' as I had in mind, as well as the attempt at validation. In the scene with the Corinthian messenger and the herdsman (*Œdipus Rex,* lines 1120, *et seq.*) the undertone lies in the extensive punning on *oida* (I know, I have seen) and on *pous* (foot, where?), as if the words were unconscious way-station associations to the answer to the question consciously and heatedly under discussion, namely, Who killed Laius?. Œdipus, as prosecutor, refuses to accept not only the prophet's vatic statement but also his own intellectual realization that he was his father's murderer. He quizzes the herdsman and overcomes that person's resistance to telling by a threat of torture and so establishes that the herdsman was an *eyewitness* to the crime. Immediately after obtaining this ocular confirmation and conviction, Œdipus attacks his own eyes.

Abraham's remarks (1913b, pp. 207, ff.) on the relation of scopophilia and obsessive doubt are relevant to problems of verification. Neurotic doubt comes from a child's curiosity,

10 See Robert Waelder (1960), *The Need for Validation* (pp. 3, ff.).

11 I am grateful to David Lewin for referring me to the passages in Knox's essay.

aroused by intimations, clues, or verbal accounts, which can be satisfied only by seeing. The child is not sure and does not 'know' unless he actually sees. He wants to know where he came from in the sense that he wants 'to see with his own eyes his own birth out of his mother's body', for instance, and other like possible or impossible events (p. 219).

The analyst's doubts are, ideally, not obsessive but Cartesian, philosophic, and methodical—'neutralized' doubts perhaps. Nevertheless, to the extent that we share with Winterstein's *type-visuel* philosopher a curiosity about the birth of our analysand's ideas and a wish to see what goes on in his head,—or what, as the figurative train rider, he sees as the landscape passes—, no camera or visual instrument will completely slake our curiosity.[12]

Not too different from our difficulties are those of our quasi colleagues, the archeologists. Niederland (1965) has recently excellently described the infantile motives in Schliemann's dogged compulsion to excavate the site of Troy. Schliemann, a country pastor's son with a churchyard for a playground and the graves as easy displacement locales for his infantile curiosity, went by a simple transition over to the exhumation of the heroes of the Greek epics his father taught him to read. Like one of Novey's patients, he searched for the heroes. There is irony in Schliemann's entire *lack* of doubt about his constructions. They aroused no doubt at all in him, but in almost everyone else.

While we are on the Homeric Greeks, it is worth noting that, according to Onians (1951, p. 18), they did not distinguish between mental faculties as we do. The word *'oida'*, etymologically 'I have seen', meant 'I know', and it lost its ocular reference only after several centuries.

The reader will recall that Freud (1937b), widening his discussion of constructions, spoke of the delusional construc-

12 For the counterpart in which an exhibitionistic patient 'shows' dreams, see. *Emergence of Hidden Ego Tendencies during Dream Analysis,* by N. L. Blitzsten, R. S. Eissler, and K. R. Eissler (1950).

As to methodical doubt, I find in Herbert Butterfield's (1949) *Origins of Modern Science,* the following: 'It was important that the methodical doubt upon which Descartes had insisted at a very high level . . . was a thing easily vulgarized . . . so that [in the eighteenth century] it had come to mean simply an unbelieving attitude, the very kind of skepticism he had tried to guard against' (p. 158).

tions as equivalents of 'attempts at explanation and cure' (p. 268). To push the analogy, all recapturing of the pictorial past, whether as dream picture, screen memory, new memory of repressed traces, etc., could include, besides the more obvious wish-fulfilments and defensive formations, an equivalent of an attempt at explanation and cure. The analyst's constructions are certainly such attempts, and in the therapeutic alliance of the analyst with the patient's 'normal ego', with its bundle of motives, it is proper to predicate an alliance or synergy of analyst's and patient's scopophilia—an unconscious looking in common, which finds expression in the common curative attempt to construct events of the forgotten infantile past.

The term, *pictorial past,* as I use it, is almost descriptive. It refers to the organized meaningful experiences of infancy that were registered as visual traces in the period that Freud[13] and Abraham had in mind when they spoke of early visually preserved memories. The 'traces' may be located nearer or further from consciousness. During the pictorial past, and not necessarily only before he learns words, the child's thinking and feeling are dominantly pictorial. Pictures precede action, sometimes closely, as children's games show, with little reflection or interposition of ideas such as the reality principle introduces; and there is little economizing purpose. Pictorial thinking is nearer the pleasure principle, and it is usually preserved in erotic fantasy, the normal sanctuary from reality. In some, pictorial thinking persists and receives training; for example, professionally in anatomists, artists, engineers, and others. It never comes to an end in the night thinking we call dreaming. It has a beginning sometime in infancy, after the period of unformed impressions of which Spitz (1965) and others have written, and it may take in, or have translated into it, some of the impressions of the previous era. Indeed, from pictures we can sometimes make assumptions about earlier impressions. Thus, the postulation of an oral triad of wishes in the nonpictorial nursing situation is derived from the

[13] Childhood memories 'are plastically visual even in people whose later function of memory has to do without any visual element. . . . In my own case the earliest childhood memories are the only ones of a visual character . . .' (Freud, 1901, p. 47).

presence of three elements in pictorial fantasies: ideas of eating, of being eaten, and of going to sleep.

Information about the child increases with his learning to speak. Yet words do not dominate his mentation for a long while, and the term *preverbal* here is ambiguous. It makes us risk imagining that there is a sharp time partition between the two ways of thinking, a partition that does not exist. Things heard get turned into pictures, as we know from certain screen memories and indeed from pictorial pseudo memories, of which Piaget (1945) supplies us with an autobiographical example.

'One of my first memories would date, if it were true, from my second year. I can still see, most clearly, the following scene, in which I believed until I was about fifteen.' Then he gives an 'ultraclear' picture of his being in a pram in the Champs Elysées, a man trying to kidnap him, his nurse defending him and getting scratched, a crowd gathering, a policeman putting the man to flight—all in minute detail (the policeman's white club, the nearby entrance to a subway station, etc.). When he was fifteen, his nurse, having got religion, wrote to confess that she had made up the whole story, faking the scratches. 'I must therefore have heard, as a child, the account of this story, which my parents believed, and projected it into the [pictorial] past in the form of a visual memory, which was a memory of a memory, but false' (p. 187).

I suppose there is a great deal more of this back-and-forth traffic between the verbal and the visual in childhood than in later life. The child's visual imagination is continually fed by stories, recited or read, much as dream imagery is later fed by nonvisual ideas. The child's first book is a picture book, subsequently, mixtures of text and illustration.

The transition of nonpictorial elements into pictures resembles an apparently unconnected phenomenon, the translation into pictures of verbally formed thoughts with the approach of sleep, as when Silberer's (1909, p. 520) idea, 'layers of consciousness and existence', turned into a picture of a *Dobostorte*. But we have many reasons for knowing that pictures of the past vary in quality and tend toward visualization with drowsiness. The mention of dreaming, hallucination, fluctuation in the analytic situation should suffice.[14] The shift from the originally formless should be related to the physiological change from nearly all-day sleeping to the final day-night rhythm, as described by Kleitman (1963) in his chapter on the duration of sleep. The turning of the unformed impression into pictures is outlined for infants by Spitz (1965, pp. 55, ff.) who utilizes Senden's comparable observations on congenitally blind persons learning to see (perceive) after their sight was restored by surgery.

Constructing, in Freud's narrower sense, the psychoanalyst seeks out the pictorial past for scenes and mental pictures. The language of memory suggests that he is looking for something active. Memory words suggest life and death. There is the dead past, recollections are revived, resurrected, unearthed, and found still dynamic or cathected—that is, alive. Among the wishes to see the past is the wish to see it alive and moving; and the quiet of the Wolf-man's dream is a denial or negation, an aversion to motility, because (I believe) of his wish to sleep. Abraham's patient, who sought his past in screen memories of his early years, also wished to see ghosts. The 'ghosts' were his parents in white nightgowns, but they were 'alive', that is, in motion and not dead (or sleeping).[15] Clinically, resistances to remembering may take the form of letting sleeping dogs lie or the dead rest. As primitive peoples still meet their dead in their dreams, so certain patients cannot sleep for fear of meeting lost kinsmen. The stirrings of ghosts, visions, and repressed memories are alarming.

I once heard the late John B. Watson, the behaviorist, tell in homey Southern language of his childhood fear of ghosts. He still could not be paid, he said, to go into a graveyard at night, even if he had in his pocket the left hind foot of a rabbit shot at midnight during the dark of the moon. Watson was notably averse to admitting the reality of visual images, for which reason Adolf Meyer used to refer to Watson's *psychophobia,* a word he used presumably in accord with

[14] See Martin H. Stein (1965). The regressive effect of drowsiness is clinically portrayed by Anna Freud (1965) in *Normality and Pathology in Childhood,* pp. 100, ff.

[15] See Jean Piaget (1926): *'La vie est assimilée à l'activité en général'* in children around eight years of age (p. 191).

Webster's definition, 'an aversion to psychological phenomena', but the word has also been used to mean a ghost phobia.

In the pictorial past, the dead, even if buried, are alive, as we know from childhood fantasies of being buried alive. We nearly say that repressed memories are buried alive; they are unseen but restless. Our language says they can be stirred up, awakened, and the like. James's analogy to rummaging is not fully appropriate when it is applied to the repressed. Repressed things have a way of coming toward one or of evading the search. Schliemann apparently was nearly convinced he would meet the Greeks and Trojans. The archeologist and the psychophile want to see a living Gradiva walking gracefully on the streets of Pompeii.

It is almost banal to add that here archeologist and psychoanalyst part company, as Freud (1909b) explained to the Rat Man, pointing to the antiques in his office: 'They were, in fact, . . . only objects found in a tomb, and their burial had been their preservation: the destruction of Pompeii was only beginning now that it had been dug up. . . . Every effort was made to preserve Pompeii, whereas people were anxious to be rid of tormenting ideas like his' (pp. 176-177). Subjected to the psychoanalytic therapeutic process, Gradiva crumbles.

IX. THE ERUDITE NURSLING AND THE MIND OF THE EMBRYO*

Ferenczi (1923b) reported on a type of dream found in psychoanalytic work, which he named in German, *Der Traum vom gelehrten Säugling,* the dream of the erudite nursling.[1] In such dreams, babes and sucklings give forth wisdom. They write and speak fluently, lecture, make profound remarks, engage in learned conversation, and propound scientific theories. The dreams are a riposte to the analyst's interpretations, and Ferenczi found at least two meanings: they show an unconscious acceptance of the interpretation, as if to say, 'I knew that long ago'; and more superficially they facetiously deride the analyst's way of attributing complicated states of mind to infants and of expressing himself in language ordinarily used when speaking of adults. In any case, cradled in the analytic couch, the nursling is annoyed and wants the analyst to shut up and let him try to sleep.

In this satire, psychoanalysts can recognize some of their own linguistic and semantic problems. It is hard to speak for the nursling. With this in mind, I tried to find a word analogous to *adultomorphic,* which would mean that the nursling's experiences were being expressed in the language and thought of a three- or four-year-old child, and after some study of Liddell and Scott's Greek Dictionary, I settled for the word *pedomorphic,* suggested by Royden Astley. As an example of pedomorphism, I once wrote that the nursing situation could be conceived as composed of three wishes: to eat, to be eaten, and to go to sleep. I took pains to explain that this vocabu-

* [Chapter 4 of No. 130 in Bibliography.]

[1] Sandor Ferenczi, The Dream of the 'Clever Baby'.

Clever for *gelehrt* is a Briticism, as in the pre-World War II remark, 'Winston will never be Prime Minister. He is too clever.' Dr. Leroy W. Earley, in England at that time, tells me that *clever* implied a quality which *der gelehrte Säugling* did show; viz., skill in opportunistic argument and advocacy. The usual word for clever in German is *gescheit.*

lary was suggested by the fantasies of a considerably older child (Lewin, 1950). To put the matter naïvely, if I were an old infant of three or four, observing a new baby and empathizing, I would think the baby had these three wishes. As for us adults, like the toddler, we get signals from the baby (Anna Freud, 1953), but between signals there are long blanks like the angelic sleep that stimulates our imagination.

A good many of us, whether or not we later become professionals, began our observation of the child with the advent of a new sibling or kinsman. Watching the baby, we were in principle guided in our understanding by an uncontrolled use of the rules stated by Spitz (1965, p. 54). We put ourselves into the infant's subjective situation and conjectured how and what he perceived, thought, and felt. We very likely also 'relate[d] these assumptions to such observable givens as [were] available' and to the data of biology, when we thought, 'He's too little; he hasn't any teeth; will she grow one?' etc. The trained professional observer readily discounts pedomorphic theories, but those of us on the fringe of such studies slip inadvertently into the role of early baby-watcher. Some of us have written in terms approximating the thoughts of the observing tot or the naïve baby-sitter. Child psychoanalysts and child psychiatrists, constantly empathizing with older children, must be constantly tempted pedomorphically, particularly because the naïve observations can be instructive.[2] In the example of the three presumed wishes in the nursing situation I tried to utilize the toddler's view of the newborn infant. The toddler, of course, may have been nursed well into the years when he was verbalizing and visualizing his ideas of his oral needs.

As professionally trained observers, we nowadays enter the nursling's mind only with extensive precautionary reality

[2] The tradition goes back to Freud (1915-1917). A student-midwife in her final examination 'was asked what it meant if meconium (excreta) made its appearance at birth in the water coming away, and she promptly replied: "it means the child's frightened". She was laughed at and failed in the examination. But silently I took her side and began to suspect that this poor woman from the humbler classes had laid an unerring finger on an important correlation' (p. 397).

Erasmus Darwin (1794, I: p. 148), a good ethologist, interpreted *fear* as a repetition of the reaction to birth of newly born animals. He compares with them a canary bird that was always overcome with fright when removed from its cage, assuming apparently that the cage was a later *simulacrum* of the eggshell.

testing. We do not, for example, transgress the conditions set by unmyelinized nerve tracts. Yet, we must unconsciously bring our own past into our creative thinking, and our more original impulse is to let ourselves go about the baby. We fluctuate (apparently we must) between the objective and the subjective. Our fluctuation has been even greater in our march from fantasy to knowledge about the embryo.

One set of ideas about prenatal psychology is combined with those about afterdeath psychology, when Eastern philosophers describe the behavior of the soul from the time of death until its next reincarnation, which, like waking too soon, is to be avoided if possible. The Tibetan Book of the Dead (Evans-Wentz, 1949) employs a perfect sleep and dream model for the transitional death-to-rebirth state. The presumed equivalents of Isakower phenomena appear while the soul is leaving the body.[3] The *Bardo* consciousness is disturbed by the intrusion of unwanted impulses such as hunger, longings for love objects, and shortly before rebirth by the œdipus complex, which is stimulated by a prenatal coitus observation.[4] Accounts of the *Bardo* states are based on experiences during the philosophers' self-absorption.

[3] The soul takes an appreciable time to leave the body, and there are attendant psychical phenomena. In the Foreword written by Sir John Woodroffe is the following observation: 'Noteworthy, too, is the description of sounds heard as (to use Dr. Evans-Wentz's language) "the psychic resultants of the disintegrating process called death". They call to mind the humming, rolling, and crackling noises heard before and up to fifteen hours after death which, recognized by Greunwaldi in 1618 and referred to by later writers, were in 1862 made the subject of special study by Dr. Collingues' (p. lxviii).

[4] *The Tibetan Book of the Dead.* 'O nobly-born, at this time thou wilt see visions of males and females in union. When thou seest them, remember to withhold thyself from going between them' (p. 177). (This is in order to keep from being reincarnated.) 'If [about] to be born as a male, the feeling of itself being a male dawneth on the Knower, and a feeling of intense hatred towards the father and of jealousy and attraction towards the mother is begotten' (p. 179). If the Knower's soul unfortunately gets in the way of the sperm or ovum, after a blissful moment comes unconsciousness, it finds itself encased as an embryo, and 'upon emerging from the womb and opening its eyes it may find itself transformed into a young dog' (or pig, ant, grub, calf, kid, lamb, or a ghost in hell, etc.) (p. 179). The list suggests doubt in the primal scene construction—whether the Knower saw the parents, or got his information from dogs, pigs, etc., and then transferred his knowledge. (*Cf.* the discussion of the Wolf-man's source of information [Freud, 1918 [1914], pp. 57, ff.].) And there is a hint of being devoured blissfully by a germ cell into a closed space or stomach.

The above is a cultivated Eastern way of understanding the mind of the embryo. A Western attempt is exemplified by Jelliffe's theory about Irving Berlin's music. Because of the conditional reflex theory, Jelliffe surmised that the composer's mother had had a cardiac arrhythmia, which subjected the embryonic composer to a continued bombardment of syncopated beats. (I heard the late Smith Ely Jelliffe present this idea several times.) Its Western quality extended to the matter of validation. Once when Jelliffe was expounding it at a meeting of the New York Academy of Medicine, a man arose from the audience and introduced himself as the doctor who had attended Mrs. Berlin during her confinement, and he announced that she had indeed suffered from a mitral valvular lesion, which was attended by a syncopated heart rhythm. I do not know whether Jelliffe checked up on this contribution.

Much that was once attributed to the embryo's mental state, in studies of schizophrenia particularly (Tausk, 1919), is now supposed to belong to early postnatal psychology. In recent years, ideas of possible fœtal impressions have been cautious (Greenacre, 1952).[5]

The wish to put ourselves in the embryo's place and to discover what was going on there instituted a branching series of later events in human sciences. When the wish was frustrated by the impenetrable barriers, we were deeply disturbed in our native feeling of scopophilic omniscience, and we developed two sets of methods and sciences to fill the gap. The subjective methods of occult science led to memories and to the images of prenatal states and of previous reincarnation as men or animals. Objective, especially laboratory, biology led to knowledge but not to memories. Biologists could not empathize or make constructions in Freud's sense or deal with the imagery of the unborn or of lower animals. In science, from Descartes on through Pavlov and Watson, animals are 'matter' and embryos without a mind.

[5] See Chapter 1, *The Biological Economy of Birth* [1945], and Chapter 2, *The Predisposition to Anxiety* [1941].

X. TRACES AND STORAGE*

The strict dualistic philosophy did not extinguish the antique wish to see images and traces of old impressions or do away with the old ways of fulfilment. The paleolithic sketch, the visual trace, of the deer and bison had been carried into the cave on a bone fragment, and this was one model for a memory trace. Words and sounds, recalled to mind by the hearer, seemed to exist somewhere as an echo or rumble in psychological space. They were perhaps allocated to the side of the head image, where air from the ears seemed to bring them in; or some Lascaux behaviorist may have insisted they were on the floor near the larynx. About taste memories there could be no doubt; tastes persisted right in the mouth.

As technology progressed, localization of memory traces became more sophisticated and the traces themselves more elusive. It was discovered that the brain was not bone marrow, although continuous with the spinal 'marrow', and that it was the important seat of consciousness and inheritor of the functions of the old picture-lined cavernous head. This and the invention of the microscope reactivated the scopophilic search for images. The new search was directed to find where in the brain they might be stored.

Said Wernicke: 'The cerebral cortex with its 600 million cells, according to Meynert's estimation, offers a sufficiently great number of storage places in which the innumerable sensory impressions provided by the outer world can be stored one by one without interference. The cerebral cortex is populated with such residues of past stimuli which we propose to call memory images.'[1]

The metaphors in this and similar writing are of interest.

* [Chapter 5 of No. 130 in Bibliography.]

[1] Cited by Freud (1891, p. 3) in *On Aphasia*. It is only fair to say that other authors, including Freud, did not agree with such 'neurologizing tautology', as Adolf Meyer called Wernicke's remarks.

A *trace* can be a mark or sign of an impression, like a footprint, or as a chemist uses the word, a minimal quantity of a substance. Neither version is suitable for preservation, though the police make cement casts from footprints and automobile tire tracks for use in court. An artist can also trace a picture and perhaps such tracings are what microscopists of the past unconsciously hoped to find. The idea of *storage* does not go along well with traces; it brings in concrete ideas of another, older category. In German, the word for *stored* is *aufgespeichert,* which refers to *Speicher,* a granary, from vulgar Latin *spicarium,* from (L.) *spica,* an ear of grain. The psychology of the mouth which Freud used for the genealogy of the function of judgment might be invoked here to help with the oral-psychological portrayal of the function of memory —as a kind of pantry.[2]

The invention of the electron microscope stimulated our neutralized scopophilia and gave new impetus to the search for the memory trace. Memories, still more elusive, are sought in RNA arrangements, and we do our stochastic best with algebraic pictures of twists and links. The memories are still somehow portrayable by Kekulé's lines and letters (Magoun, 1964).

The invention of psychoanalysis again raised scopophilic hopes. Freud's cosmic buffet to humanity's sense of omniscience, the realization that a man did not know himself, was offset by the gift of the psychoanalytic method. With Philoctetes's unhealable wound went a bow. Psychoanalytic success in constructing memories and filling in gaps in consciousness led imaginative persons to push the method and its corollaries ever further. Memories were postulated as surviving not only from before birth but as vestigial memories of glacial-period man and of the age of fishes (Ferenczi, 1924). The assumption of this extended memory, still not entirely discarded by biology, states that the cell remembers, that it develops into an organism because it remembers how to do so. This organic memory is sought in the enzymes and chromatin of the germ cells.

2 Unconsciously the good visual image should be fit for eating, as the birds were deceived by Zeuxis's grapes. For the concrete representation of images of other modalities, see Otto Isakower (1963). Also see the examples furnished by Tausk in Freud (1915a, pp. 197, ff.): *The Unconscious.*

'One rather wishes', writes Carl G. Jung in his Foreword to The Tibetan Book of the Dead (Evans-Wentz, 1949, p. xlii), 'that Freudian psycho-analysis could have happily pursued these so-called intra-uterine experiences still further back; had it succeeded in this bold undertaking . . . it would have undoubtedly led to a postulate of a pre-uterine existence, a true *Bardo* life, if only it had been possible to find at least a trace of an experiencing subject. As it was, psycho-analysis never got beyond purely conjectural traces of intra-uterine experiences.'

Betraying its tacit promise, the psychoanalytic method has failed to bring mnemic omniscience. 'It does not provide us with data (memories) about the undifferentiated phase during which the demarcation lines between the ego and the id, and between the self and the objects, are not yet drawn; and it does not provide us with direct information on the preverbal stage. Direct observation here helps first of all to discard hypotheses which are not consistent with behavioral data.' This statement, which we owe to Heinz Hartmann (1964, p. 102), also sets a limit to our knowledge, to the omniscience promised by the indefinite notion of 'recovering old memories'; at the same time, a bow goes with this wound, direct observation of children.

The futility of searching in visual archives for the nonpictorial is beautifully brought out by Anthony's (1961) analysis of Proust's herculean effort at recall. Proust's *recherche* for the picture of events that would explain the ecstasy provoked by the taste of a *madeleine* led to an enormous recall of the past, but only of the pictorial and verbal past. The nonpictorial past eluded him completely; there *were* no pictures.

Greenacre (1953a) describes the obsessional fulfilment of a patient's search: 'he had a complete collection of *Life* magazine from the earliest issue. He spoke of this at first only as a hobby, of which he seemed unduly proud. It became clear, however, that there was an extreme compulsive force back of this. Marked anger or anxiety with fear of death would arise if he seemed in danger of losing or missing one issue of his magazine. There was a neurotic need to see and to keep *Life* with all its pictorial embellishment from its very beginning' (pp. 81-82).

Greenacre's and Anthony's patients (and Marcel Proust) were Westerners. They functioned in the great tradition of objectifying the world which began with the Greeks five hundred years before the Christian era. They were Cartesians, too, who looked outward as if from a *res cogitans* to discover in an objectified world of memory and visual imagery the secrets of the earliest world. Orientals, limited differently, might have explored the cloudy world of unclear consciousness, where sensations existed that could be clothed in metaphor only.

Robert Waelder (1937) invokes the objectifying of memories to clarify the matter of the recall of those of earliest infancy. 'There is good reason for expecting that it will be quite impossible to recover conscious memories . . . of the very earliest period of life. When we remember an occurrence and know that it took place in the past, we direct our thoughts to it as an object of experience and it is natural to suppose that only those experiences can be really remembered at a later date which, at the time when they occurred, were viewed by the subject at a certain distance with "intentional" reference to them as objects. At the moment when we had a particular experience we must, as it were, have stood at a distance from it, . . . if we are to be able later to make it the object of conscious memory' (p. 415).

This statement has several implications. First of all, it says that for something to become a 'memory' it has to be objectified—treated as if it was a thing—as if it was to be found somewhere, and the examples of searching for lost memories which I have used give a vivid picture of such a search for the memory-thing. The memory-thing is projected, like a dream picture, and the system *Pcpt* (Descartes's *res cogitans*) looks at the memory as the same subject or system looks at a dream picture. I presume that Waelder had in mind pictorial images; it is hard to imagine one's self pricking up one's ears to attend to a dream or to recall an event, though the theoretical possibility is not excluded.

The second easily drawn implication is that such memories as Waelder has in mind can originate only when the infant's body image has attained sufficient form to enable the infant to objectify, to tell what is the 'I' of the moment, distinct from the current outer world, and, following Waelder, distinct also from the world of the past, which incidentally is known often to include a picture of one's past self. Memory, presumably mainly pictorial, seems to arise with the early Cartesian split of subject and objective world, and this is also when the first projected dreams, on a 'screen', might be expected. The manifest content of dreams, after all, consists entirely of memories, from one end of the psychic apparatus to the other, and all pictures in the ordinary projected dream are processed memories imposed as if on a *tabula rasa.*

There are, however, dreams and other conscious states which are not necessarily pictorial. They may be a *tabula rasa,* that is, a blank; or there may be no screen, so that the person is unable to say where his body leaves off and the cloudy, milky something in which he is as if immersed begins. He lacks the feeling of body boundary and incidentally of head boundary and mouth boundary; but his affective state is felt intensely.

Waelder (1937) defines *memories* as recalled objectified experiences. He also recognizes a related process comparable to the process of recall. 'No doubt everything . . . so experienced [without objectification] remains imprinted upon the psyche and continues to live and exert an influence, but in this case the mnemic function acts in a more primitive way: it cannot precisely be called memory. It helps to determine the subsequent life of the individual and the affect associated with it may be reproduced, or it may give rise to mental images, but it is not remembered. . . . The power to objectify experience is apparently not present from the beginning: it is rather the result of development. We are probably right in assuming that children arrive at this stage at the end of their first or the beginning of their second year' (p. 415).[3]

[3] More recent writers agree essentially with Waelder's statement. Thus Spitz (1965) holds that the experience of the mother's face, which begins in the infant's second month of life, should not be called a *percept,* and that 'some time later, the mother's face becomes a percept and then leaves a corresponding memory trace in the infant's mind' (see Cobliner's Appendix, pp. 344, ff.).

Similarly, Anna Freud (1954) writes: 'I should imagine that . . . [the object of the need or drive becomes the first love object] toward the middle of the first year, and that it happens very gradually' (p. 59).

These ideas imply the objectifying as a percept, perhaps as an image, of at least the part of the world which interests the little infant, that object of perception or memory which has become 'cathected'. The assumption also is that

By definition, Waelder distinguishes pictorial memories, I assume, from 'mnemic traces', and he calls only the first of these *memories* proper. 'Mnemic' is the adjective for memory, of course, but his distinction is clear. Later, in 1960, Waelder calls certain mnemic traces 'the imprint of the earliest experience of individual life, during the preverbal stage', and adds further on in his text, 'But there is much to suggest that unconscious imprints of this kind can influence visual experience, bodily sensation or behavior; see, e.g., the residue of early experience with the mother's breast described by Isakower (1936) and Lewin'.[4]

Most psychoanalytic writers, myself included, have at one time or another called the first part of the baby's life the *preverbal* stage or period. This term is quite proper descriptively. However, because of connotations of the word 'preverbal', especially in phrases like 'the preverbal stage' or 'the preverbal phase', etc., assumptions tacitly arise which are not appropriate. Thus, lack of words is often given as a sufficient reason or sometimes a necessary reason for one's inability to recall early events, and this needs rethinking. Offhand, words do not seem to guarantee recollection better than objectified pictures.[5] Pictorial memories are the ones best qualified to be called objectified in Waelder's sense, in his 1937 discussion.

I would posit that whatever has been put into pictorial form is theoretically capable of being recollected. Other experiences somehow return, the ones which Waelder says are not precisely 'memories'. I should like to approach the psychological problem from the standpoint of dreaming and the state of consciousness, beginning with the body image. Before a baby knows his bodily boundaries, or more precisely, before he has an image of them, his dreams probably have the quality of blank 'pure feeling' which occasionally has been reported by adults in unprojected dreams, not unlike

---

previous to this, the cathexis, shown by attention chiefly, was on bodily feelings not yet differentiated from any world—i.e., before the objectifying or Cartesian split.

[4] See, *Sleep, the Mouth, and the Dream Screen*, pp. 87-100 [Ed.].

[5] *Cf.*, Helen Schur's (1966) report of a thirty-month-old child's accurate pictorial memory of a 'red tractor' seen at the age of eighteen months.

the so-called 'oceanic feeling'. Depending on the definition one selects, one may say that the adult dreams and feelings are 'memories' of the early undifferentiated state, or one may call them 'mnemic traces' of a special kind. My own inclination is to call them nonobjectified or nonpictorial memories; that is, I prefer to use *memory* as the general, inclusive term. For me, the dreamer of an unprojected 'feeling' dream is remembering. He is also 'objectifying' the feeling, perhaps for the first time, in the form of words when he describes the dream. If he does not verbalize, he is 'registering' and recalling certain qualities as an experience.

To be concrete, I should like to quote the unprojected dream reported by Charles Rycroft (1951): 'It felt as though you [the analyst] had taken me under your wing. There was nothing to see in the dream at all. It was like a white sheet.' The patient added that this was meant as a metaphorical statement about the feeling of the dream and was not a visual description. He was 'not happy' in calling the sensation a white sheet, but that was the best he could do to convey the peculiar impression the dream made. Possibly then, for the first time, this dreamer was objectifying the dream state when he 'found' it during his analysis. We cannot be certain that this was the first time, but it seems possible.

The same question—when was a certain state of consciousness first objectified?—is relevant to a dream which Lawrence S. Kubie furnished me, reported in my paper on the dream screen. The dreamer felt immersed in a milky, endless wall and described the sense of lacking bodily boundaries between himself and the wall (B. Lewin, 1953, p. 180). This dream took off from a day residue; the dreamer had seen his sister nurse her baby. Assuming that the dream state of consciousness was a repetition of something in the dreamer's past, one cannot say for sure whether the dreamer had objectified such feelings in his pictorial past and then repressed the pictures, or whether he had never objectified them by 'standing at a distance' (as if an observer of his own state of mind) and was now objectifying them for the first time. At any rate, on awakening he was able to stand at a distance, as an experiencing subject or a *res cogitans* remembering the dream as object. Whether or not he had in his pictorial past experienced the qualities in the dream pedomorphically is uncertain. One would guess that if he had, this would be repressed and might come back to light in other ways. What we know is that as an adult the dreamer objectified the experience and put it into words which conveyed his impression very well. Memories of the experience had been created: memories of the dream feeling and elements, and the words used in their description.

The very early mental events are not yet in the head, and when they come to consciousness later as repetitions in dreams or in other states, such as half-sleep, febrile and toxic deliria, epileptic auras, ecstasies, some schizophrenic conditions, and other altered states of consciousness, they cannot be located in the body or in the head with precision. The dreams in question are described as 'like an emotion' or 'like an organic feeling', and this is what is recalled on awakening, vividly. The dreamer may specifically mention the absence of head and body boundary or may depict head and body image as broken up or indefinite or *in statu nascendi,* as it was while forming in infancy. The alteration of body feeling and the uncertainty of localization have been studied better in half-sleep states than in the dream.

The possibility of 'validating' such reminiscences of earliest childhood has been raised (Ekstein and Rangell, 1961). So far as any individual is concerned, I do not think it possible to check on such experiences by outside testimony. The interpretations we have made, for example, of elements of the nursing situation, are just that—interpretations—and not constructions in Freud's sense. His constructions were of events for which there might be visual or visualizable memories, such as the primal scene, or the appreciation of the differences between the sexes. It is quite a different matter to interpret a state of mind or sensations as repetitive of the infant's state of consciousness while nursing. Freud's rule for accepting or rejecting cannot be applied.

Rather than as a construction, interpretations of this kind were made originally because of our common-sense knowledge of childhood situations and the presumed mind of the child. Thus, Freud interpreted flying in dreams as a memory of being carried about as a child, and dreams of being nude without embarrassment in company as a memory of this situation in childhood. No doubt these examples could be 'consensually validated', but this would be trivial. They would be accepted on a plausibility basis: it is very likely that the dreamer was carried about, did appear nude in public, etc. Interpretations of the dreams reported by Rycroft and Kubie as repetitions of early states of consciousness were made in the first place because of our common-sense hunches about the baby's state of consciousness and sensations, plus certain knowledge we had from pathological states about the lack of distinction between body image and world image in early life.

Trained observers of small babies, through ingenious methods and reasoning, provide data which may substantiate our common-sense observations. They are beginning to give us new material about babies' behavior and responses, the consequences of which in later life we may come to recognize because of this alerting. Such observers and psychoanalytic students of the older child have given us a great deal to digest about the child's pictorial past, eliminating some of the restraint we felt because of the child's insufficient vocabulary.

As to the earliest experiences, it seems to me that our interpretations have held up very well. Even if they are puzzling, many psychoanalysts have called them useful for practice and for theorizing. I should say that we have accumulated 'inductive' proof, if I had not read recent logicians on the topic of induction. On this matter I take my cue from Mother Jocasta, who said life is easier if one does not bother too much about certain things.

XI. METAPHOR, MIND, AND MANIKIN*

Some of Freud's Pictures of the Mind

I am grateful to the Los Angeles Psychoanalytic Society and Institute for the honor accorded me of holding the Second Fenichel-Simmel Memorial Lecture. My relationship with these two men goes back very far, in fact forty-four years, when I was a candidate in training at the Berlin Psychoanalytic Institute. My very first lecture before a psychoanalytic body was in Berlin on January 4, 1927 and Ernst Simmel presided. I sat at his left at a long table in a not very large room and to my left sat Otto Fenichel. My admiration for the profundity of these two men was already established. With affection I recall them tonight.

The paper I read in Berlin treated of the history of the concept of consciousness, its separation from the concept of conscience, and its place in faculty psychology.[1] I am not too sure that I am not still considering an aspect of the same subject now. I came to the present topic, some of Freud's pictures of the mind, because of studies I made and published not long ago about Freud's famous metaphor of the railway journey, where he compares the analytic situation to a train ride and the free associations to remarks about the passing scenery.[2]

In some doubt about the use of such words as figure of speech, metaphor, etc., when I consulted authorities, I found that the definition was self-evident. A figure of speech was the use of one word or set of words for an object other than the one for which they were intended. (For instance, 'He married

---

* [No. 139 in Bibliography.]

1 See, *Conscience and Consciousness in Medical Psychology—A Historical Study*, pp. 307-312 [Ed.].

2 See, *The Train Ride: A Study of One of Freud's Figures of Speech*, pp. 369-384 [Ed.].

a lemon'—Hockett.) The dictionaries were clear enough, but to my astonishment I discovered that there were nineteen classical kinds of figure and that I had been using them all my life: not only the familiar simile, metaphor, personification, and hyperbole, but also litotes, prosopopoeia, and what I am now writing (for all I know) may be an oxymoron. Charles P. Hockett, a contemporary authority on linguistics, was reassuring: we inherited the names for figures of speech from Greek and Roman authors. Nobody knows whether they are valid for Chinese, Choctaw, colloquial English, or Menomini. Students of rhetoric are dealing with idioms and patterns of idiom formation when they talk of figures of speech. All that Hockett (1958) has to say about figures of rhetoric is contained in two paragraphs, although he would like to add *the pun* to the list (pp. 317, ff.). The pun that Hockett quotes is actually a joke: the classical languages department (in Ithaca) was housed on a top floor, and naturally, a wag suggested, they taught Attic Greek.

Psychoanalytic writers have usually spoken of metaphors rather than of tropes or figures of speech, perhaps using that figure which indicates the whole by a part. Ella Freeman Sharpe (1940) and Jacob Arlow (1969) agree in bringing the figure of speech to where it can be analyzed like any other manifest element. Sharpe is struck by the way the 'physical' is applied to the representation of the 'metaphysical'. Arlow says, 'I have found the examination of metaphor to lead directly to concrete representations of an unconscious fantasy'. These remarks, which put the metaphor in its proper light, permit extensions into many fields. Thus, one can apply to metaphors the practical classification that Freud (1915d) uses for dreams and say that there are metaphors 'from above', that is, near to consciousness in respect of interpretability, and metaphors 'from below', like dreams dominated by unconscious elements. The metaphor from above would be readily interpretable by its author because of elements familiar to him; the metaphor from below would offer difficulties and need 'deeper' analysis, that is, more historical information. The metaphors from above will show obvious, readily intelligible and conventional sources. Those from below may have sources that are more individual and even surprising. In a sense too the elements from above may conceal the deeper historical elements or distract attention from them.

It was indeed surprising for me to find so much history behind Freud's ostensibly practical, rather prosaic comparison of the analytic situation with a train ride. The railway journeys that determined the figure lay in Freud's infancy. What seemed on the surface a commonplace metaphor 'from above' turned out, as Freud said of proper dreams, to stand on two feet; that is, to be determined by recent material and by material from infancy.

Metaphors apparently are constructed during states of wide-awakeness, but this is not always the case. If my interpretations are correct of the metaphors that Descartes uses in the Meditations, where he debates whether he is really awake or only in a permanent dream state which seems to be real, then it is Descartes's sleepiness that makes him sensitive to messages coming from his fatigued body and leads him to somatic comparisons:

> And how could I deny that these hands and this body are mine, were it not perhaps that I compare myself to certain persons, devoid of sense, whose cerebella are so troubled and clouded by violent vapors of black bile, that they . . . [imagine] that they have an earthenware head or are nothing but pumpkins or are made of glass.

Apparently a metaphorical conscious remark may show evidence of what we know in dream psychology as 'functional phenomena'; i.e., the dreamer's (here the philosopher's) subjective state, and in the example, particularly the state of his body.[3] Descartes's comparison referred to certain changes of feeling in his hands and body due to weariness, and these came 'from below', while the scientific remarks about the cerebella and black bile came 'from above'; that is, from his medical studies.

The findings of dream interpretation help us in varying our practical attack on the interpretation of metaphors.

From another point of view, a figure of speech is an invention, and so one may inquire whether a given figure shares with many inventions an origin in the human body or the

[3] *Cf.*, Freud (1900-1901), *The Interpretation of Dreams* (p. 503), with references to Silberer's original works.

body image. It is easy to see the bodily origin of many mechanical gadgets and instruments. The rake is an imitation of and supplement to the fingers; even a computer ultimately can be reduced to counting and marking by means of the fingers, though the popular language ignores this and talks of 'memory' and 'storing'. Freud refers to the imitation and expansion of the body in many devices intended to enhance the power of our sense organs. He mentions spectacles, the photographic camera, and ear trumpets (Freud, 1924b, p. 228). The article in which he does this, A Note Upon the 'Mystic Writing Pad', is built around a kind of mechanical metaphor or as we generally say, 'model'.

The mystic writing pad is constructed in a way analogous to a part of the psychic apparatus. It consists of a flat slab of wax and a two-layered cover made up of a sheet of paper covered by a celluloid sheet on which one can write. After one writes on the celluloid, the script is seen where the wax sticks to the paper. By a simple device that separates the paper from the wax, the script may become invisible, while the traces are retained in the wax. Freud draws a limited comparison between this pad and parts of the psychic apparatus. Thus, the paper on which the writing appears transiently is (or is like) the perceptive system, *Pcpt-Cs*. Both can be 'cleared'. The celluloid is (or again *is like*) the protective barrier against stimuli (*Reizschutz*). The scratches left in the wax are like registered memory traces. This seems to be as far as the model can be carried. You will note that I include the mystic writing pad among the figures of speech by slight extension of the definition. I should also include other concrete forms, whether related to words or not, in the general theory. Plainly, metaphors may be embodied as well as derived from bodies.[4]

Freud (1924b) analyzes his mechanical metaphor from above. The device, he says, is a 'return to the ancient method of writing on tablets of clay or wax: a pointed stilus scratches the surface, the depressions upon which constitute the "writing" ' (p. 229). Given Freud's known interest in antiquity, his

[4] I do not know whether such imaginary machines were in vogue when Freud wrote this paper. But a contemporary, Felix Klein (1890-1908), consistently used adding machines and other available devices to illustrate the abstract principles taught in his lectures.

associations to the classic form are expectable and intelligible. His association is obviously 'from above', from school experience, reading, and the like; and to pursue this train of thought leads us into conventional history, particularly the history of writing. Modern letters, we know, are the remote descendants of concrete pictographs, the Phoenician letters that we use having originated from pictures. Chinese ideograms are even more obviously the remains of pictures, and if we go back thirty thousand years or so we find among the pictures in Aurignacian caves the beginnings of record keeping. All this, we note, is very much from above.

It is not safe to attribute very many bodily elements to the devices that were used in writing and drawing. The stylus used on Roman wax tablets and on contemporary 'mystic pads' is of course a finger extension or substitute. If I proceed to interpret and say that the stylus is a penis, the writing a copulation and impregnation, and that an erasure is an abortion, someone might think I was interpreting as if from below. Of course, I am doing nothing of the sort; such associations don't come from below but from a book. Coming from an analysand, they are miscalled 'intellectual resistances'. I do not agree that they show much intellect.

History covers successfully the deeper roots we should like to discover in such nowadays standard devices as the wax tablet, the slate, or pen and paper. Their unconscious origins, whether in the body or in external situations, seem at once arbitrary and obscure. Perhaps standard, so-called 'universal' symbols in dreams are the nearest analogues.

The wax tablet itself is a very old picture of the memory or the mind, or of the mind conceived as memory. Plato described the memory as a wax tablet, quite aware to be sure that he was being metaphorical. Some later writers took literally the idea that imprints or traces were made somewhere within the person, usually implicating some part of the brain (Gomulicki, 1953). *Mind* and *memory* (the words) along with *mania* originate from the same Indo-Germanic root. It is said that the great interest in memorizing that came down from the Greeks and Romans tended to equate the mind with memory. This rather restricted view of mind can easily get the upper hand, even in so precise a writer as John Locke, who says:

> Let us then suppose the mind to be, as we say, white paper, void of all characters, without any ideas [at birth]; how comes it to be furnished? Whence comes it by that vast store [of ideas] which the busy and boundless fancy of man has painted on it with an almost endless variety?[5]

Such a tabular view of the mind is a commonplace in Western thought, and the Mystic Writing Pad's genesis is lost in antiquity. Clinically I can think only of a few analogies to the idea of *tabula rasa,* and one of these is literally a blank piece of paper. When a patient brings to the analytic session a dream written down we disregard the text and call attention to the *paper* on which it is written. Sometimes a patient will trick himself, imagine that he has jotted down a dream before arising, or tell his dream into a dictaphone which he has forgotten to turn on, ending up with a blank sheet of paper, a blank tape or phonographic record. Such a *tabula rasa* is known to stand for 'uninterrupted' sleep (at the breast originally). Conceivably the experience of waking up and finding a dream as if erased or a dream fading away might lead to speculations about 'a blank mind'.[6]

Freud, I think, makes only incidental use of the traditional figure which compares mind to paper, and mental contents to something written. Thus, he speaks of a dream *text* and says that certain gaps due to repression are *erasures.* Most important, as a derivative of the idea of a written text, is the term *censorship,* which of course is the agency that governs what can be published. The Interpretation of Dreams contains many references to graphic metaphor and the publishing trade; e.g., especially in English, Strachey's word *revision* (as in 'revised edition') and Isakower's (1954) suggestion of *redaction* to translate *Bearbeitung,* that changes latent content into manifest content.

The other possible metaphor in the quotation from Locke is of possibly more direct interest. The mind is said to be 'furnished'; and Berlin (1956) tells us that Locke thought of the mind as a room. To quote Berlin's paraphrase:

> In the mind, conceived as a sort of hollow vessel or container, there are to be found a number (a 'vast store') of perfectly

[5] Quoted by Berlin (1956, p. 40).

[6] See, *Inferences from the Dream Screen,* pp. 101-114 [Ed.].

> distinct and separable entities called 'ideas'. This is taken to be self-evident (p. 43).

And before this, Berlin explains that the British empirical philosophers applied Newton's atomic concept to the mind:

> The mind was treated as if it were a box containing mental equivalents of the Newtonian particles. These were called 'ideas' (p. 18).

Looking inward, the philosopher evidently notices, i.e., sees the associations and dissociations of such ideas, 'like a contemporary chemist analyzing the ingredients and physical behavior of a compound substance'. Locke, Berlin continues, sees when he introspects.

> Thought, at least reflective thought, is for Locke a kind of inner eye, corresponding to the outer physical eye which takes in the external world. . . . Locke's reflection, then, is acting like an outer eye, which can inspect two colored objects and see whether the colors match each other or not (p. 19).

I do not know whether the preceding interpretation of Locke's position is generally accepted; however, the idea of the contents of consciousness being in a container of sorts, and the metaphor of a box are very useful. This is a one-room figure of speech; everything visible to the inner eye is in that single room. The consciousness is coextensive with the mental. The figure is better suited to portray memory and imagination than any of the other mental faculties for historic reasons, which were not considered by Professor Berlin but given extensive thought by Frances A. Yates (1966) in her book, The Art of Memory. The latter author writes about systems for improving the memory, especially those employed in classic times and later during the middle ages and early renaissance.

One method is germane to our exposition. It was known to such teachers and orators as Quintillian and Cicero, and not too many years ago a comparable method was widely advertised in this country. The subscriber to the American method never forgot a name, but could say proudly, 'You are Mr. Addison Sims of Seattle'. In the antique version what one did was imagine vividly a house of many rooms that you could go through serially. In each of these vividly visualized rooms you placed mentally the picture of some object that was to remind you of a section of the speech you were going to make at a trial, in the Senate, etc. This does not strike Professor Yates as an enormous aid to memory (and apparently Quintillian too was not too well disposed to the method), yet it was widely understood and used, with apparently a surprising development of the visual imagination.

Such housings of the contents of consciousness evidently preceded Locke by many centuries. Certainly the figure of speech by which the mind or the memory was equated to a container came readily enough. It can in effect be traced back to certain books known to the scholars of classic times. This way of looking at the sources of the metaphor is again an example of going at it 'from above'. But this one-room picture of consciousness is susceptible to a deeper analysis, and I believe that this was furnished in my book, The Image and the Past (Lewin, 1968).

In that book, I have a chapter titled Phantoms in the Head, where I discuss the physical basis of the room metaphor. From the standpoint of the individual and his development, I pointed out that the concept of consciousness as a box or room or cave, whether in Locke or in any of us, could be traced to a period in childhood which I called the *pictorial past.* At that time introspection would show the 'mind' as the subjectively sensed *head image;* that is, the subjective feeling we all have or had of our head as a cavernous part of our body image, furnished with images of several kinds, especially the visually pictorial.

Such an explanation is of course historical also, but in a different sense from the conventional one. I do not trace back the metaphor of the mind as a furnished house or a box to Simonides or to Metrodorus of Scepsis, which is what the classic teachers and Professor Yates did. I trace Locke's container back to Locke's head when he was a little boy. This is consonant with Miss Sharpe's point about the physical preceding the metaphysical and with Freud's (1923a) aphorism about the ego being primarily body ego. The metaphor is traced back in individual development to the physically based head image. The mind or consciousness is thought of as a container because that is the way it feels or felt subjectively.

The idea that the mind is in the head is not considered *au fait* by present-day philosophers of science, and much has been written about why the mind is in the head (McCulloch, 1951), including some rather sarcastic remarks about persons who picture a personality 'behind the center of the eyes' in man or animals (Schrödinger, 1956, pp. 216, ff.). The disturbing word here seems to be *in* (Berlin, 1956, p. 75; Ryle, 1949, p. 12), which is usually considered a metaphorical localization rather than a naïve intuitive reflection of the *head image*.[7] Even pre-Aristotelian Greeks naïvely thought that one of their minds, the *psyche*, was located in the head.

I should not have been so explicit about Locke's idea of the mind as a sort of box or container, his one-room metaphor for the mind, and his apparently dominant notion that mind was perception, imagination, and memory, if I had not been struck by Freud's (1915-1917) well-known comparison of the mind to a two-room suite. Freud came to see the mind, or more accurately the psychic apparatus, as being larger metaphorically than a one-room apartment. Instead he described, with some misgivings and restrictions, a mind of two rooms connected by a door guarded by a watchman (pp. 295, ff.).

One of the rooms, as we shall see, was Locke's old *Consciousness*, in which there was an 'inner eye', all quite according to tradition. But the new room that had been added beyond the door, into which the eye 'of the imagination', as it was also called, did not reach, could not be entered. In fact, no one mentions entering it. It is crowded with individuals wishing to get past the censoring guard and into consciousness. So far as I know, this two-room representation is original with Freud and the plan was never confused with the head image. My statement implies that the two-room suite cannot be modeled entirely on the subjectively felt head image, though the consciousness-room is evidently carried over from Locke's unicameral picture. Before further discussion, it would be profitable to remind ourselves of Freud's original statement, even though its familiarity may make this long quotation rather boring. Freud (1915-1917) tells us:

[7] For more discussion of the relation of head image, localization, etc., and ideas about the mind or minds, see *The Image and the Past.*

> The crudest idea of these systems [conscious and unconscious] is the most convenient for us—a spatial one. Let us therefore compare the system of the unconscious to a large entrance hall, in which the mental impulses jostle one another like separate individuals. Adjoining this entrance hall there is a second, narrower, room—a kind of drawing-room—in which consciousness, too, resides. But on the threshold between these two rooms a watchman performs his function: he examines the different mental impulses, acts as a censor, and will not admit them into the drawing-room if they displease him. You will see at once that it does not make much difference if the watchman turns away a particular impulse at the threshold itself or if he pushes it back across the threshold after it has entered the drawing-room. This is merely a question of the degree of his watchfulness and of how early he carries out his act of recognition. If we keep to this picture, we shall be able to extend our nomenclature further. The impulses in the entrance hall of the unconscious are out of sight of the conscious, which is in the other room; to begin with they must remain unconscious. If they have already pushed their way forward to the threshold and have been turned back by the watchman, then they are inadmissible to consciousness; we speak of them as *repressed*. But even the impulses which the watchman has allowed to cross the threshold are not on that account necessarily conscious as well; they can only become so if they succeed in catching the eye of consciousness. We are therefore justified in calling this second room the system of the *preconscious*. In that case becoming conscious retains its purely descriptive sense. For any particular impulse, however, the vicissitude of repression consists in its not being allowed by the watchman to pass from the system of the unconscious into that of the preconscious. It is the same watchman whom we get to know as resistance when we try to lift the repression by means of the analytic treatment (pp. 295-296).

I break into Freud's text here to make the point that one source of resistance to the idea of the unconscious is clear in those who recognize only a one-room container. Such persons suffer from a lag; they were trained to think of an inner eye and of its attention to potential conscious elements. But such critics misunderstand the idea of the unconscious because they do not allow for the functions of the watchman. They accept the preconscious, perhaps, but not the unconscious excluded by the watchman. I think that such persons had felt their mind as intimately related to their head image. In their head image they could conceive the 'dark' preconsciousness of inattention and the 'inner eye' of attention. They knew the *qualitatively* unconscious and could match it with a subjective feeling; but there was no way of introspecting and including in their head image (i.e., making conscious) the elements warded off by the watchman. Loyal to their old introspection and not seeing or feeling the watchman and the other room, they could not include it in their head image (called by them the *mind*) or more generally in their body ego (called the *personality*).

The gist of my preceding remarks is that unlike Locke's metaphorical single room, Freud's figure could not have arisen from an unmodified introspection of the head image alone. And it was this nearly unmodified native head image on which was fixed the old idea of the conscious mind. One originally sees that the earth is flat and the sky a big sphere above and only by an effort comes to accept Copernicus's view; so originally the mind is a one-room perception.

Freud, sensing the general resistance to his scheme, combats it in a different way, by an appeal to the methods of physical science, citing a comparable exposition of Ampère. He says:

> Now I know you will say that these ideas are both crude and fantastic and quite impermissible in a scientific account. I know that they are crude; and, more than that, I know that they are incorrect, and, if I am not very much mistaken, I already have something better to take their place. Whether it will seem to you equally fantastic I cannot tell. They are *preliminary working hypotheses, like Ampère's manikin swimming in the electric current* [italics by B.D.L.], and they are not to be despised in so far as they are of service in making our observations intelligible. I should like to assure you that these crude hypotheses of the two rooms, the watchman at the threshold between them and consciousness as a spectator at the end of the second room, must nevertheless be very far-reaching approximations to the real facts (*op. cit.*, p. 296).

This defense appeals to the methods of scientific thinking and is in that sense a rationalization. What strikes me in this is

Freud's choice of Ampère and the manikin, when another manikin seems much more akin to the little censor. This is Clerk-Maxwell's demon, who stands at the door that connects a two-room apartment, separating speedy molecules from slow ones, thus upsetting entropy and permitting water to turn to ice on a hot stove. True this demon is well known to be a failure at his job, and obviously the censor is not. Yet, the two homunculi have much in common. It surprises me that Freud did not use the demon in his appeal to the scientific. In any case, Freud, Clerk-Maxwell, Ampère, and many other scientists who also teach, have an appreciation of the relation of teaching and theory.

To borrow the pictorial language of colleagues in a different context, I think Freud's qualms about his metaphor may have originated in a conflict between two 'internal objects'. When Freud wrote imaginatively and pictorially, he can be thought of as paying attention to his internal Goethe; then in afterthought, scientifically, he heard (and argued with) his internal Brücke (or Helmholtz, et al.). He apparently recognized the transitional nature of his 'working hypothesis' (which is not clear to Strachey, according to a footnote). I think the character of his audience, which was not narrowly scientific, determined an excellent teaching device; his apology was to his more narrowly scientific superego. Freud was being, as we now say, 'prescientific', and he apparently felt this. Freud hesitated to elevate a blackboard diagram to a kind of reality.[8]

Freud nevertheless differs from Ampère and Clerk-Maxwell in an important respect, and this is evident in the name of his manikin, the Censorship. The homunculi of the physicists, for all the appearances, are not human and share only a purely physical quality with humanity: Ampère's stupid little fellow floats; Clerk-Maxwell's mechanically separates speedy from slow molecules and his tacit selective function (perhaps involving 'human' psychology) has been contested; Descartes's diver bobs up and down in liquids with altered specific gravity and that is all. But a Censor is not just a muscular and alert watchman or bouncer; he reads and understands the nature of the would-be intruder. As has been pointed out, his is a so-

[8] Which Kurt Lewin actually did in inventing his psychological topology. See, *Teaching and the Beginnings of Theory*, pp. 545-550 [Ed.].

cial function: as censor he keeps the reader's eye in ignorance, as gatekeeper he bounces back those who wish to crash the gate. He has human rules for this.

It is possible that the mixture of head image and social functioning does not gel, and that there is a tacit mixed metaphor. A footnote of the editors of the English translation of the Introductory Lectures makes this evident. An annotation to the phrase 'ideas that are inadmissible to consciousness' reads:

> '*Bewusstseinsunfähig*.' The term is due to Breuer, who constructed it on the model of '*hoffähig*' ('admissible to Court', 'having the *entrée*') (Freud, 1915-1917, p. 296, n.).

A reference in this footnote says: 'See Section 5 of his contribution to *Studies on Hysteria* (1895d), Standard Ed. 2, 225 n'., which reads as follows:

> This expression ['*Bewusstseinsunfähig*'] is not unambiguous and for this reason leaves much to be desired. It is, however, constructed on the analogy of '*Hoffähig*' ['admissible to Court', 'having the *entrée*'] and may in the meantime be used for lack of a better term. [Though on the analogy of '*Hoffähig*' the word is here translated '*inadmissible* to consciousness', its literal meaning is '*incapable* of consciousness'. It could equally well be translated 'incapable of being (or becoming) conscious'. The word was adopted by Freud and frequently used by him, and the context then often calls for one of these other renderings.]

The suffix *-fähig,* in terms of what is socially 'possible', appears in many comparable combinations; thus *salonfähig* = 'socially acceptable or fit for society'. The term implies not only *capable,* but *privileged.* Obviously Clerk-Maxwell's world of random particles is supposed to be anarchic; ambiguity enters when one considers whether the demon is treating rapid molecules as privileged or not.

There is no doubt at all that a censorship is backed by authority, that it is what in German is called an *Instanz,* a government agency or institution with powers to assert distinctions and determine rights and privileges. The *bewusstseinsfähig* elements in the waiting room have the privilege of becoming conscious; those that are not *fähig* do not. They would never do in the parlor; and I think a canine figure of speech would be even more apt. Some dogs are housebroken and have the privilege of entry; other dogs are not housebroken and may (but the German implies *can*) not come in. *Fähig* occupies a border position between *may* and *can*, privilege and possibility. The English 'He is an impossible person' hits this off very well: it does not mean that he cannot *exist* but that he is *vulgar*.

The unexpected switch from Locke's anatomically based container to the socially based rooms, from Ampère and electricity to imperial pomp and circumstance, raises an interesting question: Can the head image be altered by social institutions as in many ways it can be through the observation of other heads? I mean by the preceding remark about 'other heads', the knowledge that comes through the examination of the brain and the contents of the heads of other persons. So far as Freud's two-room suite is concerned, not ordinarily. So far as I know, no one introspects in a new way, taking the anteroom into the head image. Many scientists in the past have talked *as if* they could intuit the brain in their head and I am inclined to credit some very experienced brain anatomists with this talent. They somehow 'saw' a three-dimensional brain in their head—not always of course, but whenever they turned their attention to the tracts and areas of the brain.[9]

I doubt, however, whether Freud's description of the two rooms ever had or could have such an effect. Freud's great familiarity with brain anatomy and function was applied to other less intuitive schemes, for instance, the aphasia scheme in the diagram in The Ego and the Id (Freud, 1923a). Certainly, here the head image appears to be only one part of the total ego. It will be noted that in spite of its origin, Freud disclaims any anatomic locale for the elements of the ego-id scheme.

If my remarks about the head image and the social representation have validity—that is, if Freud's figure of the two rooms is a condensation of Locke's and perhaps his own picture of the inside of the head and of a picture derived say from imperial court procedure—then the metaphor shows a situation parallel to the general development of the ego from its

[9] I am not completely sure but I believe the late Adolf Meyer had this talent. I infer this from having heard him describe areas and tracts in a three-dimensional brain with tacit references to his own cranium.

pristine nature as a bodily ego into one which takes into account the environment,—other persons, other heads,—and then social customs and institutions such as the censorship. The ego and the initial intuitive basis of the metaphor develop beyond the bodily ego and the physically conditioned facts.

In this connection, it is interesting that Silberer's famous example of the hallucinated representation of a mind too tired to respond to his wishes (quoted by Freud [1900-1901, p. 503]) was also borrowed from government. The tired mind was seen as a stubborn, grouchy bureaucrat. The range of metaphor making is large, large as civilization, from the random movements of particles to the rigid movements of government officials. The mind too which began as the head image of prehistoric Aurignacian man in Lascaux, then was detached from its body as the Greek psyche, after that commingled in various ways with the body and the head image through Galenic medicine, and, with the brain and skull, emerged in Freud as something beyond head image, beyond the brain scheme and the brain mythology of moderns, to be presented as a construction partly of Locke's container, partly of social rule.

I see Freud's diagrammatic two rooms with the door between not only as a pragmatic teaching device, but also a pragmatic picture answering the needs of psychoanalytic technique, which from the beginning has had to face both the anatomical and the social; and Freud's figure mirrors this practical need. The metaphor is indeed what we stated earlier—an invention, a 'picture' which brings together the anatomical and the social in an untidy scheme, but which proves its merits, as Freud was aware. It approximates not only one set of facts; it supplies a compromise between two sets, in a brilliant didactic 'approximation'.

Science and the Homunculus

I find it difficult to estimate the influence upon my thinking of the two men for whom these lectures are named. Approximately, I think, when the topic is a psychophysical problem or the role of the body, unsuspected links with Simmel's ideas make their appearance. With Fenichel's work, I note many points of contact. When I contemplated the little watchman that guards the door in Freud's account of the two rooms, the Unconscious and the Preconscious, I thought of other little men and remembered one that Fenichel reported.

Freud's watchman was called *endopsychic,* which means that he is in the mind and by a very common mental trick, in the head or head image. The dwarf mentioned by Fenichel in his case report serves a very different function, one not ordinarily expressed in pictures. With some license this manikin can also be called endopsychic, but with many distinctions from Freud's use of the word.

Fenichel's manic-depressive patient believed that her diaphragm ached and invented an eponymous dwarf in explanation. Diaphragm in German is *Zwerchfell* and dwarf is *Zwerg* and the patient believed that the *Zwerg* was jumping around on her *Zwerchfell,* constituting a *Zwergfell,* pronounced nearly the same as the word for diaphragm. It will be noted that the dwarf functioned independently and Fenichel used him as a good clinical portrayal of an object introjected by cannibal means. Analysis showed, in Fenichel's (1932) words, that her '*Zwergfell*' was 'the same as her [recently deceased] devoured father or rather his devoured penis' (p. 370; 1945, p. 390).

My studies of Freud's metaphor led me to believe that somehow the room called the Preconscious was very close to John Locke's picture of consciousness, and that it arose from introspections about the inside of the head. The censor-watchman thus seemed to stand at an opening into the cranium, but his functions transcended those of a mechanical valve. He had many qualities that characterize a more complex being.

The creature in the belly of Fenichel's patient too seemed more than just a piece of machinery, a part of *l'homme machine.* The diaphragmatic location sounded very concrete. So, of course, did the part-soul which Homeric Greeks called the *phren* in the same concrete location, the same word that was used later on for the diaphragm (Onians, 1951). The *Zwergfell* belly dwarf more nearly resembled a Homeric part-soul than a piece of machinery. And authors in a not too distant past have speculated about 'part-souls' though in a different context; e.g., a 'soul' that might be called 'the spinal soul' and the like. One nineteenth-century physician apparently attributed something like a soul to each organ, in which I recognize echoes of Greek physiology.

A little man mentioned by Freud (1915-1917, pp. 295, ff.; B. Lewin, 1968, pp. 73, ff.) in connection with his two-room suite metaphor offers quite a contrast to the diaphragm trampler and to the little people of fairy stories. This was Ampère's manikin, who seems not to have a soul, or feeling, or ideas, and obviously no will of his own for it was his function, for which Ampère created him, only to swim in an electric current. Another related manikin, invented by a physicist, is Clerk-Maxwell's demon. He stands by a trapdoor that connects two vessels or rooms; he is the size of a molecule and it is his mission to push fast molecules into one room and keep the slow ones in the other, thus wrecking the principle of entropy. That is why he was invented—so that water might under such circumstances freeze standing on a hot stove. The demon is of course very small indeed, and this permits George Gamow (1961, pp. 112, ff.) to demonstrate that he could not obey Clerk-Maxwell's wishes. Clerk-Maxwell's demon (Ehrenberg, 1967) has to have a definite size in the world of matter and energy to serve what might be thought of as his ego purposes, entirely inculcated of course by his creator, Clerk-Maxwell. Ampère's homunculus also, one presumes, must have a definite size to float in any definite electric current. The diaphragm dwarf too must have a definite size, how large one does not know, though Fenichel's account gives us a hint and we may risk an educated guess. We note that the nursery rhyme says, 'I have a little husband/ No bigger than my thumb/' and we may also remember Gulliver's specification that the Lilliputians had the height of his middle finger. The dwarf, we could say, was of conventional size.

But we do not know and may never know the size of the little watchman in Freud's diagram. There is no reason to endow him with any size at all; nevertheless in our imagination we probably do since the two-room-suite idea evokes a picture. Here Freud's words suggest perspective but leave the matter of size ambiguous so that we may be arbitrary in our visualizing. The two rooms could remind one of a prosperous doctor's suite of waiting room and consultation room. A doctor's wish-fulfilment would fill up the waiting room with a crowd of patients, not all of them, for one reason or another, privileged to enter the consultation room. According to this particular train of thought, the watchman would be the size of an average office secretary. Yet when we introspect, we also take perspective into account and tend to reduce the size of the picture. The rooms are then pictures in our head with relative sizes only; they are labeled *large, small,* etc., but they are depicted according to scale. The secretary-size censor then becomes a homuncular model, small scale yet apparently alive; and we might reply to questioning that he was no bigger than our thumb, perhaps influenced by Freud's reference to Ampère's manikin, which might make us believe, rightly or wrongly, that Freud too saw the watchman as a little man.

On reflection, to be sure, we know that the little man and the censor in Freud's metaphor are logically what are called variables. So when we ask for their size, we are not logical. Indeed, we know we are fantastic, and that we can assign many answers none of which are right or wrong. The topography of the mind does not deal with real space. Our naïve feeling that consciousness is somewhere in our head and that consequently the manikin that stands at the entrance is proportionately small, is a remnant from our pictorial past, when we somehow 'knew' intuitively that such pictures were in our head. Later we may be able to say something about the size of the spectator who is supposed to reside in the preconscious chamber, who brings the included elements of the room into consciousness by an act of attention.

Surveying numerous examples of dwarfs and manikins we note much variety; for one reason, because of variations in the extent to which the manikin is a total person (I do not hazard the ambiguity of saying a *real* person or a *true* person). Here we have quite a range. For instance, the Cartesian diver is nothing more than a hollow tin receptacle painted like a man. By appropriate mixture of water and glycerine he can be made to float in the liquid at any level, neither rising nor sinking. He is a manikin in name only; he is replaceable by the same material in any form. Physical scientists have tackled the more difficult task of substituting theoretical, purely physical devices for Clerk-Maxwell's demon—I gather not entirely successfully. Psychoanalysts occasionally have attempted comparable replacements for parts of analytic theory, sometimes by nerve chains, sometimes by physical devices. I do not always understand the models, but the inventors seem to take entities such as the endopsychic censor and try to change them into a sort of machine, giving us not exactly an example of *l'homme machine* but instead perhaps *l'homuncule machine,* whatever that may be.

Cartesian divers and the manikins in physics do not offer us much of a psychological problem. Indeed, reading Freud's account carefully, one finds that he does not equate his watchman and Ampère's manikin. The latter only figures as a pedagogically useful idea. Freud (1915-1917, p. 296) says the *ideas* he presents by means of his two-room metaphor are preliminary working hypotheses 'like Ampère's manikin swimming in the electric current' and that such diagrams are not to be despised for pedagogic reasons, 'in so far [as they make] our observations intelligible'. He does not say the censor is such a manikin; he is teaching rather than 'theorizing', two purposes not always readily distinguishable.

Besides varying in range from the purely material to the purely human, manikins also vary in respect of their location within and without the person. There is an obvious internal manikin, of which we have seen examples. There is also an external manikin and between these extremes, manikins with ambiguous location. Though the dwarf in Fenichel's patient was inside her, he was not *of* her as we say, and in the context of Fenichel's interpretation he was undigested. In contrast, Descartes's diver seems purely external, invented to illustrate and embellish the principle of specific gravity, hence rational and utilized in the interest of exposition. I purposely said *seems* purely external, cautiously, because we did not learn what fantasies Descartes might have had in association with this toy. I venture to suggest that the grandson of two physicians, with considerable knowledge of medicine, was not unaware that a foetus floats in the uterine waters, that the position of the phallus alters with changes in its specific (or unspecific) gravity; and without much education he could have noted principles of specific gravity exemplified by the contents of a chamber pot. We should have to hold these propositions to be speculations, though not very surprising ones any more.

The notion that the homunculus is a little man with a little body and sometimes a mind reminds us of what can happen in fantasy and symptom to the body image. The literature here is rather extensive; I need no more than mention Tausk (1919), Schilder (1950), Federn (1952), Greenacre (1952, 1953a, 1955), Isakower (1936). Greenacre, who studied body image variations and developments, has also studied the homunculus, in so far as the Lilliputian arose from the creativity of Jonathan Swift. The other authors were not interested in the body image of the homunculus as such.

Freud (1923a), it is true, uses the word *homunculus,* but does not speak of its body image. Instead he uses it to demonstrate a feature of the body ego. He writes:

> The ego is first and foremost a bodily ego; it is not merely a surface entity, but is itself the projection of a surface. If we wish to find an anatomical analogy for it we can best identify it with the 'cortical homunculus' of the anatomists, which stands on its head in the cortex, sticks up its heels, faces backwards and, as we know, has its speech-area on the left-hand side (p. 26).

He adds in a footnote:

> I.e. the ego is ultimately derived from bodily sensations, chiefly from those springing from the surface of the body . . . . besides, as we have seen above, representing the superficies of the mental apparatus (*op. cit.,* 26, n.).

The scheme is of course not original with Freud, but a regular element in anatomical textbooks. It vividly explains Freud's thinking, and it is a pity that it has not been more used in psychoanalytic literature. Thus Freud (1915d) says that when persons are ready for sleep, they remove whatever is removable, such as false hair, false teeth, etc., they undress, and after that 'carry out an entirely analogous undressing of their minds and lay aside most of their psychical acquisitions' (p. 222). The homunculus gives us one idea of the state we strip down to, a stripping of which Federn and Isakower were aware when they demonstrated the possibility of further stripping, of splits and reorganizations within this diagram, as shown in partial sleep states and similar conditions.

Freud was already aware that parts of this homunculus, which somehow avoided going to sleep 'thoroughly', could be, as it were, refleshed and reclad and then appear projected into the manifest dream picture. The penis could reappear as a little man; the breasts could be projected as 'sisters'. This diagram, or what may correspond to it in the body, then would not be stripped away or flat. The aroused part gets represented in the dream. Freud and Scherner give many examples of such partial coming to life or awakening of the body in new guise, projected in dream pictures.[10]

It is not only in dreams that body parts and substance disappear. The cortical homunculus is also an example of the process called *abstraction*. The homunculus stands for an idea, or perhaps *is* an idea about the human being and the cortex. It is an abstraction, too, in the original meaning of the word, to take away from; in other words, abstraction is also a kind of undressing and removal of prosthetic devices, then a removal of what would correspond perhaps to the pictorial homuncular device itself. After stripping down to the bones, you take away the bones and have left—what? An idea of the body purely, a pure idea, a kind of ghost. In this context, the cortical homunculus seems to be a possible way station, and certain clinical findings appear to bear this out.[11] The cortical homunculus has lost its semantically superfluous parts in a way that reminds us of what happened to Miss Natalija A, Tausk's famous patient.

To refresh your memory, I must present a longish quotation from Tausk (1919). For over six years, Miss Natalija A had been under the influence of a machine, located in Berlin (while she was in Belgrade), and manipulated from there. The machine, she said, has the form of a human body, indeed, her own form.

> The trunk (torso) has the shape of a lid, resembling the lid of a coffin and is lined with silk or velvet. Regarding the limbs two significant explanations are given. At the first interview she described them as natural parts of the body. A few weeks later these limbs were not placed on the coffin lid in their natural form, but were merely drawn on it in two dimensions,

[10] Freud (1900-1901): *The Interpretation of Dreams.*

[11] All cortical homunculi are not so smooth as the one mentioned by Freud. Certain illustrations in textbooks of anatomy or physiology show monstrous homunculi in the Rolandic regions, the sensory homunculus with a gigantic tongue and lips, eyes as big as the abdomen, tiny dangling legs, etc. In politics this would be called 'proportional representation' and it indicates the density of the sensory end organs.

> in the position they would occupy in the natural state of the body. She cannot see the head—she says that she is not sure about it and she does not know whether the machine bears her own head. . . .[12] When someone strikes this machine, she feels the blow in the corresponding part of her own body. . . . At an earlier stage, sexual sensations were produced in her through manipulation of the genitalia of the machine; but now the machine no longer possesses genitalia, though why or how they disappeared she cannot tell. Ever since the machine lost its genitalia, the patient has ceased to experience sexual sensations (pp. 529-530).

Later in his discussion Tausk supposes that the change in the limbs from three dimensions to two indicates a transitional state of affairs. At least, he thought that if he had been able to follow the case for several weeks more, he would have found that the two-dimensional figure also had disappeared.

Psychoanalysts all know what an important case history this one of Miss Natalija A turned out to be. It determined many of our views about the bodily ego and gave us a remarkable peep into the psychology of schizophrenia. Its application in the present context is somewhat different and perhaps a bit subtle. For we find her three-dimensional body gradually turning into a two-dimensional figure, and in the transitional stage that Tausk was able to observe, it had turned into a kind of map of the body surface, a topography without feeling, bearing a strange resemblance to the map that Freud called the cortical homunculus. True, Miss Natalija's map was apparently body size, but the machine was nonetheless turning into a nonsentient manikin diagram. The process that we call in schizophrenia removal of cathexis from the body image has the same result as the process called abstraction in consciousness psychology in relation to cognition. Miss Natalija A is abstracting, flattening her body into an image, preparatory to its fading away, like so many forgotten 'higher abstractions'.

It is noteworthy that Miss Natalija's legs and genitalia during their transformations retain for a time the shape of the organs. After the sense of flesh and blood disappear, form and shape persist in the pictures painted on the surface of the coffin-like machine. That is, they exist as pictures of genitalia

[12] This is later explained by the remark that a dreamer also may dream of himself as faceless. In short one does not see one's own head.

and legs, then are abolished and replaced by blanks. I hesitate to speak of blanks here, for the blankness consists of the absence of pictures and feelings and Miss Natalija seems to possess the faculty of naming them. It may be that this possibility has led to the idea of word cathexis, with the words often behaving as if they had replaced the organ images, or perhaps were influenced by a resurgence with displacement of organ images, of which the best example still would be Freud's (1915a) and Tausk's example of the eye twister (*Augenverdreher*). On the other hand, the picture of the organ or the body is reduced more and more by this process and one wonders about the outcome at the limit of the reduction. It is again striking that the 'de-visualing' of the ideas about bodily parts parallels a comparable process that takes place with maturation into adulthood in many if not in most 'normal' persons, when they come to rely on 'purely verbal' or on 'imageless' thought. Again this is 'abstraction'.

Instances are known when a blank bodily part (representation), such as appeared in Miss Natalija's body image, becomes filled by a newly developed image. I am thinking of a kind of micro-restitution, and this is also to be noted in Tausk's (1919) article where he summarizes some of the symptomatology of the schizophrenic chemist Ludwig Staudenmaier.

> [Staudenmaier] described his sensations during his bowel movements from the beginning of the movement to its conclusion, and attributed every single peristaltic motion coming to his awareness to the activity of special demons allegedly located in the intestines and entrusted with the performance of each separate motion (p. 526).[13]

I am struck by the applicability of present-day thinking on the dream to explain Miss Natalija's and Dr. Staudenmaier's bodily representations. When the limb and genital representations in Miss Natalija's body image are blanked out, one is reminded of the hypnagogic reduction of mental pictures and

[13] Tausk is using the autobiographic book by Ludwig Staudenmaier (1912): *Die Magie als experimentelle Wissenschaft.* Extensive comments on Staudenmaier, with excerpts from the book, are in Karl Jaspers' (1920, pp. 220, ff.) *Allgemeine Psychopathologie.*

Staudenmaier himself says that pieces of his subconscious become independent and personified (*selbstständiggewordene Teile meines Unterbewusstseins*).

bodily representations or images that finally ends in the blankness of sleep. On the comparable blankness in Staudenmaier's intestines, the intruding equivalents of wakers—that is, intestinal sensations—get personified, much as in a dream when intruding phallic sensations are pictured as an airplane soaring into the blue. Both dream and delusion reject the waker or intruder on narcissistic regression. Breaking through into consciousness, Staudenmaier's repudiated sensations generate a homunculus in a sort of optically conditioned form; that is, as a conscious or preconscious picture. In dreams too an asleep bodily part may appear as a person (e.g., the penis as a child, the breasts as sisters, etc.).

For comparison with Freud's scientific diagram of the cortical homunculus and with Miss Natalija's psychotic analogue, we may mention the 'little men' that appear in Schreber's autobiography. M. Katan (1950) has demonstrated the connection of these little men with spermatozoa. It was indeed at one time a respectable theory that a little man (a very little man) was crouched in the head of a spermatozoon, and one scientific observer drew an allegedly objective picture of such a homunculus.

Niederland (1951, 1956, 1963) later showed how Schreber's description of the hallucinated little man was influenced by sketches to illustrate various gymnastic positions described in the books on physical exercises written by Schreber's father. Sketches of 'little men' are shown with dotted outlines of limbs or the head to indicate various positions they assume during the gymnastics.

Niederland (1951) uses these dotted-outline sketches to clarify what Schreber may have meant by *flüchtig hingemachte Männer,* which is not really translated by the phrase 'cursory contraptions'. Niederland writes:

> The German *hinmachen* means not only to make, to defecate, to kill, but also to draw or to sketch. In the last sense, it may refer to those numerous diagrams, pictures, and drawings of male figures which illustrate a book, *Ärztliche Zimmergymnastik,* written by Schreber's father . . . (p. 589).

Niederland also says that some of the detailed descriptions of the little men read 'like graphic though distorted descriptions of the anatomical illustrations included in the elder Schreber's book'.[14]

The interpretation of the Schreber case has always been attractive to psychoanalytic students. I should like to join in with only one idea that came to me reading about the little men and their origin. I should agree that they represent spermatozoa, but in view of Niederland's studies I should specify the father's spermatozoa. After Schreber's *Weltuntergang* they participate in the restitution process, in creating a new world, in which God and Schreber collaborated.

I should not like to omit from any study of body image a reference to the paper by Paul Kramer (1955), a detailed clinical report relevant not only to the development of the body image but also to the matter of location of what Federn called 'mental ego feeling', that is, the spot where one situates one's subjective self, the system *Pcpt-Cs.* Kramer's patient had a complex relation to a 'little man' who alternately was in him or with whom he identified himself. The little man was a complicated personality. The role of the mirror image in this case is also interesting, but the case is too detailed for convenient summary here.

The oral-stage problem of separation from the mother and the establishment of an independent ego, including an independent body ego, is known to give way to an anal-stage analogue; namely, the separation of feces from the body. Perhaps because of their size, the homunculi have always suggested fecal masses and derivatives of fecal masses. There are 'anal babies', an 'anal penis', and the like. The extent to which a fecal mass persists in living is a familiar childhood problem, and independence from the body image of internal homunculi figures is a problem in many accounts.

The anal quality in the homunculus was evident to that psychoanalytic pioneer, Sandor Ferenczi (1927), who made many contributions to the field of anal erotism. In his study of

[14] Staudenmaier's intestinal demons are suspiciously like personified spermatozoa. Staudenmaier describes very sensitively how he introjects objects of his admiration (or unconscious desire), such as a military commander he set up in himself and addressed as Your Highness. This personification of a part of his 'subconscious' that has become independent (to quote Staudenmaier) seems to have been exercised on a microscopic male element in the intestine. There are alchemical analogues for this fantasy (Staudenmaier, 1912, p. vi).

Gulliver Phantasies, Ferenczi matches Swift's elaborations with clinical examples, which can be summarized in the statement that the Lilliputians may represent babies, phalloi, or feces. Among the gigantic Brobdingnagians, Gulliver takes his turn at being a baby (or foetus), a phallus, or a fecal mass. Foetuses of course are 'inside' babies, located midst the feces and urine. Undefecated masses too are inside babies, foetuses.

Silberer's (1914) early paper, The Homunculus, is relevant to our present interest, especially the matter of the little man residing in the head. Silberer's interest is predominantly in the alchemist writings. Alchemy, he quotes Jung as saying, arose as a magic of fertilization, that is, to discover a means of producing babies without a mother (*'d.h., ein Mittel, wie Kinder gemacht werden könnten ohne Mutter'*). Silberer thinks this is going too far, yet he thinks there is a great deal of truth in the idea; and he certainly supplies much material to make such a theory plausible. The alchemists were interested in *sublimation* and *ennobling*. Noble metals, especially gold, were to arise from the treatment of baser metals, and the like; and scientifically, so to speak, the production of a homunculus was allegedly a preliminary run. If one could make a little man or even a monster out of such 'base' materials as the alchemists used, then this *Vorversuch* would be encouraging. The infantile fantasies here are fairly obvious.

The most striking, protoscientific, laboratory form of homunculus production is described by Paracelsus (1493-1541). Silberer's excerpt from Paracelsus's writings runs for seven pages. I shall try to make a further shortened account. Paracelsus recognizes two types of generation, the natural kind (*ohne alle Kunst*) and the artificial (*durch Kunst*). *Kunst,* he specifies, is *alchimia,* and he has in mind both science and technology. In short, the homunculus can be made as follows:

Place horse manure in a glass retort, introduce human semen, keep the vessel warm, irrigate with menstrual blood, and after forty days, signs of life will appear. Gradually during the time after that and up to forty weeks, a homunculus will develop, transparent at first, slowly taking on human form until he is born from the flask a complete man,[15] but much

[15] *Cf.*, Staudenmaier's (1912) similar process of producing his personifications, e.g., 'His Highness', 'The Child', 'Roundhead' (a rubber ball), et al., who start as pure ideas and change into independent parts that converse with him (pp. 29, ff.).

tinier. His subsequent growth is varied; he may become a dwarf, a giant, or other miraculous creature; but obviously the alchemist loses interest in this, his artificial brain child; or should one not specify the organ of thought and recognize that it is an artificial uterus or '*venter*' (belly) that comes into question.

Paracelsus marshals many current ideas to justify this procedure. It was well known that an emission on the ground might cause Mother Earth to produce an elfin creature known as the *Alraune,* an odd sort of manikin. The semen, taken literally as seed, it was thought, had to undergo putrefaction before a foetus could sprout; this thought came from agriculture, but the uterus too underwent a certain putrefaction, producing the *menstruum,* to serve as fertilizer to the planted seed. There were recorded all sorts of odd cross-fertilizations that resulted in monsters. Fertilization could also take place 'sodomitically' under certain circumstances. The word was used in the sense of animal copulation as well as anal homosexual. Apparently, a good deal of lore of this kind, not available to human scholars, was accessible to sylphs, nymphs, and other such creatures. Coprophagia after anal copulation seems to have been a recognized technique.

The retort in which the homunculus grows is called a *cucurbitula,*[16] a cucumber, but older writers suggested the use of a gourd by this name, causing confusion, which Silberer clears up.

The horse manure was symbolically called *venter equi,* since evidently the alchemists thought they were simulating the belly. So far as is known, the experiments were limited to the flask method, and did not employ animals in the ways suggested by the reasoning.

I do not know whether the alchemist's homunculus appeared later in science in the form of Descartes's diver and the others I mentioned previously. That is, I do not know whether this connection has been traced. More importantly, is it possible to connect the fantastic homunculi that were assigned to a horse's belly with those very scientific homunculi that appeared, for example, along the fissure of Rolando? Early

[16] *Cucurbitula* is not only a retort but also a cupping glass. It translates (Gr.) σικύα, a gourd something like a cucumber but eaten after it ripens, and called σπερματίας, seedy cucumber. Perhaps the name was suggestive to the early scientists.

modern science was not averse to putting homunculi of that sort into appropriate parts of the body, including the head of the spermatozoon, after that cellule was discovered by the microscope. The cortical homunculus is of course in the head, but dream psychology and the obsessions teach us that the head often gets equated with the lower abdomen or intestinal tract. Paracelsus thought of producing a homunculus as a preliminary to producing gold—we should call this latter his 'ego intention'.

Our modern homunculus along the fissure of Rolando is much reduced and comes nearer to satisfying our ego intentions; he is a little scientific map, a piece of topography and not much else, even if he arose from the medieval fantasy. He is indeed, if that is the case, an unexpected success, for he is a pure sublimation, an ennoblement of a not very salubrious starting material.

All in all, the homunculus, bred in a closed vessel, is with us 'in spirit'—returns from repression—with all the alchemical implications of male cephalic parthenogenesis, in the sublimated homuncular diagrams on the brain. The *cucurbitula* has been replaced by the cranial cavity and perhaps ultimately by the psychical apparatus in its metaphorical form of two rooms and a watchman.[17]

The two-room psychic apparatus, besides the censor-watchman, includes a part homunculus, if one wishes to scale him in this way—namely, the permanent resident of the preconscious room who is the spectator. This spectator is clearly the traditional 'inner eye' or the 'eye of the imagination' of which the philosophers have written. In Freud's metaphor he is said to become aware of some of the contents of the preconsciousness room, which makes them qualitatively conscious. Besides an eye, the spectator must have other anatomic equivalents, for instance, the muscles which permit the eyes to travel, the extraocular muscles attached to the eyeballs. This inner eye also has whatever parts it takes to permit three-dimensional vision, or accommodation. Though this eye has been portrayed, its dimensions are much more uncertain even

[17] It is an interesting coincidence perhaps that one of Freud's patients, a chemist, dreamed of himself replacing the zinc in a retort, in Grignard's synthesis. The manifest dream contains a reference to the disappearance of his body image, which is dissolving in parts (Freud, 1900-1901, p. 382).

than those of the watchman, and I suppose much more variable. Sometimes it seems to duplicate the physical eye, at other times to be very large, as if it occupied most of the inside of the cranium and coincided with the inside head image. As its concreteness diminishes, it resembles the abstract 'subject' of system *Pcpt-Cs.*

This suggests a dualism, not only in Freud's two-room diagram, but in general where the homunculus is presented. I do not know what relationship exists between such subjectively experienced actions of the 'inner eye' and the objective extraocular eye motions, observed as a presumed correlate or accompaniment of dreaming.

I should like to end by repeating the idea that I introduced earlier, namely, that of *sublimation.* Beginning with the infantile fantasy of the anal child, which was private, the idea of the homunculus received truly alchemistic treatment at the hands of Paracelsus and the other medieval and early renaissance magi. It is probably important that such work was not only imaginable but publishable, so that the recipes for making a homunculus became public, later to be used either as a fantasy in fiction (for example); or else in a further refined state *via* retorts and sophisticated chemistry and biology to serve as a sketch for real research. Even today, the idea that a baby might be produced in a test tube has been received with considerable alarm by our times, and the investigators no longer have Paracelsus's boldness. As to behavioral science, it still studies how one may best banish the little man in the head from the brain and the mind.

COMMENTS ON THE FIGURES

The first figure is from Frances Yates's book and shows literally 'the eye of the imagination'. It is taken from a book by Robert Fludd, *Ars memoria,* 1619. The second figure depicts the gymnastics described by Schreber's father, and is borrowed from William Niederland's article, *Further Data and Memorabilia Pertaining to the Schreber Case.* The human form is becoming abstract in Schreber. Figures 3 and 4 are from W. Ehrenberg's article, *Maxwell's Demon.* The demon is not seen as a bodily entity but rather as an abstraction; the accompanying text is full of references to the demon. This character is depicted in Figure 5, borrowed from George Gamow's *Biography of Physics.* Figure 6 shows the distortion of the 'little man' along the fissure of Rolando, and is borrowed from Wilder Penfield.

Figure 1.

TRACTATUS PRIMI.
SECTIONIS II.
PORTIO III.

De animæ memorativæ ſcientia, quæ vulgo ars memoriæ vocatur.

ARS MEMORIÆ.

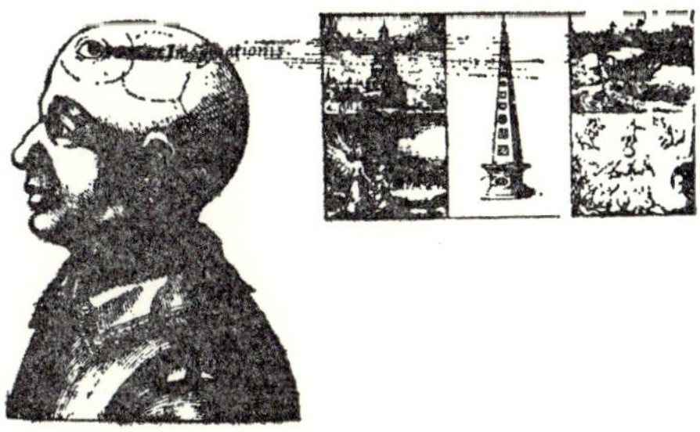

TRA

15 First page of the *Ars memoriae* in Robert Fludd's *Utriusque Cosmi . . . Historia,* Tomus Secundus, Oppenheim, 1619 (pp. 326-7).

Figure 2.

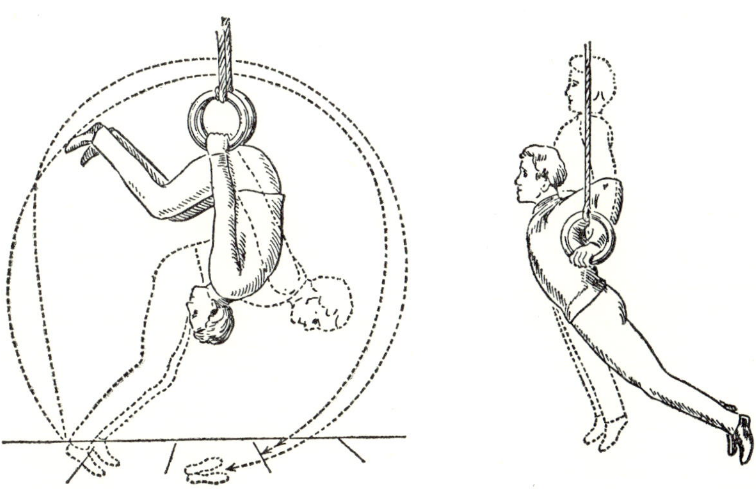

Figure 3.

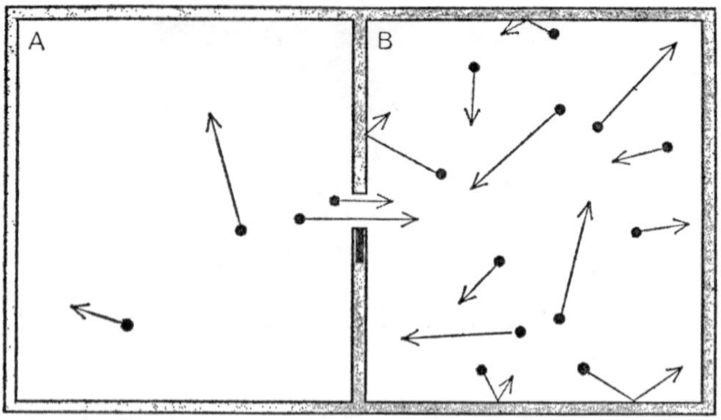

ANOTHER APPROACH to the problem of designing a perpetual-motion machine that employs the services of a sorting demon also begins with equal pressures and temperatures on both sides of the division. By opening and closing the shutter at the right times the demon could allow both swift and slow molecules to pass only from *A* to *B*. The resulting difference in pressure between the two sides could then be readily translated into mechanical work.

Figure 4.

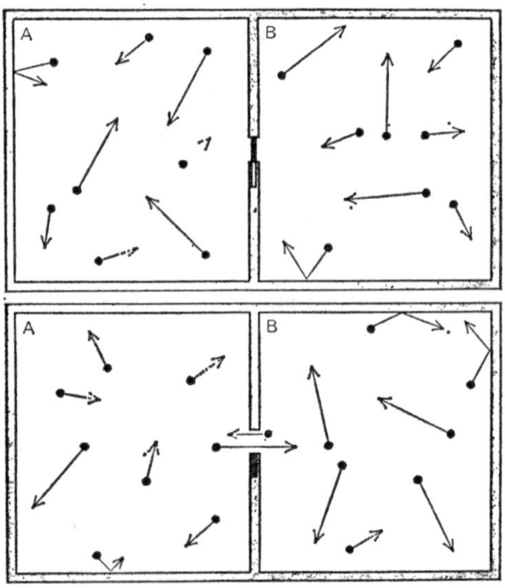

SORTING DEMON OPERATES by opening and closing a small hole in a division between two portions of a vessel full of air at a uniform temperature (*top*). The demon can see the individual molecules, which move at many different velocities. By opening and closing the hole so as to allow only the swifter molecules to pass from *A* to *B* and only the slower ones to pass from *B* to *A*, the demon could, without expenditure of work, raise the temperature of *B* and lower that of *A* (*bottom*), in contradiction to the second law of thermodynamics. It would then be an easy matter to design a perpetual-motion machine that derived its mechanical effect from the temperature difference between the two portions of the vessel.

Figure 5.

Figure 6.

MOTOR AND SENSORY

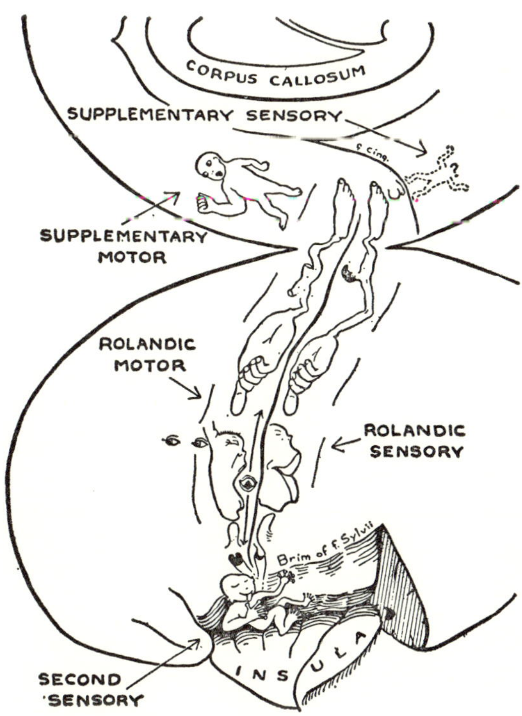

PSYCHOANALYSIS AND EDUCATION

Lewin's first article on education dealt with the training of physicians. He used what psychoanalysis had learned concerning the attitude of analysts toward analysands—the so-called countertransference—to elucidate the difficulties that physicians characteristically encounter in the treatment of their patients. The first patient the medical student encounters is a cadaver and this early clinical interchange, Lewin demonstrated, colors the future physician's approach toward all of his subsequent patients.

Genetic and historical reconstructions against the background of the dynamic influence of unconscious fantasy, were the concepts Lewin applied to the analysis of the process of education in general and of the individual in particular. Accordingly, in the survey, *Psychoanalytic Education in the United States,* which he conducted with Miss Helen Ross, the conclusions transcended mere description and evaluation of the efforts of the psychoanalytic institutes by correlating the history of the particular institute with the specific intergroup dynamics at play in each locality. Lewin and Ross functioned as analysts whose interpretations proved therapeutic. Self-consciousness concerning educational practices is for the institute what self-observation is for the patient in analysis; freed from inner conflicts, one is able to learn and to go on to create, provided one has mastered one's history.

The final contributions in this section consist of four papers which appropriately begin with the subject of historical considerations and go on to psychoanalytic education and research, from teaching to the creation of theory. The combined qualities of scientist and poet, which epitomize Lewin, are nowhere clearer than in his insights into psychoanalytic education.

J. A. A.

I. COUNTERTRANSFERENCE IN THE TECHNIQUE OF MEDICAL PRACTICE*

Transference and Countertransference

Recent medical literature has introduced many psychoanalytic concepts to the larger medical world, among others that of the transference (Dunbar, 1943; Binger, 1945).[1] Those interested in the psychosomatic approach to illness have taught that the medical patient has a relation to his medical man which resembles a psychoanalytic transference. The patient comes to the doctor with an attitude that has a history. It is a new edition of his attitudes to many previous physicians, but also to teachers, parents and other authoritative persons, or to persons who have figured in some important way in his life. Much of this attitude is unconscious, but, for all that, effective in furthering or hindering the therapeutic efforts. Hence medical men are becoming aware of its role in diagnosis and therapy.

In analytic technique, a consideration of the transference would be incomplete without, at the same time, some consideration of the countertransference, its counterpart. Broadly speaking, the countertransference is the attitude, rational or irrational, scientific or emotional, conscious or unconscious, appropriate or anachronistic, which the doctor has toward his patients. It might therefore be profitable to supplement what has been written about the 'psychosomatic' or general medical transference by a few remarks about the corresponding countertransference, so far as this topic can be treated in general and so far as it influences the common medical techniques.

Countertransference in Psychoanalysis

There are several good discussions of the countertransference in psychoanalytic literature. For simplicity and practicality,

* [No. 62 in Bibliography.]

1 Some of the ideas to be presented in this paper were expressed in my review of Binger's book. (*See*, B. Lewin, 1945b [Ed.].)

perhaps the best is that of Ferenczi (1919). Ferenczi states that in mastering the countertransference an analyst goes through a three-stage development. The first stage is due to the fact that shortly before, during his training, he was himself an analytic patient. He therefore unconsciously identifies himself with his patients, becomes their champion, and wants their wishes fulfilled. Nowadays, the analyst's teachers help him through this stage, but even by himself, the indulgent analyst learns that his attitude hampers his analytic effort. If he then resists this attitude and represses it, he goes into Ferenczi's second stage, that of 'counter-resistance'. He overcomes his identification by setting up the contrary attitude of overdetachment—a Charybdis in which he loses contact with his patients' unconscious. Instead of, so to say, understanding his patients too well, he now cannot understand them at all. Finally he strikes a balance between the two polarities: in a sublimated countertransference, the analyst identifies or detaches himself to the degree and in the manner required for his rational purposes. He becomes free to apply the appropriate, tested technique.

Countertransference in Medicine Generally

The countertransference of the physician who works in other fields of medicine, or for that matter of the analyst in his medical school days, undergoes a different development. As a medical student, the doctor begins his professional training not on the analytic couch, but as a dissector in the anatomy laboratory. He immediately has a 'patient', the cadaver. The cadaver, he recognizes, is not meant to be an individual but a type. The manual skill and knowledge he gains by dissecting are to be transferred later to living patients. The student is supposed to be emotionally detached from the cadaver and usually assumes uncritically that he is. But psychologically considered, this is hardly possible. The student derives much satisfaction from his work. His relationship to the cadaver is an outlet for many sublimated, active, libidinal drives, as well as those of mastery and power. The cadaver, completely passive and unresistant to the dissector's intentions, is an ideal object for such satisfactions. Intended to be a prototype of all future patients in certain rational respects, the cadaver easily comes to be the student's ideal of a patient in all respects.

Psychological Consequence of Anatomical Courses and Preclinical Work

To compare the medical student's initial situation with that given in Ferenczi's scheme, we find him not in an identification with his first medical object, but in a sublimated personal relationship. For our purpose it is unnecessary to discuss neurotic or perverse breakdowns of the sublimation (Brill, 1941). But it should be noted that at this stage the relationship has nothing to do with death wishes such as we encounter in psychoanalysis. The infantile wish that a scolding nurse or an inconvenient sibling should 'die'—that is, go away and leave one alone—has no bearing on the relationship to a real corpse. The deadness of the cadaver is an attribute, a quality, desirable for many subjective reasons. That the cadaver was once alive is psychologically of no importance. In the fourteenth century, the Church took care to remind students of this fact so that at the School of Salernum, when anatomy was young, the students said mass each morning for the salvation of the cadaver's soul. But in the same century, Chaucer's Doctor of Physick read 'Ypocras, old Galien', the pagans and Avicenna; and his study was but little of the Bible. It has been a long time since medical students have thought about the cadaver's soul.

Pathology and physiology follow anatomy, but neither study alters the student's relationship to his objects. In the autopsy room he sees a series of cadavers; in other laboratories a variety of small animals, frogs, cats, and dogs. But the little animals are not regarded as individuals, as pets or creatures with whom one may identify one's self. They too are partial prototypes of the future human patients; yet predominantly they are so many 'preparations'—machines and test-tubes—with which one may do what one wishes, usually after they are anesthetized or taken apart.

Transposing Preclinical Attitudes to the Clinic: The Patient as Cadaver

The preclinical studies prepare the student to apply laboratory knowledge and skills to his human patients, often directly. The scalpel he used on the cadaver is now to be used on his surgical patients; the digitalis he administered to his pharmacological laboratory 'preparation'—a frog or a cat—is to be prescribed for cardiac 'cases'. He must be as confident and as unruffled in using the knife or the drug clinically as when he worked in the laboratory. It is this calm assurance which Freud had in mind when he advised young analysts to observe their patients with the coolness of a surgeon (*mit chirurgischer Kälte*). But the surgeon too must acquire this coolness; he and other clinicians do so in part because of their preclinical state of mind. Unconsciously, along with skills and knowledge, much of the psychological relationship to the cadaver is carried over to living patients. Where these differ from preclinical objects, the clinician may feel a dissatisfaction or tension, which could be formulated as a longing for his original dead patient.

Restricting our inquiry to normal sublimations, we see that this wish—that one were working with a cadaver—has promoted many technical advances in medical practice, and has brought about important innovations. The wish that the patient might be as amenable to dissection as the cadaver led to the invention of general anesthesia. Such at any rate must have been the theory of the 'Father of Physiology', the illustrious and neurotic Magendie, who startled his colleagues by opposing the use of ether in these words:

> For some weeks, a certain number of surgeons have set themselves to experiment on man, and for an undoubtedly praiseworthy purpose—that of performing operations without pain—they intoxicate their patients to the point of reducing them, so to speak, to the state of a cadaver which one can slice and cut at will without causing pain (Olmsted, 1944, p. 244).

He added amid shocked laughter that he would never permit his wife or daughter to be anesthetized, for 'certain surgeons' might be tempted to take sexual advantage of anesthetized female patients.[2] But in the end, the normal opinion of Vel-

[2] Magendie's confession of necrophilic fantasies came rather late in life. His great teacher, Bichat, was an anatomist who dissected thousands of cadavers. In breaking with Bichat, Magendie imposed a taboo on himself against using any but living material. He rationalized his personal conflict into a theoretical schism between 'anatomists' and 'physiologists', reminiscent of many present-day pseudo conflicts. However, he treated his laboratory animals, and sometimes his patients, as if they were without life or feeling, to such an extent that after a demonstration of vivisections in London, he was attacked in Commons as a 'monster'.

peau, whom Magendie had attacked, prevailed. The usefulness of reducing patients to the 'state of a cadaver' could not be denied, regardless of the unconscious.

Another useful result of the wish to restore the dissecting room situation was the introduction into the surgical theater of the preservatives used in anatomy, as antiseptics. The first of these was phenol; its odor enhanced the illusion of the anesthetized patient's lifelessness. The gallows' humor of the anatomy table turned up on the wards as a hearty bedside manner, for which certain physicians became famous. Several of these had spent long years previous to their clinical appointment as anatomists and pathologists.

Fixation on the Cadaver and 'Therapeutic Nihilism'

The fixation on the corpse expressed itself in internal medicine as well as in the surgical specialties. In many of the best hospitals at one time, therapy, in theory, was considered irrational. Therapeutic nihilism meant that after a thorough 'examination' (Laënnec's adumbration of the autopsy) and the 'diagnosis' (the guess as to what would be found there), there was nothing to do but wait for the clinical pathological conference. In some schools the cadaver was percussed again and the findings mapped by pins just before the autopsy.

Conflict: Patient as Cadaver, or as Human Being like the Physician (Identification Mechanism)

The transition from the preclinical patients, with whom one does not identify one's self, to the human beings in the clinic with whom one does, is marked by conflict. Stage one tries to find representation in stage two. The conflict between the 'pure' anatomist's position and the humanistic one is to be found in many extensive rationalizations. The preference for the dead patient led many to insist that the dead brain alone was the real key to the living mind. 'No mental disease', it was firmly asserted, 'without brain disease'—meaning lesions—and when the lesions could not be found, unfortunately they were only too often imagined. The heat which arises from so many useless clashes between the proponents of 'organic' and 'psychological' medicine might not appear, if it were realized that the main issue was a matter of preference, an emotional preference for the dead or the live patient. The idea of psychic determinism, to leave aside its pragmatic justification, is emotionally acceptable to medical men because they appreciate the physical determinism of the inanimate.

Resolution of Conflict: Sublimated Flexible Countertransference

In view of the fruitful technical and theoretical sublimations of the wish to have a dead patient, no one will deny its great dynamic value in medical science. Yet it is clear that in the final sublimation of medical practice, the doctor must be sufficiently flexible to include both of his attitudes in his relationship to his patients, and be prepared to shift from one to the other. The surgeon treats his anesthetized patients as quasi cadavers; but in their convalescence as if they were alive. To understand them fully he must identify himself with them. As a therapist, he may need to employ (or direct that someone should employ) that refinement of the natural capacity for identification, which, as Ferenczi indicated, is psychoanalytic technique, and one might add psychological medical technique in general. The medical man's countertransference problem is in principle not different from the psychoanalyst's. In his sublimated countertransference, he identifies himself with his patients, or dissociates himself from them, in accord with the demands of the rational diagnostic and therapeutic aims.

Countertransference by Identification: The Patient as a Human Being

That the doctor reacts to his patients as human beings and considers them to be like himself sounds more banal than informative. Obviously long before the doctor learned of stethoscopes and clinical pathological conferences, he knew what it meant to be ill. One thinks immediately of many famous names in medicine, in tuberculosis for example, who were originally patients. But this is a special conspicuous example of a general situation; for there is surely no medical man who was not at one time a sick child. Like Ferenczi's analytic beginner, therefore, every doctor knows by experience what patients want and how they feel; and if this knowledge consciously recedes as his attention becomes more and more deflected to technical and scientific matters, it none the less unconsciously persists.

He will have, in other words, not only ordinary conscious sympathy with the sick, but he will unconsciously know a good deal about the patient's needs and feelings.

Illness and Aggression

A most interesting and important bit of unconscious knowledge which doctors have about the patients' conscious or unconscious minds is that sick people are aggressive, either to the environment or to themselves. Even in the 'good patient', who spares his doctor and his environment, there is somewhere at the core a howling, enraged, insulted child. The normal doctor of course does not take his patients' aggressions personally; yet he registers them unconsciously. He must cope with them somehow psychologically. Except among the most primitive peoples, the doctor distinguishes between his patient's personality and his aggressions. It is true that the Central Australians until recently, as Róheim (1945) tells us, buried their sick kinsmen alive and feared them still in the grave. But even so backward a people as the Siberian Yakuts make this distinction: the Yakut shaman works himself into a terrible rage and leaps and shouts at the patient. Not at the patient either, it seems, for the shaman believes that he is scaring a devil out of him.[3] The aggression is segregated from the patient's personality in the shaman's mind, as the 'disease entity' is segregated from the personality by more sophisticated medical thinkers. The shaman counteracts the patient's aggression by a literal counteraction: the devil scares him, he scares the devil back. The shaman was in danger. The whole history of primitive medicine testifies to the primitive unconscious feeling that in the presence of the sick, one is in danger. Clinical psychoanalysis, studying germ phobias and morbid fears of disease, substantiates the widespread existence of this thesis in the unconscious.

Countertransference Aggression and Its Sublimation in Technique

Danger engenders defensive measures, aggression counteraggression; but happily doctors no longer may conscientiously simply attack their patients, as Dr. Willis flogged the psychotic George III, with the considered approval of a good part of

[3] Korolenko, V. G.: *Makar's Dream*. This is a tale, but is based on Korolenko's experiences among the Yakuts while in exile.

the medical world of the time. Ordinarily the doctor does not need such violent measures for the illnesses he encounters. For a headache, he can prescribe aspirin, that is to say, he can poison the patient slightly, but by this very act the patient's pain vanishes and so does the doctor's danger. In the same act the patient is helped and the doctor has expressed his sublimated counteraggression. For a more severe pain the doctor could use morphine and perhaps put the patient to sleep, reducing him, as Magendie put it, to the state of a cadaver. The doctor's sublimated act, which aids the patient, nevertheless includes an unconscious regressive wish-fulfilment. For pains not amenable to drugs, he may sever nervous connections or remove organs; that is, destroy part of the patient. As a very extreme measure (but here the doctor would have much doubt and conflict) he might be tempted to think of euthanasia, which would assimilate the patient to the first object of the doctor's experience. To paraphrase Rado, the patient would then be a 'purely good' patient. Dr. Frankenstein's monster, the sick aggressive life that was added to the cadaver, is the 'purely bad' patient.

It is not the purpose of this paper to discuss the motives which may unconsciously determine the doctor's choice of a profession, nor the types of satisfaction which his practice may unconsciously furnish him. Our interest is centered on his countertransference, its nature and dynamic effect in typical therapeutic situations. The doctor's aggression was considered solely in its technical countertransference aspect.

Defense Technique: Placation

A common method of dealing with the patient is of course placation. The placating act usually takes the form of an indulgence. The doctor identifies himself with the patient, knows what he wants and symbolically gives it to him. Thus Brown-Séquard surrendered to a very simple impulse: to prescribe testis against advancing age was a direct indulging, if symbolic, response; and it is well known that Brown-Séquard was his own first patient. In the subsequent history of endocrinology something, perhaps something displaced from another matter entirely, seems to have disturbed the doctor's ability to repeat Brown-Séquard's beautiful simplicity. For, very soon in that science, there developed a massive obsessional system for giving a substance, offsetting it partially by a second, and opposing the resultant action of the two by still another. But the countertransference that develops into a neurosis is a special case beyond the scope of this paper.

Associated with the desire to placate are other identification motives for indulging the patient. Sometimes, in the prescription of certain diets, it is as if the doctor read the patient's unconscious. After the birth of a son, one of my patients developed gastric indigestion, and it was interesting and instructive to note how closely his prescribed diet paralleled that of his baby. He was put on milk; then through gruels and purees he and the baby finally worked up to solid foods.

Guilt

It would be expected that some or much of the doctor's counteraggression would take the form of unconscious guilt, which ordinarily is not hard to alleviate. Besides the rational and sublimated assuagement which comes from the proper exercise of so punishing a profession, certain elements in ordinary practice serve to clear the doctor of guilt. The taking of an anamnesis is one such method of clearing the doctor of guilt. Its effect is to throw the guilt back on the patient. The anamnesis brings home to the patient (and the doctor) that the patient was responsible for the disease. What did you eat? What did you do to cause the pain? How did you fall when you broke your arm? When were you last exposed to venereal disease? The patient's unconscious aggression turns back on himself; and if it does not the doctor has a more difficult transference problem.

Insurance. Other Aspects of Countertransference

Most of the doctor's fear of the patient's aggressions is unconscious, yet it finds rational expression in the institution of insurance against malpractice suits. Many innocent doctors have been sued, attacked, even killed, because some paranoid patient held them accountable for not curing him, or more likely for not giving him the satisfactions he unconsciously desired. The patient's aggression is rarely so effective; he is a weeping child rather than a devil. It is the aggression of one who has himself been hurt or punished; it is usually unconscious; and offset by the defensive resources of the patient's ego. Authorities referred to above (and others) have sufficiently considered the role of passive strivings in patients. Ordinarily such strivings do not set a problem in the physician's technique, but are more apt to affect him as an individual. His technical training and his sense of reality usually provide against too much concurrence in his patient's belief in his omniscience. If a physician becomes conceited, it is due to his own needs and not to his practice. Indeed, one good effect of our present preclinical education is the weakening of the student's propensity to identify himself with the Father-Doctor of Luke Fildes's well-known painting. Further discussion would lead to matters ably considered by Simmel (1926), Nunberg (1938), and others.

Value of Conscious Insight in Transference-Countertransference Relations

The doctor cannot of course master his countertransference impulses by considering them in the abstract. Psychoanalytic training courses provide that the beginning analyst shall analyze his first cases under the supervision of an experienced teacher. Under such supervision, besides being taught correct analytic technique, he is assisted in becoming aware of, and solving, some of his individual countertransference problems. The medical student might conceivably profit from a similar type of instruction. He might learn how his own personality assists or hampers his understanding and treatment of patients, or where his emotional response leads him to err. As Dunbar (1943) puts it, it is important to know not only what the doctor does to the patient, but also what the patient does to the doctor.

Without special instruction, it must be admitted, the healthy physician comes to terms somehow with his main countertransference problems. But as he becomes increasingly aware of the nature of transference he will become more aware of its counterpart or reflection in himself. The best 'bed-side manner' is not a good substitute for such awareness. Conscious insight is ultimately the best and most efficient means of solving a psychological problem.

II. EDUCATION OR THE QUEST FOR OMNISCIENCE*

This lecture marks the anniversary of the founding of the Institute for Psychoanalysis in Chicago twenty-five years ago by Franz Alexander. Fortunate Franz Alexander, *non sine honore* a prophet, who robbed Juvenal's goddess Fortuna of her divinity by his foresight. But this anniversary is not a local matter. It is a significant mark for all who esteem psychoanalysis and are concerned for its teaching and for its progress as a science. It is a moment for retrospection and reflection. I deeply appreciate the honor shown me by the invitation to deliver the First Alexander Lecture and to voice some of the thoughts appropriate to the occasion.

Many come to mind readily which relate to the rapid rise and development of psychoanalytic education. The year 1932, in which the Institute in Chicago was founded, was a good one for psychoanalysis in the United States. For some years previously, many Americans had studied psychoanalysis abroad, and the example of the new institutes there, particularly the one in Berlin, was making a strong impression on this side of the water. In several American cities the psychoanalytic groups, having grown in membership, desired and were better able to organize the education which was necessary for a psychoanalyst. Dr. Alexander was the first distinguished teacher invited to this country from one of the admired foreign institutes. Other signs of the same *élan* were the similar invitations to other teachers in the older European communities, the founding of the New York Psychoanalytic Institute in the same year 1932, and the first issue of *The Psychoanalytic Quarterly* in April of that year. In 1933 came the real beginning of the American Psychoanalytic Association as a federation of American societies. American psychoanalysis was then reaping part of a crop which had been sowed and cultivated for many years.

* [No. 108 in Bibliography.]

It is convenient to take 1932 as a midpoint in the history of psychoanalytic education. To many this will seem, as it does to me, only yesterday. Wherever we arbitrarily set the beginning of psychoanalytic education, it will still seem very recent. Psychoanalysis and psychoanalytic education are not even Tudor, as the English say when they wish to deny antiquity. In fact there was no psychoanalysis when this city of Chicago built its now historic pumping station. Twenty-five years before 1932, in 1907, the mainstream of the psychoanalytic movement was a thin trickle indeed. It was located *in posse* only, in a small discussion group which met every Wednesday evening in Freud's home, to present cases, to read papers, and particularly, to profit from Freud's presence.

Many of us are admittedly sentimental about the early days of psychoanalysis in Vienna, in Berlin, in this country. Others derogate the early enthusiasm: it was, they say, more appropriate to a 'cult'. But a religious cult is nothing more nor less than the faith of a minority. Christianity was a cult until Constantine the Great legalized it. And the enthusiasm, as I shall try to show, is only superficially to be ticketed 'emotional'; it accompanies many new discoveries, not only those which come by divine revelation. The enthusiasm, in a certain sense, is as interesting as the content of the science or belief. They are not entirely wrong who sense an irrational, or as we should prefer to say, unconscious or fantasy element in the attraction of new knowledge.

I feel I can rely on the understanding of this audience if I do not repeat facts and dates well known or easily available that have to do with the development of psychoanalytic education, and if I confine myself to general statements. From the group for study and discussion at Freud's home and others like it in the Burghölzli Hospital near Zurich, in Brill's home in New York, etc., came the early, still rather informal psychoanalytic societies and their loose union in the International Psycho-Analytical Association. The same period saw the founding of journals. Then came the demand on the societies for instruction, and gradually out of their experience arose the more formal institutes, which were at first and in many places still are the teaching arm of the society. Roughly then, psychoanalytic education has had three forms: (1) independent, empiric and unformed private teaching—the period of the *individual* seeker for knowledge; (2) loosely formal instruction ranging from nearly individual instruction to simple *society* regulation; which developed into (3) formal institutionalized instruction—the *institutes of today*. For brevity I shall arbitrarily refer to the individual, the society, and the institute periods, fully aware that the real situation did not and does not permit such categorization everywhere. There is, however, a general appreciation of this evolution. In this country, small enclaves of psychoanalytic interest, places where there are two or three psychoanalysts, look forward to the rise of a society and ultimately of a local institute. In keeping with this, symptomatically, what used to be called 'Study Groups' are now officially known as 'Training Centers' when they increase in size and approximate the second stage of development, and the term implies that 'training' will become regularized and the 'center' an institute.

Let us return to the early days of individual enthusiasm and enterprise. The enthusiasm expressed itself as an eagerness for new knowledge, and the knowledge seemed attainable; various ways of attaining it were tried out, according to temperament, varying from ambiguous self-study to devoted discipleship. It is well known that many persons were attracted to the study and practice of psychoanalysis after they had themselves been in treatment. They had personally found the new knowledge useful. Time has sobered down the enthusiasm and has permitted a more detached retrospection. The motives for studying analysis and for being psychoanalyzed are now at least superficially different from those of fifty years ago. Today, a course in psychoanalysis is a widely recognized and advantageous part of a professional training; the profession of psychoanalysis is established. The practical motives are strong. Then, there was little advantage in these respects; psychoanalysis did not lead to lucrative practice or to academic preferment. Let us keep in mind what for lack of better words we call tentatively the 'desire to know', and before trying to get at impulses concealed by this phrase, consider other historic examples of enthusiasm for new knowledge. It is impossible to treat these at all comprehensively, and we shall limit ourselves to the two aspects touched upon above: organization and motive.

On a large scale the eleventh and twelfth centuries saw a situation comparable to the rise of psychoanalysis in two vital respects: there was new knowledge and there was an enthusiastic pursuit of it. The barbarian raids against Western Europe were at an end, the political situation was more stable, travel and communication were possible, and students who had perhaps been hiding in the cloisters, or would have been so hidden during the dark ages, heard of new knowledge to be gained. In Italy the two surviving copies of the Digest of Justinian turned up; from those who had been in the Holy Land and in Spain came word of new knowledge or, better, old knowledge preserved by the Arabs in translation: the works of Aristotle, Euclid, Hippocrates, and Ptolemy the astronomer, among others, 'As early as 991', Professor Haskins writes, 'a monk of Rheims, Richer, describes the hardships of his journey to Chartres in order to study the Aphorisms of Hippocrates of Cos.' The stage of individual enterprise may be marked by this date, but before then we can readily imagine many restless individuals frustrated in their desire for knowledge by their situation. It is not precisely known when these individuals formed study groups or training centers, but they did so in several places, sometimes near the cathedral schools as at Chartres and Paris, where there were books and teachers, sometimes without such ecclesiastical proximity, as at Bologna where they could study the Digest of Justinian mentioned above. By the end of the twelfth century some of these study groups came to be known as *universities.* The dates of their founding are not definite; when the University of Paris wished to establish such a date so that it might celebrate anniversaries, it quite arbitrarily picked the year 1200.

The word *university* originally meant a guild; and in the twelfth and thirteenth centuries in Bologna this is precisely what a university was. The Bologna students united to form a guild or corporation, thereby imitating other guilds, and they did so for economic reasons, to increase their bargaining power with landlords and booksellers. The word *university,* according to Professor Haskins, came only in time to be limited to guilds of masters and students: *'universitas societas magistrorum discipulorumque'*. 'Historically, the word had no connection with the universe or the universality of learning; it denoted only the totality of a group, whether of barbers, carpenters or students did not matter.'

Social historians have shown how an organization founded for one purpose tends to expand and to include other aims not originally intended. For instance, the East India Company, which was organized for trading, incidentally conquered India for Great Britain. The students in their guilds came to possess enviable powers; they could threaten the townsmen that they would leave in a body and take the professors with them (in some instances they did so) and they came to fix the prices of lodgings and books. In Bologna, having vanquished the townsmen, they turned on the professors and in 1317 laid down statutes to govern the masters' behavior. Historically, this may be the first appearance of Training Regulations, though in a direction in reverse from the one we are now accustomed to. Our American Psychoanalytic Association's statutes look pale in comparison. A professor could not be absent from his classes even for a day, without the students' permission and then he had to deposit money as a guarantee of his return. 'If he failed to secure an audience of five for a regular lecture, he was fined as if absent. . . . He must begin with the bell and quit within one minute after the next bell. He was not allowed to skip a chapter in his commentary or postpone a difficulty to the end of the hour, and he was obliged to cover ground systematically, so much in each specific term of the year' (Haskins).

Why the students could dominate the masters admits of a very simple answer. Besides the economic power, there were more students, and they did not hesitate to use physical force. In short, they could lick them. Since all gentlemen in those days carried knives, the students gained a good many privileges. A famous fight in Paris began as a tavern brawl. The students fought not only the tavern keepers and other townsmen but also the 'provost's men' (that is, the police) and one student was killed. Besides, a good deal of property was damaged. The result of this brawl was not punishment or suppression; out of it came the Papal Bull of 1231, which granted the students extensive privileges and immunities. This was no panty raid. It is interesting to note that the elected leaders of student guilds were called *rectors,* a word still in use as an equivalent of university presidents.

When the students objected to chapters not being read to them, however, they seem to have had right on their side. Lectures in those days and for some centuries to come were literally lectures in the original etymology of the word, namely, readings. Books were rare, and the students had come to hear them read. Since many of the Bologna students intended to become lawyers and others physicians or priests, a professional interest was involved here; but as I hope to show later by means of a twelfth-century quotation, there were other, unrealistic hopes set upon book learning.

At Bologna the masters formed a guild in self-defense, with admission requirements and examinations, and no one was permitted to teach without the consent of the guild. The license to teach, to be called Master, was sought by students regardless of their future career, as a certificate of attainment; and from this and comparable procedures originated the institution of the academic degree. The word *doctor* of course means teacher, but the prestige of this word would not have been apparent to the Romans, who also used it to mean a trainer of animals and applied it to lion tamers.

The University of Paris was somewhat different from that of Bologna. Theology was its main interest, rather than jurisprudence. It originated from a school attached to the Cathedral of Notre Dame, with colleges—originally the word used for student boarding houses—that sprang up in the neighborhood which, from the students' speech, was known and is still known as the Latin Quarter. It furnished a model for Oxford (an early 'training center' dependent on Paris) and for later English and continental universities. The eloquence of Abelard is said to have been an early drawing card. He was an aggressive and popular lecturer, what Professor Haskins calls a classroom entertainer. From the beginning, the masters' guild dominated the university, in spite of the Papal Bull referred to. Much later, the theological faculty acquired extraordinary powers; for example, it could as an extreme penalty condemn to death authors of heretical books. This is already an example not of enthusiasm for new learning, but of a more complicated reaction on the part of organized learning. It is part of the universities' later response to the craving for knowledge or omniscience.

I shall have more to say of this response. Here I should like to leave it that as learning really increased, and new books were written and later printed, the field of knowledge appeared to many scholars to be closed, in much the way mathematicians used to object to new kinds of numbers—the square root of two, the negative numbers, the imaginary numbers—declaring them meaningless. A field of omniscience needs no widening. Hence, as learning 'progressed', a tacit answer came to be given to the students who wished to know more, the answer being in effect, 'We have told you everything, don't question us further'. Argument within the stated accepted field was allowable since it dealt with the known, much as an eighteenth-century geometer might use Euclidean propositions but would be reprobated for working out a non-Euclidean geometry. Historical research has shown, nevertheless, that within these limits there was a good deal of what we now call academic freedom (Mary McLaughlin). The reliance of scholars on the ancient texts, from which they had learned so much, to the exclusion of other approaches to knowledge, was to persist until later revolutions in learning came from without the universities.

To go on with the story of the universities in any comprehensive fashion would lead too far afield. In one of his essays, I think on Petrarch, Lord Macaulay is very severe with a reviewer who appears to be more interested in what the poet read than in the poet's ideas. I should not blame you if you found what I have read interesting, and I recommend the little book by Professor Haskins called The Rise of the Universities, to which I am indebted for much information, reflected erudition, and certain ideas.

Warned by Macaulay, I shall try to get on to ideas, and I shall consider more attentively the desire for knowledge to which I have referred. To most of us, this will seem to have a natural intrinsic value. If a student wishes to study the Aphorisms of Hippocrates or the books and method of Freud, we think the impulse praiseworthy. Learning is good. Knowledge is power, and there are many other epigrams. If someone wishes to be cured of a neurosis or to cure, this is right too. Let us drop the standard of praiseworthy or blameworthy and such-like values, and imitate Freud when he considered the impulse to cure. Freud pointed out, to put it more accurately, that a narcissistic desire to be a healer, when it entered the therapeutic psychoanalytic situation, could work in the opposite direction to the one intended and impede a real psychoanalytic cure. He distinguished, in other words, the narcissistic fantasy from the reality. Similarly, we have learned that there is a comparable fantasy of 'being cured', and every practicing psychoanalyst has encountered versions of this notion.

My meaning is that we need not take every stated desire to learn at its conscious face value. It is good to be wise, as it is to be healthy and wealthy. But we must remember that there exists a very widespread fantasy that heaven lay about us in our infancy and that then we were omnipotent and omniscient. The world and our knowledge of it was intuitively a priori graspable, finite, though unbounded. When we are proved otherwise than omnipotent and omniscient, there is resentment, followed by an effort through magical, real, or part-magical part-real means to restore and to repair the gaps and lesions in this primal feeling. Freud had this in mind when he remarked on the three blows delivered to narcissism by Copernicus, Darwin, and himself; and Alexander has pointed out that all three led to the efforts at repair which we know as scientific method.

A general discussion of whether such a desire for omniscience is 'neurotic' is meaningless, and we propose instead the incontestable remark that it often exists in neurotic persons. If psychoanalysis originally attracted persons with neurotic problems, it is no less true that other sciences and branches of learning have done the same. Many have sought and still seek in learning and in scientific work the restoration of an infantile confidence and sense of perfection, whether we call this variously health, security, or omniscience. In this connection, I should like to refer to Kubie's recent writings.[1]

[1] *See,* Kubie (1958) [Ed.].

Most writing on education is in terms of aim. There is no dearth of statements, but they make sense only in context. For example, Professor Whitehead writes: 'Education is the acquisition of the art of the utilization of knowledge.' This may be the most general, rational answer to the question implicit in the title of his book, which is The Aims of Education. However, in his discourse, he immediately takes up such concrete matters as methods of teaching and the function of schools as they exist today. Another, more epigrammatic statement is due to Franklin P. Mall, who said: 'The educated man is one who is able to read and to make records.' If we are looking for axioms on which to set up a deductive system, neither of these statements fills the bill. Yet they are valuable expressions. Whitehead's is an attempt to abstract ideally from practice, while Mall's is an evocative remark, whose wisdom resides in his poetic use of the word *records*. It notes the social function of education and leaves open whether records are all man-made.

The idea that education gets its meaning from what is taught was expressed, as well as by anyone, by G. K. Chesterton. He stated that both Dr. Thomas Arnold of Rugby and Fagin in Oliver Twist must be considered educators: one produced the gentleman Tom Brown, he of the Schooldays, the other the little pickpocket called The Artful Dodger. Such remarks are usually applied to elementary education, where the teacher is thought of as a designer of education if not of children. But even in the first classrooms there are little people who will educate themselves, who seek security or they know not what in learning. Veblen, rather weakly I think, called the disinterested desire of scientists and scholars for knowledge their 'idle curiosity'. But such idle curiosity in all its intensity exists even more generally in children.

Forgive me if I try my hand at a possibly more one-sided and contextually limited epigram than any quoted above: Education on the students' part is a quest for omniscience, on the teachers' part a response to the students' demands.

To illustrate one teacher's response to the desire for omniscience, I quote Hugh of St. Victor of the twelfth century, from the translation given in the Viking Portable Medieval Reader, edited by Ross and McLaughlin:

> In former times, no one seemed worthy of the name of scholar who could not profess the knowledge of these seven [liberal arts]. Pythagoras is said to have observed this custom in his schools, that for seven years, according to the number of the seven liberal arts, none of his pupils should dare to ask the reason for anything which was said to him. But the pupil should put his trust in the master's words until he has heard everything, and thus he could then discover the reason for things by himself. Certain ones are said to have learned these seven arts with such great zeal and kept them all so firmly in memory, that whatever writing they took in hand, whatever questions they proposed for solution or proof, they did not seek the pages of the book but had instantly ready by heart, one by one, rules and reasons from the liberal arts, to define whatever was in dispute. Hence it happened at that time that they wrote more books than we are able to read.

Pythagoras, who supposedly devised this effective method of dealing with inquiring students, by all accounts was a peculiar man. But his system may well have suited a certain type of student. It matches the mechanisms of those who displace their original infantile sense of omnipotence and omniscience onto adults and who remain convinced of the older generation's knowledge of everything, particularly of everything they do not themselves know. Pythagoras supplies such pupils a satisfactory substitute which will slake their thirst for omniscience. The tacit implication is that the professor knows everything, in this case because he knows the books, and that he will be glad to teach it. This point of view is no longer in the open, but where it exists under cover, it is often popular with students, and Pythagoras could have given the classroom entertainers like Abelard a run for their money.

In fact, this attitude, repudiated by the ordinarily objective teacher, may nevertheless be displaced and cling to the name and atmosphere of the school as a whole and be felt by teachers and students alike. Knowledge then is completely comprised within the school's halls of learning. It would be rather rude to name names; this type of old school loyalty is usually harmless.

Of the three classes of upper schools, as they are conventionally divided, colleges, professional schools, and 'graduate departments', it seems to me that the professional school is most liable to claim this sort of didactic omniscience, where colleges might be content with an unbeatable football team. It was as a professional school, interested in the training for the priesthood, that the theological faculty of the University of Paris in 1678 banned the physics of Descartes from university training. It found Descartes's idea, that extension is the essence of matter, to be in conflict with the theory of the Eucharist. Freud is certainly correct in regard to the deep resistance against psychoanalysis in many medical schools. But as Alexander suggested in his Harvey lecture, there are other obstacles nearer the surface. The medical schools of Freud's day, like theological and other professional schools, taught a technique, which is always a most conservative curricular area. Given the state of theology in the seventeenth century and of psychiatry around 1900, both of which purported to rest on unimpeachable evidence and principles and by inference to supply the means of professional omniscience, one can readily understand the resistance to a complete rethinking.

The thought arises that under the current argument of training versus education, the overtones of the latter word suggest that somehow education lines up with the quest for omniscience, while the concept of training pairs off with a tacit feeling that it already exists. In other words, to this extent the field of real knowledge would be confused with the field of universal fantasies and a one-to-one correspondence mistaken for an identity. Here inevitably individual inner conflicts make contact with official institutionalized fantasies, and behind the seemingly rational façade of the dispute between Descartes and the University of Paris lies the conflict referred to. Descartes has recorded for us the sense of omniscience which came to him from his inspiration. He interpreted the sensations in a dream to mean that an angel had come to illuminate him to the effect that the physical world is completely understandable through mathematics. Descartes's doubts and his fear that this omniscience will be challenged are clearly stated in his letters. The old certainty had its charm: one knew definitely the big idea and the big scheme of the universe, whether one was a theologian or a scientist.

In fact, I am persuaded by Professor Whitehead that the old formulation of the conflict between science and theology is a misstatement or at best merely an aspect of other conflicts. The theologians, as in the debate between Newton and Bishop Berkeley, often have the superior logic; the scientists are apt to have more revelation. The ostensible conflict seems to be accidental and often due to political factors.

The individual sense of omniscience that comes from a discovery, however made, conflicts with an official omniscience in many fields besides science and learning. Many persons not scientists or scholars desire omniscience and think they have attained it or know how to attain it. For example, Evelyn Underhill, in her book, Mysticism, gives as part of the psychological explanation of the mystic's motives the following:

> Now the unsatisfied psyche in her emotional aspect wants, as we have said, to love more; her curious intellect wants to know more. The awkward human creature suspects that both appetites are being kept on a low diet; that there is really more to love and more to know, somewhere in the mysterious world without, and further that its power of affection and understanding is worthy of some greater and more durable objective than that provided by the illusions of sense. Urged therefore by the cravings of feeling or of thought, consciousness is always trying to run out to encounter the Absolute, and always being forced to return. . . . Metaphysics and science seem to offer to the intellect an open window toward truth; till the heart looks out and declares the landscape to be a chill desert in which she can find no nourishment. These diverse aspects of things must be either fused or transcended if the whole self is to be satisfied. . . . When Dionysius the Areopagite divided those angels who stand nearest God into the Seraphs, who are aflame with perfect love, and the Cherubs, who are filled with perfect knowledge, he only gave expression to the two most intense aspirations of the human soul, and described under an image the twofold condition of that Beatific Vision which is her goal.

Psychoanalysts will understand, as Underhill does, the role of love and knowledge in the ecstatic states, though where a mystic might value them as progressive in tendency, the psychoanalyst, from the standpoint of his system, would call them regressive. I bring to bear on our exposition the views of the mystics, many of whom encountered the same type of theological criticism that was leveled at Descartes. Descartes was as convinced as any Saint Theresa or Ignatius de Loyola of his divine inspiration. Indeed, in the history of science, it was only in the nineteenth century that scientists became clear as to the difference between mathematical and empirical reality.

But we have got away from our own times when Cherubs are conceived differently than according to Dionysius the Areopagite. To return to education and the response of the schools to the students' demands for omniscience, the schools still have a core of anxiety about meeting this demand. There are in many places at all levels of the educational system certain counteridentifications with the students in this respect on the part of the teachers, and a wish to teach them everything. I think this state of affairs lies behind Kubie's recent remark: 'my unhappy conviction is that much of the learning which has traditionally been looked upon as an essential attribute of the educated man has almost no relevance to maturity and that many of the ingredients in the process by which men become learned tend actively to obstruct maturation'. Dr. Kubie appears to be saying that, with the best of intentions, teachers are giving students a false sense of completeness and accidentally are providing them with a fantasy which cannot, in the nature of things, satisfy them in the end.

Perhaps another version of this attempt to provide omniscience is to be found in the curricula of those universities which *as if* follow the false philology and identify themselves grandiosely with the universe of knowledge; but this fallacy has received ample discussion from Abraham Flexner in his book on American Universities.

It is time we got back to the rise of psychoanalytic education and its historic parallels. In certain respects, such a parallel is offered by the Renaissance movement known as humanism, which added the direct study of the Greek and Hebrew languages and literature to Western culture. Its high point was in the fifteenth and sixteenth centuries, by which time books were printed and a considerable number of Greek and Hebrew texts had become available. Although many humanists taught in universities and although universities differed officially in the degree to which they welcomed or rejected the new learning, nevertheless, humanism grew up generally speaking in private circles outside the framework of the universities. The humanists were often prelates of the church, Catholic or reformed, or men of private means, or they depended on the patronage of the noble and wealthy. On the whole, they showed the type of 'idle curiosity' of Veblen's terminology, a disinterested preoccupation. Dilettantes among them have been used to demonstrate them as something like intellectual playboys. The elegant Cardinal Bembo, praying in Greek to avoid the un-Ciceronian Latin of the prayer book, gives a very untrue picture of an intellectual and æsthetic snobbery which, though 'idle' enough, will not serve as a primary motive for deep scholarship. The attention given Greek and Hebrew had a very obvious practical interest. Erasmus is not explained as *homo ludens* unless we take it that he was playing a game with God. His interest in the Greek text of the Bible was not due to a craving for elegant knowledge. His own statement is that he believed the best knowledge concerning Christ's teachings must come from Greek texts since they were primary and nearer contemporary sources. According to the naïve comparative philology of his day, Latin was derived from Greek and Greek from Hebrew, and hope for salvation rested upon knowing as accurately as possible what God had revealed. Indeed, humanists are much implicated in the religious debates of those times. The humanists were seeking more knowledge; their quest for omniscience met resistance from the scholastics who were satisfied that they already had a sufficient system.

The parallel with psychoanalysis is weak. The humanists never organized but, like the first psychoanalysts, they brought knowledge unwelcome to the established order of learning. An Oxford professor was discharged for teaching the Greek pronunciation recommended by Erasmus. So far as I know, no German professor was discharged for teaching psychoanalytic principles, but also, so far as I know, none ever taught them. Ultimately after not too long a while, the humanities won over the universities, as psychoanalysis may yet win them. In fact, the humanities became so entrenched that the universities were not ready for the next great access to knowledge. It is interesting to note the opinion of the physicist

Planck on the acceptance of new knowledge. Writing as an old man, he says that when he was young he was under the misapprehension that a new theory won recognition because of proof and logical argument, but he finally realized that this was not true. New theories, he discovered, did not impress the generation which held inadequate or contrary old ones. However, the older men died, and a new generation of scientists had learned the new theories and came to accept them. The inference would be that the new student determines the validity of new knowledge, and that nobody changes his mind.

We come to the third historic parallel in our series: the rise of the natural sciences, and the role of scientific societies. It is common knowledge that the great scientists of the seventeenth and eighteenth centuries worked privately, that science and experiment were their avocation, and that this science was recorded and fostered in certain societies, of which the two most famous are the Royal Society of London, and the Académie des Sciences in Paris. Besides these two there were several short-lived precursors such as the Accademia del Cimento in Florence, and in time many imitators, especially of the Paris Académie, in Germany, Russia, and elsewhere.

Many influences determined the rise of the physical sciences in the seventeenth century. It was correlated with the discovery and exploration of new countries, which contributed so many new impressions to Europe. Another idea is that the general interest was aroused by the invention of new instruments, of which the telescope, the microscope, and the air pump are perhaps the three most important. Copernicus wrote in the sixteenth century, but only after Galileo were his writings appreciated and for a time put on the Index. Martha Ornstein, in her book, The Role of Scientific Societies in the Seventeenth Century, points out that contrary to the learning of the universities, which demanded the study of books written in the ancient tongues, this new knowledge and its tools were widely accessible to people of many callings; and it is true that the new sciences arose at the same time as the new interest in the vernaculars. The experimental method as expounded by Galileo and Bacon was readily understood and appreciated; in fact, some disgruntled conservatives referred to the movement as a cult or an affectation, and Robert Boyle's enthusiastic dedication to it furnished some grounds for the remark.

Natural science in the main was in the hands of enthusiastic amateurs. Though many of the scientists taught at universities, these were the astronomers, mathematicians, or anatomists. They were not discouraged by the universities; they were in the main ignored by them. There was occasional trouble, as the well-known story of Galileo shows us, and the university atmosphere was somewhat uncongenial to the scientist. For example, Vesalius for a long while did not dare teach what he really saw, but in his lectures at Padua repeated the erroneous and dogmatic statements of Galen. Galileo, at one point in his unhappy story, in his lectures on the planets had to expound the Ptolemaic and not the Copernican theory. In 1578, he wrote to Kepler that while he believed in Copernicus's theory, his function as a professor demanded of him nothing but to hand down the accepted wisdom of the past. Both Vesalius and Galileo became so uncomfortable that the latter retired and Vesalius resigned and took a post at the Court of Spain.

But more than any active opposition was the simple inadequacy of the universities to accommodate themselves to research and the teaching of the natural sciences. Many complaints on this score are extant, among them those of John Wallis, one of Newton's teachers. Newton's experiments were his avocation. He experimented in his kitchen and at an apothecary's shop, and his views on optics were generally unknown until a fortunate circumstance led him to publish them and, later on, his great book, the Principia. Ornstein sums up the matter after much detailed investigation: 'It thus would seem from the slight progress of the universities along lines of experimental science, from the fact that the greatest scientists of the age were not affiliated with them, from the many criticisms leveled against them, and from actual evidences of their conservatism, extending even into the eighteenth century, that the universities in the seventeenth century did not lend to science that encouragement which it needed to take root in them'.

Among the great names Ornstein mentions as unaffiliated with universities are: Bacon, Grew, Boyle, Flamsteed, Willoughby, Huygens, Leeuwenhoek, Swammerdam, Van Helmont, Hevelius, Leibnitz, Descartes, Pascal, Mariotte, Lémery, and earlier, Kepler and Guericke. Others like Robert Hooke and Gassendi held teaching appointments at institutions such as the Collège de France and Gresham College, but these cannot be counted among the regular universities. Several persons on this list, Leibnitz for instance, refused a university position because the invitation lacked the proper appeal. To summarize, the universities on the whole did not attract scientists, even when they were not unwilling to engage them. Newton turned elsewhere for the scientific contacts he desired; in Cambridge he could not get together a group interested in experimental science for lack of enthusiasm there. 'That which chiefly dasht the business was the want of persons willing to try experiments. The one we chiefly rel'd on refusing to concern himself in that kind.'

The conservative state of affairs continued, generally speaking, until in the nineteenth century, when through a revolution in their curricula, the universities became the great centers of experimental science which they are today.

What did the great and active scientists do in the seventeenth century? It is an interesting story. They formed 'study groups'. Two were to become world renowned. One of these was formed around Gresham College in London, which was not a university, but what we would call now an 'extension school', an institution which gave lectures open to the laity. As several teachers of this endowed school were interested in experimental science, they formed the nucleus for the study group, and this study group finally became incorporated as the Royal Society. Although Charles the Second gave the Society a bombastic charter, he did not supply it with any money, and the experiments performed under the Society's patronage by Boyle, Hooke, and others were at private expense, Boyle, a wealthy bachelor, being one of the financial mainstays. The Royal Society meetings sound familiar enough to modern ears. Papers were read, also letters from correspondents abroad, answered by Hooke as Curator, who also demonstrated apparatus and experiments, as did other members. Through the members' gifts, an extraordinary museum of scientific instruments was collected, among them a telescope made by Newton and Leeuwenhoek's microscopes. In fact, when the Greenwich observatory opened, the first Astronomer Royal, Flamsteed, borrowed many instruments to equip it. The Society differed from the present-day scientific societies largely in its collection and in the fact that it manned and financed a laboratory. It was not only a learned society, as we understand the term today, but also a quasi 'research institute'. It had the chartered privilege of teaching, but several times decided against doing so.

There was a lighter, fashionable side to the meetings of the Society also. Samuel Pepys tells of a visit to one meeting of the 'virtuosi' paid by the Duchess of Newcastle, at her own insistence. She was 'a good comely woman', he writes, but he 'did not like her at all . . . nor did I hear her say anything that was worth hearing, but that she was full of admiration, all admiration.' The virtuosi transformed a piece of cooked meat into pure blood for her. Pepys also tells of an evening he spent in the Duke of York's chambers at Whitehall, when the King spent two hours ribbing Sir William Petty, especially about the Royal Society. 'Gresham College he mightily laughed at, for spending time only in weighing of ayre, and doing nothing else since they sat.' Petty stood the King's rough fun 'with great discretion'. At a later date, Pepys was President of the Society, reading a very uninspired inaugural paper, helping perhaps to set a tradition for society presidents of all time; he himself comments on how badly Lord Brouncker, the first President, always spoke in public. Pepys had the distinction of satisfactorily seeing Newton's Principia into print.

In view of the present occasion, I think it worth mentioning that Sir John Cutler, a wealthy grocer, trader, and amateur of science, endowed the first annual Lectureship of the Society in June 1664.

In his book, On Understanding Science, James B. Conant makes out an excellent case for the historical continuity of humanism and the rise of experimental science. He considers such scholars, artists, and thinkers as Petrarch, Boccaccio, Brunelleschi, and Machiavelli to be the true culture-kinsmen of Galileo. Conant is equally aware of the influence of technology on the scientists and of the spur given them by problems turned up by practical workmen. The strictly experimental side seems to have dominated the earliest sessions of the Royal Society; there was as if a distrust of book learning and a more rigorous 'operational' spirit. Particularly the Society's principal mover, Robert Boyle, of whom Conant has written so revealingly, and who was very competent at explanations, was insistent on a minimum of theoretical, philosophical discussion at the meetings, and for some years there was a rule that demonstrations should not be followed by any discussion. (To digress, Freud too considered the discussion of psychoanalytic papers at meetings a futile procedure, and early meetings of the International Psycho-Analytical Association followed the same rule.) Boyle is said to have been addicted to experimentation, and is also said to have been too occupied to see to the publication of his famous law of gases, which was published by his students.

A view of experimental science more one-sided than Conant's, a historian's rather than a practicing scientist's, is represented by such authors as Farrington, who prefers the Ionian pre-Socratic sages to the Athenians among the Greeks. These authors' belief is that scientific formulations arise nearly exclusively as abstractions from practical life. Geometry they point out was a Greek translation of surveyors' and builders' rules, and they approve of the tale that Pythagoras heard the musical intervals as a smith hammered his hot iron rod at different lengths. However, the scholarly and the practical knowledge and incentive do not seem incompatible. Rather, they express differences in temperament and talent in the workers, and modern science appreciates both concept and technique.

A nineteenth-century scientist is credited with the stern injunction which used to be printed on the celluloid rulers that came with dissecting instruments: It read: 'Study nature, not books.—Agassiz.' Plainly the early virtuosi of the Royal Society were suspicious of the printed word; if we judge by some of the criticisms of university teaching, such as John Wallis's, the members of the Society may simply have been bored by the books they had to study or they were disappointed in them. If they had known Professor Mall's remark about the educated man's ability to read and to make records, they would unhesitatingly have interpreted *records* to mean those made by nature. Nevertheless, the Society itself was soon to make books. It printed its proceedings in the famous Philosophical Transactions, the records of Newton, Boyle, Hooke, Halley, and Leeuwenhoek, to name an imperishably famous few. It also printed famous books, Newton's Principia among them. Until the great revolution in university curricula in the nineteenth century, the Royal Society and some of its foreign compeers were the true centers and the shelter of science.

The Académie des Sciences in Paris began for precisely the same reasons as the Royal Society and in very much the same way. It was originally a 'study group' that met because of the amateur interest of one man and his friends. The learned Minorite friar, Marin Mersenne, famous for his friendship with Galileo, Huygens, Pascal, Hobbes, Descartes, Fermat, and other scientists, was a great amateur of science himself and invited some of these friends to his cell for evenings of discussion of experimental science. Pascal, Toricelli, Desargues, and Roberval were among Mersenne's guests. The discussions seem to have covered more ground than those of the Royal Society. The difference in the fate of Mersenne's study group and its English counterpart is an interesting commentary on the political difference of the two countries. The French King, Louis XIV, at the time was trying to centralize France and to take all of France unto himself and the French throne. When his minister Colbert became informed of the quality and probable utility of Mersenne's evenings, he arranged that they too should become royal. He turned the group into the Académie des Sciences and provided several of the members with salaries; that is, he put them on a 'full-time' basis. He had the King give them several rooms in the Royal Library so that they might there carry on experiments. Royal protection and support were very real. The names of some of the Académie members were given above. To these may be added Huygens and Roemer, who first measured the speed of light. Leibnitz and many other foreign savants, including Hobbes, were members for a time. The proceedings of the Académie were recorded in a *Journal des sçavans*. The Académie saw many ups and downs in its history. Its members were always in close relationship with those of the Royal Society. It came to serve as a model for learned academies in other countries and Leibnitz planned the ones in Berlin and St. Petersburg in direct imitation.

The literary style of several members set something of a style for French scientific papers. Bertrand Russell suggests that this was due to Descartes, who affected a cavalier attitude toward his writings, which were in graceful French and not in turgid Latin. Pascal is of course still considered a great prose writer, but this more because of his religious writings. On the other hand, the King and Colbert took the academicians very professionally and demanded team work and practical results. They found, however, that this first effort at interdisciplinary cross-fertilization ended in interdisciplinary cross-sterilization (to use Felix Frankfurter's *bon mot*), and the scientists went pretty much their own way. The Sun King deserves the gratitude of science for the example he set. It was followed into the nineteenth and twentieth centuries, in Germany, for example, where the presence of Kaiser Wilhelm Institutes attested to the effect of Louis on royal minds or at least on royal behavior. For explaining to various royal minds the advantage and prestige of such institutions, the civilized world is in debt to Leibnitz.

The sequence—individual enthusiasm, society, institutions—in all these parallels is obvious enough; the organizational analogies are easy to demonstrate. As to the matter of omniscience, there is some need for further discussion. The acceptance or rejection of new knowledge is not a black and white story. It cannot be paranoidally simplified into a fight between the forces of right and the persecutors. Psychoanalysis, when it became known through Freud's publications, by no means met with universal rejection, but in several quarters, such as Bleuler's hospital, received a very sympathetic hearing. What slowed down the understanding of psychoanalysis in many circles appears much more to be in line with Planck's remark, quoted above, that nobody changes his mind and that official teaching of a new theory begins with a new generation.

The fantasy of omniscience in the generation with which Freud's theories had to cope was different from that of the great parallels. No one thought that all knowledge was to be found in Aristotle, not even in the best and most primary Greek text. The records of books were known to be as fallible as human beings. There had taken place a switch from a faith in content to a faith in method, and the method of experiment had been trustworthy. Less openly and less clearly, however, it was believed that the inferences and assumptions as to the true nature of things were just as reliable, and it took a new and recent revolution in science to straighten out the difference between the reliability of Newton's methods and the validity of the assumptions he made concerning primary entities. Freud appeared before Einstein and before it became generally known that non-Euclidean geometry was a practical branch of mathematics. In Freud's day it was no longer thought that we had recorded everything. But it was tacitly believed that if we kept on employing the methods outlined by Bacon and Galileo, we could in time become very nearly omniscient. Ironically, science has run into facts that show the opposite to be the case. The present *Zeitgeist* is quite a *Poltergeist.* The corpuscle-wave contradiction cannot be solved in the seventeenth-century way, as an either-or proposition. Modern physicists do not feel omniscient.

The fantasy that Freud came up against was a dogmatic materialism, which seemed to follow from the empirical method. Psychiatry, determined at all costs to be scientific, had placed its stakes on brain research and on matter and energy explanations. The prestige of German university science was great. Freud's radical empiricism threatened the omniscience fantasy of the Kraepelinians, and it is significant that his theories met with their earliest official acceptance outside the German orbit—in Switzerland, in Holland, and in the United States. The present-day new insight into the conceptual nature of scientific assumptions is creating a better understanding of the position of psychoanalysis. Among psychoanalysts too there is a greater recognition of the questions they must answer as to the limits and reliability of method and the nature of fundamental assumptions, answers which should come in time.

I do not know for sure what is shown by the historic parallels. They are only rough parallels, and the more one knows of the detailed reactions to new knowledge, the more variations one discovers. Man began his quest for omniscience convinced that knowledge is finite. His consciousness, to repeat Evelyn Underhill's sentence, tries to run out to encounter the Absolute. Space and time too are, to begin with, finite; this stubborn conviction is hooked up with man's early belief in his omnipotence. A transatlantic airplane flight leads him to plan a journey to the moon in the foreseeable future and to the galaxies in his science fiction. Time too he will master with a time-machine. Knowledge is harder to force: Prometheus and not Icarus is its culture hero. Galileo, Newton, and the rest have all been fire-bringers, wresting for man some of the Olympian omniscience. Since man cannot intuit or empathize the infinite in space, time or knowledge, he will always picture just a bit more space, just a bit more time, and just a bit more knowledge—all of them ultimately measurable. He puts lines and points at infinity and measures it. Perhaps mythology proves as much as history. If either of them proves anything, it seems to be that the quest and the effort to turn the infinite into the finite, whether through mathematics and engineering or in fantasy, has survived intrenched fantasies of being already omniscient, even when the latter relied on the support and power of social institutions to which are conceded by transference some of the original narcissistic powers and functions.

The psychoanalytic institutes are too young to take on or to feel the responsibilities of omniscience. In the main, they have served as professional schools. With some twenty-five or more years of experience behind them, they have settled on a practicable course of study. But the institute system is flexible, and it has been able to serve various purposes in different localities, and to meet the various needs of faculty, students, and communities. The problems of psychoanalytic education and the university setting have not been solved, but they have been posed and scrutinized with good will and intelligence. In the institutes, moreover, there is an intellectual ferment. The imagination of teachers and students still sees the stars that descend below the horizon of knowledge as beckoning to the unexplored. The quest for omniscience is still alive.

I dare say that in the institutes it will be psychoanalyzed, so that there will be insight into what one can and what one cannot do. Let us hope so, and since this occasion calls for a special birthday sentiment, let us wish the Chicago Institute a well-psychoanalyzed, well-motivated, and well-organized future.

Appendix (in lieu of Notes, Bibliography, etc.)

Prof. Paul Lazarsfeld gave me the idea of historical parallels, remarking on the situation in social research, which has developed mainly outside the universities. Haskins's book (H. Holt, 1923) was recommended to me as a primer along with good advice by J. B. Ross and Mary M. McLaughlin; behind Haskins is Rashdall. The old meaning of *doctor* I learned from a joke of Prof. Elder of Harvard, quoting Lucretius (*De rerum natura* V, 1310). The tag about Juvenal refers to his lines (Satire 14, 315-316) that prescience is better than the Goddess Luck. Dr. Kubie, much experienced in the psychology of scientists, has published mainly in the *American Scientist* (1953, 1954). The quotation is from an address at the Bank Street School in New York. Whitehead's *The Aims of Education* (Mentor #MD 152) contains Felix Frankfurter's joke in the introduction; Whitehead's 'other' book is *Science and the Modern World* (Mentor #M 28). Veblen's *Higher Learning in America* (quite dated I think and very *ad hoc* pleading) is paper-backed by Sagamore Press, 1957. Underhill is also paper-backed, but I have the hard-backed Dutton, 1930 edition. M. M. McLaughlin's paper on academic freedom deals with thirteenth-century Siger de Brabant. (*Church History 24,* No. 3, 1955.) The facts about Erasmus come from Huizinga, Henry Osborn Taylor (*Thought and Expression in the Sixteenth Century,* Macmillan, 1920), and E. Harris Harbison (*The Christian Scholar in the Age of the Reformation,* Scribners, 1956). About Bembo I do not know; I refer to the 'tradition'. Planck's statement is in his book, *Scientific Biography* (Philosophical Library, 1949).

The Pepy's *Diary* entries are of February 1, 1663-64 (about the King) and May 30, 1667 (about the Duchess). Conant's book is Mentor #66. Information about Descartes comes from Norman Kemp Smith's book, *New Studies in the Philosophy of Descartes* (London, Macmillan, 1952), from Descartes's writings (trans. Haldane and Ross), and elsewhere. Farrington's *Greek Science* is in the Penguin series; see also Sarton. The opinion of Pascal's style is Sainte-Beuve's. The ideas on Galilean and modern relativity and on mathematics come from the Einstein-Infeld book and other scattered reading (Black, Burtt, Butterfield, Dantzig, Klein, Russell, Schrödinger, Weyl, Whitehead, and others). A Jesuit mathematician, Saccheri, did write a non-Euclidean geometry before Bolyai in 1733, but it was not published until 1889. Euclid was invested with some of the same scholastic prestige as Aristotle; he re-entered Europe on the same cultural Mayflower. Chesterton's remark is from memory, also Macaulay's. So is Prof. Mall's, made to me while I was a student in the histology laboratory. He led up to it by asking what I thought about education—my answer has been slow. The subject of this address was suggested by Dr. Gerhart Piers and Dr. Joan Fleming. The title is an Archimedean inspiration, improved by Helen Ross.

III. PSYCHOANALYTIC EDUCATION: SYNCRETISM*

WITH HELEN ROSS

> On Mondays, Wednesdays, and Fridays we adopt the one hypothesis, on Tuesdays, Thursdays, and Saturdays the other. We know that we cannot be seeing clearly and fully in either case, but are perfectly content to work and wait for the complete understanding.
>
> —Sir William Bragg

According to Webster's Unabridged Dictionary, *syncretism* originally meant (1) 'the reconciliation of conflicting beliefs, especially religious beliefs, or a movement or effort intending such: specifically, in the seventeenth century, a movement of a Lutheran party, led by George Calixtus, seeking the union of Protestant sects with each other and with the Roman Catholic Church; also the principles of such a movement'; and, more relevant here, (2) 'Egregious compromise in religion or philosophy that is illogical or leads to inconsistency; uncritical acceptance of conflicting or divergent beliefs and principles'.

Outside of religious circles the word has come to mean the *use* of conflicting and irreconcilable assumptions. In modern science several have become famous, including the 'wave-corpuscle' antinomy that applies to the nature of light. The definition errs for science when it includes the word 'uncritical'; no one is more aware than the scientist that he is willy-nilly in a syncretistic net, and that for the moment there is not much to be done about it. He is accustomed, because he has been forced to accustom himself, to living in a world with double logic, based on mutually exclusive assumptions.

Less cosmically, the psychoanalytic educator has awakened gradually to the fact that education and the psychoanalytic procedure exist in two worlds and that psychoanalytic educa-

* [Chapter IV of No. 112 in Bibliography.]

tion, as a concept, is a syncretism. As the undulatory and the corpuscular models represent the optical phenomena, so do the two models 'psychoanalytic patient' and 'student' complement, alternate with, and oppose each other. A psychoanalytic treatment is *sui generis*. The education introduces a parameter for the therapeutic procedure, and the analytic procedure an even larger one for the education. The institutes are unavoidably trying to exert two effects on the student: to 'educate' him and to 'cure' or 'change' him. Hence the student as a phenomenon fits into two conceptual frameworks: he is the pedagogic unit or object of teaching and the therapeutic unit or object of psychoanalytic procedure.

At present there is no unitary theory of psychoanalytic education. A student is presumably psychoanalyzed; he is also presumably educated at the institutes. But the two processes proceed, each according to its own canons. The training analysis has its goal and this is couched in psychoanalytic-therapeutic language. The education has its separate goal. A system which satisfactorily interdigitates the two has been at best approximated by the institutes.

Psychiatry at the present time suffers from a comparable syncretistic problem. The old Kraepelinian ideas, modeled on organic illness, are tacitly based on a physical determinism. The freudian concepts invoke a parallel psychological determinism. The psychiatrist tries to set up a partition between the two; he thinks now in one world, now in the other. Similarly the psychoanalytic teacher has tried to function dually, and variously has tried all the mechanisms and compromises inherent in dualism. The institutes are a field of a novel conflict. The principles of psychoanalysis are being tested against the demands of education; the principles of education are being tested by psychoanalysis. An experiment of nature is being carried on in institute teaching. It is conceivable that a synthesis will arise from out of the present antithesis, a new entity, 'psychoanalytic education'.

Has the psychoanalyst always been something of an educator and the educator something of a therapist? The educator, especially in modern elementary schools, has begun to look at the therapeutic side. In one such school, when the roles for a play were assigned, a youngster inquired, 'Are these therapeutic decisions?' They often are. A high school teacher, asking psychoanalytic advice on this very matter, put the question, 'Should I choose the best girl for the part, or should I think about how much good it would do Mary to have it?'

The discovery that the institutes had two goals came empirically and naturally. The first recognition of the conflict was by the training analyst, since he was at the best site for observation. In a homely everyday way, he observed that at times he was called upon to play two roles in relation to a student. The Rainbow Report (1955) states very well that 'a major difficulty in psychoanalytic training lies in the dual roles of the training analyst—as analyst and judge'. This refers to the fact that in most institutes the training analyst not only directs the analytic procedure of the student but simultaneously plays an administrative role as a faculty member, where he either may or may not be party to decisions concerning the student's progression. In different institutes, the student's personal analyst's role differs; in some he may enter into the decisions; in others, to avoid this dual role, he 'disqualifies' himself, as judges do when they are unable to give 'objective' attention in a law case because of personal relations or involvements.

The same Rainbow Report notes that an analyst or a group of analysts is tempted to adopt a 'therapeutic attitude' in regard to students. It states that 'there is a tendency in the training analyst, supervisory analyst, and the faculty to extend to the training situation in general the attitude of leniency and tolerance which forms such an important part of our therapeutic efforts'.

At first this seemed to be a problem for the individual training analyst. It was considered frequently, from his point of view naturally. Should he speak up at the meetings of the education committee or not? His conflict he first formulated as a matter of professional ethics. As the personal analyst of a given student and hence called upon to maintain a position of noninterference and 'psychoanalytic neutrality', could he properly enter into the academic decisions which had very real effect on the student's career? This may be called the *administrative* dual-role problem, and when the commission quoted above referred to the intrusion of a therapeutic attitude, it was speaking for the academic good of the institute administration.

Analysts have adopted the ameliorating device of passing on the administrative responsibility to such bodies as the education committee or the students' committee. The committee as a corporate personality has assigned to it administrative functions, and the personal training-analyst hopes to be freed of them. This official legal fiction works to some extent, but it is not unusual for the committee or 'the institute' to become the displaced object of the student's transference reactions. The fiction involves a common form of denial, and students have been known to involve committees in their personal analyses, sometimes provoking all the more the realization of the dual problem which the division between committee and training analyst was intended to settle.

More often, awareness has grown of the *technical* difficulties that arise in the training analysis, and there is a growing and helpful literature in this field. Generally the writers take the point of view of therapists and consider the technical differences that exist between an analysis of those who wish to become analysts, and an analysis which Grete Bibring calls 'the free-floating process of the therapeutic analysis of our [other] patients'.[1] Throughout this literature, there is an awareness of the patent necessity for grappling with unsatisfactory or rival conceptions of 'normality' in reference to students.

One formulation that tries to distinguish 'student' *or* 'patient' reads that the motives which impel the analysis and later propel its course are different. The patient comes to be cured; the student, to learn. But psychoanalytic thinking has not rested content with either 'the wish to be cured' or 'the wish to learn'. The survey report (Lewin and Ross, 1960) is not the place for a deep discussion or comprehensive review of what has been said about these two motives. At all events, they have themselves been analyzed (Nunberg, 1925).[2] Behind them both are unconscious fantasies of somehow attaining narcissistic perfection.

Regardless of formulation, theory, and minor points of difference, in the psychoanalytic institutes the student is pragmat-

1 The survey's (Lewin and Ross, 1960) insertion of the word 'other' in brackets may carry a false implication and may not be accurate in context. To bracket or not to bracket is the point of this chapter.

2 See also, *Education or the Quest for Omniscience*, pp. 459-483 [Ed.].

ically a patient. He is operationally a kind of 'neurotic' person, even if not classifiable. In its earliest days, psychoanalysis was rather conventional in its concept of normality and accepted the current 'disease-entity' criteria of medical thought. For the time being, so far as 'normal' persons are concerned, psychoanalysts must use one of two heuristic assumptions. Either there exist 'normal persons' (this is different from a purely ideal concept of 'normality'), who are different from 'neurotic persons', or, alternatively, the proposition would read: 'Everyone is somehow neurotic, symptoms or no symptoms, in the classical sense'. There are, in other words, at least two interpretations of Freud's remark that he thought he was analyzing hysterics but found the whole world on his couch. Certainly the alternative assumption above is the one consciously held by the majority of psychoanalysts, and it is the working assumption of all when they deal practically with the education of psychoanalytic students.

The traditions of academic bodies ignore this thesis, rightly or wrongly. Some forms of standard education exploit (as Kubie puts it) the student's defenses, and turn pathology into educational profit, as research, erudition, etc.—an epinosic gain which, like *pâté de foie gras,* may be more advantageous for the milieu than for the individual producer. The psychoanalytic schools innocently run counter to the standard consensus of 'normality'.

Supervised work, too, has been a field for the discussion of the dual role, but with fewer literary contributions. During the meetings of the Rainbow commissions, Joan Fleming and Robert Waelder debated whether the supervisor was essentially a teacher (Waelder) or must also take a therapeutic point of view (Fleming). More will be said about training analysis and supervision.[3] Here the intention is to enumerate manifestations of the academic-psychoanalytic sym- and antibiosis.

In supervised work and in the classes too, it has been noted in some committee reports . . . that teachers have carried over some of the 'passive technique' into their pedagogy and into the classroom. Jacob Arlow, in a letter, writes: '. . . This brings me to the point which I have alluded to above, namely, the philosophy of psychoanalytic teaching. Psychoanalytic teach-

[3] See, *The Training Analysis: Pedagogic,* pp. 492-503. Also, Lewin and Ross (1960), Chapters X-XIII and XV-XVII [Ed.].

ing is done, for the most part, by practicing psychoanalysts and there is a tendency, it seems to me, to carry over into the teaching situation the guiding principles which govern the therapeutic situation, i.e., a nondirective, laissez-faire, benign, passive objectivity, which has as its basis, apparently, the hope that eventually the underlying concepts will emerge like a wish from the id. While it is true that analytic students are post-graduate students, it nevertheless is a fact that a certain degree of specific guidance, of integration of concepts, of correlating data with hypotheses, is very fruitful in psychoanalytic teaching as in other preceptorial methods of learning.'

Criticisms such as this, however, may be based on pedagogic ineptitude rather than on the academic-psychoanalytic syncretism. The transposition of a specific professional point of view to an alien field has often been lauded in its form of interdisciplinary cross-fertilization. The present example, nevertheless, must be conceded to be one of interdisciplinary cross-sterilization, to use Felix Frankfurter's *bon mot.*

In spite of their reality, the double aspect in the training analysis, the possible double aspect in supervision, and the accidental displacements of patterns mentioned above, do not state completely the paradox in psychoanalytic education. These inconsistencies have been recognized; they are not always easy to resolve. But as Kubie (1958, Chapter III) remarks, in the medical sciences we are accustomed to the fact that we know problems often a long while before we can solve them; why, therefore, in education should one be expected to have the proper answers immediately upon one's recognition of the problems?

The dual nature of institute activities confronted the survey in the most unexpected areas. Ahead of time it seemed a simple enough matter to get an answer to the question, how long does psychoanalytic training last? It was not simple. Before the answer could be given, semantic problems appeared; definitions, many of them arbitrary, had to be made; and there were even problems of a metaphysical nature. Some institutes with an old and stable bureaucracy[4] knew the answer in purely academic terms: psychoanalytic education began when the

[4] The word is not used in any evaluating sense, but in accord with Max Weber's writings, to mean a permanent professional administration, operating a routine.

student paid his registration fee to the bursar's office. Less sophisticated institutes were not so sure. Student A, the institute might say, began his training analysis in 1950, but had had two years of analysis before then; so the length of his training analysis depends on what the survey wishes to consider a training analysis. Student B was still in analysis when he was graduated; when did his analysis cease to be training, or did it continue to be? Such trivial paradoxes exist because the procedures and paraphernalia of the academic world exist, with its registrations, matriculations, classes, and graduations.

For its own purposes and within its own limits, the academic procedure seems to have a precision lacking in any statistical or mathematical evaluation of the training analysis or any other kind of analysis. Here is the basic contradiction. An analysis, training or other, does not naturally run the course set down in college catalogues and proceed from A to B. Its course is something else—more like the course of a neurosis or a love affair. There is a split between the academic and the psychoanalytic conceptual worlds. Yet it is unlikely that psychoanalytic schools, teachers, or students may without harm ignore one or the other, and there is always a possibility of increasingly accurate approximation.

A suspicion arises that education in general may still be confronted with this same problem. 'Most educational situations', the Commission on Faculty[5] states, 'make use of unconscious defenses. Psychoanalytic education on the other hand tries to penetrate them, to give the student insight into them, and thus to help him free himself from dependence on his unconscious defenses.' We know something about what is demanded of psychoanalysts, consciously and unconsciously, and we have some idea of the unconscious meaning of being a doctor (Simmel, 1926). But there is little that is accepted as to the unconscious goals of education. It is regrettable that we have no formulation of the teacher game that would clarify the impulses at play in teaching. The institutes are alert to the resistances that come from the narcissistic gain of being a physician. They are not completely alert to the fact that when a student enters the institute, old school patterns and problems

[5] Rainbow Report (1955). Commission on Faculty, p. 14.

become regressively resuscitated; that they are really schools, and that their students are bringing to them many unsolved problems of educational psychology which demand, as the Commission said, to be penetrated 'to give the student insight into them, and thus to help him free himself from dependence on his unconscious defenses'. Before psychoanalytic education is fully comprehended it may be necessary to study many facts in the educational process and to test out many hypotheses and theories.[6]

[6] Some school problems in institutes are described by Lewin and Ross (1960), Chapter XXII [Ed.].

IV. THE TRAINING ANALYSIS: PEDAGOGIC*

WITH HELEN ROSS

> As is well known, the analytic situation consists in our allying ourselves with the ego of the person under treatment, in order to subdue portions of his id which are uncontrolled—that is to say to include them in the synthesis of his ego. . . . The ego, if we are to be able to make such a pact with it, must be a normal one. But a normal ego of this sort is, like normality in general, an ideal fiction. The abnormal ego, which is unserviceable for our purposes, is unfortunately no fiction. Every normal person, in fact, is only normal on the average. His ego approximates to that of the psychotic in some part or other and to a greater or lesser extent . . .
>
> —Freud

The publication of Freud's (1887-1902) letters to Wilhelm Fliess and of Jones's (1953-1957) biography of Freud has taught the psychoanalytic world to appreciate how sincerely Freud meant his statement that a personal analysis was requisite for the understanding and successful practice of psychoanalysis. Even without the inspiration of Freud's story, by the time the books were published, the psychoanalytic educational world was convinced that a personal analysis was the antecedent and the core of psychoanalytic education. The educators had themselves been analyzed. They had had, moreover, an opportunity to digest their personal analytic experience, and to judge it, like Freud, aided by continued experience with analysands. When organized psychoanalytic training began, there was little understanding that a training analysis might have special problems. An analysis was, after all, an analysis, and if the students did not present

* [Chapter XIV of No. 112 in Bibliography.]

symptoms like Charcot's patients, the principles involved, theory, rules of technique, and the like were the same. Freud, it was known even then, had analyzed his own dreams. At the beginning too, say in 1920, the structure of the institute was simple, and so was the educational curriculum. Yet, the training analysis has its own inherent peculiarities, some of them now well known, and it has been refractory to much in the academic mold.

With the growth of institute education, for many reasons it seemed proper to codify good practice into regulations; for example, concerning such matters as the minimal length of a training analysis. As in all academic number rules, this number was 'normal' in the sense of 'average', not 'ideal'. And from the start, there have been analysts who protested that all regulation was artificial—that it made what we have learned to call a 'parameter', a deviation from the good practice that a rule was supposed to enshrine. Not schoolmasters at heart, but sworn psychoanalysts, they asked why the course of classical psychoanalysis should be disturbed by an alien procedure, just because the patient happened to be a student. To the usual patient (they argued) one would not, at the beginning of treatment, state that it would last 250 or 300 hours. That would be a technical mistake, 'for which any beginner would be severely criticized by his supervising analyst' (Balint, 1947). It was feared that a minimal rule would be exploited by the resistances to a damaging extent. The student-patient, especially if he had made therapeutic progress in that length of time, could say, 'I am trained, according to the rule; the analysis is over.' Or the training analyst, also persuaded by the rule, might be content with minimal results. The analytic conscience was afraid the rule would hurt the quality of the work by interposing a factor absent in classical analysis. Supporters of regulation could grant the possibility of such 'lifemanship' with the rules. They maintained the reasonableness of some type of regulation, nevertheless. A minimal figure is only a statistical normal and estimated average, connected, as other averages are, to facts; but it is correlated with the idea of a guarantee, like a diploma. This is a social argument. As a matter of fact, the stated minimum plays little role at present among the institutes' educational problems. Gresham's law has not been effective. Other factors have seen to it that short analyses have not driven out long ones.

As to rules of this sort in general—and the above discussion was intended as a paradigm—they are aimed at an average situation and imply a 'normal' state of affairs, and they are adopted to meet a specific problem. Now, beating the rules is an old social game, and any rule can be used to create a problem, the usual sophistry being a *reductio ad absurdum.* It is probably true that for lack of understanding, certain institutes and certain individuals at one time or another have taken the stand that to meet formal requirements is sufficient—that if requirements are met, a student has 'legally' earned his graduation. This may have happened, but not often and not permanently. Psychoanalysis itself contains the correction of such constructions. At a certain point in his work, the student becomes aware of the earnestness of the psychoanalytic procedure. Where the training analyst or the institute officials have been content with less than the best, the student has often made up for lacks through further analysis, undertaken privately.

Regulation, in fact, seems to have made not for minimal training but for considerably longer analyses. At some state in his training, it is up to the student to decide for himself how much analysis he 'needs', quite apart from any rules. Often this decision is postponed until after graduation, when of course the need may be based on different premises. It is not presently possible to say how much postgraduate analysis there has been, nor to give the various motives for it. Nevertheless, in some groups, it is known, well over half of the local society members have been thus 're-analyzed'. The periodic 'postgraduate' analysis of the analyst, which Jones (1936) refers to as a common practice, was recommended by Freud (1937a) in Analysis Terminable and Interminable. In this paper, indeed, he uses his observations on the analysis of analysts, among others, to illustrate the difficulties encountered in the newer 'character analysis'.

The institute atmosphere, rather than any formal rules, plays a part in establishing the desirability of longer analyses and second analyses. An institute will develop certain mores in regard to training analyses, sometimes due to the influence of its leaders. Yet, the dominant conditions of the enveloping milieu do not necessarily determine the matter. Thus, some schools tend to stress their academic goals and attributes, yet students or graduates will enter further personal analysis on their own, without any stimulus from their institute. In the long run, analytic exigencies triumphed over the academic. The contrasting type of school would, as a type, emphasize academic attainments only minimally; its faculty would pay attention to the purely therapeutic results of its students' analyses. Hope would be pinned on the training analysis, secondarily on a type of supervision that closely approximates analysis, to give the students all that they need. Here, academic instruction might be considered a very minor issue, as if the school was devoted to therapy. The tacit assumption, let us say, would be that training analysis was a complete education in itself. All this is of course an exaggeration for the sake of exposition. But the 'types' have their occult existence, and strangely may have the same result, namely, more analysis for the student. The types are described here to bring out the horns of the dilemma on which all institutes are to a certain extent impaled, and to indicate efforts which have been made to ignore either one or the other of the lemmas of psychoanalytic education.

Various types of adjustment and arrangement have marked the practices of most institutes, where both the purely psychoanalytic and the academic goals have been recognized. One such adjustment begins with the assumption that the institute will inevitably have enrolled two general types of students. As extremes, it is assumed that certain students will not be primarily or exclusively psychoanalysts, while others will become devoted to the psychoanalytic career. Generally speaking, the former would be interested in psychoanalysis in terms of theory and tool, an extraverted interest, consistent perhaps with other traits of character. The latter type of students would be correspondingly introverted, would take more readily to self-study, and would look to psychoanalytic work in terms of personal development. These are types again, set up empirically, and there is in principle no intention at an invidious distinction. The personal analysis proceeds differently in the two types, each one encountering its own difficulties and resistances.

It can be said that there are similarly such types of members in the analytic societies and on the staffs of the institutes. It does not follow necessarily that each type would be partisan for its own kind, although the proportion between the two would affect institute admissions and progression policy. As to the institutes' general policies, it might be said that they are a mixture compounded of the two assumed elements. Some institute educators face the existence of the two types and believe that the institute should have something of a dual policy to fit its dual role. They take the position that both types belong in the institute, because nature has made both of them, and that the separate problems they present are problems for their training analyst. We are speaking again of types, with many intermediate positions. As far as the training analysis goes, the difficulties encountered have been touched upon by several writers, the first of whom was Hanns Sachs (1946). His discussion recognized, but in quotation marks, the 'normal' candidate and the neurotic. He considered the latter, with whatever shortcomings, more analyzable, and he has the following to stay about the 'normal':

> If the ego, despite repeated defeats, has kept intact its will to win insight into its conflicts and to govern its relations to reality, then the hope is justified that, with the aid that analysis can provide in supporting the ego, final victory will ensure an approvable, workable personality. Now in making such decisions, the distortions of character, the general inhibitions or diffuse anxieties which one may expect to find in the majority of 'normal' candidates offer a less favorable starting point, and decidedly more difficult technical problems, than a downright neurosis (p. 160).

There is much prejudice in various quarters both for the 'normal' and against him. Many analysts scoff at the idea of a 'normal' applicant; one jokes that normality is a form of schizophrenia; another has coined the word 'normopath'. The point seems to be that 'normal' has always in an occult way referred to an ideal statistical average. Psychiatric normality —Kraepelinian normality—is such an average of empirical findings in a wide community, judged by specific methods. With the application of the psychoanalytic method and the apparent shift in the type of patients, a new intuitive average of normality is formed but not formulated. The fact is, normality is very much a current problem, and the reader is referred to the pertinent literature, which extends beyond the present interest in institute training analysis.

Institute policies have varied and shifted in the judging of training analyses, according to some of the assumptions and views mentioned above. Difficulties in analyzing students have led to principles of selection.[1]

It is irritating that the phrases 'some institutes', 'some teachers', 'some students' must be repeated so constantly, but this necessity cannot be dodged without inaccuracy. There are institute attitudes and individual attitudes among the teachers and students, and a reading of the literature on training analysis and analytic training in general will show that the time and the place of the writing must be taken into account. There is sometimes a tendency in the literature of analytic education to assume that the situation with which the author is most familiar is also one which holds universally.

Realizing the mutual obstruction possible between the training analysis and the academic side of education, various practices have been instituted with the idea of effecting more of a separation. At Berlin, the rule was that supervised work and attendance at courses should begin only after a period of personal analysis, as a rule six months; and at first this was a common length for an official training analysis. The analyses have lengthened, but it is still the common practice of the institutes to have the student go through a period of analysis before beginning the rest of his work. Generally speaking, the idea has worked out well; students have reported in several places that their early attendance at courses was not as profitable as it might have been, and they considered their personal ('unanalyzed') unpreparedness as the source of this. At present, the institutes are generally cautious about admitting students to supervision and courses; they demand at least a year of analysis, sometimes nearly two. This rule again creates a new 'student problem' while it attempts to solve the

[1] See, Lewin and Ross (1960), Chapter IX [Ed.].

old one. The total curriculum is lengthened, and students displace conflicts about attending school onto this rule. A certain inconsistency between the position of the student as a member of a hospital staff, often entrusted with very difficult patients, and his position as a tyro analytically, is sharpened by the hesitations and cautions of the committees which judge his progress.

The rules of most institutes take into account the fact that there may be differences in analysts or in the analytic situation which cause the student to receive an unfavorable report. Hence, the student may be reassigned, where assignment to training analysts is the rule, or he may choose a new training analyst for a second (or third) attempt. Sometimes, the student is allowed to 'change the sex of his analyst', as this is drolly called; that is, a committee or the original training analyst may believe the student's psychology is such that he would do better with an analyst of the sex other than that of his original choice. The theoretic basis is partly derived from Freud's experience that women analysts, analyzing some of his ex-patients, were able to obtain results and material not accessible easily in a transference situation with a male analyst (Freud, 1931). That repeated attempts may lead to unfortunate repetitions of unsuccessful analyses with several persons has been noted. On the other hand, there have been undoubted successful second and third analyses. Individual differences in talent, temperament, and strictness in judging one's own work enter here to make final judgment on this rule inconclusive.

There have been times and places in which analysis within the institute was difficult for many persons; they often found that after graduation they were able to discover their unconscious in a way that had not been possible for them as students. Again, individual students will have had special reasons for this. At times, school policies seem to have played a role, at others the situation of certain training analysts. Such analysis after graduation, then, would come under the head of rectifying mistakes. But several very experienced training analysts have stated that in their judgment, the analysis under institute auspices is generally limited, and that many persons cannot be 'really' analyzed until they have been graduated.

Other training analysts, agreeing in general that the undergraduate situation makes for great resistances all along the way, have nevertheless tried to come to terms with the matter and believe they have been successful in individual cases. These analysts say that at a certain point in the analysis, and on the basis of the analytic material, they inform the student that the 'training' part of the analysis is over so far as they are concerned; the student, they say, is competent to analyze on his own and to go his own way. But, if he now wishes to continue, it will be as a 'free-floating' analysand: he is no longer *de facto*—only *de jure*—a student. According to their statements, this maneuver has been successful and has eliminated a good deal of irrelevant academic resistance. Other analysts say they do not need the maneuver: 'it happens'.

The time for this decision on the training analyst's part is based on clinical judgment, and the clinical signs will vary from student to student. The critical turn can be formulated in metapsychological terms approximately as follows. Appealing to Kris's well-known conception of regression in the service of the ego, and regarding the analytic process as a habituation to such a regression, we may set the moment as the one in which the student's ego has gained sufficient mastery over the regressive analytic state of mind, so that he can safely permit himself to adopt the relaxed, receptive, analyzing attitude recommended by Freud (1900-1901, p. 102) and described in The Interpretation of Dreams. The student's readiness and the training analyst's judgment will be tested by the student's success in adopting this 'analyzing position' with his first cases. This conception is influenced by Otto Isakower's ideas concerning the 'analyzing instrument'.

Ekstein (1953) has pointed out the difference between the older, small, patriarchal training groups and present-day, more professionally oriented schools. Some of the older 'patriarchal problems' are occasionally present in the professional schools, to complicate the 'reality' in which the training analysis takes place. Of former times, many bad opinions persist; 'nobody could be analyzed then' is one typical remark about this situation. It was nevertheless the case that successful training analyses did take place, and from long experience, one analyst has this to say: 'The quality of transference was the same all over, but the quantity was greater. Students, teachers and analysts met each other constantly. It was difficult for them and us to keep reality and fantasy apart. The negative transference remained in many instances unanalyzed,[2] and "reality" gave excellent rationalizations. Not only the students but we training analysts had constantly to analyze, to grasp the elements of real and fantasied situations. Even with this difficult situation, psychoanalysis worked, and I finally said to myself, "If psychoanalysis works, despite our mistakes, there must be something very solid in it." '

The point this teacher makes has a general bearing. Students and training analysts 'constantly analyzing' in this context means being aware consistently of the nature of their situation in the institute, being aware as exactly as possible of the details of their ambience and their 'ecology' as well as of their fantasies about it. Under special circumstances, our informant had been placed where such observation was a necessity; but this is a matter of degree, and knowledge concerning the workings of the school and its peculiar environment, in other words, awareness and insight—old psychoanalytic standbys—are of great service in elucidating the special local problems of the training analysis. The 'ecology' of the school is a necessary part of the 'analytic material' of a present-day training analysis. It is not always easy to sense. One thinks of Sir Oliver Lodge's mot, quoted by Alan Gregg (1956), that the last thing a deep-sea fish could discover is salt water.

It is interesting that the discussion of the training analysis entered the consciousness of analytic teachers because of a consideration of the 'termination of analysis' (Ferenczi and Rank, 1924), a subject to which several contributions have been made, mainly from the standpoint of technique. Some of the problems of termination are now spread, so that 'graduation' from the institute, usually after the analysis is over, has come to share some of the separation quality and to present some problems of its own. In the termination, much of the discussion revolves about the 'breaking of the transference'. Connected with this, and at one time a serious psy-

[2] A criticism frequently to be heard from teachers in several institutes, about their students and graduates.

chological and administrative problem, was the use of the training analyst as a model. An unresolved identification with the training analyst occurred more frequently in the 'patriarchal' days, when an institute might be dominated by one or a few persons, and is of rarer occurrence among institute students now. Here the transference may be spread as if to an institution (Reider, 1953), but ordinarily comes to be resolved by the well-known process of working through. The model taken for emulation need not be the training analyst. Ekstein (1953) remarks that a supervisor often serves as an identification model. The bit of self-analysis necessary for freedom is usually undertaken better because of the institute environment. Teachers come to be admired for their real learning and talents, i.e., for 'real' reasons, and not because of transference, *charisma* and *mana*. Some students (and patients in general) have a harder time 'finishing their analysis' than others, in this sense. Simmel, in an after-dinner speech of the 'kidding' type, at the 1929 Oxford Congress, commented on the round-table discussion on termination of analysis. So far as he was concerned, he said, only one psychoanalytic group was sure when this took place—Róheim's Central Australians. Their analysis ended either when the analyst ate up the patient or when the patient ate up the analyst.

The student's school problems are not entirely due to his 'being in analysis'. Such problems as the relation to teachers, the influence of models, and the process of superego alteration, are shared by students of many different types of schools. The fact that the student is in analysis, however, offers the teachers of the psychoanalytic institutes an exceptional opportunity to gain insight into the psychology and psychopathology of the educational process. At times, the training analysis has been given too much credit as an educational procedure. As students developed during their enrolment period and demonstrated greater and deeper understanding, their teachers tended to beam. Especially they have commented on how much the students' analysis did for them. Undoubtedly this is true in many respects. But the training analysis cannot possibly do the magic sometimes attributed to it. Adolf Meyer was fond of a joke which had to do with the benefits of hygiene, as portrayed at an exhibit of the National Tuberculosis Association. In an unhygienic room sat a suffering tuberculous man, a Negro. In the contrasting hygienic room sat a healthy man, and he was white. A sign said, 'Accomplished through hygiene'. When a sage of the analytic world was complimented on the 'wonderful result' of an analysis—the sort of obvious 'cure' for which doctors of all kinds have always been overcomplimented—he said that the qualities for which he was receiving praise had always been present, and that the analysis had had nothing to do with them.

It is again proper to point out that the teaching and the curriculum promote scholarship and the acquisition of practical expertness, and it is no aspersion on psychoanalysis to say that it alone will not produce a scholar or a professional. With the present-day interest in what it takes to make an educated and expert professional man or scientist, new knowledge will accumulate in the course of time at the institutes too. From the newer type of patients arise new problems that are being studied: the child, the psychotic, and 'the normal' are contributing to a new psychoanalytic psychiatry and a new psychoanalytic psychology. From the student 'material' at the training analysts' disposal there should arise a new psychoanalytic educational psychology and psychopathology.

The contents of this chapter have been very difficult to confine to the stated title, the training analysis. The literature, some of it very important, has dealt in large part with the problems of technique inherent in the student situation (G. Bibring, 1954) and inevitably touched upon the deeper issue of normality (Gitelson, 1954), both of which inevitably have invaded this account. It has been difficult, too, to avoid the more general problems of psychoanalytic education, which also go beyond the confines of the topic, particularly the typical school problem of reaction to rules.

It is clear, however, from several sources, that the matter of training analysis psychology in general has been progressing from that early stage when the status of student was merely regarded with annoyance, as a hindrance to analysis. Nor do the educators appear to be content with rule-making as the answer to educational problems, though this method was time-honored in the days of Isocrates, when the Athenians were building the Propylaea.

To give a realistic summary of the literature on the training analysis would involve more than the mention of papers containing the two words in their title. It runs over imperceptibly into the total matter of psychoanalytic technique and theory. The reader is referred to the series of articles on training analysis published in 1954 by G. Bibring, Gitelson, Balint, Heimann, and Lampl-de Groot; papers published in 1955 by Ekstein, Benedek, Weigert, and Windholz; and the Panel Report on Termination of Training Analysis (1955). From these papers and the bibliographies appended to them, the reader can gain access to all the relevant literature on the subject. The bibliographic references following Balint's 1947 paper include a convenient listing of Eitingon's reports as chairman of the International Training Commission from 1923 through 1938.

V. THE ORGANIZATION OF PSYCHOANALYTIC EDUCATION: HISTORICAL AND CURRENT*

The American Psychoanalytic Association approves fourteen institutes and four training centers.[1] For many years these institutes have been the standard organization for the teaching of psychoanalysis both in the United States and abroad. Historically, the older institutes originated as teaching arms of the several psychoanalytic societies which had been in existence for many years. The societies undertook the training of students in analysis informally, later with more organization. The first institute to be organized as such was in Berlin. This was in 1920, and there was considerable ambiguity in the naming. Max Eitingon, its dominant organizer and financial backer, accustomed to the European concepts of '*Ambulatorium*' and '*Poliklinik*', set up the institute (aided by Ernst Simmel and Karl Abraham) in connection with such a body. The early ideas of the teaching body were not treated very clearly from a semantic standpoint. It is not certain whether the teaching institute was considered to be a part of, or a correlated partner of, the *Poliklinik*. The polyclinic itself was opened on February 14, 1920, and on March 5, Karl Abraham gave the first lecture of a course on The Elements of Psychoanalysis.

Ambiguity enters here as to whether the organization was referred to as the institute or not, during its founding and early existence. In 1920 Eitingon's communication mentions the teaching but does not use the word 'institute'; the stress was entirely on the public service and the clinic. So far as published records are concerned, the word was used first at

* [From No. 113 in Bibliography.]

[1] In 1972, there were twenty-one approved institutes; all training centers referred to by Lewin are now approved institutes [Ed.].

a meeting of the Berlin Psychoanalytic Society on February 20, 1922, where it was called *unser poliklinisches Institut.* On June 22, 1923, the name was still unsettled; Simmel reported on the teaching at the *Poliklinik,* but at Salzburg in 1924, Simmel referred to the *Berliner Psychoanalytisches Institut.* After that this name appears regularly in the *Korrespondenzblatt* (the 'Bulletin') in the international journals.

So far as lecture courses at the *Institut* were concerned, they were open to any who wished to attend. One introduced oneself to the lecturer as a courtesy, formally asked permission to attend, and according to general convention, did not have to pay for the first lecture; the permission was formality, too. At first, there was no distinction between professional and 'extension' courses, no school enrolment, nor special prerequisites. The lectures were attended by all sorts of persons, and since they were held in the evening, and since evening extension schools of the type familiar also to New Yorkers (New School of Social Research) were popular and familiar, the *Institut* was considered loosely to fit into that category. Small groups met in the *Institut* quarters (a suite of rooms at Potsdamerstrasse 29); for larger crowds, rooms were rented from schools in the neighborhood. Among the heterogeneous listeners were included the enrolled students, who were also undergoing their didactic analyses, analyzing clinic cases under supervision, and attending the case conferences, which were not open to the public. The curriculum in principle was the same as that current today in all psychoanalytic institutes.

This somewhat informal and academically unofficial nature of institute training is reminiscent of the situation under which the Royal Society in London was established. In the seventeenth century, Gresham College was what we now call an 'extension school', with lectures open to the laity and to persons without prior university or secondary education. Among the lecturers were such famous scientists as Boyle and Hooke, and the faculty served as a nucleus around which the Royal Society was built.

In the early days it seems likely that many Berliners were more interested in the clinic than in the teaching and that the group went on for some time thinking of itself as a society with an attached outpatient clinic. However, in 1930 when the Ten Year Report appeared,[2] the *Institut,* calling itself the *Poliklinik und Lehranstalt,* claimed to be ten years old. Teaching under the aegis of the Berlin Psychoanalytic Society had gone on for some time, and it is probable that the name did not seem important. Again there is a historic parallel. The University of Paris, which has no idea really when the community of teachers and students became known as a 'university', arbitrarily decreed centuries later that its date of origin was 1200. The Royal Society and the University of Paris are not accidental analogues. The Berlin, Vienna, London, Budapest, New York, and Boston Societies were in effect teaching institutes, though not in name, for years before they adopted the name.

After several years of unincorporated society teaching, the Vienna Psychoanalytic Society opened its institute in January, 1925: an ambulatorium was already in existence. In the same year, the Institute of Psychoanalysis was founded in London, also in connection with a clinic. At the Bad Homburg Congress of the International Psycho-Analytical Association (1925) it was suggested that an International Training Commission be established to 'correlate as much as possible the methods of training candidates in the various societies and to provide opportunities for the common discussion of the technical problems concerned'. Such a body was formed and drew up a set of rules and standards of training which are essentially, except for details, still accepted today. Ives Hendrick (1961) has told how the early Boston group improved upon them. During World War II, the American Psychoanalytic Association became legislatively independent of this central International Training Commission. It had already in 1938 formulated its own minimal standards for training.

The dates and formal statements just given do not present a complete picture of psychoanalytic education in its beginnings. The reader is referred to the books by Brill (1946) and Oberndorf (1953) and to Hendrick's (1955) Presidential Address. As early as 1905, interested people met for weekly

[2] *Cf., Zehn Jahre Berliner Psychoanalytisches Institut (Poliklinik und Lehranstalt) 1920-1930.* Vienna: Internationaler Psychoanalytischer Verlag, 1930. (Reissued by the Berlin Psa. Institute. Meisenheim, Germany: Verlag Anton Hain KG, 1970 [Ed.]).

evening discussions in Freud's home. Brill describes the enthusiasm for psychoanalysis he found in 1907 in Bleuler's clinic in Zurich. Boston, too, had such informal interested groups. The pattern was the same in all cities. Discussion groups, originally informal and due to the interest of certain individuals, grew. They turned into societies and these found themselves called upon for more and more education. The New York Psychoanalytic Society was founded in 1931. What was called 'The American Psychoanalytic Association' began the same year, but the original membership and purposes of this body are still somewhat obscure. It became a 'Federation' of American psychoanalytic societies only in 1933.

Before the founding of the institutes, psychoanalytic training became organized gradually under education committees in each recognized society, particularly in those which followed the international training regulations mentioned above. In the 1920's, a large body of Americans went abroad to study at the European centers, some before and some after the formal establishment of the foreign institutes. Adolph Stern from New York is said to have been the first. In this they simply followed the customs of the time. There was then no cut-and-dried residency training in the medical specialties. If an American physician wished to become a specialist, so-called, he studied a year, more or less, as a journeyman at some important center of medical education. Vienna was, for instance, a Mecca for those who wished to be known as 'laryngologists', and it was in the mores for Americans to study abroad in this way. The first American psychiatrists who had been psychoanalyzed and trained abroad at the institutes returned to this country, and along with those older colleagues already in practice, and later with emigrating Europeans, joined our societies and set about emulating the European institutes. In the Presidential Address already mentioned, Hendrick (1955) gives an eloquent detailed description of those interesting years of development. The same paper contains a useful account of the role played by The American Psychoanalytic Association in psychoanalytic education.

Three institutes were officially opened in the United States, and a fourth was forming in 1932 and 1933, when the American Association was being reorganized into a federation. In general, usage of the word 'institute' to mean an organization for instruction in literature, arts, sciences, or education is recent. (The Oxford Dictionary gives the orginal date for this usage as 1829.) The word 'institution' used in this same sense, as in the title Smithsonian Institution, goes back only to 1800. The new usage appeared first in 1795, with the *Institut de France,* founded to promote the arts and sciences. The *Institut de France* is now a union of four previously existing *académies*. The original meaning was a code of laws, like that of Justinian. The new definition, however, employed in connection with such bodies as the Rockefeller Institute, the Institut Pasteur, and the Kaiser Wilhelm Institut, is now the more familiar one in scientific circles.

Despite a nearly uniform purpose and aim, the American psychoanalytic institutes have evolved in ways which produce differences in organization and function and in their local terminology. Local historical factors are responsible for the differences, even though ivy and moss have not dug too deeply into the walls. The most important difference in respect to organization is defined by the individual institute's relationship to a psychoanalytic society or to the medical department of a university, which naturally permits a three-way classification: 1, institutes that are university-connected; 2, society-institutes; and 3, so-called 'independent' institutes, which means independent of both society and university. Of those approved by The American Psychoanalytic Association, we have four[3] university-connected institutes, the connection in all cases being with departments of psychiatry in medical schools. They share certain original features, unknown to most other groups. For instance, the word 'institute' does not appear in the title of the two older full-grown university organizations. One is called Columbia Psychoanalytic Clinic; the other is a *Division* of the Department of Psychiatry in the University of the State of New York (Downstate). Nor does the word appear in the official university bulletins, which speak of 'graduate training programs' in psychoanalysis. The American Psychoanalytic Association, of course, recognizes them as institutes, but the Columbia organization is unique, that of an

[3] Numbers and dates in this essay have been revised by the author, as of July, 1961. (The 1972 figure for university-connected institutes is five [Ed.].)

outpatient clinic in the medical school and not the hospital. The Cleveland Psychoanalytic Institute is officially part of the Western Reserve Medical School. The psychoanalytic teachers are on the staff of this school, and in the catalogue are directly called psychoanalysts; that is, there is a Professor of Psychoanalysis and a Professor of Child Psychoanalysis, who are *not,* as in the other schools, concealing their specialty (or subspecialty) under psychiatric titles or appointments. Graduates of the Columbia and State of New York institutes join recognized psychoanalytic societies which have no official connection whatsoever with the schools. A Columbia teacher said that the 'cognate' society has no more relation to Columbia than does the New York County Medical Society. A new psychoanalytic society was formed in Cleveland in 1957, also with no official connection with the school.

In addition to these three schools, through the Western Psychiatric Institute of the State of Pennsylvania, the University of Pittsburgh had an agreement with the Philadelphia Psychoanalytic Society whereby some teachers of the University were appointed teachers of psychoanalysis at the Society's Institute. (This Institute was a society-institute type at the time, a single corporation, which became two separate corporations legally in 1956.) The education of psychoanalytic students took place partly in Pittsburgh, but under the auspices of the Philadelphia Psychoanalytic Institute. There was no Pittsburgh training center.[4]

Besides these formal arrangements and organizations, in many other 'institute cities' there are informal connections between the institutes and the local teaching hospitals and universities. Despite the lack of coöperative written agreements or any other formal arrangement, institute and society members often hold positions of top rank in other institutions of learning and in psychiatric hospitals. The students of this postgraduate type of educational organization also work and teach in these organizations. Not only members of psychoanalytic societies, but students also, very often hold high academic rank in such schools. It has been estimated that about three-quarters of the training analysts have other important teach-

[4] In May, 1961, the teaching body became the Pittsburgh Psychoanalytic Institute.

ing positions; and among the students are professors, deans, a state commissioner of mental hygiene, etc.

The two institutes connected with universities in New York City are built around outpatient clinics. One of them *is* a clinic, and its organization and working cannot be understood without taking this fact seriously. For example, psychoanalytic patients may be demonstrated before the Columbia classes, a common clinic practice. The State of New York staff runs a large psychotherapy clinic at Kings County Hospital in Brooklyn. At Columbia the word 'clinic' takes the place of the word 'institute' elsewhere. Students speak of themselves as students of the clinic; later on, graduates say they are graduates of the clinic. In an odd way, this goes back to the Berlin precedent, where there was the same institute-clinic fusion or confusion. This furnishes an interesting nuance of the meaning of psychoanalytic education in connection with a medical school. According to Dr. Howard Potter, another model for the structure of the Columbia Clinic was provided by the old New York State Psychiatric Institute on Ward's Island, which gave courses for workers in the State Hospital System. Under Meyer, Hoch, and Kirby, patients of the Manhattan State Hospital were used for research; and Brill gave lectures on psychoanalysis. When the Psychiatric Institute joined the Columbia-Presbyterian Medical Center, it was natural to think of a clinic-institute arrangement.

We now come to the more frequent arrangement for psychoanalytic institutes. These we have called the *'society-institutes'*. In Berlin, in the early days, we find Simmel and others speaking of the Institute of the Berlin Psychoanalytic Society, for the reason which Hendrick's (1961) paper on the growth of psychoanalytic teaching in Boston makes clear. The psychoanalytic society has usually been the matrix from which the institute was developed, and for a long while, except in Chicago, psychoanalytic institute and psychoanalytic society have been in effect the same body in respect of membership. Teaching began under the auspices of the Education Committees of the respective societies even before the institutes were officially formed. The Education Committee of the New York Society was set up in 1925, and by 1929 had a fairly complete educational program which included training analysis, supervisory work, lectures, and seminars. The Institute opened in September, 1931, but apparently, like all psychoanalytic organizations, it is bad at numbers, for until last year it gave this date as 1932, when it got its legal charter from the State of New York. In 1931, Sandor Rado was invited over from Berlin to be its educational director, and the new Institute adopted the standards already set up by the International Training Commission. Around this time and for some time previously, it was the custom for some Americans trained abroad, no matter where they lived over here, to join the New York Society. This gave them membership in the International Association as well, so that at one time a number of members residing in Boston, Philadelphia, and elsewhere were members of the New York Society. In many ways this promoted a more national view of the psychoanalytic movement in America.

That out-of-towners belonged to the New York Society disturbed no one. In Europe, there were members of the Berlin Society working in Dresden, Frankfurt, and Baden-Baden, and the name of the Society later was changed to *Deutsche Psychoanalytische Gesellschaft.* In those days, all members of the International felt at home in all psychoanalytic societies. Freud himself set the pattern, according to several informants, by asking members from out of town who were visiting in Vienna to remain and participate, not only in the scientific sessions, but in the business meetings as well. He stated that all psychoanalysts were members of all psychoanalytic societies; in this and in many other ways, Freud expressed his sense of the oneness of the profession.

The story of Boston in those years has been told by Ives Hendrick and needs no repetition here. About this time a number of psychoanalysts in Washington and Baltimore also decided to start an institute. Ernest Hadley discussed the matter with Brill and wished to establish an institute on the model of New York and Boston. When Dr. William Alanson White was consulted, he suggested setting up a body with a larger aim, which would teach psychiatry, anthropology, social work, and biology. Hence for some time there was confusion between the Washington School of Psychiatry and the Washington-Baltimore Psychoanalytic Institute. Some classes met together, and there was some organizational conflict in relation to the American Association, which has since been cleared up. There is now no official connection between the Washington Psychoanalytic Institute and the William Alanson White School of Psychiatry in Washington.

In this country, the impetus given by the formation of the first institutes led to the formation of new societies and institutes, and the founding of the institutes made a great impression on young psychiatrists. With European teachers of established reputation—Rado in New York, Alexander in Boston and later Chicago, Sachs in Boston, Nunberg in Philadelphia, Simmel in Los Angeles, etc.—numerous psychiatrists entered psychoanalytic training. Many of them were well along in their careers, others at what would now be called the residency level. This increased the mutual influence of psychoanalytic and psychiatric education in this country, an influence steadily growing ever since.

The Institute of Psychoanalysis in Chicago had a somewhat different organizational history. Because it is not related either to a university or to a society, it is sometimes called an 'independent' institute. It is legally a membership corporation of trustees, until recently not psychoanalysts, who elect a Director of the Institute, one of the few provisions in the brief by-laws. The Director then appoints the staff and all committees, theoretically quite independently. His independence is of course dependent on the good will of the people working with him, and in fact also on the good will of the large psychoanalytic population in the city, who coöperate with the Institute. Chicago's uniqueness lies really in its history and original conception. From the start, the Institute was designed as a research organization. It set research on a level with teaching, and immediately studied certain selected groups of patients—for example, patients with asthma and with gastric ulcers—using psychoanalysis as a research method. This was particularly important for psychiatry in Chicago. Previously, the psychiatric hospitals in Chicago had not been teaching and research hospitals, so that young psychiatrists went elsewhere for their training. The psychoanalysts were thus called upon to do what Phipps Clinic in Baltimore, or the old Boston Psychopathic, or the Psychiatric Institute in

New York did. It is astonishing for one accustomed to psychiatry in the older centers to learn what responsibility for psychoanalysis was put on the Chicago Institute, and what a success the students and graduates of the Institute made of carrying out this mission. Such names as Grinker, Levine, Brosin, Rosenbaum, Carmichael, and others immediately occur to us in this connection.

The training centers, which in Isakower's phrase are each anaclitic to one of the older institutes, are embryonic institutes. There are now two of them; they furnish part of the analytic curriculum, and the sponsoring institute tries to complete their work in whatever respect they are lacking. They differ a good deal in how much they are able to accomplish. A somewhat different method of beginning new groups with a small number of training analysts was demonstrated by the Pittsburgh situation mentioned previously. The Pittsburgh analysts were integrally part of the Philadelphia Psychoanalytic Society and Institute, were in society and institute membership 'Philadelphians' resident in Pittsburgh; the new Pittsburgh institute was formed by a sort of mitosis.

Statistics about the institutes may be deferred; there will be many in the coming reports of the Survey (Lewin and Ross, 1960). I may mention that in March, 1958, there were in the United States 259 officially designated training analysts, of whom 228 were functioning as such. There were 221 active as supervisors of students' clinical work, and 343 teachers of all kinds. At about the same time, there were 888 students, 15 of them research or special students in non-medical professions, the rest with medical degrees. For the past five years [since 1958], the student population figures were 832, 870, 910, 873, and 888. The population of the schools has not grown during these years, nor have the institutes grown very much. The main reason for the spread of psychoanalytic training has been the founding of new institutes, such as the one at the University of the State of New York in Brooklyn, the Western New England Institute, and the separation into two bodies of the original institutes in Philadelphia and Los Angeles. New psychiatric opportunities near Washington have brought about an increased student population in that city's institute. The American analysts are aging, there is an appreciable death rate, and whatever expansion may be taking place, we do not yet need birth control. The analytic population in general is at an even level, and everybody will have enough to eat. In September, 1958, there were 610 students in analysis.

Since the first American institutes were modeled on the continental European ones, especially the Berlin Institute, a few more words about the latter are in order. I mentioned the *Poliklinik* in Berlin. In Germany, a polyclinic might be connected with a university or teaching hospital, or it might be operated privately. German medicine and the public were used to this sort of 'outsider', and they used a modification of the English word to characterize it—*Aussenseiter.* For example, Ehrlich was accounted such an outsider, and there were arbitrary restrictions on appointments to the universities. However, there were none on private enterprise, once the official permission was obtained for a clinic. And in this Central European tradition, Eitingon and his colleagues saw a polyclinic organization as a hopeful center for psychoanalytic education, despite the fact that initially Eitingon's stress was on the service to the neurotically ill. It happened that American physicians were accustomed to this type of overseas graduate education.

The institutes in Berlin, later in Vienna, Budapest, and elsewhere, inaugurated all the educational methods that we still employ: the training (or 'didactic') analysis, supervised clinical work, clinical seminars, and reading courses. Though Karl Abraham had not been analyzed, Eitingon had made an attempt of this kind, after it had been recommended by Freud in 1910 as an aid to the practice of psychoanalysis. We know a good deal more about the reasons for Freud's opinion on this matter since Ernest Jones (1953-1957) published his biography and since the appearance of Freud's (1887-1902) letters to Wilhelm Fliess. By 1920 the procedure of training analysis was prevalent, though it had not yet received this name, nor was it yet a compulsory prerequisite for admission to a psychoanalytic society. It was still up to the individual, and American societies admitted unanalyzed persons to membership as late as 1925. Interestingly enough, many of the unanalyzed undertook a personal psychoanalysis on their own in consequence of their professional experience. The practice gradually turned into a tradition, and the procedure generated the special name, *Lehranalyse* or *didaktische Analyse,* training or educational analysis, preparatory analysis, etc., of which terms the most common today is 'training analysis'. In 1919 we find Ferenczi arguing its advisability, and in 1925 it was recommended by the International Training Commission. Herman Nunberg is stated by Eitingon to have been its first public exponent, at the Congress at Budapest in 1919. Eitingon, founder of the Berlin Psychoanalytic Institute, was in a way the Euclid of the movement, in that he turned common notions into axioms.

The history of the supervision of students' cases is harder to get at. It too started with the common practice of getting help by consulting an older and more experienced colleague from time to time. With no rules setting the number or the frequency of the supervisory hours, analysts working with the polyclinic cases did, in fact, report to their supervisors weekly. Again common practice became enshrined in rules. Many American students, returning from the European institutes and feeling the need for more supervision, turned for help to their more experienced American colleagues. Thus the practice of supervised work became established in this country even before any rules or any institutes were invented. It was also common for ex students of Freud to write him when they encountered a puzzling case, and they received often long and always conscientiously detailed letters in reply. The late A. A. Brill told me about such a correspondence concerning a case of fetishism, before Freud had printed anything on this subject. Freud's letter had given him the clue that solved the case. Many of these letters, from various sources, have been collected by the Sigmund Freud Archives and are deposited in the Library of Congress, awaiting eventual publication.

In the early days of the institutes, though in general procedures were rational, the students and the rules were few. In those days, though there was no formal graduation, admission to a society took place when it was known that training was complete. This and similar facts made difficulties for the Survey of Psychoanalytic Education (Lewin and Ross, 1960) when we tried to learn certain statistical facts.

Semantic traces in our vocabulary attest to our early relationship with the German-speaking countries. The word 'candidate' is used as a synonym for student in many of the institutes. It was a literal taking-over of the common German word *Kandidat. Candidate,* for *student,* is almost limited to the psychoanalytic institutes. It appears in the catalogues not only of American institutes, but is used also by the British and the Indians. In fact, the word 'student' was, so far as I know, introduced in New York to keep the students there from thinking they were candidates or nominees for membership in the Society, or that they were running for some office. A similar untranslated adoption is found in the word 'control', used in some institutes for the more usual 'supervision'. It comes from the German word *Kontrolle,* which does not mean 'control' at all. This word once caused heated argument in the League of Nations, for it appeared in the two forms just given in the Treaty of Versailles concerning armaments. The Germans thought that their arming was to be *kontrolliert,* supervised, while the English assumed it was to be *controlled,* i.e., ruled. In those institutes which used 'control' and 'candidate', the meaning of these words has been altered, just as the word 'anxiety', now generally used to translate the German word *Angst,* has gradually come to have a new meaning in American psychiatry, and indeed in the English-speaking world.

If the meaning of certain words has changed in the last three or four decades, so has the attitude of the medical profession, and to a certain extent for the same reason—that familiarity with psychoanalysts and psychoanalysis has been increasing. In the early and mid-twenties psychoanalytic procedures and societies were looked on locally with some suspicion. In 1927 the New York County Medical Society sent word to the psychoanalytic society of that city that it viewed with misgivings the presence of laymen among its members; the representative stated that even a psychoanalytically untrained member would be perfectly proper from the official point of view, provided only this person was a medical graduate and had a license. Even before this, Clarence Oberndorf had tried to establish a clinic on the Berlin model. A distinguished medical man, representing the New York State Board of

Education, explained to him that the Board had its doubts about psychoanalysis. He himself knew a happily married couple who went to Zurich to consult Carl Jung, and after only a short while they were divorced; this gave psychoanalysis a black eye with him. Dr. Oberndorf also learned that, though his informant and others had the highest respect for certain members of the psychoanalytic society individually, taken as a mass they formed a *grumus merdae* which might best be left to evaporate on the road. If there was to be a clinic, some responsible school or hospital should back it.

The magic of words! How happily the word 'institute' solved these difficulties. It seemed much more responsible than a society, even though its membership was precisely the same. A permanent address, licensing by the State Department of Education, impressive stationery with letterheads (American equivalent of the *Stempel* used by Eitingon, as he said, to impress the officials in Berlin)—all these were most reassuring. This reassurance was not limited to the official world. Young doctors also gained assurance. It became most respectable to study at an institute, instead of merely with a group of private practitioners. In every city where an institute was established, there was a notable increase in psychoanalytic training, and in respect for it at all social levels in the community. The larger body, politic and professional, began to accept some responsibility too. As everyone knows, responsibility brings with it power. Freud's (1926) book on lay analysis and the discussion in the *International Journal of Psycho-Analysis* brought organized medicine actively onto the scene, especially in New York City when the County Medical Society's Chairman of the Comitia Minora got after the New York Society. It is well to remember the good effect of organized medicine's interest, including that which came from the investigation of psychoanalysis by the British Medical Association. The report of this inquiry defined the practice of psychoanalysis as the use of Freud's concepts and techniques, and has been called by Ernest Jones the Magna Carta of psychoanalysis. Americans have shared in the results of this Runnymede, as they had in the charter signed by King John, for the approval of so powerful a body as the British Medical Association impressed the American representatives of organized medicine.

It is well, too, to recall why American medicine was so sensitive to the matter of standards at the time. Abraham Flexner's memorable book had appeared in 1910, and he had done a wonderful social-work job on American medical schools, most of which were educational slums. He visited them, exited, quickly holding his nose, and recommended the common social-work remedies: better housing, better education, more money. Flexner's standards were high, and his practicality was outstanding. He took what had been set up in Europe and at the Johns Hopkins Medical School as goals for shooting at. Because of the Flexner Report, everyone in medicine and medical education was alert to the matter of standards, and those who looked quizzically at the plans of the psychoanalysts had already been sensitized to the educational problems by these recent medical reforms.

Another concept that entered into the founding of the psychoanalytic institutes was also derived from the new look in American medical education. This is the notion of the graduate school. The requirement of a preliminary academic degree for admission to a medical school also came from the European continent and was introduced cisatlantically at the Johns Hopkins Medical School. The late Franklin P. Mall was its most consistent exponent there. He modeled his anatomy department strictly on a graduate-school plan. There were no lectures, no quizzes, no assigned reading; in fact, there were really no assignments of any kind, only daily rounds by instructors to supervise the dissections. The idea behind this system had a strong influence on the educational thinking of many members of the early institutes, particularly on those who had received their education in Europe. The book Psychoanalytic Education in the United States (Lewin and Ross, 1960) will give some interesting data concerning the medical background of our teachers, with implications of the meaning of this for the institutes' educational philosophies.

The acculturation of psychoanalytic education to the American milieu has taken an interesting and nearly foreordained path. Many alien factors were assimilated by the American schools, many older American ones transformed or accepted without always being thoroughly digested. The originators and organizers of the institutes were serious in their purpose, not always aware of the coming problems and difficulties. Through the years, the institutes have periodically realized the fact that education, and psychoanalytic education in particular, must be faced with all available intelligence. The Survey of Psychoanalytic Education in the United States, proposed many years ago, finally got under way in 1956, and is certainly testimony to this fact. The teachers at the institutes are forced to see themselves in a role beyond the boundary of therapeutic skills and competence as psychoanalytic practitioners. In other words, the practicing psychoanalyst has had slowly to develop into the psychoanalytic educator.

What this signifies would certainly astonish Abraham and Ferenczi if they were alive. Psychoanalytic training has profoundly affected the post-graduate teaching of psychiatrists. In the shape of analytically influenced 'residency training' in many parts of the country, and without especially wishing it, the analytic institutes have been used as models for residency instruction in many ways. New problems beset the institutes in relation to what has been called 'advanced study', the educational activities of their graduates which have been proceeding informally almost everywhere and have been partly organized in at least one of the older institutes.

With seventeen institutes and two training centers in this country, there has been inevitably great variety in detail. Yet the core of one astonishingly resembles the core of its contemporaries, and the over-all picture is one of solidarity. In the attainment of the present excellences, and in the striving for more, the Boston Psychoanalytic Society and Institute has been consistent, furnishing leadership and a cohesive body of the best opinion and devotion.

VI. AMERICAN PSYCHOANALYTIC EDUCATION: HISTORICAL COMMENTS*

The publication of the book, Psychoanalytic Education in the United States, has had several interesting side results. A valuable one has been to arouse the attention and thought of experienced and knowledgeable outside educators in what we are doing, and some of them have expressed their views on education and on us in writing. Among these critics, Seward Hiltner, Professor of Theology at the University of Chicago, has written an article I have been privileged to read in manuscript, which contains this flattering comment on the service to education by psychoanalysts.

> The service is plainly magnificent and munificent. . . . Even if the motives for this service are as mixed as psychoanalysis demonstrates all human motivation to be, the conclusion is plain that of him who has more, more is expected, in other words that he exercises orders of professional responsibility which are vital to the existence of the profession . . . , not even considered by the average practitioner. Psychoanalytic reluctance over claiming moral virtue ought certainly not to obscure the facts. And perhaps it would not be out of accord with psychoanalytic wisdom to suggest that inverted pride is still pride.

When we recall how often psychoanalysts have been asked to consider their evil ways and repent, it is certainly refreshing and gratifying to find a theologian, who asks us to stop and consider whether we are not repressing an unconscious sense of virtue. If Dr. Hiltner is correct, we must admit that, for all our insistent and constant need for insight, we have rarely or ever thought of the matter and have taken our

* [No. 116 in Bibliography.].

Presented at the 1961 Annual Meeting of The American Psychoanalytic Association, dedicated to the Fiftieth Anniversary of its founding [Ed.].

service in this field for granted. The duty to educate must have been built into our archaic psychoanalytic ego very early in our history, and it would indeed be proper for us to dig it up. It seems that every psychoanalyst has in his knapsack a schoolmaster's ferule. We find him teaching not only in our own institutes but in schools of social work, in psychiatric and other university departments, in hospitals and agencies, in extension courses of all sorts. In many capacities, official and unofficial, continuous and sporadic, the psychoanalyst is in fact a teacher. This fact also did not escape Dr. Hiltner's notice and gracious comment. The stereotype, which depicts the psychoanalyst as devoting full time to avaricious pursuits and extra time to an ivory-tower seclusion, is out of date, particularly, our well-disposed critics see, when it comes to education.

Within the larger educational role played by psychoanalysts, there is of course one near to their heart, namely, the training of psychoanalysts. Long before there were organized institutes indeed from the very beginning of psychoanalysis—analysts have tacitly assumed the mission to educate and to carry on the task of training new psychoanalysts. This task has become more specialized and more professional, but we still fulfil that part of the Hippocratic Oath which calls upon us to be teachers.

I began with the quotation from Dr. Hiltner and with general remarks in order to broaden the scope of the topic I was asked to present on this jubilee of our Association, and I shall not repeat many of the significant dates and events which have been well presented in Hendrick's 1955 presidential address and in Oberndorf's (1953) book. My aim is rather to present American psychoanalytic education as a dynamic substance, an ideal matter of the mind, and to give a perspective of its development in terms of the various elements, native and foreign, of which it is composed. Like so many American things, psychoanalytic education is American in its accent and development but with many European antecedents and wellsprings. For many years before NATO was formed, we have been members of the cultural Atlantic community.

In this sense, you will hear without surprise that American psychoanalytic education began in Vienna around 1905, when the first small group of interested persons met on Wednesday evenings at Freud's home in the Berggasse to learn psychoanalysis, a group prototypic of our informal and formal study groups and of our formally enrolled students. American psychoanalytic education, furthermore, can be traced to the Burghölzli Hospital near Zurich, where in 1907 A. A. Brill learned of psychoanalysis and its applications from Eugen Bleuler and Carl G. Jung. Another date and a more native one in the history of psychoanalytic education is 1909, when at G. Stanley Hall's invitation, Freud delivered his lectures at Clark University. These well-known facts and dates belong in this account because they betoken that Americans were being educated in psychoanalysis long before there were institutes and before 1911, the year we are celebrating today. In 1911, we find the opening address at the Weimar Congress given by James J. Putnam, and as if to show that psychoanalysts were from the beginning educators too, we find that, in 1914, Putnam read before the American Neurological Association a paper titled, Psychoanalysis Considered as a Phase of Education (Putnam, 1914).

Adolf Meyer, as well as Putnam, attended the Clark University lectures. Later, when he became Director of the Psychiatric Institute of the State of New York, psychoanalytic ideas began to be taught in courses given to physicians. In the State Hospital Bulletin for 1909-1910, we find his name as a reviewer and critic of Freud in an article titled, A Discussion of Some Fundamental Issues in Freud's Psycho-Analysis (Meyer, 1909-1910). Meyer and his successor at the Psychiatric Institute, August Hoch, had been interested in Freud's writings for many years—perhaps their Swiss nativity and education had kept them closely informed concerning the penetration of psychoanalysis into Swiss psychiatry—but Meyer had studied under Krafft-Ebing in Vienna and had known Freud's works for many years. He once told me that he had been attracted to Freud's thought not alone because of their common interest in aphasia (and Meyer was one of the first to do Freud justice for his point of view) but because of Freud's (1894) paper on the defense neuropsychoses with its ingenious approach to the psychology of paranoia, which for some reason Meyer read only some years later. Meyer said that this paper had impressed him more than Kraepelin's textbook, with which it was approximately contemporary.

It is a fact that so far as psychoanalytic education is concerned, 1911 is not a particularly memorable date, although the events of that year were indeed portentous. It saw the founding of the New York Psychoanalytic Society and of the old American Psychoanalytic Association, but these two were organized under the impetus of the founding of the International Psycho-Analytical Association the same year. It was a year of beginning organization, however, and psychoanalytic education became organized because of the year's events.

The moving spirit in the founding of the New York Psychoanalytic Society was A. A. Brill, but in 1911 he was engaged in what must have seemed more important tasks than the founding of the Society. I refer to his work of translating Freud's papers on hysteria and The Interpretation of Dreams. The latter book, which appeared in English in 1913,[1] provided him especially with a formidable task. Brill's translations mark real steps in psychoanalytic education. Even today many future psychoanalysts begin their analytic education, perhaps while they are in high school, by reading his translation of the book on dreams or perhaps his translation of The Psychopathology of Everyday Life or some other of Freud's works. Ernest Jones and others have criticized Brill's translations, but such criticism cannot detract from our appreciation of Brill's immense contribution. In any historic consideration of psychoanalytic education in the United States and other English-speaking countries, his place is secure. Deservedly his portrait is on the medal which each president of this Association receives on the expiration of office as a memento of service.

For all his courage and devotion, Brill was a modest man. Apropos of criticism of his translations, he once said to me, 'It's all very well for people to point out mistakes in my translations, but when I started I had nothing to go by. I had to worry whether to translate *Verdrängung* as "repression" or "suppression". I had to make the decisions myself. Because

[1] See, Abraham A. Brill's translation of *The Interpretation of Dreams*. New York: The Macmillan Co., 1913.

I worried, you fellows have it a lot easier.' And this is strictly true. Mr. Strachey—and surely no one knows better—has recently expressed his appreciation of Brill,[2] and if one examines the psychoanalytic papers written in English around 1910 one can confirm what Brill says. Writers had not decided what should be the English translation of many terms. For example, the word 'anxiety' left something to be desired as a translation of *Angst,* and our early analytic authors, who after all had studied German texts, were not thinking in English and were timid. One finds even Ernest Jones not entirely confident about the translation of *Angst* and *Zwang* and leaving them in their German form in the middle of the English text. 'Cathexis' as a term was not yet coined; there was only *Besetzung.* Many translations at that time remind one of present-day translations into the Japanese, where suddenly among the Chinese characters one comes across a word printed in Latin letters, for instance, *Überich* or *superego.*

Any historian of civilization realizes the great importance of translators. In the twelfth century, such men as Gerard of Cremona, who translated the works of the Arabs after the capture of Toledo, including Arabic translations from the Greek, were real culture-bringers. The words that had to be invented then were such important ones as *sine* and *zero.* The recent retranslation of the Bible has brought into prominence the merits and services of the translators of the King James version. Similarly, so far as the history of psychoanalytic education is concerned, and in the context of the time, the work of Brill and of later British and American translators was more valuable than the organization of the societies, portentous as this proved to be when seen in retrospect. From the point of view of education and psychoanalysis generally, the translations may be said to have led to both education and organization, for this type of education promoted gatherings and the exchange of ideas. The informal groups that met in Freud's home or in the offices of New York doctors or in hospital staff rooms were not only germinal spots of all our societies and institutes. They were also foci of education and study.

[2] See, Editor's Introduction to Freud (1901): *The Psychopathology of Everyday Life.* Standard Edition, VI, p. xi.

In the days before societies and then institutes began to organize education in psychoanalysis, the study groups and the budding societies grew out of the psychoanalytic instruction which was then available. In the main this was the personal analysis. Those who for one or another reason had undergone a personal analysis were the very persons who were to organize. And when later on, after Nunberg's prophetic remark at the Budapest Congress, we began to speak of a *Lehranalyse* and a didactic analysis, this was no more than terminological recognition—a statement of a fact well understood—that the personal analysis was an educational procedure, and that persons who had been analyzed had also received education. I have mentioned previously James J. Putnam's realization of this fact. Indeed, not long after, professional educators became interested in psychoanalysis so to say professionally, and the interaction of psychoanalysis and education is still growing.

So, historically speaking, psychoanalytic education in America was proceeding according to its own endogenous laws: future psychoanalysts were getting analyzed. From around 1910 on, several began their analysis as best they could, and at the end of the First World War Americans began to go to Vienna for this purpose. Adolph Stern was the first of these (1919), after him many others. Our European colleagues' awareness that psychoanalytic education could be organized and be made relatively systematic led to the founding of the institutes over there, the first in Berlin in 1920. So far as American education was concerned, this still consisted mainly in the contribution of American students to the new European institutes, although informally people were also being trained over here.

The European organization of education then proceeded to give a direct powerful impetus to American psychoanalytic education and organization. The International Congress at Bad Homburg on September 5, 1925, passed a fateful resolution: psychoanalytic training was no longer to be the responsibility of individual psychoanalysts but of the societies and their institutes. The International Training Commission was set up, and each society was asked to choose seven persons as members of this central committee. Locally, these persons were later to become the education committee. The societies little realized what was to come of this simple organizational move. The local education committees of the societies, later of the institutes, called thus into life were ready-made organizations when education became an increasingly important function of the local groups. As a type of organization it was on the whole well adapted to the needs of psychoanalytic education for many years in many cities. Thus, American psychoanalytic educational organization in a very important aspect dates back to 1925 and to Bad Homburg.

It is interesting to note how America responded to Eitingon's new idea of organization. The minutes of the New York Psychoanalytic Society show that nineteen members met at the office of Dr. Joseph J. Asch on October 27, 1925. Clarence P. Oberndorf reported on the proceedings of the Bad Homburg Congress. Not much attention was paid to the organizational suggestions. The main topic of interest was the controversial matter of the admission to training of nonmedical persons. There was now an international agreement to admit for training only applicants approved by the local societies, and a certain lay applicant who knew of this rule asked the approval of the New York Society so that he might properly apply for training at the Berlin Institute. The meeting did not quite know what to do about this new situation. Finally after discussion, someone suggested that the matter be referred to the new education committee, which, the minutes tell us, 'was forthwith appointed'. Thus, this important step was taken almost casually and in the context of setting up what we should now call an admissions committee. As to the American Psychoanalytic Association, which at that time was not a federation but a kind of society that met for a dinner scientific program one evening a year, with membership small and scattered, the New Yorkers unthinkingly usurped its powers and authority. They decided at the same meeting not to have a separate education committee for that body but to see to it that four of the New York committee members should also be members of the American. This provision was of course soon forgotten and the American doubtless never heard of the matter.

Odd as this seems now, the action represented the then-existing situation. For before the reorganization and federalization of the American Association in 1933, this body played no role in psychoanalytic education. It was a small dwindling group and it barely escaped being dissolved in 1919, when William Alanson White moved such action. Its life was then saved by the counterarguments of Adolf Meyer.

Dr. Oberndorf's attendance at the Bad Homburg Congress was mentioned above. American psychoanalysts had participated in such meetings from the time of the founding of the International Association in 1911. The meetings were held in beautiful and agreeable places such as Salzburg, Innsbruck, Nuremberg, and Oxford, usually in August, and Americans became well acquainted with European colleagues. American doctors of those days often went to Europe, spent a year in postgraduate work, and returning to the United States were considered specialists. It was more or less in this tradition that the first American psychoanalysts had gone to Vienna for their personal analysis. After the organization of the Berlin institute and of those in Vienna, London, and Budapest, the number increased. Organization itself seems to promote such action, and when the American institutes were opened, this too served as a stimulus to young psychiatrists to enter psychoanalytic training.

Education at the European institutes naturally led to the founding of the American schools, beginning with that of the New York Psychoanalytic Institute in 1931, of the Institute in Chicago nearly simultaneously in 1932, then of the one in Boston, and very soon after that the founding of systematic education in the Baltimore-Washington conurbation. The existence of the institutes and the sense of common aims led to the reorganization of the American into a federation. This in turn accelerated education. Even before the formal opening of the institutes, the larger groups were in fact giving fairly complete instruction. The education committees came into their own, taking over not only the functions of an admissions committee but also devising curricula, judging the progression of students, of their fitness for graduation, appointing teachers, and in general administering the school with all the incidental functions of a school faculty. There was a gradual metamorphosis of a scientific society with great educational interest into a primarily and dominantly educational body.

Among the normal steps in this evolution in those days was the invitation to distinguished foreign analysts to give their experience to the organization of the American institutes. The increasingly disturbed political situation in Europe was America's gain. Rado became the first director of education at the New York Institute. Sachs went to Boston, Alexander first to Boston then to Chicago, Nunberg to Philadelphia, and Simmel to the West Coast. Through the years to follow, such enrichment of American psychoanalytic education continued. As Professor Freud said when he first saw his beautiful house in Maresfield Gardens, 'Heil, Hitler!'.

The development of psychoanalytic education, particularly in its organizational aspects, has been well told by Ives Hendrick (1955) in the paper referred to on a previous page. There, as well as in the book, Psychoanalytic Education in the United States, are relevant information and the dates that mark the increasing interest of the Association in education from the time of its real beginning in 1933. You can also read of the great development that came with the postwar years, how the institutes faced and, after some years, partly solved the problems that came with the great popularity of psychoanalysis as science and therapy among the younger psychiatrists. I shall not repeat what has been said. Rather I should like to venture some remarks concerning the spread of psychoanalytic education, of its effects on other educational disciplines, and on particular patterns. This is, someone once said, a large country; despite our excellent and speedy systems of communication we psychoanalysts till recently knew little about what went on in psychoanalytic education in distant cities, or even in near ones. Miss Ross and I believe that many analysts first learned of the organization and policies of institutes other than their own by reading our book. We have sometimes been reminded of the way in which Boston communicated with New York during the year of the great blizzard, when the news was first cabled to London and then relayed back to the other American city.

This occasion is devoted primarily to the history of our organization and is not one for spreading news of our societies to each other. But it is history, though fairly recent, that we have now four institutes which are integral parts of university medical schools. The oldest of these is of course the institute connected with the department of psychiatry at Columbia University, known as the Psychoanalytic Clinic for Training and Research, founded in 1916. Each of the four university-connected training facilities has its own traits and experimental features, and each will contribute to solving the problem of the relation of psychoanalytic education and the university. They have learned from university organization, and reciprocally it is conceivable that some day they may bring important psychoanalytic educational principles to medical and graduate education.

In this context too, we may pride ourselves on what our colleagues have done for psychiatric education through the establishment of the Topeka Psychoanalytic Institute, from which so many have carried psychoanalytic standards to other cities. Our Boston colleagues have worked hard in the psychiatric facilities of their home city. The same is true in Washington, Philadelphia, Los Angeles, and in fact to an increasing degree in every locality where there is an institute. As a generous giver to other cities one should mention Chicago as well, which has spread its mission to so many 'geographic rule' cities; it brought not only psychoanalysis to Chicago and the Middle West but through its graduates modern psychiatry and psychiatric research as well.

Some of the activities just mentioned are of course not direct aims of institute psychoanalytic education, but they are often considered at least highly desirable secondary effects. At any rate, not only psychiatry, but social work, psychosomatic medicine, and many other disciplines first received an impetus from the extension work of our institutes and later were to use as teachers and directors members of our Association. The taking over by other institutions such as medical schools and schools of social work of these subjects has led to a more intensive curriculum in our institutes.

Of the history of psychoanalytic education in our time our memories are too fresh for proper recording. We need time for retrospection, and such a retrospect was attempted and in its context successfully by Bernard Bandler (1960) in his valedictory speech.

Looking back on the last fifty years and more, we can say with considerable assurance that since its beginnings, psychoanalysis has conceived of itself as education. From the 1905 meetings at Freud's home to this present large assembly, psychoanalysts have believed it their duty to learn and, by a simple corollary, to teach also. The spirit of inquiry and of learning came first, organization followed. Self-realization has been consistent and progressive. Our early educators stand out not only as educators. We admire them as great clinicians, as in the case of Karl Abraham, as inspired observers like Ferenczi, brilliant expositors like Ernest Jones, or remarkable disseminators like our own Brill.

Benevolent outside educators have told us they consider psychoanalytic education to be in a healthy state. As psychoanalysts, we have reservations and private opinions as to the matter of diagnosing health. At least since 1937, we know that health is an ideal, the end of a continual search. Similarly we know that education, like health, includes its own mysteries, that history has a future as well as a past, and that we cannot afford either optimism or pessimism. But as analysts, we can call on our own science and resolve to face the future of psychoanalytic education without anxiety.

VII. PSYCHOANALYTIC EDUCATION AND RESEARCH*

Dr. Wolford's[1] imaginative letter of invitation tells us to present a view of the discipline we each represent, in my case psychoanalysis. He used the word *vista* but he said a vista might be a look backward as well as a look ahead, since a retrospect is also valid. As a representative psychoanalyst therefore, and a habitual one, I immediately asked, 'What is my first association to *vista*?' It was a picture, a visual image of Hobbema's painting, the Avenue of Middelharnis in Holland—a highway, lined by handsome straight rows of old trees that converged in an evocative perspective to a dream-like infinity—a lovely representation of the sharp present leading to an ambiguous yet alluring future. Recognizing the dream quality of the vista, of course, I immediately felt at home and I knew one thing for sure, namely, that I was dealing with a wish-fulfilment.

Neither before me nor behind me, nor even where I am now, do I see such a straight road. The path behind still smokes from Freud's trail blazing and shows the soft foot-prints of the pioneers. And fully awake, I cannot call up ahead of me the mirage of a great turnpike. I, and psycho-analysis, are located on an open landscape. Nevertheless, the footprints of my predecessors and some of my own do have a certain arrangement in two intertwining trails, and imaginary signs read 'Psychoanalytic Education' and 'Psychoanalytic Science'. I shall hazard a guess as to where they may have led and where they may be extended.

Both labels are very new. It is certain that psychoanalytic education and psychoanalytic science began anonymously and simultaneously around the beginning of this century in

* [No. 122 in Bibliography.]

[1] Jack A. Wolford, M. D., Program Chairman, Fiftieth Anniversary of the Pittsburgh Neuropsychiatric Society [Ed.].

Freud's consultation room. For a long time the science was Freud's alone; nor was there thought of formal teaching. The zeal was for learning. In 1900 came Freud's paper on the anxiety neurosis and his book, The Interpretation of Dreams. Then shortly appeared his Three Essays on Sexuality and the lengthy so-called Fragment of a Case of Hysteria, an account usually referred to as the case of Dora. This was in 1905. And it was only about this date that a small number of interested persons formed a kind of study group, which met weekly in Freud's home to interchange experience and ideas and, particularly, in order to profit from Freud's presence. In 1907, this group was all there was to the psychoanalytic movement, and this was all that could be called psychoanalytic education.

This was fifty-five years ago. Let me mention a later date, 1961, to give you a sense of time passing. In this year, the Pittsburgh Psychoanalytic Institute was officially recognized by the Board on Professional Standards of the American Psychoanalytic Association and became the seventeenth institute of its kind in the United States. Besides the seventeen full-grown institutes in this country, there are now also two smaller institutes in the making, called 'training centers', and in these nineteen bodies are enrolled nearly a thousand students. The graduates of these and of foreign institutes who reside in the United States also number about a thousand. They are members of twenty-three American psychoanalytic societies and of a national American Psychoanalytic Association. Abroad there are a Mexican society, a Canadian society, five societies in South America, eleven in Europe, and three in Asia, and they all give psychoanalytic instruction either through a related institute or in less organized fashion. The numerical facts, of no intrinsic interest, do give a flash picture of the present and show by contrast the extent to which psychoanalytic practice and psychoanalytic teaching have spread and radiated from the little room at Berggasse 19 in Vienna to the four corners of the world.

In the first part of this paper, I will discuss the development of psychoanalytic education in the United States, and in the second part I propose to speak of the science. Psychoanalytic education, as a subject, was totally unnamed fifty years ago,

then unremarked for perhaps twenty more. The first formally organized institute was the one in Berlin, founded in 1920 after many years of informal society teaching. The Vienna institute was founded five years later. After years of independent teaching without formal organization, psychoanalysts in New York opened the first psychoanalytic institute in this country in 1931, followed by the establishment of a second institute in Chicago in 1932, and a third in Boston the following year.

Generally speaking, the institutes educate practitioners of a very specialized sort. They and the societies are the foci for future developments. The students, usually medical graduates, undergo a personal, so-called training analysis. For many years this procedure has been a fundamental feature of their education, so considered as far back as 1912, and since 1925 it has been an official prerequisite for admission to the psychoanalytic societies. When the American institutes began, the function of the personal analysis was considered self-evident.

In other fields than psychoanalysis, many doctors have begun their careers as specialists when they themselves were patients. It was not rare to find a doctor who was also a tuberculosis patient turning his interest into the field of his own illness and becoming an Edward Trudeau. Occasionally, a John Hunter or a Walter Reed would submit to being infected and then treated or cured, as part of an experiment. But I cannot recall any other specialty than psychoanalysis which bases its education on the doctor's going through the process of cure as a patient. Thus, all the students in the institutes all over the world are patients, or else have been recently, and all the members of the International Psycho-Analytical Association, some two thousand perhaps, have been through this therapeutic preliminary. I shall not pretend to deal with the definition of normality, but the fact that persons who by most standards would be called 'normal' have undergone this procedure has in itself furnished most interesting data and has led to much thinking about the whole problem of psychological normality. It has turned the efforts of many psychoanalysts toward extending the science into the field of general psychology. The effort to extend psychoanalysis, which constructed originally only limited theories, into a general psychology arose partly as the result of this new type of student-patient. The new propositions are usually referred to as ego psychology; it is intensively pursued today, and the chances are that it will be in the future.

The rest of the curriculum is less unique. It consists of practical instruction in psychoanalytic work with patients under faculty and individual supervision, of case discussion in seminars, and of lectures and seminars on theory, including the dream, the neuroses, and various other topics, covering as much of the science as possible. Besides the medical graduates, there are a few research students—psychologists, anthropologists, social scientists, etc.—who do not wish to become practitioners and do not usually psychoanalyze patients as part of their curriculum. They intend to apply psychoanalytic knowledge in their own discipline.

All the institutes have strictly individual features and show a healthy variety. In terms of organization, there are generally speaking two groups, the university-connected and the independent institutes. At Columbia University, at the University of the State of New York (Downstate) in Brooklyn, at Western Reserve in Cleveland, and here at the University of Pittsburgh, the psychoanalytic institutes through one or another organizational device are part of the program of graduate medical education of a university. At the Menninger Foundation in Topeka, the institute is connected in many ways with the graduate teaching program of that school. But the other thirteen psychoanalytic institutes in the United States and all the foreign ones have no connection with a university or medical school.

To give you an idea of the rather deliberate rate of development, I mention that the institute at Columbia was established in 1946, the one in Brooklyn in 1954, then six years later, in 1960, that at Western Reserve. The Pittsburgh Psychoanalytic Institute is very nearly one year old, having been recognized in May 1961. It has not been easy to adapt a psychoanalytic institute to a medical-school setting. A considerable number of teachers are necessary to serve as personal analysts and as individual supervisors of the student's analytic work. A one-man department or division of the familiar sort is impossible. The very individual nature of much of the training demands a well-trained corps. Then the simultaneity of the personal analysis and the didactic classwork provides all sorts of psychological complications and difficulties. A student must not only pass his courses in order to be graduated, but according to the regulations, he must be 'analyzed successfully', and what this phrase means empirically is not always evident and produces all sorts of academic headaches. Essentially, the personal analysis must be the same as one undertaken for therapy, and experience has shown that no matter what it is called, the psychoanalytic procedure is a potent psychological agent. The institutes do their best to select relatively normal students, but for centuries psychiatrists have been telling us that normality is an ideal, and that real people are different. So, oddly for the academic world, any real appraisal of a student's progress has to be something of a psychiatric assessment. This ordinarily would be passed over in the academic world, at least in university circles, although now elementary and secondary schools have become aware of the interlacing of psychiatric and educational problems. Child guidance clinics serving such schools are most useful, even in getting the children to 'pass their courses'.

The independent institutes in this country and abroad share some of the problems mentioned above that arise from the personal analysis. They usually follow the classic organizational pattern of the old institutes at Berlin and Vienna. That is to say, they begin as teaching arms of psychoanalytic societies of which their faculty are members, or as in Chicago they may be independent of the society. Financial support comes from the membership of the local society, as in New York, where psychoanalysts pay annual dues, most of which support the institute and the attached clinic; or, as in Chicago, the money may come from outside philanthropy.

So far as the student is concerned, he has very much the same problems, whether he attends a university school or an independent institute. Many come from the simple fact that the students are very postgraduate. They may be psychiatric residents or members of the upper staff. Indeed, among the enrolled students there have been professors of psychiatry, a medical school dean, and a state commissioner of mental health. On admission, the mean age is between thirty and thirty-one, and it is obvious that persons of this age and in this type of specialization share the problems which beset many others who in conformity with this age of scientific and technical specialty, are becoming ultraspecialists. Atomic physicists and brain and lung surgeons too are double-dosed with higher education.

Here at long last something like a vista murkily comes before my mental eye. Because of the personal analysis, there is no group of persons so carefully observed psychologically as the students of the psychoanalytic institutes. Here is an excellent situation for a study of the psychological problems of higher education. Several psychoanalytic teachers have already recognized this fact. Some long-term work in this field has been started at the Columbia institute, and I have a glimpse too of Pittsburgh psychoanalysts becoming leaders in this field of endeavor. Teaching analysts may widen the trail already somewhat cleared by recent studies. From near the beginning of psychoanalysis, it has been repeatedly stated that its main contribution might not be to medicine but to education. Here the word *education* was usually taken to mean child rearing and early education. But recent experiences in the institutes have shown that educational problems do not cease after kindergarten, grade school, college, or graduate school, and the possibility of adding to our knowledge has become widely recognized.

Before leaving organizational matters to turn to more ideal things, I should like to refer to an aspect often discussed, usually with an eye to the future. It is usually proposed as an alternative: Should psychoanalytic education and psychoanalytic institutes be merged into medical education and schools? Should there, for instance, be a department or a division of psychoanalytic education in a medical school, and would this mean that the old independent institute of the Berlin-Vienna type is obsolete and unnecessary and that in the future psychoanalytic institutes will arise only in connection with departments of psychiatry or in medical schools? These are ostensibly simple questions, but there is nothing simple about the answers, if these are to be realistic. I must repeat the word 'realistic' for I mean to imply that unrealistic ones have been proposed. Psychoanalysts, like many other people, like to play at being teacher, and a professorial life has its fantasy allure.

But aside from individual fantasies, there are many concrete facts to serve as signposts. Not only where psychoanalytic institutes are already part of psychiatric departments but also in other cities where institutes are not too far from centers of postgraduate psychiatric training—that is, residency training—such nearness has been found advantageous. The propinquity of an institute is an attraction to well-prepared graduates who are looking for residency training. In large cities with an abundance of psychoanalysts, it is not vital that the union of residency training and institute should be official. In Boston, for instance, the institute unofficially and independently educates the psychiatrists who work in many different hospitals and clinics. The same holds for the institutes in New York, Chicago, and Philadelphia. Even among the smaller institutes, more than one residency group may be served; for example in New Haven, where the Western New England Psychoanalytic Institute serves the residents of New Haven and Stockbridge, Massachusetts. On the other hand, the institutes in Cleveland and Pittsburgh tend to serve the residents and staff of one university hospital each, and these two institutes are university-connected. There are in several cities small enclaves of psychoanalysts who are insufficiently numerous to found an institute. These are all attached to universities or centered about them—in Rochester and Syracuse (New York), in St. Louis, Cincinnati, Chapel Hill, and Denver. It is possible that in time they will form institutes which like the Pittsburgh institute will be part of a university setting from the start. Nevertheless, here one should say *possibly* and not *inevitably*. An independent institute is in gestation in Detroit, and the day that the Pittsburgh university-connected institute was recognized by the American Psychoanalytic Association, a sister institute, quite independent of any university connection, was also recognized. This was the institute in New Orleans, and the psychoanalytic educators of the nation welcomed both neonates with the impartiality of approval that might exist if one of twins was a blond and the other a brunette. The older siblings were concerned only with their viability.

So there are signs pointing both ways. Some institutes will follow Pittsburgh's path, others take the older road. There is no high road as yet, no bandwagon to climb onto. To follow this vein there are still several Conestoga wagons, though luckily there seem to be fewer Indians on the warpath. University institutes and the independent ones are fraternally joined through many aims. There are not and never were really two worlds, except in those minds that habitually see an opposition in any duality. In the opinion of a professor well informed about such matters, Henry W. Brosin, the independent institutes have demonstrated competence and vitality, and if there were no such institutes the university institutes should establish and support them. I remember, a bit contrarily, that it used to be said of Austria-Hungary that if it did not exist it would have to be invented, and I vaguely recall a French remark about a more important entity. But the point is again that different signs point in different directions. Like the Buddhists, psychoanalytic educational organizers may travel by the Mahayana, the high road, or by the Hinayana, the little road, if they ever can establish which is which.

There is still an as yet untried possibility, a dream perhaps that has not come to fruition. Organizationally the American institutes have been part of a medical school and a psychiatric department, and the independent institutes have nearly solidly required of their students a previous medical degree and psychiatric training. The dream is of a specially mapped out course for psychoanalysts, regardless of medical degree and residency, or perhaps with some sort of medical background less than that covered by a degree, in a school set up, whether or not in a university, for the particular purpose of giving psychoanalytic training and producing psychoanalysts. In a university this seems to imply a separate school cognate with the law school or the medical school, a school of psychoanalysis, resembling in many ways the present institutes but with a looser tie to practice. This dream is not materializing rapidly. In some ways some institutes approach it, but even the independent institutes with good traditions of scholarship and research seem to be traveling in the opposite psychiatrically-oriented direction.

Once there was a professor of philosophy who resigned his chair and went into the business of building. His friends said that he was leaving the abstract for the concrete. I shall now do the reverse, if I can, and shall leave the formed, solid topic of educational organization and constructions to broach the more fluid topic of the future of psychoanalysis as a science and body of knowledge pure and applied, what is sometimes subsumed under the term 'research'. Here it is hard to separate psychoanalysis from those who practice it, and it is equally hard to distinguish research from those who do research. Also it is hard to view the whole landscape. One tries to speak of the world and suddenly finds it as intimate as a little town square. But in 1962, one sees that psychoanalysts and psychoanalytic theory have entered many neighboring areas. I remarked previously that a new type of psychoanalytic patient had stimulated an interest in what is called ego psychology. Psychoanalysts and psychoanalysis may have contributed a great deal to the psychologic study of the child and to child rearing. It has recently influenced the direct investigation of infants and brought new light to this field. In many undergraduate courses in sociology and anthropology, the students often hear for the first time of certain of Freud's theories and of their improvement or distortion by others. Literary criticism has been much affected by psychoanalytic thought. Philosophy and philosophers apparently have not, but there has been at least one curious meeting of professional philosophers and psychoanalysts where, unfortunately, clear psychoanalytic expositions were unintelligible to the philosophers and the philosophers' propositions mystifying to the psychoanalysts. But in many ways, including the popular ones of the press and the stage, there has been spread publicly a thin smattering of analytic ideas.

The deep appeal in this country, however, has been to psychiatrists and psychologically-minded doctors. Psychiatry and mental health work in general have been infiltrated for good by psychoanalysis and psychoanalysts. Psychoanalytically trained psychiatrists work with psychotic patients and apply psychoanalytic ideas in the understanding of the psychoses and in the various therapies. Much of modern American work with delinquents stems from August Aichhorn's teachings in the 1920's and 1930's. From the start, psychoanalysts have tried to study and treat psychotics. Their observations have often been exceedingly illuminating. Attempts to use the method devised for the treatment of neurotics have yielded varied results, but the understanding of the psychoses has been vastly increased. As an example well known to psychiatrists, I may refer to Freud's (1911a) famous study of Schreber's autobiography, which is profoundly instructive to all who wish to learn about schizophrenia. The classic method is not usually adapted to cure the schizophrenic patient but sometimes it does. The schizophrenic patient appears to have some areas of sanity, just as most 'normal' persons have an area or two of the opposite sort. Different workers are trying all sorts of methods to study the psychoses, but whatever the method, most of them employ, and usefully, at least some basic psychoanalytic concepts. In the psychiatric hospitals, the interest in psychoanalysis is still growing. Compared to psychiatry abroad and to that of former days in the United States, it may be fairly said that it has undergone a great deal of psychoanalyzation.

But when I try to carve out a perspective and peer toward the future, I must honestly say I do not know whether this trend will be abiding nor for how long. The history of psychiatry shows that it has had many moods. Methods have alternated rhythmically. Eras in which physical methods only were used were succeeded by eras dominated by psychological or moral methods. There are even now highly placed psychiatrists in this country who in a way deplore the present-day elan for psychotherapy and psychoanalysis in our residency training centers. They think that this has been correlated with a decline in psychiatric scholarship and a sacrifice of the spirit of scientific investigation. One of these teachers put it that it was too bad that psychoanalysis made people feel better, that it was unfortunate for psychoanalysis that the analysis of Freud's own dreams relieved him of certain anxieties and minor symptoms. I am sure my friend has no grudge against being healthy; he meant that the zeal to cure now may distort the inquiring spirit.

In most of the fields of learning and endeavor mentioned above, psychoanalytic theory and ideas are applied rather than the method. This method, it is well recognized, is based on the procedure of free association. For the strict application as such, there must be a person, called perhaps a patient or perhaps a dreamer or perhaps given no name, but he must be able to let himself associate freely within fairly large limits. He had best be called a 'free associator'. And he must relax and let his mind go from thought to thought, unguided and unguarded, wherever the train of thought may lead him. Free association has always been and still is the core of the psychoanalytic method. When can it be applied? For instance, to what extent can it be used by the anthropologist in the field? Oddly, more often than one would think possible. It has been used with some success by Róheim in Central Australia, and by others elsewhere, but the Bushman's capacity for coöperation is not great, and primitive informants have too many resistances as a rule and too little comprehension or interest. Children, too, rarely associate freely. Nor do psychotic patients. The word jumbles of advanced schizophrenic patients and the manic flight of ideas may sound loose and free to the casual observer, but in fact they are unfree and rigid if they are considered as associations. There may be an occasional approach to free association. Nevertheless, even when the psychotic stream of thought is not amenable to a psychoanalyst's intervention and the patients are not analyzable in the strict sense, the productions may be easily interpretable by an application of known psychoanalytic findings gleaned from the analysis of the neurotic and the near normal, that is, from people who can associate freely. Here is obviously a field that will for a long while beckon the future student, including the psychoanalytically informed.

If the classic method of free associating is still the essence of psychoanalytic investigation, how, one might ask, can one find the psychoanalytic data to compare with those that occur away from the couch and the consulting room? And where are the relevant interpretations and theory? Naturally they exist in the minds of psychoanalysts and in the ever-growing psychoanalytic literature. But, to express a personal bias, I believe the central treasury of psychoanalysis is still the dream. It will not be so much the theory of the neuroses, I think, as the theory of dreams and the accumulated knowledge about them that will help to solve the problems of other fields, including the psychoses. The comparison of dream and psychosis is ancient, and Hughlings Jackson said, 'Find out all you can about dreams, and you will have found out all about insanity'. What Freud named the manifest content of the dream, the dream as the dreamer tells it, is a normal psychosis, and the psychoanalytic knowledge of the dream has still not been completely exploited. Referring to The Interpretation of Dreams, Dr. Smith Ely Jelliffe said, 'Everything is in that book'. In a sense, a psychosis can be studied vicariously if one can find the analogous dream. The dream, thus applied, is an analogue of the test tube. The main point is that dreams can be subjected to free association and to interpretation and many have been so subjected, and there are many, as yet unclassified, types of dreams just as there are many, and already overclassified, types of psychoses. The psychosis usually cannot be subjected to free association, but it is possible that the content of a given psychosis will match the content of a dream. It is not only the manifest content of the dream that comes into question, but also what have been named dream distortion and dream elaboration, processes of which we have some understanding. Indeed, the whole psychology of the sleeping state and of states that lead to sleep, the hypnagogic ones, and states that follow sleep, the hypnopompic ones, would have to be included in this approach. Here observations, possibly of great importance, have already been made, and to look for a moment into the crystal ball, to induce in myself a vatic trancelike state, I see a path here which, pursued to its not quite visible termination, may some day put us if not upon a turnpike at least on a paved road.

The studies known as psychosomatic medicine are now so well recognized that many do not know of the role played by psychoanalysis and psychoanalysts in their introduction to this country. Out of some small interdisciplinary conferences held at the New York Psychoanalytic Institute in 1941, there developed the Society for Psychosomatic Medicine (now the American Psychosomatic Society) and its interesting journal. The term, psychosomatic medicine, indicates only the use of psychological methods for the study and treatment of organic illness. The immediate use of the psychoanalytic method as a tool is entirely possible, for many patients are able to associate freely and to undergo the regular procedure on the couch. Gastric ulcer patients and asthmatics have been ideal for such study, since the symptoms are episodic and usually not too disabling. About fifteen years ago, the lay press gave the topic considerable publicity, also considerable simplifying distortion, and I suppose there are still people who think all business executives have 'their ulcer' because of their addiction to overwork. At that time, many persons with ulcers or high blood pressure were led to consult psychoanalysts, and so did persons with other subacute or chronic illnesses, so that a good deal of information was obtained about the psychology, specific or nonspecific is still a question, of several ailments. The publicity and the interest is less nowadays. But the scientific study of the 'psychosomatic patient' goes on in the medical services of many hospitals. Other methods than free association are employed, such as the 'diagnostic interview' at the psychoanalytic institute in Chicago, and in Boston, at the institute at Columbia University, and elsewhere, there are persons especially interested in the field. They use psychoanalytic theoretical frames of reference for the statement of their findings and ideas. Despite a change of pace, it seems improbable that research here has come to an end.

In this connection I am reminded of the advice given by Adolf Meyer to a medical dean who wished every patient in his large teaching hospital, regardless of the reason for admission, to be subjected to psychiatric study. Dr. Meyer said that he did not doubt that this would uncover interesting facts, but from a practical standpoint Dr. X would need an enormous staff of psychiatrists. Then in order to hold their jobs, he reasoned, they would have to talk enormously, too, and in that case there would be an enormous amount of nonsense. Therefore, he advised that it would be well to examine psychiatrically as a starter only those patients in whom there was an indication for such study. I am sure Dr. Meyer was not disparaging mass research projects; he intended to indicate that there are limits to any expansion.

In recent years the idea of validation has appealed to some psychoanalysts, and there have been serious attempts to employ standard methods used in psychology and the sciences to psychoanalytic propositions. The analytic couch is not a well-controlled situation for this work, and the difficulty seems to have been so far in the selection of variables for study. Investigators have not known precisely what should be validated. It seems likely that work of this sort will be continued. In some localities, psychoanalysts are making use of recordings, but as yet not very extensively in terms of the analytic situation itself.

Reviewing what I have written, I feel that as a predictor I have been a very minor and uncertain prophet. Perhaps I live in too thick an atmosphere for prophetic inspiration and should emulate Zarathustra by getting above the melée on some mountain top, until the sun has given me an education. I seem to have been throughout very probabilistic in my cautious rhapsodies. I believe this is not entirely due to a personal defect. I suspect that we are now in a period of consolidation, formulation, and application, rather than discovery. Not too long ago, I heard a historian say aphoristically that for three centuries we have been living on the legacy of the seventeenth century.

But now hypnopompically, I have the image of the Avenue of Middelharnis in my mind's eye, and the obscured horizon at the infinite end of the vista is still alluring.

VIII. TEACHING AND THE BEGINNINGS OF THEORY*

For the preparation of a didactic article, I had occasion recently to reread attentively the literature on the phobias, particularly of course Freud's writings on the subject. About the same time, I was rereading the essays of Heinz Hartmann (1964) in their new format, which deal so comprehensively with the problems of theory and theorizing. Because of this dual 'actual situation', I was sensitive simultaneously to the practical problems of didactic exposition and to the role and meaning of theory-formation. Specifically, I was doubly alerted to the problem of teaching about phobias and to the development of Freud's theories of the neuroses. It occurred to me, among other things, that, in the particular writings I reviewed, there was a progressive alteration in the meaning of the words 'Little Hans'. On first acquaintance in the 1909 paper (Freud, 1909a), Little Hans is a boy of five, with many facets and interests and several prominent problems, among them the presenting fact of his fear of horses. There is much more than a 'phobia' in this paper, and its findings and interpretations have provided models for the understanding of many infantile situations, not only those connected with neurosis. Notably the paper is the foundation of child analysis. The paper is obviously useful in multiple ways and has indeed been much used and quoted.

Freud himself found it very quotable in the specific matter of neurosis-formation and neurosis-theory, and it is here that his later teaching can be thought of as giving the term 'Little Hans' new meaning. I refer particularly to the pithy summary of the horse phobia in Inhibitions, Symptoms and Anxiety (Freud, 1925a) where we encounter Little Hans at what is ordinarily called a 'different level'. Here Little Hans becomes a set of ideas, a diagram or outline, rather than a real

* [No. 125 in Bibliography.]

little boy. The metalinguistic Little Hans now consists of (1) instincts (œdipal) and (2) an ego, which can perceive danger and react with (a) anxiety, or (b) defensive measures. Similarly, the 'Wolf-man' of the same discussion is abstracted from among the many picturesque details of his personality and environment. In Inhibitions, Symptoms and Anxiety, 'he' undergoes a semantic change and for the purpose of exposition becomes defined as (1) instincts (different from Little Hans's but still œdipal) and (2) an ego which also perceives danger and reacts with (a) anxiety or (b) defenses.

For my present didactic purpose, I shall write the above in quasi-mathematical form as follows: Let I represent any (id) instinct, A any anxiety, and D any defensive measure of the ego. (Each of these letters would stand for a 'set'.) Indicate by appropriate subscripts the particular element in each set; for example, I_p = 'positive œdipal instinct', A_c = castration anxiety, and $D_1, D_2, \cdots D_n$ = the different defenses.

Then in this terminology, Little Hans's 'infantile zoophobia' $= P_z$; and $P_z = I_p + A_c + D_z$, where D_z is defined as the 'sum' of the defenses used in producing the infantile zoophobia P_z. (Or: $z = 1+2+3+ \cdots + n$; which are not to be added to make 6 or more!). D_1 could by agreement represent, say, *displacement*, D_2 *reversal of aim*, etc.

I hasten to reassure my readers, who for the moment are my 'students', that I shall not continue in this vein of mathematical parody. The above preamble may suggest that I have undertaken a mathematical formulation of the neuroses. Not at all: for didactic purposes I have translated a familiar formulation of one of Freud's theories into a form convenient for blackboard demonstration to a mathematically instructed or mathematically minded class. Doubtless my age compeers will not find equations and subscripts very illuminating. But there is no telling whether some day our grandchildren, who learn about set theory and nonparametric equations in the lower school grades, will not find such demonstrations very useful because of familiarity.

The purpose in my exposition so far has not been the teaching of psychoanalytic theory nor yet a proposal for a change in our institute teaching methods. I merely wished to lead up to the statement that teaching and theorizing coincide and that the business of teaching leads to the production of theories. I approach theorizing pragmatically as a branch of pedagogy. Equations, abbreviations, and diagrams that make for good blackboard demonstration are often good 'theory'.

I know of one instance where blackboard demonstration of diagrams presented before classes came to be regarded seriously as representing a sort of theoretical reality. In a letter to the psychologist Wolfgang Koehler, which Kurt Lewin (1936) uses as a preface to his book on topological psychology, the author writes:

> This book is the result of a very slow growth. I remember the moment when—more than ten years ago—it occurred to me that the figures on the blackboard which were to illustrate some problems for a group in psychology might after all be not merely illustrations but representations of real concepts. Much interested in the theory of science, I had already in 1912 as a student defended the thesis . . . that psychology, dealing with manifolds of coexisting facts, would be finally forced to use not only the concept of time but that of space too. Knowing something of the general theory of point sets, I felt vaguely that the young mathematical discipline, *topology*, might be of some help in making psychology a real science. I began studying topology and making use of its concepts, which soon appeared to me particularly fitted to the specific problems of psychology.

In short, Kurt Lewin's teaching methods made him assume that his diagrams were 'true', and he later applied all the machinery of topological mathematics to discover new psychological propositions. He defends such thinking in another book (K. Lewin, 1935) as the Galilean or non-Aristotelian way. The blackboard labored and produced a theory.

With no mathematical preconceptions, in several instances Freud made use of comparable 'visual aids' in propounding basic psychoanalytic ideas. The first famous diagram is that of the psychic apparatus in Chapter VII of The Interpretation of Dreams (Freud, 1900-1901); the second is the familiar drawing of the id-ego-superego topography in The Ego and the Id (Freud, 1923a) and in The New Introductory Lectures (Freud, 1932).[1]

[1] They are not exactly the same. *Cf.*, Isakower's (1939) comment on the replacement of the 'Hörkappe' by the superego-'cap'.

These diagrams were very useful to Freud as teacher and to his pupils as frames of reference for many expositions. In regard to the psychic-apparatus diagram, the didactic simplification, so admirable in its way, perhaps discouraged the construction of other possible 'models'. Colby's (1955) electronic model appears to contradict the last sentence, but his was not so much didactic in origin as it was an effort at interdisciplinary 'cross-fertilization', to establish an 'electronics of the mind' comparable to Kurt Lewin's geometry. In a certain sense, the interdisciplinary way is an attempt to teach one subject the way one has already taught another one. Freud also used an algebraic form for classroom purposes, the complementary series of etiological factors; and his 'Project' (Freud, 1895) would now be considered interdisciplinary. On this as on the other occasions, Freud was too good a historian of science and teacher to overvalue the form of statement. Freud after all was to speak of 'our mythology'.

Teaching, to be sure, is more than the use of visual aids, whether figures or equations, and I should not like to leave the impression that any diagram-formation is theory-formation. But, to teach well, one must clarify and organize ideas, and the talent which comes to fruition in the classroom as the clear, organized, and condensed presentation is very nearly related to, and often identical with, the one which produces 'theory'. The need to present material to a class and the business of teaching promotes or involves the act of theorizing.

Allowing for the presence of all types of persons in the same field of endeavor, we might take a glance at the great mathematicians and consider them as teachers and theorists. Two extreme and opposite types are well represented by Euclid and Fermat. Euclid was a pre-eminent theorist; his concepts ruled for two thousand years. He was also very obviously one of the world's great schoolmasters. Possibly it was in bringing his subject into good didactic shape that he came upon his basic ideas. At the other end of the scale, Fermat, for all his heuristic brilliance, obviously cared nothing about teaching, perhaps did not have the appropriate talent. His work comes down to us entirely from correspondence with friends or from scribblings in the margins of books. He stated theorems without troubling to show how he had proved them. And it seems a safe assumption that because of his lack of teaching interest, he left to posterity no theories, only solved puzzles or puzzles to be solved.

Somewhere between Euclid and Fermat fit in types of mathematicians or other scientists who seem to have hit upon theories, but for one reason or another were not able to present them intelligibly or to hit the mark in the classroom. In some instances such persons' ideas get 'retrieved', as we now say. A probable example is the mathematician, Grassman, whose invention of what was later called 'vector analysis' was completely neglected because of his obscure language. In despair he gave up his profession and turned to the study of Indian culture, a field in which he attained fame. It happened later that Hamilton, the Irish mathematician, understood Grassman, which in itself may have represented a sort of genius, and put Grassman's ideas into generally intelligible terminology. In fact he introduced the term 'vector analysis'. Though not quite the same thing, this resembles the rediscovery of Willard Gibbs's and Mendel's basic papers. Hamilton was not a simple commentator but also an independent and original teacher himself—a 'theorist'. There are other familiar instances where what started out as a commentary on another person's works,—that is, a teaching of them—, turned into an independent and by that time 'original' system or theory.

In some languages, the analogies or equalities I have drawn between teaching and theory would become etymologically evident in the writing itself. Thus, in German for 'theory' I could use the word '*Lehre*'. Freud's theory of the instincts in that language is called his '*Trieblehre*'. A '*Lehre*' (from '*lehren*', to teach) could be a 'teaching' or a theory. Here the two nearly coincide.

Helen Ross (1965) has recently written an account of what she calls the 'teaching game', by analogy with what psychoanalysts have called for many years the 'doctor game' in small children, and has indicated how its varieties parallel some later methods used in the classroom. Such a study may also lead to insight into theorizing and theories. It could be that our adult theorizing is related to the omniscience-urge manifest in some of the teaching games. At times a sort of regression can lead to an undesired reductionism both in theorizing and in teaching. Heinz Hartmann has stated this incisively in a remark he has often used in teaching.[2] The quantum theory, he said, undoubtedly holds throughout the whole realm of mechanics, but one would not wish to invoke it when giving instruction in bridge-building. Hartmann here registers no objection to quantum-mechanics theory;[3] and it is even conceivable that somehow there is a genetic link between early (perhaps Ionian) instruction in bridge-building and quantum mechanics by way of countless classrooms and section foremen.

Much can be said about teaching and much about theory. One thinks of Freud's 'classroom' use of the amoeba as a picture of narcissistic investment,[4] and of other teaching devices he borrowed from biology. In this paper, however, I wished to limit myself to the bit of theorizing and teaching directly relevant to the single point of their close coincidence.

[2] Confirmed in a letter from Dr. Hartmann. At other times he used the theory of relativity and the repair of one's car.

[3] *Cf.*, for example, his argument for the utility of general formulations (Hartmann, 1964).

[4] 'Thus we form the idea of there being an original libidinal cathexis of the ego, from which some is later given off to objects, but which fundamentally persists and is related to the object-cathexes much as the body of an amoeba is related to the pseudopodia which it puts out' (Freud, 1914b, p. 75). Later in *Beyond the Pleasure Principle* (Freud, 1920b), other unicellular animals furnish both teaching and theorizing purposes in relation to instinct theory.

CURRICULUM VITAE

BIBLIOGRAPHY

REFERENCES

INDEX

CURRICULUM VITAE OF BERTRAM D. LEWIN

Born:	November 30, 1896, Victoria, Texas
Education:	University of Texas, B.A., 1916 Johns Hopkins Medical School, M.D., 1920
Languages:	French, German, Greek, Italian, Latin, Portuguese, Spanish, Swedish, Russian

Medical Training:

1920-1922	Intern and Resident in Psychiatry Phipps Psychiatric Clinic, Johns Hopkins Hospital, Baltimore, Maryland
1922-1924	Assistant in Neuropathology New York Psychiatric Institute New York, N. Y.
1922-1925	Assistant Psychiatrist and Assistant Instructor in Medicine Cornell Clinic New York, N. Y.
1924-1925	Senior Assistant Physician New York Psychiatric Institute New York, N. Y.
1925-1927	Courses and clinical work in Neurology Oppenheim Clinic and Friedrich Wilhelm Hospital Berlin
	Candidate Berlin Psychoanalytic Institute Berlin

Professional Affiliations:

1930-1933	Secretary-Treasurer New York Psychoanalytic Society
1932-1971	Staff Member New York Psychoanalytic Institute

1936-1939	President New York Psychoanalytic Society
1942-1947	Advisory Board Member Chicago Institute for Psychoanalysis
1946-1947	President The American Psychoanalytic Association
1951-1971	Charter Member and President Sigmund Freud Archives, Inc.
1956-1959	Director, Survey of Psychoanalytic Education The American Psychoanalytic Association
1959-1962	Consultant, Psychoanalytic Education The American Psychoanalytic Association
1962-1971	Visiting Professor of Psychoanalysis University of Pittsburgh School of Medicine

Editorial Affiliations:

1932-1971	Co-founder and Editor The Psychoanalytic Quarterly
1945-1971	Member Editorial Board The Psychoanalytic Study of the Child
1950-1971	Member Advisory Board The Annual Survey of Psychoanalysis

Member:

American Medical Association
American Orthopsychiatric Association
American Psychiatric Association
American Psychoanalytic Association
American Psychosomatic Association
New York Psychoanalytic Society

Honorary Member:

Centro psícosomático, Lima, Peru
New Jersey Psychoanalytic Society
Philadelphia Psychoanalytic Society
Pittsburgh Psychoanalytic Society

BIBLIOGRAPHY OF BERTRAM D. LEWIN*

1926

1. INTERSTITIAL GLAND CELLS IN THE HUMAN OVARY. Amer. J. Med. Science, CLXXI, pp. 518-521.

1927

2. A STUDY OF THE ENDOCRINE ORGANS IN THE PSYCHOSES. Amer. J. Psychiatry, VII, pp. 391-458.

1928

3. HISTOPATHOLOGY OF THE ENDOCRINE ORGANS. In: *Schizophrenia.* Research Proceedings of Assn. for Research in Nervous and Mental Diseases. New York: Paul B. Hoeber, Inc.
4. ZUR GESCHICHTE DER GEWISSENSPSYCHOLOGIE. Imago, XIV, pp. 441-446. [*Conscience and Consciousness in Medical Psychology.* Psa. Review, XVII, 1930, pp. 20-25. Reprinted in *Psychoanalysis in America: Historical Perspectives.* Ed. by M. H. Sherman. Springfield, Ill.: Charles C Thomas, 1966, pp. 431-437.]

1930

5. THE COMPULSIVE CHARACTER. Med. Rev. of Reviews, XXXVI, pp. 191-199.
6. KOTSCHMIEREN, MENSES UND WEIBLICHES UBER-ICH. Int. Ztschr. f. Psa., XVI, pp. 43-56. [*El Ensuciarse con Matéria Fecal, la Menstruación y el Superyo Feminino.* Rev. Psicoanálisis, III, 1945, pp. 240-253.]
7. REPORT OF THE NEW YORK PSYCHOANALYTIC SOCIETY. Int. Ztschr. f. Psa., XVI, pp. 541-543.
8. TRANSLATION (with B. Glueck) of Alexander, Franz: *The Psychoanalysis of the Total Personality; the Application of Freud's Theory of the Ego to the Neuroses.* New York: Nervous & Mental Disease Publishing Co.
9. WHEN ADULTS TEASE. Child Study Magazine, VII, p. 106. [*Warum Kinder von den Erwachsenen geneckt Werden.* Psa. Paedagogik., IV, 1930, pp. 312-316.]

* Bertram D. Lewin's complete works are in the custody of the Pittsburgh Psychoanalytic Society, to which they were presented by his heirs, David B. Lewin and Barbara L. Schwartz.

1932

10. ANAL EROTISM AND THE MECHANISM OF UNDOING. Psa. Quart., I, pp. 343-344.
11. ANALYSIS AND STRUCTURE OF A TRANSIENT HYPOMANIA. Psa. Quart., I, pp. 43-58. [*Analyse und Struktur einer passagèren Hypomanie.* Int. Ztschr. f. Psa., XX, 1934, pp. 73-84; *Análisis y Estructura de una Hipomania Transitoria.* Rev. Psicoanálisis, IV, 1946, pp. 782-796; reprinted as Chap. XXIII in *Psicoanálisis de la Melancolia.* Ed. by A. Garma and L. Rascovsky. Buenos Aires: El Ateneo, 1948.]
12. REVIEW of Froeschels, E.: *Psychological Elements in Speech.* Psa. Quart., I, pp. 740-741.
13. REVIEW of Hrdlička, Aleš: *Children Who Run on All Fours and Other Animal-Like Behavior in the Human Child.* Psa. Quart., I, pp. 366-368.
14. REVIEW of Paget, R.: *Human Speech. Some Observations, Experiments, and Conclusions as to the Nature, Origin, Purpose and Possible Improvement of Human Speech.* Psa. Quart., I, pp. 350-355.
15. REVIEW of Ramos, A.: *Estudos de Psychanalyse.* Psa. Quart., I, pp. 743-744.
16. TRANSLATION (with G. Zilboorg) of Fenichel, Otto: *Outline of Clinical Psychoanalysis.* Psa. Quart., I, pp. 121-165, 292-342, 545-652; II, pp. 94-122, 260-308, 563-591; III, pp. 42-127, 223-302. [Published in book form with W. W. Norton & Co., Inc., New York, and by Kegan Paul, Trench, Trubner & Co. Ltd., London, 1934.]

1933

17. THE BODY AS PHALLUS. Psa. Quart., II, pp. 24-47.
18. OBSESSIONAL NEUROSES. In: *Psychoanalysis Today.* Ed. by S. Lorand. New York: Covici-Friede; London: Allen & Unwin. [Second edition, 1944, published by International Universities Press, Inc., New York.]
19. REVIEW of Weiss, E.: *Elementi di Psicoanalisi.* Psa. Quart., II, pp. 336-337.
20. REVIEW of Whytt, R.: *Observations on the Nature, Causes, and Cure of Those Disorders which have been Commonly Called Nervous, Hypochondriac, or Hysteric.* Psa. Quart., II, pp. 615-618.
21. TRANSLATION of Rado, Sandor: *Fear of Castration in Women.* Psa. Quart., II, pp. 425-475.

1934

22. REVIEW of Campbell, C. M.: *Towards Mental Health: The Schizophrenic Problem.* Psa. Quart., III, pp. 317-324.

1935

23. CLAUSTROPHOBIA. Psa. Quart., IV, pp. 227-233. [*Claustrofobia.* Rev. Psicoanálisis, IX, 1952, pp. 123-128.]

1936

24. FOOTNOTES (with L. S. Kubie) to Hoskins, R. G.: *An Endocrine Approach to Psychodynamics.* Psa. Quart., V, pp. 87-100, 104.

1937

25. EXPLORERS OF THE MIND. Sat. Rev. of Literature, *16,* Sept. 11, pp. 3-4, 16.
26. IN MEMORIAM: DORIAN FEIGENBAUM. Psa. Quart., VI, pp. 1-3.
27. A TYPE OF NEUROTIC HYPOMANIC REACTION. Arch. Neurology & Psychiatry, XXXVII, pp. 868-873.

1939

28. SOME OBSERVATIONS ON KNOWLEDGE, BELIEF, AND THE IMPULSE TO KNOW. Int. J. Psa., XX, pp. 426-431.

1940

29. REVIEW of Strecker, E. A.: *Beyond the Clinical Frontiers.* Sat. Rev. of Literature, *21,* March 23.

1941

30. COMMENTS ON HYPOMANIC AND RELATED STATES. Psa. Rev., XXVIII, pp. 86-91.
31. THE EMERGENCY COMMITTEE ON RELIEF AND IMMIGRATION OF THE AMERICAN PSYCHOANALYTIC ASSOCIATION (with B. Warburg and L. S. Kubie). J. Nervous & Mental Disease, XCIII, p. 416.

1942

32. COMMENTS ON CH. DOLF VON HOLLERBORN. The Shepherd Dog Rev., May. (Organ of The Shepherd Dog Club of New England.)
33. REVIEW of Alexander, F.: *Our Age of Unreason.* Sat. Rev. of Literature, *25,* Oct. 24.
34. REVIEW of Garma, A.: *El Psicoanálisis, Presente y Perspectivas.* Psa. Quart., XI, p. 561.

35. REVIEW of Garma, A.: *Psicoanálisis de los Sueños.* Psa. Quart., XI, pp. 98-99.
36. REVIEW of Hayakawa, S. I.: *Language in Action.* Psa. Quart., XI, pp. 436-437.
37. REVIEW of Horney, K.: *Self-Analysis.* Sat. Rev. of Literature, *25,* June 13.
38. REVIEW of Korzybski, A., et al.: *General Semantics.* Psa. Quart., XI, p. 595.
39. REVIEW of Menninger, K.: *Love against Hate.* Sat. Rev. of Literature, *25,* Dec. 19.
40. REVIEW of Wertham, F.: *Dark Legend.* Sat. Rev. of Literature, *25,* Jan. 31.
41. REVIEW of Zilboorg, G.: *A History of Medical Psychology.* Sat. Rev. of Literature, *25,* Jan. 17.

1943

42. REVIEW of Austregésilo, A.: *Fames, Libido, Ego.* Psa. Quart., XII, pp. 408-409.
43. REVIEW of Berman, L.: *Behind the Universe.* Sat. Rev. of Literature, *26,* Jan. 8.
44. REVIEW of Castiglione, T.: *A Eugenia no direito de Familia.* Psa. Quart., XII, pp. 424-425.
45. REVIEW of Sachs, H.: *Creative Unconscious.* Psa. Quart., XII, pp. 106-107.
46. REVIEW of Zilboorg, G.: *Mind, Medicine and Man.* Sat. Rev. of Literature, *26,* May 15.

1944

47. COLLABORATOR in Langer, W. C.: *A Psychological Analysis of Adolf Hitler.* 'Secret' document of Office of Strategic Services. (Pub. as *The Mind of Adolf Hitler.* New York: Basic Books, Inc., 1972.)
48. REVIEW of Garma, A.: *Sadismo y Masoquismo en la Conducta.* Psa. Quart., XIII, pp. 363-364.
49. REVIEW of Krapf, E. E.: *Tomás de Aquino y la Psicopatologia.* Psa. Quart., XIII, pp. 223-224.
50. REVIEW of Mira, E.: *Psychiatry in War.* Psa. Quart., XIII, pp. 376-377.
51. REVIEW of Selling, L. S.: *Synopsis of Neuropsychiatry.* Psa. Quart., XIII, pp. 507-508.

1945

52. COMMENTS on Bateson, G. and Mead, M.: Balinese Character. A Photographic Analysis. In: *The Psychoanalytic Study of the Child, Vol. I.* New York: International Universities Press, Inc., pp. 379-387.

53. REVIEW of Binger, C.: *The Doctor's Job.* Psa. Quart., XIV, pp. 394-397.
54. REVIEW of Child, I. L. and van de Water, M., Editors: *Psychology for the Returning Serviceman.* Sat. Rev. of Literature, *28,* May 5.
55. REVIEW of Grinker, R. and Spiegel, J.: *Men Under Stress.* Sat. Rev. of Literature, *28,* Nov. 3.
56. REVIEW of Hall, J. K., Editor: *One Hundred Years of American Psychiatry.* Psa. Quart., XIV, pp. 99-103.
57. REVIEW of Hunt, J. M., Editor: *Personality and the Behavior Disorders.* Psa. Quart., XIV, pp. 545-547.
58. REVIEW of Kardiner, A., et al.: *The Psychological Frontiers of Society.* Psa. Quart., XIV, pp. 535-540.
59. REVIEW of Kupper, H. I.: *Back to Life.* Sat. Rev. of Literature, *28,* Nov. 17.
60. REVIEW of Rees, J. R.: *The Shaping of Psychiatry by War.* Sat. Rev. of Literature, *28,* April 28.
61. REVIEW of Reik, T.: *The Unknown Murderer.* Sat. Rev. of Literature, *28,* Nov. 17.

1946

62. COUNTERTRANSFERENCE IN THE TECHNIQUE OF MEDICAL PRACTICE. Psychosomatic Med., VIII, pp. 195-199.
63. REVIEW of Cooke, E. D.: *All But Me and Thee.* Sat. Rev. of Literature, *29,* Dec. 21.
64. REVIEW of Hobman, J. B., Editor: *David Eder. Memoirs of a Modern Pioneer.* Psa. Quart., XV, p. 106.
65. REVIEW of Montagu, M. F. A.: *Man's Most Dangerous Myth: The Fallacy of Race.* Psa. Quart., XV, pp. 120-121.
66. SLEEP, THE MOUTH, AND THE DREAM SCREEN. Psa. Quart., XV, pp. 419-434. [*El Dormir, la Boca y la Pantalla del Sueño.* Rev. Psicoanálisis, V, 1948, pp. 180-195.]
67. TRAINING IN PSYCHOANALYSIS. In: *Symposium: Preparation of Psychiatrists for Practice, Teaching and Research.* Amer. J. Orthopsychiatry, XVI, pp. 427-429.

1947

68. REVIEW of Abrahamsen, D.: *The Mind and Death of a Genius.* Sat. Rev. of Literature, *30,* p. 27.
69. REVIEW of Flugel, J. C. and I.: *Men and Their Motives.* Psa. Quart., XVI, pp. 401-404.
70. REVIEW of Marcondes, D., et al.: *Noções Gerais de Higiene Mental da Criança.* Psa. Quart., XVI, p. 255.

1948

71. INFERENCES FROM THE DREAM SCREEN. Int. J. Psa., XXIX, pp. 224-231. [*Inferencias sobre la Pantalla del Sueño.* Rev. Psicoanálisis, VI, 1949, pp. 330-346.]

72. THE NATURE OF REALITY, THE MEANING OF NOTHING, WITH AN ADDENDUM ON CONCENTRATION. Psa. Quart., XVII, pp. 524-526.

73. THE NEUROSES AND THEIR ACCOMPANIMENT IN PHYSICAL DYSFUNCTION. In: *Synopsis of Psychosomatic Diagnosis and Treatment.* Ed. by F. Dunbar. St. Louis: C. V. Mosby, pp. 393-408.

74. REVIEW of Alves Garcia, J.: *Psicoanalise e Psiquiatria.* Amer. J. Psychiatry, CV, p. 238.

75. REVIEW of Angel Bustamente, J.: *Las Enfermedades mentales en Cuba. Estudio estadistico.* Amer. J. Psychiatry, CV, p. 476.

76. REVIEW of Du Noüy, L.: *Human Destiny.* Psa. Quart., XVII, p. 124.

77. REVIEW of Katz, S., Editor: *Freud: On War, Sex and Neurosis.* Psa. Quart., XVII, p. 104.

78. REVIEW of Rosen, G. and Caspari-Rosen, B.: *Four Hundred Years of a Doctor's Life.* Sat. Rev. of Literature, *31,* Apr. 10.

79. REVIEW of Schwarz, F.: *Probleme des Selbstmordes.* Psa. Quart., XVII, p. 104.

80. REVIEW of Weaver, W., Editor: *The Scientists Speak.* Psa. Quart., XVII, p. 124.

81. REVIEW of Weinstein, A. A.: *A Barbed Wire Surgeon.* Sat. Rev. of Literature, *31,* June 26.

1949

82. CHILD PSYCHIATRY IN THE 1830'S—THREE LITTLE HOMICIDAL MONOMANIACS (Excerpt from Esquirol's *Maladies mentales*). In: *The Psychoanalytic Study of the Child, Vol. III/IV.* New York: International Universities Press, Inc., pp. 489-493.

83. MANIA AND SLEEP. Psa. Quart., XVIII, pp. 419-433.

84. PSYCHOANALYSIS: A SUPPLEMENT TO FREUD'S 1925 ARTICLE (with L. S. Kubie). In: *Encyclopedia Britannica, Vol. XVIII.* Chicago: Encyclopedia Britannica, Inc., pp. 672-674.

85. REVIEW of Kafka, F.: *Diaries 1910-1913.* Psa. Quart., XVIII, pp. 97-98.

86. REVIEW of Mullahy, P.: *Œdipus Myth and Complex.* Sat. Rev. of Literature, *32,* July 9.
87. REVIEW of Oberndorf, C. P.: *Which Way Out; Stories Based on the Experience of a Psychiatrist.* Sat. Rev. of Literature, *32,* Feb. 5.

1950

88. IN MEMORIAM: PAUL FEDERN. Psa. Quart., XIX, pp. 295-297.
89. THE PSYCHOANALYSIS OF ELATION. New York: W. W. Norton & Co., Inc.; reprinted by The Psychoanalytic Quarterly, Inc., 1961. [*Psicoanálisis de la Exaltación.* Trans. by José Remus Araico. Buenos Aires: Editorial Nova, 1953.]
90. REVIEW of Nobre de Melo, A. L.: *O Problema das Neuroses na Clinica.* Psychosomatic Med., XII, p. 68.

1951

91. MANKIND DISCOVERS MAN (with L. S. Kubie). New York Evening Post, November 12.
92. A PSYCHOANALYTIC NOTATION ON THE ROOT GN, KN, CN (with H. A. Bunker). In: *Psychoanalysis and Culture.* Ed. by G. Wilbur and W. Muensterberger. New York: International Universities Press, Inc., pp. 363-367.

1952

93. PHOBIC SYMPTOMS AND DREAM INTERPRETATION. Psa. Quart., XXI, pp. 295-322.

1953

94. DISCUSSION of Kubie, L. S.: *Some Implications for Psychoanalysis of Modern Concepts of the Organization of the Brain.* Psa. Quart., XXII, pp. 61-63.
95. THE FORGETTING OF DREAMS. In: *Drives, Affects, Behavior, Vol. I.* Ed. by R. M. Loewenstein. New York: International Universities Press, Inc., pp. 191-202.
96. INTRODUCTION to Fenichel, O.: *Collected Papers.* New York: W. W. Norton & Co., Inc., pp. vii-xii.
97. RECONSIDERATION OF THE DREAM SCREEN. Psa. Quart., XXII, pp. 174-199.
98. REVIEW of Jones, E.: *The Life and Works of Sigmund Freud, Vol. I.* Sat. Rev. of Literature, *36,* Oct. 24.

1954

99. PROBLEMS OF INFANTILE NEUROSIS. A DISCUSSION. In: *The Psychoanalytic Study of the Child, Vol. IX.* New York: International Universities Press, Inc., p. 44.

100. REVIEW of Róheim, G.: *The Gates of the Dream.* Psa. Quart., XXIII, pp. 98-102.

101. SLEEP, NARCISSISTIC NEUROSIS, AND THE ANALYTIC SITUATION. Psa. Quart., XXIII, pp. 487-510.

1955

102. CLINICAL HINTS FROM DREAM STUDIES. Bull. Menninger Clinic, XIX, pp. 73-85.

103. DREAM PSYCHOLOGY AND THE ANALYTIC SITUATION. Psa. Quart., XXIV, pp. 169-199. [*Psicología del Sueño y la Situación Analítica.* Rev. Uruguaya Psicoanálisis, IV, 1958, pp. 86-115.]

104. EDWARD HITSCHMANN—AN APPRECIATION. J. Amer. Psa. Assn., III, pp. 711-714.

105. REVIEW of Seguin, C. A.: *Bases de la psicoterapia.* Psychosomatic Med., XVII, p. 332.

1958

106. DISCUSSION of Loomie, L. S., et al.: Ernst Kris and the Gifted Adolescent Project. In: *The Psychoanalytic Study of the Child, Vol. XIII.* New York: International Universities Press, Inc., pp. 58-60.

107. DREAMS AND THE USES OF REGRESSION. FREUD ANNIVERSARY LECTURE. New York: International Universities Press, Inc.

108. EDUCATION OR THE QUEST FOR OMNISCIENCE. J. Amer. Psa. Assn., VI, pp. 389-412.

109. INTRODUCTION to Ekstein, R. and Wallerstein, R. S.: *The Teaching and Learning of Psychotherapy.* New York: Basic Books, Inc.

1959

110. THE ANALYTIC SITUATION: TOPOGRAPHIC CONSIDERATIONS. Psa. Quart., XXVIII, pp. 455-469.

111. SOME PSYCHOANALYTIC IDEAS APPLIED TO ELATION AND DEPRESSION. Amer. J. Psychiatry, CXVI, pp. 38-43.

1960

112. PSYCHOANALYTIC EDUCATION IN THE UNITED STATES (with H. Ross). New York: W. W. Norton & Co., Inc.

1961

113. THE ORGANIZATION OF PSYCHOANALYTIC EDUCATION. HISTORICAL AND CURRENT. In: *The Birth of an Institute.* Ed. by I. Hendrick. Freeport, Maine: The Bond Wheelwright Co., pp. 95-118.

114. REFLECTIONS ON DEPRESSION. In: *The Psychoanalytic Study of the Child, Vol. XVI.* New York: International Universities Press, Inc., pp. 321-331.

115. REVIEW of Guillain, G.: *J. M. Charcot 1825-1893. His Life—His Work.* Psa. Quart., XXX, pp. 111-113.

1962

116. AMERICAN PSYCHOANALYTIC EDUCATION: HISTORICAL COMMENTS. J. Amer. Psa. Assn., X, pp. 119-126.

117. THE CONSULTATION SERVICE. J. Amer. Psa. Assn., X, pp. 139-144.

118. KNOWLEDGE AND DREAMS. Bull. Phila. Assn. Psa., XII, pp. 97-111.

119. REMINISCENCE AND RETROSPECT. In: *Fruition of an Idea: Fifty Years of Psychoanalysis in New York.* Ed. by M. Wangh. New York: International Universities Press, Inc., pp. 35-42.

120. REVIEW of Scheflen, A. E.: *Psychotherapy of Schizophrenia: Direct Analysis.* J. Nervous & Mental Disease, CXXXIV, pp. 578-581.

121. SUPERVISION: A REPORT BASED ON THE RESPONSES OF 192 SUPERVISORS TO A QUESTIONNAIRE (with H. Ross). New York: American Psychoanalytic Assn., Inc.

1964

122. PSYCHOANALYTIC EDUCATION AND RESEARCH. In: *Vistas in Neuropsychiatry.* Ed. by Y. D. Koskoff and R. J. Shoemaker. Pittsburgh: Univ. of Pittsburgh Press, pp. 83-94.

123. REVIEW of Kleitman, N.: *Sleep and Wakefulness.* Psa. Quart., XXXIII, pp. 430-432.

1965

124. REFLECTIONS ON AFFECT. In: *Drives, Affects, Behavior, Vol. II.* Ed. by M. Schur. New York: International Universities Press, Inc., pp. 23-37.

125. TEACHING AND THE BEGINNINGS OF THEORY. Int. J. Psa., XLVI, pp. 137-139.

1966

126. EDITOR of and INTRODUCTION to *On Character and Libido Development. Six Essays by Karl Abraham.* New York: W. W. Norton & Co., Inc.
127. IN MEMORIAM: JOHN D. BENJAMIN. Psa. Quart., XXXV, pp. 125-126.
128. INTRODUCTION to Garma, A.: *The Psychoanalysis of Dreams.* Chicago: Quadrangle Books, Inc., pp. 15-17.

1967

129. THE PAST AND FUTURE OF PSYCHIATRY. Psychiatric Communications, Western Psychiatric Inst. & Clinic, IX, pp. 1-12.

1968

130. THE IMAGE AND THE PAST. New York: International Universities Press, Inc.
131. UN DETALLE DE LAS ESCENA PRIMARIA (Chapter II of The Image and the Past). Rev. Psicoanálisis (Argentine), XXV, pp. 809-813.
132. PHOBIAS. International Encyclopedia of the Social Sciences, XII, pp. 81-85.
133. IN MEMORIAM: ROBERT WÄLDER. Bull. Phila. Assn. Psa., XVIII, pp. 8-9.
134. FOREWORD to Novey, Samuel A.: *The Second Look, the Reconstruction of Personal History in Psychiatry and Psychoanalysis.* Baltimore: The Johns Hopkins Press.

1969

135. DIALOGO CIENTIFICO: CARTA DEL DOCTOR BERTRAM LEWIN AL DOCTOR LEON GRINBERG, 16 DE AGOSTO DE 1968. Rev. Psicoanálisis (Argentine), XXVI, pp. 227-228.
136. REMARKS ON CREATIVITY, IMAGERY AND THE DREAM. J. Nervous & Mental Disease, CXLIX, pp. 115-121 (Lawrence S. Kubie Festschrift).

1970

137. THE TRAIN RIDE: A STUDY OF ONE OF FREUD'S FIGURES OF SPEECH. Psa. Quart., XXXIX, pp. 71-89.
138. OBITUARY: HERMAN NUNBERG, 1884–1970. Int. J. Psa., LI, pp. 421-423.

1971

139. METAPHOR, MIND, AND MANIKIN. Psa. Quart., XL, pp. 6-39.

REFERENCES

ABERCROMBIE, MINNIE L. J. (1960): *The Anatomy of Judgment. An Investigation into the Processes of Perception and Reasoning.* New York: Basic Books, Inc.

ABRAHAM, KARL (1911): Notes on the Psychoanalytical Investigation and Treatment of Manic-Depressive Insanity and Allied Conditions. In: *Selected Papers of Karl Abraham, M.D., Vol. I.* New York: Basic Books, Inc., 1953, pp. 137-156.

——— (1913a): Should Patients Write Down Their Dreams? In: *Clinical Papers and Essays on Psycho-Analysis. Selected Papers of Karl Abraham, M.D., Vol. II.* New York: Basic Books, Inc., 1955, pp. 33-35.

——— (1913b): Restrictions and Transformations of Scoptophilia in Psycho-Neurotics; with Remarks on Analogous Phenomena in Folk-Psychology. In: *Selected Papers of Karl Abraham, M.D., Vol. I.* New York: Basic Books, Inc., 1953, pp. 169-234.

——— (1913c): A Constitutional Basis of Locomotor Anxiety. In: *Ibid.,* pp. 235-243.

——— (1913d): On the Psychogenesis of Agoraphobia in Childhood. In: *Clinical Papers and Essays on Psycho-Analysis. Selected Papers of Karl Abraham, M.D., Vol. II.* New York: Basic Books, Inc., 1955, pp. 42-43.

——— (1916): The First Pregenital Stage of the Libido. In: *Selected Papers of Karl Abraham, M.D., Vol. I.* New York: Basic Books, Inc., 1953, pp. 248-279.

——— (1924a): A Short Study of the Development of the Libido, Viewed in the Light of Mental Disorders. In: *Ibid.,* pp. 418-501.

——— (1924b): The Influence of Oral Erotism on Character-Formation. In: *Ibid.,* pp. 393-406.

ALEXANDER, FRANZ (1925): Dreams in Pairs and Series. In: *The Psychoanalytic Reader, Vol. I.* Edited by Robert Fliess. New York: International Universities Press, Inc., 1948, pp. 371-377.

——— (1927a): *Zur Theorie der Zwangneurosen und der Phobien.* Int. Ztschr. f. Psa., XIII, pp. 20-35.

——— (1927b): *The Psychoanalysis of the Total Personality; The Application of Freud's Theory of the Ego to the Neuroses.* New York and Washington: Nervous and Mental Disease Publishing Co., 1930.

——— (1932): *The Medical Value of Psychoanalysis.* New York: W. W. Norton & Co., Inc.; London: Allen & Unwin.

ANTHONY, E. JAMES (1961): A Study of 'Screen Sensations'. In: *The Psychoanalytic Study of the Child, Vol. XVI.* New York: International Universities Press, Inc., pp. 211-245.

ARLOW, JACOB A. (1969): *Unconscious Fantasy and Disturbances of Conscious Experience.* Psa. Quart., XXXVIII, pp. 1-27.

ASHBY, W. ROSS (1952): *Design for a Brain.* New York: John Wiley & Sons, Inc.

BALDWIN, J. M., Editor (1940): *Dictionary of Philosophy and Psychology.* New York: Peter Smith.

BALINT, MICHAEL (1947): *On the Psycho-Analytic Training System.* Int. J. Psa., XXIX, pp. 163-173.

——— (1954): *Analytic Training and Training Analysis.* Int. J. Psa., XXXV, pp. 157-162.

BANDLER, BERNARD (1960): *The American Psychoanalytic Association 1960.* J. Amer. Psa. Assn., VIII, pp. 389-406.

BATESON, GREGORY and MEAD, MARGARET (1942): *Balinese Character. A Photographic Analysis.* New York: The New York Academy of Sciences.

BENEDEK, THERESE (1955): *A Contribution to the Problem of Termination of Training Analysis.* J. Amer. Psa. Assn., III, pp. 615-629.

BENJAMIN, JOHN D. (1961): *Some Developmental Observations Relating to the Theory of Anxiety.* J. Amer. Psa. Assn., IX, pp. 652-668.

BERES, DAVID (1957): *Communication in Psychoanalysis and in the Creative Process: A Parallel.* J. Amer. Psa. Assn., V, pp. 408-423.

BERLIN, ISAIAH (1956): *The Age of Enlightenment.* New York: Mentor Books.

BIBRING, EDWARD (1953): The Mechanism of Depression. In: *Affective Disorders. Psychoanalytic Contribution to Their Study.* Edited by Phyllis Greenacre. New York: International Universities Press, Inc., pp. 13-48.

BIBRING, GRETE L. (1954): *The Training Analysis and Its Place in Psycho-Analytic Training.* Int. J. Psa., XXXV, pp. 169-173.

BINGER, CARL (1945): *The Doctor's Job.* New York: W. W. Norton & Co., Inc.

BLALOCK, J. R. (1936): *Psychology of the Manic Phase of the Manic-Depressive Psychoses.* Psychiat. Quart., X, 1936, pp. 262-344.

BLITZSTEIN, N. LIONEL; EISSLER, RUTH S.; EISSLER, K. R. (1950): Emergence of Hidden Ego Tendencies during Dream Analysis. In: *The Yearbook of Psychoanalysis, Vol. VII.* Edited by Sandor Lorand. New York: International Universities Press, Inc., 1951, pp. 71-80.

BONAPARTE, MARIE (1933): *The Life and Works of Edgar Allan Poe. A Psychoanalytic Interpretation.* London: Imago Publishing Co., Ltd., 1949.

——— (1945): Notes on the Analytic Discovery of the Primal Scene. In: *The Psychoanalytic Study of the Child, Vol. I.* New York: International Universities Press, Inc., pp. 119-125.

BONHOEFFER, KARL (1910): *Die symptomatischen Psychosen.* Leipzig and Vienna: Deuticke.

BORNSTEIN, BERTA (1936): *Ein Beispiel für die Leugnung durch die Phantasie.* Ztschr. f. psa. Päd., X, pp. 269-275.

——— (1949): The Analysis of a Phobic Child. Some Problems of Theory and Technique in Child Analysis. In: *The Psychoanalytic Study of the Child, Vol. III/IV.* New York: International Universities Press, Inc., pp. 181-226.

BREUER, JOSEF and FREUD (1893-1895): *Studies on Hysteria.* Standard Edition, II.

BRILL, A. A. (1928a): *The Application of Psychoanalysis to Psychiatry.* J. Nervous & Mental Disease, LXVIII, pp. 561-577.

——— (1928b): The Schizoid Concept in the Neuroses and Psychoses. In: *Schizophrenia (Dementia Praecox). Proceedings of the Assn. for Research in Nervous and Mental Disease for 1925, Vol. V.* New York: Paul Hoeber, Inc., pp. 31-43.

——— (1941): *Necrophilia.* J. Criminal Psychopathol., II, pp. 433-443; III, pp. 51-73.

(1946): *Lectures on Psychoanalytic Psychiatry.* New York: Alfred A. Knopf.

BRITTAIN, FREDERICK (1962): *Introduction to the Penguin Book of Latin Verse.* Baltimore: Penguin Books.

BROMBERG, WALTER and SCHILDER, PAUL (1933): *Psychologic Considerations in Alcoholic Hallucinosis—Castration and Dismembering Motives.* Int. J. Psa., XIV, pp. 206-224.

BRUNSWICK, RUTH MACK (1928a): *The Analysis of a Case of Paranoia (Delusions of Jealousy).* J. Nervous & Mental Disease, LXX, 1929, pp. 1-22, 155-178.

——— (1928b): *A Supplement to Freud's 'History of an Infantile Neurosis'.* Int. J. Psa., IX, pp. 439-476.

——— (1929): *A Note on the Childish Theory of Coitus a Tergo.* Int. J. Psa., X, pp. 93-95.

BURTT, EDWIN ARTHUR (1954): *The Metaphysical Foundation of Modern Physical Science.* Garden City, N.Y.: Doubleday & Co., Inc.

BUTTERFIELD, HERBERT (1949): *The Origins of Modern Science.* London: G. Bell & Sons, Ltd.

CHANDLER, R. and SCHWARTZ, K., Editors (1967): *A New Anthology of Spanish Literature, Vol. II.* Baton Rouge: Louisiana State University Press.

CHAPPELL, V. C., Editor (1962): *The Philosophy of Mind.* Englewood Cliffs, N.J.: Prentice-Hall, Inc.

COHN, FRANZ (1928): *Aus der Analyse eines Falles von Strassenangst.* Int. Ztschr. f. Psa., XIV, pp. 387-400.

COLBY, KENNETH MARK (1955): *Energy and Structure in Psychoanalysis.* New York: The Ronald Press Co.

CORIAT, ISADOR (1928): *Stammering. A Psychoanalytic Interpretation.* (Nervous and Mental Disease Monograph No. 47.) Washington, D.C.: Nervous and Mental Disease Publishing Co.

DARWIN, ERASMUS (1794): *Zoonomia, Vols. I, II.* London: J. Johnson.

DAVISON, CHARLES (1945): *Psychological and Psychodynamic Aspects of Disturbances in the Sleep Mechanism.* Psa. Quart., XIV, pp. 478-497.

DE SAUVAGES, F. B. (1768): *Nosologia Methodica.* Amstelodami: Frates de Tournes.

DEUTSCH, HELENE (1925): *Zur Psychoanalyse der weiblichen Sexualfunktionen.* Leipzig, Vienna: Internationaler Psychoanalytischer Verlag.

——— (1928): *The Genesis of Agoraphobia.* Int. J. Psa., X, 1929, pp. 51-69.

——— (1930): *Psychoanalysis of the Neuroses.* London: The Hogarth Press and The Institute of Psycho-Analysis, 1932.

——— (1932): *On Female Homosexuality.* Psa. Quart., I, pp. 484-510.

——— (1933): *Psychologie der manisch-depressiven Zustände insbesondere der chronischen Hypomanie.* Int. Ztschr. f. Psa., XIX, pp. 358-371.

——— (1937): *Absence of Grief.* Psa. Quart., VI, pp. 12-22.

DODDS, E. R. (1951): *The Greeks and the Irrational.* Boston: Beacon Press.

DUNBAR, FLANDERS (1943): *Psychosomatic Diagnosis.* New York: Paul Hoeber, Inc.

EDER, M. D. (1930): *Dreams—as Resistance.* Int. J. Psa., XI, pp. 40-47.

EHRENBERG, W. (1967): *'Maxwell's Demon'.* Scientific American, CCXVII, pp. 103-111.

EISLER, MICHAEL J. (1921): *Pleasure in Sleep and Disturbed Capacity for Sleep.* Int. J. Psa., III, 1922, pp. 30-42.

EISSLER, K. R. (1943): *Some Psychiatric Aspects of Anorexia Nervosa, Demonstrated by a Case Report.* Psa. Rev., XXX, pp. 121-145.

EISSLER, K. R. (cont'd.) (1951): *Remarks on the Psycho-Analysis of Schizophrenia.* Int. J. Psa., XXXII, pp. 139-156.

——— (1963): *Goethe. A Psychoanalytic Study, 1775-1786, Vol. I.* Detroit: Wayne State University Press.

——— (1965): *Medical Orthodoxy and the Future of Psychoanalysis.* New York: International Universities Press, Inc.

EKSTEIN, RUDOLF (1953): On Current Trends in Psychoanalytic Technique. In: *Explorations in Psychoanalysis. Essays in Honor of Theodor Reik on the Occasion of His Sixty-Fifth Birthday, May 12, 1953.* Edited by Robert M. Lindner. New York: The Julian Press, Inc.

——— (1955): *Termination of the Training Analysis within the Framework of Present-Day Institutes.* J. Amer. Psa. Assn., III, pp. 600-614.

——— and RANGELL, LEO (1961): *Reconstruction and Theory Formation.* J. Amer. Psa. Assn., IX, pp. 684-697.

EVANS-WENTZ, W. Y., Editor (1949): *The Tibetan Book of the Dead or The After-Death Experiences on the Bardo Plane, according to Lāma Kazi Dawa-Samdup's English Rendering.* London: Oxford University Press.

FARROW, E. PICKWORTH (1945): *Psychoanalyze Yourself. A Practical Method of Self-Analysis Enabling a Person to Remove Unreasoning Fears and Depressions from His Mind.* New York: International Universities Press, Inc.

FEDERN, PAUL (1913): *Ein Fall von Pavor Nocturnus mit Subjektiven Lichterscheinungen.* Int. Ztschr. f. Psa., I, pp. 556-559.

——— (1926): Some Variations in Ego-Feeling. In: *Ego Psychology and the Psychoses.* Edited by Edoardo Weiss. New York: Basic Books, Inc., 1952, pp. 25-37.

——— (1932): Ego Feeling in Dreams. In: *Ibid.*, pp. 60-89.

——— (1934): The Awakening of the Ego in Dreams. In: *Ibid.*, pp. 90-96.

——— (1936): On the Distinction between Healthy and Pathological Narcissism. In: *Ibid.*, pp. 323-364.

——— (1952): *Ego Psychology and the Psychoses.* Edited by Edoardo Weiss. New York: Basic Books, Inc.

FEIGENBAUM, DORIAN (1926): *A Case of Hysterical Depression. Mechanisms of Identification and Castration.* Psa. Rev., XIII, pp. 404-423.

FENICHEL, OTTO (1927): The Economic Function of Screen Memories. In: *Collected Papers of Otto Fenichel, Vol. I.* New York: W. W. Norton & Co., Inc., 1953, pp. 113-116.

FENICHEL, OTTO (cont'd.) (1928a): The Dread of Being Eaten. In: *Ibid.*, pp. 158-159.

——— (1928b): On the Inner Injunction to 'Make a Mental Note'. In: *Ibid.*, pp. 153-154.

——— (1932): *Outline of Clinical Psychoanalysis.* New York: W. W. Norton & Co., Inc.

——— (1934): On the Psychology of Boredom. In: *Collected Papers of Otto Fenichel, Vol. I.* New York: W. W. Norton & Co., Inc., 1953, pp. 292-302.

——— (1936): The Symbolic Equation: Girl = Phallus. In: *Collected Papers of Otto Fenichel, Vol. II.* New York: W. W. Norton & Co., 1954, pp. 3-18.

——— (1942): Participant in *Symposium on Neurotic Disturbances of Sleep.* Int. J. Psa., XXIII, pp. 49, 62-64.

——— (1944): Remarks on the Common Phobias. In: *Collected Papers of Otto Fenichel, Vol. II.* New York: W. W. Norton & Co., Inc., 1954, pp. 278-287.

——— (1945): *The Psychoanalytic Theory of Neurosis.* New York: W. W. Norton & Co., Inc.

FERENCZI, SANDOR (1909): Introjection and Transference. In: *Sex in Psychoanalysis.* (First titled *Contributions to Psychoanalysis.*) New York: Basic Books, Inc., 1950, pp. 35-93.

——— (1916): Interchange of Affect in Dreams. In: *Further Contributions to the Theory and Technique of Psychoanalysis. The Selected Papers of Sandor Ferenczi, M.D., Vol. II.* New York: Basic Books, Inc., 1952, p. 345.

——— (1916/1917a): Composite Formations of Erotic and Character Traits. In: *Ibid.*, pp. 257-258.

——— (1916/1917b): Disease—or Patho-Neuroses. In: *Ibid.*, pp. 78-89.

——— (1916/1917c): Pollution without Dream Orgasm and Dream Orgasm without Pollution. In: *Ibid.*, pp. 297-304.

——— (1919): On the Technique of Psycho-Analysis. In: *Ibid.*, pp. 177-189.

——— (1922): Bridge Symbolism and the Don Juan Legend. In: *Ibid.*, pp. 356-358.

——— (1923a): An 'Anal Hollow-Penis' in Woman. In: *Ibid.*, p. 317.

——— (1923b): The Dream of the 'Clever Baby'. In: *Ibid.*, pp. 349-350.

——— (1924): *Thalassa. A Theory of Genitality.* New York: W. W. Norton & Co., Inc., 1968. (Originally published by The Psychoanalytic Quarterly, Inc., 1938.)

FERENCZI, SANDOR (cont'd.) (1925): Psychoanalysis of Sexual Habits. In: *Further Contributions to the Theory and Technique of Psychoanalysis. The Selected Papers of Sandor Ferenczi, M.D., Vol. II.* New York: Basic Books, Inc., 1952, pp. 259-297.

——— (1927): Gulliver Phantasies. In: *Final Contributions to the Theory and Technique of Psychoanalysis. The Selected Papers of Sandor Ferenczi, M.D., Vol. III.* New York: Basic Books, Inc., 1955, pp. 41-60.

——— (1931): On the Revision of the Interpretation of Dreams. In: *Ibid.,* pp. 238-243.

——— and RANK, OTTO (1924): *The Development of Psychoanalysis.* New York and Washington: Nervous and Mental Disease Publishing Co., 1925.

FISHER, CHARLES (1953): *Studies on the Nature of Suggestion, Part I. Experimental Induction of Dreams by Direct Suggestion.* J. Amer. Psa. Assn., I, pp. 222-255.

FLIESS, ROBERT (1953): *The Revival of Interest in the Dream. A Critical Study of Post-Freudian Psychoanalytic Contributions.* New York: International Universities Press, Inc.

FLUGEL, J. C. (1930): *The Psychology of Clothes.* London: Hogarth Press, 1950.

FRENCH, THOMAS M. (1929): *Psychogenic Material Related to the Semicircular Canals.* Int. J. Psa., X, pp. 398-410.

——— (1937): *Reality Testing in Dreams.* Psa. Quart., VI, pp. 62-77.

——— (1952): *The Integration of Behavior. Basic Postulate, Vol. I.* Chicago: University of Chicago Press.

FREUD, ANNA (1936): *The Ego and the Mechanisms of Defence.* New York: International Universities Press, Inc., 1948.

——— (1953): Some Remarks on Infant Observation. In: *The Psychoanalytic Study of the Child, Vol. VIII.* New York: International Universities Press, Inc., pp. 9-19.

——— (1954): Discussant: Problems of Infantile Neurosis. A Discussion. In: *The Psychoanalytic Study of the Child, Vol. IX.* New York: International Universities Press, Inc., pp. 16-71.

——— (1965): *Normality and Pathology in Childhood. Assessments of Development.* New York: International Universities Press, Inc.

FREUD, SIGMUND (1887-1902): *The Origins of Psycho-Analysis. Letters to Wilhelm Fliess, Drafts and Notes: 1887-1902.* Edited by Marie Bonaparte, Anna Freud, Ernst Kris. New York: Basic Books, Inc., 1954.

——— (1888-1892): *Papers on Hypnotism and Suggestion.* Standard Edition, I, pp. 75-172.

FREUD, SIGMUND (cont'd.) (1891): *On Aphasia, a Critical Study*. New York: International Universities Press, Inc.; London: Imago Publishing Co., 1953.

——— (1894): *The Neuro-Psychoses of Defence*. Standard Edition, III, pp. 45-61.

——— (1895): *Project for a Scientific Psychology*. Standard Edition, I, pp. 295-397.

——— (1899): *Screen Memories*. Standard Edition, III, pp. 303-322.

——— (1900-1901): *The Interpretation of Dreams*. Standard Edition, IV/V.

——— (1901): *The Psychopathology of Everyday Life*. Standard Edition, VI.

——— (1905 [1901]): *Fragment of an Analysis of a Case of Hysteria*. Standard Edition, VII, pp. 7-122.

——— (1908a): *Character and Anal Erotism*. Standard Edition, IX, pp. 169-175.

——— (1908b): *Some General Remarks on Hysterical Attacks*. Standard Edition, IX, pp. 229-234.

——— (1909a): *Analysis of a Phobia in a Five-Year-Old Boy*. Standard Edition, X, pp. 5-149.

——— (1909b): *Notes upon a Case of Obsessional Neurosis*. Standard Edition, X, pp. 155-318.

——— (1911a): *Psycho-Analytic Notes on an Autobiographical Account of a Case of Paranoia (Dementia Paranoides)*. Standard Edition, XII, pp. 9-82.

——— (1911b): *The Handling of Dream-Interpretation in Psycho-Analysis*. Standard Edition, XII, pp. 91-96.

——— (1913a): *The Disposition to Obsessional Neurosis. A Contribution to the Problem of Choice of Neurosis*. Standard Edition, XII, pp. 317-326.

——— (1913b): *On Beginning the Treatment. (Further Recommendations on the Technique of Psycho-Analysis)*. Standard Edition, XII, pp. 123-144.

——— (1914a): *On the History of the Psycho-Analytic Movement*. Standard Edition, XIV, pp. 7-66.

——— (1914b): *On Narcissism: An Introduction*. Standard Edition, XIV, pp. 73-102.

——— (1915a): *The Unconscious*. Standard Edition, XIV, pp. 166-215.

——— (1915b): *Instincts and Their Vicissitudes*. Standard Edition, XIV, pp. 117-140.

——— (1915c): *Mourning and Melancholia*. Standard Edition, XIV, pp. 243-258.

FREUD, SIGMUND (cont'd.) (1915d): *A Metapsychological Supplement to the Theory of Dreams.* Standard Edition, XIV, pp. 222-235.

——— (1915/1917): *Introductory Lectures on Psycho-Analysis.* Standard Edition, XV/XVI.

——— (1917): *On Transformations of Instinct as Exemplified in Anal Erotism.* Standard Edition, XVII, pp. 127-133.

——— (1918 [1914]): *From the History of an Infantile Neurosis.* Standard Edition, XVII, pp. 7-122.

——— (1919): *'A Child is Being Beaten': A Contribution to the Study of the Origin of Sexual Perversions.* Standard Edition, XVII, pp. 179-204.

——— (1920a): *A Note on the Prehistory of the Technique of Analysis.* Standard Edition, XVIII, pp. 263-265.

——— (1920b): *Beyond the Pleasure Principle.* Standard Edition, XVIII, pp. 7-64.

——— (1921): *Group Psychology and the Analysis of the Ego.* Standard Edition, XVIII, pp. 69-143.

——— (1923a): *The Ego and the Id.* Standard Edition, XIX, pp. 12-66.

——— (1923b): *Neurosis and Psychosis.* Standard Edition, XIX, pp. 149-153.

——— (1924a): *The Economic Problem of Masochism.* Standard Edition, XIX, pp. 159-170.

——— (1924b): *A Note upon the 'Mystic Writing-Pad'.* Standard Edition, XIX, pp. 227-232.

——— (1925a): *Inhibitions, Symptoms and Anxiety.* Standard Edition, XX, pp. 87-174.

——— (1925b): *Negation.* Standard Edition, XIX, pp. 235-239.

——— (1926): *The Question of Lay Analysis. Conversations with an Impartial Person.* Standard Edition, XX, pp. 183-258.

——— (1927): *Fetishism.* Standard Edition, XXI, pp. 152-157.

——— (1929a): *Some Dreams of Descartes'. A Letter to Maxime Leroy.* Standard Edition, XXI, pp. 203-204.

——— (1929b): *Civilization and Its Discontents.* Standard Edition, XXI, pp. 64-145.

——— (1931): *Female Sexuality.* Standard Edition, XXI, pp. 225-243.

——— (1932): *New Introductory Lectures on Psycho-Analysis.* Standard Edition, XXII, pp. 5-182.

——— (1937a): *Analysis Terminable and Interminable.* Standard Edition, XXIII, pp. 216-253.

——— (1937b): *Constructions in Analysis.* Standard Edition, XXIII, pp. 257-269.

FREUD, SIGMUND (cont'd.) (1938): *Splitting of the Ego in the Process of Defence.* Standard Edition, XXIII, pp. 275-278.

FRIEDMAN, PAUL (1949): *Some Aspects of Concentration Camp Psychology.* Amer. J. Psychiat., CV, pp. 601-605.

——— (1952): *The Bridge: A Study in Symbolism.* Psa. Quart., XXI, pp. 49-80.

FUCHS, EDWARD (1909-1912): *Illustrierte Sittengeschichte vom Mittelalter bis zur Gegenwart.* München: Albert Langen.

GAMOW, GEORGE (1961): *Biography of Physics.* New York: Harper & Row, Publishers, Inc.

GARCÍA LORCA, FEDERICO (1955): *Poet in New York.* New York: Grove Press, Inc.

GARDINER, MURIEL M. (1953): *Meetings with the Wolf-Man.* Bull. Menninger Clinic, XVII, pp. 41-48.

——— (1958): Introduction to *How I Came into Analysis with Freud* (By the Wolf Man). J. Amer. Psa. Assn., VI, p. 348.

GARMA, ANGEL (1947): *Morfologia y fisiologia genital en sueños.* Rev. Psicoanálisis, V, pp. 31-92.

GERO, GEORGE (1936): *The Construction of Depression.* Int. J. Psa., XVII, pp. 423-461.

——— (1939): *Zum Problem der oralen Fixierung.* Int. Ztschr. f. Psa., XXIV, pp. 239-257.

——— (1951): *Defenses in Symptom Formation.* J. Amer. Psa. Assn., I, pp. 87-103.

GITELSON, MAXWELL (1954): *Therapeutic Problems in the Analysis of the 'Normal' Candidate.* Int. J. Psa., XXXV, pp. 174-183.

GLOVER, EDWARD (1925): *Notes on Oral Character Formation.* Int. J. Psa., VI, pp. 131-154.

——— (1950): *Freud or Jung.* New York: W. W. Norton & Co., Inc.

GOMULICKI, BRONISLAW (1953): *The Development and Present Status of the Trace Theory of Memory.* Brit. J. Psychol. Monograph Supplement 29. London and New York: Cambridge University Press.

GRABER, GUSTAV HANS (1937): *Die zweierlei Mechanismen der Identifizierung.* Imago, XXIII, pp. 24-48.

GREENACRE, PHYLLIS (1949): A Contribution to the Study of Screen Memories. In: *The Psychoanalytic Study of the Child, Vol. III/IV.* New York: International Universities Press, Inc., pp. 73-84.

——— (1952): *Trauma, Growth and Personality.* New York: International Universities Press, Inc., 1969.

GREENACRE, PHYLLIS (cont'd.) (1953a): Certain Relationships between Fetishism and Faulty Development of the Body Image. In: *The Psychoanalytic Study of the Child, Vol. VIII.* New York: International Universities Press, Inc., pp. 79-98.

——— (1953b): Penis Awe and Penis Envy. In: *Drives, Affects, Behavior, Vol. I.* Edited by Rudolph M. Loewenstein. New York: International Universities Press, Inc., pp. 176-190.

——— (1955): *Swift and Carroll. A Psychoanalytic Study of Two Lives.* New York: International Universities Press, Inc.

GREENSON, RALPH R. (1949): *The Psychology of Apathy.* Psa. Quart., XVIII, pp. 290-302.

GREGG, ALAN (1956): *Challenges to Contemporary Medicine.* New York: Columbia University Press.

GRIESINGER, WILHELM (1867): *Mental Pathology and Therapeutics.* London: Sydenham Society.

GROTJAHN, MARTIN (1938): *Dream Observations in a Two-Year-Four-Months-Old Baby.* Psa. Quart., VII, pp. 507-513.

——— (1942): *The Process of Awakening.* Psa. Rev., XXIX, pp. 1-19.

——— (1945): *Laughter in Dreams.* Psa. Quart., XIV, pp. 221-227.

——— and FRENCH, THOMAS M. (1938): *Akinesia after Ventriculography. A Contribution to Ego Psychology and the Problem of Sleep.* Psa. Quart., VII, pp. 319-328.

HÁRNIK, J. (1923): *The Various Developments Undergone by Narcissism in Men and Women.* Int. J. Psa., V, 1924, pp. 66-83.

——— (1928): *The Economic Relations between the Sense of Guilt and Feminine Narcissism.* Psa. Rev., XV, pp. 94-95.

——— (1931): *Introjection and Projection in the Mechanism of Depression.* Int. J. Psa., XIII, 1932, pp. 425-432.

——— (1932): *Pleasure in Disguise, the Need for Decoration, and the Sense of Beauty.* Psa. Quart., I, pp. 216-264.

HARTMANN, HEINZ (1939): *Ego Psychology and the Problem of Adaptation.* New York: International Universities Press, Inc., 1958.

——— (1947): On Rational and Irrational Action. In: *Psychoanalysis and the Social Sciences, Vol. I.* Edited by Géza Róheim. New York: International Universities Press, Inc., pp. 359-392.

——— (1950): Comments on the Psychoanalytic Theory of the Ego. In: *The Psychoanalytic Study of the Child, Vol. V.* New York: International Universities Press, Inc., pp. 74-96.

——— (1964): *Essays on Ego Psychology. Selected Problems in Psychoanalytic Theory.* New York: International Universities Press, Inc.

HARTMANN, HEINZ; KRIS, ERNST; LOEWENSTEIN, RUDOLPH M. (1951): Some Psychoanalytic Comments on 'Culture and Personality'. In: *Psychoanalysis and Culture. Essays in Honor of Géza Róheim.* Edited by George B. Wilbur and Warner Muensterberger. New York: International Universities Press, Inc., pp. 3-31.

——— ——— ——— (1953): The Function of Theory in Psychoanalysis. In: *Drives, Affects, Behavior, Vol. I.* Edited by Rudolph M. Loewenstein. New York: International Universities Press, Inc., pp. 13-37.

HEILBRUNN, GERT (1953): *Fusion of the Isakower Phenomenon with the Dream Screen.* Psa. Quart., XXII, pp. 200-204.

HEIMANN, PAULA (1954): *Problems of the Training Analysis.* Int. J. Psa., XXXV, pp. 163-168.

HEINROTH, JOHANN (1818): *Lehrbuch der Störungen des Seelenliebens oder der Seelenstörungen und ihrer Behandlung.* Leipzig: F. C. W. Vogel.

HENDRICK, IVES (1931): *Ego Defence and the Mechanism of Oral Ejection in Schizophrenia: The Psycho-Analysis of a Pre-Psychotic Case.* Int. J. Psa., XII, pp. 298-325.

——— (1955): *Presidential Address: Professional Standards of the American Psychoanalytic Association.* J. Amer. Psa. Assn., III, pp. 561-599.

———, Editor (1961): *The Birth of an Institute. Twenty-fifth Anniversary of the Boston Psychoanalytic Institute, 1958.* Freeport, Maine: The Bond Wheelwright Co.

HOCH, AUGUST (1921): *Benign Stupors. A Study of a New Manic-Depressive Reaction Type.* New York: The Macmillan Co.

HOCKETT, CHARLES P. (1958): *A Course in Modern Linguistics.* New York: The Macmillan Co.

HODGES, H. A. (1952): *The Philosophy of Wilhelm Dilthey.* London: Routledge and Kegan Paul, Ltd.

HOFFER, WILLI (1952): The Mutual Influences in the Development of Ego and Id: Earliest Stages. In: *The Psychoanalytic Study of the Child, Vol. VII.* New York: International Universities Press, Inc., pp. 31-41.

ISAKOWER, OTTO (1936): *A Contribution to the Patho-Psychology of Phenomena Associated with Falling Asleep.* Int. J. Psa., XIX, 1938, pp. 331-345.

——— (1939): *On the Exceptional Position of the Auditory Sphere.* Int. J. Psa., XX, pp. 340-348.

——— (1954): *Spoken Words in Dreams. A Preliminary Communication.* Psa. Quart., XXIII, pp. 1-6.

——— (1963): *Minutes of the Faculty Meeting, New York Psychoanalytic Institute, November 20.*

JACOBSON, EDITH (1943): *Depression. The Œdipus Conflict in the Development of Depressive Mechanisms.* Psa. Quart. XII, pp. 541-560.

——— (1953): The Affects and Their Pleasure-Unpleasure Qualities in Relation to the Psychic Discharge Processes. In: *Drives, Affects, Behavior, Vol. I.* Edited by Rudolph M. Loewenstein. New York: International Universities Press, Inc., pp. 38-66.

——— (1954): *Contribution to the Metapsychology of Psychotic Identifications.* J. Amer. Psa. Assn., II, pp. 239-262.

JAMES, WILLIAM (1890): *Principles of Psychology, Vols. I and II.* New York: Dover Publications, Inc., 1972.

——— (1902): *The Varieties of Religious Experience.* London: Longmans, Green, 1928.

——— (1909): *A Pluralistic Universe.* New York: Longmans, Green, 1915.

JASPERS, KARL (1920): *Allgemeine Psychopathologie.* Berlin: Julius Springer.

JEKELS, LUDWIG (1945): *A Bioanalytical Contribution to the Problem of Sleep and Wakefulness.* Psa. Quart., XIV, pp. 169-189.

——— and BERGLER, EDMUND (1940): *Instinct Dualism in Dreams.* Psa. Quart., IX, pp. 394-414.

JONES, ERNEST (1910): Simulated Foolishness in Hysteria. In: *Papers on Psycho-Analysis.* (Third Edition.) London: Baillière, Tindall & Cox; Baltimore: William Wood & Co., 1925, pp. 475-486.

——— (1911): Some Instances of the Influence of Dreams on Waking Life. In: *Ibid.,* pp. 247-254.

——— (1912): A Forgotten Dream. Note on the Œdipus Saving Phantasy. In: *Ibid.,* pp. 255-265.

——— (1916): The Theory of Symbolism. In: *Papers on Psycho-Analysis.* (Second Edition.) London: Baillière, Tindall & Cox; Baltimore: William Wood & Co., 1918, pp. 129-186.

——— (1933): The Psychology of Religion. In: *Psychoanalysis Today.* Edited by Sandor Lorand. New York: Covici-Friede, pp. 323-337.

——— (1936): *The Future of Psycho-Analysis.* Int. J. Psa., XVII, pp. 269-277.

——— (1953-1957): *The Life and Work of Sigmund Freud, 3 Vols.* New York: Basic Books, Inc.

JUNG, CARL GUSTAV (1916): *Psychology of the Unconscious. A Study of the Transformations and Symbolisms of the Libido. A Contribution to the History of the Evolution of Thought.* New York: Dodd, Mead & Co., 1944; London: Kegan Paul, Trench, Trubner & Co., Ltd., 1946.

KAGAN, J., Editor (1968): *Creativity and Learning.* Boston: Beacon Press.

KANZER, MARK (1958): *Image Formation during Free Association.* Psa. Quart., XXVII, pp. 465-484.

KATAN, ANNY (1934): *Einige Bemerkungen über den Optimismus.* Int. Ztschr. f. Psa., XX, pp. 191-199.

——— (1937): *The Role of 'Displacement' in Agoraphobia.* Int. J. Psa., XXXII, 1951, pp. 41-50.

KATAN, MAURITS (1950): *Schreber's Hallucinations about the 'Little Men'.* Int. J. Psa., XXXI, pp. 32-35.

——— (1953): Mania and the Pleasure Principle: Primary and Secondary Symptoms. In: *Affective Disorders. Psychoanalytic Contribution to Their Study.* Edited by Phyllis Greenacre. New York: International Universities Press, Inc., pp. 140-209.

KEPECS, JOSEPH G. (1952): *A Waking Screen Analogous to the Dream Screen.* Psa. Quart., XXI, pp. 167-171.

KIRBY, GEORGE H. (1913): *The Catatonia Syndrome and Its Relation to Manic-Depressive Insanity.* J. Nervous and Mental Disease, XL, pp. 694-704.

KLEIN, FELIX (1890-1908): *Elementary Mathematics from an Advanced Standpoint, 2 Vols.* New York: Dover Publications, Inc., 1959.

KLEIN, MELANIE (1932): *The Psychoanalysis of Children.* New York: Grove Press, Inc., 1960.

——— (1935): A Contribution to the Psychogenesis of Manic-Depressive States. In: *Contributions to Psycho-Analysis, 1921-1945.* London: The Hogarth Press, Ltd., and the Institute of Psycho-Analysis, 1948, pp. 282-310.

KLEITMAN, NATHANIEL (1963): *Sleep and Wakefulness.* Chicago: The University of Chicago Press.

KNOX, BERNARD (1960): Sophocles' Œdipus. In: *Tragic Themes in Western Literature.* Edited by Cleanth Brooks. New Haven: Yale University Press, pp. 7-29.

KRAMER, PAUL (1955): On Discovering One's Identity: A Case Report. In: *The Psychoanalytic Study of the Child, Vol. X.* New York: International Universities Press, Inc., pp. 47-74.

KRAMKE, E. (1950): *Theory of Sets.* New York: Dover Publications, Inc.

KRIS, ERNST (1950a): *The Significance of Freud's Earliest Discoveries.* Int. J. Psa., XXXI, pp. 108-116.

—— (1950b): On Preconscious Mental Processes. In: *Psychoanalytic Explorations in Art.* New York: International Universities Press, Inc., 1952, pp. 303-320.

——— (1952): *Psychoanalytic Explorations in Art.* New York: International Universities Press, Inc.

KUBIE, LAWRENCE S. (1930): *A Theoretical Application to Some Neurological Problems of the Properties of Excitation Waves Which Move in Closed Circuits.* Brain, LIII, pp. 166-177.

——— (1948): Instincts and Homeostasis. In: *The Yearbook of Psychoanalysis, Vol. V.* Edited by Sandor Lorand. New York: International Universities Press, Inc., 1949, pp. 157-188.

——— (1958): *The Neurotic Distortion of the Creative Process.* Lawrence: University of Kansas Press.

LAMPL-DE GROOT, JEANNE (1954): *Problems of Psycho-Analytic Training.* Int. J. Psa., XXXV, pp. 184-187.

LEWIN, BERTRAM D. (1945a): Comments on Bateson, G. and Mead, M.: Balinese Character, A Photographic Analysis. In: *The Psychoanalytic Study of the Child, Vol. I.* New York: International Universities Press, Inc., pp. 379-387.

——— (1945b): Review of Binger, Carl: *The Doctor's Job.* Psa. Quart., XIV, pp. 394-397.

——— (1950): *The Psychoanalysis of Elation.* New York: The Psychoanalytic Quarterly, Inc., 1961.

——— (1953): *Reconsideration of the Dream Screen.* Psa. Quart., XXII, pp. 174-199.

——— (1959): *Some Psychoanalytic Ideas Applied to Elation and Depression.* Amer. J. Psychiat., CXVI, pp. 38-43.

——— (1968): *The Image and the Past.* New York: International Universities Press, Inc.

——— and ROSS, HELEN (1960): *Psychoanalytic Education in the United States.* New York: W. W. Norton & Co., Inc.

LEWIN, KURT (1935): *A Dynamic Theory of Personality.* New York: McGraw-Hill Book Co.

——— (1936): *Principles of Topological Psychology.* New York: McGraw-Hill Book Co.

LOEWENSTEIN, RUDOLPH M. (1954): *Some Remarks on Defences, Autonomous Ego and Psycho-Analytic Technique.* Int. J. Psa., XXXV, pp. 188-193.

LORAND, SANDOR (1948): *On the Meaning of Losing Teeth in Dreams.* Psa. Quart., XVII, pp. 529-530.

MAC CURDY, JOHN T. (1925): *The Psychology of Emotion.* New York: Harcourt Brace.

MAENCHEN, ANNA (1942): Participant in *Symposium on Neurotic Disturbances of Sleep.* Int. J. Psa., XXIII, pp. 59-62.

MAGOUN, HORACE W. (1964): Recent Concepts of the Memory Process. In: *Vistas in Neuropsychiatry.* Edited by Y. D. Koskoff and R. J. Shoemaker. Pittsburgh: University of Pittsburgh Press, pp. 25-50.

MALCOVE, LILLIAN (1933): *Bodily Mutilation and Learning to Eat.* Psa. Quart., II, pp. 557-561.

MC CULLOCH, WARREN S. (1951): Why the Mind Is in the Head. In: *Cerebral Mechanisms in Behavior.* (The Hixon Symposium.) Edited by Lloyd A. Jeffress. New York: John Wiley & Sons, Inc., pp. 42-57.

MEYER, ADOLF (1909-1910): *A Discussion of Some Fundamental Issues in Freud's Psycho-Analysis.* State Hospital Bull., II, pp. 827-848.

——— (1917): *The Aims and Meaning of Psychiatric Diagnosis.* Amer. J. Insanity, LXXIV, pp. 163-168.

MEYER, MONROE A. (1922): *Die Traumform als Inhaltsdarstellung.* Int. Ztschr. f. Psa., VIII, pp. 475-477.

——— (1933): Dream Mechanisms and Interpretations. In: *Psychoanalysis Today.* Edited by Sandor Lorand. New York: International Universities Press, Inc., 1944, pp. 151-173.

MITTELMANN, BELA (1940): *Euphoric Reactions in the Course of Psychoanalytic Treatment.* Psa. Rev., XXVII, pp. 27-44.

——— (1949): *Ego Functions and Dreams.* Psa. Quart., XVIII, pp. 434-448.

NEWBOLD, W. R. (1897): *Subconscious Reasoning.* London: Proceedings of the Society for Psychical Research, Vol. XII, pp. 11-20.

NIEDERLAND, WILLIAM G. (1951): *Three Notes on the Schreber Case.* Psa. Quart., XX, pp. 579-591.

——— (1956): Clinical Observations on the 'Little Man' Phenomenon. In: *The Psychoanalytic Study of the Child, Vol. XI.* New York: International Universities Press, Inc., pp. 381-395.

——— (1963): *Further Data and Memorabilia Pertaining to the Schreber Case.* Int. J. Psa., XLIV, pp. 201-207.

——— (1965): An Analytic Inquiry into the Life and Work of Heinrich Schliemann. In: *Drives, Affects, Behavior, Vol. II. Essays in Memory of Marie Bonaparte.* Edited by Max Schur. New York: International Universities Press, Inc., pp. 369-396.

NOVEY, SAMUEL (1966): *Why Some Patients Conduct Actual Investigations of Their Biographies.* J. Amer. Psa. Assn., XIV, pp. 376-387.

——— (1968): *The Second Look: The Reconstruction of Personal History in Psychiatry and Psychoanalysis.* Baltimore: The Johns Hopkins Press.

NUNBERG, HERMAN (1920): On the Catatonic Attack. In: *Practice and Theory of Psychoanalysis.* New York: Nervous and Mental Disease Publishing Co., 1948, pp. 3-23.

——— (1925): The Will to Recovery. In: *Ibid.,* pp. 75-88.

NUNBERG, HERMAN (cont'd.) (1926): The Sense of Guilt and the Need for Punishment. In: *Ibid.*, pp. 89-101.

——— (1932): *Allgemeine Neurosenlehre auf Psychoanalytischer Grundlage.* Bern and Berlin: Hans Huber Verlag.

——— (1938): Psychological Interrelations between Physician and Patient. In: *Practice and Theory of Psychoanalysis.* New York: Nervous and Mental Disease Publishing Co., 1948, pp. 174-184.

——— (1949): *Problems of Bisexuality as Reflected in Circumcision.* London: Imago Publishing Co.

——— (1951): *Transference and Reality.* Int. J. Psa., XXXII, pp. 1-9.

OBERNDORF, CLARENCE P. (1915): *Analysis of a Claustrophobia.* Medical Record, LXXXVIII, pp. 349-353.

——— (1929): *Submucous Resection as a Castration Symbol.* Int. J. Psa., X, pp. 228-241.

——— (1953): *A History of Psychoanalysis in America.* New York: Grune & Stratton, Inc.

OLMSTED, J. M. D. (1944): *François Magendie.* New York: Henry Schuman, Inc.

ONIANS, RICHARD BROXTON (1951): *The Origins of European Thought about the Body, the Mind, the Soul, the World, Time and Fate.* London and New York: Cambridge University Press.

Panel Report (1955): *Scientific Proceedings of the American Psychoanalytic Association. Special Problems in Connection with Termination of Training Analysis.* J. Amer. Psa. Assn., III, pp. 314-323.

PANOFSKY, ERWIN (1939): *Studies in Iconography.* New York: Oxford University Press.

PIAGET, JEAN (1926): *La représentation du monde chez l'enfant.* Paris: Alcan. English edition: *The Child's Conception of the World.* London: Routledge & Kegan Paul, 1960.

——— (1945): *Play, Dreams and Imitation in Childhood.* New York: W. W. Norton & Co., Inc., 1962.

PÖTZL, OTTO (1917): The Relationship between Experimentally Induced Dream Images and Indirect Vision. In: *Preconscious Stimulation in Dreams, Associations, and Images.* Edited by Charles Fisher. (Psychological Issues, II, No. 3, Monograph 7.) New York: International Universities Press, Inc., 1960, pp. 41-120.

PUTNAM, JAMES JACKSON (1914): *Psychoanalysis Considered as a Phase of Education.* J. Nervous and Mental Disease, XLI, pp. 666-669.

RADO, SANDOR (1925): *The Economic Principle in Psychoanalytic Technique.* Int. J. Psa., VI, pp. 35-44.

——— (1926): *The Psychical Effects of Intoxication: Attempt at a Psycho-Analytical Theory of Drug-Addiction.* Int. J. Psa., IX, 1928, pp. 301-317.

——— (1927): *The Problem of Melancholia.* Int. J. Psa., IX, 1928, pp. 420-438.

——— (1933a): *Fear of Castration in Women.* Psa. Quart., II, pp. 425-475.

——— (1933b): *The Psychoanalysis of Pharmacothymia (Drug Addiction).* Psa. Quart., II, pp. 1-23.

Rainbow Report (1955): *Report of the Survey Steering Committee to the Board on Professional Standards of the American Psychoanalytic Association.*

RANK, OTTO (1924a): *The Trauma of Birth.* New York: Basic Books, Inc., 1952.

——— (1924b): *Eine Neurosenanalyse in Träumen. Neue Arbeiten zur ärztlichen Psychoanalyse, III.* Leipzig, Vienna, Zurich: Internationaler Psychoanalytischer Verlag.

RAPAPORT, DAVID (1942): *Emotions and Memory.* New York: International Universities Press, Inc., 1950.

——— (1953): *On the Psycho-Analytic Theory of Affects.* Int. J. Psa., XXXIV, pp. 177-198.

REICH, ANNIE (1954): *Early Identifications as Archaic Elements in the Super-Ego.* J. Amer. Psa. Assn., II, pp. 218-238.

REIDER, NORMAN (1953): A Type of Transference to Institutions. In: *The Yearbook of Psychoanalysis, Vol. X.* Edited by Sandor Lorand. New York: International Universities Press, Inc., 1954, pp. 170-176.

REIK, THEODOR (1931): *Ritual: Psychoanalytic Studies.* New York: W. W. Norton & Co., Inc.

REISS, EDUARD (1910): *Konstitutionelle Verstimmung und manisch-depressives Irresein.* Berlin: J. Springer.

ROBITSEK, ALFRED (1912): *Symbolisches Denken in der Chemischen Forschung.* Imago, I, pp. 83-90.

ROCHLIN, GREGORY (1953): *The Disorder of Depression and Elation. A Clinical Study of the Changes from One State to the Other.* J. Amer. Psa. Assn., I, pp. 438-457.

RÓHEIM, GÉZA (1932): *Animism and Religion.* Psa. Quart., I, pp. 59-112.

——— (1942): *Transition Rites.* Psa. Quart., XI, pp. 336-374.

——— (1945): *War, Crime and the Covenant.* Monticello, N.Y.: Medical Journal Press.

RORSCHACH, H. (1927): *Zwei schweizerische Sektenstifter.* Imago, XIII, pp. 395-441.

ROSEN, JOHN (1953): *Direct Analysis. Selected Papers.* New York: Grune & Stratton, Inc.

ROSEN, VICTOR H. (1955): *The Reconstruction of a Traumatic Childhood Event in a Case of Derealization.* J. Amer. Psa. Assn., III, pp. 211-221.

ROSS, HELEN (1965): The Teacher Game. In: *The Psychoanalytic Study of the Child, Vol. XX.* New York: International Universities Press, Inc., pp. 288-297.

ROSS, W. DONALD and KAPP, FREDERIC T. (1962): *A Technique for Self-Analysis of Countertransference. Use of the Psychoanalyst's Visual Images in Response to Patients' Dreams.* J. Amer. Psa. Assn., X, pp. 643-657.

RYCROFT, CHARLES (1951): *A Contribution to the Study of the Dream Screen.* Int. J. Psa., XXXII, pp. 178-184.

RYLE, GILBERT (1949): *The Concept of Mind.* New York: Barnes & Noble, Inc., 1965.

SACHS, HANNS (1924): *Gemeinsame Tagträume.* In: *Gemeinsame Tagträume.* Leipzig, Vienna and Zurich: Internationaler Psychoanalytischer Verlag.

——— (1928): *One of the Motive Factors in the Formation of the Super-Ego in Women.* Int. J. Psa., X, 1929, pp. 39-50.

——— (1946): *Observations of a Training Analyst.* Psa. Quart., XVI, 1947, pp. 157-168.

SADGER, J. [ISIDOR] (1911): *Haut-, Schleimhaut- und Muskelerotik.* Jahrb. f. psa. und psychopathologische Forschungen, III, pp. 525-556.

SCHILDER, PAUL (1950): *The Image and Appearance of the Human Body.* New York: International Universities Press, Inc.

SCHMIDEBERG, MELITTA (1948): *A Note on Claustrophobia.* Psa. Rev., XXXV, pp. 309-311.

SCHRÖDINGER, ERWIN (1956): *What is Life?* Garden City, N.Y.: Doubleday & Co., Inc.

SCHUR, HELEN (1966): An Observation and Comments on the Development of Memory. In: *The Psychoanalytic Study of the Child, Vol. XXI.* New York: International Universities Press, Inc., pp. 468-479.

SCHUR, MAX (1953): The Ego in Anxiety. In: *Drives, Affects, Behavior, Vol. I.* Edited by Rudolph M. Loewenstein. New York: International Universities Press, Inc., pp. 67-103.

SCOTT, W. CLIFFORD M. (1952): *Patients Who Sleep or Look at the Psycho-Analyst during Treatment—Technical Considerations.* Int. J. Psa., XXXIII, pp. 465-469.

SEROTA, HERMAN (1964): *Home Movies in Early Childhood.* Sciences, CXLIII, p. 1195.

SHARPE, ELLA FREEMAN (1930): Certain Aspects of Sublimation and Delusion. In: *Collected Papers on Psycho-Analysis.* London: The Hogarth Press and the Institute of Psycho-Analysis, 1950, pp. 125-136.

——— (1940): Psycho-Physical Problems Revealed in Language. An Examination of Metaphor. In: *Ibid.,* pp. 155-169.

SHERFEY, MARY JANE (1966): *The Evolution and Nature of Female Sexuality in Relation to Psychoanalytic Theory.* J. Amer. Psa. Assn., XIV, pp. 28-128. (Discussion of this paper by Marcel Heiman, Judith S. Kestenberg, Therese Benedek, and Sylvia Keiser, *ibid.,* XVI, 1968, pp. 406-456.)

SILBERER, HERBERT (1909): *Bericht über eine Methode, gewisse symbolische Halluzinations-Erscheinungen hervorzurufen und zu beobachten.* Jahrb. f. psa. und psychopathologische Forschungen, I, pp. 513-525.

——— (1911): *Symbolik des Erwachens und Schwellensymbolik überhaupt.* Jahrb. f. psa. und psychopathologische Forschungen, III, pp. 621-660.

——— (1914): *Der Homunculus.* Imago, III, pp. 37-79.

SIMMEL, ERNST (1926): *The 'Doctor-Game', Illness and the Profession of Medicine.* Int. J. Psa., VII, pp. 470-483.

——— (1942): Participant in *Symposium on Neurotic Disturbances of Sleep.* Int. J. Psa., XXIII, pp. 65-68.

——— (1944): *Self-Preservation and the Death Instinct.* Psa. Quart., XIII, pp. 160-185.

SMITH, NORMAN KEMP (1952): *New Studies in the Philosophy of Descartes.* London: Macmillan & Co., Ltd.

SPENDER, STEPHEN (1956): *Notes from a Diary.* Encounter, VI, pp. 82-83.

SPITZ, RENÉ A. (in collaboration with Cobliner, W. Godfrey) (1965): *The First Year of Life. A Psychoanalytic Study of Normal and Deviant Development of Object Relations.* New York: International Universities Press, Inc.

SPRING, WILLIAM J. (1939): *Observations on World Destruction Fantasies.* Psa. Quart., VIII, pp. 48-56.

STAUDENMAIER, LUDWIG (1912): *Die Magie als experimentelle Wissenschaft.* Leipzig: Akademische Verlagsgesellschaft.

STEIN, MARTIN (1965): States of Consciousness in the Analytic Situation. In: *Drives, Affects, Behavior, Vol. II. Essays in Memory of Marie Bonaparte.* Edited by Max Schur. New York: International Universities Press, Inc., pp. 60-86.

STERBA, RICHARD (1946): *Dreams and Acting Out.* Psa. Quart., XV, pp. 175-179.

STONE, LEO (1947): *Transference Sleep in a Neurosis with Duodenal Ulcer.* Int. J. Psa., XXVIII, pp. 18-32.

Symposium (1942): *Symposium on Neurotic Disturbances of Sleep.* Int. J. Psa., XXIII, pp. 49-68.

TAUSK, VICTOR (1919): *On the Origin of the 'Influencing Machine' in Schizophrenia.* Psa. Quart., II, 1933, pp. 519-556.

TRILLING, LIONEL (1950): *The Liberal Imagination. Essays on Literature and Society.* New York: Viking Press, Inc.

UNDERHILL, EVELYN (1948): *Mysticism.* London: Methuen.

VINACKE, W. EDGAR (1968): Thinking—The Field. In: *International Encyclopedia of Social Sciences, Vol. XV.* Edited by David Sills, et al. New York: Macmillan-Free Press, pp. 608-614.

VON SIEBENTHAL, W. (1953): *Die Wissenschaft vom Traum.* Berlin: Springer Verlag.

VON SYDOW, ECKART (1927): *Primitive Kunst und Psychoanalyse; eine Studie über die sexuelle Grundlage der bildenden Künste der Naturvölker.* Leipzig, Vienna, and Zurich: Internationaler Psychoanalytischer Verlag.

WAELDER, ROBERT (1926): *Schizophrenic and Creative Thinking.* Int. J. Psa., VII, pp. 366-376.

——— (1930): *The Principle of Multiple Function: Observations on Over-Determination.* Psa. Quart., V, 1936, pp. 45-62.

——— (1937): *The Problem of the Genesis of Psychical Conflict in Earliest Infancy. Remarks on a Paper by Joan Riviere.* Int. J. Psa., XVIII, pp. 406-473.

——— (1960): *Basic Theory of Psychoanalysis.* New York: International Universities Press, Inc.

WARREN, MAX (1961): *The Significance of Visual Images during the Analytic Session.* J. Amer. Psa. Assn., IX, pp. 504-518.

WATSON, J. B. (1919): *Psychology from the Standpoint of a Behaviorist.* Philadelphia: J. B. Lippincott & Co.

WEIGERT, EDITH (1955): *Special Problems in Connection with Termination of Training Analysis.* J. Amer. Psa. Assn., III, pp. 630-640.

WEISS, EDOARDO (1935): *Agoraphobia and Its Relation to Hysterical Attacks and to Traumas.* Int. J. Psa., XVI, pp. 59-83.

——— (1936): *Agorafobia, Isterismo d'Angoscia.* Rome: Paolo Cremonese.

WILDER, THORNTON (1948): *Ides of March.* New York and London: Harper & Brothers.

WINDHOLZ, EMANUEL (1942): Participant in *Symposium on Neurotic Disturbances of Sleep.* Int. J. Psa., XXIII, pp. 49-52.

——— (1955): *Problems of Termination of the Training Analysis.* J. Amer. Psa. Assn., III, pp. 641-650.

WINTERSTEIN, ALFRED (1913): *Psychoanalytische Anmerkungen zur Geschichte der Philosophie.* Imago, II, pp. 175-237.

——— (1929): *Motorisches Erleben im schöpferischen Vorgang.* Psa. Bewegung, I, pp. 299-317.

WINTERSTEIN, HANS (1932): *Schlaf und Traum.* Berlin: Springer Verlag.

WISDOM, J. O. (1947): *Three Dreams of Descartes.* Int. J. Psa., XXVIII, pp. 11-18.

WITTELS, FRITZ (1931): *Freud and His Time.* (Second edition.) New York: Liveright Publishing Corp., 1948.

WOODS, RALPH L., Editor (1947): *The World of Dreams.* New York: Random House.

WOOLLEY, LEONARD (1930): *Digging Up the Past.* Baltimore: Penguin Books, 1953.

YATES, FRANCES A. (1966): *The Art of Memory.* Chicago: University of Chicago Press.

ZETZEL, ELIZABETH R. (1953): The Depressive Position. In: *Affective Disorders. Psychoanalytic Contribution to Their Study.* Edited by Phyllis Greenacre. New York: International Universities Press, Inc., pp. 84-116.

ZILBOORG, GREGORY (1930): *Affective Reintegration in the Schizophrenias.* Arch. of Neurology and Psychiatry, XXIV, p. 335-345.

——— (1933): *Anxiety without Affect.* Psa. Quart., II, pp. 48-67.

——— (1937): *Considerations on Suicide with Particular Reference to That of the Young.* Amer. J. Orthopsychiat., VII, pp. 15-31.

——— (1952): *Some Sidelights on Free Association.* Int. J. Psa., XXXIII, pp. 489-495.

——— (in collaboration with Henry, George W.) (1941): *A History of Medical Psychology.* New York: W. W. Norton & Co., Inc.

INDEX